READINGS IN
HISTORICAL
THEOLOGY

READINGS IN HISTORICAL THEOLOGY

PRIMARY SOURCES OF THE CHRISTIAN FAITH

Robert F. Lay

Kregel
Academic & Professional

Readings in Historical Theology: Primary Sources of the Christian Faith

© 2009 by Robert F. Lay

Published by Kregel Publications, a division of Kregel, Inc., P.O. Box 2607, Grand Rapids, MI 49501.

The Greek font used in this book is SymbolGreekU and is available from www.linguistsoftware.com/lgku.htm, +1-425-755-1130.

Pictured on the cover is the Cross of the Scriptures near the tenth-century ruins of the cathedral at Clonmacnoise, County Offaly, Ireland. Carved of a single piece of sandstone thirteen feet tall, the cross depicts scenes of the crucifixion, the last judgment, and Christ in the tomb.

ISBN: 978-0-8254-3067-1

Printed in the United States of America

09 10 11 12 13 / 5 4 3 2 1

"Take up and read!"
—Augustine's *Confessions*, viii:12

Contents

CONTENTS

Foreword

It is not unusual for students of history, reading a textbook for the first time, or even subsequent times, to long to reach beyond the story delineated on the pages to the primary sources that have defined and shaped the telling. Something is lost in the secondhand telling of a story, even by our most outstanding historians who synthesize a vast amount of material into a cohesive story line and central thesis of progressive movement through the centuries.

Though gathering, synthesizing, and summarizing can promote the understanding of history immensely, the shortcomings are readily apparent. The interpreter's situated perspective, the impossibility of re-creating past situations with precision, and the incompleteness of our knowledge of the past hamper scholarly efforts to adequately and accurately mirror the original sources for the reader. In the art of historical writing, there is no escaping the personal biases of the writer or observer and, therefore, the subjective selection of materials.

Thus a particular perspective has informed the selecting and gathering of historical sources in this volume. It must be declared that compiling sources is not an easy endeavor because finding sources that reflect the main currents of opinion and discussion in various eras of the past requires a significant degree of familiarity with the broader field of inquiry and the expertise to accurately select material. However, if this task is not performed, the student is left with a secondary telling of the story.

The purpose of the work is to provide students of history access to the original sources (whether creeds, treatises, ecclesiastical decrees, and so forth) that make

the writing of history possible. General survey texts are important, yet the texts can distance students from the past that they are seeking to make available. A good survey text by a competent scholar combined with a sourcebook holds significant promise of promoting historical awareness in students. Sourcebooks allow the student to directly interact with the material. The student can experience history, interact with the voices of the past, and form his or her own judgments concerning the great issues that have occupied the best minds of church history.

In *Readings in Historical Theology*, the selection of sources clearly emphasizes the church's development through the centuries from the perspective of conservative orthodoxy in general and conservative Protestantism in particular. This is not to fault the editor since it is his purpose to create a text that functions to promote traditional Protestant faith. It does suggest, however, that the editor carries a consistently executed perspective in the selection and non-selection of materials.

This caveat should not dampen the important accomplishment of this work. The selections are judicious and quite complete. Some of the sources, particularly Medieval sources, rarely appear in history sourcebooks and yet are important in documenting our heritage and its development. *Readings in Historical Theology* is truly a valuable work that makes available to a new generation of students the "real stuff"—the real sources of our written history.

I believe this work is an important contribution and a fine supplement for those who seek to understand our past. Without an understanding of our past, stability in the contemporary swirl of events is precarious and a future hope rendered uncertain. The rootlessness of the postmodern mind-set and its rejection of the past as offering helpful insights to provide guidance makes the work of presenting a usable past increasingly important in the life of the contemporary church. It is only to the detriment of the church's health that we neglect to instruct the new generation of Christ-followers.

An acquaintance with the past can give us a sense of calm in turbulent times and a knowledge that the Lord's church will ultimately triumph. The Devil has employed every strategy to destroy the church: armies have marched against it, faithless scholarship has relentlessly assaulted it, internal bickering has rent it, and martyrdom has depleted its ranks from time to time. Yet the church marches forward in triumphal anticipation of the day when the kingdoms of this world will be put under Christ's feet and the bride, without spot or wrinkle, will be given to the king.

—John D. Hannah
Distinguished Professor of Historical Theology
Research Professor of Theological Studies
Dallas Theological Seminary

Preface

Why This Sourcebook?

Many sourcebooks have been published. This one is the product of over a decade of introducing undergraduate students to primary source readings. I began self-publishing my sourcebook in 1996 in order to discourage overdependence (my students' and my own) on textbooks. While textbooks have their place, my aim is to encourage critical reading and thinking skills while fostering appreciation for the classical Christian authors such as Augustine, Anselm, and Aquinas. I want my students to read the church fathers for themselves, and I have seen their confidence in tackling challenging reading grow along with their comprehension. At some point along the way, I augmented my sourcebook with less familiar voices of the Christian tradition, such as those of the Alexandrian Catechetical School and the monastic movement. Since it was necessary to help students understand the theological contexts emerging from the Protestant Reformation and the Great Awakening, I added a few representative documents. Admittedly, no collection spanning the centuries can include more than a tiny fraction of the extant documents. The selection offered here represents the interests of an ecumenically minded evangelical who teaches in a liberal arts setting.

This sourcebook differs from others. Most readings included here are longer than is typical of such publications, and where possible several chapters or even entire documents are included, offering a continuity of reading and avoiding the choppy nature of most primary source readers. A student need not read all of an early church document in order to follow its basic thrust, but key passages of the church fathers taken out of context are notoriously oblique and subject to misinterpretation. Savvy readers always rely on material in the surrounding passages in order to make good sense of a valued quotation, and they will not be disappointed here. Second, most of the ancient and Medieval texts included in this sourcebook have been (conservatively) modernized to allow for smoother reading. This has become necessary since public domain translations, though readily available online, are nonetheless not very accessible in their antiquated English translations. However, the pieces originally written in English have not been modernized and original spellings and punctuation are mostly preserved. Third, most of the readings are introduced with a bit of historical background information, many include questions for guided reading, and some offer suggested assignments.

Though few of these venerable documents fall neatly into familiar genres, they have been arranged in thematic sections, and are chronologically arranged within each section. Additional, unedited documents are presented in the CD that accompanies this volume; they provide examples from the classical tradition as well as from the broader theological tradition, and their length requires an electronic format for easy access. Both the book and the CD texts preserve traditional chapter and section numbers found in standard published editions; ellipses are used to indicate omitted passages. Since it is often impossible to determine at what stage of the transmission of the text or translation Scripture citations were added, all are uniformly placed in parentheses in this volume.

My heartfelt thanks for assistance in bringing this reader to its present stage of refinement belong first of all to Chris Collins Lay—a "woman of excellence" (Ruth 3:11) as everyone who knows her will attest, and a wife whose many virtues I find conveniently catalogued in Proverbs 31. She patiently listens and offers valuable feedback on my projects, and her steadfast love through the years has formed the daily context of my work. It was a delight to have our daughter, Rebekah, as a student in the class for which this text was assigned. The way she valued and preserved her copy of my self-published sourcebook has been a great source of motivation for me!

In the fall of 2000 I began sharing my sourcebook with faculty colleagues at academic conferences, and soon after I began receiving orders. Since then I have distributed several hundred copies, and the reader has been used in courses at Asbury Theological Seminary, Moody Bible Institute, Nazarene Theological Seminary, Ohio Christian University, and elsewhere. Equally gratifying is the interest shown in this reader by college graduates who want to renew their studies, advanced homeschoolers looking for curricula, ministers, homemakers, and others who simply want to become more conversant with the Christian tradition. Faculty colleagues at Taylor University have always been supportive. Dr. Ted Ewing regularly implored me to publish the reader and Dr. Paul House convinced me to submit the manuscript to Kregel, which turned out to be great advice as Jim Weaver and Stephen Barclift have made the process of publication easier and more encouraging than I could have imagined.

Thanks also belong to hundreds of students who have read these documents, more or less thoroughly, have interacted with them by way of the suggested assignments, and have freely shared their impressions with me. Special thanks to Ashley Pikel who tirelessly tracked down the typographical errors in my self-published reader, and to Kelsey Warren who helped extensively with the preparation of the manuscript for submission. Finally, I am grateful to my sister, Belinda, for the reminder that one may pursue a publication project in order to learn, and not because one knows everything about the subject. My limited knowledge of the Christian tradition will be all too apparent to those who make use of this volume, and its ongoing usefulness will depend on their encouragement and constructive feedback.

Acknowledgments

Excerpts from Luther's Works used with permission of Concordia House. All rights reserved. From Vol. 2 *Lectures on Genesis* © 1960, 1988. From Vol. 10 *First Lectures on the Psalms, I, Psalms 1–75* © 1974. From Vol. 14 *Psalms 1 and 2* © 1958, 1986. From Vol. 16 *Lectures on Isaiah* © 1968. From Vol. 26 *Lectures on Galatians* © 1963, 1991.

The excerpt from Spener's *Pia Desideria* translated by Theodore G. Tappert, © 1964, and used with permission of Fortress Press.

Most of the ancient and early Medieval texts included in this reader are my own paraphrased versions of translations now in the public domain, many of which are found in the *Ante-Nicene, Nicene and Post Nicene Christian Library*, ed. Alexander Roberts and James Donaldson (Edinburgh: T & T Clark, 1867–70; with later reprints). Libraries of later Medieval and modern texts are more difficult to find, but online repositories now provide a rich source of these texts, for example the Internet Medieval Sourcebook of Paul Halsall (http://www.fordham.edu/halsall/Sbook.html) and the Christian Classics Ethereal Library (http://www.ccel.org/). Excerpts of Martin Luther's *Ninety-five Theses*, *Shorter Catechism*, and "Three Walls of the Romanists" included in this reader are based on the translations of Martin Luther's works by Henry Wace (1836–1924), first published in 1885 by the Lutheran Publication Society, and now in the public domain. The translations of Calvin's works included here are those of Henry Beveridge (1799–1863), first published in 1879 by T & T Clark, and now in the public domain. The translation of Turretin's writings on the atonement (originally "A Historical Sketch of Opinions on the Atonement . . .") was first published by James R. Wilson in Philadelphia in 1817, and is also in the public domain.

Introduction
On Learning to Read, Again

Reading and learning from the primary sources of the Christian tradition requires a diligence that is increasingly rare. Like the reading of Scripture—and the earliest of these documents were once seen as Scripture—reading these documents is a cross-cultural experience that requires long-term investment. Navigating Greek or Latin prose has always been difficult due to the complexity of thought that lies behind the writing. English translators (or in this case, paraphrasers) do the best they can, but something is inevitably "lost in translation." It is good discipline, in such reading, to distinguish the main clause or thought from all subordinate clauses (even by marking it), and thereby to grasp the message in its simplified form. The following example comes from the early church letter of Mathetes to Diognetus. It is a single, lengthy sentence for which I have **highlighted** the main thought, and <u>underlined</u> the most important subordinate thought, thus revealing the reason amidst the rhetoric:

> <u>Since</u> I see that <u>you</u>, most excellent Diognetus, <u>are zealous to learn the way of</u> worship prevalent among <u>Christians</u>, and that you are inquiring very carefully and earnestly concerning them: what God they trust in, and what form of religion they observe; how they disregard the world and fear not death, while esteeming neither those gods held sacred by the Greeks, nor holding to Jewish superstitions; and what affection they cherish among themselves; and why, this new practice [of piety] has only now entered into the world, and not long ago; **I** cordially **welcome this inquiry of yours, and implore God**, who enables us both to speak and to hear, <u>to grant to me so to speak, so that</u>, above all, I may learn that <u>you</u> have been <u>edified</u>, and that you may discover that I who speak may have no cause of regret for having done so.

Essentially the author is saying, "Diognetus, I welcome your inquiry (since you are sincerely eager to learn about Christians) and I ask God to grant me speak so that you may be edified." Now, why didn't Mathetes simply say that? In truth, he *did* say it. For while today's readers find this prose to be dense, for the original author and reader it was respectful, educated speech. The sooner we grant that, the sooner we may understand and appreciate what has been written in ages past.

A second example leads us into deeper waters:

> Therefore, if Christ came so that we might learn how much God loves us, and that we might grow fervent in our love for Him who first loved us, but also that we might love our neighbor at the command of Him who became our neighbor (loving us while He was still afar off); and if all divine Scripture written before (i.e., prior to Christ's coming) was written to announce His coming, and if whatever has since been written and established by divine authority tells of Christ and admonishes us to love, then is obvious that **on the** two great **commandments**—to love God and our

neighbor—**depend** not only the law and the prophets (which comprised all scripture at the time when the Lord taught this) but also **whatever books of divine teaching were later written** for our health and committed to our remembrance.

This statement from Augustine on the aim of Christian teaching (*On the Instruction of the Beginner* 4, 8) leaves even determined readers mired in parenthetical clauses and missing the main point. In this case it is necessary to wade through the several "if" clauses (i.e., the compound protasis or subordinate part of an "if . . . then" statement) in order to identify the main "then" clause (the apodosis). Thus the complex sentence simplifies as follows:

If Christ came so that we might learn how much God loves us, etc.
    and if (the) Scriptures written beforehand . . . announced His coming and
    those written since tell of Christ and admonish us to love,

then all Scripture depends on the two great commandments, to love God and neighbor.

Not everything you will read between these covers requires this kind of effort; some statements are very concise. Immediately following Augustine's statement above, for example, we read his conclusion concerning the Testaments:

In the Old the New is hidden, and in the New the Old is revealed.

As you read and reread the documents in this sourcebook, you are engaging the foundational authors of our faith and thinking their thoughts after them. In them you will discover the diverse and rich threads of Christian doctrine. All that remains to be said, at this point, was already said by Mathetes to Diognetus many centuries ago: Since you are sincerely eager to learn about Christians, I welcome your inquiry and ask God to grant me speak so that you may be edified.

Timeline
Select Events and Writings

THE CLASSICAL HERITAGE

FIFTH CENTURY B.C.

Birth of Socrates (470 B.C.)

Birth of Plato (427 B.C.)

Plato becomes a student of Socrates (407 B.C.)

FOURTH CENTURY B.C.

Socrates condemned to death by the Athenian Assembly (399 B.C.)

Plato establishes the *Academy* in Athens (387 B.C.)

Birth of Aristotle (384 B.C.)

Aristotle enrolls in Plato's *Academy* (367 B.C.)

Death of Plato (348–347 B.C.)

Aristotle is named tutor for Alexander the Great (343 B.C.)

The *Hellenistic Period*: the spread of the Greek language and culture (336–31 B.C.)

Aristotle establishes a rival to the *Academy*, the *Lyceum* (335 B.C.)

The conquests of Alexander the Great (333 B.C.)

The death of Aristotle (322 B.C.)

THE ANCIENT PERIOD

A.D. FIRST CENTURY

Crucifixion of Jesus of Nazareth (c. 30)

Birth of Ignatius of Antioch (c. 35)

Disciples are first called Christians at Antioch (c. 40–44)

Paul's first missionary journey (c. 46)

Jerusalem Council (c. 50)

Burning of Rome, persecution by Emperor Nero (64)

Birth of Polycarp (69)

Jerusalem temple destroyed by Rome (70)

Expulsion of Christians from Jewish synagogues (c. 75)

Didache (c. 70–90)

Domitian persecution (81–96)

A.D. SECOND CENTURY

Persecution of Christians under Emperor Trajan (98–117)

Upsurge in Gnosticism (117 and following)

Birth of Irenaeus (130)

Justin the Martyr's *First Apology* (155)

Montanist movement begins in Phrygia (c. 172)

Pantaenus heads the Alexandrian Catechetical School (179)

Clement of Alexandria heads the Alexandrian Catechetical School (190–202)

Tertullian of Carthage's *Against Heretics* (200)

A.D. THIRD CENTURY

Origen heads the Alexandrian Catechetical School (202–230)

Monarchian controversy, ransom theory of atonement (c. 225)

Alexandrian Catechetical School falls under ecclesiastical scrutiny (231)

Beginning of the demise of the Roman empire (234–284)

Goths attack Rome (248)

Birth of Athanasius (c. 296)

A.D. FOURTH CENTURY

Great Persecution under Diocletian (303)
Donatist controversy (c. 312)
Edict of Milan (313)
(First) Council of Nicaea (325)
Birth of John Chrysostom (c. 347)
Augustine of Hippo: Birth (354) and conversion to
   Christianity (386)
(Second Ecumenical) Council of Constantinople
   (381)
Jerome's *Vulgate* translation (382)
Augustine becomes bishop of Hippo (395)

A.D. FIFTH CENTURY

Beginning of the rise of papal power (early 400s)
Fall of Rome (410)
Augustine's *City of God* (413–426)
Pelagianism takes hold in Britain (c. 419)
Death of Augustine (430)
(Third Ecumenical) Council of Ephesus (431)
(Fourth Ecumenical) Council of Chalcedon (451)
Birth of Benedict of Nursia (480)
Monophysite schism between East and West begins
   (c. 482)
Latin replaces Greek as the language of the western
   church (late fifth century)

THE MEDIEVAL PERIOD

EARLY MIDDLE AGES: TIME OF MONASTIC INFLUENCE

Sixth Century

Apollinarianism and Nestorianism; debate over the
   two natures of Christ (520s)
Dionysius introduces a Christian Chronology
   (c. 525)
Platonic Academy in Athens closes; paganism passes
   off the scene (c. 530s)
Benedict of Nursia's *Rule* (543)
Fifth Ecumenical Council (II Constantinople, 553)
Emergence of four streams of the Christian
   tradition (c. 570s)
   • Western (Roman) Christianity
   • Antioch Nestorianism

   • Byzantine Orthodoxy
   • Alexandrian Monophysites
Debate on the *filioque* clause (c. 590s)

Seventh Century

Mohammed and the rise of Islam (570–632)
Death of Gregory the Great (604)
Monothelitism controversy (647)
Birth of the Venerable Bede (673)
Sixth Ecumenical Council (III Constantinople,
   680–681)

Eighth Century

Iconoclastic controversy (725)
Donation of Constantine grants Western Roman
   Empire to the pope (750s)
Seventh Ecumenical Council (II Nicaea, 787)
Alcuin becomes master of the Carolingian Palace
   School (790)

Ninth Century

Charlemagne and the Carolingian Revival (781–814)
Johann Scotus Erigena heads the Palace School at
   Paris (850s)
Cyril and Methodius evangelize the Slavic people;
   Slavic Bible translation (863)

HIGH MIDDLE AGES: TIME OF SCHOLASTIC INFLUENCE

Tenth Century

Monastery of Cluny founded (910)
University of Al-Azhar (970)

Eleventh Century

Monastic reforms under Pope Leo IX (1049)
Final (formal) schism between Eastern and Western
   churches (1054)
Anselm's *Proslogion* (1079)
First Crusade (1096–1099)
Founding of the Cistercian Order at Citeaux (1098)

Twelfth Century

Bernard of Clairvaux joins the Cistercians (1112)
Abelard's *Sic et Non* (1120)
Lombard's *Sentences* (1147)
University of Paris founded (1160), many others
   thereafter

Thirteenth Century

University of Paris adopts Aristotle syllabus (1255)

Aquinas's *Summa Theologica* (1265)

THE PERIOD OF RENAISSANCE AND REFORMATION

FOURTEENTH CENTURY

Beginning of the decline of the papacy (early 1300s)

Death of William of Ockham (1349)

Julian of Norwich's *Showings* (1373)

FIFTEENTH CENTURY

Thomas à Kempis joins the Brethren of the Common Life (early 1400s) and writes *The Imitation of Christ* (1441)

Invention of the printing press (1439)

Devotio Moderna movement (late 1400s)

SIXTEENTH CENTURY

Erasmus's *In Praise of Folly* (1509)

Martin Luther's *Ninety-Five Theses* (1517) and German Bible (1534)

John Calvin's *Institutes of the Christian Religion* (1536)

Teresa of Avila establishes her Convent of the Barefoot Nuns (1562)

THE MODERN PERIOD

SEVENTEENTH CENTURY

Francis Bacon's *Advancement of Learning* (1608)

The Colonial *Old Deluder Satan Act* (1647)

Quaker movement begins (1648)

Comenius's *Great Didactic* (1657)

Death of Roger Williams, English theologian for the separation of church and state (1683)

John Locke's *Essay Concerning Human Understanding* (1690)

EIGHTEENTH CENTURY

Births of John Wesley and Jonathan Edwards (1703)

Welsh Methodist revival (1735)

Israel Baal Shem Tov founds the Jewish Hasidism (1736)

The Great Awakening peaks in New England (1740–1742)

Jean Jacques Rousseau's *Social Contract* (1762)

Emanuel Swedenborg founds Swedenborgianism (1772)

The first Sunday school, Gloucester, England (1780)

First Amendment to the Constitution (1791)

Age of Reason (advocating Deism) written by Thomas Paine (1795)

Friedrich Schleiermacher's *Speeches on Religion* (1799)

NINETEENTH CENTURY

Cane Ridge revival, the beginning of the Second Great Awakening (1801)

Restoration Movement begins (1811)

Richard Allen founds the African Methodist Episcopal Church (1816)

American Sunday School Union formed (1824)

Plymouth Brethren founded (1828)

Charles Finney revivals (1830)

Southern Baptist Convention formed (1845)

Horace Bushnell's *Christian Nurture* (1846)

YMCA established in America (1851)

Hudson Taylor arrives in China (1854)

Bible Institute Movement (beginning in the 1880s)

Student Volunteer Missions Movement (1886–1936)

CHAPTER 1

Ancient Creeds, Confessions, and Catechisms

A creed is concise statement of belief affirmed by a particular community. The earliest creeds included here are those that were affirmed in ancient Israel—for example, the Shema of Deuteronomy 6, "Hear, O Israel! The LORD is our God, the LORD is one!"—and those declared among ancient Christians—such as the one Paul includes in his first letter to Timothy, "For there is one God, and one mediator also between God and men, the man Christ Jesus, who gave Himself as a ransom for all, the testimony given at the proper time" (1 Tim. 2:5–6). The term *creed* itself, in its Christian usage, is somewhat later and comes from the Latin *credo*, meaning "I believe," and so begins each section of the *Credo in Deum*, the Apostles' Creed, "I believe in God . . . in Jesus Christ . . . in the Holy Spirit." Biblical and later Christian creeds come first in this reader (1) because of their foundational relation to the other documents included here, (2) because they are or should be the basis of Christian unity, and (3) because it is the creeds and other ancient Christian documents to which each generation returns in its quest to define faith for itself and to find direction for the Church. In addition to the best-known creeds, several key documents from the history of the Church—such as *Didache*, baptismal and catechetical rites, and canonical lists are included here.

OLD TESTAMENT COVENANTS AND CREEDS
New American Standard Bible, 1995 Update

The Creation Mandate (Gen. 1:26–28)

Then God said, "Let Us make man in Our image, according to Our likeness; and let them rule over the fish of the sea and over the birds of the sky and over the cattle and over all the earth, and over every creeping thing that creeps on the earth." God created man in His own image, in the image of God He created him; male and female He created them. God blessed them; and God said to them, "Be fruitful and multiply, and fill the earth, and subdue it; and rule over the fish of the sea and over the birds of the sky and over every living thing that moves on the earth."

The Union of Man and Woman (Gen. 2:23–24)

The man said, "This is now bone of my bones, and flesh of my flesh; She shall be called Woman, because she was taken out of Man." For this reason a man shall leave his father and his mother, and be joined to his wife; and they shall become one flesh.

God Curses the Serpent (Gen. 3:14–15)

The LORD God said to the serpent, "Because you have done this, cursed are you more than all cattle, and more than every beast of the field; on your belly you will go, and dust you will eat all the days of your life; and I will put enmity between you and the woman, and between your seed and her seed; He shall bruise you on the head, and you shall bruise him on the heel.

God's Covenant with Noah (Gen. 9:1–15)

And God blessed Noah and his sons and said to them, "Be fruitful and multiply, and fill the earth. The fear of you and the terror of you will be on every beast of the earth and on every bird of the sky; with everything that creeps on the ground, and all the fish of the sea, into your hand they are given. Every moving thing that is alive shall be food for you; I give all to you, as I gave the green plant. Only you shall not eat flesh with its life, that is, its blood. Surely I will require your lifeblood; from every beast I will require it. And from every man, from every man's brother I will require the life of man. Whoever sheds man's blood, by man his blood shall be shed, for in the image of God He made man. As for you, be fruitful and multiply; populate the earth abundantly and multiply in it." Then God spoke to Noah and to his sons with him, saying, "Now behold, I Myself do establish My covenant with you, and with your descendants after you; and with every living creature that is with you, the birds, the cattle, and every beast of the earth with you; of all that comes out of the ark, even every beast of the earth. I establish My covenant with you; and all flesh shall never again be cut off by the water of the flood, neither shall there again be a flood to destroy the earth." God said, "This is the sign of the covenant which I am making between Me and you and every living creature that is with you, for all successive generations; I set My bow in the cloud, and it shall be for a sign of a covenant between Me and the earth. It shall come about, when I bring a cloud over the earth, that the bow will be seen in the cloud, and I will remember My covenant, which is between Me and you and every living creature of all flesh; and never again shall the water become a flood to destroy all flesh.

The Call of Abraham (Gen. 12:1–3)

Now the LORD said to Abram, "Go forth from your country, and from your relatives and from your father's house, to the land which I will show you; and I will make you a great nation, and I will bless you, and make your name great; and so you shall be a blessing; and I will bless those who bless you, and the one who curses you I will curse. And in you all the families of the earth will be blessed."

The Faith of Abraham (Gen. 15:6)

Then he believed in the LORD; and He reckoned it to him as righteousness.

The Ten Commandments (Exod. 20:1–17)

Then God spoke all these words, saying, "I am the LORD your God, who brought you out of the land of Egypt, out of the house of slavery. You shall have no other gods before Me. You shall not make for yourself an idol, or any likeness of what is in heaven above or on the earth beneath or in the water under the earth. You shall not worship them or serve them; for I, the LORD your God, am a jealous God, visiting the iniquity of the fathers on the children, on the third and the fourth generations of those who hate Me, but showing lovingkindness to thousands, to those who love Me and keep My commandments. You shall not take the name of the LORD your God in vain, for the LORD will not leave him unpunished who takes His name in vain. Remember the Sabbath day, to keep it holy. Six days you shall labor and do all your work, but the seventh day is a sabbath of the LORD your God; in it you shall not do any work, you or your son or your daughter, your male or your female servant or your cattle or your sojourner who stays with you. For in six days the LORD made the heavens and the earth, the sea and all that is in them, and rested on the seventh day; therefore the LORD blessed the sabbath day and made it holy. Honor your father and your mother, that your days may be prolonged in the land which the LORD your God gives you. You shall not murder. You shall not commit adultery. You shall not steal. You shall not bear false witness against your neighbor. You shall not covet your neighbor's house; you shall not covet your neighbor's wife or his male servant or his female servant or his ox or his donkey or anything that belongs to your neighbor."

The Shema (Deut. 6:4–9)

Hear, O Israel! The LORD is our God, the LORD is one! You shall love the LORD your God with all your heart and with all your soul and with all your might. These words, which I am commanding you today, shall be on your heart. You shall teach them diligently to your sons and shall talk of them when you sit in your house and when you walk by the way and when you lie down and when you rise up. You shall bind them as a sign on your hand and they shall be as frontals on your forehead. You shall write them on the doorposts of your house and on your gates.

First Fruits (Deut. 26:5–10a)

You shall answer and say before the LORD your God, "My father was a wandering Aramean, and he went down to Egypt and sojourned there, few in number; but there he became a great, mighty and populous nation. And the Egyptians treated us harshly and afflicted us, and imposed hard labor on us. Then we cried to the LORD, the God of our fathers, and the LORD heard our voice and saw our affliction and our toil and our oppression; and the LORD brought us out of Egypt with a mighty hand and an outstretched arm and with great terror and with signs and wonders; and He has brought us to this place and has given us this land, a land flowing with milk and honey. Now behold, I have brought the first of the produce of the ground which You, O LORD have given me."

Ruth's Steadfast Love (Ruth 1:16–17)

"Do not urge me to leave you or turn back from following you; for where you go, I will go, and where you lodge, I will lodge. Your people shall be my people, and your God, my God. Where you die, I will die, and there I will be buried. Thus may the LORD do to me, and worse, if anything but death parts you and me."

Job's Profession (Job 1:20–22)

Then Job arose and tore his robe and shaved his head, and he fell to the ground and worshiped. He said, "Naked I came from my mother's womb, and naked I shall return there. The LORD gave and the LORD has taken away. Blessed be the name of the LORD." Through all this Job did not sin nor did he blame God.

Job's Faith (Job 19:25)

"As for me, I know that my Redeemer lives, and at the last He will take His stand on the earth."

Living by Faith (Hab. 2:4)

Behold, as for the proud one, his soul is not right within him; but the righteous will live by his faith.

NEW TESTAMENT CREEDS AND COMMISSIONS

New American Standard Bible, 1995 Update

The Beatitudes (Matt. 5:1–12)

When Jesus saw the crowds, He went up on the mountain; and after He sat down, His disciples came to Him. He opened His mouth and began to teach them, saying, "Blessed are the poor in spirit, for theirs is the kingdom of heaven. Blessed are those who mourn, for they shall be comforted. Blessed are the gentle, for they shall inherit the earth. Blessed are those who hunger and thirst for righteousness, for they shall be satisfied. Blessed are the merciful, for they shall receive mercy. Blessed are the pure in heart, for they shall see God. Blessed are the peacemakers, for they shall be called sons of God. Blessed are those who have been persecuted for the sake of righteousness, for theirs is the kingdom of heaven. Blessed are you when people insult you and persecute you, and falsely say all kinds of evil against you because of Me. Rejoice and be glad, for your reward in heaven is great; for in the same way they persecuted the prophets who were before you.

Pater Noster: Our Father (Matt. 6:9–13, with the Latin, Textum Vaticanum)

Our Father who is in heaven, hallowed be Your name.
Pater noster qui es in caelis, sanctificetur nomen tuum.

Your kingdom come, Your will be done, on earth as it is in heaven.
Adveniat regnum tuum. Fiat voluntas tua, sicut in caelo et in terra.

Give us this day our daily bread.
Panem nostrum quotidianum da nobis hodie.

And forgive us our debts as we also have forgiven our debtors.
Et dimitte nobis debita nostra, sicut et nos dimittimus debitoribus nostris.

And do not lead us into temptation,
Et ne passus nos fueris induci in tentationem

but deliver us from evil. [. . . Amen.]
Sed libera nos a malo. Amen.

The Great Commandment (Matt. 22:37–40)

And He [Jesus] said to him, "'You shall love the Lord your God with all your heart, and with all your soul, and with all your mind.' This is the great and foremost commandment. The second is like it, 'You shall love your neighbor as yourself.' On these two commandments depend the whole Law and the Prophets."

The Great Commission (Matt. 28:18–20)

And Jesus came up and spoke to them, saying, "All authority has been given to Me in heaven and on earth. Go therefore and make disciples of all the nations, baptizing them in the name of the Father and the Son and the Holy Spirit, teaching them to observe all that I commanded you; and lo, I am with you always, even to the end of the age."

The Word (John 1:1)

In the beginning was the Word, and the Word was with God, and the Word was God.

You Will Be My Witnesses (Acts 1:7–8)

He [Jesus] said to them, "It is not for you to know times or epochs which the Father has fixed by His own authority; but you will receive power when the Holy Spirit has come upon you; and you shall be My witnesses both in Jerusalem, and in all Judea and Samaria, and even to the remotest part of the earth."

The Ingathering and Promise (Acts 2:38–39)

Peter said to them, "Repent, and each of you be baptized in the name of Jesus Christ for the forgiveness of your sins; and you will receive the gift of the Holy Spirit. For the promise is for you and your children and for all who are far off, as many as the Lord our God will call to Himself."

The Heart of the Gospel (Rom. 3:19–26)

Now we know that whatever the Law says, it speaks to those who are under the Law, so that every mouth may be closed and all the world may become accountable to God; because by the works of the Law no flesh will be justified in His sight; for through the Law comes the knowledge of sin. But now apart from the Law the righteousness of God has been manifested, being witnessed by the Law and the Prophets, even the righteousness of God through faith in Jesus Christ for all those who believe; for there is no distinction; for all have sinned and fall short of the glory of God, being justified as a gift by His grace through the redemption which is in Christ Jesus; whom God displayed publicly as a propitiation in His blood through faith. This was to demonstrate His righteousness, because in the forbearance of God He passed over the sins previously committed; for the demonstration, I say, of His righteousness at the present time, so that He would be just and the justifier of the one who has faith in Jesus.

Paul's Tradition (1 Cor. 15:3–8)

For I delivered to you as of first importance what I also received, that Christ died for our sins according to the Scriptures, and that He was buried, and that He was raised on the third day according to the Scriptures, and that He appeared to Cephas, then the twelve. After that He appeared to more than five hundred brethren at one time, most of whom remain until now, but some have fallen asleep; then He appeared to James, then to all the apostles; and last of all, as to one untimely born, He appeared to me also.

Paul's Benediction (2 Cor. 13:14)

The grace of the Lord Jesus Christ, and the love of God, and the fellowship of the Holy Spirit, be with you all.

The Christ Hymn (Phil. 2:5–11)

Have this attitude in yourselves which was also in Christ Jesus, who, although He existed in the form of God, did not regard equality with God a thing to be grasped, but emptied Himself, taking the form of a bond-servant, and being made in the likeness of men. Being found in appearance as a man, He humbled Himself by becoming obedient to the point of death, even death on a cross. For this reason also, God highly exalted Him, and bestowed on Him the name which is above every name, so that at the name of Jesus every knee will bow, of those who are in heaven and on earth and under the earth, and that every tongue will confess that Jesus Christ is Lord, to the glory of God the Father.

The Ephesians Blessing (Eph. 1:3–14)

Blessed be the God and Father of our Lord Jesus Christ, who has blessed us with every spiritual blessing in the heavenly places in Christ, just as He chose us in Him before the foundation of the world, that we would be holy and blameless before Him. In love He predestined us to adoption as sons through Jesus Christ to Himself, according to the kind intention of His will, to the praise of the glory of His grace, which He freely bestowed on us in the Beloved. In Him we have redemption through His blood, the forgiveness of our trespasses, according to the riches of His grace which He lavished on us. In all wisdom and insight He made known to us the mystery of His will, according to His kind intention which He purposed in Him with a view to an administration suitable to the fullness of the times, that is, the summing up of all things in Christ, things in the heavens and things on the earth. In Him also we have obtained an inheritance, having been predestined according to His purpose who works all things after the counsel of His will, to the end that we who were the first to hope in Christ would be to the praise of His glory. In Him, you also, after listening to the message of truth, the gospel of your salvation—having also believed, you were sealed in Him with the Holy Spirit of promise, who is given as a pledge of our inheritance, with a view to the redemption of God's own possession, to the praise of His glory.

The Unity of the Spirit (Eph. 4:1–13)

Therefore I, the prisoner of the Lord, implore you to walk in a manner worthy of the calling with which you have been called, with all humility and gentleness, with patience, showing tolerance for one another in love, being diligent to preserve the unity of the Spirit in the bond of peace. There is one body and one Spirit, just as also you were called in one hope of your calling; one Lord, one faith, one baptism, one God and Father of all, who is over all and through all and in all. But to each one of us grace was given according to the measure of Christ's gift. Therefore it says, "When He ascended on high, He led captive a host of captives, and He gave gifts to men." (Now this expression, "He ascended," what does it mean except that He also had descended into the lower parts of the earth? He who descended is Himself also He who ascended far above all the heavens, so that He might fill all things.) And He gave some as apostles, and some as prophets, and some as evangelists, and some as pastors and teachers, for the equipping of the saints for the work of service, to the building up of the body of Christ; until we all attain the unity of the faith, and of the knowledge of the Son of God, to a mature man, to the measure of the stature which belongs to the fullness of Christ.

One God (1 Tim. 2:5–6)

For there is one God, and one mediator also between God and men, the man Christ Jesus, who gave Himself as a ransom for all, the testimony given at the proper time.

Confession (1 Tim. 3:16)

By common confession, great is the mystery of godliness: He who was revealed in the flesh, was vindicated in the Spirit, seen by angels, proclaimed among the nations, believed on in the world, taken up in glory.

Scripture (2 Tim. 3:16–17)

All Scripture is inspired by God and profitable for teaching, for reproof, for correction, for training in righteousness; so that the man of God may be adequate, equipped for every good work.

DIDACHE: THE TEACHING OF THE TWELVE APOSTLES
Greek, Early Second Century A.D.

Aside from the New Testament writings, this is the earliest known summary of apostolic teaching prepared for Christian instruction and addressed to individual believers (notice "My child" at the beginning of chapters 3 and 4; cf. 1 John 2:1). The document combines gospel teachings with themes found in Jewish texts of the first century A.D. and earlier, together with directions for Christian discipline and sacramental practice. Harshly worded directives contained in this teaching, for example, "do not be like the hypocrites who fast on Mondays and Thursdays," may be aimed at Judaizing Christians—those who insisted that adherence to the law of Moses was necessary for salvation. Guidelines on itinerate prophets and the admonition to honor local bishops and deacons suggest that this document may have circulated prior to the establishment of the threefold church order (bishop, elder, and deacon).

Questions for Guided Reading

1. This entire teaching is based on a contrast between two "ways" of life; summarize each.
2. Identify as many scriptural references or allusions in chapters 1–5 as you can.
3. Compare the form of the Lord's Prayer found in the *Didache* to those found in the Gospels of Matthew and Luke.
4. Describe the procedures for baptism, fasting, and Eucharist prescribed by the *Didache*.
5. How was the behavior of itinerant Christian teachers or prophets to be regulated?
6. What directions are given regarding bishops (*episkopoi*) and deacons (*diakonos*)?
7. With what cautions and directives for the church does the *Didache* conclude?
8. In your view, what sort of Christian life and practice does the *Didache* prescribe?
9. Why do you think the *Didache* is rigorous and detailed in its regulation of the sacraments?
10. Why do you think "the prophets" are allowed by this document to vary its regulations?
11. How does the restriction on who may take communion compare with your church?
12. Elders (*presbuteroi*) are mentioned in the New Testament and in documents written later than the *Didache* but not in the *Didache* itself; what are some possible reasons for this?

✦

PART I: THE TWO PATHS

Chapter I: The path of life

There are two paths, one of life and one of death, and there is a great difference between the two.

Now this is the path of life: first, you shall love the Lord who made you; secondly, your neighbor as yourself; and whatever you do not wish to be done to you, do not do that to others. Here is the instruction (*didache*): Bless those who curse you, and pray for your enemies. Fast for those who persecute you. What good is it if you love only those who love you? Don't the Gentiles do this? But love those that hate you and you will have no enemies. Abstain from fleshly and worldly lusts. If anyone strikes you on your right cheek, turn the left one to him and you will be perfect. If anyone makes you march with him a mile, then go with him two. If anyone takes your coat, give him your tunic as well; and if someone takes anything of yours from you, do not ask for it back. Give to everyone who asks, and do not ask for it back, for the Father wants all to share in His gifts. Blessed, then, is he who gives generously according to this commandment, for he is free from guilt; but woe to those who receive and do not give. Those who receive things they actually need are free from guilt, but those who take things they do not need shall account for what they have done, and shall pay a penalty, not leaving until every penny is paid back. As someone has said, let your donation stay put in your hand until you know who should receive it.

Chapter II: Remember the commandments

Now the second commandment of the teaching is this: You shall not murder; you shall not commit adultery; you shall not corrupt a young person; you shall not commit fornication; you shall not steal; you shall not use magic; you shall not kill a child by abortion, nor slay it when born. You shall not covet your neighbor's possessions; you shall not commit perjury, nor bear false witness; you shall not speak evil; you shall not bear malice; you shall not be double-minded or double-tongued, for to be double-tongued is the snare of death. Your speech shall not be false or empty, but concerned with action. You shall not be one who covets or extorts, hypocritical, malicious, or proud; you shall not plan evil against your neighbor. Do not hate anyone. Rather, rebuke some, pray for others, and love still others more than your own soul.

Chapter III: Various warnings

My child, flee from everything that is evil and wicked. Do not become too angry, for anger can lead to murder. Do not be jealous or argumentative for murder comes from all these things as well. My child, do not lust, for lust leads to fornication. Do not use filthy language or gaze on others lustfully, for from all these things come adulteries. My child, do not investigate the occult or subscribe to the signs of astrology because these things lead to idolatry. My child, do not be a liar, for lying leads one to steal. Do not be envious or conceited, for these things also lead to stealing. My child, be not a complainer, since that leads to blasphemy; and do not be stubborn or evil-minded, because those things lead to blasphemy as well. But you be humble, for the meek shall inherit the earth. Be patient and compassionate, too, and blameless, and peaceable, and good, having respect always for this teaching (*didache*). Never exalt yourself or think more highly of yourself than you ought. Do not accompany the proud but prefer rather to walk with the meek and the righteous. Accept whatever happens to you for the best, knowing that nothing happens outside of the providence of God.

Chapter IV: Generosity

My child, remember always and with great respect those who teach you the Word of God; honor them as you honor the Lord, for where the teaching of the Lord is given, there is the Lord. Seek daily conversation with the saints that you may rest in their words. Despise divisions, but work peacefully among those who fight with one another. Judge righteously and do not show favoritism. Make a decision and stick with it, do not be double-minded. Don't be like those who are glad to receive but unwilling to give to those in need. If you have earnings, then by all means give something in redemption for your sins. Do not hesitate to give, and do not murmur when giving; for you know Who repays rewards. Do not neglect those who are in need, but willingly share everything with your brother as if your possessions were his; after all, if you share in what is imperishable, how much more should you share things that perish? Do not neglect your responsibilities toward your son or your daughter, but teach them to fear God from their earliest days. Do not treat your men and women servants too severely, who place their trust in the same God as you, lest they lose their respect of both God and you. When the Lord returns He will show no favoritism but will call those whom the Spirit has prepared. And you servants submit yourselves to your masters with reverence and fear, as you would God. Hate all hypocrisy and everything that is not pleasing to God. Never reject the commandments of the Lord but guard the teaching you have received, neither adding anything to them or reducing the importance of any one of them. Confess your sins in the church and do not come to prayer with unconfessed sin on your conscience for this is the path of life.

Chapter V: The path of death

Now the path of death is this: First of all, it is evil and full of cursing; in that path one finds murder, adultery, lust, fornication, stealing, idolatry, occult practices, witchcraft, larceny, lies, hypocrisy, double-mindedness, scheming, pride, hatred, arrogance, envy, filthy language, jealousy, and audacity. Also in that path are found those who persecute the good, who love to lie, not knowing the reward of righteousness, seeking neither the good nor righteous judgment, but the bad only. Those found in this way are far from meekness and patience; they love meaningless things and seek rewards for themselves while having no compassion on the needy, nor lifting a finger for those in trouble. Neither do they seek to know Him who made them; they are murderers of children, corrupters of God's image, oppressors, unjust judges who err in all things. From all these types, my children, may you be delivered!

PART II: CONCERNING CHURCH PRACTICES

Chapter VI: Meat sacrificed to idols

Let no one lead you away from the path of this teaching (*didache*); whoever attempts to do so is godless. For whoever would bear the entire yoke of the Lord would be perfect; but whoever cannot, must do as much as they are able. Concerning the eating of meat do what you must, but take care not to eat meat sacrificed to idols, for it is the worship of the infernal deities.

Chapter VII: Baptism

Baptize in this way: having first recited all these things [the preceding teachings], baptize "in the name of the Father, and of the Son, and of the Holy Spirit," in living water. However, if you have no living water, baptize in other water—preferably cold water, but a warm pond will do if no cold water is available. If neither pool nor living water is available, then pour water three times over the head, saying, "in the name of the Father, and of the Son, and of the Holy Spirit." Let the baptizer and the one being baptized fast before the baptism, and any others who are able. But require the one being baptized to fast one or two days before the baptism.

Chapter VIII: Fasting and prayer

When you fast, do not be like the hypocrites who fast on Mondays and Thursdays, but you fast on Wednesdays and Fridays. Do not pray as the hypocrites pray, but like the Lord commanded in His Gospel: "Our Father, who art in heaven, hallowed be Thy name, Thy kingdom come, Thy will be done as in heaven so also on earth. Give us this day our daily bread. And forgive us our debt as we also forgive our debtors. And lead us not into temptation, but deliver us from the Evil One, for Thine is the power and the glory, for ever." Pray this way three times a day.

Chapter IX: The Eucharist

Concerning the Eucharist, give thanks in prayer in this manner: First, concerning the cup. "We give thanks to Thee, our Father, for the holy vine of David Thy child, which Thou didst make known to us through Jesus, Thy child; to Thee be glory forever." And concerning the broken bread: "We give Thee thanks, our Father, for the life and knowledge which Thou didst make known to us through Jesus, Thy Child. To Thee be the glory forever. As this broken bread was scattered on the mountains, but was brought together and became one, so let Thy Church be gathered together from the ends of the earth unto Thy kingdom, for Thine is the glory and the power through Jesus Christ for ever." But let none eat or drink of Your Eucharist except those who have been baptized in the name of the Lord. For concerning this, too, the Lord said: "Do not give what is holy to the dogs."

Chapter X: Prayer after the Lord's Supper

After you are filled, give thanks in this manner: "We thank Thee, Holy Father, for Thy holy name which Thou didst make to dwell in our hearts, and for the knowledge and faith and immortality which Thou didst make known to us through Jesus Thy child; to Thee be the glory for ever. Thou Lord Almighty, didst create all things for Thy name's sake, and did give food and drink to all for their enjoyment, that they might give thanks to Thee, but us Thou hast blessed with spiritual food and drink, and eternal life through Thy Child. Above all we give thanks to Thee for Thou art mighty; to Thee be glory forever. Remember Thy Church, O Lord, to redeem it from every evil and to perfect it in Thy love, and gather it together in its holiness from the four winds to Thy kingdom for which Thou hast prepared it. For Thine is the power and the glory forever. Let grace come and let this world pass away. Hosanna to the God of David. Whoever is sanctified, let him come! Whoever is not, let him repent: Maranatha. Amen." But allow the prophets to conduct the Eucharist in their own way.

Chapter XI: Itinerate teachers

Welcome anyone who comes to you teaching these things. But do not listen to one who turns from this way to teach subversive things; listen only to those who come to add to your knowledge of the Lord and of righteousness, and receive them as the Lord. But concerning apostles and prophets, follow the Gospel guidelines: Let every apostle who comes to you be received as the Lord. Let him stay a day or two as needed; but if he wants to stay longer he is a false prophet. And when an apostle leaves, let him depart with nothing more than bread to keep him until he reaches his next destination; if he asks for money he is a false prophet. Do not test or examine any prophet who is speaking in a spirit, for every sin shall be forgiven except that. But not everyone who speaks in the spirit is a prophet, but only those whose actions are of the Lord; "By their fruit they shall be known," both the false and the true prophet. And no prophet who while in the spirit directs that a table be set for a meal should eat of it himself—if he does he is a false prophet. And every prophet who teaches the truth but fails to live it out is a false prophet. Every prophet who is approved and true, and who acts in the visible mystery of the Church, yet does not teach others to imitate his ways—he shall not be judged by you, for his judgment rests with God and this is how it was with the ancient prophets. But whoever says in a spirit, "give me money" or "give me this or that," do not listen to him; but if he asks you to give for the sake of others in need, then let no one judge him.

Chapter XII: Christian visitors

Anyone coming to you in the name of the Lord shall be received, but examine him so you may know his character, for you can judge right from wrong. If he is traveling help him as much as you are able, but let him stay no more than two days or if necessary three. Now if he wants to settle among you and is a craftsman by trade, let him work for his bread. But if he has no craft then provide work suited for him according to your best judgment, so that no one lives among you in idleness just because he is a Christian. If he is unwilling to accept the job you offer him then he is a slacker in Christ and you should stay away from him.

Chapter XIII: The first fruits are for true teachers and prophets

Now every true prophet who is willing to dwell among you is worthy of support. The same goes for a true teacher who like the workman is worthy of his hire. Therefore, take a portion of the first fruits of every harvest of the grapes, of the threshing-floor, and of the oxen and sheep, and give it to the prophets, for they are your chief priests. And if you have no prophet among you, then give it to the poor. If you make bread then take and give a portion of the first fruits as an offering as it is commanded. Likewise, whenever you open a new jar of wine or of oil, give some of it to the prophets. Take also a portion of the first fruits of any money, clothes, or all your possessions and give according to the commandment.

Chapter XIV: The Lord's Day

On the Lord's day, when you have assembled together, break the bread and hold the Eucharist, after confessing your transgressions, that your offering may be pure. Let no one who has a quarrel with his companion join with you in your meeting until they be reconciled, so that your sacrifice may not be corrupted, as the Lord said, "In every place and time offer unto Me a pure sacrifice, for I am a great King, and My name is wonderful among the Gentiles."

Chapter XV: Appoint leaders

Appoint for yourselves bishops (*episkopoi*) and deacons (*diakonoi*) who are worthy of the Lord, men who are meek and not lovers of money, truthful and approved, for they minister to you in the ministry of prophets and teachers. Therefore, do not despise them, for they are to be honored among you along with the prophets and teachers. Rebuke one another, not in your anger but peacefully, as the Gospel says; but do not fellowship with anyone who has wronged his neighbor, do not even listen to him until he repents. Pray, give, and do all according to the commandments given in the Gospel of our Lord.

Chapter XVI: Keep watch

Keep a close watch over your life; do not let your lamp go out and do not be found undressed, but be ready at all times for you do not know the hour in which our Lord comes. Gather together frequently for the building up of your souls; for your entire life of faith will do you little good unless you are found to be perfect in the last times. For in the last days there will be many false prophets and seducers; sheep will be turned into wolves, and love will be turned into hate. And as lawlessness abounds they will hate each other, and persecute each other, and deliver each other up; and then shall the Deceiver of the world appear as the Son of God, and shall do signs and wonders, and the earth shall be delivered into his hands; and he shall do unlawful things, such as have never happened since the beginning of the world. Then shall the creation of mankind come to the final tribulation; many will stumble and be lost but those who endure in their faith shall be saved by the curse itself. Next will appear signs of the truth: First, the sign displayed in the heavens; Second, the sound of the trumpet; and Third, the resurrection of the dead—though not of all the dead. And, as it is written, "The Lord shall come and all His saints with Him. . . . Then the world too will behold the Lord coming on the clouds of heaven."

TERTULLIAN: *ON BAPTISM* (EXCERPTS)
Latin, Late Second Century

Tertullian was born of pagan parents (A.D. 160) and converted as an adult (A.D. 197). A highly educated and gifted lawyer, Tertullian was one of the most able defenders of the Christian faith and the first to employ the Latin language, coining theological terms such as *sacramentum*, *trinitas*, and *persona* which became standard Christian vocabulary. In *On Baptism* (*De Baptismo*), Tertullian writes to counter the charges of a Gnostic sect that Christian baptism is powerless compared to pagan mystery rites. The following paraphrase is based on the translation of the Reverend Sydney Thelwall first published in 1869 and reprinted in the Ante-Nicene Fathers series, volume 4 (Grand Rapids: Eerdmans).

◆

Chapter I: Introduction

Blessed is our sacrament of water, in that, by washing away the sins of our early blindness, we are set free and admitted into eternal life! A treatise on this matter will not be superfluous; instructing not only those just becoming formed [in the faith], but also those who, content with having simply believed, without full examination of the grounds of the traditions, carry [in mind], through ignorance, an untried though probable faith. The consequence is, that a viper of the Cainite heresy, lately conversant in this quarter, has carried away a great number with her most venomous doctrine, making it her first aim to destroy baptism. Which is quite in accordance with nature; for vipers and asps themselves generally do affect arid and waterless places. But we, little fishes, after the example of our *Ichthus*, Jesus Christ, are born in water, nor have we safety in any other way than by permanently abiding in water; so that most monstrous creature, who had no right to teach even sound doctrine, knew full well how to kill the little fishes, by taking them away from the water!

Chapter II: The simplicity of God's means of working is a stumbling-block to the carnal mind

Well, but how great is the force of perversity for so shaking the faith or entirely preventing its reception, that it impugns it on the very principles of which the faith consists! There is absolutely nothing which makes men's minds more obdurate than the simplicity of the divine works which are visible in the act, when compared with the grandeur which is promised thereto in the effect; so that from the very fact, that with so great simplicity, without pomp, without any considerable novelty of preparation, finally, without expense, a man is dipped in water, and amid the utterance of some few words, is sprinkled, and then rises again, not much [or not at all] the cleaner, the consequent attainment of eternity is esteemed the more incredible. I am a deceiver if, on the contrary, it is not from their circumstance, and preparation, and expense, that idols' solemnities or mysteries get their credit and authority built up.

Oh, miserable incredulity, which quite denies to God His own properties, simplicity and power! What, then? Is it not wonderful, too, that death should be washed away by bathing? But it is the more to be believed if the wonderfulness be the reason why it is not believed. For what must divine works be in their quality, but above all wonder? We also ourselves wonder, but it is because we believe. Incredulity, on the other hand, wonders, but does not believe: for the simple acts it wonders at, as if they were vain; the grand results, as if they were impos-

sible. And grant that it be just as you think sufficient to meet each point in the divine declaration, "The foolish things of the world hath God elected to confound its wisdom," and "The things very difficult with men are easy with God." For if God is wise and powerful (which even they who pass Him by do not deny), it is with good reason that He lays the material causes of His own operation in the contraries of wisdom and of power, that is, in foolishness and impossibility; since every virtue receives its cause from those things by which it is called forth.

Chapter III: Water is prominent in all creation and was chosen for divine use in the sacrament

Mindful of this declaration as of a conclusive prescript, we nevertheless proceed to treat the question, "How foolish and impossible it is to be formed anew by water. In what respect, pray, has this material substance merited an office of so high dignity?" The authority, I suppose, of the liquid element has to be examined. This however, is found in abundance, and that from the very beginning. For water is one of those things which, before all the furnishing of the world, was quiescent with God in a yet unformed state. "In the first beginning," says Scripture, "God made the heaven and the earth. But the earth was invisible, and unorganized, and darkness was over the abyss; and the Spirit of the Lord was hovering over the waters." The first thing, O man, which you have to venerate, is the age of the waters in that their substance is ancient; the second, their dignity, in that they were the seat of the Divine Spirit, more pleasing to Him, no doubt, than all the other then existing elements. For the darkness was total thus far, shapeless, without the ornament of stars; and the abyss gloomy; and the earth unfurnished; and the heaven unwrought: water alone—always a perfect, delightful, simple material substance, pure in itself—supplied a worthy vehicle to God. What of the fact that waters were in some way the regulating powers by which the disposition of the world thenceforward was constituted by God? For the suspension of the celestial firmament in the midst He caused by "dividing the waters"; the suspension of "the dry land" He accomplished by "separating the waters." After the world had been hereupon set in order through its elements, when inhabitants were given it, "the waters" were the first to receive the precept "to bring forth living creatures." Water was the first to produce that which had life, that it might be no wonder in baptism if waters know how to give life. For was not the work of fashioning man himself also achieved with the aid of waters? Suitable material is found in the earth, yet not apt for the purpose unless it be moist and juicy; which (earth) "the waters," separated the fourth day before into their own place, temper with their remaining moisture to a clay consistency. If, from that time onward, I go forward in recounting universally, or at more length, the evidences of the "authority" of this element which I can adduce to show how great is its power or its grace; how many ingenious devices, how many functions, how useful an instrumentality, it affords the world, I fear I may seem to have collected rather the praises of water than the reasons of baptism; although I should thereby teach all the more fully, that it is not to be doubted that God has made the material substance which He has disposed throughout all His products and works, obey Him also in His own peculiar sacraments; that the material substance which governs terrestrial life acts as agent likewise in the celestial.

Chapter IV: The hovering of the Spirit of God over the waters typified baptism

But it will suffice to have thus called at the outset those points in which withal is recognized that primary principle of baptism—which was even then fore-noted by the very attitude assumed for a type of baptism—that the Spirit of God, who hovered over [the waters] from the beginning, would continue to linger over the waters of the baptized. But a holy thing, of course, hovered over a holy; or else, from that which hovered over that which was hovered over borrowed a holiness, since it is necessary that in every case an underlying material substance should catch the quality of that which overhangs it, most of all a corporeal of a spiritual, adapted [as the spiritual is] through the subtleness of its substance, both for penetrating and insinuating. Thus the nature of the waters, sanctified by the Holy One, itself conceived withal the power of sanctifying. Let no one say, "Why then, are we, pray, baptized with the very waters which then existed in the first beginning?" Not with those waters, of course, except in so far as the genus indeed is one, but the species very many. But what is an attribute to the genus reappears likewise in the species. And accordingly it makes no difference whether a man be washed in a sea or a pool, a stream or a fount, a lake or a trough; nor is there any distinction between those whom John baptized in the Jordan and those whom Peter baptized in the Tiber, unless withal the eunuch whom Philip baptized in the midst of his journeys with chance water, derived [therefrom] more or less of salvation than others. All waters, therefore, in virtue of the pristine privilege of their origin, do, after invocation of God, attain the sacramental power of sanctification; for the Spirit immediately supervenes from the heavens, and rests over the waters, sanctifying them from Himself; and being thus sanctified, they imbibe at the same time the power of sanctifying. Albeit the similitude may be admitted to be suitable to the simple act; that, since we are defiled by sins, as it were by dirt, we should be washed from those stains in waters. But as sins do not show themselves in our flesh [inasmuch as no one carries on his skin the spot of idolatry, or fornication, or fraud], so persons of that kind are foul in the spirit, which is the author of the sin; for the spirit is lord, the flesh servant. Yet they each mutually share the guilt: the spirit, on the ground of command; the flesh, of subservience. Therefore, after the waters have been in a manner endued with medicinal virtue through the intervention of the angel, the spirit is bodily washed in the waters, and the flesh is in the same spiritually cleansed.

Chapter V: The use made of water by the heathen and the type of the angel at the pool of Bethsaida

"Well, but the nations, who are strangers to all understanding of spiritual powers, ascribe to their idols the imbuing of waters with the self-same efficacy." [So they do] but they cheat themselves with waters which are widowed. For washing is the channel through which they are initiated into some sacred rites—of some notorious Isis or Mithras. The gods themselves likewise they honor by washings. Moreover, by carrying water around, and sprinkling it, they everywhere expiate country-seats, houses, temples, and whole cities: at all events, at the Apollinarian and Eleusinian games they are baptized; and they presume that the effect of their doing that is their regeneration and the remission of the penalties due to their perjuries. Among the ancients, again, whoever had defiled himself with murder, was wont to go in quest of purifying waters. Therefore, if the mere nature of water, in that it is the appropriate material for washing away, leads men to flatter themselves with a belief in omens of purification, how much more truly will waters render that service through the authority of God, by whom all their nature has been constituted! If men think that water is endued with a medicinal virtue by religion, what religion is more effectual than that of the living God? Which fact being acknowledged, we recognize here also the zeal of the devil rivaling the things of God, while we find him, too, practicing baptism in his subjects. What similarity is there? The unclean cleanses! The ruiner sets free! The damned absolves! He will, indeed, destroy his own work, by washing away the sins which himself inspires! These [remarks] have been set down by way of testimony against such as reject the faith; if they put no trust in the things of God, the spurious imitations of which, in the case of God's rival, they do trust in. Are there not other cases too, in which, without any sacrament, unclean spirits brood on waters, in spurious imitation of that brooding of the Divine Spirit in the very beginning? Witness all shady founts, and all unfrequented brooks, and the ponds in the baths, and the conduits in private houses, or the cisterns and wells which are said to have the property of "spiriting away," through the power, that is, of a hurtful spirit. Men whom waters have drowned or affected with madness or with fear, they call nymph-caught, or "lymphatic," or "hydro-phobic." Why have we adduced these instances? Lest any think it too hard for belief that a holy angel of God should grant his presence to waters, to temper them to man's salvation; while the evil angel holds frequent profane commerce with the selfsame element to man's ruin. If it seems a novelty for an angel to be present in waters, an example of what was to come to pass has forerun. An angel, by his intervention, was wont to stir the pool at Bethsaida. They who were complaining of ill-health used to watch for him; for whoever had been the first to descend into them, after his washing, ceased to complain. This figure of corporeal healing sang of a spiritual healing, according to the rule by which things carnal are always antecedent as figurative of things spiritual. And thus, when the grace of God advanced to higher degrees among men, an accession of efficacy was granted to the waters and to the angel. They who were wont to remedy bodily defects, now heal the spirit; they who used to work temporal salvation now renew eternal; they who did set free only once a year, now save peoples in a body daily, death being done away through ablution of sins. The guilt being removed, of course the penalty is removed too. Thus man will be restored for God to His "likeness," who in days bygone had been conformed to "the image" of God [the "image" is counted (to be) in his form: the "likeness" in his eternity]; for he receives again that Spirit of God which he had then first received from His afflatus, but had afterward lost through sin.

Chapter VI: The meaning of the baptismal formula

Not that in the waters we obtain the Holy Spirit; but in the water, under [the witness of] the angel, we are cleansed, and prepared for the Holy Spirit. In this case also a type has preceded; for thus was John beforehand the Lord's forerunner, "preparing His ways." Thus, too, does the angel, the witness of baptism, "make the paths straight" for the Holy Spirit, who is about to come upon us, by the washing away of sins, which faith, sealed in [the name of] the Father, and the Son, and the Holy Spirit, obtains. For if "in the mouth of three witnesses every word shall stand": while, through the benediction, we have the same [three] as witnesses of our faith whom we have as sureties of our salvation too—how much more does the number of the divine names suffice for the assurance of our hope likewise! Moreover, after the pledging both of the attestation of faith and the promise of salvation under "three witnesses," there is added, of necessity, mention of the Church; inasmuch as, wherever there are three [that is, the Father, the Son, and the Holy Spirit], there is the Church, which is a body of three.

Chapter VII: The unction

After this, when we have issued from the font, we are thoroughly anointed with a blessed unction—[a practice derived] from the old discipline, wherein on entering the priesthood, men were anointed with oil from a horn, ever since Aaron was anointed by Moses. Whence Aaron is called "Christ," from the "chrism," which is "the unction"; which, when made spiritual, furnished an appropriate name to the Lord, because He was "anointed" with the Spirit by God the Father; as written in the Acts: "For truly they were gathered together in this city against Thy Holy Son whom Thou hast anointed." Thus, too, in our case, the unction runs carnally [i.e., on the body], but profits spiritually; in the same way as the act of baptism itself too is carnal, in that we are plunged in water, but the effect spiritual, in that we are freed from sins.

Chapter VIII: The laying on of hands, types of the flood, and the dove

In the next place the hand is laid on us, invoking and inviting the Holy Spirit through benediction. Shall it be granted possible for human ingenuity to summon a spirit into water, and, by the application of hands from above, to animate their union into one body with another spirit of so clear sound; and shall it not be possible for God, in the case of His own organ, to produce, by means of "holy hands," a sublime spiritual modulation? But this, as well as the former, is derived from the old sacramental rite in which Jacob blessed his grandsons, born of Joseph, Ephraim and Manasseh; with his hands laid on them and interchanged, and indeed so transversely slanted one over the other, that, by delineating Christ, they even portended the future benediction into Christ. Then, over our cleansed and blessed bodies willingly descends from the Father that Holiest Spirit. Over the waters of baptism, recognizing as it were His primeval seat, He reposes: [He who] glided down on the Lord "in the shape of a dove," in order that the nature of the Holy Spirit might be declared by means of the creature [the emblem] of simplicity and innocence, because even in her bodily structure the dove is without literal gall. And accordingly He says, "Be simple as doves." Even this is not without the supporting evidence of a preceding figure. For just as, after the waters of the deluge, by which the old iniquity was purged-after the baptism, so to say, of the world—a dove was the herald which announced to the earth the assuagement of celestial wrath, when she had been sent her way out of the ark, and had returned with the olive branch, a sign which even among the nations is the foretoken of peace; so by the selfsame law of heavenly effect, to earth—that is, to our flesh—as it emerges from the font, after its old sins flies the dove of the Holy Spirit, bringing us the peace of God, sent out from the heavens where is the Church, the typified ark. But the world returned unto sin; in which point baptism would ill be compared to the deluge. And so it is destined to fire; just as the man too is, who after baptism renews his sins: so that this also ought to be accepted as a sign for our admonition.

Chapter IX: The Red Sea and water from the rock

How many, therefore, are the pleas of nature, how many the privileges of grace, how many the solemnities of discipline, the figures, the preparations, the prayers, which have ordained the sanctity of water? First, indeed, when the people, set unconditionally free, escaped the violence of the Egyptian king by crossing over through water, it was water that extinguished the king himself, with his entire forces. What figure more manifestly fulfilled in the sacrament of baptism? The nations are set free from the world by means of water, to wit: and the devil, their old tyrant, they leave quite behind, overwhelmed in the water. Again, water is restored from its defect of "bitterness" to its native grace of "sweetness" by the tree of Moses. That tree was Christ, restoring, to wit, of Himself, the veins of sometime envenomed and bitter nature into the all-salutary waters of baptism. This is the water which flowed continuously down for the people from the "accompanying rock"; for if Christ is "the Rock," without doubt we see baptism blest by the water in Christ. How mighty is the grace of water, in the sight of God and His Christ, for the confirmation of baptism! Never is Christ without water: if, that is, He is Himself baptized in water; inaugurates in water the first rudimentary displays of His power, when invited to the nuptials; invites the thirsty, when He makes a discourse, to His own water; approves, when teaching concerning love, among works of charity, the cup of water offered to a poor [child]; recruits His strength at a well; walks over the water; willingly crosses the sea; ministers water to His disciples. Onward even to the passion does the witness of baptism last: while He is being surrendered to the cross, water intervenes; witness Pilate's hands: when He is wounded, forth from His side bursts water; witness the soldier's lance!

Chapter XV: Unity of baptism and heretical baptism

There is to us one, and but one, baptism; as well according to the Lord's gospel as according to the Apostle's letters, inasmuch as he says, "One God, and one baptism, and one church in the heavens." But it must be admitted that the question, "What rules are to be observed with regard to heretics?" is worthy of being treated. For it is to us that that assertion refers. Heretics, however, have no fellowship in our discipline, whom the mere fact of their excommunication testifies to be outsiders. I am not bound to recognize in them a thing which is enjoined on me, because they and we have not the same God, nor one—that is, the same—Christ. And therefore their baptism is not one with ours either, because it is not the same; a baptism which, since they have it not duly, doubtless they have not at all; nor is that capable of being counted which is not had. Thus they cannot receive it either, because they have it not. But this point has already received a fuller discussion from us in Greek. We enter, then, the font once: once are sins washed away, because they ought never to be repeated. But the Jewish Israel bathes daily, because he is daily being defiled: and, for fear that defilement should be practiced among us also, therefore was the definition touching the one bathing made. Happy water, which once washes away; which does not mock sinners [with vain hopes]; which does not, by being infected with the repetition of impurities, again defile them whom it has washed!

Chapter XVI: The second baptism—of blood

We have indeed, likewise, a second font, of blood, concerning which the Lord said, "I have to be baptized with a baptism," when He had been baptized already. For He had come "by means of water and blood," just as John has written; that He might be baptized by the water, glorified by the blood; to make us, in like manner, called by water, chosen by blood. These two baptisms He sent out from the wound in His pierced side, in order that they who believed in His blood might be bathed with the water; they who had been bathed in the water might likewise drink the blood. This is the baptism which both stands in place of the fontal bathing when that has not been received, and restores it when lost.

Chapter XVII: The power of conferring baptism

For concluding our brief subject, it remains to put you in mind also of the due observance of giving and receiving baptism. Of giving it, the chief priest [who is the bishop] has the right: in the next place, the presbyters and deacons, yet not without the bishop's authority, on account of the honor of the Church, which being preserved, peace is preserved. Beside these, even laymen have the right; for what is equally received can be equally given. Unless bishops, or priests, or deacons, be on the spot, other disciples are called, i.e., to the work. The word of the Lord ought not to be hidden by any: in like manner, too, baptism, which is equally God's property, can be administered by all. But how much more is the rule of reverence and modesty incumbent on laymen—seeing that these powers belong to their superiors—lest

they assume to themselves the specific function of the bishop! Emulation of the Episcopal office is the mother of schisms. The most holy Apostle has said, that "all things are lawful, but not all expedient." Let it suffice, in cases of necessity, to avail yourself of that rule, for then the courage of the helper, when the situation of the endangered one is urgent, is exceptionally admissible; inasmuch as he will be guilty of a human creature's loss if he shall refrain from bestowing what he had free liberty to bestow. But the woman of pertness, who has usurped the power to teach, will of course not give birth for herself likewise to a right of baptizing, unless some new beast shall arise like the former; so that, just as the one abolished baptism, so some other should in her own right confer it! But if the writings which wrongly go under Paul's name, claim Thecla's example as a license for women's teaching and baptizing, let them know that, in Asia, the presbyter who composed that writing, as if he were augmenting Paul's fame from his own store, after being convicted, and confessing that he had done it from love of Paul, was removed from his office. For how credible would it seem, that he who has not permitted a woman even to learn with over-boldness, should give a female the power of teaching and of baptizing! "Let them be silent," he says, "and at home consult their own husbands."

Chapter XVIII: Who is to receive baptism and when

But they whose office it is, know that baptism is not rashly to be administered. "Give to every one who asks thee," has a reference of its own, appertaining especially to almsgiving. On the contrary, this precept is rather to be looked at carefully: "Give not the holy thing to the dogs, nor cast your pearls before swine"; and, "Lay not hands easily on any; share not other men's sins." If Philip so "easily" baptized the Ethiopian Official, let us reflect that a manifest and conspicuous evidence that the Lord deemed him worthy had been interposed. The Spirit had enjoined Philip to proceed to that road: the eunuch himself, too, was not found idle, nor as one who was suddenly seized with an eager desire to be baptized; but, after going up to the temple for prayer's sake, being intently engaged on the divine Scripture, was thus suitably discovered—to whom God had, unasked, sent an apostle, which one, again, the Spirit bade adjoin himself to the chamberlain's chariot. The Scripture which he was reading falls in opportunely with his faith: Philip, being requested, is taken to sit beside him; the Lord is pointed out; faith lingers not; water needs no waiting for; the work is completed, and the apostle snatched away. "But Paul too was, in fact, 'speedily' baptized": for Simon, his host, speedily recognized him to be "an appointed vessel of election." God's approbation sends sure premonitory tokens before it; every "petition" may both deceive and be deceived. And so, according to the circumstances and disposition, and even age, of each individual, the delay of baptism is preferable; principally, however, in the case of little children. For why is it necessary—if [baptism itself] is not so necessary—that the sponsors likewise should be thrust into danger? Who both themselves, by reason of mortality, may fail to fulfill their promises, and may be disappointed by the development of an evil disposition, in those for whom they stood? The Lord does indeed say, "Forbid them not to come unto me." Let them "come," then, while they are growing up; let them "come" while they are learning, while they are learning whither to come; let them become Christians when they have become able to know Christ. Why does the innocent period of life hasten to the "remission of sins?" More caution will be exercised in worldly matters: so that one who is not trusted with earthly substance is trusted with divine! Let them know how to "ask" for salvation, that you may seem [at least] to have given "to him that asks." For no less cause must the unwedded also be deferred—in whom the ground of temptation is prepared, alike in such as never were wedded by means of their maturity, and in the widowed by means of their freedom—until they either marry, or else be more fully strengthened for continence. If any understand the weighty import of baptism, they will fear its reception more than its delay: sound faith is secure of salvation.

Chapter XIX: Suitable times for baptism

The Passover affords a more than usually solemn day for baptism; when, withal, the Lord's passion, in which we are baptized, was completed. Nor will it be incongruous to interpret figuratively the fact that, when the Lord was about to celebrate the last Passover, He said to the disciples who were sent to make preparation, "You will meet a man bearing water." He points out the place for celebrating the Passover by the sign of water. After that, Pentecost is a most joyous space for conferring baptisms; wherein, too, the resurrection of the Lord was repeatedly proved among the disciples, and the hope of the advent of the Lord indirectly pointed to, in that, at that time, when He had been received back into the heavens, the angels told the Apostles that "He would so come, as He had withal ascended into the heavens"; at Pentecost, of course. But, moreover, when Jeremiah says, "And I will gather them together from the extremities of the land in the feast day," he signifies the day of the Passover and of Pentecost, which is properly a "feast day." However, every day is the Lord's; every hour, every time, is apt for baptism: if there is a difference in the solemnity, distinction there is none in the grace.

Chapter XX: Preparation for, and conduct following, baptism

They who are about to enter baptism ought to pray with repeated prayers, fasts, and bendings of the knee, and vigils all the night through, and with the confession of all bygone sins, that they may express the meaning even of the baptism of John: "They were baptized," says [the Scripture], "confessing their own sins." To us it is matter for thankfulness if we do now publicly confess our iniquities or our turpitudes: for we do at the same time both make satisfaction for our former sins, by mortification of our flesh and spirit, and lay beforehand the foundation of defenses against the temptations which will closely follow. "Watch and pray," says [the Lord], "lest you fall into temptation." And the reason, I believe, why they were tempted was, that they fell asleep; so that they deserted the Lord when apprehended, and he who continued to stand by Him, and used the sword, even denied Him thrice: for withal the word had gone before, that "no one untested should attain the celestial kingdoms." The Lord Himself forthwith after baptism temptations surrounded, when in forty days He had kept fast. "Then," someone will say," it becomes us, too, rather to fast after baptism." Well, and who forbids you, unless it be the necessity for joy, and the thanksgiving for salvation? But so far as I, with my poor powers, understand, the Lord figuratively retorted upon Israel the reproach they had cast on the Lord. For the people, after crossing the sea, and being carried about in the desert during forty years, although they were there nourished with divine supplies, nevertheless were more mindful of their belly and their gullet than of God. Thereupon the Lord, driven apart into desert places after baptism, showed, by maintaining a fast of forty days, that the man of God lives "not by bread alone," but "by the word of God"; and that temptations incident to fullness or immoderation of appetite are shattered by abstinence. Therefore, blessed ones, whom the grace of God awaits, when you ascend from that most sacred font of your new birth, and spread your hands for the first time in the house of your mother, together with your brethren, ask from the Father, ask from the Lord, that His own specialties of grace and distributions of gifts may be supplied you. "Ask," says He, "and You shall receive." Well, you have asked, and have received; you have knocked, and it has been opened to you. Only, I pray that, when you are asking, you be mindful likewise of Tertullian the sinner.

HIPPOLYTUS: "TEACHING ON BAPTISM AND CHRISMATION"
Greek, Early Third Century A.D.

Hippolytus (A.D. 170–253) was a presbyter (elder) in the church at Rome. Already by the late second century A.D., baptism had become a somewhat elaborate ritual, and was preceded by a lengthy *catechesis*—a procedure designed to prepare and test those desiring to join the church. The principles outlined here were for admission to the *catechumenate*; that is, to the class of candidates preparing for baptism. *Chrismation* refers to the anointing with oil of the newly baptized by the elders of the church and symbolized infilling by the Holy Spirit. Only those who successfully completed the catechesis and baptism were invited to participate in the Lord's Supper.

Questions for Guided Reading

1. What terms are used for *learning* and *learner* in this text?
2. What sorts of questions were asked of those seeking baptism?
3. According to this particular document, how long was the period of hearing (inquiry and testing) prior to baptism? Was this length of time mandated (with no exceptions)?
4. Explain the threefold baptismal process described here.
5. What ceremony happens after baptism and what is its significance?
6. How do the baptismal themes and ceremonies described here compare with those you have experienced?

Newcomers to the Faith

Those who present themselves for the first time to hear the word shall first of all be brought to the teachers before the congregation arrives. They shall be asked about the reason for coming to the faith, and those who have brought them [i.e., their sponsors] will testify about whether they are "capable of hearing the word." Each shall be asked about the kind of life he leads: whether he has a wife or whether he is a slave. And if a slave, then is he the slave of one of the faithful, and whether he has his master's approval for taking hearing. If his master does not testify that he is a good man, let him be rejected. If his master is a pagan, teach him to please his master lest scandal arise. If, however, one of the candidates has a wife, or a wife has a husband, let them be taught to be content, husband with wife and wife with husband. If however, someone does not have a wife, let him be taught not to fornicate but to take a wife according to the law, or to remain as he is [i.e., single]. Should someone be possessed of a demon, he is not to be instructed in the teaching until he is pure.

Unacceptable Occupations and Professions

Moreover, inquiry shall be made about the jobs and occupations of those seeking to be instructed. If anyone runs a house of prostitution, let him cease or be sent away. If anyone is a sculptor or paints let him be taught not to make idols: let him either cease or repent. If anyone is an actor or is engaged in theatrical presentations, let him cease or be rejected. As for him who teaches children, it is best that he cease, yet if he has no skill, let him be allowed to continue. Likewise, the charioteer who competes in the games and those who take part in them, let them cease or be rejected. The gladiator, or one who trains gladiators to fight, or one who engages in the arena hunt, or any official in the gladiatorial enterprise, let him cease or be rejected. He who is a priest of idols, or an idol attendant, let him cease or be rejected. A military man shall not kill anyone. If he is ordered to, he shall not carry out the order, nor shall he take the [military] oath. He who has the power of the sword [i.e., to execute] or the city magistrate who wears the purple, let him cease or be rejected. A catechumen, or one of the faithful who wants to become a soldier, let them be rejected, because they have shown contempt for God. The prostitute, or the profligate, or the eunuch, or one who does unspeakable things, let them be rejected; they are impure. A magician is not to be brought to the inquiry. The maker of charms, or the astrologer, or the diviner, or the interpreter of dreams, or the charlatan, or the fringe-cutter, or the phylactery-maker, let them either cease or be rejected. Someone who is a concubine, if she is a slave and if she brings up her children, remaining faithfully to one man, let her hear the word; otherwise let her be sent away. The man who has a concubine, let him cease and take a wife according to the law; if, however, he refuses, let him be rejected. If we have omitted anything, the occupations [in question] will instruct you; for all of us have the Spirit of God.

Length of the Catechesis

Catechumens will be under the hearing [i.e., instruction] for a period of three years. If anyone is zealous and applies himself, it is not the period of time but the evidence of conversion that shall be judged.

Prayer and Baptism

When the teacher has finished his instruction [for the day], the catechumens should pray apart from the faithful [i.e., full church members]. The women—whether catechumens or faithful—should stand and pray together in a specially designated place in the church. And when the catechumens have finished praying, they are not to offer one another the kiss of peace, because their mouths are not [yet] holy. The faithful, however, will greet each other in this way: men greeting men and women greeting women; the men will not greet the women. Moreover, let the women cover their heads with a mantle, and not just with linen, for that is not a veil. When he who is to be baptized goes down to the water, let him who baptizes lay hands on him and ask, "Do you believe in God the Father Almighty?" And he who is being baptized will say, "I believe." Then let him be baptized once, with hands laid on his head. Next let him ask, "Do you believe in Jesus Christ, the Son of God, Who was born of the Holy Spirit and the Virgin Mary, was crucified in the days of Pontius Pilate, and Who died and was buried; And He rose the third day living from the dead and ascended into heaven; And sat down at the right hand of the Father; And will come to judge the living and the dead?" And when he says, "I believe," let him baptized a second time. And finally let him ask, "Do you believe in the Holy Spirit in the Holy Church and the resurrection of the flesh?" And he who is being baptized will say, "I believe." And so let him baptize him the third time. And afterward when he comes up from the water, he shall be anointed by the presbyter with the Oil of Thanksgiving saying, "I anoint thee with holy oil in the Name of Jesus Christ." And so each one drying himself with a towel, they shall now put on their clothes, and after this let them be together in the assembly [Church]. Then the Bishop will lay his hand on them, invoking and saying, "Lord God, who deems these your servants worthy of the forgiveness of sins by the bath of regeneration, make them worthy to be filled with your Holy Spirit and send upon them your grace, that they may serve you according to your will; for to you is the glory, to the Father and to the Son with the Holy Ghost in the Holy Church, both now and ever and world without end. Amen." After this, pouring the consecrated oil from his hand and laying his hand on his head, he shall say, "I anoint thee with holy oil in the name of God the Father Almighty and Christ Jesus and the Holy Spirit." And sealing him on the forehead, he shall give him the kiss of peace and say, "The Lord be with you." And he who has been sealed will say, "And with your spirit."

And so on for each one. From then on they will pray together with all the people. But they are not to pray with the faithful until they have undergone all these things. And after the prayers, let them give the kiss of peace.

EUSEBIUS AND ATHANASIUS: EARLY CANON LISTS
Greek, Fourth Century A.D.

At least two important factors contributed to the formal selection of books to be included in the canon of Holy

Scripture. First, some books, such as the *Wisdom of Solomon* and *Ecclesiasticus* (not to be confused with *Ecclesiastes*), were included in the Old Testament by Greek-speaking Jews but rejected by other Jews. During the first three centuries of the church these works were accepted as Scripture, but when in the fourth century the Bible scholar Jerome labeled them "apocrypha" (*hidden* or *excluded*) this signaled a decline in their use as Scripture.[1] Second, some early heresies were based on a rejection of portions of Scripture. Marcion, for example, rejected the entire Old Testament and accepted only Luke's Gospel and Paul's letters from the New. Therefore, it became necessary for church leaders to declare which books should be accepted as the authoritative word of God. As is evident from the lists quoted here, some of the general epistles and Revelation were slow to gain acceptance as Scripture. Thus the canon (which refers both to the list of books included in Scripture and the books themselves) was "born." In fact, however, earlier (partial) lists of accepted books have come to light (the Muratorian Canon, the Canon of Origen, etc.), most containing at least the names of the four Gospels, Acts, and Paul's letters.[2]

> ## Questions for Guided Reading
> 1. Define canon and apocrypha.
> 2. What are Eusebius's three lists and which books are included in each?
> 3. How do the lists of Eusebius and Athanasius compare?

♦

FROM THE CHURCH HISTORY OF EUSEBIUS (3.25.1–7)

It is reasonable to sum up . . . the writings of the New Testament. Indeed the holy *quatern* of the Gospels must be arranged among the first [books] which the book of the Acts of the Apostles follows. After this the Epistles of Paul must be enumerated, following which the extant former Epistle of John and likewise the Epistle of Peter

must be pronounced authoritative. To these must be added, if it would seem [permissible], the Apocalypse of John. These, then are among the recognized [writings].

Those (books) that are questioned but familiar to many, include the epistles known as James, Jude, second Peter and those called second and third John, whether they are written by the Evangelist or another of the same name.

Among the rejected books must be placed the books of The Acts of Paul, the Shepherd, and The Apocalypse of Peter, the epistle of Barnabas, and the Teaching of the Apostles (*Didache*), and the Apocalypse of John which, as I have said, some reject but others accept. Moreover, although some would include the Gospel according to the Hebrews in the list (a book in which Hebrew Christians rejoice) it too should be considered rejected. So, then, we have a list of writings which, according to church tradition, are to be acknowledged as true and genuine (Scripture), and a separate list of those not in the canon (because) they are disputed but still recognized by most Christians. These lists are necessary and must not be confused with writings produced by heretics in the name of the Apostles, such as the Gospels of Peter and Thomas and Matthias, the Acts of Andrew and John and the other Apostles; none of which were ever deemed worthy. Indeed their style of writing clearly distinguishes them from the apostolic style and their thought and choice of quotation is absolutely out of harmony with true orthodoxy, and this confirms that they are forgeries of heretical men, and must be denounced as altogether foul and impious.

FROM THE THIRTY-NINTH EASTER LETTER OF ATHANASIUS

There must be no hesitation to state . . . the [books] of the New Testament; for they are these: Four Gospels: according to Matthew, according to Mark, according to Luke, and according to John. Further, after these, also the Acts of the Apostles, and the seven so-called catholic epistles of the Apostles, as follows: One of James, but two of Peter, then, three of John, and after these, one of Jude. In addition to these there are fourteen Epistles of the Apostle Paul put down in the following order: The first to the Romans, then two to the Corinthians, and after these, [the Epistles] to the Galatians, and then to the Ephesians; further, [the Epistles] to Philippians and

---

1. E. A. Livingston, ed., *The Oxford Dictionary of the Christian Church*, 3rd ed. (Oxford: Oxford University Press, 1997), 84.
2. These can be viewed online at http://www.bible-researcher.com/canon8.html. Daniel J. Theron's *Evidence of Tradition* (first published in 1957 and reprinted by Baker in 1980) offers a complete survey of canon lists.

to the Colossians and two to the Thessalonians, and the [Epistle] to the Hebrews. And next two [letters] to Timothy, but one to Titus, and the last [being] the one to Philemon. Moreover, also the Apocalypse of John.

Of necessity I add this for the sake of completeness, that there are other books besides these, which although not canonized, were recommended by the Fathers to be read by the novices and by those who desire to be instructed in the learning of piety: The Wisdom of Solomon, and the Wisdom of Sirach, and Esther, and Judith, and Tobit, and the so-called Teaching of the Apostles [*Didache*], and The Shepherd. And, beloved, the former being canonized and the later being read, nevertheless there is no mention of the apocrypha,[3] but they are a device of the heretics, [who], writing them when they desire, approve them and assign [early] dates to them so that, presenting [them] as ancient, they may have a pretense to lead astray the simple by these [writings].

CYRIL OF JERUSALEM: "CATECHETICAL LECTURES" (EXCERPT)
Greek, Mid Fourth Century A.D.

It has long been my wish, true-born and long-desired children of the church, to discourse to you upon these spiritual, heavenly mysteries.

—Cyril

Cyril, Bishop of Jerusalem from A.D. 349 to 389, composed a series of catechetical lectures especially for pilgrims traveling to Jerusalem for "hearing" and baptism. These lectures include an introductory sermon, eighteen "hearings" delivered during the season of Lent (the forty days preceding Easter) to those who were preparing for baptism, and five *mystagogical* hearings offered during Easter week to the same persons after their baptism. The *mystagogical* catechesis explained the renunciation of Satan (which preceded baptism) as well as the importance and effects of baptism, confirmation, and communion. The guarded approach to initiation into the church via this instruction is indicated by the fact that hearers are instructed to repeat nothing of what they have heard to unbelievers or new initiates. As written, these lectures served as authoritative commentary on the baptismal liturgy, and may have become a model catechetical instruction for those living far from Jerusalem.

Questions for Guided Reading

1. What are some benefits and some symbolic references of baptism mentioned here?
2. Why, according to Cyril, are these truths necessary?
3. Why are some catechetical lectures delayed until after baptism?
4. Describe the first step in this process (changes in directions, the renunciation of Satan, etc.).
5. Describe the second step in the baptismal process (moving to another building, disrobing, immersion, etc.). What do each of the steps signify?
6. What role and significance does *chrismation* play in baptism? Is this a biblical practice?

Procatechesis (Sermon Preceding the Catechism)

Great indeed is the baptism offered to you. It is a ransom to captives; the remission of offences; the death of sin; the regeneration of the soul; the garment of light; the holy seal indissoluble; the chariot to heaven; the luxury of paradise; a procuring of the kingdom; the gift of adoption. But a serpent by the wayside is watching the passengers; beware lest he bite you with unbelief; he sees so many receiving salvation, and seeks to devour some of them. You are going to the Father of Spirits, but you are going past that serpent; how then must you pass him? Have your feet shod with the preparation of the gospel of peace; that even if he bite, he may not hurt you. Having faith indwelling, strong hope, a sandal of power, with which to pass the enemy, and enter the presence of your Lord. Prepare your own heart to receive doctrine, to have fellowship in holy mysteries. Pray more often, that

---

3. *Apocrypha* originally meant *concealed* or *hidden* books but in Christian usage came to refer to those books excluded from the official canon of Scripture. Athanasius does not name those books he considers apocryphal, but very likely some are found in the list of spurious works mentioned in the canon list of Eusebius (e.g., the Gospel of Thomas). In fact, works that are on Athanasius's "recommended reading list" (e.g., Judith) are now called apocryphal by Protestants, though Catholics still include seven of these books in their canon of Scripture.

God may make you worthy of the heavenly and immortal mysteries. Let neither day be without its work, nor night, but when sleep fails your eyes, at once abandon your thoughts to prayer. And should any crude imagination arise in your thoughts, reflect on God's judgment, to remind you of salvation; give up your mind to sacred studies, that it may forget wicked things. If anyone may say to you, "Why are you going to be baptized when the city has baths?" Be aware that he is the dragon who is plotting against you; pay no attention to him, but to God who is doing the work. Guard your own soul, so that you may escape the snare, and so that abiding in hope, you may become heir of everlasting salvation. . . .

Baptismal Catechesis I: Renunciation and Profession

[The Bishop reads from 1 Peter 5:8ff. . . . "Be sober, be watchful . . ."]

1. It has long been my wish, true-born and long-desired children of the Church, to discourse to you upon these spiritual, heavenly mysteries. On the principle, however, that seeing is believing, I delayed until the present occasion, calculating that after you saw what you saw on that night I should find you a readier audience now when I am to be your guide to the brighter and more fragrant meadows of this second Eden. In particular, you are now capable of understanding the diviner mysteries of divine, life-giving baptism. The time being now come to spread for you the board of more perfect hearing, let me explain the significance of what was done for you on that evening of your baptism.

2. First you entered the antechamber of the baptistery and faced toward the west. On the command to stretch out your hand, you renounced Satan as though he were there in person. This moment, you should know, is prefigured in ancient history. When that tyrannous and cruel despot, Pharaoh, was oppressing the noble, free-spirited Hebrew nation, God sent Moses to deliver them from the hard slavery imposed upon them by the Egyptians. The doorposts were anointed with the blood of a lamb that the destroyer might pass over the houses signed with the blood;

so the Jews were miraculously liberated. After their liberation the enemy gave chase, and, on seeing the sea part miraculously before them, still continued in hot pursuit, only to be overwhelmed and engulfed in the Red Sea.

3. Pass, pray, from the old to the new, from the figure to the reality. There Moses sent by God to Israel; here Christ sent from the Father into the world. Moses' mission was to lead out from Egypt a persecuted people; Christ's, to rescue all the people of the world who were under the tyranny of sin. There the blood of a lamb was the charm against the destroyer; here the blood of the unspotted Lamb, Jesus Christ, is appointed your inviolable sanctuary against demons. Pharaoh pursued that people of old right into the sea; this outrageous spirit, the impudent author of all evil, followed you, each one, up to the very verge of the saving streams. The other tyrant is engulfed and drowned in the Red Sea; this one is destroyed in the saving water.

4. You are told, however, to address him as personally present, and with arm outstretched to say: "I renounce you, Satan." Allow me to explain the reason of your facing west, for you should know it. Because the west is the region of visible darkness, Satan, who is himself darkness, has his empire in darkness—that is the significance of your looking steadily toward the west while you renounce that gloomy Prince of night. What was it that each of you said, standing there? "I renounce you, Satan, you wicked and cruel tyrant." In effect you were saying, "I no longer fear your power. For Christ broke that power by sharing flesh and blood with me, planning through their assumption to break, by his death, the power of death, to save me from subjugation to perpetual bondage. I renounce you, crafty scoundrel of a serpent; I renounce you, traitor, perpetrator of every crime, who inspired our first parents to revolt. I renounce you, Satan, agent and abettor of all wickedness."

5. Then, in a second phrase you are taught to say, "and all your works." All sin is "the works of Satan"; and sin, too, you must renounce, since

he who has escaped from a tyrant has also cast off the tyrant's livery. Sin in all its forms, then, is included in the works of the devil. Only let me tell you this: all your words, particularly those spoken at that awful hour, are recorded in the book of God. Whenever, therefore, you are caught in conduct contrary to your profession, you will be tried as a renegade. Renounce, then, the works of Satan, that is, every . . . deed and thought [contrary to your baptismal promise].

6. Next you say, "and all his pomp." The pomp of the devil is the craze for the theatre, the horse races in the circus, the wild-beast hunts, and all such vanity, from which the saint prays to God to be delivered in the words, "Turn away my eyes that they may not behold vanity." Avoid addiction to the theatre, with its spectacle of the licentious, the lewd and unseemly antics of actors and the frantic dancing of degenerates. Not for you, either, the folly of those who, to gratify their miserable appetite, expose themselves to wild beasts in the amphitheater. They pamper their belly at the cost of becoming themselves, in the event, food for the mouths of savage beasts; of these gladiators it is fair to say that in the service of the belly which is their God they court death in the arena. Shun also the bedlam of the races, a spectacle in which souls as well as riders come to grief. All these follies are the pomp of the Devil.

7. The food, also, which is sometimes hung up in pagan temples and at festivals—meat, bread, and so forth—since it is defiled by the invocation of abominable demons, may be included in "the pomp of the Devil." For as the bread and wine of the Eucharist before the holy invocation of the adorable Trinity were ordinary bread and wine, while after the invocation the bread and wine becomes the Body of Christ, and the wine his Blood, so these foods of the pomp of Satan, though of their own nature ordinary food, become profane through the invocation of evil spirits.

8. After this you say, "and all your service." The service of the Devil is prayer in the temples of idols, the honoring of lifeless images, the lighting of lamps or the burning of incense by

springs or streams; there have been cases of persons who, deceived by dreams or evil spirits, have gone to this length in the hope of being rewarded by the cure of even bodily ailments. Have nothing to do with these practices. . . . For if you should succumb to such practices after renouncing Satan and transferring your allegiance to Christ, you will find the usurper more cruel than ever . . . so you will lose Christ and taste Satan's fury.

9. When you renounce Satan, trampling underfoot every covenant with him, then you annul that ancient league with Hell (Isa. 28:15), and God's paradise opens before you, that Eden, planted in the east, from which for his transgression our first father was banished. Symbolic of this is your facing about from the west to the east, the place of light. It was at this point that you were told to say, "I believe in the Father, and in the Son, and in the Holy Spirit, and in one baptism of repentance." All these things were done in the outer chamber. When we enter, God willing, in the succeeding discourses on the mysteries, into the Holy of Holies, we shall receive the key to the rites performed there.

Baptismal Catechesis II: Baptism

[The Bishop reads from Rom. 6:3–14: "Do you not know that all who have been baptized into Christ Jesus have been baptized into his death?"]

1. Instruction, daily, into these mysteries and declarations of truth are beneficial for us and especially for you, who are being renewed. With the symbols of those previous lessons heard in the inner chambers, therefore, will I refresh your memories, as often as needed.

2. Immediately, upon entering, you removed your tunics. This was a figure of the "stripping off of the old man with his deeds" (Col. 3:9). Having stripped you were naked, in this also imitating Christ, who was naked on the cross, by his nakedness "throwing off the cosmic powers and authorities like a garment and publicly upon the cross leading them in triumphal procession" (Col. 2:15). For as the forces of the enemy made their lair in our members, you may no longer

wear the old garment. I do not, of course, refer to the visible garment, but to "the old man which, deluded by its lusts, is sinking towards death" (Eph. 4:22). May the soul that has once put off that old self never put it on again, but say with the Bride of Christ in the Song of Solomon: "I have put off my garment: how shall I put it on?" (Song 5:13). Marvelous! You were naked in the sight of all and were not ashamed! Truly you bore the image of the first-born Adam, who was naked in the garden and "was not ashamed" (Gen. 2:25).

3. Then, when stripped, you were anointed with exorcised olive oil from the topmost hairs of your head to the soles of your feet, and became partakers of the good olive tree, Jesus Christ. Cuttings from the wild olive tree, you were grafted into the good olive tree and became partakers of the fatness of the true olive tree (cf. Rom. 2:17–24). The exorcised olive oil, therefore, symbolized the partaking of the richness of Christ; its effect is to disperse every concentration of the cosmic forces arrayed against us. For as the breath of the saints upon you [i.e., the exorcists], with the invocation of the name of God, burns the devils like fierce fire and expels them, so this exorcised olive oil receives, through prayer and the invocation of God, power so great as not only to burn and purge away the traces of sin but also to put to rout all the invisible forces of the Evil One.

4. After this you were conducted to the sacred pool of divine baptism, as Christ passed from the cross to the sepulcher you see before you. You were asked, one by one, whether you believed in the name of the Father and of the Son and of the Holy Spirit; you made that saving confession, and then you dipped thrice under the water and thrice rose up again, therein mystically signifying Christ's three day burial. For as our Savior passed three days and three nights in the bowels of the earth, so you by your first rising out of the water represented Christ's first day in the earth, and by your descent the night. For as in the night one no longer sees, while by day one is in the light, so you during your immersion, as in a night, saw

nothing, but on coming up found yourselves in the day. In the same moment you were dying and being born, and that saving water was at once your grave and your mother. What Solomon said in another context is applicable to you: "A time for giving birth, a time for dying" (Eccl. 3:2); although for you it is a case of "a time for dying and a time for being born." One time brought both, and your death coincided with your birth.

5. The strange, the extraordinary, thing is that we did not really die, nor were really buried or really crucified; nor did we really rise again: this was figurative and symbolic; yet our salvation was real. Christ's crucifixion was real, his burial was real, and his resurrection was real; and all these he has freely made ours, that by sharing his sufferings in a symbolic enactment we may really and truly gain salvation. Oh, too generous love! Christ received the nails in his immaculate hands and feet; Christ felt the pain: and on me without pain or labor, through the fellowship of his pain, he freely bestows salvation.

6. Let no one imagine, then, that baptism wins only the grace of remission of sins plus adoption, as John's baptism conferred only the remission of sins. No; we know full well that baptism not only washes away our sins and procures for us the gift of the Holy Spirit, but is also the antitype of the passion of Christ. That is why Paul proclaimed: "Do you not know that all we who have been baptized into Christ Jesus have been baptized into his death? For through baptism we were buried along with him" (Rom. 6:3–4). Perhaps this was directed against those who supposed that baptism procures only the remission of sins and the adoption of sons and does not, beyond this, really make us imitatively partakers of the sufferings of Christ.

7. So that we might learn that whatever Christ endured, He did so for us and for our salvation, and that in reality, and not merely in appearance, we are also made partakers of His sufferings. Paul truely declared that "For if we have become united with Him in the likeness of His death, certainly we shall also be in the likeness of his resurrection" (Rom. 6:5).

Well he has said, "united with Him." For by partaking in the Baptism of His death we have been united with Him. Attend closely to the Apostle's words: he did not say "For if we have become united with him in His death," but "in the likeness of his death." For to Christ death came in reality, His soul truly separating from His body, and His burial was true, for His holy body was wrapped in linen. But in your case, the reality of salvation has been experienced, but only the likeness of death and suffering.

8. I urge you to keep in your memory that I too, though unworthy, may be able to say to you: "I love you because at all times you keep me in mind and maintain the tradition I handed on to you" (1 Cor. 11:2). God, "who has presented you as those who have come alive from the dead," is able to grant to you to "walk in newness of life," because His is the glory and the power, now and forever. Amen.

Baptismal Catechesis III: Chrismation

[The bishop reads from 1 John 2:20–28: "But you have an anointing from God and you know all things."]

1. Baptized in Christ and clothed with Christ (Gal. 3:27) you have been shaped to the likeness of the Son of God. For God, in "predestining us to be adopted as his sons" (Eph. 1:5) has "conformed us to the body of the glory" (Eph.3:21) of Christ. As "partakers of Christ" (Heb. 3:14), therefore, you are rightly called "Christs," that is "anointed ones": it was of you that God said: "Touch not my Christs" [Ps. 104:15—Greek Translation of the Old Testament]. Now you became Christs by receiving the antitype of the Holy Spirit; everything has been wrought in you "likewise" because you are likenesses of Christ. He bathed in the river Jordan and, after imparting the fragrance of His Godhead to the waters, came up from them. Him the Holy Spirit visited in essential presence, *like* resting on *like*. Similarly for you, after you had ascended from the sacred streams, there was an anointing with *chrism*, the antitype of that with which Christ was anointed, that is, of the Holy Spirit. Concerning this Spirit the blessed Isaiah . . . said, speaking in the person of the Lord: "The Spirit of the Lord is upon me because he has anointed me. He has sent me to preach glad tidings to the poor" (Isa. 61:1).

2. For Christ was not anointed by men with material oil or balsam; his Father, appointing him Savior of the whole world, anointing him with the Holy Spirit, as Peter says: "Jesus of Nazareth, whom God anointed with the Holy Spirit" (Acts 10:38). The prophet David also made proclamation: "Your throne, O God, is forever and ever: the scepter of your kingdom is the scepter of uprightness. You have loved justice, and hated iniquity: therefore God, your God, has anointed you with the oil of gladness above your fellows" (Ps. 44:7–8). As Christ was really crucified and buried and rose again, and you at baptism are privileged to be crucified, buried, and raised along with him in a likeness, so also with the chrism. Christ was anointed with a mystical oil of gladness; that is with the Holy Spirit, called the "oil of gladness" because He is the cause of spiritual gladness; so you, being anointed with ointment, have become partakers and fellows of Christ.

3. Beware of supposing that this ointment is mere ointment. Just as after the invocation of the Holy Spirit the Eucharistic bread is no longer ordinary bread, but the body of Christ, so this holy oil, in conjunction with the invocation, is no longer simple or common oil, but becomes the gracious gift of Christ and the Holy Spirit, producing the advent [presence?] of his Deity. With this ointment your forehead and sense organs are sacramentally anointed, in such as way that while your body is anointed with the visible oil, your soul is sanctified by the holy, quickening Spirit.

4. You are anointed first upon the forehead to rid you of the shame which the first human transgressor bore about with him everywhere; so you may "reflect as in a mirror the splendor of the Lord" (2 Cor. 3:18). Then upon the ears, to receive ears quick to hear the divine mysteries, the ears of which Isaiah said: "The Lord gave me also an ear to hear" (Isa. 50:4) and the Lord Jesus in the Gospels: "He who has

ears to hear, let him hear" (Matt. 11:15). Then upon the nostrils, that, scenting the divine oil, you may say: "We are the incense offered by Christ to God" (2 Cor. 2:15) . . . then on the breast, that "putting on the breastplate of righteousness you may be able to withstand the wiles of the Devil" (Eph. 6:14). For as Christ after his baptism and visitation by the Holy Spirit went forth and overthrew the adversary, so must you after holy baptism and the mystical chrism, clad in the armor of the Holy Spirit, stand firm against the forces of the Enemy and overthrow them, saying: "I can do all things in the Christ who strengthens me" (Phil. 4:13).

5. Once privileged to receive the holy chrism, you are called *Christians* and have a name that bespeaks your new birth. Before admission to baptism and the grace of the Holy Spirit you were not strictly entitled to this name but were like people on the way toward being Christians.

6. You must know that this chrism is prefigured in the Old Testament. When Moses, conferring on his brother the divine appointment, was ordering him as high priest, he anointed him after he had bathed in water, and thenceforth he was called "christos" ["anointed"—Lev. 8:5, 12; 4:5], clearly after the figurative chrism. . . .

7. Keep this chrism unsoiled, for it shall teach you all things if it abides in you . . . [as] both a heavenly protection of the body and salvation for the soul . . . anointed with this holy oil . . . making progress through good works and becoming well-pleasing to the "trail-blazer of our salvation" (Heb. 2:10), Christ Jesus, to whom be glory forever and ever. Amen.

THE NICENE (NICENO-CONSTANTINOPOLITAN) CREED
Greek, 381 A.D.

What the Apostles' Creed was to Western (Catholic) churches, the Nicene Creed was to Eastern and Russian Orthodox churches. The Nicene Creed was first composed to counter heretical Arian teachings (that Jesus was *not* fully God) by emphasizing the deity of Christ and the Holy Spirit.

However, as the variant forms of the creed show, there was a basic disagreement between the churches of Eastern and Western Christendom regarding the Holy Spirit: did he proceed from the Father alone as the Eastern Church insists, or did he come "from the Father and the Son" as the Western Church believes? Examine the biblical evidence for yourself and summarize your conclusions: See, for example, Mark 1:8; John 3:34, 14:26, 15:26, 20:22; Acts 2:17–18, 33. The view of the Eastern Church (that the Holy Spirit proceeded from the Father alone and not from the Father *and* the Son) was probably intended to protect the doctrine of the Holy Spirit as a full member of the Trinity (i.e., to avoid teaching that the Spirit was somehow lesser than or derived from the Son). The inclusion of the phrase "and the Son" in the Western version of this creed is known as the *"filioque"* which is Latin for "and the Son," and it is sometimes placed in brackets (as below). The original language of the Nicene Creed is a reminder that Eastern Orthodox Christians spoke Greek while Western, Catholic Christians spoke Latin. These and other differences led to the formal division of Christendom in A.D. 1054. The form of the Nicene Creed reprinted here (known as the Niceno-Constantinopolitan Creed of A.D. 381) evolved from a briefer and more ancient form of this creed, developed at the first ecumenical Council held at Nicaea in A.D. 325, and is taken from Philip Schaff, *The Creeds of Christendom: With a History and Critical Notes* (Grand Rapids: Baker, 1998).

✦

We believe in one God, the Father Almighty,
Πιστεύομεν εἰς ἕνα Θεὸν, πατέρα παντοκράτορα,

Maker of heaven and earth, of all things visible and invisible;
ποιητὴν οὐρανοῦ καὶ γῆς, ὁρατῶν τε πάντων καὶ ἀοράτων·

And in one Lord Jesus Christ, the only begotten Son of God,
Καὶ εἰς ἕνα κύριον Ἰησοῦν Χριστὸν τὸν υἱὸν τοῦ θεοῦ τὸν μονογενη·

Begotten of the Father before all worlds; Light from Light,

τὸν ἐκ τοῦ πατρὸς γεννηθέντα πρὸ
πάντων τῶν αἰώνων· φῶς ἐκ
φωτὸς,

True God from true God, begotten,
not made,
θεὸν ἀληθινὸν ἐκ θεοῦ ἀληθινοῦ,
γεννηθέντα, οὐ ποιηθέντα,

being of one substance (*homoousion*)
with the Father, through him all
things were made.
ὁμοούσιον τῷ πατρί· δι᾽ οὗ τὰ πάντα
ἐγένετο·

Who for us and for our salvation came
down from heaven:
τὸν δι᾽ ἡμᾶς τοὺς ἀνθρώπους καὶ
διὰ τὴν ἡμετέραν σωτηρίαν
κατελθόντα ἐκ τῶν οὐρανῶν,

And was incarnate by the Holy Spirit
of the Virgin Mary, and was made
man,
καὶ σαρκωθέντα ἐκ πνεύματος ἁγίου
καὶ Μαρίας τῆς παρθένου, καὶ
ἐνανθρωπήσαντα·

and was crucified also for us under
Pontius Pilate; He suffered and
was buried,
σταυρωθέντα τε ὑπὲρ ἡμῶν ἐπὶ
Ποντίου Πιλάτου, καὶ παθόντα,
καὶ ταφέντα,

And the third day he rose again
according to the Scriptures,
καὶ ἀναστάντα τῇ τρίτῃ ἡμέρᾳ κατὰ
τὰς γραφὰς,

And ascended into heaven, and sitteth
at the right hand of the Father.
καὶ ἀνελθόντα εἰς τοὺς οὐρανοὺς,
καὶ καθεζόμενον ἐκ δεξιῶν τοῦ
πατρὸς,

And he shall come again with glory to
judge both the quick and the dead,
καὶ πάλιν ἐρχόμενον μετὰ δόξης
κρῖναι ζῶντας καὶ νεκρούς·

Whose kingdom shall have no end.
οὗ τῆς βασιλείας οὐκ ἔσται τέλος.

And we believe in the Holy Spirit, the
Lord and giver of life,
Καὶ εἰς τὸ πνεῦμα τὸ ἅγιον, τὸ
κύριον, (καὶ) τὸ ζωοποιὸν,

Who proceedeth from the Father [*and
the Son*].
τὸ ἐκ τοῦ πατρὸς ἐκπορευόμενον,
[*filioque*]

Who with the Father and the Son
together is worshiped and
glorified,
τὸ σὺν πατρὶ καὶ υἱῷ [συν]
προσκυνούμενον καὶ
συνδοξαζόμενον,

Who spoke by the prophets.
τὸ λαλῆσαν διὰ τῶν προφητῶν·

We believe in one holy catholic and
apostolic Church.
εἰς μίαν ἁγίαν καθολικὴν καὶ
ἀποστολικὴν ἐκκλησίαν·

We acknowledge one baptism for the
remission of sins.
ὁμολογοῦμεν ἓν βάπτισμα εἰς ἄφεσιν
ἁμαρτιῶν·

We look for the resurrection of the
dead,
προσδοκῶμεν ἀνάστασιν νεκρῶν

and the life of the world to come.
Amen.
καὶ ζωὴν τοῦ μέλλοντος αἰῶνος.
Ἀμήν.

THE ANATHASIAN CREED
Latin, About 500 A.D.

This creed is particularly concerned with an orthodox formulation of Trinitarian doctrine, for example, "in this Trinity, no one is before or after, greater or less than the other; but all three persons are in themselves, coeternal and coequal." It was also written to rightly express the two natures of Christ, who "although he is God and man, he is not divided, but is one Christ." Although the creed is attributed to the great fourth century Eastern Church Bishop Athanasius of Alexandria, it was not accepted by the Eastern Church and in fact reflects Latin or Western Church theology in some particulars, for example, "the Spirit was neither made nor created, but is proceeding from the Father and the Son" (see comments on page 44 regarding the Nicene Creed).

✦

Whoever wants to be saved should above all cling to the catholic faith.
Quicumque vult salvus esse, ante omnia opus est, ut teneat catholicam fidem:

Whoever does not guard it whole and inviolable will doubtless perish eternally.
Quam nisi quisque integram inviolatamque servaverit, absque dubio in aeternam peribit.

Now this is the catholic faith: We worship one God in trinity and the Trinity in unity,
Fides autem catholica haec est: ut unum Deum in Trinitate, et Trinitatem in unitate veneremur.

neither confusing the persons nor dividing the divine being.
Neque confundentes personas, neque substantiam seperantes.

For the Father is one person, the Son is another, and the Spirit is still another.
Alia est enim persona Patris alia Filii, alia Spiritus Sancti:

But the deity of the Father, Son, and Holy Spirit is one, equal in glory, coeternal in majesty.

Sed Patris, et Fili, et Spiritus Sancti una est divinitas, aequalis gloria, coeterna maiestas.

What the Father is, the Son is, and so is the Holy Spirit.
Qualis Pater, talis Filius, talis Spiritus Sanctus.

Uncreated is the Father; uncreated is the Son; uncreated is the Spirit.
Increatus Pater, increatus Filius, increatus Spiritus Sanctus.

The Father is infinite; the Son is infinite; the Holy Spirit is infinite.
Immensus Pater, immensus Filius, immensus Spiritus Sanctus.

Eternal is the Father; eternal is the Son; eternal is the Spirit:
Aeternus Pater, aeternus Filius, aeternus Spiritus Sanctus.

And yet there are not three eternal beings, but one who is eternal;
Et tamen non tres aeterni, sed unus aeternus.

as there are not three uncreated and unlimited beings, but one who is uncreated and unlimited.
Sicut non tres increati, nec tres immensi, sed unus increatus, et unus immensus.

Almighty is the Father; almighty is the Son; almighty is the Spirit:
Similiter omnipotens Pater, omnipotens Filius, omnipotens Spiritus Sanctus.

And yet there are not three almighty beings, but one who is almighty.
Et tamen non tres omnipotentes, sed unus omnipotens.

Thus the Father is God; the Son is God; the Holy Spirit is God:
Ita Deus Pater, Deus Filius, Deus Spiritus Sanctus.

And yet there are not three gods, but one God.
Et tamen non tres dii, sed unus est Deus.

Thus the Father is Lord; the Son is Lord; the Holy Spirit is Lord:

Ita Dominus Pater, Dominus Filius, Dominus Spiritus Sanctus.

And yet there are not three lords, but one Lord.

Et tamen non tres Domini, sed unus est Dominus.

As Christian truth compels us to acknowledge each distinct person as God and Lord,

Quia, sicut singillatim unamquamque personam Deum ac Dominum confiteri christiana veritate compelimur:

so catholic religion forbids us to say that there are three gods or lords.

ita tres Deos aut Dominos dicere catholica religione prohibemur.

The Father was neither made nor created nor begotten;

Pater a nullo est factus: nec creatus, nec genitus.

the Son was neither made nor created, but was alone begotten of the Father;

Filius a Patre solo est: non factus, nec creatus, sed genitus.

the Spirit was neither made nor created, but is proceeding from the Father and the Son.

Spiritus Sanctus a Patre et Filio: non factus, nec creatus, nec genitus, sed procedens.

Thus there is one Father, not three fathers; one Son, not three sons; one Holy Spirit, not three spirits.

Unus ergo Pater, non tres Patres: unus Filius, non tres Filii: unus Spiritus Sanctus, non tres Spiritus Sancti.

And in this Trinity, no one is before or after, greater or less than the other;

Et in hac Trinitate nihil prius aut posterius, nihil maius aut minus:

but all three persons are in themselves, coeternal and coequal;

sed totae tres personae coaeternae sibi sunt et coaequales.

and so we must worship the Trinity in unity and the one God in three persons.

Ita ut per omnia, sicut iam supra dictum est, et unitas in Trinitate, et Trinitas in unitate veneranda sit.

Whoever wants to be saved should think thus about the Trinity.

Qui vult ergo salvus esse, ita de Trinitate sentiat.

It is necessary for eternal salvation that one also faithfully believe that our Lord Jesus Christ became flesh.

Sed necessarium est ad aeternam salutem, ut incarnationem quoque Domini nostri Iesu Christi fideliter credat.

For this is the true faith that we believe and confess: That our Lord Jesus Christ, God's Son, is both God and man.

Est ergo fides recta ut credamus et confiteamur, quia Dominus noster Iesus Christus, Dei Filius, Deus et homo est.

He is God, begotten before all worlds from the being of the Father, and he is man, born in the world from the being of his mother;

Deus est ex substantia Patris ante saecula genitus: et homo est ex substantia matris in saeculo natus.

existing fully as God, and fully as man with a rational soul and a human body;

Perfectus Deus, perfectus homo: ex anima rationali et humana carne subsistens.

equal to the Father in divinity, subordinate to the Father in humanity.

Aequalis Patri secundum divinitatem: minor Patre secundum humanitatem.

Although he is God and man, he is not divided, but is one Christ.

Qui licet Deus sit et homo, non duo tamen, sed unus est Christus.

He is united because God has taken humanity into himself; he does not transform deity into humanity.

Unus autem non conversione divinitatis in carnem, sed assumptione humanitatis in Deum.

He is completely one in the unity of his person,
without confusing his natures.
Unus omnino, non confusione substantiae, sed unitate personae.

For as the rational soul and body are one person, so the one Christ is God and man.
Nam sicut anima rationalis et caro unus est homo: ita Deus et homo unus est Christus.

He suffered death for our salvation.
Qui passus est pro salute nostra:

He descended into hell and rose again from the dead.
descendit ad inferos: tertia die resurrexit a mortuis.

He ascended into heaven and is seated at the right hand of the Father.
Ascendit ad caelos, sedet ad dexteram Dei Patris omnipotentis:

He will come again to judge the living and the dead.
inde venturus est iudicare vivos et mortuos.

At his coming all people shall rise bodily to give an account of their own deeds.
Ad cuius adventum omnes homines resurgere habent cum corporibus suis: et reddituri sunt de factis propriis rationem.

Those who have done good will enter eternal life,
Et qui bona egerunt, ibunt in vitam aeternam:

those who have done evil will enter eternal fire.
qui vero mala, in ignem aeternum.

This is the catholic faith.
Haec est fides catholica,

One cannot be saved without believing this firmly and faithfully. Amen.
quam nisi quisque fideliter firmiterque crediderit, salvus esse non poterit. Amen.

THE APOSTLES' CREED
Latin, Fourth Through Eighth Centuries A.D.

The *Credo* (Latin for "I believe") *in Deum* is the most concise and universally accepted summary of Christian belief. Known as the Apostles' Creed, it was the standard baptismal confession of the ancient Roman (Western) church. Its name suggests that it was a summary of the Apostles' teaching and there is indeed a legend that the Apostles themselves composed it on the day of Pentecost. Various forms of the Apostles' Creed developed from the fourth to the eighth centuries, based on confessional statements found in the New Testament and in the early church Fathers (e.g., Irenaeus, Cyprian, Tertullian).

Questions for Guided Reading

1. Noting the Creed's threefold organization around the three Persons of the Trinity, describe (1) the central trait and work attributed to Father, (2) the way and works of the Son, and (3) the gifts of the Holy Spirit.
2. Many theologians and teachers have employed the *Credo* as a teaching outline (e.g., Karl Barth, *Credo*, 1935). Following in their footsteps, expound on the various statements (e.g., "the Father almighty") by citing supporting scriptures and by writing a basic biblical explanation for each phrase.
3. Reciting the Apostles' Creed is a part of Sunday worship in many churches today. Is this true of your church?

✦

I believe in God
Credo in Deum

The Father almighty
Patrem omnipotentem;

Creator of heaven and earth.
Creatorem coeli et terrae.

And in Jesus Christ,
Et in Jesum Christum,

His only son, our Lord;
Filium ejus unicum, Dominum nostrum;

Who was conceived by the Holy Spirit,
qui conceptus est de Spiritu Sancto,

born of the virgin Mary
natus ex Maria virgine;

suffered under Pontius Pilate
passus sub Pontio Pilato,

was crucified, dead, and buried
crucifixus, mortuus, et sepultus;

He descended to hell;
descendit ad iferna;

the third day he rose again from the dead
teria die resurrexit a mortuis;

He ascended to heaven
ascendit ad coelos;

and is seated at the right hand of God, the Father
  almighty;
sedt ad dexteram Dei Patris omnipotentis;

From there He will come to judge the living and the
  dead.
inde venturus (est) judicare vivos et mortuos.

I believe in the Holy Spirit
Credo in Spiritum Sanctum;

the holy catholic church,
sanctam ecclesiam catholicam;

the communion of saints,
sanctorum communionem;

the forgiveness of sins,
remissionem peccatorum;

the resurrection of the body,
carnis resurrectionem;

(and) the life everlasting. Amen.
vitam oeteram. Amen.

Ancient Apologetics

Among the earliest Christian teachers were the apologists, whose literary gifts and life circumstances required them to represent Christianity to a hostile culture. With great zeal and ability, apologists such as Justin Martyr offered reasoned explanations of the faith "once for all delivered to the saints" and thereby gained a wider hearing for the gospel in the Roman Empire. As the apologists studied how best to communicate truth to people of the Greco-Roman culture, they did so with the knowledge that the success of their teaching was a matter of life and death.

For the first three centuries of the Church's existence, Christianity was illegal.[1] To confess to being a Christian, to possess a copy of the Scriptures, or to teach Christian truths to one's own children were all capital offences. The Christian martyrs (from the Greek *marturios*, witness) were those who publicly declared *Christos Kurios* ("Christ is Lord") rather than *Caesar Kurios* ("Caesar is Lord"). As a voice for the martyrs, the apologists served as a living conscience for a corrupt society and the voice of reason crying out on behalf of those whose faithfulness to Christ had cost them their lives.

Zeal for God's people and the courage to speak up were not enough to fulfill this special calling. Apologists were first of all Christian philosophers who read widely in classical literature and thought deeply about the meaning of the gospel in relation to Greco-Roman thought. No ivory-tower philosophers, the apologists pursued truth with the aim of presenting that truth to nonbelievers at the very highest educational and social levels. Even the open-

ing words of the *First Apology* illustrate how remarkable an investment and how great a risk was undertaken by Justin Martyr and others like him.

Apologetics could be described as teaching in relation to society, by which is meant that all truth claims are investigated and presented in an ongoing dialogue with the contrary perspective—the unconvinced, the uninitiated. The apologist's work is not finished once a truth has been discovered; rather, it succeeds only as it finds expression in words familiar to and definitions common with the dialogue partner. This form of teaching did not originate with Christian authors but was adapted from Greek and Jewish models. In an empire where all philosophies and practices were embraced or at least tolerated, and in a society in which Romans could exclaim "I consider nothing human to be alien from me,"[2] the Christian story, nevertheless, was despised, and its followers were ridiculed and widely rejected.

As spokespersons for Christianity, the Apologists faced the enormous challenge of representing the views of a despised and powerless minority with no voice or representation in society. Like voices "crying in the wilderness" (Isa. 40:3), they represented Christian belief and practice honestly and accurately in relation to the Empire. Declaring the truth about Christ and his followers, the Apologists opened a dialogue between Christians and the philosophers of the day, and increased the potential for reconciliation between disparate groups of Christians. Although they called themselves philosophers, their success with communicating faith under fire won the apologists a place among "the Fathers," as later generations of Christians called them.

---

1. An edict known as the Edict of Milan declaring Christianity to be *religio licita* (legal religion) was issued in 313 by Emperor Constantine.

2. The Latin playwright Terence (190–158 B.C.).

JUSTIN MARTYR: *FIRST APOLOGY* (EXCERPTS)
Greek, Mid Second Century

According to the ancient church historian Eusebius, Justin Martyr appeared in the cloak of a philosopher, preaching the divine word and contending for the faith in his writings (iv.11.11).

Of the many works attributed to Justin, only three—the first and second *Apologies* and the *Dialogue with Trypho*—were known to Eusebius (viii.3, cxli.5) and are thought to be his authentic writings. Justin described himself as being raised a Gentile and educated in the Greek classics (*Dialogue with Trypho* xxix and ii respectively). Again according to Eusebius, Justin taught at Rome during the reign of Antonius Pius and was martyred under Marcus Aurelius, suggesting that he may have been born in the late first or early second century. Justin wrote his *First Apology* in order to demand justice for Christians based on a careful examination of their lives and doctrine. He systematically addresses the many false charges against them and demonstrates the reasonableness of the Christian faith. In the concluding chapters of his *First Apology*, Justin describes the Christian worship of the period.

Questions for Guided Reading
1. What does Justin ask of the Emperor, and on what basis does he make his request?
2. What are some of the charges against Christians?
3. How does Christian worship differ in manner and intent from pagan worship?
4. Who is Marcion and how do his teachings differ from those which are truly Christian?
5. How does the Christian worship of Justin Martyr's time compare with our own?

✦

1. To the Emperor Titus Aelius Adrianus Antoninus Pius Augustus Caesar, and to his son Verissimus the Philosopher, and to Lucius the Philosopher, the natural son of Caesar, and the adopted son of Pius, a lover of learning, and to the sacred Senate together with the entire Roman nation, on behalf of those of every nation who are unjustly hated and abused, myself among them; I, Justin, offer this petition.

2. Reason requires those who are truly pious and philosophical to honor and love truth alone, rejecting the traditions of the fathers if these are shown to be groundless. For not only does reason lead us to refuse the guidance of those who did or taught anything wrong, but it is required of the lover of truth, by all means, even if his own life be threatened, to do and say what is right. Since then you are called pious and philosophers, guardians of justice and lovers of learning (and if you are indeed this will be manifest), pay close attention to my address; for we have come not to merely flatter you by this writing nor to please you by our speech, but to implore you to judge rightly, after an accurate and thorough investigation, not prejudiced toward superstitious men, nor influenced by rash thoughts or evil lies long standing (lest by it you judge yourselves). As for us [Christians], no evil can harm us unless we are convicted as criminals or shown to be sinful persons. You may indeed be able to kill us, but you cannot finally harm us.

3. So that no one will consider this request unreasonable or impulsive, we petition that the charges against the Christians be investigated. If these charges prove to be true then let them be punished as required. If however, there turns out to be no way to prove these accusations, sane reason forbids you to punish innocent men (indeed you yourselves are judged when you act on the basis of passion and not sound judgment). . . .

4. Nothing good or evil is usually implied in the mere use of a name, that is, apart from any actions associated with that name. If this were the case then, to judge from our name (*Christianoi*), we are indeed a most excellent (*chrestotaoi*) people, and to hate what is excellent is unjust! . . .[3]

5. Rashly you punish those of us who are not atheists and who are pledged to do no

---

3. A play on words.

wickedness, and you do this at the prompting of demons. For the truth will be told: from ancient times these evil demons appeared, defiling women, corrupting boys, and showing such bizarre sights to men, that those who were not led by reason in judging these demonic acts were thunder struck. Not knowing they were demons they mistook them for gods, calling them by whatever names the demon had chosen. Now when Socrates attempted, by true reason and examination, to bring these things to light, and to draw men away from the demons, these very demons, working through men who delight in evil, planned his execution as an atheist and sinful, on the charge that "he was teaching about new gods." And they seek to do the same to us. For not only among the Greeks did reason (*Logos*) appear in order to condemn these things through Socrates, but also among the non-Greeks were they condemned by the Logos Himself, who took shape and became man, and was called Jesus Christ; and in obedience to Him, we deny that these are gods but affirm that they are wicked and impious demons, whose actions are incomparable with those who seek virtue.

6. So we are called atheists. And we could admit to that charge as far as false gods are concerned, but not with respect to the most true God, the Father of righteousness and temperance and of all the other virtues, who is free from all impurity. We worship and adore Him and the Son who came forth from Him who taught us these things, and also the angels who attend Him, reflecting these virtues, and the Prophetic Spirit. We honor these in reason and truth, and accurately convey His doctrine to everyone who wishes to learn.

7. Someone may object on the basis of legal precedent: "Christians have already been arrested and convicted as evil-doers." But the fact that you condemn many men after they are investigated does not justify condemning anyone on account of others previously convicted. This much we affirm: among the Greeks all who teach their own theories are called "Philosopher," though they may all disagree with one another. Likewise among the non-Greeks those who are wise and those who merely seem wise go by the name Christian. This is why we ask that all those accused before you be judged on the basis of their deeds, and that the convicted be punished on account of wickedness, not because he is a Christian. And if he is found to be blameless, let him be acquitted as a Christian who has done no wrong. And we do not require our accusers be punished because their sinful state and their ignorance of what is fine and noble is punishment enough.

8. Be assured therefore that we say these things for your benefit. After all, we could simply deny that we are Christians whenever examined, yet we would not live by lying. Desiring an eternal and holy life, we seek a dwelling place with God, the Father and Creator of all, and eagerly confess our faith, being absolutely persuaded that no sin can keep those who long for God's love from that dwelling. This, in brief, is what we look for, what we have learned from Christ, and what we pass on to others. Now, Plato taught that Rhadamanthus and Minos would punish the wicked who came before them. We declare that the very same thing will happen, only that it will be Christ who punishes sinners, and that in their bodies reunited with their souls, they will endure everlasting torment, and not merely for a thousand years, as Plato said. If any one says this is incredible or impossible, the "error" remains ours and does no one any harm, so long as we are not charged with any wickedness.

9. We do not worship with sacrifices and garlands those objects that men make, place in their temples, and call gods, since we know them to be lifeless and not the form of God. Indeed, we do not believe God has the sort of form that craftsmen may reproduce in order, as some claim, to honor Him; rather, they take the names and forms of demons who have appeared. No description is needed (since you already know) of the shapes these artisans fashion by carving, cutting, molding, and hammering their materials. From vessels

destined for dishonor, by merely changing their form into the desired shape, they make what they call a god. The name of Him who is of ineffable glory and form is thus dishonored, once bestowed on that which is corruptible and requires maintenance. Not to mention the fact that these artists live thoroughly sinful lives (without dwelling unnecessarily on details), even corrupting the girls who assist them in their trade. How ridiculous—the lustful men who make gods for your worship you appoint as guardians of the very temples wherein the gods are enshrined, conveniently forgetting the blasphemy of the notion that a man might be considered a keeper of the gods.

10. That God requires no material offerings men can give, seeing that He Himself is the provider of all things—this is the teaching handed down to us (cf. Acts 17:25). And we are convinced that He accepts only those who imitate the excellences which dwell in Him, namely temperance, justice, and love of man, and any other virtue proper to a God who is called by no proper name. We have been taught how, in the beginning, God, in His goodness created all things out of unformed matter. Now if men prove themselves worthy of His plan, they will be found to dwell and even reign with Him, free from all corruption and suffering. For as in the beginning He created us when we were not, so do we consider that, in like manner, those who choose what is pleasing to Him are, on account of their choice, deemed worthy of incorruption and of fellowship with Him. For our creation was not in our own power; and in order that we may follow those things which please Him, choosing them by means of the rational faculties He has Himself endowed us with, He both persuades us and leads us to faith. And it for the advantage of all men that none are prevented from learning these truths but are rather urged to consider them. For what human laws could never achieve, the Divine Word would have accomplished, had not wicked demons in league with the sinful nature of every man spread much false gossip and many profane accusations, though none applies to us.

11. When you hear that we look forward to a kingdom, you assume that we speak of a human kingdom, whereas we mean a kingdom that is with God. This is also evident from our confession that we are Christians, though such a profession of faith is punishable by death. For if we looked for a human kingdom we would deny Christ in order to avoid execution, and would flee from you to that kingdom. But since our thoughts are not fixed on the present, we are not concerned when men cut us off. Death is a debt which, sooner or later, everyone must pay.

12. More than all other men, we are your helpers and allies in promoting peace because we believe it is impossible for the wicked, the covetous, the treacherous, and for the virtuous alike to escape God's notice, and that each man goes to everlasting punishment or salvation according to the merit of his actions. If every man realized this, no one would choose sin even for a little while, knowing himself to be destined for everlasting fire. He would rather by any means control himself, and put on virtue, that he might obtain the good gifts of God, and escape the punishment. There are some who merely try to conceal their wrongdoing because of the laws and punishments which you decree, knowing that since you are only men it is possible for wrongdoers to escape you; if they learned and were convinced that our thoughts as well as our actions cannot be hidden from God they would certainly lead orderly lives, if only because of the consequences; as you must agree. But it seems as if you were afraid of having all men well-behaved, and nobody left for you to punish; this would be the conduct of public executioners, not of good rulers. Such things, we are convinced, are brought about by the evil demons, the ones who demand sacrifices and service from men who live irrationally; but we have not learned [to expect] any unreasonable conduct from you, who aim at piety and philosophy. Yet, if as thoughtless men you prefer custom to truth, then go ahead and do whatever is in your power to do. A ruler who follows popular

opinion rather than truth has no more power than a thief in the wilderness. That you will not succeed in exterminating Christians is declared by the Word, for no ruler is more kingly and just than the Father who begot Him. Just as men avoid the poverty, pain, and obscurity of their fathers, so a reasonable man avoids whatever the Word forbids him to choose. That all these things should happen, I say, was foretold by our Teacher, who is both Son and Apostle of God the Father and Ruler of all, and from whom we take our name, Christians. So then we are assured of everything He taught us, because it has all come to pass, even as He foretold; and this is after all God's practice, to foretell an event before its occurrence, and then to demonstrate how it has unfolded just as predicted. . . .[4]

13. What rational man will not admit that we are not atheists, since we worship the Maker of this universe, and affirm, as we have been taught, that He needs no blood sacrifice, no libations, and no incense? Yet we praise to the utmost of our power through prayer and thanksgiving for all He supplies. We have been instructed the only honor worthy of Him is not to consume by fire what He has created for our nurture, but to use it for the good of ourselves and the needy, and, with thankful voices, to offer Him thanks through prayers and hymns for our creation, for preserving our health, for the changes of the seasons, and petition Him for eternal life through faith in Him. Our teacher in these things is Jesus Christ, who was born for this purpose, who was crucified under Pontius Pilate, procurator of Judea during the reign of Tiberius Caesar. And we will demonstrate that our worship of Him is reasonable, since we have learned that He is the Son of the living God Himself, second only to the Father, after whom is the prophetic Spirit.[5] On account of this they

say we are deranged: that we hold a crucified man up next to the unchangeable and eternal God, Creator of everything, yet this because they cannot discern the mystery that lies herein. To this mystery, then, we ask now ask you to turn your attention as we endeavor to clarify it for you.

15. Concerning purity, He said, "Whoever looks at a woman with lust has already committed adultery with her in his heart before God" (Matt. 5:28). And, "If your right eye offends you, pluck it out, for it is better for you to enter the kingdom of heaven with one eye than, with both, to be cast into everlasting fire" (Matt. 5:29). And, "Whoever marries a woman who has been divorced from another husband commits adultery" (Matt. 5:32). And, "There are eunuchs who were born eunuchs, some who were made eunuchs by men, and some who have made themselves eunuchs for the kingdom of heaven's sake; but not everyone can receive this saying" (Matt. 19:12). And therefore, all who remarry according to human law are, in the eyes of our Master, sinners, and those who look lustfully on a woman not only commit adultery but are also rejected by Him: Indeed, not only those who actually commit adultery but also those who wish to do so, because not only our deeds but also our inner thoughts are open before God. Many, both men and women, who have been Christ's disciples from childhood, remain virgin at the age of sixty or seventy years, and of such, I am proud to say, there are examples in every nation. And what shall I say of the countless numbers who have mastered uncontrollable habits? Indeed, Christ has not called only the righteous or the virgin to repentance, but the ungodly, the licentious, and the unjust; in His own words, "I came not to call the righteous, but sinners to repentance" (Matt. 9:13). The heavenly Father desires the repentance of the sinner rather than his punishment. Concerning the love we should have for all, He taught, "If you love those who love you, what new thing do you do? Even fornicators do this. But I say to you, pray for

---

4. Recall, for example, the admonitions of the angels and of Jesus in Luke 24 where the disciples must be repeatedly reminded of their Lord's words to them regarding what will happen at the crucifixion and following.

5. *Prophetic Spirit* refers to the *Holy Spirit.* Justin's formulation here seems to subordinate Christ and the Holy Spirit in a manner which later trinitarian writings are careful to avoid.

your enemies and love those that hate you; bless those that curse you, and pray for those who abuse you" (Luke 6:27–28). He taught us also to share our possessions with the needy and to do nothing for personal glory, saying, "Give to everyone who asks of you and do not turn away from him who would. If you lend only to those who can repay, what new thing do you do? Even sinners do this" (Luke 6:34). "Do not store up for yourselves treasure on earth, where moth and rust corrupts, and where thieves break in; but store up for yourselves treasures in heaven, where neither moth nor rust corrupts" (Matt. 6:19–20). "For what does it profit a man if he gains the whole world and lose his own soul? Or what shall a man give in exchange for his own soul? Therefore, store up treasure in heaven, where neither moth nor rust corrupts" (Matt. 6:20). And, "Be kind and merciful as your heavenly Father is also kind and merciful, who makes His sun to rise on sinners, and on the righteous and the wicked (Matt. 5:45). Don't be anxious about what you will eat or what you will wear. Are you not better than the birds and the beasts, and God feeds them. So don't be anxious about what you eat or wear; for your heavenly Father knows you have need of these things. But seek first the kingdom of heaven and all these things will be added to you (Matt. 6:25–26, 33). For where his treasure is, there also is the mind of a man" (cf. Matt. 6:21). And, "Do not do these things to be seen by men; otherwise you will have no reward from your Father who is in heaven" (Matt. 6:1).

16. Concerning our patient suffering, our willingness to serve all, and to be free from anger, He said, "Whoever strikes you on the one cheek, offer him the other; and whoever takes your cloak or coat, do not resist (Matt. 5:39–40). Whoever is subject to anger is in danger of the fire (Matt. 5:22). Whoever compels you to go with him a mile, go with him two (Matt. 5:41). And let your good works shine before men, that they, seeing them, may glorify your Father which is in heaven" (Matt. 5:16). For we should not strive; nor does He desire us to imitate wicked men, but He has

exhorted us to lead all men, by patience and gentleness, from shame and the love of evil. And this indeed is proved in the case of many who once were of your way of thinking, but have changed their violent and tyrannical disposition, being overcome either by the constancy which they have witnessed in their neighbors' lives, or by the extraordinary patience they have observed in their fellow-travelers who are defrauded, or by the honesty of those with whom they have transacted business. And with regard to our not swearing at all, and always speaking the truth, He taught as follows: "Do not swear but let your yea be yea, and your nay, nay; for anything more than these come from the evil one" (Matt. 5:34, 37). And convincing us to worship God alone, He taught, "The greatest commandment is this: Love the Lord your God and serve only Him, with all your heart and with all your strength, the Lord God who made you" (Mark 12:30). And when a certain man came to Him and said, "Good Master," He answered and said, "There is none good but God only, who made all things" (cf. Matt. 19:16–17). Now then, may those who do *not* live as He taught realize that they are no Christians, even though they profess with the lip the commandments of Christ, for it is not those who merely profess His word but those who practice it who will be saved. For He said, "Not all who say to Me, 'Lord, Lord,' shall enter the kingdom of heaven, but he that does the will of My Father is in heaven. For whoever hears my word and does it, obeys Him who sent Me. Many will say to Me, 'Lord, Lord, have we not eaten and drunk and done wonders in your name?' Then will I say unto them, Depart from Me, all evil doers (Matt. 7:21–23). Then shall there be weeping and gnashing of teeth, when the righteous shall shine as the sun and the wicked are sent into everlasting fire (Matt. 13:42–43). For many shall come in My name, clothed outwardly in sheep's clothing, but inwardly being ravening wolves. By their works you will know them. Every tree that does not bring forth good fruit is cut down and thrown into the fire (Matt.

7:15, 16, 19).” We ask that you punish all those who falsely call themselves Christians but who do not live according to His teachings.

17. We, more than all others, endeavor to pay your appointed officials both the regular and special taxes, just as He taught us. For someone came to Him and asked if it were necessary to pay tribute to Caesar, to which He answered, “Tell Me, whose image does the coin bear?” And they said, “Caesar’s.” And again He answered them, “Give therefore to Caesar the things that are Caesar’s, and to God the things that are God’s” (Matt. 22:20–21). Therefore to God alone we offer worship, while in other things we gladly serve you, acknowledging you as kings and rulers of men, and praying that with your kingly power you be also found to possess sound judgment. Nevertheless, if you pay no regard to our prayers and clear explanations, we experience no loss, because we believe— indeed, are certain—that every man will suffer punishment in eternal fire according to his misdeeds, and will give an account in proportion to the power he received from God, as Christ explained when He said, “To whom God has given more, of him more will be required” (Luke 12:48).

18. Reflect on the end of the past emperors, how they died a death common to all, which death, if it led to a state of insensibility, would be a blessing to all the wicked. But since sensation remains to all who have ever lived, and eternal punishment is reserved for the wicked, see that you neglect not to be convinced, and to hold as your belief, that these things are true. Let these familiar practices convince you that after death, souls retain their senses: sorcery and divination performed through the sacrifice of innocent children, the evoking of the souls of the dead, the practices of those known as magi, dream-senders, familiar spirits and everything else done by those who are skilled in such matters. Be convinced, likewise, by those who are possessed by the spirits of the dead, demoniacs or madmen, and also by what you call the oracles of Amphilochus, Dodana, Pytho, and by the teaching of writers Empedocles and

Pythagoras, Plato and Socrates, the pit of Homer,[6] and the descent of Ulysses, to inspect these things. As you give the benefit of the doubt to all these traditions, give also to us Christians who believe more, not less, in God. For we expect our own bodies, though dead and buried in the earth, to be revived; for we hold that with God nothing is impossible.

19. What is more incredible to a reasonable person, than the idea that from a small drop of human seed bones, muscle, and flesh might take shape as in fact happens? Now suppose that you yourselves were neither of your present form nor born from parents in the usual manner. If someone were to show you both a human seed and a portrait of a man, affirming with confidence that from such seed a being could be produced, would you believe it before seeing the actual production? No one will dare to deny that such a miracle surpasses all belief. In the same way, you doubt the resurrection since you have never seen a dead man rise. But just as initially you would not have believed it possible that a person could be produced from so small a seed, and yet now you see them so produced, so also consider that it is not impossible that the bodies of men, after they have been dissolved, and like seeds planted in the earth, they should in God’s appointed time rise again and put on incorruption. We can hardly imagine what power worthy of God is attributed to Him by those who say everything returns to its source. But this we see clearly, that no one would believe it possible that from similar matter has been produced both themselves and the whole world. Indeed, we have learned, it is better for us to believe in things impossible for man, than to be unbelieving like the rest of the world. For we know that our Master Jesus Christ said, that “what is impossible with men is possible with God,” and, “Do not fear those who kill the body and can do no more; rather, fear Him who after death is able to cast both soul and body into hell” (Matt. 19:26; 10:28). For hell is the place of

---

6. See the Odyssey 11.24–25, where Ulysses digs a pit with his sword and fills it with blood to attract the souls of the dead.

punishment for those who have lived wickedly and who have refused to believe that what God has taught us by Christ will come to pass.

20. According to the (Greek myths of) Sibyl and Hystaspes, all corruptible things will be consumed by fire. Likewise the philosophers called Stoics teach that even God will be transformed into fire, and that by this process the world will be reformed. We believe, on the other hand, that God, the Creator of all things, is superior to what is changeable. So, if on some points we teach things similar to your honored poets and philosophers, and on other points we offer a more complete and supernatural teaching—if we alone prove our assertions, then why are we unjustly hated more than all others? For when we claim that all things in this world have been created and arranged by God, we say no more than Plato.[7] When we proclaim the final destruction by fire of all things, we follow the doctrine of the Stoics. And when we affirm that the souls of the wicked will experience sensation even after death and will be punished, and that the souls of the good will be rescued from punishment and will enjoy a blessed afterlife, we seem to follow the teachings of your poets and philosophers. For while we believe that men ought not to worship the works of their hands, we also say things similar to the comic poet Menander and other writers, for they too declare that "the workman is greater than the work."

21. When we say that the Word, who is the first-begotten of God, was produced without human union, and that He, Jesus Christ, our Teacher, was crucified and died, and rose again, and ascended into heaven, we teach nothing different from what you believe regarding about the sons of Jupiter. You know how many sons your esteemed writers ascribed to Jupiter: Mercury, the interpreting word and teacher of all; Aesculapius, who, though he was a great physician, was struck by a thunderbolt, and so ascended to heaven; and Bacchus too, after he

had been torn limb from limb; and Hercules, when he had committed himself to the flames to escape his labor; and the sons of Leda, and Dioscuri; and Perseus, son of Danae; and Bellerophon, who, though descended from mortals, rose to heaven on the horse Pegasus. And what shall we say of Ariadne and those like her who are said to be set among the stars? And what about the emperors who die among you, yet whom you consider worthy to be deified, and bring out a false witness who claims to have seen Caesar rise from the funeral pyre and ascend unto heaven? And you are well aware of the deeds attributed to the sons of Jupiter, written for the profit and instruction of young students, since everyone considers it honorable to imitate the gods. But may such beliefs about the gods be far from every reasonable mind. For to believe as you do that the ruler and creator of all things (i.e., Jupiter), was both a murderer of his kinsman and the son of a murderer of kinsman, and that he, seized by the lust of carnal and shameful pleasures, fell on Ganymede and many other women he had violated and that his sons did likewise. But, as we said above, wicked demons have done these things. And we have been taught that only those who draw close to God in holiness and virtue will live in eternal bliss, while those who live wickedly and do not repent are punished with everlasting fire.

22. Moreover, this Jesus, were he only an ordinary man, yet, on account of His wisdom, is worthy to be called the Son of God. For all writers call God the Father of men and also of gods. So if we assert that the Word of God was born of God in a manner different from ordinary men, this should hardly seem surprising to those who say that Mercury is the angelic word of God. But if any one objects on the basis of the teaching about his crucifixion, here too the sons of Jupiter are said to have suffered, though not in the same (but in an inferior) way. As promised earlier in this discourse, we will now demonstrate Him superior—though indeed we have already begun to do so since superiority is revealed by His actions. And if we further

---

7. See Plato's dialogue, the *Timaeus*, for the classic Greek doctrine of creation.

claim that He was born of a virgin, then we say no more than is commonly believed of Perseus. When we claim that He healed the lame, the paralytic, and those born blind, we attribute to Him deeds similar to those said to have been performed by Aesculapius.

23. To present our case before you, then, we assert first of all, that whatever has been taught us by Christ, was first taught by the prophets before Him, whose teachings alone are true and are older than any other writers who have ever lived; Secondly, that Jesus Christ is the only proper Son who has been begotten by God, being His Word and first-begotten, and power; and, becoming man according to His will, He taught us these things for the conversion and restoration of the human race. Thirdly, before He assumed human nature and dwelt among men, some, influenced by the demons already mentioned, invented false prophecies about Him and spread them abroad through the poets, as if the things they made up were actually true, though they have no witnesses and can offer no proofs for them.

24. First, although we say things similar to what the Greeks say, we alone are despised for the name of Christ, and though we do no wrong, we are put to death as criminals. Others worship trees, rivers, cats, crocodiles, and all manner of non-rational animals. Nor do they all worship the same animals but consider to be profane those who worship different animals than themselves. We need not tell you (since you well know), the very same animals that are revered by some men as gods, are seen merely as wild beasts by other men, and are employed as sacrificial animals by still others. And you accuse us because we do not revere the same gods as you, nor do we offer sacrifices and libations to the dead or decorate their statues with jewels!

25. Secondly, because we—who are from every race of men—used to worship Bacchus the son of Semele, and Apollo the son of Latona (who in their love of men did such things as it is shameful even to mention), and Proserpine and Venus (who were maddened with love of Adonis, and whose mysteries also you celebrate),

or Aesculapius, and many other so-called gods—have now, through Jesus Christ, learned to despise all these, though we are threatened with death, and have dedicated ourselves to the un-begotten and impassible God; Who never condescended to the lust of Antiope or Ganymede or any such women (as did the so-called gods); nor was associated with (myths such as) the giant with one hundred hands whose help was conjured through Thetis; nor curried favor with these so that Achilles might destroy many Greeks. We pity those who believe these things and hold that demons invented them.

26. Third, after Christ's ascension into heaven demons prompted certain men who claimed themselves to be gods. Now these were not persecuted by you but were rather deemed worthy of honors. For there was a Samaritan, Simon of Gitto, who, in the reign of Claudius Caesar and in your royal city of Rome, did mighty acts of magic, by the demonic power within him. He was considered a god, and as a god was honored by you with a statue erected on the river Tiber, between the two bridges, and bearing this inscription, in the language of Rome, "*Simoni Deo Sancto*," (To Simon, the holy God). Now many Samaritans and others worship him as the first god, and his consort, Helena (who formerly was a prostitute) as his first principle emanation. Menander, another man Samaritan and a disciple of Simon, likewise deceived many while in Antioch by his magical art. He persuaded those who followed him that they would never die, and some still believe this. Then there is Marcion, a man of Pontus, still living and teaching his disciples to believe in some other god greater than the Creator. And he, with the help of demons, has caused many from every nation to blaspheme, denying that God is the maker of this universe, and asserting that another, greater being than He has done greater works. Even some of these have been labeled Christians, although it is they and not us, who are guilty of the shameful deeds of orgies in darkened rooms and human cannibalism with infants (of which we have been accused). Now on the subject of these

heresies I have written another thesis which, if you wish to read, I will send to you.

65. After we have baptized those convinced of our teaching, we bring them to the place where the brethren are assembled so that we may offer prayers for ourselves, for the illuminated, and for everyone everywhere, that we may be counted worthy, now that we have learned the truth, and by our deeds to be good citizens and keepers of the commandments, so that we may be saved with an everlasting salvation. When the prayers are concluded, we greet one another with a kiss. Then bread and a cup of wine mixed with water are brought to the one who presides over the brethren. He takes these and, giving praise and glory to the Father of the universe through the name of the Son and of the Holy Ghost, he offers lengthy prayers in the name of those to whom He granted such favors. After this the people agree by saying "amen," Hebrew for "so be it." Now when thanks have been offered and the people have agreed, then the deacons distribute the bread and wine mixed with water to all who are present, and also carry a portion to those who are absent.

66. Among us this food is called the *Eukaristia* [the Eucharist]. And no one is allowed to partake of it except those who believe that what we teach is true, and who have been washed with the washing for the forgiveness of sins and for regeneration, and who are living in accordance with Christ's commands. For it is no ordinary bread and drink we receive. Just as Jesus Christ our Savior became incarnate, taking on himself flesh and blood for our salvation, so we are taught that the food which is blessed by the prayer of His word, and which nourishes our flesh and blood and by assimilation, is both the flesh and blood of that Jesus who was made flesh. Now the apostles, in their writings called the Gospels, have passed on to us what was commanded to them; that Jesus took bread and when he had given thanks, said, "Do this in remembrance of me" and "this is My body." In the same manner, having taken the cup and given thanks, he said, "This is my blood,"

and gave it to them alone (see Matt. 26:26–27; Mark 14:22; Luke 22:19). Demons have imitated this practice in the mysteries of Mithras, commanding the same thing to be done. For, as you know or can easily learn, the bread and a cup of water are placed with certain incantations in the mystic rites of one who is being initiated.

67. From then on we continually encourage one another with these truths. The wealthy among us help the needy, and in all things we stay together. For all the blessings with which we are supplied, we bless the Maker of all things through His Son Jesus Christ, and through the Holy Ghost. On the day called Sunday, all who live in cities or in the country gather together to one place, and the writings of the apostles or of the prophets are read, as long as time permits. Then, after the reading, the one presiding over the assembly teaches, admonishing everyone to live according the teachings. Then we all stand together and pray, after which bread and wine mixed with water are brought, and the leader offers prayers of thanksgiving. Once the people assent, saying amen, there is a distribution to each, and a participation in that over which thanks have been given, with the absent being taken a portion by the deacons. Those who are well off and willing to give offer what each has decided. Whatever is collected is given to the leader, who then helps the orphans and widows, the sick and needy, those in bonds and the strangers traveling among us—in a word, anyone in need. Now Sunday is the day on which we all hold our common assembly, since it is also the first day on which God, having transformed darkness and (prime) matter, created the world; and also the day on which Jesus Christ our Savior rose from the dead. For he was crucified on the day of Saturn (Saturday); and on the day after that—the day of the Sun—having appeared to his apostles and disciples, he taught them all these things that we have offered for your consideration.

68. Now if these things seem to you reasonable and true, then honor them. But if they seem irrational then treat them as nonsense. In either case, do not decree death to those who have

done no wrong, as you would do to enemies. For we forewarn you, that you will not escape the coming judgment of God if you continue in your injustice, and we declare, "Let God's will be done."

JUSTIN MARTYR: *DIALOGUE WITH TRYPHO* (CHAPTERS 1–15)
Greek, c. 160

See page 52 for an introduction to Justin Martyr. Here in the *Dialogue* the reader encounters a personal narrative of Justin's beliefs. While on a walk one day, Justin encounters an old man who recognizes Justin as a philosopher and invites him to expound on his philosophy. Justin complies by telling of his conversion to Christ.

✦

Chapter I: Introduction

While I was walking in the Xystus[8] one morning, someone called out to me, "Hail, O philosopher!" I turned to find a certain old man and his companions following me, so I greeting them, asking, "What is the matter?" He replied, "I was taught by Corinthus the Socratic in Argos, not to despise anyone wearing the philosopher's gown, but to show him kindness and to associate with him so that, perchance, one of us might benefit from the discussion. Therefore we have called to you, hoping for something beneficial from you. But who are you, most excellent man?" I replied, half in jest. He told me honestly his name and family. "I am Trypho," he said, "a man of the circumcision—a Hebrew—spending my days in Greece, mainly here at Corinth, since fleeing the recent war." "How do you expect," I asked, "to benefit from philosophy more than from your own lawgiver and the prophets?" "Why not?" he replied, "don't the philosophers speak constantly of God, of his unity and providence? Is the duty of philosophy not to investigate the Deity?" "Certainly," I replied, "but most do not speak of this, whether there be one or more gods, or whether they care for us humans or not, as if this knowledge

contributed nothing to our happiness. Others try to persuade us that God cares for the universe with its many species, but not us, else why would we need to pray to him night and day? This talk is hardly surprising, coming from those who neither fear God's punishment nor expect any blessing from him. And how could they, since they believe that nothing ever changes and that our lives are lived again and again yet without improvement. There are still others who believe that the soul is immortal and immaterial, and that therefore it needs nothing from God and needs fear no punishment for wickedness since what is immaterial knows no pain." Trypho smiled. "Tell us your thoughts on these matters, what you believe about God and what your philosophy is."

Chapter II: Justin Martyr's study of philosophy

"I will," I told them, "for philosophy is, in fact, the greatest possession, and most honorable before God, to whom it leads us and alone commends us; and these are truly holy men who have bestowed attention on philosophy. What philosophy is, however, and the reason why it has been sent down to men, have escaped the observation of most; otherwise there would be no Platonists, Stoics, Peripatetics, Theoretics, or Pythagoreans, this knowledge being *one*. I will tell you why it has become manifold: those who first philosophized and who were therefore greatly esteemed, were followed by those who never bothered themselves with seeking truth, but only admired the perseverance and self-discipline of their teachers, as well as the novelty of their doctrines. Each doctrine came to be known by the name of its father. Desirous of conversing with one of these men, I surrendered myself to a certain Stoic. But after spending much time with him, since I acquired no knowledge of God from him (indeed he said such instruction was unnecessary), I left him and followed another, who was called a Peripatetic, and who thought himself clever. This man, after having entertained me for the first few days, requested me to settle the fee, so that our discussion might not be unprofitable. I left him also, believing him to be no philosopher at all. Then, as my soul was eager to hear the peculiar and choicest of philosophies, I came to a Pythagorean, a famous man who greatly esteemed his own wisdom. After I had interviewed with him and was willing to become his hearer and disciple, he asked, 'Are you acquainted with music, astronomy,

---

8. A covered walkway.

and geometry? Do you expect to learn what leads to a happy life if you have not first learned those lessons that wean the soul from sensible objects, and prepare it for that which relates to the mind, so that it can contemplate what is honorable and good in its essence?' Having commended these branches of learning, and telling me that they were necessary, he dismissed me when I confessed to him my ignorance. After this I grew impatient; this last teacher clearly had some knowledge, but what a lengthy preparation I would need if I were to follow him! In this state of mind I sought out the Platonists, spending as much of my time as possible with a sagely man, recently settled in our city, who held a high position among them. I progressed, making enormous strides every day. The perception of immaterial things quite overpowered me, and the contemplation of ideas furnished my mind with wings, so that in a little while I supposed that I had become wise; and such was my stupidity, I expected forthwith to look upon God, for this is the aim of Plato's philosophy."

Chapter III: Justin narrates the manner of his conversion

"Continuing on like this I wanted only solitude and, shunning all company, I would walk in a certain field next to the sea. One day, while believing myself to be all alone there, a certain old man of no mean appearance, meek and venerable in manner, followed me a little ways off. As I turned to stare at him he asked, 'Do you know me?' To which I replied in the negative. 'Then why are you looking at me like that?' 'I was surprised,' I said, 'because I had not expected to see anyone here.' To this the old man replied, 'I am worried about some of my household which have left me, so I came to search for them. But why are you here?' 'I love to walk where my attention is not distracted, and where my thoughts will not be interrupted, since such places are best for philology.' 'So you are a *philologian*,[9] he said, 'but not a lover of deeds or of truth? A sophist, but not a practical man?' To this I rejoined, 'What greater work could one accomplish than to show the reason which governs all, and having laid hold of it, to look down on the errors of others, and their pursuits? But without philosophy and right reason, prudence would not be available

to anyone. So everyone must philosophize, since other things are only of second-rate or third-rate importance.' 'Does philosophy, then, make happiness?' he asked, interrupting me. 'Certainly,' I answered, 'and that alone.' To this he replied, 'What, then, is philosophy and what is happiness? Tell me, if you can!' 'Philosophy,' I said, 'is the knowledge of that which really exists, and a clear perception of the truth; and happiness is the reward of such knowledge and wisdom.' 'So, what do you call God?' he asked. 'That which always maintains the same nature, and is the cause of all other things—that, indeed, is God.' So I answered him, and he listened to me with pleasure, and asked me further, 'Isn't it true that knowledge is a term applicable to all kinds of matters? For example, one skilled in any art—whether in military tactics, in governing, or healing—is called "skillful"; and yet, there can be no generally applicable knowledge for both divine and human affairs can there, such that acquaints us with the very righteousness of the Divinity?' 'I believe there is,' I replied. 'What, then?' he rejoined, 'Do we "know" God or even men, in the same way we know music, arithmetic, astronomy, or subject?' 'Not at all,' I replied. 'You have not answered correctly, then,' he said, 'for some subjects come to us by investigation, while others we know only by sight. Now, if I were to tell you of an animal in India with an entirely unique nature, you would not know it before you saw it; neither could you describe it, unless you heard my description.' 'True enough,' I agreed. 'So then, how can philosophers judge correctly about God, or speak any truth, when they have no knowledge of Him, having neither seen Him at any time, nor heard Him?' 'But, father,' I said, 'the Deity cannot be seen merely by the eyes, as other living beings can, but is discernible to the mind alone, as Plato says; and I believe him!'"

Chapter IV: The soul of itself cannot see God

"Well then," the old man asked, "are our minds really so powerful, don't we perceive things more readily through our senses? And can the mind of man see God at any time, if it is uninstructed by the Holy Spirit?" To this I replied, "Plato does say, that the mind's eye, when pure, is designed to see that very Being Who is the cause of everything else the mind may know, though Being itself has no color, form, or size—in fact it has nothing the natural eye can see. It is, rather, beyond all essence, unutterable and inexplicable, and alone honorable and

---

9. A lover of reason.

good, coming suddenly into souls well-dispositioned, on account of their desire to see Him." "What affinity," he continued, "is there between us and God? Is the soul also divine and immortal, and a part of the Divine Mind? Does it also conceive of and comprehend God, and are we thereby made happy?" "Certainly," I answered. "And do the souls of all living beings comprehend Him?" he asked, "or are human souls one type and the souls of horses or donkeys another?" "No," I answered, "a soul is a soul." "In that case," he continued, "do horses and donkeys also see God?" "No indeed," I said, "and most humans will not, unless they are purified by righteousness, and by every other virtue." "So, it is not because of the mind, or any affinity between us and God, but on account of temperance and righteous that one sees God?" "Exactly," I replied, "but also because he has what is necessary to perceive God." "Well then," he continued, "do goats or sheep harm anyone?" "Not at all," I replied. "So then, by what you say, these animals will see God." "No," I answered, "their bodies deter them from this." "But if these animals could only speak," he exclaimed, "they would be entitled to ridicule our bodies! Even so, for now, I will have to be content with your explanations, except for one thing: Does the soul see God while it is in the body, or after it has left?" "So long as a soul is in human form," I answered, "it can achieve this, but all the more so when set free from the body and, of its own, possesses what it has continually desired." "So," he said, "will it remember the appearance of God when it returns to the body?" "It doesn't seem so to me," I replied. "But then what benefit is it," he continued, "for anyone to have seen God who cannot remember what he has seen, or what advantage does he have over anyone else?" "I cannot say," I answered. "And what do those endure who are judged unworthy to see?" he asked. "It is as if they are imprisoned in the bodies of wild beasts," I said—"and this is their punishment." "Do they comprehend," he asked, "that they are this way because of some sin they have committed?" "I don't think so." "Then it seems they gain no advantage from their punishment; I would even say that they are not punished unless they are conscious of the punishment." "No, indeed"—I had to agree. "That is why I conclude," he said, "that souls neither see God nor transmigrate into other bodies, because then they would know they are punished and be afraid to commit even the smallest sin afterward. But I would agree that they can perceive that God exists, and that righteousness and piety are honorable."

Chapter V: The soul is not in its own nature immortal

The old man continued, "It seems to me these philosophers know nothing all, since they cannot explain what a soul is." "So it would seem," I agreed. "Nor should the soul be called immortal; if it is immortal, it is obviously uncreated." "According to those known as Platonist," I said, "the soul is both uncreated and immortal." He then asked, "Do you believe that the world is also uncreated?" "No," I said. "You are right," he agreed, "because why would anyone believe that our bodies—tangible, solid, composite, changeable, decaying, and renewed every day—have not arisen from some cause? But if the world is created, souls must also be created. Perhaps at one time they were not in existence, for they were made for humans and other living creatures, that is, if you believe they were created distinctly, and not together with their respective bodies." "Yes," I agreed, "so souls are not immortal?" "No," he said, "not if we also believe the world is created." "But I am not claiming that all souls die," he continued, "for that would benefit the evil. We conclude, then, that the souls of the righteous go to a better place, and those of the wicked go to a worse place, awaiting judgment. And so, some who are worthy of God never die, but others are punished as long as God wills them to exist and to be punished." "What you are saying then," I replied, "is like that which Plato, in *The Timaeus*, hints about the world, when he says that it is subject to decay, because it has been created, but that it will never be destroyed by God's will. And doesn't it seem to you the very same could be said of the soul, and generally of all things? Because, besides God, all created things decay, and will cease to exist; God alone is uncreated and imperishable, and therefore He is God, but all other things are created by Him and, so, are perishable. So then, souls both die and are punished, because if they were uncreated they would never sin—being foolish one moment, cowardly the next, and violent the next. Nor would anyone agree to be changed into pigs, snakes, or dogs, and it would not be just to make them so, for everything uncreated ought to be treated alike, with no one uncreated thing preferred over another—this is why there cannot be many uncreated things. And even if there were differences between uncreated things, you could hardly find out why. You might puzzle about this from now on, but in the end you must conclude that there can be only One Uncreated, and that that One is the cause of everything else. And these things did not escape the observation of Plato and Pythagoras, those wise men," I said, "who have been as a wall and fortress of philosophy to us."

Chapter VI: These things were unknown to Plato and other philosophers

"Not that I care," the old man said, "whether Plato or Pythagoras or anyone else held such opinions. For the truth is obvious—that the soul is not life itself, but that life is in the soul, otherwise it would give life to something else, just as motion moves something other than itself. And no one denies that the soul lives, but if it lives, it does so not as being itself, but as that which partakes of being. Now then, the soul partakes of life if God so wills, and not if He does not. For life is not its own attribute, as it is God's. But if no one lives forever, and also the soul is not forever joined with the body, then whenever the union between body and soul is broken, the soul leaves the body and the person no longer exists; then there also can be no more soul, but it returns to wherever it was taken from."

Chapter VII: The knowledge of truth is found in the prophets alone

"If no help is found in these teachers" (i.e., the philosophers), I asked, "then who can help anyone to find this way?" "Long ago," he replied, "there were ancients, esteemed philosophers, both righteous and loved by God, who spoke by the Divine Spirit and foretold events that would take place and which, indeed, are now taking place. They are called prophets. These alone both saw and announced the truth to men, neither reverencing nor fearing any man, not influenced by a desire for glory, but speaking those things alone which they saw and which they heard, being filled with the Holy Spirit. Their writings are still extant, and he who has read them is very much helped in his knowledge of the beginning and end of all things—those matters the philosophers ought to know, if they would believe. For the prophets did not use (philosophical) demonstration in their writings, but were witnesses to the truth superseding all demonstration, and worthy of belief. And those things which have happened and are happening prove the va-lidity of their utterances, even though they were entitled to credit on account of the miracles which they themselves performed. These prophets glorified the Creator, the God and Father of all things, and proclaimed His Son, the Christ sent by Him. But all false prophets, filled with lying, unclean spirits, are not like this, but they work miracles for the purpose of astonishing people, and they glorify the spirits and demons of error. So pray that, above all things, the gates of light may be opened to you; for these things cannot be perceived or understood by all, but only by the one to whom God and His Christ have imparted wisdom."

Chapter VIII: Justin by his colloquy is kindled with love to Christ

"When the old man had explained all this, and much more than I have time to share now, he left with me with the admonition to reflect on it, and I have not seen him since. But immediately a flame ignited within my soul, and a love of the prophets and of everyone who is a friend of Christ, possessed me. Reflecting on his message, I discovered the only safe and profitable philosophy. Therefore, I am a philosopher of this way, and I desire that everyone would resolve, as I, to not avoid the message of the Savior. His words are powerful and sufficient to inspire those who turn aside from the right path; and the sweetest rest is offered to those who diligently practice them. You, then, if you care about yourself at all and are eagerly looking for salvation, and if you believe in God, you may—since you are not lax about this—become acquainted with the Christ of God, and, after having been perfected, come to live a blessed life."

After saying this, those who were with Trypho laughed. He, smiling, said, "I approve of your remarks, and admire the eagerness with which you study divine things; but it would be better for you stay with the philosophy of Plato, or of some other philosopher, cultivating endurance, self-control, and moderation, than to be deceived by false words and the opinions of men of no reputation. For if you continue following that philosophy and live blamelessly, a hope of a better destiny is still open to you. Yet if you forsake God and put your confidence in man, what safety still awaits you? So then, if you accept my message (for I have already considered you a friend), then be circumcised and observe the ordinances have been enacted with respect to the Sabbath, and the feasts, and the new moons of God; and, in a word, do all things which have been written in the law: and then perhaps you shall obtain mercy from God. But Christ—if He has indeed been born—is unknown, and does not even know Himself, and has no power until Elias comes to anoint Him, and makes Him manifest to all. And in that case you, having accepted a groundless report, invent a Christ for yourselves, and for his sake are inconsiderately perishing."

Chapter IX: Christians do not believe groundless stories

"I excuse and forgive you, my friend," I said. "For you do not know what you are talking about but have merely been persuaded by teachers who do not understand the Scriptures; you speak, like a prophet, whatever comes into your mind. But if you are willing to listen to a true account of Him and shall confess Him—though reproach is heaped on us and tyrants compel us to deny Him—I shall prove to you that we have not believed empty fables, or words without any foundation but words filled with the Spirit of God and power, flourishing with grace." Once more those in his company laughed. So I got up and began to leave. But Trypho, grasping my garment, refused me until I should do what I had promised. "In that case tell your companions not to behave so disgracefully," I said. "Let them listen in silence or else go away, so that we may find a place to rest and finish our discourse." That seemed good to Trypho and so we found another quiet space in the Xystus. Two of his companions who ridiculed us, left. Finding a place we sat down, Trypho and I, together with the companions of his that stayed behind.

Chapter X: Trypho blames Christians for the non-observance of the law

Trypho's companions bantered for a while about the wars waged in Judea. When they finally stopped, I began again, "So, is this all we are blamed for, my friends, that we do not live according to the Law and are not circumcised in the flesh as your forefathers were, and do not observe Sabbaths as you do? Are our lives and customs also slandered among you? Do you believe the myths told of us, that we are cannibals and that after our feasts we put out the lights and engage in promiscuity? Or do you blame us merely for our views?" "With your views alone we take issue," Trypho answered, "and not for the things the rabble accuses you of, which are not

at all worthy of consideration. Moreover, your precepts in the so-called Gospel are so wonderful and so great, that I suspect no one can keep them, for I have carefully read them. But this is what is most troubling to us: that you, professing holiness, and supposing yourselves to be better than others, in no way separate from them, and do not change your manner of living from that of the heathen, in that you observe no festivals or Sabbaths, and yes, you do not circumcise. Resting your hopes on a man who was crucified, you expect something good from God, yet you do not obey His commandments. Have you not read that soul shall be cut off from his people who is not circumcised on the eighth day (Gen. 17:12–14)? And this was ordained for strangers and for slaves as well as for Israelites. But you, despising this covenant rashly, reject the consequent duties, and attempt to persuade yourselves that you know God, when, however, you perform none of those things which they do who fear God. If, therefore, you can defend yourself on these points and explain how you can hope for anything whatsoever from God, though you do not observe the law, this we would like to know, and we have other questions for you as well."

Chapter XI: The law abrogated; the New Testament promised and given by God

"There is no other God, O Trypho, nor was there any from eternity, but He who made and arrayed the entire universe. Nor do we believe that there is one God for us and another for you. But He alone is God who led your fathers out from Egypt with a strong hand and a high arm. Nor have we trusted in any other, for there is no other, but only in Him whom you also have trusted—the God of Abraham, Isaac, and Jacob. However, we do not trust through Moses or through the law; for then we would live just as yourselves. But I have read that there will be a final law and covenant, the chief of all, which all must now observe who are seeking the inheritance of God. For the law transmitted on Mount Horeb is now old, and belongs to yourselves alone; but *that to which I refer* is for all universally. Now, once law is placed against law, the latter abolishes the former, and any covenant that comes after, likewise puts an end to the previous one. Thus, an eternal and final law—namely, Christ—has been given to us, and that covenant is trustworthy, after which there will be no further law, commandment, or ordinance. Have you not read what

Isaiah says, 'Listen to Me, my people; and you kings, heed Me, for a law will go forth from Me, and My judgment will be for a light to the nations. My righteousness comes swiftly and My salvation shall go forth, and nations shall trust in My arm'? And Jeremiah, concerning this same new covenant, says, 'Behold, the days come, says the Lord, that I will make a new covenant with the house of Israel and with the house of Judah, not like the covenant I made with their fathers, in the day that I took them by the hand, to bring them out of the land of Egypt.' If, therefore, God proclaimed a new covenant that was to be instituted, and this for a light of the nations, we see and are persuaded that men approach God, leaving their idols and other unrighteousness, through the name of Him who was crucified, Jesus Christ, and abide by their confession even unto death, and maintain piety. Moreover, by the works and by the attendant miracles, it is possible for all to understand that He is the new law, and the new covenant, and the expectation of those who out of every people wait for the good things of God. For the true spiritual Israel, and descendants of Judah, Jacob, Isaac, and Abraham (who in uncircumcision was approved of and blessed by God on account of his faith, and called the father of many nations), are we who have been led to God through this crucified Christ, as shall be demonstrated while we proceed."

Chapter XII: The Jews violate the eternal law and misinterpret the law of Moses

"I also add another passage in which Isaiah exclaims: 'Hear My words, and your soul shall live; and I will make an everlasting covenant with you, even the sure mercies of David. Behold, I have given Him for a witness to the people: nations which know not You shall call on You; peoples who know not You shall escape to You, because of your God, the Holy One of Israel; for He has glorified You.' This same law you have despised, and His new holy covenant you have slighted; and now you neither receive it, nor repent of your evil deeds. 'For your ears are closed, your eyes are blinded, and the heart is hardened,' as Jeremiah cries out, yet not even then do you listen. The Lawgiver is present, yet you do not see Him; to the poor the Gospel is preached, the blind see, yet you do not understand. You now need a second circumcision, though you glory greatly in the flesh. The new law requires you to keep perpetual sabbath, and you, because you are idle for one day, suppose you are pious, not discerning why this has been commanded you. And if you eat unleavened bread, you say the will of God has been fulfilled. The Lord our God does not take pleasure in such observances: if there is any perjured person or a thief among you, let him cease to be so; if any adulterer, let him repent; then he has kept the sweet and true sabbaths of God. If any one has impure hands, let him wash and be pure."

Chapter XIII: Isaiah teaches that sins are forgiven through Christ's blood

"Isaiah did not send you to a bath to wash away murder and other sins, which all the water of the sea is insufficient to purge. But, this was that saving bath of ancient times which followed those who repented, and who were no longer purified by the blood of goats and of sheep or the ashes of an heifer or the offerings of fine flour, but by faith through the blood of Christ and through His death. For this very reason Christ died, as Isaiah explained, saying 'The Lord will show His holy arm before the eyes of all the nations, and all the nations and the ends of the earth shall see the salvation of God. Depart, go out from here and touch no unclean thing; go out of the midst of here, be clean those of you who carry the vessels of the Lord, for you do not leave in haste. For the Lord goes before you; and the Lord, the God of Israel, will gather you together. Behold, my Servant will deal wisely and He will be exalted and greatly glorified. Just as many were astonished at You, so Your form and Your glory will be marred more than men. So will many nations be astonished at Him, and the kings will shut their mouths; for that which had not been told them concerning Him shall they see, and that which they had not heard shall they consider. Lord, who hath believed our report? and to whom is the arm of the Lord revealed? We have announced Him as a child before Him, as a root in a dry ground. He has no form or beauty, and when we saw Him He had no form or beauty; but His form is dishonored, and fails more than the sons of men. He is a man in affliction, and acquainted with bearing sickness, because His face has been turned away; He was despised, and we esteemed Him not. He bears our sins, and is distressed for us; and we esteemed Him to be in toil and in affliction, and in evil treatment. But He was wounded for our transgressions, He was bruised for our iniquities; the chastisement of our peace was upon Him. With His stripes we are healed. All we, like sheep, have gone astray. Every man has turned to his own way; and the Lord laid on Him our iniquities, and by reason of His oppression He opens not His mouth. He was brought as a sheep to the slaughter; and as a lamb before her shearer is dumb, so He opened not His mouth. In His humiliation His judgment was taken away. And who shall declare His generation? For His life is taken from the earth. Because of the transgressions of my people He came to death. And I will give the wicked for His grave, and the rich for His death, because He committed no iniquity, and deceit was not found in His mouth. And the Lord wills to purify Him from affliction. If he has been given for sin, your soul will see a long-lived seed. And the Lord wills to take His soul away from trouble, to show Him light, and to form Him in understanding, to justify the righteous One who serves many well. And He shall bear our sins; therefore He will inherit many, and will divide the spoil of the strong, because His soul was delivered to death; and He was numbered with the transgressors, and He bore the sins of many, and was delivered for their transgression. Sing, O barren; break forth and cry aloud, you who do not travail in pain, for more are the children of the desolate than the children of the married wife. For the Lord said, 'Enlarge the place of your tent and of your curtains; fix them and spare not, lengthen your cords and strengthen your stakes; stretch forth to your right and your left, and your seed will inherit the Gentiles, and you will make the desolate cities to be inherited. Fear not if you are ashamed, nor be dismayed if you have been reproached; for you will forget everlasting shame and will not remember the reproach of your widowhood, because the Lord has made a name for Himself, and He who has redeemed you will be called the God of Israel, throughout the whole earth. The Lord has called you as a woman forsaken and grieved in spirit, as a woman hated from her youth.'"

Chapter XIV: Righteousness is not placed in Jewish rites, but in the conversion of the heart given in baptism by Christ

"By this washing of repentance and knowledge of God, ordained on account of the transgression of God's people, Isaiah cries out, we have believed, and testify that the very baptism which he announced is alone able to purify those who have repented—this is the water of life. But the cisterns which you have dug for yourselves are broken and profitless to you. For what is the use of that baptism which cleanses the flesh and body alone? Baptize the soul from wrath and from covetousness, from envy and from hatred, and behold, your body is pure. Here is the symbolic significance of unleavened bread, that you do not commit the old deeds of wicked leaven. But you understand things in a fleshly sense, and you suppose it pious if you perform these things, all the while your souls are filled with deceit and every wickedness. Accordingly, after the seven days of eating unleavened bread, God commanded them to mingle new leaven, that is, the performance of other works, and not the imitation of the old and evil works. And because this is what this new Lawgiver demands of you, I shall again refer to the words which have been quoted by me, and to others also which have been passed over. They are related by Isaiah to the following effect: 'Hearken to me, and your soul will live, and I will make with you an everlasting covenant, even the sure mercies of David. Behold, I have given Him for a witness to the people, a leader and commander to the nations. Nations that do not know you will call on you; peoples whom you do not know will come to you, because of your God, the Holy One of Israel. For He has glorified You. Seek God, and when you find Him call on Him, as long as He is near. Let the wicked forsake his ways and the unrighteous man his thoughts; and let him return to the Lord and he will obtain mercy, because He abundantly pardons sins. For my thoughts are not your thoughts, nor are your ways my ways. But as far as the heavens are from the earth, so far is my way removed from your way, and your thoughts from my thoughts. For as the snow or rain descend from heaven and shall not return till it waters the earth, and makes it bring forth and bud and gives seed to the sower and bread for food, so too is My word that goes forth out of My mouth: it will not return until it has accomplished all that I desired, and I will make My commandments prosperous. For you will go out with joy and be taught with gladness. For the mountains and the hills will leap while they expect you, and all the trees of the fields will applaud with their branches. Instead of the thorn, the cypress will grow; and instead of the brier, the myrtle. And the Lord shall be for a name and for an everlasting sign, and He shall not fail!' These and many similar words were written by the prophets, O Trypho," I said, "some of which are in reference to the first advent of Christ, in which He is preached as inglorious, obscure, and of mortal appearance; but others in reference to His second advent, when He will appear in glory and above the clouds; and those of your own nation will see and know Him whom they have pierced. Just as Hosea, one of the twelve prophets, and Daniel, foretold."

Chapter XV: True fasting

"Learn, therefore, to keep the true fast of God, as Isaiah says, that you may please God. Isaiah has cried out, 'Shout vehemently, and do not spare: lift up your voice as a trumpet, and show My people their transgressions and the house of Jacob their sins. They seek Me from day to day, and desire to know My ways as a nation that did righteousness, and did not forsake the judgment of God. They ask for righteous judgment and desire to draw near to God, saying, "Why have we fasted, and You do not see? And have afflicted our souls and You have not known?" Because in the days of your fasting you find your own pleasure, and oppress all those who are subject to you. Behold, you fast for strife and debate, and strike the humble with your fists. Why do you fast for Me, as today, so that your voice is heard aloud? This is not the fast which I have chosen: the day in which a man afflicts his soul. And even if you strain, clothing yourself in sackcloth and ashes—this is not the fast I have chosen, says the Lord. Rather, loose unrighteous bonds, dissolve wrong covenants, free the oppressed and avoid every sinful contract. Give your bread to the hungry and bring the homeless poor under your roof; if you see him naked, clothe him; and do not hide yourself from your own flesh. Then will your light break forth as the morning and you will rise up quickly, and your righteousness will go before you and the glory of God will cover you. Then You will cry out and the Lord will hear you while you are still speaking. He will say, "Behold, I am here." And if you will remove the yoke, the abusive hand, and the murmuring, and give your bread generously to the hungry, and will satisfy the afflicted, then your light will arise in the darkness, and your darkness will be as the noon-day. God will be continually with you, and you will be satisfied with what your soul desires, and your bones shall grow strong. You will become like a well-watered garden, as a fountain of water, as a land where the water never fails. So, circumcise the foreskin of your heart,' as the words of God in all these passages demand."

IRENAEUS: *THE DEMONSTRATION OF THE APOSTOLIC PREACHING* (EXCERPT)
Originally in Greek, Late Second Century A.D.

Irenaeus was probably born in Smyrna, a city mentioned in Revelation 2:8, though he is known as Irenaeus of Lyon, having moved from Asia Minor to Gaul in his adulthood. In his letter to a Roman presbyter, Florinus, Irenaeus explains that, as a boy in Smyrna, he heard the preaching of Polycarp (a disciple of the Apostle John). Thus, this second century theologian provides readers with an important link to the apostolic age. The first few chapters of the hundred-chapter work are reprinted here and include one of the first Christian reflections on the Trinity (see chapter 5). The following paraphrase is based on J. A. Robinson's translation (1920).

◆

1. Knowing, my beloved Marcianus, your desire to walk in godliness, which alone leads man to life eternal, I rejoice with you and make my prayer that you may preserve your faith entire and so be pleasing to God who made you. Would that it were possible for us to be always together, to help each other and to lighten the labor of our earthly life by continual discourse together on the things that profit. But, since at this present time we are parted from one another in the body, yet according to our power we will not fail to speak with you a little by writing, and to show forth in brief the preaching of the truth for the confirmation of your faith. We send you as it were a manual of essentials, that by little you may attain to much, learning in short space all the members of the body of the truth, and receiving in brief the demonstration of the things of God. So shall it be fruitful to your own salvation, and you shall put to shame all who inculcate falsehood, and bring with all confidence our sound and pure teaching to everyone who desires to understand it. For one is the way leading upward for all who see, lightened with heavenly light, but many and dark and contrary are the ways of them that see not. This way leads to the kingdom of heaven, uniting man to God, but those ways

bring down to death, separating man from God. Wherefore it is needful for you and for all who care for their own salvation to make your course unswerving, firm and sure by means of faith, that you falter not, nor be retarded and detained in material desires, nor turn aside and wander from the right.

2. Now, since man is a living being compounded of soul and flesh, he must exist by both of these: and, whereas from both of them offences come, purity of the flesh is the restraining abstinence from all shameful things and all unrighteous deeds, and purity of the soul is the keeping faith toward God entire, neither adding thereto nor diminishing therefrom. For godliness is obscured and dulled by the soiling and the staining of the flesh, and is broken and polluted and no more entire, if falsehood enter into the soul; but it will keep itself in its beauty and its measure, when truth is constant in the soul and purity in the flesh. For what profit is it to know the truth in words, and to pollute the flesh and perform the works of evil? Or what profit can purity of the flesh bring, if truth be not in the soul? For these rejoice with one another, and are united and allied to bring man face to face with God. Wherefore the Holy Spirit says by David, *Blessed is the man who hath not walked in the counsel of the ungodly*, that is, the counsel of the nations which know not God: for those are ungodly who worship not the God that truly is. And therefore the Word says to Moses: *I am He that is*, but they that worship not the God that is, these are the ungodly. *And hath not stood in the way of sinners*, but sinners are those who have the knowledge of God and keep not His commandments; that is, disdainful scorners. *And hath not sat in the seat of the pestilential*, now the pestilential are those who by wicked and perverse doctrines corrupt not themselves only, but others also. For the seat is a symbol of teaching. Such then are all heretics: they sit in the seats of the pestilential, and those are corrupted who receive the venom of their doctrine.

3. Now, that we may not suffer anything of this kind, we must hold the rule of the faith without deviation, and do the commandments of God, believing in God and fearing Him as Lord and loving Him as Father. Now this doing is produced by faith: for Isaiah (7:9) says: *If ye believe not, neither shall ye understand*. And faith is produced by the truth, for faith rests on things that truly are. For in things that are, as they are, we believe; and believing in things that are, as they ever are, we keep firm our confidence in them. Since then faith is the perpetuation of our salvation, we must maintain it, in order that we may have a true comprehension of the things that are. Faith makes this possible for us, even as the Elders, the disciples of the Apostles, have handed it down to us. First of all it bids us bear in mind that we have received baptism for the remission of sins, in the name of God the Father, and in the name of Jesus Christ, the Son of God, who was incarnate and died and rose again, and in the Holy Spirit of God. And that this baptism is the seal of eternal life, and is the new birth unto God, that we should no longer be the sons of mortal men, but of the eternal and perpetual God; and that what is everlasting and continuing is made God; and is over all things that are made, and all things are put under Him; and all the things that are put under Him are made His own; for God is not ruler and Lord over the things of another, but over His own; and all things are God's, and therefore God is Almighty, and all things are of God.

4. For it is necessary that things that are made should have their beginning from some great cause, and the beginning of all things is God. For He Himself was not made by any, and by Him all things were made. And therefore it is right first of all to believe that there is One God, the Father, who made and fashioned all things, and made what was not, that it should be, and who, containing all things, alone is uncontained. Now among all things is this world of ours, and in the world is man, so then this world also was formed by God.

5. Thus then there is shown forth One God, the Father, not made, invisible, Creator of all things, above whom there is no other God, and

after whom there is no other God. And, since God is rational, therefore by [the] Word He created the things that were made; and God is Spirit, and by (the) Spirit He adorned all things, as also the prophet says, *By the word of the Lord were the heavens established, and by his spirit all their power.* Since then the Word establishes, that is to say, gives body and grants the reality of being, and the Spirit gives order and form to the diversity of the powers; rightly and fittingly is the Word called the Son, and the Spirit the Wisdom of God. Well also does Paul His apostle say: *One God, the Father, who is over all and through all and in us all.* For *over all* is the Father; and *through all* is the Son, for through Him all things were made by the Father; and *in us all* is the Spirit, who cries *Abba Father,* and fashions man into the likeness of God. Now the Spirit shows forth the Word, and therefore the prophets announced the Son of God; and the Word utters the Spirit, and therefore is Himself the announcer of the prophets, and leads and draws man to the Father.

6. This then is the order of the rule of our faith, and the foundation of the building, and the stability of our conversation: God, the Father, not made, not material, invisible; one God, the Creator of all things, this is the first point of our faith. The second point is this: The Word of God, Son of God, Christ Jesus our Lord, who was manifested to the prophets according to the form of their prophesying and according to the method of the dispensation of the Father, through whom all things were made; who also at the end of the times, to complete and gather up all things, was made man among men, visible and tangible, in order to abolish death and show forth life and produce a community of union between God and man. And the third point is this: The Holy Spirit, through whom the prophets prophesied and the fathers learned the things of God, and the righteous were led forth into the way of righteousness, and who in the end of the times was poured out in a new way upon mankind in all the earth, renewing man unto God.

7. And for this reason the baptism of our

regeneration proceeds through these three points: God the Father bestowing on us regeneration through His Son by the Holy Spirit. For as many as carry (in them) the Spirit of God are led to the Word that is to the Son; and the Son brings them to the Father; and the Father causes them to possess incorruption. Without the Spirit it is not possible to behold the Word of God, nor without the Son can any draw near to the Father: for the knowledge of the Father is the Son, and the knowledge of the Son of God is through the Holy Spirit; and, according to the good pleasure of the Father, the Son ministers and dispenses the Spirit to whomsoever the Father wills and as He wills.

8. And by the Spirit the Father is called Most High and Almighty and Lord of hosts; that we may learn concerning God that He is creator of heaven and earth and all the world, and maker of angels and men, and Lord of all, through whom all things exist and by whom all things are sustained; merciful, compassionate and very tender, good, just, the God of all, both of Jews and of Gentiles, and of them that believe. To them that believe He is as Father, for in the end of the times He opened up the covenant of adoption; but to the Jews as Lord and Lawgiver, for in the intermediate times, when man forgot God and departed and revolted from Him, He brought them into subjection by the Law, that they might learn that the Lord was their maker and creator, who also gives the breath of life, and whom we ought to worship day and night: and to the Gentiles as maker and creator and almighty: and to all alike sustainer and nurturer and king and judge; for none shall escape and be delivered from His judgment, neither Jew nor Gentile, nor believer that has sinned, nor angel: but they who now reject His goodness shall know His power in judgment, according to that which the blessed apostle says: Not knowing that the goodness of God leadeth thee to repentance; but according to thy hardness and impenitent heart thou treasurest up for thyself wrath in the day of wrath and of the revelation of the righteous judgment of God, who shall render to every man according

to his works. This is He who is called in the Law the God of Abraham and the God of Isaac and the God of Jacob, the God of the living; although the sublimity and greatness of this God is unspeakable.

9. Now this world is encompassed by seven heavens, in which dwell powers and angels and archangels, doing service to God, the Almighty and Maker of all things; not as though He was in need, but that they may not be idle and unprofitable and ineffectual. Wherefore also the Spirit of God is manifold in (His) indwelling, and in seven forms of service is He reckoned by the prophet Isaiah, as resting on the Son of God, that is the Word, in His coming as man. *The Spirit of God*, he says, *shall rest upon him, the Spirit of wisdom and of understanding, the Spirit of counsel and of might (the Spirit of knowledge) and of godliness; the Spirit of the fear of God shall fill him.* Now the heaven which is first from above, and encompasses the rest, is (that of) wisdom; and the second from it, of understanding; and the third, of counsel; and the fourth, reckoned from above, (is that) of might; and the fifth, of knowledge; and the sixth, of godliness; and the seventh, this firmament of ours, is full of the fear of that Spirit which gives light to the heavens. For, as the pattern (of this), Moses received the seven-branched candlestick, that shined continually in the holy place; for as a pattern of the heavens he received this service, according to that which the Word spake unto him: *Thou shalt make (it) according to all the pattern of the things which thou hast seen in the mount.*

10. Now this God is glorified by His Word who is His Son continually, and by the Holy Spirit who is the Wisdom of the Father of all: and the power(s) of these, (namely) of the Word and Wisdom, which are called Cherubim and Seraphim, with unceasing voices glorify God; and every created thing that is in the heavens offers glory to God the Father of all. He by His Word has created the whole world, and in the world are the angels; and to all the world He has given laws wherein each several thing should abide, and according to that which

is determined by God should not pass their bounds, each fulfilling his appointed task.

AUGUSTINE: *CITY OF GOD* (EXCERPTS)
Latin, A.D. 413–426

Augustine (354–430), Bishop of Hippo (North Africa), is arguably the most influential Christian theologian in all of church history. In this, the most widely read and influential of his later works, Augustine responds to pagan charges that Christians are to be blamed for the downfall of the Roman Empire. His apology (defense and explanation of Christian belief and practice) presents all of history as a "tale of two cities"—the temporal city of man and the eternal city of God. In his description of the latter city, Augustine rejected the widely taught premillennial view of a literal, future reign of Christ on earth for a thousand years (then known as *chiliasm*) in favor of amillennialism (which Augustine was the first to teach), which rejects altogether the idea of an earthly reign of Christ and sees the final judgment as immediately following his second coming. In his description of true worship, Augustine critiques the teaching of the Platonists, philosophers who followed Plato and his idealism. Brief selections from three sections of *City of God* are included here. Chapters 1–6 and 20 from Book 10 address the definition and nature of true worship of a supreme God. Chapter 1 of Book 15 and chapter 17 of Book 19 summarize the famous two-cities thesis of Augustine's work.

Questions for Guided Reading: Book 10

1. What is the ultimate human purpose and what common origin is held for this purpose?
2. What term, according to Augustine, best expresses the idea of true worship and why?
3. What do Platonist philosophers believe in common with Christians about enlightenment?
4. Where did the Platonists go wrong in their understanding of *latreia* (worship)?
5. What was the point of Old Testament sacrifices and how do these relate to sacraments?

6. What is the supreme sacrifice, and how could God have offered *and* received that sacrifice?

Questions for Guided Reading: Book 15

1. The account of Cain and Abel helps us understand our origins and destiny: What is our *natural* lineage (from which biblical ancestor do we "naturally" descend), and what is his impact on us?

2. What is our *spiritual* lineage, and how does that come about?

3. To which ancestor does Augustine trace the origin of the earthly city? The heavenly city?

Questions for Guided Reading: Book 19

1. Contrast the two cities: what are their essential differences?

2. What, if anything, do they have in common?

✦

FROM BOOK 10

Chapter I: Platonists say God alone bestows blessedness, but do those beings they themselves worship desire sacrifice, or that sacrifice should be made to God alone?

It is the opinion of those who reason, that all men desire to be happy. But who are happy, or how they become so, these are questions about which the weakness of human understanding stirs endless and angry controversies, in which philosophers have wasted their strength and expended their leisure. To discuss their opinions would be tedious and unnecessary. The reader may remember what we said in the eighth book, while making a selection of the philosophers with whom we might discuss the question regarding the future life of happiness, whether we can reach it by paying divine honors to the one true God, the Creator of all gods, or by worshipping many gods. For we choose the Platonists, noblest of the philosophers, because they perceived that the human soul, immortal and rational as it is, cannot be happy except by partaking of the light of that God by whom

both itself and the world were made; and also that the happy life which all men desire cannot be reached by any who does not hold with pure and holy love to that one supreme good, the unchangeable God. But since even these philosophers, whether accommodating to the folly and ignorance of the people, or as the apostle says, "becoming vain in their imaginations," supposed that many gods should be worshipped, so some of them considered that divine honor by worship and sacrifice should be rendered even to the demons (an error I have already refuted), we must now, by God's help, ascertain what is thought about our religious worship and reverence by those immortal and blessed spirits who dwell in the heavenly places among those dominions, principalities, and powers, whom the Platonists call gods, and some either good demons, or like us, angels. In other words, we must find out whether angels desire our sacrifice and worship, consecrating our possessions and ourselves to them, or only to God—theirs and ours—alone.

This worship due to the Deity is best expressed in the Greek term, *latreia*, used in Scripture to mean *service*. Now, service due to men—where the apostle writes that servants must be subject to their own masters (Eph. 6:5)—is called by a different Greek term, but the service to God by worship is most always called *latreia*. This word could not simply be *cultus*, because then it would not be due exclusively to God; for the same word is applied to the respect we pay either to the memory or the living presence of men. From that word also we derive *agriculture*, *colonist*, and other words. And the gods themselves are called *caelicolae*, simply because they dwell in caelum—heaven—where the verbal form of this word means to inhabit, not worship. So they are "inhabitants of heaven."

Now, the word *religion* might seem to express more definitely the worship due to God alone, and so our translators have used this word to express the Greek term *threskeia*. However, in Latin *religion* is something displayed in human relationships, in the family, and between friends, so using this word does not help reduce our ambiguity. Piety (*eusebeia* in Greek) is commonly understood as the proper designation for the worship of God. Yet we also use this word to speak of one's duty to his parents, and for kind works—the sort God commands and is pleased with in place of (formal) sacrifices. Even God himself is described as *pius*, though the Greeks never describe God as *eusebes*, in their language, although they do commonly use *eusebeia* as a synonym for *compassion*. To make the distinction clear and precise in their translations of Scripture, they use *theo-sebia* (God-worship) in place of *eu sebia* (good-worship). We Latin speakers, on the other hand, cannot express either of these ideas in a single word. The attitude of worship, then, is *latreia* in Greek and is translated *servitus* in Latin, meaning the service of the worship of God. Or, it may be called *threskia* in Greek, but in Latin *religio*, the religion which binds us to God; and also, as mentioned, Greeks call it *theo-sebeia*, which, for lack of a better word, is *worship of God*. Those words, then express worship which is due only to the true God, who transforms his worshipers into gods. And whatever blessed and immortal beings inhabit the heavens, they have no right to our worship if they do not love us and wish us to be blessed. If, however, they do love us and desire our happiness, then they must want our happiness to come from the same source of joy as theirs—how could our happiness come from any other source than theirs?

Chapter II: Views on enlightenment from the Platonist philosopher, Plotinus

With the distinguished philosophers we agree. For they write that these spirits have the same source of happiness as ourselves—a certain intelligible light which is their God. One who is different from themselves, illuminating them until they are penetrated with light, enjoying perfect happiness in the participation of God. Indeed, Plotinus, in his commentary on Plato, asserts that not even the being whom they believe to be the "Soul of the Universe" derives its blessedness from any other source than we do, that is, from the Light which is distinct from the Soul, by which it was created, and by whose intelligent illumination it shines with intelligible light. Plotinus compares these invisible heavenly realities with the heavenly spheres visible to us—where God is the sun and the soul the moon; for they suppose that the moon derives its light from the sun. The great Platonist, therefore, believes that the souls of the immortal, blessed beings who inhabit heaven, belong to the class of rational souls. There is nothing higher than the rational soul in all creation, he says, except God—the Creator of the world and the soul itself. From no other source but this the heavenly spirits derive their blessed life and light of truth, just as we read in the gospel, "There was a man sent from God whose name was John; he came

as a witness to bear witness to the Light, that through Him all might believe. He himself was not the Light but he came to witness to the Light—the true Light that enlightens everyone, coming into the world" (John 1:6–9). This distinction proves that a rational soul, like John had, cannot be its own light, but needs to receive illumination from another, the true Light. This is what John affirms through his witness, "We have all received of His fullness" (John 1:16).

Chapter III: Platonists abandoned the true worship of God by worshiping angels

Platonists, if they had not become vain in their thinking would certainly acknowledge that neither could angels keep nor could we mortals reach, a state of blessedness without worshiping the one God of gods—both their God and ours. To Him alone we owe that service called *latreia*, whether through the sacraments or inwardly. For we are all His temple, individually and collectively, since He condescends to dwell in each one and in the whole body, being no greater in all than in each, since He is neither expanded nor divided. Our heart when it rises to Him is His altar. The priest who intercedes for us is His Only-begotten Son. We sacrifice blood-stained victims to Him when we fight for His truth at the loss of our own blood (cf. Heb. 12:4). To Him we offer the sweetest incense when we come before Him burning with holy and pious love; to Him we devote and surrender ourselves and His gifts in us; to Him, by solemn feasts and on appointed days, we sanctify the memory of His benefits, so that neither time nor ungratefulness should creep up on us; to Him we offer on the altar of our heart the sacrifice of humility and praise, kindled by the fire of burning love. This is all so we may see Him, as far as He may be seen, and that we may cling to Him, cleansed from all stain of sins and evil passions, being consecrated in His name. Therefore, he is the fountain of our happiness, and the aim of all our desires; being attached to Him—or rather reattached since we formerly detached ourselves and lost hold of Him—being, I say, reattached to Him, we are drawn toward Him by love, that we may rest in Him, and find our blessedness by attaining that goal. Our good, about which philosophers debate, is found in nothing other than being united with God. And by spiritually embracing Him, the intellectual soul is also filled and inspired with true virtues.

We are commanded to love this good with all our heart, with all our soul, and with all our strength. To this good we should be led by those who love us, just as we should lead those we love. In this way will be fulfilled those two commandments on which hang all the law and the prophets, "Love the Lord your God with all your heart, and with all thy mind, and with all thy soul," and "Love your neighbor as yourself" (Matt. 22:37–40). In order that we may know how to love ourselves, there was commanded for us an ultimate purpose—the aim of all our actions, by which we may be blessed (for if anyone loves himself, his goal is to achieve that blessedness)—and that purpose is "to draw near to God" (Ps. 73:28). So then, for the one who knows how to love himself in this way, the commandment requires him to do all he can to bring his neighbor to this love. This *is* the worship of God, this *is* true religion and right piety, the service due to God alone. Any immortal power, therefore, no matter how powerful it may be, if he loves us as he loves himself, must desire that we find our happiness by submitting ourselves to God, to whom in submission he also finds happiness. If he does not worship God then he is miserable because he is God-deprived. If he worships God, then he cannot wish to be worshiped in God's place. On the contrary, these higher powers gladly follow the divine decree which says, "He that sacrifices to any god except the Lord will be utterly destroyed" (Exod. 22:20).

Chapter IV: Sacrifice is due the true God only

Aside from other religions, no one dares claim that sacrifice is due to any but God. To be sure, some aspects of worship have been used to honor men either through excessive humility or vain flattery. Yet, those who are venerated or even adored are still human, and who ever sacrificed to that which is not a god? Now the antiquity of sacrifice in worship is sufficiently proved by the brothers Cain and Abel, of whom God rejected the older brother's sacrifice, while looking favorably on the younger.

Chapter V: God requires no sacrifice—a sacrifice is a symbol of what is required

No one is foolish enough to believe that God actually needs the things offered to Him. Scripture refutes this notion in many places, for example, "I said to the Lord, You are my God, for You need none of my posses-

sions" (Ps. 16:2). We must believe that God has no need of cattle or any other earthly and material thing, or our righteousness—indeed even our worship of God does not profit Him, but benefits us. Would anyone claim he has benefited a fountain by drinking from it? Do we benefit light by seeing?

If in times past our fathers offered animal sacrifices—of which we read today without imitating—this merely signifies things we do to draw near to God, and to encourage our neighbor to do the same. Thus, the visible sacrifice is the sacrament—the sacred sign of an invisible sacrifice. So the Psalmist implores God's mercies for his sins, saying, "If You desired sacrifice, I would give it, but You do not delight not in whole burnt offerings. The sacrifice of God is a broken heart; a contrite and humble heart God will not reject" (Ps. 51:16–17). Note how in the very words expressing God's refusal of sacrifice, he shows that God requires sacrifice—not the sacrifice of a slaughtered beast but of a contrite heart. Thus, the very sacrifice which God does not desire is the symbol of that sacrifice God does desire. Now God does not desire sacrifices in the way that the foolish may suppose, that is, in order to gratify His own pleasure. No, He would never have commanded those Old Covenant sacrifices unless He wanted to symbolize those things, such as a repentant heart, that He does desire. And both these realities—the external and the internal—were destined to merge into one, so that we might understand it was not the formal sacrifices themselves but the things symbolized by them, that were pleasing to God. So also it says, in another Psalm, "If I were hungry, I would not tell you; for the world is mine and its fullness. Will I eat the flesh of bulls or drink the blood of goats?" (Ps. 50:12–13). It is as if He is saying, 'Suppose such things were necessary to me, I would never need to ask you for what I already possess.' Then He explains what these things signify, "Offer to God the sacrifice of praise, pay your vows to the Most High, call on me in the day of trouble and I will deliver you, and you will glorify me" (Ps. 50:14–15). And then there is this passage from the prophet, "By what means will I come before the Lord, bowing myself before the Most High God? Shall I come before Him with burnt offerings, the sacrifice of a yearling? Will the Lord be pleased with thousands of rams or with ten thousands of rivers of oil? Shall I give my first born for my transgression, the fruit of my body for the sin of my soul? Has He not showed you, O man,

what is good and what the Lord requires of you—to do justly, to love mercy, and to walk humbly with your God?" (Mic. 6:6ff.). In the prophet's words these two realities are again distinguished and set forth clearly, that God does not require sacrifices for their own sakes, but that He does require the sacrifices which they symbolize. In the epistle titled Hebrews it is said, "Don't forget to do good and to give to others, for with such sacrifices God is pleased" (Heb. 13:16). So, when we read, "I desire mercy and not a sacrifice" (Hos. 6:6), this simply means that one type of sacrifice is preferred to another; for what goes by the name sacrifice is merely a symbol of true sacrifice. And mercy *is* the true sacrifice, so it said, "with such sacrifices God is well pleased." Therefore, all the worship regulations we read about in reference to the (Old Testament) tabernacle or temple point ultimately to the love of God and our neighbor, since "on these two commandments," as it is written, "depend all the law and the prophets" (Matt. 22:40).

Chapter VI: The true and perfect sacrifice

A true sacrifice is one by which we may be united to God in holy fellowship, and which points to that supreme good and ultimate goal by which alone we may be truly blessed. Therefore, even compassion, if not shown for God's sake, is not a sacrifice. For sacrifice is, to use the old Latin expression, a *divine thing*, even though it is offered by human hands. Hence a man consecrated in the name of God, and vowed to God, is himself a sacrifice in that he dies to the world so that he may live for God (Rom. 6:11). And this is also related to compassion—the kind that one shows to oneself, as it is written, "Have compassion on thy soul by pleasing God" (Ecclesiasticus 30:23). Our own bodies also become a sacrifice when disciplined by self-control—if we do so for the sake of God—so that we do not offer our bodies as instruments of unrighteousness but of righteousness unto God (Rom. 6:16). Exhorting us to this sacrifice, the apostle says, "I implore you, therefore, brethren, by the mercies of God, that you present your bodies as a living sacrifice, holy and acceptable to God, which is your reasonable service" (Rom. 12:1). So just as the body—inferior as it is to the soul and employed by the soul as a servant or instrument—is a sacrifice when it is used rightly, how much more so is the soul a fitting sacrifice, offering itself to God, so that, inflamed by His love, it may receive of His beauty and become pleasing to Him,

ot

"Be

the re

is that g

(Rom. 12:.

Therefore

sion toward o

reference to Go

relieve our distre

is only acquired by

me, the nearness of G

lows then that the wh

is congregation and fello

to God as a universal sacri

Priest who offered Himself to

so that we might be the body

pearing in the form of a servant.

offered, in this form He was offere

this form He is Mediator, in this for

and in this form He is the Sacrifice.

exhorts us first of all to present our bo

sacrifice, holy, acceptable to God, as the re

vice we owe to Him, and not to be confor

age, but to be transformed by the renewing of

to prove what is good, what is acceptable, and

perfect, for we are that sacrifice. He continues, "

say, through the grace of God given to me, to everyo

do not think more highly of yourselves than you ough

to think; rather, think soberly, as God has dealt to each

one a measure of faith. Just as we have many members

in one body, and not all members have the same function, so we who are many are one body in Christ, and individually members of one another. Since we have gifts that differ according to the grace given to us..." (Rom. 12:3–6). This is the sacrifice of Christians, who, being many, are one body in Christ. And this also is the sacrifice which the Church continually celebrates in the sacrament of the altar, known to the faithful, in which she teaches that she herself is offered in the offering she presents to God...

Chapter XX: The supreme and true sacrifice accomplished by the mediator between God and man

So it is that the true Mediator—in so far as he took the form of a servant and thus was made "the Mediator

mankind, the man Christ Jesus"
...es the sacrifice 'in the form of God,'
...Father, with whom He is one God.
...m of a servant' He Himself chose to be
...er than to receive it, and so to prevent
...suming that sacrifice, even in this case,
...d to any created being. Thus He is both
...presents the offering and the Sacrifice
...is the reality, and He intended the daily
...e church to be the sacramental symbol of
...urch is the body of which He is the head,
...to offer itself through him. This true sacri-
...efigured by various ancient sacrifices even as
...g is signified by various words—the variety of
...lows us to speak without being redundant. To
...reme and true sacrifice all false sacrifices have
...vay.

FROM BOOK 15

Chapter I: Two lines of the human race

Of the bliss of Paradise, of Paradise itself, and of
the life of our first parents there, and of their sin and
punishment, many have thought much, spoken much,
written much. We ourselves, too, have spoken of these
things in the foregoing books, and have written either
what we read in the Holy Scriptures, or what we could
reasonably deduce from them. And were we to enter
into a more detailed investigation of these matters, an
endless number of endless questions would arise, which
would involve us in a larger work than the present occasion admits. We cannot be expected to find room for
replying to every question that may be posed by idle
quibblers who ask more questions than they are really
able to understand. Yet I trust we have already done justice to these great and difficult questions regarding the
beginning of the world, or of the soul, or of the human
race itself.

This race we have distributed into two parts, the one
consisting of those who live according to man, the other
of those who live according to God. And these we also
mystically call the two cities, or the two communities
of men, of which the one is predestined to reign eternally with God, and the other to suffer eternal punishment with the devil. That, however, concerns their final
end, and that we will address later. At present, since we

have described the origin of these societies (whether it
happened among the angels whose numbers we know
not or with the two first human beings), it seems suitable to describe their development, from the time when
our two first parents began to produce offspring up until the time when human reproduction will cease. For
this whole time or world-age, in which the dying make
room for those who are born, is the career of these two
cities, which we now describe.

Now Cain was the first born of the two parents of
the human race, and he belonged to the city of men.
After him came Abel, who belonged to the city of God.
It was in Abel that the Apostle's truth was realized,
"However, the spiritual is not first, but the natural;
then the spiritual" (1 Cor. 15:46). So it is the case that
each one of us, being the offspring of a condemned
lineage, is first of all descended of Adam, evil and
fleshly. And only later, if grafted into Christ by regeneration, do we become good, spiritual—thus it is with
the entire human race. When these two cities began to
develop by the progression of deaths and births, citizens of this world were first-born, as it were, and later
some became strangers in the world but citizens of the
city of God: by grace predestinated, by grace elected,
by grace a stranger below, and by grace a citizen above.
They have their origin from the same lump that was
condemned, as a whole lump, from the beginning. But
God, like a potter (for this figure is wisely used by the
Apostle), from the same lump some vessels for honor
and others for dishonor. Now in the case of Cain, who
was first, a vessel for dishonor was made; but after
him a vessel of honor was made. In both there was
first of all that which is fallen—that from which all
of us must begin but in which we need not remain—
and afterward, that which is well-approved, to which
we advance to attain, and after attaining in which we
may abide. Not that all the wicked will attain this to
be sure, but surely no one will become good who was
not first of all wicked. In any case, the sooner one becomes good, the quicker he receives his new title, the
old name being abolished by the new. So it is written
of Cain that he founded a city, but that Abel, being
a pilgrim, founded none. For the city of the saints is
above, although it produces citizens here below, and
in them the city continues on its pilgrimage until the
time of its kingdom arrives. At that time it will gather
all its citizens together in the day of their resurrection.

Then the promised kingdom will be theirs, in which they will rule with their Prince, the King of the ages, throughout eternity.

FROM BOOK 19

Chapter XVII: Conflict and common grace between the two cities

Now families that do not live by faith seek their peace in the material advantages of this life. Families that live by faith, on the other hand, look for the promised eternal blessings. They use time and material advantages (at least those that do not captivate them or divert their attention from God), to help them to endure and to ease the burdens that a corruptible body loads on the soul. So the necessities for this mortal life are used by both kinds of families alike, but each has its own aim in using them. The earthly city, which does not live by faith, seeks earthly peace, aiming for a well-ordered harmony of civic obedience and rule. The heavenly city—that portion which sojourns on earth and lives by faith, uses this peace as required until all mortality passes away. It lives as a captive and stranger in the earthly city (though it has received the promise of redemption and the gift of the Spirit as a down payment), not opposing the (just) laws necessary for prolonging the administration of mortal life. As long as this life is common to both cities, there is harmony between them. Yet, the earthly city has had philosophers whose doctrine is condemned by divine teaching and who were deceived by speculation or by demons—believing in many gods that dabble in human affairs, assigning each a separate sphere (one to the body, another to the soul, and on and on). The celestial city, on the other hand, knew that one God was to be worshiped and that to Him alone was due that service which the Greeks call *latreia*. So it came about that the two cities could never have common laws of religion, and so the heavenly city has been made out to be the objector and obnoxious to those who believe differently. Moreover, they must endure anger, hatred, and persecutions, limited only by the sheer numbers of Christians and quieted by God's protection.

This heavenly city, then, while it sojourns on earth, calls citizens out of all nations, and gathers together a society of pilgrims of all languages, customs, laws, and institutions whereby earthly peace is secured and maintained, recognizing these as tending to the same purpose of earthly peace. Therefore the heavenly city does not oppose this diversity, but preserves and adopts it so long as it does not hinder the worship of the one supreme and true God. And even the heavenly city, while on its pilgrimage, takes full advantage of the peace of earth, earnestly keeping peace with all regarding the necessaries of life, and desiring this earthly peace to reflect the peace of heaven, so long as it does no harm to faith and godliness. This alone should be magnified as the peace of the reasonable creatures, consisting in the orderly and harmonious enjoyment of God and of one another in God. When we finally reach that peace, this mortal life will give way to the eternal, and our material bodies will no longer burden the soul but will become spiritual, experiencing no needs and having all its members perfectly obeying the will. As long as it is a pilgrim, the heavenly city possesses this peace by faith, and by this faith it lives righteously, enjoying the peace and harmony between itself and God and also in relation to its neighbor. For the life of the city is a social life.

AUGUSTINE: "AUGUSTINE'S CONVERSION" (FROM *THE CONFESSIONS*)
Latin, A.D. 400

For you have made us for yourself, and our heart is restless until it rests in You.
—Confessions 1.1

Augustine's *Confessions*, written when he was about forty years of age, is a unique autobiographical work "in praise of memory" in which the Bishop of Hippo (North Africa) testifies about how his life-purpose and direction was transformed into a single-minded pursuit of God. Augustine's reflections frequently break forth in spontaneous praise. In Book 8 of the *Confessions*, Augustine describes his remarkable conversion at age thirty-two. Augustine's *Confessions*, a wonderful model for Christian journaling, is one of the most widely read books in Western literature.

Questions for Guided Reading

1. Who was Simplicianus, and what role did he play in the lives of the two prominent church fathers, Ambrose and Augustine?

2. How does the transformation of Victorinus foreshadow that of Augustine?

3. Explain the principle that says "greater pain precedes greater joy."

4. Of what significance is the salvation of well-known, as opposed to unknown, persons?

5. What did Augustine learn about the difficulty of overcoming fleshly habits, and how does he relate Galatians 5:17 to this struggle?

6. Who was St. Anthony, and how did his story influence Augustine?

7. What is Augustine's understanding of the disobedient will, and how does it differ from the explanation given by the Manichees?

8. What is the meaning of the Latin phrase, *tolle lege, tolle lege*, and how did it play into Augustine's transformation?

9. Write a description of your own spiritual journey in a confession-style essay patterned after Augustine.

✦

Chapter I: Struggling, Augustine seeks a mentor

1. Unto You, O God, I call to mind and profess with gratitude those abundant mercies you have extended to me. Let my very bones bask in your love; let them sing out, Who is like You, O Lord? Now that you have broken my chains I offer up thanks and praise to You, declaring to one and all how You have liberated me! All who bow before You, as soon as they hear this, will say "Blessed is the Master of heaven and earth, how magnificent is His name!" Your words were planted deep in my inner man; You laid siege to me on every side. I had come to see life everlasting, though 'through a glass darkly.' No longer did I doubt the existence of an Incorruptible Being from which all other being derived its being; nor did I now require further proof of You, but began to grow steadfast in You. As for my earthly life, nothing was as it had been and my inner man longed to be purified from the old yeast. The Way, my Salvation, called sweetly to me but the narrowness of the passage gave me pause. Now the thought occurred to me (though it was planted by you) that I ought to visit Simplicianus, in whom Your grace shone forth—a shining example of a faithful servant. I knew he had been faithfully devoted to you since a child; and, now, years of closely following You had brought him to great wisdom and maturity. Sharing my struggles with him, I hoped by his experience to find direction, for one so tortured as I, to Your path.

2. Observing the many types of people that come and go from the church, I grew discontent with my materialistic life. Even my passions—honor, wealth, and the like—ceased to excite me as they used to, and actually began to feel like a great burden to which I was enslaved; compared with You—Your great loveliness and the beauty of Your dwelling place—these things no longer held any delight for me. Nevertheless, I was still captivated by a woman. For although the Apostle never commanded me *not* to marry, he encouraged me to a better way, hoping that all men would follow his example (1 Cor. 7:7). In my weakness I chose not to follow him in this, yet in my hesitation to submit to conjugal duties I vacillated, so all my decisions were on hold. Now I had heard "The Truth" himself say that "there are eunuchs who were born that way from their mother's womb; and there are eunuchs who were made eunuchs by men; and there are also eunuchs who made themselves eunuchs for the sake of the kingdom of heaven. He who is able to accept this, let him accept it" (Matt. 19:12). How lost are those who have no knowledge of God! So much good appears before them that they cannot discover Him who is truly good! Not that I was so lost at this time: rising above all the hype and hearing finally the harmonious testimony of Your creation, I found You, the Creator, and Your Word—Who, together with the Holy Spirit was with you in the beginning, and by Whom You created all

things. Others, "when they knew God, glorified Him not as God, neither were thankful" (Rom. 1:21). To this I had indeed fallen prey, yet Your right hand lifted me and carried me away, hiding me in a place where I could recover. You have told us, "Behold, the fear of the Lord—that is wisdom" (Job 28:28) and "Be not wise in your own eyes" (Prov. 26:5) for "professing to be wise they became fools" (Rom. 1:22). By this time I had uncovered the 'pearl of great price,' for which I should immediately have sold everything, that I might purchase it; yet I hesitated.

Chapter II: The conversion of a pagan professor

3. So I went to Simplicianus—whom even the great Bishop Ambrose loved as a father in the faith—and confessed all my straying. I also described some of the books of the Platonists (translated by Professor Victorinus of Rome whom, as we shall see, died a Christian) which I had been reading. To my surprise, he congratulated me for reading these instead of other, false philosophers, whose writings were filled with the principles of this world (Col. 2:8), and since those Platonists' writings pointed, though imperfectly, to the truth of God and His word. Then, in order to encourage me in the humility of Christ—hidden from the wise and revealed to little ones—he told me about Victorinus himself, for while he was at Rome, Simplicianus had known him intimately. Now, I will not be silent about this, for it testifies to Your great grace, which ought to be confessed to You—Oh, accomplished Victorinus! Gifted in all the liberal arts; knowledgeable critic of philosophical writings; teacher of many noble senators, whose excellence was honored with the dedication of his statue in the Roman Forum. At that time he was still an idol worshipper and participant in pagan rites involving most of the Roman nobility, and had even inspired the adoration of certain Eastern gods whose homelands Rome had conquered. This same old Victorinus, for many years the most eloquent spokesman of paganism, had now become an unabashed child of Christ, a little one seeking a drink at Your fountain, bending his neck to the yoke of humility, and bowing his forehead to the shame of the Cross.

4. Oh Lord, Lord, You who made the very heavens bow down, Who touched the mountains and cause them to smoke, by what means did You invade the heart of Victorinus? Simplicianus explained that he used to read Holy Scripture and diligently study Christian writings. To Simplicianus he would confide, "You know I am a Christian." To this Simplicianus would reply, "I will not believe it, nor will I call you a Christian until I see you in Christ's Church." To this Victorinus would respond, mockingly, "Is it the walls of the church that make Christians?" He said this often and continued to claim to be Christian before Simplicianus, only in private, for he was afraid of offending his proud, demon-worshipping friends—like mighty cedars of Lebanon not yet felled by the Lord—lest by his confession he might unleash a storm of enmity on his head from the heights of Babylonian pomp. Later, however, from his reading and study Victorinus drew strength, realizing that he would be denied by Christ before His holy angels if he now feared to confess Him before men. He also realized the guilt of his shame toward the sacraments established by Your word, while feeling no shame on account of those same proud demons whose pride he imitated and whose rites he practiced. At that time he boldly rejected his former vanity and became humble before the truth. Unexpectedly and all at once he insisted, "Let us go to the church, for I wish to become a Christian." Hardly able to contain his joy, Simplicianus accompanied him. Victorinus was soon admitted to the first sacraments of instruction, and not long after he submitted his name as a candidate to be regenerated by baptism. All of Rome marveled and all the Church rejoiced. The proud witnessed his transformation and became enraged, gnashing their teeth and melting in anger! But by then the Lord God had become the hope of Your servant so that he "turned not to the proud" (Ps. 40:4).

5. Finally, the hour arrived for Victorinus to profess his faith. Now at Rome, those who are about to approach Your grace make their profession from an elevated platform in view of all the faithful, and by reciting a creed learned by heart. The elders, Simplicianus recalled, offered for Victorinus to make his profession in private, for they commonly offered this to the shy. But he chose instead to profess his salvation openly, in the presence of the holy assembly. For it was not salvation that he professed openly as a teacher of rhetoric, so now he would publicly profess salvation. Why should he who never feared to proclaim his own words to the deranged mob, fear to declare Your word to Your gentle flock? So, as he climbed the platform in order to make his profession and was quickly recognized—who would not have recognized the great Victorinus?—a murmur arose throughout the congregation "Victorinus! Victorinus!" And just as suddenly as the sight of him had raised a ruckus, a greater desire to hear his profession of faith brought a hush over the crowd. Then he articulated the true faith with such excellent boldness, that all present responded with love and joy and Victorinus was swallowed up in loving embraces.

Chapter III: The principle of joyful restoration

6. Oh Lord, what is it in man that causes him to rejoice more at the salvation of one who was feared lost and then rescued from great danger, than for one whose hope was more sure and whose situation less precarious? For You also, O merciful Father, "rejoice more joy over one sinner that repents than over ninety-nine who are justified and need no repentance" (Luke 15:7). We rejoice as often as we hear how a lost sheep has been brought home again on the Shepherd's shoulders, and how a lost coin is returned to your treasury, as the neighbors rejoice with the woman who found it (Luke 15:8–9). And the joy of holy worship in Your house brings tears to the eyes, whenever it is read of the younger son, that he "was dead but is alive again, was lost but is now found" (Luke 15:24, 32). For You rejoice in us and in Your angels, who are sanctified by holy charity. For You Who are always the same, all things which do change and are not enduring, nonetheless are known forever by You.

7. Why is it, then, that we delight more in finding or restoring something we love and which has been lost, than if it had never been lost in the first place? Indeed, many things testify to this reality—the victorious commander triumphs but would never have conquered had he not fought (and the more intense the battle the greater the triumph); the storm upsets voyagers and threatens shipwreck, all on board faint at the nearness of death; but when the sky and sea grow calm, they rejoice as much as they formerly feared; a loved one's illness make those who love him sick at heart, yet even before he regains full strength they rejoice more than when he was well. Even the common pleasures of life come to us by way of distress, and that not just by accident but also through discomforts we intentionally undergo. There is hardly any pleasure in eating and drinking unless the discomfort of hunger and thirst come before. Drunks eat salty meat in order to create a burning thirst that they will quench by drinking to excess. It is also customary that the bride, once betrothed, should not be handed over to the groom immediately, that he will not undervalue that for which he never had to sigh and wait.

8. So then, this principle holds true for shameful and illicit pleasures as well as for those that are accepted and lawful; also for sincere and honest friendship, and for that same younger son who "was dead but is alive again, was lost but is now found." Greater joy is always preceded by greater agony. How can this be, O Lord my God, when You are Yourself Your own everlasting joy, and all that surrounds You in heaven eternally rejoices in You? Why is it that our earthly portion ebbs and flows between pain and reconciliation? Is this the rule You have assigned from highest heaven to the lowest earth, from the beginning of the world to its end, from the angel to the worm, from first to last, appointing each to its place and time, each

good after its own kind? Ah, me! How awesome You are in majesty, how deep in mystery! Nowhere are You absent, yet we are slow to return to You.

Chapter IV: When famous men are enlightened, others follow

9. Arouse us, O Lord, lure us back to You and rekindle our flame; reignite our passion for You, that in loving You, we may begin to pursue You! Are not many who are more hellishly blind than Victorinus reconciled to You? And once enlightened, do they not welcome Your light and gladly receive power to become Your sons? Yet these, since they are not famous, stir up less enthusiasm (even among those who know them well). For when many people rejoice together over the salvation of a celebrity, their mutual excitement fans the flame of enthusiasm for one who may lead the way for others—so those who were in the faith before him rejoice not merely for the sake of that celebrity, but also for those who will surely follow his lead. However, may the rich never go before the poor into your Tabernacle, nor the noble before the lowly. Just as the one known as the "least of the apostles" said, "you have chosen the foolish things of this world to shame the wise, and the weak things to shame the strong" (1 Cor. 1:27). Now, when the Roman official, Paulus, was vanquished by the Apostle's bold message and became yoked together with Christ and a common subject of the Great King (see Acts 13:7–12), from that point on Saul (as he was formerly called) preferred to be called Paulus, in testimony to this great victory. So the enemy suffers a greater loss from one over whom he formerly had a greater hold, or who formerly led many astray; for the proud he dominates by reason of the pride of their nobility, and the strong because of their pride in their authority. How much more welcome then was Victorinus regarded, in whom the devil formerly had a stronghold, and by whose tongue he wielded a deadly weapon by which many were slain. Therefore, all the more do your children rejoice seeing that our king has bound the strong man (Matt. 12:29), capturing and cleansing his weapons for the use and honor of the Master's purpose.

Chapter V: The charms and chains of the flesh

10. After Simplicianus had told me all about Victorinus I was very eager to imitate him (and this, of course, is why he had told me). But he added that in the time of the (pagan) Emperor Julian, a law was passed forbidding Christians to teach literature and rhetoric. Victorinus obeyed this law, preferring your word which makes infants eloquent to the wordy school in which he formerly taught. I considered his act more blessed than brave, since it freed him up to wait entirely on You—the very thing I longed for as someone bound not by the irons chains of others but by his own iron will. In fact, my will had become the tool of the enemy and by it he kept me bound. Now lust is born of a perverted will, and once indulged lust becomes habit; and habit, if not checked, becomes a compulsion. These links joined together and hardened into a chain that held me tightly. But a new will had begun to form in me, a will free to worship and to enjoy You, O God, the only sure enjoyment. Yet, at this point, I could not overcome my former willfulness which was strengthened by being indulged for so long. So my two wills fought within me—the old and the new, the carnal and the spiritual—and their battle tore apart my soul.

11. In this way I learned from my own experience what I had read that "the flesh opposes the Spirit and the Spirit opposes the flesh" (Gal. 5:17). I battled both ways, at times more successfully in the spirit since my new will was so opposed to the flesh. Yet, by my own former willingness, the force of habit had grown very strong in me. And who can rightly complain about the consequences that follow a sinful life? I had become so accustomed to letting my flesh win out, and I excused it by denying that anyone could prove that we are truly engaged in a spiritual battle. Now I no longer doubted that a war was on, but still I hesitated to enlist as your soldier. Instead of fearing the further consequences of fleshly bondage, as I should

have, I was more afraid of what life might be like if I were free of such compulsions.

12. So I slept on, hopelessly intoxicated with worldly desire, my irregular meditations of You sometimes arousing me from slumber, while at other times I was overpowered by heavy drowsiness and fell back to sleep. Now, no one wants to sleep all the time, and most sensible people prefer waking to sleeping, yet we hesitate to shake off the drowsiness whenever its weight pulls us toward deeper sleep, even if it's time to get up. I understood well enough that surrender to your love would be far better than continued surrender to my lust; yet while your love had begun to draw me my lust continued to ensnare me. You called out, "Awake, O sleeper, and rise from the dead, and Christ shall rise on thee" (Eph. 5:14), but I did not reply. You demonstrated the truth of your word with so many proofs that I was completely convicted. Still my only response was, "Just a minute," and "One more minute," and "In a little while," but the little while continued on and on. To delight in your law in my inner man was of no use to me since "another law was waging war against the law of my mind, and bringing me into captivity to the law of sin in my members." For the law of sin is the force of habit, by which the mind is attracted and held against its will (and it deserves to be, for this is all it wants). "Wretched man that I am! who will deliver me from this body of this death" but Your grace alone, through Jesus Christ our Lord? (Rom. 7:24–25).

Chapter VI: Augustine's companions and the two converted court officials

13. Now let me confess and declare to your glory, O Lord, my strength and my Redeemer, how you freed me from the trap of fleshly desire and enslavement to worldly labor. Keeping up my usual routine, although with mounting anxiety, I spent as much time in your church as my continued bondage would allow. My friend, Alypius, was with me, now freed from his third tour of duty as a government assessor, and looking for clients to whom he could sell his legal counsel (just as I peddled the art of speaking, as if that could be bought and sold). And we persuaded Nebridius to serve as teaching assistant to Verecundus, a citizen and schoolmaster of Milan whom we all knew and liked and who needed our help. Nebridius agreed to this position not so much for the career advantages it might bring (with his learning he could have started in a better position), but as a genuine friend who would not ignore our request for help. He accepted his new position discreetly, avoiding the temptation to spend time with those who could advance his career and leaving himself free to read and to do research and to attend lectures for himself.

14. One day when Nebridius was away (I can't remember why) something interesting happened. Ponticianus—a man who held high office in the Emperor's court—came to visit Alypius and I. As an African he was our fellow countryman, and wanted something from us, though I could not guess what it was. When we sat down together to talk, he noticed a book lying on the gaming table and picked it up expecting that it was one of my textbooks. To his surprise he found that it was a copy of Paul's letters. At this he smiled and expressed his delight, for he himself was both a Christian and baptized, often bowing himself before You, our God, in the church and in constant daily prayers. When I told him that I was now diligently studying Scriptures, he began to tell us about Anthony, an Egyptian monk whose name was highly regarded among Your servants, though unfamiliar to us at that time. Astonished that we were ignorant about Anthony, Ponticianus went on and on about this great man. We listened in rapt amazement at the wonders You worked through the true faith of the catholic Church, and he could hardly get over the fact that we had never heard of Anthony!

15. From there he began to describe the many monasteries springing up, and that sweet aroma rising up to You from the lives of the monks in the fertile wastelands of the desert. We knew nothing about all this (although there was a monastery of good brothers at Milan outside

the walls of the city, under the watchful care of Ambrose, but we did not know it then). Ponticianus continued on about life in the monastery as we drank it all in. Finally he told the story of how one afternoon at Triers when the Emperor was attending the Circensian games, he and three friends went for a walk in the gardens next to the city walls. Eventually the four split up into two pairs, one companion following Ponticianus and the other two wandering off together in another direction. As it happened, those two came upon a cottage inhabited by some of Your servants—those poor in spirit, like those to whom belongs the kingdom of heaven—and there they discovered the book *The Life of St. Anthony*. One of them began to read it and was completely taken with it, imagining what it would be like to give up public life in order to serve You as a monk (he was an administrative officer). His reading filled him with passion for a life of holy devotion and a disgust for his own life. Turning to his friend he demanded, "Tell me, what good are our lives? Why do we strive and for what purpose? At best we might hope to be promoted as counselors to the Emperor, but even if we make it, such a position will surely be full of risks and dangerous duties. On the other hand, we could commit our lives to God right here and now!" As if he were in the pains of labor bringing forth new life, he went on talking for some time before returning to his reading. Soon his transformation was complete (that inward change in the place of the soul that You alone can see) and his mind was emptied of worldly ambition. The more he read, it seems, the more his heart resolved on a better course of life; now he belonged entirely to You. He told his friend, "I will no longer pursue my old ambitions but will serve God from this moment on: go with me or else get out of my way!" His friend quickly agreed to stick with him and to share in this great service and reward; both of them now belonged to you. Enlisting in your service and counting the cost of building their tower (Luke 14:28), they gave up everything to pursue You. Meanwhile Ponticianus and his friend

were strolling in another part of the garden and came in search of the others; it was getting late and time to return to their duties. Meeting up again their companions shared their discovery and new life resolution, inviting Porticianus and the other to join them or, at least, to wish them well and not to oppose their plans. As Porticianus then explained, neither him nor his companion felt compelled to join them, but bid them a tearful congratulations and farewell, asking for their prayers. So, the two whose hearts were now set on heaven took up residence in the cottage, sending their farewells to their fiancées, both of whom took holy vows in response to the news, dedicating themselves to you. Porticianus and his companion meanwhile returned to the palace, their eyes still fixed on the world.

Chapter VII: Augustine's honest self-examination

16. Even while Porticianus went on with his story, O Lord, You were speaking to me, first catching me off guard by way of his story, and then calling me to examine myself face to face, as it were, so that I might see clearly just how ambitious, self-centered, and completely corrupted I had become. This sight caused me to tremble and to try turning my attention away, but Porticianus went on with more of the story as I was confronted with example after example from my own sinful life. Not that I had not known all these things about myself before, but somehow I managed to ignore and bury the truth about myself.

17. Inwardly I delighted in the story of the two court officials and their experience with God, especially at the ease with which they entrusted themselves to you for their healing. Yet the more I identified with them, the more disgusted I became with myself. How many years had gone to waste (and I with them)—at least a dozen—since I, as a nineteen year old, had been aroused to pursue wisdom (*sapientia*) after being inspired by reading Cicero's *Hortensius*? Now in my thirties I was still putting off my plan to give up worldly pursuits and devote

myself to wisdom, the mere pursuit of which (to say nothing of possibly finding it) would have been more precious to me than possessing all the world's treasures and pleasures. Miserably given-over even in my youth, I had cried out, "Grant me purity, O Lord, and self control, but not just yet!" For I was really afraid you might answer my prayer immediately and free me from my lust—a fire I preferred to fuel rather than put out. And so I wandered the crooked paths of blasphemous superstitions, not believing in such views but preferring them to other beliefs which I was not seriously investigating but only opposing maliciously.

18. Every time the issue of my call to pursue wisdom came up, I would tell myself that I had received no clear sign to direct my course. But the day finally came when I could not longer cling to this excuse, my conscience convicting me, "Now that you have glimpsed truth clearly enough, what keeps you from at last throwing off the weight of worldly pursuits? Others have gone free without investing ten years in the search! How much longer will you deceive yourself? In this way I inwardly burned with shame while Pontitianus went on. At last, when he had finished the story and the business he had come to conduct, he went his way. How I wrestled within myself after this! Even as part of me demanded that I begin to follow You faithfully, the other part of me fought to resist but could find no more excuses in which to hide. I was exhausted and numb from the battle, and could only think of escape into the disgusting habits that were causing me to waste away.

Chapter VIII: Augustine's struggle in the garden

19. The conflict raged on within the dwelling of my soul, and I knew I must do something or die. At once I went to my friend Alyupius and took hold of him. "What is happening with us," I cried, "What does all this mean and what do you make of it? The unlearned are rising up and storming the kingdom of God while we, for all our wisdom and learning, are still wallowing in flesh and blood! Are we ashamed to follow just because people like these court officials take the lead? Should we not be more ashamed at lacking the courage to follow them?" I went on and on like this until in a frenzy I stormed out, leaving Alypius gazing at me silently and in utter astonishment (my face and mannerisms surely communicated more than my words). Next to our house was a small garden which our landlord, who did not reside with us, permitted us to use and into which I was now driven in order to get away from anything that might disrupt the storm within me until it be resolved (only You knew how this would happen). I had become like a madman but only that I might be made whole, dying that I might have life, and understanding how corrupt I had become but completely unaware of the good I would finally become. So I blew into the garden with Alypius following close behind—his presence was no bother to my solitude and he could hardly desert me when I was so troubled. We sat down as far as possible from the house. I was groaning in my spirit and everything within me was agonizing over my inability to commit to Your will and way, O my God. My journey to You was not one requiring a ship, a chariot, or even the ability to walk from the house to the place I was now sitting. To undertake and complete this journey required the wholehearted and unmixed desire to go, not a double-minded stumbling in Your direction, with half of me rising up even as the other half sinks back down.

20. Even as I floundered in my inability to commit to you, I twitched and fidgeted and did a great many things which the sick or impaired are unable to do, even if they willed it. For I was tearing at my hair, striking myself on the forehead, wrapping my arms around my knees and rocking—all because I willed it so. Indeed, I might have wanted to do these things but would have been prevented from doing them if my limbs lacked the power to respond. So then, there were many actions I performed where willing something was not the same as being able. Yet I was not doing the one thing I desired to do with infinitely greater desire—the thing

I would be able to do as soon as I willed it, because to will this thing is to do it! For in this case the ability to act and the will to do so are one and the same. But this was not happening for me; because, while my body instantly obeyed my every whim, my soul would not join what must be accomplished in the realm of the will alone.

Chapter IX: The sin-sick will

21. How does such a thing happen, and why? May your grace shine on my inquiry, so that an answer may be found to the mysterious questions of humanity's struggles—the perplexing sickness of Adam's children. So, again, how does such a thing happen, and why? Whenever the mind commands the body to move, it immediately obeys; yet when the mind commands itself it hesitates and resists. When the mind commands the hand to move, it obeys so quickly one can hardly tell the difference between the command and the obedience (even though the mind and the body are distinct). On the other hand, if the mind commands itself to will something, it does not always obey. Once more I ask, how does such a thing happen, and why? Whenever the mind commands itself to will something, surely it would not give the order if it did not want what it asked for; so why does it not immediately do what it commands? Apparently it does not want this thing with the whole of itself, and therefore the command issues from a divided mind. It commands only insofar as it wills; to whatever degree it is unwilling the command is not fully carried out. It is, after all, *the will* that commands all *acts* of the will; so it commands itself, not some other will. Therefore, *the will* does not command with its entire self since part of the will is busy *willing itself to will*. If *the will* were fully engaged in *willing*, there would be no need for it to command itself since, obviously it would already be fully willing. Nor is it surprising for anyone to be partly willing and partly unwilling at the same time. This has to do with a kind of sickness of the mind, in that it is unable to rise to the truth, weighted down as

it is by sinful habits. And so, it is as if there were two wills; neither is whole, and what the one lacks the other supplies.

Chapter X: The false teaching of the two natures

22. Now there are those (the Manichees) who teach that this battle of the two wills is really a battle between a good nature and a bad nature, each with its own mind and each pulling us in the opposite directions in our inner man. May such teachers, and all who lead us astray, perish from your presence, O God! For they do indeed reflect a bad nature when they teach such things, yet if they embrace the truth they will become good and even deserving of the Apostle's good words, "you were formerly in darkness but now you are Light in the Lord" (Eph. 5:8a). But they desire to be light: not just *light in the Lord* but light in themselves. Believing the nature of the soul to be of the same substance as God, they become darkened in their understanding, and through their outrageous arrogance, they wander farther from You, the "true Light which, coming into the world, enlightens every man" (John 1:9). Consider carefully what you are saying! Be ashamed and draw near to God that you may be truly enlightened and not ashamed. Now then, as I was at last making up my mind to commit to fully serve the Lord (as I had intended to do for a long time) I was *both* the one who wanted to fully commit and the one who held back and resisted commitment. I myself, the only person involved, was neither entirely willing nor entirely unwilling. So, of course I appeared to be at odds with myself and was in fact tearing myself apart. Yet, while none of this happened by my own choosing, it was not because I had two alien natures warring within me, but that my one nature was suffering the consequences of punishment, in other words, not an evil nature dwelling in me but a sinful principle at work in me (Rom. 7:17). This sinful principle, in turn, resulted as a penalty for a sin freely committed by Adam, whose son I am.

23. Indeed, if we are to believe that conflicting urges are a sign of conflicting natures, then

we must have more than two! And if someone ponders about whether to attend a meeting of the Manichees or to go to the theatre, the Manichees themselves will point to this as evidence of two natures, saying, "The bad nature is pulling him away to the theatre, for what else can account for this indecision and conflict of the wills?" I say that both are bad—that which draws anyone to such a meeting and that which draws him back again to the theatre. Yet they insist that that will which draws anyone to themselves must be good. But what if one of our members was struggling with the decision about whether to go to our church (*ecclesiam*) or to the theatre, won't our opponents also be undecided on what to think about this? Either they have to admit that a good will leads a person to our church, just as good as that which leads to theirs the people who are initiated into their sacred rites and trapped there (which they are unwilling to admit); or else they will have to conclude that two evil natures were found to conflict within a single person, in which case their doctrine of one good and one evil nature within each person is proved false; or, finally they will have to accept the truth, that whenever anyone is conflicted about what to do, this is the result of conflicting impulses within a single nature, one soul.

24. So whenever they see two conflicting impulses struggling within one person, may they no longer teach that this results from competing natures within the same person, and that these result from two opposing substances, and ultimately from two opposing principles, one good and the other bad. For You are true, O God, and so you punish and rebuke the wrong. So how can the Manichees answer the possibility that a choice may lie between two impulses, both of which are evil, for example: one may deliberate whether to kill someone by poison or a sword; whether to take this or that parcel of someone else's land when he cannot both; whether he should purchase as much pleasure as he can afford or else hoard his money because of greed; whether he should go

to the circus or to the theatre, if both are open on the same day. Or add a third impulse—whether to go and steal from someone else's house while he has have the opportunity; or even a fourth—whether to commit adultery while he is committing the robbery. All these impulses may occur simultaneously even though they cannot all be acted on at the same time. Thus, in light of the variety of impulses that drives a person, his mind may be torn between four or even more battling natures, but the Manichees do not teach that there are this many disparate substances. Now the same holds true for good impulses. So I ask them, is it good to delight in reading the apostle, or to meditate on a psalm, or to discuss a gospel passage? To each of these questions they will answer, "It is good." But what if they all equally delight us at the same time? Isn't it true that as long as he cannot make up his mind he is torn between several good desires? All these desires are good, yet they conflict with each other until a decision is made and the will is thereby unified. Therefore, since the joys of eternity draw our thoughts higher while worldly pleasures weigh us down, our soul is unable to embrace the highest good with its entire will, and is torn between the options, preferring truth but enslaved by habit.

Chapter XI: The sirens of sin and the vision of self-control

25. Still sick and now feeling tormented in my soul, I accused myself mercilessly, writhing in those chains which I still wore, though these were now weakening. You were beside me, O Lord, there in my inward self, reinforcing the work of repentance in me, so that I would not give up the struggle to be free and allow my chains to be re-fastened. I was saying to myself, "Now is the time, let it be done now!" and as I said this I felt as if I had almost broken through—almost but not quite! This time, however, I did not lapse back into my old condition, but stood firm for a moment as I caught my breath. Gathering my strength I began to wrestle once more, and once more felt as if I had nearly subdued the

old man . . . almost but not quite, not quite dominating him! I fought on in suspense, wondering all the while what would happen to me if I succeeded. Could I really die entirely to my old self and I live entirely for You?

26. All the old obsessions—my "mistresses"—now whispered in my ear. Plucking the strings of my flesh as if I was their instrument, they cooed seductively, "You are not really leaving us behind, are you? Will we never again enjoy what we have shared together? If you leave now, just imagine what you will be missing!" Briefly, my imagination stirred up some intensely alluring thoughts. But just as quickly they began to fade—and may those memories of what I would be missing, O my God, be forever erased from my soul by your mercy. Now the voices also began to fade and I could hear them, as it were, calling to me from a distance, hoping to entice me look back, as I walked away. My departure was slow, it seems I could not run as I ought, and still an audible voice cried, "Do you really think you can live without them?"

27. As this last voice faded I could see myself climbing a wall and peering over—a wall I had seen before but had never approached for fear of what lay on the other side. Now I saw: it was Self Control in all her dignity and serenity, extending holy hands, encouraging me to fear no longer, offering me a comforting embrace. And there was a multitude of boys and girls, of young people and old, venerable widows and women grown old in their virginity. Self Control herself was not at all barren, but the fertile mother of children conceived in joy by You, O Lord, her Husband. She smiled on me teasingly, as if to say, "So you thought that in your strength you could do what all these have done? And would any of these be with me had they not relied on the Lord, their God who granted them to me? Why struggle in your own strength only to fail? Throw yourself on His mercy and be not afraid; He will never withdraw, leaving you to fall. Call confidently on Him and He will support and heal you." Hearing this I was greatly ashamed for the memory of my temptations was still fresh in my

mind, I was not still holding back, or was I? To this it seemed as if she responded, "Close your ears to the unclean whispers of your earthly flesh, and they will die. For while they may promise delight, they have no delight to offer in comparison to those described in the law of the Lord, your God!" Now both the vision and my struggle had been completely internal; but Alypisus remained at my side in silence, awaiting the outcome of my unique ordeal.

Chapter XII: *"Tolle lege, tolle lege"*

28. My heart nearly fainted at the sight of the mountain of my sinful misery, piled high before me. At once a storm flood of my own tears began to overflow and I moved away from Alypius, giving myself room to sob without concern for what he might think. He understood, for I managed to excuse myself and my voice was choked with emotion. He stayed behind, still stunned and wondering what had come over me. I walked a little farther and then flung myself down, somehow, beneath a fig tree, letting go of my emotions entirely and releasing another flood of tears—an acceptable sacrifice to You. Then I prayed something like this, "How long, O Lord, how long? Will you be angry forever? Dismiss the long record of our sins" (Ps. 79:5, 8). For by now I understood well that I had become a prisoner of my own iniquities.

29. I continued in my bitter weeping for a long while. Suddenly, something interrupted my sobbing: a voice—maybe that of a young boy or girl, I'm not sure—coming from a nearby house and singing over and over again, "You take it, you read it! You take it, you read it!" (*tolle lege, tolle lege*). This struck me: when had I ever heard a children's game with these lines? I stopped crying and got up, thinking that this must be a sign from heaven to get my copy of Scriptures and to read the first passage I opened to. (Now I had just heard the story of Anthony and how he, on coming into the church, heard the passage read, "Go and sell all that you have and give it to the poor and you will have treasure in heaven; then come and

follow me." By this he was immediately won to You.) Quickly I went back to where Alypius was sitting (I had left my copy of Paul's letters there on the ground). Taking it in my hands I opened it up and read silently the first passage my eyes fell on—"Not in carousing and drunkenness, not in sexual promiscuity and sensuality, not in strife and jealousy; but put on the Lord Jesus Christ, and make no provision for the flesh in regard to its lusts" (Rom. 13:13–14). There was no need for me to read any further; instantly, a brilliant light flooded every dark corner of my imprisoned soul! My captivity was over and the chains of doubt fell away!

30. After marking the passage I set down the book and gazed at Alypius; my peaceful face said it all. He told me what he had been pondering, and asked to see the passage I had marked. When I passed him the book open to the place I had read, he overlooked my passage and read the next verse which says "Now accept the one who is weak in faith, but not for the purpose of passing judgment on his opinions" (Rom. 14:1). Immediately he took this passage to heart, applying it to me and resolving to encourage my new direction, for such was the strength of his character, and he had always been stronger than I. Next we went in to tell my mother what had happened so that she could rejoice. As we explained what had happened she listened intently at first and then leaped to her feet to praise and bless You, who are "able to do exceeding abundantly above all that we ask or think," (Eph. 3:10), for she realized that You had given her even more than she had cried out for in regards to me. Years before, You had given her a vision of me standing on the *Rule of Faith* (*regula fidei*). And here I was, now standing solidly on that *Rule*—and no longer seeking a wife or harboring any other worldly hopes. In this way you transformed her sorrow into joy and gave her more to delight in than if I had given her many grandchildren!

[CHAPTER 3]

Faith and Learning

In his highly regarded book, *The Scandal of the Evangelical Mind*, Mark Noll charges that "modern American evangelicals have failed notably in sustaining serious intellectual life." For Noll the situation is especially peculiar in light of evangelical sponsorship of many seminaries and colleges (but not a single research university) and the fact that evangelicals "are the spiritual descendants of leaders and movements distinguished by probing, creative, fruitful attention to the mind."[1] Indeed, the anti-intellectualism found in some Christian circles is without Scriptural warrant and would have been foreign to the church fathers, many of whom saw rationality as the surest evidence for the image of God in humanity. In the writings of Augustine, for example, the intellect "even if not defining the human, is our best part" since "by it we participate in the divine" and "it ought to dominate in us." It is also the case, however, that the view of reason held by ancient Christian scholars "has been obscured to us" by the modern tendency to dichotomize reason and revelation and to compartmentalize philosophy, theology, and religion.[2] In modernity, faith is portrayed as something entirely distinct from, and inferior to, reason—a view that would have been ridiculous to the great Christian thinkers. For, while faith is "being sure of what we hope for and certain of what we do not see" (Heb. 11:1 NIV), nevertheless it is God who "endows the heart with wisdom and gives understanding to the mind" (see Job 38:36 NIV). Anselm, like Augustine, considered faith to be the basis of clear reasoning, and Clement of Alexandria found faith grounded in reason to be preferable to simple faith (i.e., assent). Of course, these Christian thinkers acknowledged the negative impact of sin on human rationality as do the Scriptures themselves—which are rich in the vocabulary of rationality (see, for example, Job 12:3; 17:4; Luke 24:45; Acts 26:24–25; Rom 1:28; 2 Cor 2:13). None of these passages condemns rationality, but they uphold it to the degree that it is sustained by God, and even Paul's familiar question to the Corinthians, "Has not God made foolish the wisdom of the world?" (1 Cor. 1:20b) must be viewed in light of its polemical context, where his opponents' sophistical arguments masqueraded as wisdom. Documents included in this section reveal just how early (second century) Christian thinkers were aware of the importance of reason in articulating the faith, and how their efforts were sustained throughout the Middle Ages. The idea that "all truth is God's truth," wherever it may be found, was universally affirmed, and even those, like Tertullian, who questioned "what has Jerusalem to do with Athens?" (i.e., what has faith to do with philosophy), demonstrated their reliance on philosophical reasoning even as they warned against its use.

---

1. Mark A. Noll, *The Scandal of the Evangelical Mind* (Grand Rapids: Eerdmans, 1994), 3, 4.
2. Allan D. Fitzgerald, *Augustine Through the Ages: An Encyclopedia* (Grand Rapids: Eerdmans, 1999), 710.

CLEMENT OF ALEXANDRIA: "PHILOSOPHY, THE HANDMAID OF THEOLOGY" (FROM *STROMATEIS*)
Greek, Late Second Century A.D.

Clement was probably born in Athens and was certainly cosmopolitan in his outlook, strongly favoring the use of philosophy for Christian learning. He taught students to interpret Scripture allegorically in order to discover its deepest and most spiritual meanings. As a teacher at the Alexandrian Catechetical School (c. A.D. 190–202), Clement published a trilogy of works on higher Christian learning, *Protreptikos* (An Exhortation to the Greeks), *Paidagogos* (Christ the Educator), and *Stromateis* (Miscellanies). In the following selection from *Stromateis* (Book I, chapters 5–8), Clement makes a case for the value of Greek philosophy as a propaedeutic—a preparatory school or course of study—for the gospel. For Clement, the idea that "all truth is God's truth" (see page 89) meant that the search for truth need not avoid pagan literature and philosophy.

Questions for Guided Reading

1. Does Clement refer to "many paths to the way of truth" to mean more than one way of salvation?
2. What is the "preliminary stage of education" and what is its function in salvation?
3. Why is philosophy necessary (what is its role) for the true initiate?
4. If it is possible to have faith without literacy, what is the role of studies?
5. If helpful knowledge originates in the intellect; where does sophistry begin?
6. What do (or should) teachers of the word and farmers of vineyards have in common?
7. What is a "Christian Gnostic," and why is he equipped to avoid being deceived?
8. Do you see Clement's perspective as strengthening or weakening faith, and why?

◆

Before the Lord's coming, philosophy was an essential guide to righteousness for the Greeks. At the present time, it is a useful guide toward reverence for God—a kind of preliminary education for those who are trying to gather faith through demonstration. "Your foot will not stumble" (Prov. 3:23), says Scripture, if you attribute good things, whether Greek or Christian, to Providence. God is responsible for all good things, of some, like the blessings of the Old and New Covenants, directly; of others, like the riches of philosophy, indirectly. Perhaps philosophy, too, was a direct gift of God to the Greeks before the Lord extended his appeal to the Greeks. For philosophy was to the Greek world what the Law was to the Hebrews, a tutor escorting them to Christ. So philosophy is a preparatory course; it opens the way for those whom Christ brings to his final destination. Solomon says, "Guard Wisdom and she will exalt you; she will shield you with a rich crown" (Prov. 4:8–9), because once you have fortified her with a fence by means of the true riches of philosophy, you will keep her inaccessible to the sophists. There is only one path of truth, but different ways lead up to it, just as various tributaries flow into a river. So these are truly inspired words: "Hear, my son, and accept my words, to have many paths of life. I am teaching you the ways of wisdom, so that its springs may never fail you" (Prov. 4:10–11, 21), that is, those which spring from the same soil. He is not merely affirming that there is more than one path of salvation for a single righteous person. He adds that there are plenty of righteous people and plenty of routes for them. He explains this as follows: "The paths of the righteous shine like light" (Prov. 4:18). The commandments and the preliminary stages of education would seem to be paths, starting-points for life. "Jerusalem, Jerusalem, how often have I wished to gather your children together to me like a bird with her fledglings!" (Matt. 23:37). "Jerusalem" means "vision of peace." He is showing us prophetically that those who have grasped the vision of peace have had a large variety of different tutors leading to their calling. . . . So from this we make the simple assertion that philosophy includes questions concerning truth and the nature of the universe (the truth of which the Lord himself says, "I am the truth" [John 14:6]); I also assert that the stage of education preliminary to resting in Christ exercises the mind, awakens the understanding, and produces a sharpness of intellect which uses true philosophy for its investigations. Those who discover this, or rather who have received it from Truth herself and hold on to it, are the true initiates.

Philosophy Is Excellent Training

Our readiness to see what we ought to see is largely due to this preliminary training. This training must be in perceiving intelligible objects with the mind. Their nature is of three kinds, considered in number, size, and definition. Definition on the basis of demonstrations implants in the soul of one who follows the argument a faith which is precise and incapable of coming to any other conclusion about the subject of the demonstration; such a definition does not allow us to succumb to those who seek to deceive and undermine us. In the course of these studies, the soul is purified from its sense perceptions and rekindled with the power of discerning the truth. For the preservation of a good diet of education forms virtuous natures, and those naturally excellent latch on to education of this sort and grow even better than they were before, particularly in the production of offspring, as with the rest of the animal creation. That is why Scripture says, "Go to the ant, you sluggard, and become wiser than he" (Prov. 6:6). The ant at the time of harvest lays up an ample and varied store of food against the threat of winter. Or go to the bee and learn her diligence. For she feeds over the whole meadow to produce a single honeycomb. If you pray in your inner room, as the Lord taught, in a spirit of adoration, then your domestic economy would no longer be confined to your domicile, but would extend to your soul. What should it feed on? How? In what quantity? What should we store in its treasury? When should these treasures be produced? For whom? Those who live by virtue emerge, not naturally but by education, like doctors or pilots. We all alike can see a vine or a horse. Only the cultivator will know whether the vine is good for bearing grapes or not; only the groom will readily distinguish a sluggish from a speedy horse. Admittedly some people are naturally more inclined to virtue than others; this is shown by the practices of those so endowed compared with the rest. But this by no means proves perfection in virtue on the part of those better endowed, since those less inclined to virtue by nature have been known through the enjoyment of appropriate education to achieve personal excellence in every regard, and again by contrast, those favorably endowed become wicked through neglect. God has created us sociable and righteous by nature. It follows that we may not say that righteousness appears simply to be a divine dispensation. We are to understand that the good of creation is rekindled by the commandment, when the soul learns by instruction to be willing to choose the highest. But just as we say that it is possible to have faith without being literate, so we assert that it is not possible to understand the statements contained in the faith without study. To assimilate the right affirmations and reject the rest is not the product of simple faith, but of faith engaged in learning. Ignorance involves a lack of education and learning. It is teaching which implants in us the scientific knowledge of things divine and human. It is possible to live uprightly in poverty. It is also possible in wealth. We admit that it is easier and quicker to track down virtue if we have a preliminary education. It can be hunted down without these aids, although even then those with learning, "with their faculties trained by practice," have an advantage. "Hatred," says Solomon, "stirs up strife, but education guards the paths of life" (Prov. 10:12, 17). There is no possibility of being deceived or kidnapped by those who engage in evil artifices to injure their listeners. Yet, "education without refutation goes astray" (Prov. 10:19). We must claim our share in the pattern of refutation in order to repress the false views of the sophists. Anaxarchus the Endaemonist wrote well in his book *On Sovereignty*: "Wide learning is both of great advantage and great disadvantage to its possessor. It benefits the person of skill but damages the person who speaks out without thinking. You must know the limits of the appropriate moment. That is the definition of wisdom. Those who make speeches at the wrong moment, even if they are full of sense, are not counted wise and have a reputation for folly." Hesiod too says, "The Muses who make one rich in thoughts, inspired, vocal." By "rich in thoughts" he means one who is fluent in the use of words, wise, and knowing of truth.

Each Philosophy Has Some Truth

Clearly, Greek philosophy has come from God not as an ultimate goal but as rainstorms bursting on fertile soil, manure heaps, and houses alike. Grass and wheat sprout alike, fig trees and other less respectable trees grow on top of graves, and these growths emerge in the pattern of the genuine articles, because they enjoy the same power of the rain; but they do not have the same charm as those which grow in rich soil; they either wither or are torn up. Yes, and the parable of the seed as explained by the Lord has its place here too. There is only one cultivator of the soil within human beings. It is the One who from the first, from the foundation of the universe, has been sowing the seeds with potential growth, Who has produced rain on every appropriate occasion in the form of His sovereign Word. Differences arise from the times and places which receive the Word. Besides, the farmer does not confine his sowing to wheat (and there are plenty of varieties of that), but sows other seeds as well—barley, beans, peas, vetches, seeds of vegetables and flowers. Care of plants is part of the same process of cultivation appropriate to nurseries, parks, orchards, and, in general, the growth and nurture of trees of all kinds. Similarly, farm care involves more than sheep; the skills are also needed for cattle, horses, hounds, bees, and, in general, the maintenance of flocks and herds, and the nurture of life, differ from one another to a greater or smaller extent, apart from the fact that they are all helpful to life. When I speak of philosophy, I do not mean Stoic, Platonic, Epicurean or Aristotelian. I apply the term philosophy to all that is rightly said in each of these schools, all that teaches righteousness combined with a scientific knowledge of religion, the complete eclectic unity. I do not know how I could call divine, likenesses made from human calculations. Let us now consider this. However admirably people live, if they do so without real knowledge of what they are doing, their good actions go for nothing. They have stumbled into doing good works by accident, whereas there are people who hit the target of the Word of truth by means of understanding. "Abraham was accounted just for his faith, not his actions" (Rom. 4). So whatever good actions they perform today will be of no benefit to them after life's close, unless they have faith. This is why the Scriptures were translated into the language of the Greeks, so that the later could never offer a plea of ignorance; they are perfectly capable of hearing all that we have to say if they are only willing. Contrast someone's talk about truth with that account Truth gives of herself: these are very different matters. The first is a shot at truth, the second is Truth. The first is a likeness, the second the actuality. The first survives by learning and discipline, the second by power and faith. Instruction in religion is a gift, faith is a grace. We know the will of God by doing the will of God. "Open to me the gates of righteousness," Scripture says, "I shall enter through them, I shall give thanks to the Lord" (Ps. 118:19). God offers salvation in many different ways (for He is good) and the roads to righteousness are many and various and lead to the master road and master gate. If you are looking for the authentic royal entrance, you will hear this: "This is the Lord's gate; righteous people will enter by it" (Ps. 118:20). Many gates are open but only one—that is Christ—is righteous. Blessed are all those who enter by it, keeping a straight course in holiness and revealed knowledge. Paul, in his letter to the Corinthians, expounds the differences between those of repute in the Church. I am quoting: "To one is given the word of wisdom through the Spirit, to another the word of knowledge according to the same Spirit; to another faith by the same Spirit; and to another gifts of healing by the one Spirit" (1 Cor. 12:8–9).

Sophistry Is Deceitful

Skill in sophistry, an enthusiasm of the Greeks, is a power operating on the imagination, using arguments to implant false opinions as if they were true. It produces rhetoric for persuasion, heuristic for controversy. If the skillful speaker lacks philosophy then he is harmful. Plato himself opposed sophistry, calling it "immoral practice," and Aristotle showed it to be "skill in banditry," in that it uses persuasion to imitate the practice of wisdom, promising a wisdom it has never practiced. To put it briefly, just as persuasiveness is the starting point of rhetoric, argument its practice, and persuasion its goal, so with heuristic the starting point is opinion, its practice contention, its goal victory. Similarly with sophistry, the starting point is the world of the senses. Its practice is twofold: one, derived from rhetoric, is expository: the other, from dialectic, is interrogatory. Its goal is to shock. Dialectic, which the schools of philosophy are always preoccupied about, is revealed as a philosopher's exercise in the field of conjecture, to acquit the power of refutation. Truth does not lie in any of this. So, the admirable Apostle was right to play down these appalling excesses in language skills when he says, "If anyone does not agree with these sound words, but with some other doctrine, he is proud and ignorant; he has a morbid craving for asking questions and for verbal disputation. From these emerge strife, jealousy, slander, wicked suspicions, and altercations between men who are intellectually depraved and have lost all contact with truth" (1 Tim. 6:3–4). You see how worked up he is, how he calls their skill in arguments a disease, although the sophists, Greek and non-Greek alike, pride themselves in these skills.

Faith Grounded in Reason Is Preferable to Simple Faith

There are some people who imagine they are fully equipped by nature, and do not consider it right to have anything to do with philosophy or dialectic. Moreover, these refuse to engage in the consideration of the natural world at all. All they ask for is simply and solely faith. It is as if they expected to gather grapes from the very first without taking any care of the vine. The vine is allegorically the Lord. From Him, with care and an agricultural skill that follows the Word, we can harvest the fruit. We have to prune, dig, fasten, and all the rest. We need the pruning-knife, the mattock, and all the other tools of agriculture for the care of the vine, if we want it to produce edible fruit for us. In farming or medicine, the expert is the person who has grasped a wide variety of lessons to enable him to become a better farmer or doctor. So here I affirm that the expert is the one who brings everything to bear on the truth. He culls whatever is useful from mathematics, the fine arts, literary studies, and, of course, philosophy, and protects the faith from all attacks. No one bothers about the athlete whose only contribution to the community is his physical strength. We approve of the sea-captain who has had plenty of experience and has visited "the cities of many peoples," and the doctor who has treated many patients. This is how some people form the idea of "the empirical doctor." Anyone who brings every experience to bear on right action, taking models from Greeks and non-Greeks alike, is a highly skilled hunter of truth. He really is multi-talented. Like the testing stone (a stone from Lydia that was believed to distinguish genuine from false gold), our "man of many skills," our Christian Gnostic, is also competent to distinguish sophistry from philosophy, superficial adornment from athletics, cookery from pharmacy, rhetoric from dialectic, and then in Christian thought, heresies from the actual truth. The person who yearns to touch the fringes of God's power must of necessity become a philosopher to have a proper conception about intellectual objects. He must be able also to distinguish the ambiguities and nominally similar terms in the two Testaments. It is in fact by an ambiguity that the Lord outwits the devil at the time of the temptation, and I no longer understand how the inventor of philosophy and dialectic can be deceived by the method of ambiguity and led astray, as some people suppose.

ORIGEN: "ON SPOILING THE EGYPTIANS" (LETTER TO GREGORY)
Greek, Late Second Century A.D.

Origen (185–232 A.D.) was surely one of the most gifted and colorful teachers of the early church. Probably born in Alexandria, Origen was raised in a Christian home and given a thorough Christian education. Prompted by the martyrdom of his father, Origen declared his intention to make a public declaration of his faith and face death as well. However, according to the ancient church historian, Eusebius, Origen's mother had other ideas for her gifted son and hid his clothing to prevent him from leaving the house! By his eighteenth birthday, Origen's considerable knowledge of Scripture was recognized, and he was appointed head of the Catechetical School of Alexandria in the place of Clement, who had left the city to avoid persecution. Origen's zealous obedience to the words of Jesus in the gospel led him to a strict ascetic lifestyle and even to a literal interpretation of Matthew 19:12, thus, according to Eusebius, he castrated himself! Ironically, Origen later taught the importance of moving beyond a literal translation to a moral and finally a spiritual level of understanding. He makes a case for his threefold understanding of Scripture in his major theological work *On First Principles*, of which a brief selection follows here from the Latin translation of Rufinus. Next, in his Letter to Gregory, Origen argues for the importance of appropriating philosophical wisdom in service to Christian education.

Questions for Guided Reading
1. What is the role of philosophy in Christian education?
2. How does the account of the Israelite exodus foreshadow the Christian use of philosophy?

♦

Greetings in God, most excellent sir, and venerable son Gregory, from Origen. A natural readiness of comprehension, as you well know, may contribute to any goal one wishes to achieve. So, for example, one's natural abilities may enable one to become an excellent Roman lawyer or even a philosopher in an outstanding school.

Yet I am anxious that you, Gregory, should devote all the strength of your gifts to Christianity in order to reach your goal; and to this end, I wish to ask you to extract from the philosophy of the Greeks whatever may serve as a course of study or a preparation for Christianity, and from geometry and astronomy whatever will serve to explain the sacred Scriptures, in order that all which the sons of the philosophers are inclined to say about geometry and music, grammar, rhetoric, and astronomy, we, as ministrants to philosophy, may apply to Christianity itself.

Perhaps something like this is foreshadowed in Exodus, where the children of Israel were commanded to ask from their neighbors and those who dwelt with them, vessels of silver and gold, and raiment, in order that, by spoiling the Egyptians, they might have material for the preparation of the things which pertained to the service of God. For from the things which the children of Israel took from the Egyptians the vessels in the holy of holies were made—the ark with its lid, and the cherubim, and the mercy seat, and the golden coffer, where was the manna, the angels' bread. These things were probably made from the best Egyptian gold. A lesser quality gold than might have been used for the solid golden candlestick near the inner veil, and its branches, and the golden table on which were the pieces of showbread, and the golden censer between them. And if there was a third and a fourth quality of gold, from it would be made still lesser vessels, all incidental pieces being made from Egyptian silver. For when the children of Israel dwelt in Egypt, they gained this from their dwelling there, and they had no lack of such precious material for the utensils of the service of God. And the Egyptian raiment were probably made of all those things which, as Scripture mentions, required embroidered work, sewn with the wisdom of God, that the veils might be made for the inner and outer courts. And need I go on in this untimely digression, to explain how useful to the children of Israel were the things brought from Egypt, which the Egyptians had not put to proper use, but which the Hebrews, guided by the wisdom of God, used for God's service?

Now, it is also true that some are harmed by their sojourn in Egypt, meddling with the knowledge of this world, after they have lived according to the law of God. I may tell you from my own experience that some take from Egypt not only the useful for the service of God, but also that which is detrimental. For just as Aaron fashioned the golden calf from Egyptian gold, some produce heretical notions from their study of Greek philosophy.

ANSELM: *PROSLOGION* (CHAPTERS 1–4)
Latin, A.D. 1078–1079

The fool said in his heart, "There is no God."
—Psalm 14:1

At age twenty-six Anselm crossed the Alps and entered the monastic school of Bec at Normandy, France. His strong faith and intellectual gifts soon gained Anselm a reputation as a teacher and spiritual mentor; within a few years of his arrival he was appointed prior (spiritual director, assistant to the abbot) of the monastery and in time became abbot. While holding these positions Anselm wrote *Prayers and Meditations*, *Proslogion*, and *Monologion*. After being promoted to the politically powerful position of Archbishop of Canterbury, Anselm wrote his best known work, *Cur Deus Homo* (*Why the God-Man?*), on the incarnation of Christ. This was a period of intense spiritual and interpersonal struggles for Anselm.

The prologue to Anselm's *Proslogion* broaches the question of the relationship between faith and learning. His best known and most concise statement on the matter follows Augustine of Hippo, *credo ut intelligam* (I believe in order that I may understand), and shows that Anselm considered faith a necessary prerequisite to the proper use of reason. Faith, then, is prior to reason. Still it is the Christian's duty to exercise his or her mind in the work of understanding revealed (scriptural) truth. *Proslogion* was written, Anselm said, from the perspective of one trying to "raise his mind to the contemplation of God, who is seeking to understand what he believes." In this particular writing, the belief in question is the existence of God. Here Anslem introduces readers to what has become known as the *ontological argument* for the existence of God. Various forms of the *ontological argument* (literally, the argument for the existence of something) have been developed; the effect of Anselm's argument is to demonstrate that if one can think about the possible existence of God—and of course anyone can—then it is logically impossible to think of God as not existing. Anselm's argument, in sum, is that whenever someone thinks about God, he or she is contemplating "that-than-which-no-greater-can-be-thought" (his expression for the highest possible concept or thought, i.e., God). Once this notion is introduced, Anselm raises a question, namely, "Is it possible for a person to conceive of *that-than-which-no-greater-can-be-thought* [God] as not existing?" The answer, logically speaking, must be "no," because if it did *not* exist, then an existing being (God) would be greater than *that* thought. So then, if one acknowledges that it is possible to think such a thought as that-than-which-no-greater-can-be-thought, then one is bound by logic to admit that it exists (or else he or she has not been thinking about that-than-which-no-greater-can-be-thought!).

Questions for Guided Reading

1. What is the quest, and what are some of the requests of Anselm in chapter 1?
2. What does Anselm believe about the relationship between faith and learning?
3. What is the alternative(s) to Anselm's view of faith and learning?
4. Do you follow Anselm's view or the alternative? Why?
5. How would you describe Anselm's proof for God's existence? What sort of proof is it?
6. Explain Anselm's proof to someone else.

✦

Chapter I

Come now, busy bee, forget your busyness for a bit,
Silence your hurtful thoughts;
Put away your cares, pack-off your troubles;
Allow time for God and rest in Him.
Take cover in your soul,
Shut out absolutely everything except God alone,
then seek Him, praying,
"I seek your face, Oh Lord,
Your face I seek." (Ps. 27:8)
Come near, Oh Lord my God,
Teach my heart how to seek you and where to find you.
If you are not with me, Lord, then where am I to look
      for you?
If you are everywhere, why can I not perceive you?
Truly you dwell in inapproachable light.

But where is such light and how could I possibly
      approach it?
Who shall lead me to this light and bring me into it
      that I may perceive you?
In what form or dimension will I discover you?
I have never seen you, Oh Lord my God; I do not know
      your shape.
What is an exile far from God, Most High, to do?
Your servant who longs for you lovingly but does not
      see your face?
Your servant . . .
    Gasps to see your countenance and longs to
      approach you,
      Yet your dwelling-place is far removed;
      Anxiously looks for you but knows not your place;
      Desires to come upon you,
        but how would your servant recognize you?
Even so, you are my God; even so, my Lord.
First You formed me, then You reformed me, endowing
      me with all the blessings I enjoy.
You have blessed me and still I do not know you;
I was made to see you, yet I have not accomplished that
      for which I was created.
Oh the miserable situation of humanity: losing that for
      which they were made!
Oh cruel and unthinkable destiny!
What riches they have lost and what little they have
      found.
What great value is that which left them, what little
      remains,
Gone is the very blessedness for which they were
      created;
Discovered is the misery for which they were not made.
At one time they feasted on the bread of angels (for
      which they still hunger);
Now they eat the bread of sorrows, which formerly
      they did not know.
Hear, then, the dirge of all humanity, the world-wide
      lamentation of the sons of perdition:
    Those who stuffed themselves now groan in
      hunger;
    Those rich in everything now go about begging.
    Those possessed of happiness; are now miserable
      destitutes;
Why?
He could have prevented the loss we bear as weight;
Immersed in darkness we are kept from light;

Robbed of life we know the sting of death;
 Refugees, we are driven out to somewhere
  unknown, sent into ruin.
 But why?
From homeland to exile;
From kingdom light to cursed blindness;
From everlasting joy to horrible wasting;
Robbed of all good and stuck with all evil;
Crushed with the weigh of loss, of grief, of such a fate!
But listen, I am the victim-son of Eve, orphaned of
  God;
What have I done? What did I expect to accomplish?
What did I hope to gain?
See here, fumbling toward ecstasy I stumbled over
  myself;
Seeking peace I encountered only grief of failure;
How I hoped to laugh again but choking on my tears, I
  sigh, and again, I sigh.
How long, Oh Lord, will you forget us forever?
How long will you turn your face away?
When will you give light to our eyes once more?
Once more turn your gaze on us?
When will we have you again?
Look on us and give us life again!
Reveal yourself to us, restore our lives;
Have compassion on our labor since without you it
  profits nothing.
May we breathe hope afresh and no longer lose breath
  in sighing;
My heart's drink is bitter desolation, but you know
  how to sweeten it;
I seek the comfort of your consolation;
Hungry, I go looking for you that I might be fed.
Poor, I come to the Rich in mercy: do not send me
  away empty!
Bent over, my Lord, my face is fallen: Lift my eyes to
  Thee!
Sunk in sin I drown: Rescue me!
As the pit around me caves in, I cry out: "Excavate me
  Oh my God!"
Permit me to look upon your light, even if as a distant
  star, even if from ocean floor.
Teach me to search for you again for I have forgotten
  how; Reveal yourself to my forgetfulness;
As I look for you in longing, let me long for you in
  looking;

Let me encounter you in love, and love you in the
  encounter;
It is true, an icon of God You made me to be—
 This is how I am mindful of You,
 This how I am able to conceive of You,
 This is how I can love you, and give thanks.
It is also true, this icon is rusty,
 Misshapened by sin,
 Tarnished by wrong-doing,
No longer good for what it was made, unless . . .
You renew and make me anew!
Finally, Oh Lord, while I do not expect to fathom your
  mysterious depths,
I want to taste your wisdom—for this my heart is
  starving!
Not that I need the wisdom to know you are there,
  no—
I know you are there, and so I want to taste your
  wisdom;
For *I believe* that if I did *not believe*, I would never, ever
  understand.

Chapter II

Grant me, Lord, to comprehend my faith, so far as it may profit me, to truly know that You are all we have believed You to be. Yes, we believe You are a being *than which nothing greater can be conceived*. Or is the fool correct who believes there is no God (Ps. 14:1)? Yet when this fool hears of a being *than which nothing greater can be conceived* he must acknowledge the sense of it in his mind, even though he will not admit to its existence. It is, after all, one thing to have an idea in mind and something else altogether to know for certain that it really exists. For example, when a painter gets an idea for a painting then we say he has it in mind, though he knows it does not yet exist because he has not yet painted it. But once he has painted it, he not only has it mind but also in fact since he has made it. Therefore, even the fool must acknowledge that *than which nothing greater can be conceived* exists as an idea in the mind, and that he understands it.

Now then, how can *that than which nothing greater can be conceived* exist only in the mind? It is not possible! Because if *than which nothing greater can be conceived* existed only in the mind and not in reality, then it would indeed be possible to think of something

96

greater—namely, *that than which nothing greater can be conceived* existing in reality! Therefore if *that than which nothing greater can be conceived* exists in the mind alone, an actual Being *than which nothing greater can be conceived* is greater than the thought itself. And therefore there can be no doubt that *that than which nothing greater can be conceived* exits both in the mind and in reality.

Chapter III

So then, it is not possible to conceive of God as not existing—that is, as *that than which nothing greater can be conceived*. Because that which can be conceived not to exist is not God. And certainly that *than which nothing greater can be conceived* cannot be conceived of as not existing. For, it is possible to conceive of a being which cannot be conceived of as not existing; and such a being would be greater than one which can be conceived not to exist. Therefore, if *that than which nothing greater can be conceived* can be conceived of as not existing, then it is not *that than which nothing greater can be conceived*. But this is an impossible contradiction! So there truly is a being *than which nothing greater can be conceived* to exist, such that it cannot even be conceived of as not existing, and You, Oh Lord, our God, are that Being. And so truly do You exist, Oh Lord my God, that You cannot be conceived of as not existing, and rightly so. For if any mind could conceive of a better being than You—that mind would rise above the Creator (which is absurd). Indeed, everything else, except You alone, can be conceived of as not existing. And yes, existence itself belongs to you more than all other beings, and therefore in higher degree in You than in all others. Whatever else exists does not exist as certainly as You; only to a lesser degree does it have its existence. So then, why has the fool said in his heart there is no God (Ps. 14:1)? since it is obvious to the rational mind that You do exist and in the highest degree of all? Why else, but that he is a foolish fool.

Chapter IV

How could even a fool seriously claim that such a thing as God cannot exist? A thing can be conceived of in two ways: (1) We can simply think about the word that signifies it—in this case "God." (2) We ponder the "thing" referred to whenever the word ("God") is used. Now the fool imagines that God can be conceived of as not existing, as easily as if the word "God" itself could simply be said not to exist, but that makes no sense—how could the fool express anything which he has not already conceived? Or how could he not conceive of anything he expresses? To express anything one must first conceive of it. The fool cannot have it both ways—denying the existence of a thing whose reality he has just verified by naming it. Once again, there is more than one way something can be conceived: First, something is conceived whenever the word signifying it comes to mind; Second, when the very thing itself—and not just the word—comes to mind. Even if "God" as a word could be conceived of as not existing, God as a reality cannot be.

After all, no one who understands what fire and water are would mistake fire for water in reality: even though one might mix up the words he would never mistake actual fire with water or visa versa. So, then, no one who understands what God is can conceive that God does not exist; although he says these words in his heart. For, God is that *than which a greater cannot be conceived*. He who thoroughly understands this will know for certain that this being truly exists, and that He cannot be nonexistent. Therefore, he who understands "God" as a word cannot conceive that he does not exist.

Thank You, gracious Lord, thank You: What I formerly believed by your grace, I now understand by your illumination—that if I were unwilling to believe that You exist, I would have to acknowledge by understanding that such a thing were impossible.

ANSELM: *WHY THE GOD-MAN?* (FROM *CUR DEUS HOMO*)
Latin, A.D. 1098

See pages 94–95 for an introduction to Anselm of Lyon. Anselm wanted Christians to meditate on their beliefs—especially God's existence (see *Proslogion*) and the doctrine of the incarnation (*Cur Deus Homo*)—and to this end he composed a dialogue between himself and "Boso" (Latin for "ox"). Chapters 1–9 follow.

Questions for Guided Reading

1. According to Boso in chapter 2, which comes first, faith or reason, and why?

2. In chapter 2, what opening question does Boso ask, and why does he ask about such things?

3. Why does Anselm hesitate to answer Boso, and what encouragement does he offer him to pursue the answer?

4. According to chapter 2, how do the questions of the faithful compare with those of infidels, and how do their approaches to reason differ?

5. Give an example or two of what Anselm in chapter 3 calls the "indescribable beauty of our redemption."

6. According to chapter 5, why couldn't redemption be accomplished through a sinless man, that is, not a God-man?

7. The basic and interrelated questions raised by Boso in chapters 6 and 7 are essentially one question: *If God is all-powerful, why was the work of redemption so difficult or laborious for God?* What is Anselm's reply in chapter 8?

8. Based on chapter 8, how could a just God punish a just man (his own Son, Jesus) for the sins of the unjust (us)?

9. Is it accurate to say that God mandated the death of his Son? Why or why not?

✦

Chapter I: The question on which the whole work rests

I have been often and most earnestly requested by many, both personally and by letter, that I would hand down in writing the proofs of a certain doctrine of our faith, which I am accustomed to give to inquirers; for they say that these proofs gratify them, and are considered sufficient. This they ask, not for the sake of attaining to faith by means of reason, but that they may be gladdened by understanding and meditating on those things which they believe; and that, as far as possible, they may be always ready to convince anyone who demands of them a reason of that hope which is in us (1 Peter 3:15). And this question, both infidels are accustomed to bring up against us, ridiculing Christian

simplicity as absurd; and many believers ponder it in their hearts; for what cause or necessity, God became man, and by his own death, as we believe and affirm, restored life to the world; when he might have done this, by means of some other being, angelic or human, or merely by his will. Not only the learned, but also many unlearned persons interest themselves in this inquiry and seek for its solution. Therefore, since many desire to consider this subject, and, though it seems very difficult in the investigation, it is yet plain to all in the solution, and attractive for the value and beauty of the reasoning; although what ought to be sufficient has been said by the holy fathers and their successors, yet I will take pains to disclose to inquirers what God has seen fit to lay open to me. And since investigations, which are carried on by question and answer, are thus made more plain to many, and especially to less quick minds, and on that account are more gratifying, I will take to argue with me one of those persons who agitate this subject; one, who among the rest impels me more earnestly to it, so that in this way Boso may question and Anselm reply.

Chapter II: How those things which are to be said should be received

BOSO. As the right order requires us to believe the deep things of Christian faith before we undertake to discuss them by reason; so to my mind it appears a neglect if, after we are established in the faith, we do not seek to understand what we believe. Therefore, since I thus consider myself to hold the faith of our redemption, by the prevenient grace of God, so that, even were I unable in any way to understand what I believe, still nothing could shake my constancy; I desire that you should discover to me, what, as you know, many besides myself ask, for what necessity and cause God, who is omnipotent, should have assumed the littleness and weakness of human nature for the sake of its renewal?

ANSELM. You ask of me a thing which is above me, and therefore I tremble to take in hand subjects too lofty for me, lest, when some one may have thought or even seen that I do not satisfy him, he will rather believe that I am in error with regard to the substance of the truth, than that my intellect is not able to grasp it.

BOSO. You ought not so much to fear this, because you should call to mind, on the other hand, that it often happens in the discussion of some question that God opens what before lay concealed; and that you should hope for the grace of God, because if you liberally impart those things which you have freely received, you will be worthy to receive higher things to which you have not yet attained.

ANSELM. There is also another thing on account of which I think this subject can hardly, or not at all, be discussed between us comprehensively; since, for this purpose, there is required a knowledge of Power and Necessity and Will and certain other subjects which are so related to one another that none of them can be fully examined without the rest; and so the discussion of these topics requires a separate labor, which, though not very easy, in my opinion, is by no means useless; for ignorance of these subjects makes certain things difficult, which by acquaintance with them become easy.

BOSO. You can speak so briefly with regard to these things, each in its place, that we may both have all that is requisite for the present object, and what remains to be said we can put off to another time.

ANSELM. This also much disinclines me from your request, not only that the subject is important, but as it is of a form fair above the sons of men, so is it of a wisdom fair above the intellect of men. On this account, I fear, lest, as I am wont to be incensed against sorry artists, when I see our Lord himself painted in an unseemly figure; so also it may fall out with me if I should undertake to exhibit so rich a theme in rough and vulgar diction.

BOSO. Even this ought not to deter you, because, as you allow any one to talk better if he can, so you preclude none from writing more elegantly if your language does not please him. But, to cut you off from all excuses, you are not to fulfill this request of mine for the learned but for me, and those asking the same thing with me.

ANSELM. Since I observe your earnestness and that of those who desire this thing with you, out of love and pious zeal, I will try to the best of my ability with the assistance of God and your prayers, which, when making this request, you have often promised me, not so much to make plain what you inquire about, as to inquire with you. But I wish all that I say to be received with this understanding, that, if I shall have said anything which higher authority does not corroborate, though I appear to demonstrate it by argument, yet it is not to be received with any further confidence, than as so appearing to me for the time, until God in some way make a clearer revelation to me. But if I am in any measure able

to set your inquiry at rest, it should be concluded that a wiser than I will be able to do this more fully; nay, we must understand that for all that a man can say or know still deeper grounds of so great a truth lie concealed.

BOSO. Suffer me, therefore, to make use of the words of infidels; for it is proper for us when we seek to investigate the reasonableness of our faith to propose the objections of those who are wholly unwilling to submit to the same faith, without the support of reason. For although they appeal to reason because they do not believe, but we, on the other hand, because we do believe; nevertheless, the thing sought is one and the same. And if you bring up anything in reply which sacred authority seems to oppose, let it be mine to urge this inconsistency until you disprove it.

ANSELM. Speak on according to your pleasure.

Chapter III: Objections of infidels and replies of believers

BOSO. Infidels ridiculing our simplicity charge upon us that we do injustice and dishonor to God when we affirm that he descended into the womb of a virgin, that he was born of woman, that he grew on the nourishment of milk and the food of men; and, passing over many other things which seem incompatible with Deity, that he endured fatigue, hunger, thirst, stripes and crucifixion among thieves.

ANSELM. We do no injustice or dishonor to God, but give him thanks with all the heart, praising and proclaiming the ineffable height of his compassion. For the more astonishing a thing it is and beyond expectation, that he has restored us from so great and deserved ills in which we were, to so great and unmerited blessings which we had forfeited; by so much the more has he shown his more exceeding love and tenderness toward us. For if they carefully considered how fitly in this way human redemption is secured, they would not ridicule our simplicity, but would rather join with us in praising the wise beneficence of God. For, as death came upon the human race by the disobedience of man, it was fitting that by man's obedience life should be restored. And, as sin, the cause of our condemnation, had its origin from a woman, so ought the author of our righteousness and salvation to be born of a woman. And so also was it proper that the devil, who, being man's tempter, had conquered him in eating of the tree, should be vanquished by man in the suffering of the tree which man bore. Many other things also, if we carefully examine them, give a certain indescribable beauty of our redemption as thus procured.

Chapter IV: These things appear indecisive and unsubstantial to infidels

BOSO. These things must be admitted to be beautiful, and like so many pictures; but, if they have no solid foundation, they do not appear sufficient to infidels, as reasons why we ought to believe that God wished to suffer the things which we speak of. For when one wishes to make a picture, he selects something substantial to paint it upon, so that his picture may remain. For no one paints in water or in air, because no traces of the picture remain in them. Wherefore, when we hold up to infidels these harmonious proportions which you speak of as so many pictures of the real thing, since they do not think this belief of ours a reality, but only a fiction, they consider us, as it were, to be painting upon a cloud. Therefore the rational existence of the truth must first be shown, I mean, the necessity, which proves that God ought to or could have condescended to those things which we affirm. Afterward, to make the body of the truth, so to speak, shine forth more clearly, these harmonious proportions, like pictures of the body, must be described.

ANSELM. Does not the reason why God ought to do the things we speak of seem absolute enough when we consider that the human race, that work of his so very precious, was wholly ruined, and that it was not seemly that the purpose which God had made concerning man should fall to the ground; and, moreover, that this purpose could not be carried into effect unless the human race were delivered by their Creator himself?

Chapter V: Only God could accomplish the redemption of man

BOSO. If this deliverance were said to be effected somehow by any other being than God (whether it were an angelic or a human being), the mind of man would receive it far more patiently. For God could have made some man without sin, not of a sinful substance, and not a descendant of any man, but just as he made Adam, and by this man it should seem that the work we speak of could have been done.

ANSELM. Do you not perceive that, if any other being should rescue man from eternal death, man would rightly be adjudged as the servant of that being? Now

if this be so, he would in no wise be restored to that dignity which would have been his had he never sinned. For he, who was to be through eternity only the servant of God and an equal with the holy angels, would now be the servant of a being who was not God, and whom the angels did not serve.

Chapter VI: Infidels doubt God loves us

BOSO. This they greatly wonder at, because we call this redemption a release. For, say they, in what custody or imprisonment, or under whose power were you held, that God could not free you from it, without purchasing your redemption by so many sufferings, and finally by his own blood? And when we tell them that he freed us from our sins, and from his own wrath, and from hell, and from the power of the devil, whom he came to vanquish for us, because we were unable to do it, and that he purchased for us the kingdom of heaven; and that, by doing all these things, he manifested the greatness of his love toward us; they answer: If you say that God, who, as you believe, created the universe by a word, could not do all these things by a simple command, you contradict yourselves, for you make him powerless. Or, if you grant that he could have done these things in some other way, but did not wish to, how can you vindicate his wisdom, when you assert that he desired, without any reason, to suffer things so unbecoming? For these things which you bring up are all regulated by his will; for the wrath of God is nothing but his desire to punish. If, then, he does not desire to punish the sins of men, man is free from his sins, and from the wrath of God, and from hell, and from the power of the devil, all which things are the sufferings of sin; and, what he had lost by reason of these sins, he now regains. For, in whose power is hell, or the devil? Or, whose is the kingdom of heaven, if it be not his who created all things? Whatever things, therefore, you dread or hope for, all lie subject to his will, whom nothing can oppose. If, then, God were unwilling to save the human race in any other way than that you mention, when he could have done it by his simple will, observe, to say the least, how you disparage his wisdom. For, if a man without motive should do, by severe toil, a thing which he could have done in some easy way, no one would consider him a wise man. As to your statement that God has shown in this way how much he loved you, there is no argument to support this, unless it be proved that he could not otherwise have saved man. For, if he could not have done it otherwise, then it was, indeed, necessary for him to manifest his love in this way. But now, when he could have saved man differently, why is it that, for the sake of displaying his love, he does and suffers the things which you enumerate? For does he not show good angels how much he loves them, though he suffer no such things as these for them? As to what you say of his coming to vanquish the devil for you, with what meaning dare you allege this? Is not the omnipotence of God everywhere enthroned? How is it, then, that God must needs come down from heaven to vanquish the devil? These are the objections with which infidels think they can withstand us.

Chapter VII: The devil had no justice on his side against man

BOSO. Moreover, I do not see the force of that argument, which we are wont to make use of, that God, in order to save men, was bound, as it were, to try a contest with the devil in justice, before he did in strength, so that, when the devil should put to death that being in whom there was nothing worthy of death, and who was God, he should justly lose his power over sinners; and that, if it were not so, God would have used undue force against the devil, since the devil had a rightful ownership of man, for the devil had not seized man with violence, but man had freely surrendered to him. It is true that this might well enough be said, if the devil or man belonged to any other being than God, or were in the power of any but God. But since neither the devil nor man belong to any but God, and neither can exist without the exertion of Divine power, what cause ought God to try with his own creature (*de suo, in suo*), or what should he do but punish his servant, who had seduced his fellow-servant to desert their common Lord and come over to himself; who, a traitor, had taken to himself a fugitive; a thief, had taken to himself a fellow-thief, with what he had stolen from his Lord. For when one was stolen from his Lord by the persuasions of the other, both were thieves. For what could be more just than for God to do this? Or, should God, the judge of all, snatch man, thus held, out of the power of him who holds him so unrighteously, either for the purpose of punishing him in some other way than by means of the devil, or of sparing him, what injustice would there be in this? For, though man deserved to be tormented by the devil, yet the devil tormented him unjustly. For

man merited punishment, and there was no more suitable way for him to be punished than by that being to whom he had given his consent to sin. But the infliction of punishment was nothing meritorious in the devil; on the other hand, he was even more unrighteous in this, because he was not led to it by a love of justice, but urged on by a malicious impulse. For he did not do this at the command of God, but God's inconceivable wisdom, which happily controls even wickedness, permitted it. And, in my opinion, those who think that the devil has any right in holding man, are brought to this belief by seeing that man is justly exposed to the tormenting of the devil, and that God in justice permits this; and therefore they suppose that the devil rightly inflicts it. For the very same thing, from opposite points of view, is sometimes both just and unjust, and hence, by those who do not carefully inspect the matter, is deemed wholly just or wholly unjust.

Suppose, for example, that one strikes an innocent person unjustly, and hence justly deserves to be beaten himself; if, however, the one who was beaten, though he ought not to avenge himself, yet does strike the person who beat him, then he does it unjustly. And hence this violence on the part of the man who returns the blow is unjust, because he ought not to avenge himself; but as far as he who received the blow is concerned, it is just, for since he gave a blow unjustly, he justly deserves to receive one in return. Therefore, from opposite views, the same action is both just and unjust, for it may chance that one person shall consider it only just, and another only unjust. So also the devil is said to torment men justly, because God in justice permits this, and man in justice suffers it. But when man is said to suffer justly, it is not meant that his just suffering is inflicted by the hand of justice itself, but that he is punished by the just judgment of God. But if that written decree is brought up, which the Apostle says was made against us, and cancelled by the death of Christ; and if any one thinks that it was intended by this decree that the devil, as if under the writing of a sort of compact, should justly demand sin and the punishment of sin, of man, before Christ suffered, as a debt for the first sin to which he tempted man, so that in this way he seems to prove his right over man, I do not by any means think that it is to be so understood. For that writing is not of the devil, because it is called the writing of a decree of the devil, but of God. For by the just judgment of God it was decreed, and, as it were, confirmed by writing, that, since man had sinned, he should not henceforth of himself have the power to avoid sin or the punishment of sin; for the spirit is out-going and not returning (*est enim spiritus vadens et non rediens*); and he who sins ought not to escape with impunity, unless pity spare the sinner, and deliver and restore him. Wherefore we ought not to believe that, on account of this writing, there can be found any justice on the part of the devil in his tormenting man. In fine, as there is never any injustice in a good angel, so in an evil angel there can be no justice at all. There was no reason, therefore, as respects the devil, why God should not make use of his own power against him for the liberation of man.

Chapter VIII: Infidels reject the notion of condescension even for men; they cannot believe Christ died willingly

ANSELM. The will of God ought to be a sufficient reason for us, when he does anything, though we cannot see why he does it. For the will of God is never irrational.

BOSO. That is very true, if it be granted that God does wish the thing in question; but many will never allow that God does wish anything if it be inconsistent with reason.

ANSELM. What do you find inconsistent with reason, in our confessing that God desired those things which make up our belief with regard to his incarnation?

BOSO. This in brief: that the Most High should stoop to things so lowly, that the Almighty should do a thing with such toil.

ANSELM. They who speak thus do not understand our belief. For we affirm that the Divine nature is beyond doubt impassible, and that God cannot at all be brought down from his exaltation, nor toil in anything which he wishes to effect. But we say that the Lord Jesus Christ is very God and very man, one person in two natures, and two natures in one person. When, therefore, we speak of God as enduring any humiliation or infirmity, we do not refer to the majesty of that nature, which cannot suffer; but to the feebleness of the human constitution which he assumed. And so there remains no ground of objection against our faith. For in this way we intend no debasement of the Divine nature, but we teach that one person is both Divine and human. In the incarnation of God there is no lowering of the Deity; but the nature of man we believe to be exalted.

BOSO. Be it so; let nothing be referred to the Divine nature, which is spoken of Christ after the manner of human weakness; but how will it ever be made out a just or reasonable thing that God should treat or suffer to be treated in such a manner, that man whom the Father called his beloved Son in whom he was well pleased, and whom the Son made himself? For what justice is there in his suffering death for the sinner, who was the most just of all men? What man, if he condemned the innocent to free the guilty, would not himself be judged worthy of condemnation? And so the matter seems to return to the same incongruity which is mentioned above. For if he could not save sinners in any other way than by condemning the just, where is his omnipotence? If, however, he could, but did not wish to, how shall we sustain his wisdom and justice?

ANSELM. God the Father did not treat that man as you seem to suppose, nor put to death the innocent for the guilty. For the Father did not compel him to suffer death, or even allow him to be slain, against his will, but of his own accord he endured death for the salvation of men.

BOSO. Though it were not against his will, since he agreed to the will of the Father; yet the Father seems to have bound him, as it were, by his injunction. For it is said that Christ "humbled himself, being made obedient to the Father even unto death, and that the death of the cross. For which cause God also hath highly exalted him"; and that "he learned obedience from the things which he suffered"; and that God "spared not his own Son, but gave him up for us all." And likewise the Son says: "I came not to do my own will, but the will of him that sent me." And when about to suffer, he says; "As the Father hath given me commandment, so I do." Again: "The cup which the Father hath given me, shall I not drink it?" And, at another time: "Father, if it be possible, let this cup pass from me; nevertheless, not as I will, but as thou wilt." And again: "Father, if this cup may not pass from me except I drink it, thy will be done." In all these passages it would rather appear that Christ endured death by the constraint of obedience, than by the inclination of his own free will.

Chapter IX: He died of his own accord

ANSELM. It seems to me that you do not rightly understand the difference between what he did at the demand of obedience, and what he suffered, not demanded by obedience, but inflicted on him, because he kept his obedience perfect.

BOSO. I need to have you explain it more clearly.

ANSELM. Why did the Jews persecute him even unto death?

BOSO. For nothing else, but that, in word and in life, he invariably maintained truth and justice.

ANSELM. I believe that God demands this of every rational being, and every being owes this in obedience to God.

BOSO. We ought to acknowledge this.

ANSELM. That man, therefore, owed this obedience to God the Father, humanity to Deity; and the Father claimed it from him.

BOSO. There is no doubt of this.

ANSELM. Now you see what he did, under the demand of obedience.

BOSO. Very true, and I see also what infliction he endured, because he stood firm in obedience. For death was inflicted on him for his perseverance in obedience and he endured it; but I do not understand how it is that obedience did not demand this.

ANSELM. Ought man to suffer death, if he had never sinned, or should God demand this of him?

BOSO. It is on this account that we believe that man would not have been subject to death, and that God would not have exacted this of him; but I should like to hear the reason of the thing from you.

ANSELM. You acknowledge that the intelligent creature was made holy, and for this purpose, viz., to be happy in the enjoyment of God.

BOSO. Yes.

ANSELM. You surely will not think it proper for God to make his creature miserable without fault, when he had created him holy that he might enjoy a state of blessedness. For it would be a miserable thing for man to die against his will.

BOSO. It is plain that, if man had not sinned, God ought not to compel him to die.

ANSELM. God did not, therefore, compel Christ to die; but he suffered death of his own will, not yielding up his life as an act of obedience, but on account of his obedience in maintaining holiness; for he held out so firmly in this obedience that he met death on account of it. It may, indeed be said, that the Father commanded him to die, when he enjoined that upon him on account of which he met death. It was in this sense, then, that "as the Father gave him the commandment, so he did, and the cup which He gave to him, he drank; and he was made obedient to the Father, even unto death"; and thus "he learned obedience from the things which he suffered," that is, how far obedience should be maintained.

Now the word *didicit* (he learned), which is used, can be understood in two ways. For either *didicit* (he learned) is written for this: he caused others to learn; or it is used, because he did learn by experience what he had an understanding of before. Again, when the Apostle had said: "he humbled himself, being made obedient even unto death, and that the death of the cross," he added: "wherefore God also hath exalted him and given him a name, which is above every name." And this is similar to what David said: "he drank of the brook in the way, therefore did he lift up the head." For it is not meant that he could not have attained his exaltation in any other way but by obedience unto death; nor is it meant that his exaltation was conferred on him, only as a reward of his obedience (for he himself said before he suffered, that all things had been committed to him by the Father, and that all things belonging to the Father were his); but the expression is used because he had agreed with the Father and the Holy Spirit, that there was no other way to reveal to the world the height of his omnipotence, than by his death. For if a thing does not take place, except on condition of something else, it is not improperly said to occur by reason of that thing. For if we intend to do a thing, but mean to do something else first by means of which it may be done; when the first thing which we wish to do is done, if the result is such as we intended, it is properly said to be on account of the other; since that is now done which caused the delay; for it had been determined that the first thing should not be done without the other.

If, for instance, I propose to cross a river only in a boat, though I can cross it in a boat or on horseback, and suppose that I delay crossing because the boat is gone; but if afterward I cross, when the boat has returned, it may be properly said of me: the boat was ready, and therefore he crossed. And we not only use this form of expression, when it is by means of a thing which we desire should take place first, but also when we intend to do something else, not by means of that thing, but only after it. For if one delays taking food because he has not today attended the celebration of mass; when that has been done which he wished to do first, it is not improper to say to him: now take food, for you have now done that for which you delayed taking food. Far less, therefore, is the language strange, when Christ is said to be exalted on this account, because he endured death; for it was through this, and after this, that he determined to accomplish his exaltation. This may be understood also in the same way as that passage in which it is said that our Lord increased in wisdom, and in favor with God; not that this was really the case, but that he deported himself as if it were so. For he was exalted after his death, as if it were really on account of that. Moreover, that saying of his: "I came not to do mine own will, but the will of him that sent me," is precisely like that other saying: "My doctrine is not mine"; for what one does not have of himself, but of God, he ought not to call his own, but God's. Now no one has the truth which he teaches, or a holy will, of himself, but of God. Christ, therefore, came not to do his own will, but that of the Father; for his holy will was not derived from his humanity, but from his divinity. For that sentence: "God spared not his own Son, but gave him up for us all," means nothing more than that he did not rescue him. For there are found in the Bible many things like this.

Again, when he says: "Father, if it be possible, let this cup pass from me; nevertheless not as I will, but as thou wilt"; and "If this cup may not pass from me, except I drink it, thy will be done"; he signifies by his own will the natural desire of safety, in accordance with which human nature shrank from the anguish of death. But he speaks of the will of the Father, not because the Father preferred the death of the Son to his life; but because the Father was not willing to rescue the human race, unless man were to do even as great a thing as was signified in the death of Christ. Since reason did not demand of another what he could not do, therefore, the Son says that he desires his own death. For he preferred to suffer, rather than that the human race should be lost; as if he were to say to the Father: "Since thou dost not desire the reconciliation of the world to take place in any other way, in this respect, I see that thou desirest my death; let thy will, therefore, be done, that is, let my death take place, so that the world may be reconciled to thee." For we often say that one desires a thing, because he does not choose something else, the choice of which would preclude the existence of that which he is said to desire; for instance, when we say that he who does not choose

to close the window through which the draft is admitted which puts out the light, wishes the light to be extinguished. So the Father desired the death of the Son, because he was not willing that the world should be saved in any other way, except by man's doing so great a thing as that which I have mentioned. And this, since none other could accomplish it, availed as much with the Son, who so earnestly desired the salvation of man, as if the Father had commanded him to die; and, therefore, "as the Father gave him commandment, so he did, and the cup which the Father gave to him he drank, being obedient even unto death."

PETER ABELARD: "SHOULD FAITH BE BASED ON REASON?" (FROM *SIC ET NON*)
Latin, Early Twelfth Century

In the twelfth century A.D., few Christian teachers were more popular with their students than Peter Abelard. However, influential church leaders suspected Abelard of heresy and viewed him with contempt. Bernard of Clairvaux, for example, opposed his teaching because of Abelard's controversial approach to disputation, one that involved a critical examination of the Scripture and the writings of the Church Fathers. Abelard's method is best seen in his book *Sic et Non* (Yes and No), a list of over 150 philosophical and theological questions followed by answers from Scripture and the writings of various church authorities—many of which apparently contradict one another. Abelard's stated aims were to stimulate his students to (1) think for themselves and not merely accept traditional church teachings on the basis of authority and (2) work to resolve apparent contradictions between authorities. Although in his own day Abelard's methods were considered to undermine church authority, these same methods were later freely adopted by Scholastic teachers (such as Thomas Aquinas) for use in Christian classrooms.

Questions for Guided Reading
1. With what encouragement and what caution does Abelard advise a critical appraisal?
2. What are some reasons Abelard gives for the appearance of apparent contradictions?

> 3. What distinction does Abelard make between Scripture and the "later authors"?

✦

From the Introduction to *Sic et Non*

Among the innumerable words written by the holy Fathers, there appear variations and even contradictions among their sayings. Now it is hardly disrespectful to inquire about such differences in the writings of those "by whose wisdom the world shall be judged," as it is written, "They shall judge nations" (Prov. 3:8) and, again, "You shall sit and judge" (Luke 22:30). Nor do we rebuke as untruthful or denounce as erroneous those to whom the Lord said, "He who hears you hears me; he who despises you despises me" (Luke 10:16).

Keeping in mind our own limitations, we acknowledge that it is our understanding which is defective, and not the writings of those to whom the Truth Himself said, "It is not you who speak but the spirit of your Father who speaks in you" (Matt. 10:20). It is hardly surprising that we, lacking the guidance of the Holy Spirit through whom these things were originally impressed on the writers, fail to understand them. Our understanding is moreover inhibited by unusual expressions and by the various meanings attached to the same word—a word that can used by one writer in one way, and another writer in another. As there are many words, there may be many meanings for a single word. As Tully says, "sameness is the mother of boredom in all things," so it is appropriate to use a variety of words in discussing the same thing and not to express everything with a few common words.

We must also understand that some sayings are falsely attributed to the fathers, since many apocryphal writings were written in the name of a saint, just to enhance their authority, and even the text of divine Scripture is corrupted by the errors of scribes. That most faithful writer and true interpreter, Jerome, accordingly warned us, "Beware of apocryphal writings . . ." If in the Gospels themselves some things are corrupted by the ignorance of scribes, we should not be surprised that the same thing has sometimes hap-pened in the writings of later Fathers who are of much less authority. . . .

It is no less important in my opinion to ascertain whether texts quoted from the Fathers may be ones that they themselves have retracted and corrected after they came to a better understanding of the truth as the blessed Augustine did on many occasions; or whether they are giving the opinion of another rather than their own opinion . . . or whether, in inquiring into certain matters, they left them open to question rather than settled them with a definitive solution . . .

In order that the way be not blocked and posterity deprived of the healthy labor of treating and debating difficult questions of language and style, a distinction must be drawn between the work of later authors and the supreme canonical authority of the Old and New Testaments. If, in Scripture, anything seems absurd, one does not say, "The author is in error"—but rather that the manuscript is defective or that the interpreter is mistaken or, more simply, that you do not understand. But if anything seems contrary to truth in the works of later authors, which are contained in innumerable books, the reader is free to judge, so that he may approve what is pleasing and reject what gives offense, unless the matter is established by certain reason or by canonical authority (of the Scriptures) . . .

In light of all this, we have undertaken here to collect various sayings of the Fathers that give rise to questioning because of their apparent contradictions (as we recall). Such questioning stimulates and sharpens young minds in the pursuit of truth. Indeed, rigorous questioning is the first key to wisdom. Aristotle, that most exacting of philosophers, exhorted the studious to practice it eagerly, saying, "It is difficult to express oneself with confidence on any matter that is not thoroughly discussed, and entertaining doubts on the particulars will indeed be profitable." For by doubting we come to inquiry; through inquiring we perceive the truth, according to the Truth Himself. "Seek and you shall find," Christ says, "Knock and it shall be opened to you." After all, it was He who, as our chief example, was found at age twelve sitting among the doctors and questioning them, appearing as a disciple by questioning rather than as a master by teaching, although there was already in Him the complete and perfect wisdom of God. Where we have quoted Scripture, the greater the authority attributed to Scripture, the more they should stimulate the reader and attract him to the search for truth. Hence I have prefixed to this my book, compiled in one volume from the sayings of the saints, the decree of Pope Gelasius concerning authentic books, from which it may be known that I have cited nothing from apocryphal books. I have also added excerpts from the Retractions of St. Augustine, from which it will be clear that nothing is included which he later retracted and corrected.

[Abelard next presents 156 questions dealing with pro and con topics such as "That God is one—and that God is a plurality," "That the Son of God has existed from eternity—and that he was created," "That God can do all things—and that he cannot." Question #1 is given below.]

Should Faith Be Based on Reason or Not?

First: Support for the idea that faith should not be based on human reason

From Gregory's Twenty-sixth Sermon: "We know that the works of the Lord would not excite wonder if they were understood by reason; nor is there any merit in faith where human reason offers proof."

A similar point in Gregory's Letter to Theodoric: "Faith and a good life are chosen by priests; if a good life is lacking so is faith."

A similar point in Gregory's Fifth Sermon: "At one word of command Peter and Andrew left their nets and followed the Redeemer. They had seen him work no miracles; they had heard nothing from him about eternal retribution; and nevertheless, at one command of the Lord, they forgot what they had seemed to possess . . ."

From the Life of St. Sylvester: When disputing with the Jews, St. Sylvester said to the Rabbi Roasus, "Faith is not submitted to human reason, and faith teaches us that this God, whom you confess to be God, is Father, Son, and Holy Spirit."

Augustine, On the Morals of the Church against the Manicheans: "The order of nature is such that, when we state anything, authority precedes reason for a reason might seem weak if, after it has been presented, authority is cited to confirm it . . ."

Ambrose: "If I am convinced by reason I give up faith . . ."

Second: Support for the idea that faith must be based on human reason

From the First Book of Augustine against Faustus: "Faustus: It is a weak profession of faith if one does not believe in Christ without evidence and argument. You yourself are accustomed to say that Christian belief is simple and absolute and should not be inquired into too curiously. Why then are you destroying the simplicity of the faith by buttressing it with judgments and evidences?"

Gregory to Bishop Dominicus: "I would that all heretics be held in check by Catholic priests vigorously and always by reasoning."

Gregory, On Pastoral Care: "The wise of this world and the dull are to be admonished differently. The former are for the most part converted by the arguments of reason, the latter sometimes better by examples. Doubtless it profits the former to be defeated in their arguments; it is sometimes sufficient for the latter to know of the praiseworthy deeds of other men . . ."

Hilary, On the Trinity, Book XII: "It is fitting for those who preach Christ to the world to refute the irreligious and unsound doctrines of the world through their knowledge of omnipotent wisdom, according as the Apostle says, 'Our weapons are not carnal but mighty before God for the destruction of strongholds and the destroying of arguments and of every obstacle raised up against the knowledge of God . . .'" (2 Cor. 10:4).

Augustine to Count Valerian: "It is good to know how to support what we believe by defending it; for the Apostle Peter commanded us to be always ready to give satisfaction to anyone asking us the reason for our faith and hope . . . We should always explain the just grounds of our faith and hope to questioners . . ."

PETER LOMBARD: "ON THE UNITY AND TRINITY OF GOD" (FROM *FOUR BOOKS OF SENTENCES*)
Latin, 1155–1158

Peter Lombard's *Four Books of Sentences* (*Sententiarum Libri Quattuor*) served as the standard textbook of Catholic theology during the Middle Ages. *Sententiae* (sentences) were reasoned propositions concerning various aspects of the Christian faith. Many composed such sentences in the interest of theology, but Peter Lombard became known as Master of the Sentences due to his clear, systematic, and authoritative presentation. Rather than expressing new ideas or opinions, Peter Lombard systematized theology by organizing sayings of the church fathers. In time his textbook would be superseded by Thomas Aquinas's *Summa Theologica*.

✦

Distinction 2: On the Unity and Trinity of God

Chapter 1: On the Trinity and unity

One must believe by a genuine faith, that the Trinity is the One and Only True God. As Augustine, in his book *On the Trinity*, says, "the Father and the Son and the Holy Spirit—the Trinity—is said, believed, and understood to be of one substance or essence (*substantiae vel essentiae*), which is the most high Good (*summum bonum*), discerned by cleansed minds. For the feeble ability of human intelligence, the mind is not so wonderfully illumined except it be purged by the justice of faith. This is recounted in Book One of Augustine's *Retractions*, "I amend what I (formerly) prayed: God wills only the cleansed to know truth," because one could observe that many who are unclean have some truth. Therefore one ought to approach this lofty subject in fear and humility. And with devout and attentive listening one inquires about the unity of the Trinity—Father, Son, and Holy Spirit—because in this study any errors are grave, any true findings require great effort and bear great fruit. So then, anyone who hears and reads of our awesome God should follow the venerable doctor Augustine who said, "If I do not understand I will not hesitate to ask for help, nor will I be ashamed to learn (from someone else) when I have made a mistake." So then, whoever reads the following should continue as long as he understands, and should stop to ask when he is puzzled or errs, and should correct me where I err. In this way let us follow the path of love together, pondering the One of whom it is said, "Always seek His face."

Chapter 2: The aim of those writing about the Trinity

As with Augustine, all catholic exegetes writing about the Trinity aim to teach in accordance with Scripture, that the Father and the Son and the Holy Spirit are of one Substance and inseparables equal with One God,

there is therefore a "unity in the essence" and a "plurality in the persons" of God. This, however, does not mean there are three gods, but One. Since the Father "begot the Son," the Son is not the Father but is begotten of the Father, and so the Father is not the Son. The Holy Spirit is neither the Father nor the Son, but only the Father's and the Son's Spirit, equal to both in relation to the Unity of the Trinity. Therefore we believe that the Father, and the Son, and the Holy Spirit are by nature (*naturaliter*) just as Augustine says in his book *The Trinity*. For indeed, Father, Son and Holy Spirit are One essence (or *ousios* as the Greeks say), even though the Father is one Person, and the Son is another Person, and the Holy Spirit is yet another Person.

THOMAS AQUINAS: "THE ACT OF FAITH" (FROM *SUMMA THEOLOGICA*)
Latin, Late Thirteenth Century

In formulating the rational approach to faith known as Scholasticism, Aquinas combined Christian doctrine and Greek philosophy with such success that he became known as the greatest of the "Schoolmen." Aquinas, like Peter Lombard, quotes authoritative sources in order to substantiate his claims, but unlike Lombard, Aquinas draws his own final conclusions. Aquinas often quotes Aristotle, whom he calls "the Philosopher." Aristotle's exacting observations and methodical logic provided the most widely adopted approach to systematic thinking in the Middle Ages. The Schoolmen developed exhaustive answers to theological questions. The following example from *Summa Theologica*[3] illustrates Aquinas's dialogical style known as the "disputed question." It helps to imagine Aquinas standing before his students, responding to questions and opposing views prior to reaching his conclusions. His initial points (labeled objection I, objection II, objection III, etc.) are those that Aquinas intends to defeat.

Aquinas raises opposing evidence in order to give it a careful hearing. After this he cites opposing evidence ("in

---

3. The most widely used text and translation of the *Summa* is the sixty-volume set published by Blackfriars in the 1960s. A popular paraphrase is that of Timothy McDermott, published by Christian Classics ([Westminster, MD], 1989). The translation offered here is that of the Fathers of the English Dominican Province, 1920, now in the public domain.

contrast") and draws his conclusion: "My answer is as follows." Before moving on to another (related) question, Aquinas responds to each of the initial points, completing his analysis with "reply to objection #1" and so on.

✦

Question 2: The Act of Faith

What is "to believe," which is the internal act of faith?

In how many ways is it expressed?

Is it necessary for salvation to believe in anything above natural reason?

Is it necessary to believe those things that are attainable by natural reason?

Is it necessary for salvation to believe certain things explicitly?

Are all equally bound to explicit faith?

Is explicit faith in Christ always necessary for salvation?

Is it necessary for salvation to believe in the Trinity explicitly?

Is the act of faith meritorious?

Does human reason diminish the merit of faith?

Article I: Whether to believe is to think with assent

Objection I

It would seem that to believe is not to think with assent. Because the Latin word "cogitatio" [thought] implies a research, for "cogitare" [to think] seems to be equivalent to "coagitare," i.e., "to discuss together." Now Damascene says that faith is "an assent without research." Therefore thinking has no place in the act of faith.

Objection II

Further, faith resides in the reason, as we shall show further on (4, 2). Now to think is an act of the cogitative power, which belongs to the sensitive faculty, as stated in I, 78, 4. Therefore thought has nothing to do with faith.

Objection III

Further, to believe is an act of the intellect, since its object is truth. But assent seems to be an act not of the intellect, but of the will, even as consent is, as stated above (I–II, 15, 1, Reply to 3). Therefore to believe is not to think with assent.

On the contrary, this is how "to believe" is defined by Augustine (*On the Predestination of the Saints*, 2).

I answer that "To think" can be taken in three ways. First, in a general way for any kind of actual consideration of the intellect, as Augustine observes (*The Trinity*, 14, 7): "By understanding I mean now the faculty whereby we understand when thinking." Secondly, "to think" is more strictly taken for that consideration of the intellect, which is accompanied by some kind of inquiry, and which precedes the intellect's arrival at the stage of perfection that comes with the certitude of sight. On this sense Augustine says (*The Trinity*, 15, 16) that "the Son of God is not called the Thought, but the Word of God. When our thought realizes what we know and takes form therefrom, it becomes our word. Hence the Word of God must be understood without any thinking on the part of God, for there is nothing there that can take form, or be unformed." In this way thought is, properly speaking, the movement of the mind while yet deliberating, and not yet perfected by the clear sight of truth. Since, however, such a movement of the mind may be one of deliberation either about universal notions, which belongs to the intellectual faculty, or about particular matters, which belongs to the sensitive part, hence it is that "to think" is taken secondly for an act of the deliberating intellect, and thirdly for an act of the cogitative power.

Accordingly, if "to think" be understood broadly according to the first sense, then "to think with assent," does not express completely what is meant by "to believe": since, in this way, a man thinks with assent even when he considers what he knows by science [Science is certain knowledge of a demonstrated conclusion through its demonstration.], or understands. If, on the other hand, "to think" be understood in the second way, then this expresses completely the nature of the act of believing. For among the acts belonging to the intellect, some have a firm assent without any such kind of thinking, as when a man considers the things that he knows by science, or understands, for this consideration is already formed. But some acts of the intellect have unformed thought devoid of a firm assent, whether they incline to neither side, as in one who "doubts"; or incline to one side rather than the other, but on account of some slight motive, as in one who "suspects"; or incline to one side yet with fear of the other, as in one who "opines." But this act "to believe," cleaves firmly to one side, in which respect belief has something in common with science and understanding; yet its knowledge does not attain the perfection of clear sight, wherein it agrees with doubt, suspicion and opinion. Hence it is proper to the believer to think with assent: so that the act of believing is distinguished from all the other acts of the intellect, which are about the true or the false.

Reply to Objection I

Faith has not that research of natural reason which demonstrates what is believed, but a research into those things whereby a man is induced to believe, for instance that such things have been uttered by God and confirmed by miracles.

Reply to Objection II

"To think" is not taken here for the act of the cogitative power, but for an act of the intellect, as explained above.

Reply to Objection III

The intellect of the believer is determined to one object, not by the reason, but by the will, wherefore assent is taken here for an act of the intellect as determined to one object by the will.

Article II: Whether the act of faith is suitably distinguished as believing God, believing in a God, and believing in God

Objection I

It would seem that the act of faith is unsuitably distinguished as believing God, believing in a God, and believing in God. For one habit has but one act. Now faith is one habit since it is one virtue. Therefore it is unreasonable to say that there are three acts of faith.

Objection II

Further, that which is common to all acts of faith should not be reckoned as a particular kind of act of faith. Now "to believe God" is common to all acts of faith, since faith is founded on the First Truth. Therefore it seems unreasonable to distinguish it from certain other acts of faith.

Objection III

Further, that which can be said of unbelievers, cannot be called an act of faith. Now unbelievers can be said to believe in a God. Therefore it should not be reckoned an act of faith.

Objection IV

Further, movement toward the end belongs to the will, whose object is the good and the end. Now to believe is an act, not of the will, but of the intellect. Therefore "to believe in God," which implies movement toward an end, should not be reckoned as a species of that act. On the contrary is the authority of Augustine who makes this distinction.

I answer that the act of any power or habit depends on the relation of that power or habit to its object. Now the object of faith can be considered in three ways. For, since "to believe" is an act of the intellect, in so far as the will moves it to assent, as stated above (1, Reply to 3), the object of faith can be considered either on the part of the intellect, or on the part of the will that moves the intellect.

If it be considered on the part of the intellect, then two things can be observed in the object of faith, as stated above (1, 1). One of these is the material object of faith, and in this way an act of faith is "to believe in a God"; because, as stated above nothing is proposed to our belief, except in as much as it is referred to God. The other is the formal aspect of the object, for it is the medium on account of which we assent to such and such a point of faith; and thus an act of faith is "to believe God," since, as stated above (1, 1) the formal object of faith is the First Truth, to Which man gives his adhesion, so as to assent to its sake to whatever he believes.

Thirdly, if the object of faith be considered in so far as the intellect is moved by the will, an act of faith is "to believe in God." For the First Truth is referred to the will, through having the aspect of an end.

Reply to Objection I

These three do not denote different acts of faith, but one and the same act having different relations to the object of faith. This suffices for the Reply to the Second Objection.

Reply to Objection III

Unbelievers cannot be said "to believe in a God" as we understand it in relation to the act of faith. For they do not believe that God exists under the conditions that faith determines; hence they do not truly imply belief in a God, since, as the Philosopher observes (*Metaphysics*, 9, text. 22) "to know simple things defectively is not to know them at all."

Reply to Objection IV

As stated above (I–II, 9, 1) the will moves the intellect and the other powers of the soul to the end: and in this respect an act of faith is "to believe in God."

Article III: Whether it is necessary for salvation to believe anything above the natural reason

Objection I

It would seem unnecessary for salvation to believe anything above the natural reason. For the salvation and perfection of a thing seem to be sufficiently insured by its natural endowments. Now matters of faith surpass man's natural reason, since they are things unseen as stated above (1, 4). Therefore to believe seems unnecessary for salvation.

Objection II

Further, it is dangerous for man to assent to matters, wherein he cannot judge whether that which is proposed to him be true or false, according to Job 12:11: "Doth not the ear discern words?" Now a man cannot form a judgment of this kind in matters of faith, since he cannot trace them back to first principles, by which all our judgments are guided. Therefore it is dangerous to believe in such matters. Therefore to believe is not necessary for salvation.

Objection III

Further, man's salvation rests on God, according to Psalm 36:39: "But the salvation of the just is from the Lord." Now "the invisible things" of God "are clearly seen, being understood by the things that are made; His eternal power also and Divinity," according to Romans 1:20: and those things which are clearly seen by the understanding are not an object of belief. Therefore it is not necessary for man's salvation, that he should believe certain things.

On the contrary, it is written (Heb. 11:6): "Without faith it is impossible to please God."

I answer that wherever one nature is subordinate to another, we find that two things concur toward the perfection of the lower nature, one of which is in respect of that nature's proper movement, while the other is in respect of the movement of the higher nature. Thus water by its proper movement moves toward the center (of the earth), while according to the movement of the moon, it moves round the center by ebb and flow. On like manner the planets have their proper movements from west to east, while in accordance with the movement of the first heaven, they have a movement from east to west. Now the created rational nature alone is immediately subordinate to God, since other creatures do not attain to the universal, but only to something particular, while they partake of the Divine goodness either in "being" only, as inanimate things, or also in "living," and in "knowing singulars," as plants and animals; whereas the rational nature, in as much as it apprehends the universal notion of good and being, is immediately related to the universal principle of being.

Consequently the perfection of the rational creature consists not only in what belongs to it in respect of its nature, but also in that which it acquires through a supernatural participation of Divine goodness. Hence it was said above (I–II, 3, 8) that man's ultimate happiness consists in a supernatural vision of God: to which vision man cannot attain unless he be taught by God, according to John 6:45: "Every one that hath heard of the Father and hath learned cometh to Me." Now man acquires a share of this learning, not indeed all at once, but by little and little, according to the mode of his nature: and every one who learns thus must needs believe, in order that he may acquire science in a perfect degree; thus also the Philosopher remarks (*On Sophistic Refutations*, 1, 2) that "it behooves a learner to believe."

Hence in order that a man arrive at the perfect vision of heavenly happiness, he must first of all believe God, as a disciple believes the master who is teaching him.

Reply to Objection I

Since man's nature is dependent on a higher nature, natural knowledge does not suffice for its perfection, and some supernatural knowledge is necessary, as stated above.

Reply to Objection II

Just as man assents to first principles, by the natural light of his intellect, so does a virtuous man, by the habit of virtue, judge aright of things concerning that virtue; and in this way, by the light of faith which God bestows on him, a man assents to matters of faith and not to those which are against faith. Consequently "there is no" danger or "condemnation to them that are in Christ Jesus," and whom He has enlightened by faith.

Reply to Objection III

In many respects faith perceives the invisible things of God in a higher way than natural reason does in proceeding to God from His creatures. Hence it is written (Sirach 3:25): "Many things are shown to thee above the understandings of man."

Article IV: Whether it is necessary to believe those things which can be proved by natural reason

Objection I

It would seem unnecessary to believe those things which can be proved by natural reason. For nothing is superfluous in God's works, much less even than in the works of nature. Now it is superfluous to employ other means, where one already suffices. Therefore it would be superfluous to receive by faith, things that can be known by natural reason.

Objection II

Further, those things must be believed, which are the object of faith. Now science and faith are not about the same object, as stated above (1, 4, 5). Since therefore all things that can be known by natural reason are an object of science, it seems that there is no need to believe what can be proved by natural reason.

Objection III

Further, all things knowable scientifically [Science is certain knowledge of a demonstrated conclusion through its demonstration] would seem to come under one head: so that if some of them are proposed to man as objects of faith, in like manner the others should also be believed. But this is not true. Therefore it is not necessary to believe those things which can be proved by natural reason.

On the contrary, it is necessary to believe that God is one and incorporeal: which things philosophers prove by natural reason.

I answer that it is necessary for man to accept by faith not only things which are above reason, but also those which can be known by reason: and this for three motives. First, in order that man may arrive more quickly at the knowledge of Divine truth. Because the science to whose province it belongs to prove the existence of God, is the last of all to offer itself to human research, since it presupposes many other sciences: so that it would not be until late in life that man would arrive at the knowledge of God. The second reason is, in order that the knowledge of God may be more general. For many are unable to make progress in the study of science, either through dullness of mind, or through having a number of occupations, and temporal needs, or even through laziness in learning, all of whom would be altogether deprived of the knowledge of God, unless Divine things were brought to their knowledge under the guise of faith. The third reason is for the sake of certitude. For human reason is very deficient in things concerning God. A sign of this is that philosophers in their researches, by natural investigation, into human affairs, have fallen into many errors, and have disagreed among themselves. And consequently, in order that men might have knowledge of God, free of doubt and uncertainty, it was necessary for Divine matters to be delivered to them by way of faith, being told to them, as it were, by God Himself Who cannot lie.

Reply to Objection I

The researches of natural reason do not suffice mankind for the knowledge of Divine matters, even of those that can be proved by reason: and so it is not superfluous if these others be believed.

Reply to Objection II

Science and faith cannot be in the same subject and about the same object: but what is an object of science for one, can be an object of faith for another, as stated above (1, 5).

Reply to Objection III

Although all things that can be known by science are of one common scientific aspect, they do not all alike lead man to beatitude: hence they are not all equally proposed to our belief.

Article V: Whether man is bound to believe anything explicitly

Objection I

It would seem that man is not bound to believe anything explicitly. For no man is bound to do what is not in his power. Now it is not in man's power to believe a thing explicitly, for it is written (Rom. 10:14–15): "How shall they believe Him, of whom they have not heard? And how shall they hear without a preacher? And how shall they preach unless they be sent?" Therefore man is not bound to believe anything explicitly.

Objection II

Further, just as we are directed to God by faith, so are we by charity. Now man is not bound to keep the precepts of charity, and it is enough if he be ready to fulfil them: as is evidenced by the precept of Our Lord (Matt. 5:39): "If one strike thee on one [Vulgate: 'thy right'] cheek, turn to him also the other"; and by others of the same kind, according to Augustine's exposition (*The Sermon on the Mount*, 19). Therefore neither is man bound to believe anything explicitly, and it is enough if he be ready to believe whatever God proposes to be believed.

Objection III

Further, the good of faith consists in obedience, according to Romans 1:5: "For obedience to the faith in all nations." Now the virtue of obedience does not require man to keep certain fixed precepts, but it is enough that his mind be ready to obey, according to Psalm 118:60: "I am ready and am not troubled; that I may keep Thy commandments." Therefore it seems enough for faith, too, that man should be ready to believe whatever God may propose, without his believing anything explicitly.

On the contrary, It is written (Heb. 11:6): "He that cometh to God, must believe that He is, and is a rewarder to them that seek Him."

I answer that the precepts of the Law, which man is bound to fulfil, concern acts of virtue which are the means of attaining salvation. Now an act of virtue, as stated above (I–II, 60, 5) depends on the relation of the habit to its object. Again two things may be considered in the object of any virtue; namely, that which is the proper and direct object of that virtue, and that which is accidental and consequent to the object properly so

called. Thus it belongs properly and directly to the object of fortitude, to face the dangers of death, and to charge at the foe with danger to oneself, for the sake of the common good: yet that, in a just war, a man be armed, or strike another with his sword, and so forth, is reduced to the object of fortitude, but indirectly.

Accordingly, just as a virtuous act is required for the fulfillment of a precept, so is it necessary that the virtuous act should terminate in its proper and direct object: but, on the other hand, the fulfillment of the precept does not require that a virtuous act should terminate in those things which have an accidental or secondary relation to the proper and direct object of that virtue, except in certain places and at certain times. We must, therefore, say that the direct object of faith is that whereby man is made one of the Blessed, as stated above (1, 8): while the indirect and secondary object comprises all things delivered by God to us in Holy Writ, for instance that Abraham had two sons, that David was the son of Jesse, and so forth.

Therefore, as regards the primary points or articles of faith, man is bound to believe them, just as he is bound to have faith; but as to other points of faith, man is not bound to believe them explicitly, but only implicitly, or to be ready to believe them, in so far as he is prepared to believe whatever is contained in the Divine Scriptures. Then alone is he bound to believe such things explicitly, when it is clear to him that they are contained in the doctrine of faith.

Reply to Objection I

If we understand those things alone to be in a man's power, which we can do without the help of grace, then we are bound to do many things which we cannot do without the aid of healing grace, such as to love God and our neighbor, and likewise to believe the articles of faith. But with the help of grace we can do this, for this help "to whomsoever it is given from above it is mercifully given; and from whom it is withheld it is justly withheld, as a punishment of a previous, or at least of original, sin," as Augustine states (*On Admonition and Grace* 5, 6 [cf. *Epistle*, 190; *The Predestination of the Saints*, 8]).

Reply to Objection II

Man is bound to love definitely those lovable things which are properly and directly the objects of charity, namely, God and our neighbor. The objection refers to those precepts of charity which belong, as a consequence, to the objects of charity.

Reply to Objection III

The virtue of obedience is seated, properly speaking, in the will; hence promptness of the will subject to authority, suffices for the act of obedience, because it is the proper and direct object of obedience. But this or that precept is accidental or consequent to that proper and direct object.

Article VI: Whether all are equally bound to have explicit faith

Objection I

It would seem that all are equally bound to have explicit faith. For all are bound to those things which are necessary for salvation, as is evidenced by the precepts of charity. Now it is necessary for salvation that certain things should be believed explicitly. Therefore all are equally bound to have explicit faith.

Objection II

Further, no one should be put to test in matters that he is not bound to believe. But simple reasons are sometimes tested in reference to the slightest articles of faith. Therefore all are bound to believe everything explicitly.

Objection III

Further, if the simple are bound to have, not explicit but only implicit faith, their faith must needs be implied in the faith of the learned. But this seems unsafe, since it is possible for the learned to err. Therefore it seems that the simple should also have explicit faith; so that all are, therefore, equally bound to have explicit faith.

On the contrary, It is written (Job 1:14): "The oxen were ploughing, and the asses feeding beside them," because, as Gregory expounds this passage (*Moral.* 2, 17), the simple, who are signified by the asses, ought, in matters of faith, to stay by the learned, who are denoted by the oxen.

I answer that the unfolding of matters of faith is the result of Divine revelation: for matters of faith surpass natural reason. Now Divine revelation reaches those of lower degree through those who are over them, in a certain order; to men, for instance, through the angels, and to the lower angels through the higher, as Dionysius explains (*The Celestial Hierarchy*, 4, 7). On like manner therefore the unfolding of faith must needs reach men of lower degree through those of higher degree. Consequently, just as the higher angels, who enlighten those who are below them, have a fuller knowledge of Divine things than the lower angels, as Dionysius states (*The Celestial Hierarchy*, 12), so too, men of higher degree, whose business it is to teach others, are under obligation to have fuller knowledge of matters of faith, and to believe them more explicitly.

Reply to Objection I

The unfolding of the articles of faith is not equally necessary for the salvation of all, since those of higher degree, whose duty it is to teach others, are bound to believe explicitly more things than others are.

Reply to Objection II

Simple persons should not be put to the test about subtle questions of faith, unless they be suspected of having been corrupted by heretics, who are wont to corrupt the faith of simple people in such questions. If, however, it is found that they are free from obstinacy in their heterodox sentiments, and that it is due to their simplicity, it is no fault of theirs.

Reply to Objection III

The simple have no faith implied in that of the learned, except in so far as the latter adhere to the Divine teaching. Hence the Apostle says (1 Cor. 4:16): "Be ye followers of me, as I also am of Christ." Hence it is not human knowledge, but the Divine truth that is the rule of faith: and if any of the learned stray from this rule, he does not harm the faith of the simple ones, who think that the learned believe aright; unless the simple hold obstinately to their individual errors, against the faith of the universal Church, which cannot err, since Our Lord said (Luke 22:32): "I have prayed for thee," Peter, "that thy faith fail not."

Article VII: Whether it is necessary for the salvation of all that they should explicitly believe in the mystery of Christ

Objection I

It would seem that it is not necessary for the salvation of all that they should believe explicitly in the mystery of Christ. For man is not bound to believe explicitly what the angels are ignorant about: since the unfolding of faith is the result of Divine revelation, which reaches man by means of the angels, as stated above (6; I, 111, 1). Now even the angels were in ignorance of the mystery of the Incarnation: hence, according to the commentary of Dionysius (*The Celestial Hierarchy*, 7), it is they who ask (Ps. 23:8): "Who is this king of glory?" and (Isa. 63:1): "Who is this that cometh from Edom?" Therefore men were not bound to believe explicitly in the mystery of Christ's Incarnation.

Objection II

Further, it is evident that John the Baptist was one of the teachers, and most nigh to Christ, Who said of him (Matt. 11:11) that "there hath not risen among them that are born of women, a greater than" he. Now John the Baptist does not appear to have known the mystery of Christ explicitly, since he asked Christ (Matt. 11:3): "Art Thou He that art to come, or look we for another?" Therefore even the teachers were not bound to explicit faith in Christ.

Objection III

Further, many gentiles obtained salvation through the ministry of the angels, as Dionysius states (*The Celestial Hierarchy*, 9). Now it would seem that the gentiles had neither explicit nor implicit faith in Christ, since they received no revelation. Therefore it seems that it was not necessary for the salvation of all to believe explicitly in the mystery of Christ.

On the contrary, Augustine says (*On Admonition and Grace*, 7; *Epistle*, 190): "Our faith is sound if we believe that no man, old or young is delivered from the contagion of death and the bonds of sin, except by the one Mediator of God and men, Jesus Christ."

I answer that as stated above (5; 1, 8), the object of faith includes, properly and directly, that thing through which man obtains beatitude. Now the mystery of Christ's Incarnation and Passion is the way by which men obtain beatitude; for it is written (Acts 4:12): "There is no other name under heaven given to men, whereby we must be saved." Therefore belief of some kind in the mystery of Christ's Incarnation was necessary at all times and for all persons, but this belief differed according to differences of times and persons. The reason of this is that before the state of sin, man believed, explicitly in Christ's Incarnation, in so far as it was intended for the consummation of glory, but not as it was intended to deliver man from sin by the Passion and Resurrection, since man had no foreknowledge of his future sin. He does, however, seem to have had foreknowledge of the Incarnation of Christ, from the fact that he said (Gen. 2:24): "Wherefore a man shall leave father and mother, and shall cleave to his wife," of which the Apostle says (Eph. 5:32) that "this is a great sacrament . . . in Christ and the Church," and it is incredible that the first man was ignorant about this sacrament.

But after sin, man believed explicitly in Christ, not only as to the Incarnation, but also as to the Passion and Resurrection, whereby the human race is delivered from sin and death: for they would not, else, have foreshadowed Christ's Passion by certain sacrifices both before and after the Law, the meaning of which sacrifices was known by the learned explicitly, while the simple folk, under the veil of those sacrifices, believed them to be ordained by God in reference to Christ's coming, and thus their knowledge was covered with a veil, so to speak. And, as stated above (1, 7), the nearer they were to Christ, the more distinct was their knowledge of Christ's mysteries.

After grace had been revealed, both learned and simple folk are bound to explicit faith in the mysteries of Christ, chiefly as regards those which are observed throughout the Church, and publicly proclaimed, such as the articles which refer to the Incarnation, of which we have spoken above (1, 8). As to other minute points in reference to the articles of the Incarnation, men have been bound to believe them more or less explicitly according to each one's state and office.

Reply to Objection I

The mystery of the Kingdom of God was not entirely hidden from the angels, as Augustine observes (*On the Literal Interpretation of Genesis*, 19), yet certain aspects thereof were better known to them when Christ revealed them to them.

Reply to Objection II

It was not through ignorance that John the Baptist inquired of Christ's advent in the flesh, since he had clearly professed his belief therein, saying: "I saw, and I gave testimony, that this is the Son of God" (John 1:34). Hence he did not say: "Art Thou He that hast come?"

but "Art Thou He that art to come?" thus saying about the future, not about the past. Likewise it is not to be believed that he was ignorant of Christ's future Passion, for he had already said (John 1:39): "Behold the Lamb of God, behold Him who taketh away the sins [Vulgate: "sin"] of the world," thus foretelling His future immolation; and since other prophets had foretold it, as may be seen especially in Isaiah 53. We may therefore say with Gregory (*Sermons in the Gospels*, 26) that he asked this question, being in ignorance as to whether Christ would descend into hell in His own Person. But he did not ignore the fact that the power of Christ's Passion would be extended to those who were detained in Limbo, according to Zechariah 9:11: "Thou also, by the blood of Thy testament hast sent forth Thy prisoners out of the pit, wherein there is no water"; nor was he bound to believe explicitly, before its fulfillment, that Christ was to descend thither Himself.

It may also be replied that, as Ambrose observes in his commentary on Luke 7:19, he made this inquiry, not from doubt or ignorance but from devotion: or again, with Chrysostom (*Sermon on Matthew*, 36), that he inquired, not as though ignorant himself, but because he wished his disciples to be satisfied on that point, through Christ: hence the latter framed His answer so as to instruct the disciples, by pointing to the signs of His works.

Reply to Objection III

Many of the gentiles received revelations of Christ, as is clear from their predictions. Thus we read (Job 19:25): "I know that my Redeemer liveth." The Sibyl too foretold certain things about Christ, as Augustine states (*Against Faustus,* 13, 15). Moreover, we read in the history of the Romans, that at the time of Constantine Augustus and his mother Irene a tomb was discovered, wherein lay a man on whose breast was a golden plate with the inscription: "Christ shall be born of a virgin, and in Him, I believe. O sun, during the lifetime of Irene and Constantine, thou shalt see me again" [Cf. Baron, Annal., A.D. 780]. If, however, some were saved without receiving any revelation, they were not saved without faith in a Mediator, for, though they did not believe in Him explicitly, they did, nevertheless, have implicit faith through believing in Divine providence, since they believed that God would deliver mankind in whatever way was pleasing to Him, and according to the revelation of the Spirit to those who knew the truth,

as stated in Job 35:11: "Who teacheth us more than the beasts of the earth."

Article VIII: Whether it is necessary for salvation to believe explicitly in the trinity

Objection I

It would seem that it was not necessary for salvation to believe explicitly in the Trinity. For the Apostle says (Heb. 11:6): "He that cometh to God must believe that He is, and is a rewarder to them that seek Him." Now one can believe this without believing in the Trinity. Therefore it was not necessary to believe explicitly in the Trinity.

Objection II

Further our Lord said (John 17:5–6): "Father, I have manifested Thy name to men," which words Augustine expounds (*Tractate on the Gospel of John*, 106) as follows: "Not the name by which Thou art called God, but the name whereby Thou art called My Father," and further on he adds: "In that He made this world, God is known to all nations; in that He is not to be worshipped together with false gods, God is known in Judea; but, in that He is the Father of this Christ, through Whom He takes away the sin of the world, He now makes known to men this name of His, which hitherto they knew not." Therefore before the coming of Christ it was not known that Paternity and Filiation were in the Godhead: and so the Trinity was not believed explicitly.

Objection III

Further, that which we are bound to believe explicitly of God is the object of heavenly happiness. Now the object of heavenly happiness is the sovereign good, which can be understood to be in God, without any distinction of Persons. Therefore it was not necessary to believe explicitly in the Trinity.

On the contrary, in the Old Testament the Trinity of Persons is expressed in many ways; thus at the very outset of Genesis it is written in manifestation of the Trinity (Gen. 1:26): "Let us make man to Our image and likeness." Therefore from the very beginning it was necessary for salvation to believe in the Trinity.

I answer that it is impossible to believe explicitly in the mystery of Christ, without faith in the Trinity, since the mystery of Christ includes that the Son of God took flesh; that He renewed the world through the grace of the Holy Ghost; and again, that He was conceived by the Holy Ghost. Wherefore just as, before Christ, the mystery of Christ was believed explicitly by the learned, but implicitly and under a veil, so to speak, by the simple, so too was it with the mystery of the Trinity. And consequently, when once grace had been revealed, all were bound to explicit faith in the mystery of the Trinity: and all who are born again in Christ, have this bestowed on them by the invocation of the Trinity, according to Matthew 28:19: "Going therefore teach ye all nations, baptizing them in the name of the Father, and of the Son and of the Holy Ghost."

Reply to Objection I

Explicit faith in those two things was necessary at all times and for all people: but it was not sufficient at all times and for all people.

Reply to Objection II

Before Christ's coming, faith in the Trinity lay hidden in the faith of the learned, but through Christ and the apostles it was shown to the world.

Reply to Objection III

God's sovereign goodness as we understand it now through its effects, can be understood without the Trinity of Persons: but as understood in itself, and as seen by the Blessed, it cannot be understood without the Trinity of Persons. Moreover the mission of the Divine Persons brings us to heavenly happiness.

Article IX: Whether to believe is meritorious

Objection I

It would seem that to believe is not meritorious. For the principle of all merit is charity, as stated above (I–II, 114, 4). Now faith, like nature, is a preamble to charity. Therefore, just as an act of nature is not meritorious, since we do not merit by our natural gifts, so neither is an act of faith.

Objection II

Further, belief is a mean between opinion and scientific knowledge or the consideration of things scientifically known [Science is a certain knowledge of a demonstrated conclusion through its demonstration.].

Now the considerations of science are not meritorious, nor on the other hand is opinion. Therefore belief is not meritorious.

Objection III

Further, he who assents to a point of faith, either has a sufficient motive for believing, or he has not. If he has a sufficient motive for his belief, this does not seem to imply any merit on his part, since he is no longer free to believe or not to believe: whereas if he has not a sufficient motive for believing, this is a mark of levity, according to Sirach 19:4: "He that is hasty to give credit, is light of heart," so that, seemingly, he gains no merit thereby. Therefore to believe is by no means meritorious.

On the contrary, it is written (Heb. 11:33) that the saints "by faith . . . obtained promises," which would not be the case if they did not merit by believing. Therefore to believe is meritorious.

I answer that as stated above (I–II, 114, 3, 4), our actions are meritorious in so far as they proceed from the free-will moved with grace by God. Therefore every human act proceeding from the free-will, if it be referred to God, can be meritorious. Now the act of believing is an act of the intellect assenting to the Divine truth at the command of the will moved by the grace of God, so that it is subject to the free-will in relation to God; and consequently the act of faith can be meritorious.

Reply to Objection I

Nature is compared to charity which is the principle of merit, as matter to form: whereas faith is compared to charity as the disposition which precedes the ultimate form. Now it is evident that the subject or the matter cannot act save by virtue of the form, nor can a preceding disposition, before the advent of the form: but after the advent of the form, both the subject and the preceding disposition act by virtue of the form, which is the chief principle of action, even as the heat of fire acts by virtue of the substantial form of fire. Accordingly neither nature nor faith can, without charity, produce a meritorious act; but, when accompanied by charity, the act of faith is made meritorious thereby, even as an act of nature, and a natural act of the free-will.

Reply to Objection II

Two things may be considered in science: namely the scientist's assent to a scientific fact and his consideration of that fact. Now the assent of science is not subject to free-will, because the scientist is obliged to assent by force of the demonstration, wherefore scientific assent is not meritorious. But the actual consideration of what a man knows scientifically is subject to his free-will, for it is in his power to consider or not to consider. Hence scientific consideration may be meritorious if it be referred to the end of charity, i.e., to the honor of God or the good of our neighbor. On the other hand, in the case of faith, both these things are subject to the free-will so that in both respects the act of faith can be meritorious: whereas in the case of opinion, there is no firm assent, since it is weak and infirm, as the Philosopher observes (*Posterior Analytics*, 1, 33), so that it does not seem to proceed from a perfect act of the will: and for this reason, as regards the assent, it does not appear to be very meritorious, though it can be as regards the actual consideration.

Reply to Objection III

The believer has sufficient motive for believing, for he is moved by the authority of Divine teaching confirmed by miracles, and, what is more, by the inward instinct of the Divine invitation: hence he does not believe lightly. He has not, however, sufficient reason for scientific knowledge, hence he does not lose the merit.

Article X: Whether reasons in support of what we believe lessen the merit of faith

Objection I

It would seem that reasons in support of what we believe lessen the merit of faith. For Gregory says (*Sermons on the Gospels*, 26) that "there is no merit in believing what is shown by reason." If, therefore, human reason provides sufficient proof, the merit of faith is altogether taken away. Therefore it seems that any kind of human reasoning in support of matters of faith, diminishes the merit of believing.

Objection II

Further, whatever lessens the measure of virtue, lessens the amount of merit, since "happiness is the reward of virtue," as the Philosopher states (*Nicomachean Ethics*, 1, 9). Now human reasoning seems to diminish the measure of the virtue of faith, since it is essential to faith to be about the unseen, as stated above (1, 4, 5).

Now the more a thing is supported by reasons the less is it unseen. Therefore human reasons in support of matters of faith diminish the merit of faith.

Objection III

Further, contrary things have contrary causes. Now an inducement in opposition to faith increases the merit of faith whether it consist in persecution inflicted by one who endeavors to force a man to renounce his faith, or in an argument persuading him to do so. Therefore reasons in support of faith diminish the merit of faith.

On the contrary, It is written (1 Peter 3:15): "Being ready always to satisfy every one that asketh you a reason of that faith [Vulgate: "Of that hope which is in you." St. Thomas's reading is apparently taken from Bede.] and hope which is in you." Now the Apostle would not give this advice, if it would imply a diminution in the merit of faith. Therefore reason does not diminish the merit of faith.

I answer that as stated above (9), the act of faith can be meritorious, in so far as it is subject to the will, not only as to the use, but also as to the assent. Now human reason in support of what we believe may stand in a twofold relation to the will of the believer. First, as preceding the act of the will; as, for instance, when a man either has not the will, or not a prompt will, to believe, unless he be moved by human reasons: and in this way human reason diminishes the merit of faith. On this sense it has been said above (I–II, 24, 3, ad 1; 77, 6, ad 2) that, in moral virtues, a passion which precedes choice makes the virtuous act less praiseworthy. For just as a man ought to perform acts of moral virtue, on account of the judgment of his reason, and not on account of a passion, so ought he to believe matters of faith, not on account of human reason, but on account of the Divine authority. Secondly, human reasons may be consequent to the will of the believer. For when a man's will is ready to believe, he loves the truth he believes, he thinks out and takes to heart whatever reasons he can find in support thereof; and in this way human reason does not exclude the merit of faith but is a sign of greater merit. Thus again, in moral virtues a consequent passion is the sign of a more prompt will, as stated above (I–II, 24, 3, ad 1). We have an indication of this in the words of the Samaritans to the woman, who is a type of human reason: "We now believe, not for thy saying" (John 4:42).

Reply to Objection I

Gregory is referring to the case of a man who has no will to believe what is of faith, unless he be induced by reasons. But when a man has the will to believe what is of faith on the authority of God alone, although he may have reasons in demonstration of some of them, e.g., of the existence of God, the merit of his faith is not, for that reason, lost or diminished.

Reply to Objection II

The reasons which are brought forward in support of the authority of faith, are not demonstrations which can bring intellectual vision to the human intellect, wherefore they do not cease to be unseen.

But they remove obstacles to faith, by showing that what faith proposes is not impossible; wherefore such reasons do not diminish the merit or the measure of faith. On the other hand, though demonstrative reasons in support of the preambles of faith [The Leonine Edition reads: "in support of matters of faith which are however, preambles to the articles of faith, dimin-ish," etc.], but not of the articles of faith, diminish the measure of faith, since they make the thing believed to be seen, yet they do not diminish the measure of charity, which makes the will ready to believe them, even if they were unseen; and so the measure of merit is not diminished.

Reply to Objection III

Whatever is in opposition to faith, whether it consist in a man's thoughts, or in outward persecution, increases the merit of faith, in so far as the will is shown to be more prompt and firm in believing. Hence the martyrs had more merit of faith, through not renouncing faith on account of persecution; and even the wise have greater merit of faith, through not renouncing their faith on account of the reasons brought forward by philosophers or heretics in opposition to faith. On the other hand things that are favorable to faith, do not always diminish the promptness of the will to believe, and therefore they do not always diminish the merit of faith.

[CHAPTER 4]

The Church and Church Councils

The Church is the fellowship of those who worship the triune God, Father, Son, and Holy Spirit (John 3.16; 1 Thess. 1:1), who have received the forgiveness of their sins, and who thereby are saved through the grace of Christ (Acts 15:11). The Greek New Testament word *ekklesia* (most often translated *church*) refers to the assembly of God's people, and in the context of Greek cities, the *ekklesia* was the duly authorized gathering of free citizens assembled to make decisions. In the Septuagint (the Greek translation of the Hebrew Scriptures or Old Testament), *ekklesia* refers to God's people gathered to receive the law from Moses (Deut. 5:22). It is notable that our English word *church* does not derive from *ekklesia* but from *kuriakon*, a Greek New Testament word meaning "of the Lord," (as in "the Lord's supper," 1 Cor. 11:20). Unfortunately, then, at some point in history—perhaps in Medieval times—the significance of the name *church* changed from a people to a place. The New Testament letters of Paul were addressed to specific *ekklesia* or their leaders in answer to their specific questions, concerns, and circumstances. The Catholic or General letters were probably written to circulate among a group of churches in a specific region. The very first church council was held at Jerusalem (c. A.D. 49) over the question of requirements for Gentile membership in the Church.

Within a generation or two after Paul warned the Corinthian church about their divisiveness (1 Cor. 1), Clement of Rome was addressing the same church about a similar matter (see below). Beginning early in the fourth century, a series of ecumenical councils assembled (at irregular intervals) to address critical issues related to the Church's unity, testimony, and polity. While all the documents in this volume relate in some way to the Church, this chapter in-

cludes several early church encyclicals (circulating letters), a treatise (Cyprian's) on the unity of the Church, the first Roman edicts that legalized the Church and guaranteed her safety, a selection of writings from several of the ecumenical councils, the Vincentian Canon on church authority and unity, and also the thoughts of a Protestant Reformer—John Calvin—on the Church.

IGNATIUS: LETTER TO THE MAGNESIANS
Greek, Late First Century A.D.

Ignatius, early church bishop of Antioch, is believed to have been born soon after Christ's crucifixion and to have been martyred about A.D. 107. Enroute to his martyrdom in Rome, Ignatius wrote letters of encouragement to seven churches, including the following to the Church at Magnesia, in Greece.

Ignatius, who is also called Theophorus, to the [Church] blessed in the grace of God the Father, in Jesus Christ our Savior, in whom I salute the Church which is at Magnesia, near the Moeander, and wish it abundance of happiness in God the Father, and in Jesus Christ.

Chapter I: Reason for writing the epistle

Having been informed of your godly love, so well-ordered, I rejoiced greatly, and determined to commune with you in the faith of Jesus Christ. For as one who has been thought worthy of the most honorable of all names, in those bonds which I bear about, I commend the Churches, in which I pray for a union both of the flesh and spirit of Jesus Christ, the constant source of our life, and of faith and love, to which nothing is to be preferred, but especially of Jesus and the Father, in whom, if we endure all the assaults of the prince of this world, and escape them, we shall enjoy God.

Chapter II: I Rejoice in your messengers

Since, then, I have had the privilege of seeing you, through Damas your most worthy bishop (*episkopos*), and through your worthy presbyters (*presbuterous*) Bassus and Apollonius, and through my fellow-servant the deacon Sotio, whose friendship may I ever enjoy, inasmuch as he is subject to the bishop as to the grace of God, and to the presbytery as to the law of Jesus Christ, [I now write to you].

Chapter III: Honor your youthful bishop

Now it becomes you also not to treat your bishop too familiarly on account of his youth, but to yield him all reverence, having respect to the power of God the Father, as I have known even holy presbyters to, not judging rashly, from the manifest youthful appearance [of their bishop], but as being themselves prudent in God, submitting to him, or rather not to him, but to the Father of Jesus Christ, the bishop of us all. It is therefore fitting that you should, after no hypocritical fashion, obey [your bishop], in honor of Him who has written us [to do so], since he that disobeys deceives not the bishop who is visible, but mocks Him that is invisible. And all such conduct has reference not to man, but to God, who knows all secrets.

Chapter IV: Some wickedly act independently of the bishop

It is fitting, then, not only to be called Christians, but to be so in reality: as some indeed acknowledge the bishop, but do all things without him. Now such persons are not possessed of a good conscience, seeing they are not steadfastly gathered together according to the commandment.

Chapter V: Death is the fate of all such

Seeing, then, all things have an end, these two things are simultaneously set before us—death and life; and ev-ery one shall go unto his own place. For as there are two kinds of coins, the one of God, the other of the world, and each of these has its special character stamped upon it. The unbelieving are of this world; but the believing have, in love, the character of God the Father by Jesus Christ, by whom, if we are not in readiness to die into His passion, His life is not in us.

Chapter VI: Preserve harmony

Since therefore I have, in the persons before mentioned, beheld the whole multitude of you in faith and love, I exhort you to study to do all things with a divine harmony, while your bishop presides in the place of God, and your presbyters in the place of the assembly of the apostles, along with your deacons, who are most dear to me, and are entrusted with the ministry of Jesus Christ, who was with the Father before the beginning of time, and in the end was revealed. Do you all then, imitating the same divine conduct, pay respect to one another, and let no one look upon his neighbor after the flesh, but do you continually love each other in Jesus Christ. Let nothing exist among you that may divide you ; but be you united with your bishop, and those that preside over you, as a type and evidence of your immortality.

Chapter VII: Do nothing without the bishop and presbyters

As therefore the Lord did nothing without the Father, being united to Him, neither by Himself nor by the apostles, so neither do you anything without the bishop (*episkopos*) and presbyters (*presbuterous*). Neither endeavor that anything appear reasonable and proper to yourselves apart; but being come together into the same place, let there be one prayer, one supplication, one mind, one hope, in love and in joy undefiled. There is one Jesus Christ, than whom nothing is more excellent. Do, therefore, run together as into one temple of God, as to one altar, as to one Jesus Christ, who came forth from one Father, and is with and has gone to one.

Chapter VIII: Caution against false doctrines

Be not deceived with strange doctrines, nor with old fables, which are unprofitable. For if we still live according to the Jewish law, we acknowledge that we have not received grace. For the divine prophets lived according to Christ Jesus. On this account also they were persecuted, being inspired by His grace to fully convince the unbelieving that there is one God, who has manifested Himself by Jesus Christ His Son, who is His eternal Word, not proceeding forth from silence, and who in all things pleased Him that sent Him.

Chapter IX: Let us live with Christ

If, therefore, those who were brought up in the ancient order of things have come to the possession of a new hope, no longer observing the Sabbath, but living in the observance of the Lord's Day, on which also our life has sprung up again by Him and by His death—whom some deny, by which mystery we have obtained faith, and therefore endure, that we may be found the disciples of Jesus Christ, our only Master—how shall we be able to live apart from Him, whose disciples the prophets themselves in the Spirit did wait for Him as their Teacher? And therefore He whom they rightly waited for, being come, raised them from the dead.

Chapter X: Beware of Judaizing

Let us not, therefore, be insensible to His kindness. For were He to reward us according to our works, we should cease to be. For "if You, Lord, shall mark iniquities, O Lord, who shall stand?" Let us therefore prove ourselves worthy of that name which we have received. For whosoever is called by any other name besides this, he is not of God; for he has not received the prophecy which speaks thus concerning us: "The people shall be called by a new name, which the Lord shall name them, and shall be a holy people." This was first fulfilled in Syria; for "the disciples were called Christians at Antioch," when Paul and Peter were laying the foundations of the Church. Lay aside, therefore, the evil, the old, the corrupt leaven, and be you changed into the new leaven of grace. Abide in Christ, that the stranger may not have dominion over you. It is absurd to speak of Jesus Christ with the tongue, and to cherish in the mind a Judaism that has now come to an end. For where there is Christianity there cannot be Judaism. For Christ is one, in whom every nation that believes, and every tongue that confesses, is gathered unto God. And those that were of a stony heart have become the children of Abraham, the friend of God; and in his seed all those have been blessed who were ordained to eternal life in Christ.

Chapter XI: I write these things to warn you

These things [I address to you], my beloved, not that I know any of you to be in such a state; but, as less than any of you, I desire to guard you beforehand, that you fall not upon the hooks of vain doctrine, but that you may rather attain to a full assurance in Christ, who was begotten by the Father before all ages, but was afterward born of the Virgin Mary without any intercourse with man. He also lived a holy life, and healed every kind of sickness and disease among the people, and wrought signs and wonders for the benefit of men; and to those who had fallen into the error of polytheism He made known the one and only true God, His Father, and underwent the passion, and endured the cross at the hands of the Christ-killing Jews, under Pontius Pilate the governor and Herod the king. He also died, and rose again, and ascended into the heavens to Him that sent Him, and is sat down at His right hand, and shall come at the end of the world, with His Father's glory, to judge the living and the dead, and to render to every one according to his works. He who knows these things with a full assurance, and believes them, is happy; even as you are now the lovers of God and of Christ, in the full assurance of our hope, from which may no one of us ever be turned aside!

Chapter XII: You are superior to me

May I enjoy you in all respects, if indeed I be worthy! For though I am bound, I am not worthy to be compared to one of you that are at liberty. I know that you are not puffed up, for you have Jesus in yourselves. And all the more when I commend you, I know that you cherish modesty of spirit; as it is written, "The righteous man is his own accuser"; and again, "First declare your iniquities, that you may be justified"; and again, "When you shall have done all things that are commanded you, say, We are unprofitable servants"; "for that which is highly esteemed among men is abomination in the sight of God." For says [the Scripture], "God be merciful to me a sinner." Therefore those great ones, Abraham and Job, styled themselves "dust and ashes" before God. And David says, "Who am I before You, O Lord, that You have glorified me?" And Moses, who was "the meekest of all men," said to God, "I am of a feeble voice, and of a slow tongue." Therefore you, too, should be of humble spirit, that you may be exalted; for "he that abases himself shall be exalted, and he that exalts himself shall be abased."

Chapter XIII: Be established in faith and unity

Study, therefore, to be established in the doctrines of the Lord and the apostles, so that all things, whatever you do, may prosper both in the flesh and spirit; in faith and love; in the Son, and in the Father, and in the Spirit; in the beginning and in the end; with your most admirable bishop, and the well-compacted spiritual crown of your presbytery (*presbuteroi*), and the deacons who are according to God. Be you subject to the bishop, and to one another, as Jesus Christ to the Father, according to the flesh, and the apostles to Christ, and to the Father, and to the Spirit; that so there may be a union both fleshly and spiritual.

Chapter XIV: Your prayers requested

Knowing as I do that you are full of God, I have but briefly exhorted you. Be mindful of me in your prayers, that I may attain to God; and of the Church which is in Syria, whence I am not worthy to derive my name: for I stand in need of your united prayer in God, and your love, that the Church which is in Syria may be "deemed worthy of being refreshed by your Church.

Chapter XV: Salutations

The Ephesians from Smyrna (from where I am writing), who are here for the glory of God, as you also are, who have in all things refreshed me, salute you, along with Polycarp, the bishop of the Smyrnaeans. The rest of the Churches, in honor of Jesus Christ, also salute you. Farewell in the harmony of God, you who have obtained the inseparable Spirit, who is Jesus Christ, by the will of God.

CLEMENT OF ROME: FIRST EPISTLE TO THE CORINTHIANS (ABRIDGED)
Greek, c. A.D. 100

Many years after the Apostle Paul wrote the Corinthian church to avoid schisms, Clement, Bishop of Rome, sent another "Epistle to the Corinthians" (c. A.D. 100), this time to condemn the church for expelling its ministers and installing new ones more to their liking. Few details of the offense that caused the expulsion are apparent from the letter. What is clear in the letter are Clement's appeal to apostolic succession (those chosen by the apostles and

their successors in turn "cannot be dismissed from the ministry," chap. xliv) and his condemnation of the independent Corinthian spirit. Clement's frequent use of biblical examples demonstrates the early Father's approach to scriptural exegesis, and his use of literary allusions (e.g., the phoenix as a symbol of resurrection) provides evidence of his classical education. The early church historian Eusebius mentions the letter, noting that "it is acknowledged to be genuine and is of considerable length and of remarkable merit. He wrote it in the name of the Church of Rome to the Church of Corinth, when a rebellion had arisen in the latter church. We know that this epistle also has been publicly used in a great many churches both in former times and in our own. Hegesippus, a reliable witness, also confirms that the rebellion took place in the Church of Corinth at that time."[1]

◆

Chapter I: Greetings—Praise was due the Corinthians prior to their schism

The Church of God which sojourns at Rome, to the Church of God sojourning at Corinth, to them that are called and sanctified by the will of God, through our Lord Jesus Christ: Grace to you, and peace, from Almighty God through Jesus Christ, be multiplied.

Owing, dear brethren, to the sudden and successive calamitous events which have happened to ourselves, we feel that we have been somewhat tardy in turning our attention to the points respecting which you consulted us; and especially to that shameful and detestable rebellion, utterly abhorrent to the elect of God, which a few rash and self-confident persons have kindled to such a pitch of frenzy, that your venerable and illustrious name, worthy to be universally loved, has suffered grievous injury. For whoever dwelt even for a short time among you, and did not find your faith to be as fruitful of virtue as it was firmly established? Who did not admire the sobriety and moderation of your godliness in Christ? Who did not proclaim the magnificence of your habitual hospitality? And who did not rejoice over your perfect and well-grounded knowledge? For you did all things without respect of persons, and walked in the commandments of God, being obedient to those who had the rule over you, and giving all fitting honor to the

---

1. *Church History*, 3.16.

presbyters among you. You enjoined young men to be of a sober and serious mind; you instructed your wives to do all things with a blameless, becoming, and pure conscience, loving their husbands as in duty bound; and you taught them that, living in the rule of obedience, they should manage their household affairs becomingly, and be in every respect marked by discretion.

Chapter II: Formerly they were distinguished by humility

Moreover, you were all distinguished by humility, and were in no respect puffed up with pride, but yielded obedience rather than extorted it, and were more willing to give than to receive. Content with the provision which God had made for you, and carefully attending to His words, you were inwardly filled with His doctrine, and His sufferings were before your eyes. Thus a profound and abundant peace was given to you all, and you had an insatiable desire for doing good, while a full outpouring of the Holy Spirit was upon you all. Full of holy designs, you did, with true earnestness of mind and a godly confidence, stretch forth your hands to God Almighty, beseeching Him to be merciful unto you, if you had been guilty of any involuntary transgression. Day and night you were anxious for the whole brotherhood that the number of God's elect might be saved with mercy and a good conscience. You were sincere and uncorrupted, and forgetful of injuries between one another. Every kind of faction and schism was abominable in your sight. You mourned over the transgressions of your neighbors: their deficiencies you deemed your own. You never grudged any act of kindness, being "ready to every good work." Adorned by a thoroughly virtuous and religious life, you did all things in the fear of God. The commandments and ordinances of the Lord were written upon the tablets of your hearts.

Chapter III: After this, a rebellion arose from envy

Every kind of honor and happiness was bestowed upon you, but then happened that which is written, "My beloved did eat and drink, and was enlarged and became fat, and kicked." With this came emulation and envy, strife and rebellion, persecution and disorder, war and captivity. So the worthless rose up against the honored, those of no reputation against such as were renowned, the foolish against the wise, the young against those advanced in years. For this reason righteousness and peace are now far departed from you, inasmuch as every one abandons the fear of God, and is become blind in his faith, neither walks in the ordinances of His appointment, nor acts a part becoming a Christian, but walks after his own wicked lusts, resuming the practice of an unrighteous and ungodly envy, by which death itself entered into the world.

Chapter IV: This evil arose in ancient times

For thus it is written: "And it came to pass after certain days that Cain brought of the fruits of the earth a sacrifice unto God; and Abel also brought of the firstlings of his sheep, and of the fat thereof. And God had respect to Abel and to his offerings, but Cain and his sacrifices He did not regard. And Cain was deeply grieved, and his countenance fell. And God said to Cain, "Why are you grieved, and why is your countenance fallen? If you offer rightly but do not divide rightly, have you not sinned? Be at peace, your offering returns to you, and you shall again possess it. And Cain said to Abel his brother, 'Let us go into the field.' And it came to pass, while they were in the field, that Cain rose up against Abel his brother, and slew him." You see, brethren, how envy and jealousy led to the murder of a brother. Through envy, also, our father Jacob fled from the face of Esau his brother. Envy caused Joseph to be murderously persecuted and to come into bondage. Envy compelled Moses to flee from the face of Pharaoh king of Egypt, when he heard these words from his fellow-countryman, "Who made you a judge or a ruler over us? Will you kill me, as you killed the Egyptian yesterday?" On account of envy, Aaron and Miriam had to make their dwelling place outside the camp. Envy brought down Dathan and Abiram alive to Hades, through the rebellion which they excited against God's servant Moses. Through envy, David underwent the hatred not only of foreigners, but was also persecuted by Saul king of Israel.

Chapter V: From the same source came the martyrdom of Peter and Paul

But not to dwell upon ancient examples, let us come to the most recent spiritual heroes. Let us take the noble examples furnished in our own generation. Through envy and jealousy, the greatest and most righteous pillars of the Church have been persecuted and put to death. Let us set before our eyes the illustrious apostles.

Peter, through unrighteous envy, endured not one or two, but numerous labors and when he had at length suffered martyrdom, departed to the place of glory due to him. Owing to envy, Paul also obtained the reward of patient endurance, after being seven times thrown into captivity, compelled to flee, and stoned. After preaching both in the east and west, he gained the illustrious reputation due to his faith, having taught righteousness to the whole world, and come to the extreme limit of the west, and suffered martyrdom under the prefects. Thus was He removed from the world, and went into the holy place, having proved himself a striking example of patience.

Chapter VII: Exhortation to repentance

These things, beloved, we write unto you, not merely to admonish you of your duty, but also to remind ourselves. For we are struggling in the same arena and the same conflict is assigned to both of us. Wherefore let us give up vain and fruitless cares and approach to the glorious and venerable rule of our holy calling. Let us attend to what is good, pleasing, and acceptable in the sight of Him who formed us. Let us look steadfastly to the blood of Christ, and see how precious that blood is to God, which, having been shed for our salvation, has set the grace of repentance before the whole world. Let us turn to every age that has passed, and learn that, from generation to generation, the Lord has granted a place of repentance to all such as would be converted to Him. Noah preached repentance, and as many as listened to him were saved. Jonah proclaimed destruction to the Ninevites; but they, repenting of their sins, propitiated God by prayer, and obtained salvation, although they were aliens to the covenant of God.

Chapter VIII: The benfits of repentance

The ministers of the grace of God have, by the Holy Spirit, spoken of repentance; and the Lord of all things has Himself declared with an oath regarding it, "As I live, says the Lord, I desire not the death of the sinner, but rather his repentance"; adding, moreover, this gracious declaration, "Repent O house of Israel, of your iniquity. Say to the children of my people, though your sins reach from earth to heaven, and though they be more red than scarlet, and blacker than sackcloth, if you turn to Me with your whole heart, and say, Father! I will listen to you, as to a holy people." And in another place

He speaks thus: "Wash and become clean; put away the wickedness of your souls from before mine eyes; cease from your evil ways, and learn to do well; seek out judgment, deliver the oppressed, judge the fatherless, and see that justice is done to the widow; and come, and let us reason together. He declares, though your sins be like crimson, I will make them white as snow; though they be like scarlet, I will whiten them like wool. And if you be willing and obey Me, you shall eat the good of the land; but if you refuse, and will not hearken unto Me, the sword shall devour you, for the mouth of the Lord hath spoken these things." Desiring, therefore, that all His beloved should be partakers of repentance, He has, by His almighty will, established these declarations.

Chapter IX: Examples of the saints

Therefore, let us yield obedience to His excellent and glorious will; and imploring His mercy and lovingkindness, while we forsake all fruitless labors, and strife, and envy, which lead to death, let us turn and have recourse to His compassions. Let us steadfastly contemplate those who have perfectly ministered to His excellent glory. Let us take for example Enoch, who, being found righteous in obedience, was translated, and death was never known to happen to him. Noah, being found faithful, preached regeneration to the world through his ministry; and the Lord saved by him the animals which, with one accord, entered into the ark.

Chapter X: Abraham

Abraham, called "the friend," was found faithful, inasmuch as he rendered obedience to the words of God. He, in the exercise of obedience, went out from his own country, and from his kindred, and from his father's house, in order that, by forsaking a small territory, and a weak family, and an insignificant house, he might inherit the promises of God. For God said to him, "Leave your country, your kindred, and your father's house, and go to the land I will show you. And I will make you a great nation and will bless you; I will make your name great and you will be blessed. And I will bless those who bless you and curse those who curse you; and in you shall all the families of the earth be blessed." And again, on his departing from Lot, God said to him, "Lift up your eyes, and look from the place where you now are, northward and southward, eastward, and westward; for all the land you see I will give to you, and to your seed forever. And I will make your seed as the dust of the earth, so that if a man can number the dust of the earth, then your seed shall also be numbered." And again the Scripture says, "God brought forth Abram and spoke to him, "Look up now to heaven, and count the stars if you can number them; so numerous shall your seed also be." And Abram believed God, and it was counted to him for righteousness." On account of his faith and hospitality, a son was given to him in his old age; and in the exercise of obedience he offered him as a sacrifice to God on one of the mountains which He showed him.

Chapter XI: Lot

On account of his hospitality and godliness, Lot was saved out of Sodom when all the country round was punished by means of fire and brimstone, the Lord thus making it manifest that He does not forsake those that hope in Him, but gives up such as depart from Him to punishment and torture. For Lot's wife, who went forth with him, being of a different mind from himself and not continuing in agreement with him as to the command which had been given them, was made an example so as to be a pillar of salt to this day. This was done that all might know that those who are of a double mind, and who distrust the power of God, bring down judgment on themselves and become a sign to all succeeding generations.

Chapter XII: Rahab

On account of her faith and hospitality, Rahab the harlot was saved. For when spies were sent by Joshua, the son of Nun, to Jericho, the king of the country ascertained that they were come to spy out their land, and sent men to seize them, in order that, when taken, they might be put to death. But the hospitable Rahab, receiving them, concealed them on the roof of her house under some stalks of flax. And when the men sent by the king arrived and said, "Men came to you who are to spy out our land; bring them forth, for so the king commands," she answered them, "The two men whom you seek came to me, but quickly departed again and are gone," thus not disclosing the spies to them. Then she said to the men, "I know assuredly that the Lord your God has given you this city, for the fear and dread of you have fallen on its inhabitants. When therefore you shall have taken it, keep me and the house of my father in safety." And they said to her, "It shall be as you have

spoken to us. As soon, therefore, as you know that we are at hand, you shall gather all your family under your roof, and they shall be preserved, but all found outside of your dwelling shall perish." Moreover, they gave to her a sign, that she should hang from her house a scarlet thread. And thus they made it manifest that redemption should flow through the blood of the Lord to all them that believe and hope in God. You see, beloved, that there was not only faith, but prophecy, in this woman.

Chapter XIII: Exhortation to humility

Let us therefore, brethren, be of humble mind, laying aside all haughtiness, and pride, and foolishness, and angry feelings; and let us act according to that which is written. For the Holy Spirit says, "Let not the wise man glory in his wisdom, neither let the mighty man glory in his might, neither let the rich man glory in his riches; but let him that glories glory in the Lord, in diligently seeking Him, and doing judgment and righteousness," being especially mindful of the words the Lord Jesus spoke, teaching us meekness and long-suffering. For He said, "Be merciful, so that you may obtain mercy; forgive, that you may also be forgiven; as you do, so shall it be done to you; as you judge, so shall you be judged; as you are kind, so shall kindness be shown to you; with what measure you mete, with the same it shall be measured to you." By this precept and by these rules let us establish ourselves that we may walk with all humility in obedience to His holy words. For the holy word says, "On whom shall I look, but on him that is meek and peaceable, and that trembles at My words?"

Chapter XIV: We must obey God, not the rebellious

It is right and holy therefore, men and brethren, rather to obey God than to follow those who, through pride and rebellion, have become the leaders of a detestable emulation. For we shall incur no slight injury, but rather great danger, if we rashly yield ourselves to the inclinations of men who aim at exciting strife and tumults, so as to draw us away from what is good. Let us be kind one to another after the pattern of the tender mercy of our Creator. For it is written, "The kind-hearted shall inhabit the land, and the guiltless shall be left upon it, but transgressors shall be destroyed from off the face of it." And again the Scripture says, "I saw the ungodly highly exalted, and lifted up like the cedars of Lebanon: I passed by, and, behold, he was not; and I diligently sought his place, and could not find it. Preserve innocence, and look on equity, for there shall be a remnant to the peaceful man."

Chapter XV: Follow those who advocate peace

Let us cleave, therefore, to those who cultivate peace with godliness, and not to those who hypocritically profess to desire it. For the Scripture says in a certain place, "This people honors Me with their lips, but their heart is far from Me." And again: "They bless with their mouth, but curse with their heart." And again it says, "They loved Him with their mouth, and lied to Him with their tongue; but their heart was not right with Him, neither were they faithful in His covenant." "Let the deceitful lips become silent," and "let the Lord destroy all lying lips, and the boastful tongue of those who have said, Let us magnify our tongue; our lips are our own; who is lord over us? For the oppression of the poor, and for the sighing of the needy, will I now arise, says the Lord: I will place him in safety; I will deal confidently with him."

Chapter XVI: Christ's example of humility

For Christ is of those who are humble-minded, and not of those who exalt themselves over His flock. Our Lord Jesus Christ, the Scepter of the majesty of God, did not come in the pomp of pride or arrogance, although He might have done so, but in a lowly condition, as the Holy Spirit had declared regarding Him. For He says, "Lord, who hath believed our report, and to whom is the arm of the Lord revealed? We have declared our message in His presence: He is, as it were, a child, and like a root in thirsty ground; He has neither form nor glory; we saw Him, and He had neither form nor beauty; His form was without eminence, deficient in comparison with the ordinary form of men. He is a man exposed to stripes and suffering, acquainted with the endurance of grief: for His countenance was turned away; He was despised, and not esteemed. He bears our iniquities, and is in sorrow for our sakes; we supposed that on His own account He was exposed to labor, and stripes, and affliction. But He was wounded for our transgressions, and bruised for our iniquities. The chastisement of our peace was upon Him, and by His stripes we were healed. All we, like sheep, have gone astray; every man has wandered in his own way; and the Lord has delivered Him

up for our sins, while He in the midst of His sufferings opens not His mouth. He was brought as a sheep to the slaughter, and as a lamb before its sheerer is dumb, so He opens not His mouth. In His humiliation His judgment was taken away; who shall declare His generation? For His life is taken from the earth. For the transgressions of my people was He brought down to death. And the Lord is pleased to purify Him by stripes. If you make an offering for sin, your soul shall see a long-lived seed. And the Lord is pleased to relieve Him of the affliction of His soul, to show Him light, and to form Him with understanding, to justify the Just One who ministers well to many, and who carry their sins. On this account He shall inherit many, and shall divide the spoil of the strong; because His soul was delivered to death, and He was reckoned among the transgressors, and He bore the sins of many, and for their sins was He delivered." And again He says, "I am a worm, and no man; a reproach of men, and despised of the people. All that see me have derided me; they have spoken with their lips; they have wagged their head, saying, He hoped in God, let Him deliver Him, let Him save Him, since He delights in Him." You see, beloved, what is the example which has been given us; for if the Lord thus humbled Himself, what shall we do who have through Him come under the yoke of His grace?

Chapter XXXVIII: Submit to one another

Let our whole body, then, be preserved in Christ Jesus; and let every one be subject to his neighbor, according to the special gift bestowed upon him. Let the strong not despise the weak, and let the weak show respect unto the strong. Let the rich man provide for the wants of the poor; and let the poor man bless God, because He hath given him one by whom his need may be supplied. Let the wise man display his wisdom, not by mere words, but through good deeds. Let the humble not bear testimony to himself, but leave witness to be borne to him by another. Let him that is pure in the flesh not grow proud of it, and boast, knowing that it was another who bestowed on him the gift of continence. Let us consider, then, brethren, of what matter we were made, who and what manner of beings we came into the world, as it were out of a sepulchre, and from utter darkness. He who made us and fashioned us, having prepared His bountiful gifts for us before we were born, introduced us into His world. Since, therefore, we receive all these things from Him, we ought for everything to give Him thanks; to whom be glory for ever and ever. Amen.

Chapter XL: Preserve God's order in the church

These things therefore being manifest to us, and since we look into the depths of the divine knowledge, we must do all things in order, which the Lord has commanded us to perform at stated times. He has commanded offerings and service to be performed, not thoughtlessly or irregularly, but at the appointed times and hours. Where and by whom He desires these things to be done, He Himself has fixed by His own supreme will, in order that all things being piously done according to His good pleasure, may be acceptable unto Him. Those, therefore, who present their offerings at the appointed times, are accepted and blessed; for inasmuch as they follow the laws of the Lord, they sin not. For his own peculiar services are assigned to the high priest, and their own proper place is prescribed to the priests, and their own special ministrations devolve on the Levites. The layman is bound by the laws that pertain to laymen.

Chapter XLII: The order of ministers in the church

The apostles have preached the Gospel to us from the Lord Jesus Christ; Jesus Christ has done so from God. Christ therefore was sent forth by God, and the apostles by Christ. Both these appointments, then, were made in an orderly way, according to the will of God. Having therefore received their orders, and being fully assured by the resurrection of our Lord Jesus Christ, and established in the Word of God, with full assurance of the Holy Ghost, they went forth proclaiming that the kingdom of God was at hand. And thus preaching through countries and cities, they appointed the first-fruits of their labors, having first proved them by the Spirit, to be bishops and deacons of those who should afterward believe. Nor was this any new thing, since indeed many ages before it was written concerning bishops and deacons. For thus says the Scripture a certain place, "I will appoint their bishops in righteousness, and their deacons in faith."

Chapter XLIII: Moses guarded priestly dignity

And what wonder is it if those in Christ who were entrusted with such a duty by God, appointed those ministers before mentioned, since the blessed Moses also, "a faithful servant in all his house," noted down in the sacred books all the injunctions which were given him, and since the other prophets also followed him bearing witness with one consent to the ordinances which he had appointed? For, when rivalry arose concerning the priesthood, and the tribes were contending among themselves as to which of them should be adorned with that glorious title, he commanded the twelve princes of the tribes to bring him their rods, each one being inscribed with the name of the tribe. And he took them and bound them together, and sealed them with the rings of the princes of the tribes, and laid them up in the tabernacle of witness on the table of God. And having shut the doors of the tabernacle, he sealed the keys, as he had done the rods, and said to them, "Men and brethren, the tribe whose rod shall blossom has God chosen to fulfil the office of the priesthood, and to minister unto Him." And when the morning was come, he assembled all Israel, six hundred thousand men, and showed the seals to the princes of the tribes, and opened the tabernacle of witness, and brought forth the rods. And the rod of Aaron was found not only to have blossomed, but to bear fruit upon it. What think you, beloved? Did not Moses know beforehand that this would happen? Undoubtedly he knew; but he acted thus, that there might be no rebellion in Israel, and that the name of the true and only God might be glorified; to Whom be glory forever and ever. Amen.

Chapter XLIV: The apostles guarded the episcopate

Our apostles also knew, through our Lord Jesus Christ, and there would be strife on account of the office of the episcopate. For this reason, therefore, inasmuch as they had obtained a perfect fore-knowledge of this, they appointed those ministers already mentioned, and afterward gave instructions, that when these should fall asleep, other approved men should succeed them in their ministry. We are of opinion, therefore, that those appointed by them, or afterward by other eminent men, with the consent of the whole Church, and who have blamelessly served the flock of Christ in a humble, peaceable, and disinterested spirit, and have for a long time possessed the good opinion of all, cannot be justly dismissed from the ministry. For our sin will not be small, if we eject from the episcopate those who have blamelessly and holily fulfilled its duties. Blessed are those presbyters who, having finished their course before now, have obtained a fruitful and perfect departure from this world; for they have no fear lest any one deprive them of the place now appointed them. But we see that you have removed some men of excellent behavior from the ministry, which they fulfilled blamelessly and with honor.

Chapter XLVI: Cleave to the holy, avoid all strife

Such examples therefore, brethren, it is right that we should follow; since it is written, "Cleave to the holy, for those that cleave to them shall themselves be made holy." And again, "With a harmless man you shall prove yourself harmless, and with an elect man you shall be elect, and with a perverse man you shall show yourself perverse." Let us cleave, therefore, to the innocent and righteous, since these are the elect of God. Why is there strife, tumults, divisions, schisms, and wars among you? Have we not all one God and one Christ? Is there not one Spirit of grace poured out upon us? And have we not one calling in Christ? Why do we divide and tear to pieces the members of Christ, and raise up strife against our own body, and have reached such a height of madness as to forget that "we are members one of another?" Remember the words of our Lord Jesus Christ, how He said, "Woe to that man by whom offenses come! It were better for him that he had never been born, than that he should cast a stumbling-block before one of my elect. It were better for him that a millstone should be hung about his neck, and he should be sunk in the depths of the sea, than that he should cast a stumbling-block before one of My little ones." Your schism has subverted the faith of many, has discouraged many, has given rise to doubt in many, and has caused grief to us all. And still your rebellion continues.

Chapter XLVII: The Apostle Paul's warning

Take up the epistle of the blessed Apostle Paul. What did he write to you at the time when the Gospel first began to be preached? Truly, under the inspiration of the Spirit, he wrote to you concerning himself, and Cephas, and Apollos, because even then parties had been formed among you. But that inclination for one above another entailed less guilt upon you, inasmuch as your partialities were then shown toward apostles, already of high reputation, and toward a man whom they had approved. But now reflect who those are that have perverted you, and lessened the renown of your far-famed brotherly love. It is disgraceful, beloved, highly disgraceful, and unworthy of your Christian profession, that such a thing should be heard of as that the most steadfast and ancient Church of the Corinthians should, on account of one or two persons, engage in rebellion against its presbyters. And this rumor has reached not only us, but those also who are unconnected with us; so that, through your error, the name of the Lord is blasphemed, while danger is also brought upon yourselves.

Chapter XLVIII: Let us return to brotherly love

Let us therefore, with all haste, put an end to this; and let us fall down before the Lord, and beseech Him with tears, that He would mercifully be reconciled to us, and restore us to our former seemly and holy practice of brotherly love. For such is the gate of righteousness, which is set open for the attainment of life, as it is written, "Open to me the gates of righteousness; I will go in by them, and will praise the Lord: this is the gate of the Lord: the righteous shall enter in by it." Although, therefore, many gates have been set open, yet this gate of righteousness is that gate in Christ by which blessed are all they that have entered in and have directed their way in holiness and righteousness, doing all things without disorder. Let a man be faithful: let him be powerful in the utterance of knowledge; let him be wise in judging of words; let him be pure in all his deeds; yet, the more he seems to be superior to others the more humble-minded he ought to be, and to seek the common good of all, and not merely his own advantage.

Chapter XLIX: In praise of love

Let him who has love for Christ keep the commandments of Christ. Who can describe the blessed bond of the love of God? What man is able to tell the excellence of its beauty, as it ought to be told? The height to which love exalts is unspeakable. Love unites us to God. Love covers a multitude of sins. Love bears all things, is long-suffering in all things. There is nothing base, nothing arrogant in love. Love admits of no schisms: love gives rise to no rebellions: love does all things in harmony. By love have all the elect of God been made perfect; without love nothing is well-pleasing to God. In love has the Lord taken us to Himself. On account of the Love he bore us,

Jesus Christ our Lord gave His blood for us by the will of God; His flesh for our flesh, and His soul for our souls.

Chapter L: Let us pray to be worthy of love

You see, beloved, how great and wonderful a thing is love, and that there is no declaring its perfection. Who is fit to be found in it, except such as God has vouchsafed to render so? Let us pray, therefore, and implore of His mercy, that we may live blameless in love, free from all human partialities for one above another. All the generations from Adam even unto this day have passed away; but those who, through the grace of God, have been made perfect in love, now possess a place among the godly, and shall be made manifest at the revelation of the kingdom of Christ. For it is written, "Enter into thy secret chambers for a little time, until my wrath and fury pass away; and I will remember a propitious day, and will raise you up out of your graves." Blessed are we, beloved, if we keep the commandments of God in the harmony of love; that so through love our sins may be forgiven us. For it is written, "Blessed are they whose transgressions are forgiven, and whose sins are covered. Blessed is the man whose sin the Lord will not impute to him, and in whose mouth there is no guile." This blessedness comes upon those who have been chosen by God through Jesus Christ our Lord; to Whom be glory forever and ever. Amen.

Chapter LI: Let the rebellious confess their sin

Let us therefore implore forgiveness for all those transgressions which through any suggestion of the adversary we have committed. And those who have been the leaders of rebellion and disagreement ought to have respect to the common hope. For such as live in fear and love would rather that they themselves than their neighbors should be involved in suffering. And they prefer to bear blame themselves, rather than that the concord which has been well and piously handed down to us should suffer. For it is better that a man should acknowledge his transgressions than that he should harden his heart, as the hearts of those were hardened who stirred up rebellion against Moses the servant of God, and whose condemnation was made manifest to all. For they went down alive into Hades, and death swallowed them up. Pharaoh with his army and all the princes of Egypt, and the chariots with their riders, were sunk in the depths of the Red Sea, and perished, for no other reason than that

their foolish hearts were hardened, after so many signs and wonders had been wrought in the land of Egypt by Moses the servant of God.

Chapter LII: Confession pleases God

The Lord, brethren, stands in need of nothing; and He desires nothing of any one, except that confession be made to Him. For David, the elect, says, "I will confess unto the Lord, and that will please Him more than a young bullock that hath horns and hoofs. Let the poor see it and be glad." And again he says, "Offer to God the sacrifice of praise, pay your vows to the Most High. Call on Me in the day of trouble and I will deliver you, and you shall glorify Me." Now, "the sacrifice of God is a broken spirit."

Chapter LIV: Love bears all that peace may be restored to the Church

Who among you is noble-minded? Who compassionate? Who full of love? Let him declare, "If on my account rebellion and disagreement and schisms have arisen, I will depart, I will go away wherever you desire, and I will do whatever the majority commands; only let the flock of Christ live on terms of peace with the presbyters set over it." He that acts thus shall acquire great glory in the Lord; and every place will welcome him. For "the earth is the Lord's, and the fullness thereof." These things they who live a godly life, that is never to be repented of, both have done and always will do.

Chapter LVI: Let us admonish one another

Let us then also pray for those who have fallen into any sin, that meekness and humility may be given to them, so that they may submit, not unto us, but to the will of God. For in this way they shall secure a fruitful and perfect remembrance from us, with sympathy for them, both in our prayers to God, and our mention of them to the saints. Let us receive correction, beloved, on account of which no one should feel displeased. Those exhortations by which we admonish one another are both good in themselves and highly profitable, for they tend to unite us to the will of God. For thus says the holy Word: "The Lord hath severely chastened me, yet hath not given me over to death." "For whom the Lord loves He chastens, and scourges every son whom He receives." "The righteous," it says, "shall chasten me in mercy, and reprove me; but let not the oil of sinners make fat my head." And again, "Blessed is the man whom the Lord reproves, and reject not the warning of the Almighty. For He causes sorrow, and again restores to gladness; He wounds, and His hands make whole. He shall deliver you from six disasters, and in the seventh no evil will touch you. In famine He shall rescue you from death, and in war He shall free you from the power of the sword. From the scourge of the tongue will He hide you, and you shall not fear when evil comes. You shall not fear the unrighteous and the wicked, and shall not be afraid of the beasts of the field. For the wild beasts shall be at peace with you. Then you will know that your house shall be at peace, and your dwelling place shall not fail. You also will know that your seed will be great, and your children like the grass of the field. And you will come to the grave like ripened corn harvested in its season, or like a heap on the threshing-floor, gathered together at the proper time." You see, beloved, that protection is afforded to those that are chastened of the Lord; for since God is good, He corrects us, that we may be admonished by His holy chastisement.

Chapter LVII: Let the rebellious submit

You therefore, who laid the foundation of this rebellion, submit yourselves to the presbyters, and receive correction so as to repent, bending the knees of your hearts. Learn to be subject, laying aside the proud and arrogant self-confidence of your tongue. For it is better for you that you should occupy a humble but honorable place in the flock of Christ, than that, being highly exalted, you should be cast out from the hope of His people. For thus speaks all-virtuous Wisdom: "Behold, I will bring forth to you the words of My Spirit, and I will teach you My speech. Since I called, and you did not hear; I held forth My words, and you regarded not, but set at naught My counsels, and yielded not at My reproofs; therefore I too will laugh at your destruction; I will rejoice when ruin comes upon you, and when sudden confusion overtakes you, when overturning presents itself like a tempest, or when tribulation and oppression fall upon you. For it shall come to pass, that when you call upon Me, I will not hear you; the wicked shall seek Me, and they shall not find Me. For they hated wisdom, and did not choose the fear of the Lord; nor would they listen to My counsel, but despised My reproof. Therefore they shall eat the fruits of their own way, and they shall be filled with their own ungodliness."

Chapter LVIII: Blessings on all who call on God

May God, Who sees all things, and who is the Ruler of all spirits and the Lord of all flesh—who chose our Lord Jesus Christ and us through Him to be a peculiar people—grant to every soul that calls on His glorious and holy Name, faith, fear, peace, patience, long-suffering, self-control, purity, and sobriety, to the well-pleasing of His Name, through our High Priest and Protector, Jesus Christ, by whom be to Him glory, and majesty, and power, and honor, both now and for evermore. Amen.

Chapter LIX: Send news of peace soon

Send back quickly to us in peace and with joy these messengers of ours—Claudius Ephebus and Valerius Bito, with Fortunatus—that they may announce to us the peace and harmony we so earnestly desire and long for among you, and that we may the more quickly rejoice over the good order re-established among you. The grace of our Lord Jesus Christ be with you, and with all everywhere that are the called of God through Him, by whom be to Him glory, honor, power, majesty, and eternal dominion, from everlasting to everlasting. Amen.

POLYCARP: LETTER TO THE PHILIPPIANS
Greek, c. A.D. 150

I could describe the very place in which the blessed Polycarp sat and taught; his going out and coming in; the whole tenor of his life; his personal appearance; how he would speak of the conversations he had held with John and with others who had seen the Lord. How he did make mention of their words and of whatever he had heard from them respecting the Lord.

—Irenaeus

In addition to the above quotation, Irenaeus's writings tells of Polycarp's visit to Rome and of his rebuke of the heretic, Marcion. Polycarp's Epistle to the Philippians (the "firstborn" of European churches) abounds in practical wisdom and is rich in Scripture citations and allusions.

✦

Polycarp, and the presbyters with him, to the Church of God sojourning at Philippi: Mercy to you, and peace from God Almighty, and from the Lord Jesus Christ, our Savior, be multiplied.

Chapter I: Praise of the Philippians

I have greatly rejoiced with you in our Lord Jesus Christ, because you have followed the example of true love [as displayed by God], and have accompanied, as became you, those who were bound in chains, the fitting ornaments of saints, and which are indeed the diadems of the true elect of God and our Lord; and because the strong root of your faith, spoken of in days long gone by, endures even until now, and brings forth fruit to our Lord Jesus Christ, who for our sins suffered even unto death, [but] "whom God raised froth the dead, having loosed the bands of the grave." "In whom, though now you see Him not, you believe, and believing, rejoice with joy unspeakable and full of glory"; into which joy many desire to enter, knowing that "by grace you are saved, not of works," but by the will of God through Jesus Christ.

Chapter II: An exhortation to virtue

"Wherefore, girding up your loins, serve the Lord in fear" and truth, as those who have forsaken the vain, empty talk and error of the multitude, and "believed in Him who raised up our Lord Jesus Christ from the dead, and gave Him glory," and a throne at His right hand. To Him all things in heaven and on earth are subject. Him every spirit serves. He comes as the Judge of the living and the dead. His blood will God require of those who do not believe in Him. But He who raised Him up from the dead will raise up us also, if we do His will, and walk in His commandments, and love what He loved, keeping ourselves from all unrighteousness, covetousness, love of money, evil speaking, false witness; "not rendering evil for evil, or railing for railing," or blow for blow, or cursing for cursing, but being mindful of what the Lord said in His teaching: "Judge not, that you be not judged; forgive, and it shall be forgiven unto you; be merciful, that ye may obtain mercy; with what measure you measure, it shall be measured to you again; and once more, "Blessed are the poor, and those that are persecuted for righteousness' sake, for theirs is the kingdom of God."

Chapter III: Expressions of personal unworthiness

These things, brethren, I write to you concerning righteousness, not because I take anything upon myself, but because you have invited me to do so. For neither I, nor any other such one, can come up to the wisdom of the blessed and glorified Paul. He, when among you, accurately and steadfastly taught the word of truth in the presence of those who were then alive. And when absent from you, he wrote you a letter, which, if you carefully study, you will find to be the means of building you up in that faith which has been given you, and which, being followed by hope, and preceded by love toward God, and Christ, and our neighbor, "is the mother of us all." For if any one be inwardly possessed of these graces, he hath fulfilled the command of righteousness, since he that hath love is far from all sin.

Chapter IV: Various exhortations

"But the love of money is the root of all evils." Knowing, therefore, that "as we brought nothing into the world, so we can carry nothing out," let us arm ourselves with the armor of righteousness; and let us teach, first of all, ourselves to walk in the commandments of the Lord. Next, [teach] your wives [to walk] in the faith given to them, and in love and purity tenderly loving their own husbands in all truth, and loving all [others] equally in all chastity; and to train up their children in the knowledge and fear of God. Teach the widows to be discreet as respects the faith of the Lord, praying continually for all, being far from all slandering, evil-speaking, false-witnessing, love of money, and every kind of evil; knowing that they are the altar of God, that He clearly perceives all things, and that nothing is hid from Him, neither reasoning, nor reflection, nor any one of the secret things of the heart.

Chapter V: The duties of deacons, youths, and virgins

Knowing, then, that "God is not mocked," we ought to walk worthy of His commandment and glory. In like manner should the deacons be blameless before the face of His righteousness, as being the servants of God and Christ, and not of men. They must not be slanderers, double-tongued, or lovers of money, but temperate in all things, compassionate, industrious, walking according to the truth of the Lord, who was the servant of all.

If we please Him in this present world, we shall receive also the future world, according as He has promised to us that He will raise us again from the dead, and that if we live worthy of Him, "we shall also reign together with Him," provided only we believe. In like manner, let the young men also be blameless in all things, being especially careful to preserve purity, and keeping themselves in, as with a bridle, from every kind of evil. For it is well that they should be cut off from the lusts that are in the world, since "every lust wars against the spirit"; and "neither fornicators, nor effeminate, nor abusers of themselves with mankind, shall inherit the kingdom of God," nor those who do things inconsistent and unbecoming. Wherefore, it is needful to abstain from all these things, being subject to the presbyters and deacons, as unto God and Christ. The virgins also must walk in a blameless and pure conscience.

Chapter VI: The duties of presbyters and others

And let the presbyters be compassionate and merciful to all, bringing back those that wander, visiting all the sick, and not neglecting the widow, the orphan, or the poor, but always "providing for that which is becoming in the sight of God and man"; abstaining from all wrath, respect of persons, and unjust judgment; keeping far off from all covetousness, not quickly crediting [an evil report] against any one, not severe in judgment, as knowing that we are all under a debt of sin. If then we entreat the Lord to forgive us, we ought also ourselves to forgive; for we are before the eyes of our Lord and God, and "we must all appear at the judgment-seat of Christ, and must every one give an account of himself." Let us then serve Him in fear, and with all reverence, even as He Himself has commanded us, and as the apostles who preached the Gospel unto us, and the prophets who proclaimed beforehand the coming of the Lord [have alike taught us]. Let us be zealous in the pursuit of that which is good, keeping ourselves from causes of offence, from false brethren, and from those who in hypocrisy bear the name of the Lord, and draw away vain men into error.

Chapter VII: Avoid the docetics and persevere in fasting and prayer

"For whosoever does not confess that Jesus Christ has come in the flesh, is antichrist"; and whosoever does not confess the testimony of the cross, is of the devil; and whosoever perverts the oracles of the Lord to his own lusts, and says that there is neither a resurrection nor a judgment, he is the first-born of Satan. Wherefore, forsaking the vanity of many, and their false doctrines, let us return to the word which has been handed down to us from the beginning; "watching unto prayer," and persevering in fasting; beseeching in our supplications the all-seeing God "not to lead us into temptation," as the Lord has said: "The spirit truly is willing, but the flesh is weak."

Chapter VIII: Persevere in hope and patience

Let us then continually persevere in our hope, and the earnest of our righteousness, which is Jesus Christ, "who bore our sins in His own body on the tree," "who did no sin, neither was guile found in His mouth," but endured all things for us, that we might live in Him. Let us then be imitators of His patience; and if we suffer for His name's sake, let us glorify Him. For He has set us this example in Himself, and we have believed that such is the case.

Chapter IX: Patience inculcated

I exhort you all, therefore, to yield obedience to the word of righteousness, and to exercise all patience, such as you have seen [set] before your eyes, not only in the case of the blessed Ignatius, and Zosimus, and Rufus, but also in others among yourselves, and in Paul himself, and the rest of the apostles. [This do] in the assurance that all these have not run in vain, but in faith and righteousness, and that they are [now] in their due place in the presence of the Lord, with whom also they suffered. For they loved not this present world, but Him who died for us, and for our sakes was raised again by God from the dead.

Chapter X: Exhortation to the practice of virtue

Stand fast, therefore, in these things, and follow the example of the Lord, being firm and unchangeable in the faith, loving the brotherhood, and being attached to one another, joined together in the truth, exhibiting the meekness of the Lord in your intercourse with one another, and despising no one. When you can do good, defer it not, because "alms delivers from death." Be all of you subject one to another having your conduct blameless among the Gentiles," that you may both receive praise for your good works, and the Lord may not be blasphemed through you. But woe to him by whom the name of the Lord is blasphemed! Teach, therefore, sobriety to all, and manifest it also in your own conduct.

Chapter XI: Expression of grief on account of Valens

I am greatly grieved for Valens, who was once a presbyter among you, because he so little understands the place that was given him [in the Church]. I exhort you, therefore, that you abstain from covetousness, and that you be chaste and truthful. "Abstain from every form of evil." For if a man cannot govern himself in such matters, how shall he enjoin them on others? If a man does not keep himself from covetousness, he shall be defiled by idolatry, and shall be judged as one of the heathen. But who of us are ignorant of the judgment of the Lord? "Do we not know that the saints shall judge the world?" as Paul teaches. But I have neither seen nor heard of any such thing among you, in the midst of whom the blessed Paul labored, and who are commended in the beginning of his Epistle. For he boasts of you in all those Churches which alone then knew the Lord; but we [of Smyrna] had not yet known Him. I am deeply grieved, therefore, brethren, for him (Valens) and his wife; to whom may the Lord grant true repentance! And be you then moderate in regard to this matter, and "do not count such as enemies," but call them back as suffering and straying members, that you may save your whole body. For by so acting you shall edify yourselves.

Chapter XII: Exhortation to various graces

For I trust that you are well versed in the Sacred Scriptures, and that nothing is hid from you; but to me this privilege is not yet granted. It is declared then in these Scriptures, "Be angry, and sin not," and, "Let not the sun go down upon your wrath." Happy is he who remembers this, which I believe to be the case with you. But may the God and Father of our Lord Jesus Christ, and Jesus Christ Himself, who is the Son of God, and our everlasting High Priest, build you up in faith and truth, and in all meekness, gentleness, patience, longsuffering, forbearance, and purity; and may He bestow on you a lot and portion among His saints, and on us with you, and on all that are under heaven, who shall believe in our Lord Jesus Christ, and in His Father, who "raised Him from the dead. Pray for all the saints. Pray also for kings, and potentates, and princes, and for those that persecute and hate you, and for the enemies of the cross, that your fruit may be manifest to all, and that you may be perfect in Him.

Chapter XIII: Concerning the transmission of Epistles

Both you and Ignatius wrote to me, that if any one went [from this] into Syria, he should carry your letter with him; which request I will attend to if I find a fitting opportunity, either personally, or through some other acting for me, that your desire may be fulfilled. The Epistles of Ignatius written by him to us, and all the rest [of his Epistles] which we have by us, we have sent to you, as you requested. They are subjoined to this Epistle, and by them you may be greatly profited; for they treat of faith and patience, and all things that tend to edification in our Lord. Any more certain information you may have obtained respecting both Ignatius himself, and those that were with him, have the goodness to make known to us.

Chapter XIV: Conclusion

These things I have written to you by Crescens, whom up to the present time I have recommended unto you, and do now recommend. For he has acted blamelessly among us, and I believe also among you. Moreover, you will hold his sister in esteem when she comes to you. Be you safe in the Lord Jesus Christ. Grace be with you all. Amen.

CYPRIAN: "THE UNITY OF THE CATHOLIC CHURCH" (CHAPTERS 3–8)
Latin, A.D. 251

Prior to his conversion to Christ, Cyprian was a teacher of pagan rhetoric. In his role as Bishop of Carthage (North Africa), Cyprian wrote in response to the divisive issues of his day, such as the readmission of the lapsed (those who fled persecution). Cyprian is believed to have died about A.D. 258.

Chapter III

But not only must we guard against things which are open and manifest but also against those which deceive with the subtlety of clever fraud. Now what is more clever, or what more subtle than that the enemy, detected and cast down by the coming of Christ, after light had come to the Gentiles, and the saving splendor had shone forth for the preservation of man, that the deaf might receive the hearing of spiritual grace, the blind open their eyes to the Lord, the weak grow strong with eternal health, the lame run to the church, the dumb supplicate with clear voices and prayers, seeing the idols abandoned and his shrines and temples deserted because of the great populace of believers, devise a new fraud, under the very title of Christian name to deceive the incautious? He invented heresies and schisms with which to overthrow the faith, to corrupt the truth, to divide unity. Those whom he cannot hold in the blindness of the old way, he circumvents and deceives by the error of a new way. He snatches men from the Church itself, and, while they seem to themselves to have already approached the light and to have escaped the night of the world, he again pours forth other shadows upon the unsuspecting, so that, although they do not stand with the Gospel of Christ and with the observation of Him and with the law, they call themselves Christians, and, although they walk in darkness, they think that they have light, while the adversary cajoles and deceives, who, as the Apostle says, transforms himself into an angel of light, and adorns his ministers as those of justice who offer night for day, death for salvation, despair under the offer of hope, perfidy under the pretext of faith, antichrist under the name of Christ, so that while they tell plausible lies, they frustrate the truth by their subtlety. This happens, most beloved brethren, because there is no return to the source of truth, and the Head is not sought, and the doctrine of the heavenly Master is not kept.

Chapter IV

If anyone considers and examines these things, there is no need of a lengthy discussion and arguments. Proof for faith is easy in a brief statement of the truth. The Lord speaks to Peter: "I say to thee," He says, "thou art Peter, and upon this rock I will build my church, and the gates of hell shall not prevail against it. And I will give thee the keys of the kingdom of heaven; and whatever thou shalt bind on earth shall be bound also in heaven, and whatever thou shalt loose on earth shall be loosed also in heaven." Upon him, being one, He builds His Church, and although after His resurrection He bestows equal power upon all the Apostles, and says: "As the Father has sent me, I also send you. Receive ye the Holy Spirit: if you forgive the sins of anyone, they will be forgiven him; if you retain the sins of anyone, they will be retained," yet that He might display unity, He established by His authority the origin of the same unity as beginning from one. Surely the rest of the Apostles also were that which Peter was, endowed with an equal partnership of office and of power, but the beginning proceeds from unity, that the Church of Christ may be shown to be one. This one Church, also, the Holy Spirit in the Canticle of Canticles designates in the person of the Lord and says: "One is my dove, my perfect one is but one, she is the only one of her mother, the chosen one of her that bore her." Does he who does not hold this unity think that he holds the faith? Does he who strives against the Church and resists her think that he is in the Church, when too the blessed Apostle Paul teaches this same thing and sets forth the sacrament of unity saying: "One body and one Spirit, one hope of your calling, one Lord, one faith, one baptism, one God"?

Chapter V

This unity we ought to hold firmly and defend, especially we bishops who watch over the Church, that we may prove that also the episcopate itself is one and undivided. Let no one deceive the brotherhood by lying; let no one corrupt the faith by a perfidious prevarication of the truth. The episcopate is one, the parts of which are held together by the individual bishops. The Church is one which with increasing fecundity extend far and wide into the multitude, just as the rays of the sun are many but the light is one, and the branches of the tree are many but the strength is one founded in its tenacious root, and, when many streams flow from one source, although a multiplicity of waters seems to have been diffused from the abundance of the overflowing supply nevertheless unity is preserved in their origin. Take away a ray of light from the body of the sun, its unity does not take on any division of its light; break a branch from a tree, the branch thus broken will not be able to bud; cut off a stream from its source, the stream thus cut off dries up. Thus too the Church bathed in the light of the Lord projects its rays over the whole world, yet there is one light which is diffused everywhere, and the unity of the body is not separated. She extends her branches over the whole earth in fruitful abundance; she extends her richly flowing streams far and wide; yet her head is one, and her source is one, and she is the one mother copious in the results of her fruitfulness. By her womb we are born; by her milk we are nourished; by her spirit we are animated.

Chapter VI

The spouse of Christ cannot be defiled; she is uncorrupted and chaste. She knows one home; with chaste modesty she guards the sanctity of one couch. She keeps us for God; she assigns the children whom she has created to the kingdom. Whoever is separated from the Church and is joined with an adulteress is separated from the promises of the Church, nor will he who has abandoned the Church arrive at the rewards of Christ. He is a stranger; he is profane; he is an enemy. He cannot have God as a father who does not have the Church as a mother. If whoever was outside the ark of Noah was able to escape, he too who is outside the Church escapes.

The Lord warns, saying: "He who is not with me is against me, and who does not gather with me, scatters." He who breaks the peace and concord of Christ acts against Christ; he who gathers somewhere outside the Church scatters the Church of Christ. The Lord says: "I and the Father are one." And again of the Father and Son and the Holy Spirit it is written: "And these three are one." Does anyone believe that this unity which comes from divine strength, which is closely connected with the divine sacraments, can be broken asunder in the Church and be separated by the divisions of colliding wills? He who does not hold this unity, does not hold the law of God, does not hold the faith of the Father and the Son, does not hold life and salvation.

Chapter VII

This sacrament of unity, this bond of concord inseparably connected is shown, when in the Gospel the tunic of the Lord Jesus Christ is not at all divided and is not torn, but by those who cast lots for the garment of Christ, who rather might have put on Christ, a sound garment is received, and an undamaged and undivided tunic is possessed. Divine Scripture speaks and says: "Now of the tunic, since it was woven throughout from the upper part without seam, they said to one another: 'Let us not tear it, but let us cast lots for it, whose it shall be.'" He bore the unity that came down from the upper part, that is, that came down from heaven and the Father, which could not all be torn by him who received

and possessed it, but he obtained it whole once for all and a firmness inseparably solid. He cannot possess the garment of Christ who tears and divides the Church of Christ. Then on the other hand when at the death of Solomon his kingdom and people were torn asunder, Ahias the prophet met King Jeroboam in the field and tore his garment into twelve pieces, saying: "Take to thee ten pieces, for thus saith the Lord: 'Behold I rend the kingdom out of the hand of Solomon, and will give thee ten scepters, but two scepters shall remain to him for the sake of my servant David and for the sake of Jerusalem the city which I have chosen, that I may place my name there.'" When the twelve tribes of Israel were torn asunder, the prophet Ahias rent his garment. But because the people of Christ cannot be torn asunder, His tunic woven and united throughout was not divided by those who possessed it. Undivided, joined, connected it shows the coherent concord of us who have put on Christ. By the sacrament and sign of His garment, He has declared the unity of the Church.

Chapter VIII

Who then is so profane and lacking in faith, who so insane by the fury of discord as either to believe that the unity of God, the garment of the Lord, the Church of Christ, can be torn asunder or to dare to do so? He Himself warns us in His Gospel, and teaches saying: "And there shall be one flock and one shepherd." And does anyone think that there can be either many shepherds or many flocks in one place? Likewise the Apostle Paul insinuating this same unity upon us beseeches and urges us in these words: "I beseech you, brethren," he says, "by the name of our Lord Jesus Christ, that you all say the same thing, and that there be no dissensions among you: but that you be perfectly united in the same mind and in the same judgment." And again he says: "Bearing with one another in love, careful to preserve the unity of the Spirit, in the bond of peace." Do you think that you can stand and live, withdrawing from the Church, and building for yourself other abodes and different dwellings, when it was said to Rahab, in whom the Church was prefigured: "You shall gather your father and your mother and your brethren and the entire house of your father to your own self in your house, and it will be that everyone who goes out of the door of your house shall be his own accuser"; likewise, when the sacrament of the Passover contains nothing else in the law of the Exodus than that the lamb which is slain in the figure of Christ be eaten in one house? God speaks, saying: "In one house it shall be eaten, you shall not carry the flesh outside of the house." The flesh of Christ and the holy of the Lord cannot be carried outside, and there is no other house for believers except the one Church. This house, this hospice of unanimity the Holy Spirit designates and proclaims, when He says: "God who makes those of one mind to dwell in his house." In the house of God, in the Church of Christ, those of one mind dwell; they persevere in concord and simplicity.

EDICTS OF TOLERATION
Latin, Early Fourth Century

The official end to state-sponsored persecution of Christianity came with the dispatch of these official circulars to the provincial governors of the Roman Empire. The content of these documents comes down to us from a work by Lactantius (*On the Death of Persecutions*, 48) and in the *Church History* of Eusebius (10.5).

GALERIUS'S EDICT OF TOLERATION, A.D. 311

The great persecution of Christians (c. A.D. 300–311) under Galerius officially ended when that Roman ruler fell prey to disease and to political defeat by Constantine in the latter's quest to become supreme emperor of the Roman Empire. The tone of the edict suggests that Galerius took seriously the Christian claim that he had been stricken by God on account of the persecution.

✦

Among other accommodations that we have always made for the prosperity and welfare of the Republic, we sought to bring all things into harmony with the ancient laws and public order of the Romans, and to exhort Christians, who abandoned the religion of their fathers, to return to reason. For they, on a whim, disobeyed the institutes of antiquity which their own ancestors first established, and at their own will and pleasure made laws for themselves, gathering diverse multitudes into congregations. Finally, after our law demanded they

should conform to the institutes of antiquity, many were subdued by the fear of danger, many even suffered death. However, since most of them persevered in their ways, and as we noticed that they neither revered the gods nor worshiped the God of the Christians; in view of our mercies and tendency to grant forgiveness to all, we permit that they may again be Christians and may hold their meetings, provided they do nothing contrary to good order. But we shall tell the magistrates in another letter what they ought to do. Therefore, for this our indulgence, they ought to pray to their God for our safety, for that of the Republic and for their own, so that the Republic may continue uninjured on every side, and that they may be able to live securely in their homes. This edict is published at Nicomedia on the day before the Kalends of May, in our eighth consulship and the second of Maximinus

EDICT OF MILAN, A.D. 313

The successor to Galerius, Constantine, was sympathetic toward Christianity and eventually became a Christian himself, declaring Christianity the official religion of the Roman Empire.

✦

When I, Constantine Augustus, as well as I, Licinius Augustus, fortunately met near Mediolanurn (Milan), and were considering everything that pertained to the public welfare and security, we thought, among other things which we saw would be for the good of many, those regulations pertaining to the reverence of the Divinity ought certainly to be made first, so that we might grant to the Christians and others full authority to observe that religion which each preferred; whence any Divinity whatsoever in the seat of the heavens may be propitious and kindly dispose to us and all who are placed under our rule. And thus by this wholesome counsel and most upright provision we thought to arrange that no one whatsoever should be denied the opportunity to give his heart to the observance of the Christian religion, of that religion which he should think best for himself, so that the Supreme Deity, to whose worship we freely yield our hearts may show in all things His usual favor and benevolence. Therefore, your Worship should know that it has pleased us to remove all conditions whatsoever, which were in the rescripts formerly given to you officially, concerning the Christians and now any one of these who wishes to observe Christian religion may do so freely and openly, without molestation. We thought it fit to commend these things most fully to your care that you may know that we have given to those Christians free and unrestricted opportunity of religious worship. When you see that this has been granted to them by us, your Worship will know that we have also conceded to other religions the right of open and free observance of their worship for the sake of the peace of our times, that each one may have the free opportunity to worship as he pleases; this regulation is made that we may not seem to detract from any dignity or any religion. Moreover, in the case of the Christians especially we esteemed it best to order that if it happens anyone heretofore has bought from our treasury from anyone whatsoever, those places where they were previously accustomed to assemble, concerning which a certain decree had been made and a letter sent to you officially, the same shall be restored to the Christians without payment or any claim of recompense and without any kind of fraud or deception. Those, moreover, who have obtained the same by gift, are likewise to return them at once to the Christians. Besides, both those who have purchased and those who have secured them by gift, are to appeal to the vicar if they seek any recompense from our bounty, that they may be cared for through our clemency. All this property ought to be delivered at once to the community of the Christians through your intercession, and without delay. And since these Christians are known to have possessed not only those places in which they were accustomed to assemble, but also other property, namely the churches, belonging to them as a corporation and not as individuals, all these things which we have included under the above law, you will order to be restored, without any hesitation or controversy at all, to these Christians, that is to say to the corporations and their conventicles: providing, of course, that the above arrangements be followed so that those who return the same without payment, as we have said, may hope for an indemnity from our bounty. In all these circumstances you ought to tender your most efficacious intervention to the community of the Christians, that our command may be carried into effect as quickly as possible, whereby, moreover, through our clemency, public order may be secured. Let this be done so that, as we have said above, Divine favor toward us, which, under the most important circumstances we have already experienced, may, for all time, preserve and prosper our successes together with the good of the state. Moreover, in order that the statement of this decree of our good will may come to the notice of all, this rescript, published by your decree, shall be announced everywhere and brought to the knowledge of all, so that the decree of this, our benevolence, cannot be concealed.

THE ECUMENICAL CHURCH COUNCILS (EXCERPTS)
Latin, A.D. Fourth to Eighth Centuries

From the fourth to the eighth centuries A.D., councils of ruling bishops assembled in order to settle matters of church controversy. While in theory these councils were ecumenical—representative of all the churches in the empire—practical and political realities made broad representation impossible. So, for example, when in A.D. 325 the Emperor Constantine convened a Church Council at Nicaea to address heretical views of Christ introduced by Arius, the majority of the 220 bishops in attendance were from Greek-speaking Eastern churches, with relatively few from the Latin West. The creeds and canons (ecclesiastical laws) formulated by the seven ecumenical councils nevertheless became authoritative for all Christendom. The Nicene Creed is the best known product of the Council of Nicaea. In addition to creeds, the council documents also include authoritative letters, "anathamas" (formal condemnations), and excerpts from theological writings. Excerpts cited here are from several councils and relate to the formulation of the doctrines of the Trinity and the two natures of Christ.

The Second Ecumenical Council: The First Council of Constantinople, A.D. 381

The Creed Found in Epiphanius's Ancoratus

We believe in one God, the Father Almighty, maker of all things, invisible and visible.[2] And in one Lord

---

2. Philip Schaff and Henry Wace, eds., *The Seven Ecumenical Councils*, The Nicene and Post-Nicene Fathers, 2nd ser., 14 (Grand Rapids: Eerdmans, 1974) 164–65.

Jesus Christ the Son of God, begotten of God the Father, only begotten, that is of the substance of the Father, God of God, Light of Light, very God of very God, begotten not made, being of one substance with the Father, by whom all things were made, both which be in heaven and in earth, whether they be visible or invisible. Who for us men and for our salvation came down, and was incarnate, that is to say was conceived perfectly through the Holy Ghost of the holy ever-virgin Mary, and was made man, that is to say a perfect man, receiving a soul, and body, and intellect, and all that make up a man, but without sin, not from human seed, nor [that he dwelt] in a man, but taking flesh to himself into one holy entity; not as he inspired the prophets and spake and worked [in them], but was perfectly made man, for the Word was made flesh; neither did he experience any change, nor did he convert his divine nature into the nature of man, but united it to his one holy perfection and Divinity.

For there is one Lord Jesus Christ, not two, the same is God, the same is Lord, the same is King. He suffered in the flesh, and rose again, and ascended into heaven in the same body, and with glory he sat down at the right hand of the Father, and in the same body he will come in glory to judge both the quick and the dead, and of his kingdom there shall be no end. And we believe in the Holy Ghost, who spake in the Law, and preached in the Prophets, and descended at Jordan, and spake in the Apostles, and indwells the Saints. And thus we believe in him, that he is the Holy Spirit, the Spirit of God, the perfect Spirit, the Spirit the Comforter, uncreate, who proceedeth from the Father, receiving of the Son, and believed on

[We believe] in one Catholic and Apostolic Church. And in one baptism of penitence, and in the resurrection of the dead, and the just judgment of souls and bodies, and in the Kingdom of heaven and in life everlasting. And those who say that there was a time when the Son was not, or when the Holy Ghost was not, or that either was made of that which previously had no being, or that he is of a different nature or substance, and affirm that the Son of God and the Holy Spirit are subject to change and mutation; all such the Catholic and Apostolic Church, the mother both of you and of us, anathematizes. And further we anathematize such as do not confess the resurrection of the dead, as well as all heresies which are not in accord with the true faith.

Finally, you and your children thus believing and keeping the commandments of this same faith, we trust that you will always pray for us, that we may have a share and lot in that same faith and in the keeping of these same commandments. For us make your intercessions, you and all who believe thus, and keep the commandments of the Lord in our Lord Jesus Christ, through whom and with whom, glory be to the Father with the Holy Spirit forever and ever. Amen.

An Excerpt from the Synodical Letter of the Council of Constantinople, A.D. 382 (on the Trinity)

Through them we wish to make it plain that our disposition is all for peace with unity for its sole object, and that we are full of zeal for the right faith.[3] For we, whether we suffered persecutions, or afflictions, or the threats of emperors, or the cruelties of princes, or any other trial at the hands of heretics, have undergone all for the sake of the evangelic faith, ratified by the three hundred and eighteen fathers at Nicaea in Bithynia. This is the faith which ought to be sufficient for you, for us, for all who wrest not the word of the true faith; for it is the ancient faith; it is the faith of our baptism; it is the faith that teaches us to believe in the name of the Father, of the Son, and of the Holy Ghost. According to this faith there is one Godhead, Power and Substance of the Father and of the Son and of the Holy Ghost; the dignity being equal, and the majesty being equal in three perfect hypostases, i.e., three perfect persons. Thus there is no room for the heresy of Sabellius by the confusion of the hypostases, i.e., the destruction of the personalities; thus the blasphemy of the Eunomians, of the Arians, and of the Pneumatomachi is nullified, which divides the substance, the nature, and the Godhead, and superinduces on the uncreated consubstantial and co-eternal Trinity a nature posterior, created and of a different substance. We moreover preserve unperverted the doctrine of the incarnation of the Lord, holding the tradition that the dispensation of the flesh is neither soulless nor mindless nor imperfect; and knowing full well that God's Word was perfect before the ages, and became perfect man in the last days for our salvation.

---

3. Ibid., 189.

The Third Ecumenical Council: The Council of Ephesus, A.D. 431

The XII Anathematisms of St. Cyril Against Nestorius (Complete)

I. If anyone will not confess that the Emmanuel is very God, and that therefore the Holy Virgin is the Mother of God, inasmuch as in the flesh she bore the Word of God made flesh [as it is written, "The Word was made flesh"] let him be anathema.

II. If anyone shall not confess that the Word of God the Father is united hypostatically to flesh, and that with that flesh of his own, he is one only Christ both God and man at the same time: let him be anathema.

III. If anyone shall after the [hypostatic] union divide the hypostases in the one Christ, joining them by that connection alone, which happens according to worthiness, or even authority and power, and not rather by a coming together, which is made by natural union: let him be anathema.

IV. If anyone shall divide between two persons or subsistences those expressions which are contained in the Evangelical and Apostolical writings, or which have been said concerning Christ by the Saints, or by himself, and shall apply some to him as to a man separate from the Word of God, and shall apply others to the only Word of God the Father, on the ground that they are fit to be applied to God: let him be anathema.

V. If anyone shall dare to say that the Christ is a Theophorus [that is, God-bearing] man and not rather that he is very God, as an only Son through nature, because "the Word was made flesh," and "hath a share in flesh and blood as we do": let him be anathema.

VI. If anyone shall dare say that the Word of God the Father is the God of Christ or the Lord of Christ, and shall not rather confess him as at the same time both God and Man, since according to the Scriptures, "The Word was made flesh": let him be anathema.

VII. If anyone shall say that Jesus as man is only energized by the Word of God, and that the glory of the Only-begotten is attributed to him as something not properly his: let him be anathema.

VIII. If anyone shall dare to say that the assumed man ought to be worshipped together with God the Word, and glorified together with him, and recognized together with him as God, and yet as two different things, the one with the other (for this "Together with" is added [i.e., by the Nestorians] to convey this meaning); and shall not rather with one adoration worship the Emmanuel and pay to him one glorification, as [it is written] "The Word was made flesh": let him be anathema.

IX. If any man shall say that the one Lord Jesus Christ was glorified by the Holy Ghost, so that he used through him a power not his own and from him received power against unclean spirits and power to work miracles before men and shall not rather confess that it was his own Spirit through which he worked these divine signs, let him be anathema.

X. Whosoever shall say that it is not the divine Word himself, when he was made flesh and had become man as we are, but another than he, a man born of a woman, yet different from him, who is become our Great High Priest and Apostle; or if any man shall say that he offered himself in sacrifice for himself and not rather for us, whereas, being without sin, he had no need of offering or sacrifice: let him be anathema.

XI. Whosoever shall not confess that the flesh of the Lord giveth life and that it pertains to the Word of God the Father as his very own, but shall pretend that it belongs to another person who is united to him [i.e., the Word] only according to honor, and who has served as a dwelling for the divinity; and shall not rather confess, as we say, that that flesh giveth life because it is that of the Word who giveth life to all: let him be anathema.

XII. Whosoever shall not recognize that the Word of God suffered in the flesh, that he was crucified in the flesh, and that likewise in that same flesh he tasted death and that he is become the first-begotten of the dead, for, as he is God, he is the life and it is he that giveth life: let him be anathema.

The Fourth Ecumenical Council: The Council of Chalcedon, A.D. 451

Excerpts from the Letter of Cyril to John of Antioch

. . . Concerning the Virgin Mother of God, we thus think and speak; and of the manner of the Incarnation of the Only Begotten Son of God, necessarily, not by way of addition but for the sake of certainty, as we have received from the beginning from the divine Scriptures and from the tradition of the holy fathers, we will speak briefly, adding nothing whatever to the Faith set forth by the holy Fathers in Nice.[4] For, as we said before, it suffices for all knowledge of piety and the refutation of all false doctrine of heretics. But we speak, not presuming on the impossible; but with the confession of our own weakness, excluding those who wish us to cling to those things which transcend human consideration.

We confess, therefore, our Lord Jesus Christ, the Only Begotten Son of God, perfect God, and perfect Man of a reasonable soul and flesh consisting; begotten before the ages of the Father according to his Divinity, and in the last days, for us and for our salvation, of Mary the Virgin according to his humanity, of the same substance with his Father according to his Divinity, and of the same substance with us according to his humanity; for there became a union of two natures. Wherefore we confess one Christ, one Son, one Lord.

According to this understanding of this unmixed union, we confess the holy Virgin to be Mother of God; because God the Word was incarnate and became Man, and from this conception he united the temple taken from her with himself. For we know the theologians make some things of the Evangelical and Apostolic teaching about the Lord common as pertaining to the one person, and other things they divide as to the two natures, and attribute the worthy ones to God on account of the Divinity of Christ, and the lowly ones on account of his humanity [to his humanity].

These being your holy voices, and finding ourselves thinking the same with them ("One Lord, One Faith, One Baptism"), we glorified God the Savior of all, congratulating one another that our churches and yours have the Faith which agrees with the God-inspired Scriptures and the traditions of our holy Fathers . . .

We remember too, the Savior himself saying, "And no man hath ascended up to heaven, but he that came down from heaven, even the Son of Man." Although he was born according to his flesh, as just said, of the holy Virgin, yet God the Word came down from above and from heaven. He "made himself of no reputation, and took upon him the form of a servant," and was called the Son of Man, yet remaining what he was, that is to say God. For he is unchanging and unchangeable according to nature; considered already as one with his own Flesh, he is said to have come down from heaven. He is also called the Man from heaven, being perfect in his Divinity and perfect in his Humanity, and considered as in one Person. For one is the Lord Jesus Christ, although the difference of his natures is not unknown, from which we say the ineffable union was made.

Will your holiness vouchsafe to silence those who say that a *crasis*, or mingling, or mixture took place between the Word of God and flesh. For it is likely that certain also gossip about me as having thought or said such things.

But I am far from any such thought as that, and I also consider them wholly to rave who think a shadow of change could occur concerning the Nature of the Word of God. For he remains that which he always was, and has not been changed, nor can he ever be changed, nor is he capable of change. For we all confess in addition to this, that the Word of God is impassible, even though when he dispenses most wisely this mystery, he appears to ascribe to himself the sufferings endured in his own flesh. To the same purpose the all-wise Peter also said when he wrote of Christ as having "suffered in the flesh," and not in the nature of his ineffable Godhead. In order that he should be believed to be the Savior of all, by an economic appropriation to himself, as just said, he assumed the sufferings of his own Flesh. . . .

Excerpt from the Tome of St. Leo

. . . If, then, he (Eutyches) knew not what he ought to think about the Incarnation of the Word of God, and was not willing, for the sake of obtaining the light of intelligence, to make laborious search through the whole extent of the Holy Scriptures, he should at least have received with heedful attention that general Confession common to all, whereby the whole body of the faithful

---

4. Ibid., 251–53.

profess that they "believe in God the Father Almighty, and in Jesus Christ his only Son our Lord, who was born of the Holy Ghost and the Virgin Mary."[5] By which three clauses the engines of almost all heretics are shattered. For when God is believed to be both "Almighty" and "Father," it is proved that the Son is everlasting together with himself, differing in nothing from the Father, because he was born as "God from God," Almighty from Almighty, Coeternal from Eternal; not later in time, not inferior in power, not unlike him in glory, not divided from him in essence, but the same Only-begotten and Everlasting Son of an Everlasting Parent was "born of the Holy Ghost and the Virgin Mary." This birth in time in no way detracted from, in no way added to, that divine and everlasting birth; but expended itself wholly in the work of restoring man, who had been deceived; so that it might both overcome death, and by its power "destroy the devil who had the power of death." For we could not have overcome the author of sin and of death, unless he who could neither be contaminated by sin, nor detained by death, had taken upon himself our nature, and made it his own. For, in fact, he was "conceived of the Holy Ghost" within the womb of a Virgin Mother, who bore him as she had conceived him, without loss of virginity.

But if he (Eutyches) was not able to obtain a true conception from this pure fountain of Christian faith because by his own blindness he had darkened for himself the brightness of a truth so clear, he should have submitted himself to the Evangelist's teaching; and after reading what Matthew says, "The book of the generation of Jesus Christ, the Son of David, the Son of Abraham," he should also have sought instruction from the Apostle's preaching; and after reading in the Epistle to the Romans, "Paul, a servant of Jesus Christ, called an Apostle, separated unto the gospel of God, which he had promised before by the prophets in the Holy Scriptures, concerning his Son, who was made unto him of the seed of David according to the flesh," he should have bestowed some devout study on the pages of the Prophets; and finding that God's promise said to Abraham, "in thy seed shall all nations be blessed," in order to avoid all doubt as to the proper meaning of this "seed," he should have attended to the Apostle's words, "To Abraham and to his seed were the promises made.

He saith not, 'and to seeds,' as in the case of many, but as in the case of one, 'and to thy seed,' which is Christ." He should also have apprehended with his inward ear the declaration of Isaiah, "Behold, a Virgin shall conceive and bear a Son, and they shall call his name Emmanuel, which is, being interpreted God with us," and should have read with faith the words of the same prophet, "Unto us a Child has been born, unto us a Son has been given, whose power is on his shoulder; and they shall call his name Angel of great counsel, Wonderful, Counselor, Strong God, Prince of Peace, Father of the age to come." And he should not have spoken idly to the effect that the Word was in such a sense made flesh, that the Christ who was brought forth from the Virgin's womb had the form of a man, and had not a body really derived from his Mother's body.

Possibly his reason for thinking that our Lord Jesus Christ was not of our nature was this—that the Angel who was sent to the blessed and ever Virgin Mary said, "The Holy Ghost shall come upon thee, and the power of the Highest shall overshadow thee, and therefore also that holy thing which shall be born of thee shall be called the Son of God"; as if, because the Virgin's conception was caused by a divine act, therefore the flesh of him whom she conceived was not of the nature of her who conceived him. But we are not to understand that "generation," peerlessly wonderful, and wonderfully peerless, in such a sense as that the newness of the mode of production did away with the proper character of the kind. For it was the Holy Ghost who gave fecundity to the Virgin, but it was from a body that a real body was derived; and "when Wisdom was building herself a house," the "Word was made flesh, and dwelt among us," that is, in that flesh which he assumed from a human being, and which he animated with the spirit of rational life.

Accordingly while the distinctness of both natures and substances was preserved, and both met in one Person, lowliness was assumed by majesty, weakness by power, mortality by eternity; and, in order to pay the debt of our condition, the inviolable nature was united to the passible, so that as the appropriate remedy for our ills, one and the same "Mediator between God and man, the Man Christ Jesus," might from one element be capable of dying and also from the other be incapable. Therefore in the entire and perfect nature of very man was born very God, whole in what was his, whole in what was ours. By

---

5. Ibid., 254–58.

"ours" we mean what the Creator formed in us at the beginning and what he assumed in order to restore; for of that which the deceiver brought in, and man, thus deceived, admitted, there was not a trace in the Savior; and the fact that he took on himself a share in our infirmities did not make him a partaker in our transgressions. He assumed "the form of a servant" without the defilement of sin, enriching what was human, not impairing what was divine: because that "emptying of himself," whereby the Invisible made himself visible, and the Creator and Lord of all things willed to be one among mortals, was a stooping down in compassion, not a failure of power. Accordingly, the same who, remaining in the form of God, made man, was made man in the form of a servant. For each of the natures retains its proper character without defect; and as the form of God does not take away the form of a servant, so the form of a servant does not impair the form of God.

For since the devil was glorying in the fact that man, deceived by his craft, was bereft of divine gifts and, being stripped of his endowment of immortality, had come under the grievous sentence of death, and that he himself, amid his miseries, had found a sort of consolation in having a transgressor as his companion, and that God, according to the requirements of the principle of justice, had changed his own resolution in regard to man, whom he had created in so high a position of honor; there was need of a dispensation of secret counsel, in order that the unchangeable God, whose will could not be deprived of its own benignity, should fulfill by a more secret mystery his original plan of lovingkindness toward us, and that man, who had been led into fault by the wicked subtlety of the devil, should not perish contrary to God's purpose. Accordingly, the Son of God, descending from his seat in heaven, and not departing from the glory of the Father, enters this lower world, born after a new order, by a new mode of birth. After a new order; because he who in his own sphere is invisible, became visible in ours; He who could not be enclosed in space, willed to be enclosed; continuing to be before times, he began to exist in time; the Lord of the universe allowed his infinite majesty to be overshadowed, and took upon him the form of a servant; the impassible God did not disdain to be passible Man and the immortal One to be subjected to the laws of death. And born by a new mode of birth; because inviolate virginity, while ignorant of concupiscence, sup-

plied the matter of his flesh. What was assumed from the Lord's mother was nature, not fault; nor does the wondrousness of the nativity of our Lord Jesus Christ, as born of a Virgin's womb, imply that his nature is unlike ours. For the selfsame who is very God, is also very man; and there is no illusion in this union, while the lowliness of man and the loftiness of Godhead meet together. For as "God" is not changed by the compassion [exhibited], so "Man" is not consumed by the dignity [bestowed]. For each "form" does the acts which belong to it, in communion with the other; the Word, that is, performing what belongs to the Word, and the flesh carrying out what belongs to the flesh; the one of these shines out in miracles, the other succumbs to weaknesses. And as the Word does not withdraw from equality with the Father in glory, so the flesh does not abandon the nature of our kind. For, as we must often be saying, he is one and the same, truly Son of God, and truly Son of Man. God, inasmuch as "in the beginning was the Word, and the Word was with God, and the Word was God." Man, inasmuch as "the Word was made flesh, and dwelt among us." God, inasmuch as "all things were made by him, and without him nothing was made." Man, inasmuch as he was "made of a woman, made under the law." The nativity of the flesh is a manifestation of human nature; the Virgin's childbearing is an indication of Divine power. The infancy of the Babe is exhibited by the humiliation of swaddling clothes: the greatness of the Highest is declared by the voices of angels. He whom Herod impiously designs to slay is like humanity in its beginnings; but he whom the Magi rejoice to adore on their knees is Lord of all. Now when he came to the baptism of John his forerunner, lest the fact that the Godhead was covered with a veil of flesh should be concealed, the voice of the Father spake in thunder from heaven, "This is my beloved Son, in whom I am well pleased." Accordingly, he who, as man, is tempted by the devil's subtlety, is the same to whom, as God, angels pay duteous service. To hunger, to thirst, to be weary, and to sleep, is evidently human. But to satisfy five thousand men with five loaves, and give to the Samaritan woman that living water, to draw which can secure him that drinks of it from ever thirsting again; to walk on the surface of the sea with feet that sink not, and by rebuking the storm to bring down the "uplifted waves," is unquestionably Divine. As then—to pass by many points—it does not belong to the same nature to weep with feelings of pity over a dead friend and, after the mass of stone had been removed from the grave where he had lain four days, by a voice of command to raise him up to life again; or to hang on the wood, and to make all the elements tremble after daylight had been turned into night; or to be transfixed with nails, and to open the gates of paradise to the faith of the robber; so it does not belong to the same nature to say, "I and the Father are one," and to say, "the Father is greater than I." For although in the Lord Jesus Christ there is one Person of God and man, yet that whereby contumely attaches to both is one thing, and that whereby glory attaches to both is another; for from what belongs to us he has that manhood which is inferior to the Father; while from the Father he has equal Godhead with the Father. Accordingly, on account of this unity of Person which is to be understood as existing in both the natures, we read, on the one hand, that "the Son of Man came down from heaven," inasmuch as the Son of God took flesh from that Virgin of whom he was born; and on the other hand, the Son of God is said to have been crucified and buried, inasmuch as he underwent this, not in his actual Godhead; wherein the Only-begotten is coeternal and consubstantial with the Father, but in the weakness of human nature. Wherefore we all, in the very Creed, confess that "the only-begotten Son of God was crucified and buried," according to that saying of the Apostle, "for if they had known it, they would not have crucified the Lord of Majesty."

But when our Lord and Savior himself was by his questions instructing the faith of the disciples, he said, "Whom do men say that I the Son of Man am?" And when they had mentioned various opinions held by others, he said, "But whom say ye that I am?" that is, "I who am Son of Man, and whom you see in the form of a servant, and in reality of flesh, whom say ye that I am?" Whereupon the blessed Peter, as inspired by God, and about to benefit all nations by his confession, said, "Thou art the Christ, the Son of the living God." Not undeservedly, therefore, was he pronounced blessed by the Lord, and derived from the original Rock that solidity which belonged both to his virtue and to his name, who through revelation from the Father confessed the selfsame to be both the Son of God and the Christ; because one of these truths, accepted without the other, would not profit unto salvation, and it was equally dangerous to believe the Lord Jesus Christ to be merely God and not man, or merely man and not God. But after the resurrection of the Lord—which was in truth the resurrection of a real body, for no other person was raised again than he who had been crucified and had died— what else was accomplished during that interval of forty days than to make our faith entire and clear of all darkness? For while he conversed with his disciples, and dwelt with them, and ate with them, and allowed himself to be handled with careful and inquisitive touch by those who were under the influence of doubt, for this end he came in to the disciples when the doors were shut, and by his breath gave them the Holy Ghost, and opened the secrets of Holy Scripture after bestowing on them the light of intelligence, and again in his selfsame person showed to them the wound in the side, the prints of the nails, and all the flesh tokens of the Passion, saying, "Behold my hands and my feet, that it is I myself; handle me and see, for a spirit hath not flesh and bones, as ye see me have": that the properties of the Divine and the human nature might be acknowledged to remain in him without causing a division, and that we might in such sort know that the Word is not what the flesh is, as to confess that the one Son of God is both Word and flesh. On which mystery of the faith this Eutyches must be regarded as unhappily having no hold, who does not recognize our nature to exist in the Only-begotten Son of God, either by way of the lowliness of mortality, or of the glory of resurrection. Nor has he been overawed by the declaration of the blessed Apostle and Evangelist John, saying, "Every spirit that confesses that Jesus Christ has come in the flesh is of God; and every spirit which diminishes Jesus is not of God, and this is Antichrist." Now what is to diminish Jesus, but to separate the human nature from him, and to make void by shameless inventions that mystery by which alone we have been saved? Moreover, being in the dark as to the nature of Christ's body, he is entangled in the senseless blindness with regard to his Passion also. For if he does not think the Lord's crucifixion to be unreal, and does not doubt that he really accepted suffering, even unto death, for the sake of the world's salvation; as he believes in his death, let him acknowledge his flesh also, and not doubt that he whom he recognizes as having been capable of suffering is also Man with a body like ours; since to deny his true flesh is also to deny his bodily sufferings. If then he accepts the Christian faith, and does not turn away his ear from the preaching of the Gospel, let him see what nature it was that was transfixed with nails and hung on the wood of the cross; and let him understand whence it was that, after the side of the Crucified had been pierced by the soldier's spear, blood and water flowed out, that the Church of God might be refreshed both with a Laver and with a Cup. Let him listen also to the blessed Apostle Peter when he declares, that "sanctification by the Spirit" takes place through the "sprinkling of the blood of Christ," and let him not give a mere cursory reading to the words of the same Apostle, "Knowing that ye were not redeemed with corruptible things, as silver and gold, from your vain way of life received by tradition from your fathers, but with the precious blood of Jesus Christ as of a Lamb without blemish and without spot." Let him also not resist the testimony of Blessed John the Apostle, "And the blood of Jesus the Son of God cleanses us from all sin." And again, "This is the victory which overcomes the world, even our faith"; and, "Who is he that overcomes the world, but he that believeth that Jesus is the Son of God? This is He that came by water and blood, even Jesus Christ; not in water only, but in water and blood; and it is the Spirit that bears witness, because the Spirit is truth. For there are three that bear witness—the Spirit, the water, and the blood; and the three are one." That is, the Spirit of sanctification, and the blood of redemption, and the water of baptism; which three things are one, and remain undivided, and not one of them is disjoined from connection with the others; because the Catholic Church lives and advances by this faith, that Christ Jesus we should believe neither manhood to exist without true Godhead, nor Godhead without true manhood. But when Eutyches, on being questioned in your examination of him, answered, "I confess that our Lord was of two natures before the union, but after the union I confess one nature"; I am astonished that so absurd and perverse a profession as this of his was not rebuked by a censure on the part of any of his judges, and that an utterance extremely foolish and extremely blasphemous was passed over, just as if nothing had been heard which could give offense: seeing that it is as impious to say that the Only-begotten Son of God was of two natures before the Incarnation as it is shocking to affirm that, since the Word became flesh, there has been in him one nature only. But lest Eutyches should think that what he said was correct, or was tolerable, because it was not confuted by any assertion of yours, we exhort your earnest solicitude, dearly beloved brother, to see that, if by God's merciful inspiration the case is brought to a satisfactory issue, the inconsiderate and inexperienced man be cleansed also from this pestilent notion of his; seeing that, as the record of the proceedings has clearly shown, he had fairly begun to abandon his own opinion when on being driven into a corner by authoritative words of yours, he professed himself ready to say what he had not said before, and to give his adhesion to that faith from which he had previously stood aloof. But when he would not consent to anathematize the impious dogma you understood, brother, that he continued in his own misbelief, and deserved to receive a sentence of condemnation. For which if he grieves sincerely and to good purpose, and understands, even though too late, how properly the Episcopal authority has been put in motion, or if, in order to make full satisfaction, he shall condemn viva voce, and under his own hand, all that he has held amiss, no compassion, to whatever extent, which can be shown him when he has been set right, will be worthy of blame, for our Lord, the true and good Shepherd, who laid down his life for his sheep, and who came to save men's souls and not to destroy them, wills us to imitate his own loving kindness; so that justice should indeed constrain those who sin, but mercy should not reject those who are converted. For then indeed is the true faith defended with the best results, when a false opinion is condemned even by those who have followed it. But in order that the whole matter may be piously and faithfully carried out, we have appointed our brethren, Julius, Bishop, and Reatus, Presbyter (of the title of St. Clement) and also my son Hilarus, Deacon, to represent us; and with them we have associated Dulcitius, our Notary, of whose fidelity we have had good proof: trusting that the Divine assistance will be with you, so that he who has gone astray may be saved by condemning his own unsound opinion. May God keep you in good health, dearly beloved brother. Given on the Ides of June, in the Consulate of the illustrious men, Asterius and Protogenes.

The Fifth Ecumenical Council: The Second Council of Constantinople, A.D. 553

The Capitula of the Council (I–X of XII Capitula)

I. If anyone shall not confess that the nature or essence of the Father, of the Son, and of the Holy Ghost is one, as also the force and the power; [if anyone does not confess] a consubstantial Trinity, one Godhead to be worshipped in three subsistences or Persons: let him be anathema.[6] For there is but one God even the Father of whom are all things, and one Lord Jesus Christ through whom are all things, and one Holy Spirit in whom are all things.

II. If anyone shall not confess that the Word of God has two nativities, the one from all eternity of the Father, without time and without body; the other in these last days, coming down from heaven and being made flesh of the holy and glorious Mary, Mother of God and always a virgin, and born of her: let him be anathema.

III. If anyone shall say that the wonder-working Word of God is one [Person] and the Christ that suffered another; or shall say that God the Word was with the woman-born Christ, or was in him as one person in another, but that he was not one and the same our Lord Jesus Christ, the Word of God, incarnate and made man, and that his miracles and the sufferings which of his own will he endured in the flesh were not of the same [Person]: let him be anathema.

IV. If anyone shall say that the union of the Word of God to man was only according to grace or energy, or dignity, or equality of honor, or authority, or relation, or effect, or power, or according to good pleasure in this sense that God the Word was pleased with a man, that is to say, that he loved him for his own sake, as says the senseless Theodorus, or [if anyone pretends that this union exists only] so far as likeness of name is concerned, as the Nestorians understand, who call also the Word of God Jesus and Christ, and even accord to the man the names of Christ and of Son, speaking thus clearly of two persons, and only designating disingenuously one Person and one Christ when the reference is to his honor, or his dignity, or his worship; if anyone shall not acknowledge as the Holy Fathers teach, that the union of God the Word is made with the flesh animated by a reasonable and living soul, and that such

union is made synthetically and hypostatically, and that therefore there is only one Person, to wit: our Lord Jesus Christ, one of the Holy Trinity: let him be anathema. As a matter of fact the word "union" has many meanings, and the partisans of Apollinaris and Eutyches have affirmed that these natures are confounded inter se, and have asserted a union produced by the mixture of both. On the other hand the followers of Theodorus and of Nestorius rejoicing in the division of the natures, have taught only a relative union. Meanwhile the Holy Church of God, condemning equally the impiety of both sorts of heresies, recognizes the union of God the Word with the flesh synthetically, that is to say, hypostatically. For in the mystery of Christ the synthetical union not only preserves unconfusedly the natures which are united, but also allows no separation.

V. If anyone understands the expression "one only Person of our Lord Jesus Christ" in this sense, that it is the union of many hypostases, and if he attempts thus to introduce into the mystery of Christ two hypostases, or two Persons, and, after having introduced two persons, speaks of one Person only out of dignity, honor or worship, as both Theodorus and Nestorius insanely have written; if anyone shall speak ill of the holy Council of Chalcedon, pretending that it made use of this expression [one hypostasis] in this impious sense, and if he will not recognize rather that the Word of God is united with the flesh hypostatically, and that therefore there is but one hypostasis or one only Person, and that the holy Council of Chalcedon has professed in this sense the one Person of our Lord Jesus Christ: let him be anathema. For since one of the Holy Trinity has been made man, namely, God the Word, the Holy Trinity has not been increased by the addition of another person or hypostasis.

VI. If anyone shall not call in a true acceptation, but only in a false acceptation, the holy, glorious, and ever-virgin Mary, the Mother of God, or shall call her so only in a relative sense, believing that she bare only a simple man and that God the word was not incarnate

---

6. Ibid., 312–14.

of her, but that the incarnation of God the Word resulted only from the fact that he united himself to that man who was born [of her]; if he shall calumniate the Holy Synod of Chalcedon as though it had asserted the Virgin to be Mother of God according to the impious sense of Theodore; or if anyone shall call her the mother of a man or the Mother of Christ, as if Christ were not God, and shall not confess that she is exactly and truly the Mother of God, because God the Word, Who before all ages was begotten of the Father, was in these last days made flesh and born of her, and if anyone shall not confess that in this sense the holy Synod of Chalcedon acknowledged her to be the Mother of God: let him be anathema.

VII. If anyone using the expression, "in two natures," does not confess that our one Lord Jesus Christ has been revealed in the divinity and in the humanity, so as to designate by that expression a difference of the natures of which an ineffable union is unconfusedly made, [a union] in which neither the nature of the Word was changed into that of the flesh, nor that of the flesh into that of the Word, for each remained that it was by nature, the union being hypostatic; but shall take the expression with regard to the mystery of Christ in a sense so as to divide the parties, or recognizing the two natures in the only Lord Jesus, God the Word made man, does not content himself with taking in a theoretical manner the difference of the natures which compose him, which difference is not destroyed by the union between them, for one is composed of the two and the two are in one, but shall make use of the number [two] to divide the natures or to make of them Persons properly so called: let him be anathema.

VIII. If anyone uses the expression "of two natures," confessing that a union was made of the Godhead and of the humanity, or the expression "the one nature made flesh of God the Word," and shall not so understand those expressions as the holy Fathers have taught, to wit: that of the divine and human nature there was made an hypostatic union, whereof is one Christ; but from these expressions shall try to introduce one nature or substance [made by a mixture] of the Godhead and manhood of Christ: let him be anathema. For in teaching that the only-begotten Word was united hypostatically [to humanity] we do not mean to say that there was made a mutual confusion of natures, but rather each [nature] remaining what it was, we understand that the Word was united to the flesh. Wherefore there is one Christ, both God and man, consubstantial with the Father as touching his Godhead, and consubstantial with us as touching his manhood. Therefore they are equally condemned and anathematized by the Church of God, who divide or part the mystery of the divine dispensation of Christ, or who introduce confusion into that mystery.

IX. If anyone shall take the expression, Christ ought to be worshipped in his two natures, in the sense that he wishes to introduce thus two adorations, the one in special relation to God the Word and the other as pertaining to the man; or if anyone to get rid of the flesh, [that is of the humanity of Christ,] or to mix together the divinity and the humanity, shall speak monstrously of one only nature or essence of the united (natures), and so worship Christ, and does not venerate, by one adoration, God the Word made man, together with his flesh, as the Holy Church has taught from the beginning: let him be anathema.

X. If anyone does not confess that our Lord Jesus Christ who was crucified in the flesh is true God and the Lord of Glory and one of the Holy Trinity: let him be anathema.

The Sixth Ecumenical Council: The Third Council of Constantinople, A.D. 680–681

Excerpt from the Letter of Pope Agatho

. . . as we confess the holy and inseparable Trinity, that is, the Father, the Son and the Holy Ghost, to be of one deity, of one nature and substance or essence, so we will profess also that it has one natural will, power, operation, domination, majesty, potency, and glory.[7] And whatever is said of the same Holy Trinity essentially in singular number we understand to refer to the one nature of the three consubstantial Persons, having been so taught by canonical logic. But when we make a confession concerning one of the same three Persons of that Holy Trinity, of the Son of God, or God the Word, and of the mystery of his adorable dispensation according to the flesh, we assert that all things are double in the one and the same our Lord and Saviour Jesus Christ according to the Evangelical tradition, that is to say, we confess his two natures, to wit the divine and the human, of which and in which he, even after the wonderful and inseparable union, subsists. And we confess that each of his natures has its own natural propriety, and that the divine, has all things that are divine, without any sin. And we recognize that each one (of the two natures) of the one and the same incarnated, that is, humanated (*humanati*) Word of God is in him unconfusedly, inseparably and unchangeably, intelligence alone discerning a unity, to avoid the error of confusion. For we equally detest the blasphemy of division and of commixture. For when we confess two natures and two natural wills, and two natural operations in our one Lord Jesus Christ, we do not assert that they are contrary or opposed one to the other (as those who err from the path of truth and accuse the apostolic tradition of doing. Far be this impiety from the hearts of the faithful!), nor as though separated (*per se* separated) in two persons or subsistences, but we say that as the same our Lord Jesus Christ has two natures so also he has two natural wills and operations, to wit, the divine and the human: the divine will and operation he has in common with the coessential Father from all eternity: the human, he has received from us, taken with our nature in time. This is the apostolic and evangelic tradition, which the spiritual mother of your most felicitous empire, the Apostolic Church of Christ, holds.

Those that confound the mystery of the holy Incarnation, inasmuch as they say that there is one nature of the deity and humanity of Christ, contend that he has one will, as of one, and (one) personal operation. But they who divide, on the other hand, the inseparable union, unite the two natures which they acknowledge that the Savior possesses, not however in union which

is recognized to be hypostatic; but blasphemously join them by concord, through the affection of the will, like two subsistences, i.e., two somebodies. Moreover, the Apostolic Church of Christ, the spiritual mother of your God-founded empire, confesses one Jesus Christ our Lord existing of and in two natures, and she maintains that his two natures, to wit, the divine and the human, exist in him unconfused even after their inseparable union, and she acknowledges that each of these natures of Christ is perfect in the proprieties of its nature, and she confesses that all things belonging to the proprieties of the natures are double, because the same our Lord Jesus Christ himself is both perfect God and perfect man, of two and in two natures: and after his wonderful Incarnation, his deity cannot be thought of without his humanity, nor his humanity without his deity. Consequently, therefore, according to the rule of the holy Catholic and Apostolic Church of Christ, she also confesses and preaches that there are in him two natural wills and two natural operations.

For if anybody should mean a personal will, when in the holy Trinity there are said to be three Persons, it would be necessary that there should be asserted three personal wills, and three personal operations (which is absurd and truly profane). Since, as the truth of the Christian faith holds, the will is natural, where the one nature of the holy and inseparable Trinity is spoken of, it must be consistently understood that there is one natural will, and one natural operation.

But when in truth we confess that in the one person of our Lord Jesus Christ the mediator between God and men, there are two natures (that is to say the divine and the human), even after his admirable union, just as we canonically confess the two natures of one and the same person, so too we confess his two natural wills and two natural operations. But that the understanding of this truthful confession may become clear to your Piety's mind from the God-inspired doctrine of the Old and the New Testament (for your Clemency is incomparably more able to penetrate the meaning of the sacred Scriptures, than our littleness to set it forth in flowing words), our Lord Jesus Christ himself, who is true and perfect God, and true and perfect man, in his holy Gospels shows forth in some instances human things, in others, divine, and still in others both together, making a manifestation concerning himself in order that he might instruct his faithful to believe and preach that he

---

7. Ibid., 330–35.

is both true God and true man. Thus as man he prays to the Father to take away the cup of suffering, because in him our human nature was complete, sin only excepted, "Father, if it be possible, let this cup pass from me; nevertheless not as I will, but as thou wilt." And in another passage: "Not my will, but thine be done." If we wish to know the meaning of which testimony as explained by the holy and approved Fathers, and truly to understand what "my will," what "thine" signify, the blessed Ambrose in his second book to the Emperor Gratian, of blessed memory, teaches us the meaning of this passage in these words, saying: "He then, receives my will, he takes my sorrow, I confidently call it sorrow as I am speaking of the cross, mine is the will, which he calls his, because he bears my sorrow as man, he spoke as a man, and therefore he says: 'Not as I will but as thou wilt.'" Mine is the sadness which he has received according to my affection. See, most pious of princes, how clearly here this holy Father sets forth that the words our Lord used in his prayer, "Not my will," pertain to his humanity; through which also he is said, according to the teaching of Blessed Paul the Apostle of the Gentiles, to have "become obedient unto death, even the death of the Cross." Wherefore also it is taught us that he was obedient to his parents, which must piously be understood to refer to his voluntary obedience, not according to his divinity (by which he governs all things), but according to his humanity, by which he spontaneously submitted himself to his parents. St. Luke the Evangelist likewise bears witness to the same thing, telling how the same our Lord Jesus Christ prayed according to his humanity to his Father, and said, "Father, if it be possible let the cup pass from me; nevertheless not my will but thine be done,"—which passage Athanasius, the Confessor of Christ, and Archbishop of the Church of Alexandria, in his book against Apollinaris the heretic, concerning the Trinity and the Incarnation, also understanding the wills to be two, thus explains: And when he says, "Father, if it be possible, let this cup pass from me, nevertheless not my will but thine be done," and again, "The spirit is willing, but the flesh is weak"; he shows that there are two wills, the one human which is the will of the flesh, but the other divine. For his human will, out of the weakness of the flesh was fleeing away from the passion, but his divine will was ready for it. What truer explanation could be found? For how is it possible not to acknowledge in him two wills, to wit, a human

and a divine, when in him, even after the inseparable union, there are two natures according to the definitions of the synods? For John also, who leaned upon the Lord's breast, his beloved disciple, shews forth the same self-restraint in these words: "I came down from heaven not to do mine own will but the will of the Father that sent me." And again: "This is the will of him that sent me, that of all that he gave me I should lose nothing, but should raise it up again at the last day." Again he introduces the Lord as disputing with the Jews, and saying among other things: "I seek not mine own will, but the will of him that sent me." On the meaning of which divine words blessed Augustine, a most illustrious doctor, thus writes in his book against Maximinus the Arian. He says, "When the Son says to the Father 'Not what I will, but what you will,' what doth it profit you, that you brought thy words into subjection and say, It shows truly that his will was subject to his Father, as though we would deny that the will of man should be subject to the will of God? For that the Lord said this in his human nature, anyone will quickly see who studies attentively this place of the Gospel. For therein he says, 'My soul is exceeding sorrowful even unto death.' Can this possibly be said of the nature of the One Word? But, O man, who thinkest to make the nature of the Holy Ghost to groan, why do you say that the nature of the Only-begotten Word of God cannot be sad? But to prevent anyone arguing in this way, he does not say 'I am sad' (and even if he had so said, it could properly only have been understood of his human nature), but he says 'My soul is sad,' that is, the soul he has as a man; however in saying also, 'Not what I will' he showed that he willed something different from what the Father did, which he could not have done except in his human nature, since he did not introduce our infirmity into his divine nature, but would transfigure human affection. For had he not been made man, the Only Word could in no way have said to the Father, 'Not what I will.' For it could never be possible for that immutable nature to will anything different from what the Father willed. If you would but make this distinction, O ye Arians, ye would not be heretics."

In this disputation this venerable Father shows that when the Lord says "his own" he means the will of his humanity, and when he says not to do "his own will," he teaches us not chiefly to seek our own wills but that through obedience we should submit our wills to the

Divine Will. From all which it is evident that he had a human will by which he obeyed his Father, and that he had in himself this same human will immaculate from all sin, as true God and man. Which thing St. Ambrose also thus treats of in his explanation of St. Luke the Evangelist.

Excerpt from the Definition of Faith

. . . Following the five holy Ecumenical Councils and the holy and approved Fathers, with one voice defining that our Lord Jesus Christ must be confessed to be very God and very man, one of the holy and consubstantial and life-giving Trinity, perfect in Deity and perfect in humanity, very God and very man, of a reasonable soul and human body subsisting;[8] consubstantial with the Father as touching his Godhead and consubstantial with us as touching his manhood; in all things like unto us, sin only excepted; begotten of his Father before all ages according to his Godhead, but in these last days for us men and for our salvation made man of the Holy Ghost and of the Virgin Mary, strictly and properly the Mother of God according to the flesh; one and the same Christ our Lord the only-begotten Son of two natures unconfusedly, unchangeably, inseparably indivisibly to be recognized, the peculiarities of neither nature being lost by the union but rather the proprieties of each nature being preserved, concurring in one Person and in one subsistence, not parted or divided into two persons but one and the same only-begotten Son of God, the Word, our Lord Jesus Christ, according as the Prophets of old have taught us and as our Lord Jesus Christ himself hath instructed us, and the Creed of the holy Fathers hath delivered to us; defining all this we likewise declare that in him are two natural wills and two natural operations indivisibly, inconvertibly, inseparably, inconfusedly, according to the teaching of the holy Fathers. And these two natural wills are not contrary the one to the other (God forbid!) as the impious heretics assert, but his human will follows and that not as resisting and reluctant, but rather as subject to his divine and omnipotent will. For it was right that the flesh should be moved but subject to the divine will, according to the most wise Athanasius. For as his flesh is called and is the flesh of God the Word, so also the natural will of his flesh is called and is the proper will of God the Word, as he himself says: "I came down from heaven, not that I might do mine own will but the will of the Father which sent me!" where he calls his own will the will of his flesh, inasmuch as his flesh was also his own. For as his most holy and immaculate animated flesh was not destroyed because it was deified but continued in its own state and nature, so also his human will, although deified, was not suppressed, but was rather preserved according to the saying of Gregory Theologus: "His will [i.e., the Saviour's] is not contrary to God but altogether deified." We glorify two natural operations indivisibly, immutably, inconfusedly, inseparably in the same our Lord Jesus Christ our true God, that is to say a divine operation and a human operation, according to the divine preacher Leo, who most distinctly asserts as follows: "For each form does in communion with the other what pertains properly to it, the Word, namely, doing that which pertains to the Word, and the flesh that which pertains to the flesh."

For we will not admit one natural operation in God and in the creature, as we will not exalt into the divine essence what is created, nor will we bring down the glory of the divine nature to the place suited to the creature. We recognize the miracles and the sufferings as of one and the same [Person], but of one or of the other nature of which he is and in which he exists, as Cyril admirably says. Preserving therefore the inconfusedness and indivisibility, we make briefly this whole confession, believing our Lord Jesus Christ to be one of the Trinity and after the incarnation our true God, we say that his two natures shone forth in his one subsistence in which he both performed the miracles and endured the sufferings through the whole of his economic conversation, and that not in appearance only but in very deed, and this by reason of the difference of nature which must be recognized in the same Person. For although they are joined together, each nature wills and does the things proper to it, indivisibly and inconfusedly. For this reason we confess two wills and two operations, concurring most fitly in him for the salvation of the human race.

These things, therefore, with all diligence and care having been formulated by us, we define that it be permitted to no one to bring forward, or to write, or to compose, or to think, or to teach a different faith. Whosoever shall presume to compose a different faith, or to propose, or teach, or hand to those wishing to be

---

8. Ibid., 334–46.

converted to the knowledge of the truth, from the Gentiles or Jews, or from any heresy, any different Creed; or to introduce a new voice or invention of speech to subvert these things which now have been determined by us, all these, if they be Bishops or clerics let them be deposed, the Bishops from the Episcopate, the clerics from the clergy; but if they be monks or laymen: let them be anathematized.

VINCENT OF LERINS: "THE VINCENTIAN CANON" (FROM *COMMONITORIUM*)
Latin, Fifth Century A.D.

"Vincentian Canon" refers to the concise rule laid down by Vincent of Lerins (c. early fifth century) for distinguishing orthodox belief from heresy, namely, "what has been believed everywhere, always, and by all" (*quod ubique, quod semper, quod ab omnibus, credium est*; see paragraph 6. After becoming a monk at the Abbey of Lerinum, Vincent wrote his *Commonitorium*, or "Aid to Memory" for clarifying the orthodox faith, under the pseudonym of Peregrinus ("stranger").

Questions for Guided Reading

1. Vincent's "canon" or rule is certainly concise, but what is the merit of judging a potentially heretical belief against the idea of "what has been believed everywhere [i.e., in all Christendom], always [since the time of Christ], and by all [authoritative Christian teachers]"?
2. Many Protestants hesitate to accept the idea that the Church (any church) possesses inherent authority to interpret Scripture. Why does Vincent appeal to such authority (see [5.])?
3. Does this canon teach that truth lies with the majority of believers (see [6.])?
4. Does the work of authoritative interpretation ultimately depend on official church counsels (i.e., [7.])?

Chapter II: The Vincentian Canon

[4.] I have often asked men who are known for their great faith and learning whether there is a universal rule by which we are able to distinguish the truth of catholic faith from false teachings and, in most cases, I receive an answer like this: That whoever desires to detect false doctrine, avoid deception, and continue to be strong in the catholic faith must, with the Lord's assistance, fortify his belief in two ways; first, by the authority of the Divine Law, and then, by the Tradition of the catholic Church.

[5.] But someone may ask, *since the canon of Scripture is complete and sufficient of itself for everything—and more than sufficient—why add the authority of the Church's interpretation?* Because Scripture is deep and not everyone agrees on all interpretations—some understand a passage one way and others another. Indeed, some passages seem to have as many interpretations as there are interpreters. For Novatian expounds it one way, Sabellius another, Donatus another, Arius, Eunomius, Macedonius, another, Photinus, Apollinaris, Priscillian, another, Iovinian, Pelagius, Celestius, another, lastly, Nestorius another.[9] Therefore it is necessary, especially because of the great complexities involved in such disagreements, that we develop a rule for the correct understanding of the prophets and apostles and that we do so according to the catholic Church and faith.

[6.] Specifically, in the Church itself, we must be careful to believe that which has been believed everywhere, always, by all. For that is truly "catholic," which as the name itself implies encompasses universality. And, indeed, we follow this rule by observing universality, antiquity, and consent. First, we follow universality if we confess as true the one faith which the whole Church throughout the world confesses. Second, we follow antiquity, if we do not depart from those interpretations known to have been held by our holy ancestors and fathers. Finally, we have consent if in the ancient interpretation we follow to the consensus of all, or at the least most, priests and doctors.

Chapter III: What if some choose to separate themselves from the Church?

[7.] *What should Christians do when a few members of the Church cut themselves off from communion with the*

---

9. Names of those who fostered heresies in the church.

universal faith? They should prefer the security of the entire body to the unsoundness of pestilent and corrupt members.

What if some false and innovative teaching threatens to infect the entire Church? Then it is his duty to hold on to ancient and genuine belief which cannot be corrupted by modern heresies.

[8.] *But what if we were to discover some error in an ancient doctrine?* In that case a decree of a General Council of the Church must always be accepted over the word of a rash and ignorant few.

But what if no decree is forthcoming? In that case a Christian must carefully collect and examine all the writings of the ancient Christians who, though they lived in many times and places, maintained the communion and faith of the one catholic Church, and who agree with many other Christian authorities on the matter at hand.

JOHN CALVIN: "ON THE CHURCH" (FROM *INSTITUTES OF THE CHRISTIAN RELIGION*, BOOK 4, CHAPTER I)
Latin, 1530s

Born in 1509 in France, John Calvin was raised in the Catholic Church and from a young age was favored by the Bishop of Noyon (his home town) with ecclesiastical benefits and the hope of a prosperous career in the church. However, his education in law (beginning in 1528) and later in humanities (1532) led him to identify with the writings of Martin Luther and the ideals of the growing Reformation movement. By 1533 those ideals were attacked by the Catholic Church, and anyone advocating them was persecuted. Calvin abandoned his church benefits and left his homeland for Switzerland. There, in 1536, he wrote the first edition of his *Institutes* in which he sermonized on the Ten Commandments, the Apostles' Creed, the Lord's Prayer, the sacraments, and church government. Although this first edition (in Latin) of the *Institutes* was patterned after Luther's *Shorter Catechism*, over time Calvin expanded the work to eighty chapters of biblical-doctrinal description uniquely his own and translated it into French. For its simple organization, clarity, and thoroughness, the *Institutes* became a far more effective tool in the hands of Calvinist teachers than its German counterpart, Philip

Melanchthon's *Loci Communes* ("Commonplaces"). The *Institutes* have been called "the most important theological text of the Reformation."[10] Even today, Calvin's *Institutes*, along with his commentaries on nearly every book of the Bible, serve as a basis of Christian teaching and faith for millions of Reformed Christians worldwide. Book 4, chapter I of the *Institute* follows.

Section 1: The necessity of the church

In the last Book, it has been shown, that by the faith of the gospel Christ becomes ours, and we are made partakers of the salvation and eternal blessedness procured by him. But as our ignorance and sloth (I may add, the vanity of our mind) stand in need of external helps, by which faith may be begotten in us, and may increase and make progress until its consummation, God, in accommodation to our infirmity, has added much helps, and secured the effectual preaching of the gospel, by depositing this treasure with the Church. He has appointed pastors and teachers, by whose lips he might edify his people (Eph. 4:11); he has invested them with authority, and, in short, omitted nothing that might conduce to holy consent in the faith, and to right order. In particular, he has instituted sacraments, which we feel by experience to be most useful helps in fostering and confirming our faith. For seeing we are shut up in the prison of the body, and have not yet attained to the rank of angels, God, in accommodation to our capacity, has in his admirable providence provided a method by which, though widely separated, we might still draw near to him.

Wherefore, due order requires that we first treat of the Church, of its Government, Orders, and Power; next, of the Sacraments; and, lastly, of Civil Government;—at the same time guarding pious readers against the corruptions of the Papacy, by which Satan has adulterated all that God had appointed for our salvation.

I will begin with the Church, into whose bosom God is pleased to collect his children, not only that by her aid and ministry they may be nourished so long as they are babes and children, but may also be guided by her maternal care until they grow up to manhood, and, finally, attain to the perfection of faith. What God has thus

---

10. E. A. Livingston, ed., *The Oxford Dictionary of the Christian Church*, 3rd ed. (Oxford: Oxford University Press, 1997), 838.

joined, let not man put asunder (Mark 10:9): to those to whom he is a Father, the Church must also be a mother. This was true not merely under the Law, but even now after the advent of Christ; since Paul declares that we are the children of a new, even a heavenly Jerusalem (Gal. 4:26).

Section 2: What is the relationship of church and creed?

When in the Creed we profess to believe the Church, reference is made not only to the visible Church of which we are now treating, but also to all the elect of God, including in the number even those who have departed this life. And, accordingly, the word used is "believe," because oftentimes no difference can be observed between the children of God and the profane, between his proper flock and the untamed herd. The particle *in* is often interpolated, but without any probable ground. I confess, indeed, that it is the more usual form, and is not unsupported by antiquity, since the Nicene Creed, as quoted in Ecclesiastical History, adds the preposition. At the same time, we may perceive from early writers, that the expression received without controversy in ancient times was to believe "the Church," and not "in the Church." This is not only the expression used by Augustine, and that ancient writer, whoever he may have been, whose treatise, *De Symboli Expositione*, is extant under the name of Cyprian, but they distinctly remark that the addition of the preposition would make the expression improper, and they give good grounds for so thinking. We declare that we believe in God, both because our mind reclines upon him as true, and our confidence is fully satisfied in him. This cannot be said of the Church, just as it cannot be said of the forgiveness of sins, or the resurrection of the body. Wherefore, although I am unwilling to dispute about words, yet I would rather keep to the proper form, as better fitted to express the thing that is meant, than affect terms by which the meaning is ceaselessly obscured.

The object of the expression is to teach us, that though the devil leaves no stone unturned in order to destroy the grace of Christ, and the enemies of God rush with insane violence in the same direction, it cannot be extinguished—the blood of Christ cannot be rendered barren, and prevented from producing fruit. Hence, regard must be had both to the secret election and to the internal calling of God, because he alone "knoweth them that are his" (2 Tim. 2:19); and as Paul expresses it, holds them as it were enclosed under his seal (Eph.1:13), although, at the same time, they wear his insignia, and are thus distinguished from the reprobate. But as they are a small and despised number, concealed in an immense crowd, like a few grains of wheat buried among a heap of chaff, to God alone must be left the knowledge of his Church, of which his secret election forms the foundation. Nor is it enough to embrace the number of the elect in thought and intention merely. By the unity of the Church we must understand a unity into which we feel persuaded that we are truly ingrafted. For unless we are united with all the other members under Christ our head, no hope of the future inheritance awaits us.

Hence the Church is called Catholic or Universal (August. Ep. 48), for two or three cannot be invented without dividing Christ; and this is impossible. All the elect of God are so joined together in Christ, that as they depend on one head, so they are as it were compacted into one body, being knit together like its different members; made truly one by living together under the same Spirit of God in one faith, hope, and charity, called not only to the same inheritance of eternal life, but to participation in one God and Christ. For although the sad devastation which everywhere meets our view may proclaim that no Church remains, let us know that the death of Christ produces fruit, and that God wondrously preserves his Church, while placing it as it were in concealment. Thus it was said to Elijah, "Yet I have left me seven thousand in Israel," (1 Kings 19:18).

Section 3: "The communion of saints"

Moreover this article of the Creed relates in some measure to the external Church, that every one of us must maintain brotherly concord with all the children of God, give due authority to the Church, and, in short, conduct ourselves as sheep of the flock. And hence the additional expression, the "communion of saints"; for this clause, though usually omitted by ancient writers, must not be overlooked, as it admirably expresses the quality of the Church; just as if it had been said, that saints are united in the fellowship of Christ on this condition, that all the blessings which God bestows upon them are mutually communicated to each other. This, however, is not incompatible with a diversity of graces, for we know that the gifts of the Spirit are variously distributed; nor is it incompatible with civil order, by which each is permitted privately to possess his own means, it being necessary for the preservation of peace among men that distinct rights of property should exist among them. Still a community is asserted, such as Luke describes when he says, "The multitude of them that believed were of one heart and of one soul" (Acts 4:32); and Paul, when he reminds the Ephesians, "There is one body, and one Spirit, even as ye are called in one hope of your calling" (Eph. 4:4). For if they are truly persuaded that God is the common Father of them all, and Christ their common head, they cannot but be united together in brotherly love, and mutually impart their blessings to each other.

Then it is of the highest importance for us to know what benefit thence redounds to us. For when we believe the Church, it is in order that we may be firmly persuaded that we are its members. In this way our salvation rests on a foundation so firm and sure, that though the whole fabric of the world were to give way, it could not be destroyed. First, it stands with the election of God, and cannot change or fail, any more than his eternal providence. Next, it is in a manner united with the stability of Christ, who will no more allow his faithful followers to be dissevered from him, than he would allow his own members to be torn to pieces. We may add that so long as we continue in the bosom of the Church, we are sure that the truth will remain with us.

Lastly, we feel that we have an interest in such promises as these, "In Mount Zion and in Jerusalem shall be deliverance" (Joel 2:32; Obad. 17). "God is in the midst of her, she shall not be moved" (Ps. 46:5). So available is communion with the Church to keep us in the fellowship of God. In the very term, communion, there is great consolation; because, while we are assured that every thing which God bestows on his members belongs to us, all the blessings conferred upon them confirm our hope.

But in order to embrace the unity of the Church in this manner, it is not necessary, as I have observed, to see it with our eyes, or feel it with our hands. Nay, rather from its being placed in faith, we are reminded that our thoughts are to dwell upon it, as much when it escapes our perception as when it openly appears. Nor is our faith the worse for apprehending what is unknown, since we are not enjoined here to distinguish between the elect and the reprobate (this belongs not to us, but to God only), but to feel firmly assured in our minds, that all those who, by the mercy of God the Father, through the efficacy of the Holy Spirit, have become partakers with Christ, are set apart as the proper and peculiar possession of God, and that as we are of the number, we are also partakers of this great grace.

Section 4: The visible church as mother of believers

But as it is now our purpose to discourse of the visible Church, let us learn, from her single title of Mother, how useful, nay, how necessary the knowledge of her is, since there is no other means of entering into life unless she conceive us in the womb and give us birth, unless she nourish us at her breasts, and, in short, keep us under her charge and government, until, divested of mortal flesh, we become like the angels (Matt. 22:30). For our weakness does not permit us to leave the school until we have spent our whole lives as scholars. Moreover, beyond the pale of the Church no forgiveness of sins, no salvation, can be hoped for, as Isaiah and Joel testify (Isa. 37:32; Joel 2:32). To their testimony Ezekiel subscribes, when he declares, "They shall not be in the assembly of my people, neither shall they be written in the writing of the house of Israel" (Ezek. 13:9); as, on the other hand, those who turn to the cultivation of true piety are said to inscribe their names among the citizens of Jerusalem. For which reason it is said in the psalm, "Remember me, O Lord, with the favor that thou bearest unto thy people: O visit me with thy salvation; that I may see the good of thy chosen, that I may rejoice in the gladness of thy nation, that I may glory with thine inheritance" (Ps. 106:4–6). By these words the paternal favor of God and the special evidence of spiritual life are confined to his peculiar people, and hence the abandonment of the Church is always fatal.

CHAPTER 5

The Monastic Tradition

Monastic practices predate Christianity. The legalization of Christianity in the fourth century prompted some Christians to flee from what they saw as the corrupting effects of society on the Church. Some of these became hermits and lived in caves, others wandered about begging, and still others formed small, self-sufficient communities (both male and female orders). Common to most forms of monastic life were the practices of prayer and asceticism, or depriving oneself of the comforts, distractions, and pursuits of this life in order to focus entirely on the next. Members of monastic communities ordered their lives around daily worship. Over time these communities became centers of Christian scholarship, disseminating Christian literature and liturgy.

Developments within Christian monasticism often have paralleled events in the history of the Church, and Church reform and reformers have often arisen from the cloistered ranks of monks. The writings in this chapter are entirely from the pens of Monastics and include a story about the life of a famous monk (Anthony), advice from a monk (Jerome) on raising a Christian daughter, two "rules" for monastic community life (those of Augustine and Benedict), a set of spiritual exercises (Ignatius), and a spiritual vision recorded by Teresa of Avila, who founded monastic houses for women.

ATHANASIUS: *LIFE OF ST. ANTHONY* (EXCERPT)
Greek, Fourth Century

Known as the father of Christian monasticism, Anthony of Egypt (A.D. c. 251–356) renounced all his earthly possessions as a young man and moved to the desert, where he lived in solitude. Anthony's extreme self-denial (motivated by his desire to free himself of fleshly desires) reportedly led to Satanic attacks, described by Athanasius and depicted in Christian art in terms of bizarre apparitions and intense spiritual agitation, and through which Anthony remained steadfast. By 305 Anthony had left the desert in order to found a monastic community, and was among the first to develop guidelines for cenobitic life (monastic life in community). During the Arian controversy, Anthony lent his considerable influence and support to Athanasius and the orthodox cause. Athanasius (295–373), the great Eastern Church bishop and champion of orthodoxy learned about the life of Anthony through his acquaintance with monastic founder Pachomius. His biography of Anthony—an excerpt of which is reprinted here—was one of the most read and loved works from late antiquity throughout the Middle Ages.

✦

The life and conversation of our holy Father, Anthony, written and sent to the monks in foreign parts by our Father among the Saints, Athanasius, Bishop of Alexandria. Athanasius, bishop to the brethren in foreign parts:

You have entered upon a noble rivalry with the monks of Egypt by your determination either to equal or surpass them in your training in the way of virtue. For by this time there are monasteries among you, and the name of monk receives public recognition. With reason, therefore, all men will approve this determination, and in answer to your prayers God will give its fulfillment. Now since you asked me to give you an account of the blessed Anthony's way of life, and are wishful to learn how he began the discipline, who and what manner of man he was previous to this, how he closed his life, and whether the things told of him are true, that you also may bring yourselves to imitate him, I very readily accepted your behest, for to me also the bare recollection of Anthony is a great accession of help. And I know that you, when you have heard, apart from your admiration of the man, will be wishful to emulate his determination; seeing that for monks the life of Anthony is a sufficient pattern of discipline. Wherefore do not refuse credence to what you have heard from those who brought tidings of him; but think rather that they have told you only a few things, for at all events they scarcely can have given circumstances of so great import in any detail. And because I at your request have called to mind a few circumstances about him, and shall send as much as I can tell in a letter, do not neglect to question those who sail from here: for possibly when all have told their tale, the account will hardly be in proportion to his merits. On account of this I was desirous, when I received your letter, to send for certain of the monks, those especially who were wont to be more frequently with him, that if I could learn any fresh details I might send them to you. But since the season for sailing was coming to an end and the letter carrier urgent, I have decided to write to your piety what I myself know, having seen him many times, and what I was able to learn from him, for I was his attendant for a long time, and poured water on his hands; in all points being mindful of the truth, that no one should disbelieve through hearing too much, nor on the other hand by hearing too little should despise the man.

1. Anthony you must know was by descent an Egyptian: his parents were of good family and possessed considerable wealth, and as they were Christians he also was reared in the same Faith. In infancy he was brought up with his parents, knowing nothing else but them and his home. But when he was grown and arrived at boyhood, and was advancing in years, he could not endure to learn letters, not caring to associate with other boys; but all his desire was, as it is written of Jacob, to live a plain man at home. With his parents he used to attend the Lord's House, and neither as a child was he idle nor when older did he despise them; but was both obedient to his father and mother and attentive to what was read, keeping in his heart what was profitable in what he heard. And though as a child brought up in moderate affluence, he did not trouble his parents for varied or luxurious fare, nor was this a source of pleasure to him; but was content simply with what he found nor sought anything further.

2. After the death of his father and mother he was left alone with one little sister: his age was about eighteen or twenty, and on him the care both of home and sister rested. Now it was not six months after the death of his parents, and going according to custom into the Lord's House, he communed with himself and reflected as he walked how the Apostles left all and followed the Savior; and how they in the Acts sold their possessions and brought and laid them at the Apostles' feet for distribution to the needy, and what and how great a hope was laid up for them in heaven. Pondering over these things he entered the church, and it happened the Gospel was being read, and he heard the Lord saying to the rich man, "If you would be perfect, go and sell that you have and give to the poor; and come follow Me and you shall have treasure in heaven." Anthony, as though God had put him in mind of the Saints, and the passage had been read on his account, went out immediately from the church, and gave the possessions of his forefathers to the villagers—they were three hundred acres, productive and very fair—that they should be no more a clog upon himself and his sister. And all the rest that was movable he sold, and having got together much money he gave it to the poor, reserving a little however for his sister's sake.

3. And again as he went into the church, hearing

the Lord say in the Gospel, "be not anxious for the morrow," he could stay no longer, but went out and gave those things also to the poor. Having committed his sister to known and faithful virgins, and put her into a convent to be brought up, he henceforth devoted himself outside his house to discipline, taking heed to himself and training himself with patience. For there were not so many monasteries in Egypt, and no monk at all knew of the distant desert; but all who wished to give heed to themselves practiced the discipline in solitude near their own village. Now there was then in the next village an old man who had lived the life of a hermit from his youth up. Anthony, after he had seen this man, imitated him in piety. And at first he began to abide in places outside the village. Then if he heard of a good man anywhere, like a prudent bee he went forth and sought him nor turned back to his own place until he had seen him. And once he returned, he received from the good man "supplies for his journey," as it were, in the way of virtue. So dwelling there at first, he confirmed his purpose not to return to the abode of his fathers nor to the remembrance of his kinsfolk, but to keep all his desire and energy for perfecting his discipline. He worked, however, with his hands, having heard, "he who is idle let him not eat," and part he spent on bread and part he gave to the needy. And he was constant in prayer, knowing that a man ought to pray in secret unceasingly. For he had given such heed to what was read that none of the things that were written fell from him to the ground, but he remembered all, and afterward his memory served him for books.

4. Thus conducting himself, Anthony was beloved by all. He subjected himself in sincerity to the good men whom he visited, and learned thoroughly where each surpassed him in zeal and discipline. He observed the graciousness of one; the unceasing prayer of another; he took knowledge of another's freedom from anger and another's loving-kindness; he gave heed to one as he watched, to another as he studied; one he admired for his endurance, another

for his fasting and sleeping on the ground; the meekness of one and the long-suffering of another he watched with care, while he took note of the piety toward Christ and the mutual love which animated all. Thus filled, he returned to his own place of discipline, and henceforth would strive to unite the qualities of each, and was eager to show in himself the virtues of all. With others of the same age he had no rivalry; save this only, that he should not be second to them in higher things. And this he did so as to hurt the feelings of nobody, but made them rejoice over him. So all they of that village and the good men in whose intimacy he was, when they saw that he was a man of this sort, used to call him God-beloved. And some welcomed him as a son, others as a brother.

5. But the devil, who hates and envies what is good, could not endure to see such a resolution in a youth, but endeavored to carry out against him what he had been wont to effect against others. First of all he tried to lead him away from the discipline, whispering to him the remembrance of his wealth, care for his sister, claims of kindred, love of money, love of glory, the various pleasures of the table and the other relaxations of life, and at last the difficulty of virtue and the labor of it; he suggested also the infirmity of the body and the length of the time. In a word he raised in his mind a great dust of debate, wishing to debar him from his settled purpose. But when the enemy saw himself to be too weak for Anthony's determination, and that he rather was conquered by the other's firmness, overthrown by his great faith and falling through his constant prayers, then at length putting his trust in the weapons which are "in the navel of his belly" and boasting in them— for they are his first snare for the young—he attacked the young man, disturbing him by night and harassing him by day, so that even the onlookers saw the struggle which was going on between them. The one would suggest foul thoughts and the other counter them with prayers: the one fire him with lush the other, as one who seemed to blush, fortify his body with

faith, prayers, and fasting. And the devil one night even took on the shape of a woman and imitated all her acts simply to beguile Anthony. But he, his mind filled with Christ and the nobility inspired by Him, and considering the spirituality of the soul, quenched the coal of the other's deceit. Again the enemy suggested the ease of pleasure. But he like a man filled with rage and grief turned his thoughts to the threatened fire and the gnawing worm, and setting these in array against his adversary, passed through the temptation unscathed. All this was a source of shame to his foe. For he, deeming himself like God, was now mocked by a young man; and he who boasted himself against flesh and blood was being put to flight by a man in the flesh. For the Lord was working with Anthony—the Lord who for our sake took flesh and gave the body victory over the devil, so that all who truly fight can say, "not I but the grace of God which was with me."

6. At last when the dragon could not even thus overthrow Anthony, but saw himself thrust out of his heart, gnashing his teeth as it is written, and as it were beside himself, he appeared to Anthony like a boy, taking a visible shape in accordance with his mind. And cringing to him, as it were, he plied him with thoughts no longer, for guileful as he was, he had been worsted, but at last spoke in human voice and said, "Many I deceived, many I cast down; but now attacking you and your labors as I had many others, I proved weak." When Anthony asked, "Who are you who speaks thus with me?" He answered with a lamentable voice, "I am the friend of whoredom, and have taken upon me incitements which lead to it against the young. I am called the spirit of lust. How many have I deceived who wished to live soberly, how many are those who, by my incitements, I have persuaded! I am he of whom also the prophet reproves those who have fallen, saying, 'You have been caused to err by the spirit of whoredom.' For by me they have been tripped up. I am he who has so often troubled you and have so often been overthrown by you." But Anthony having given thanks to the Lord, with good courage said to him, "You are very despicable then, for you are weak as a child. Henceforth I shall have no trouble from you, 'for the Lord is my helper, and I shall look down on mine enemies.'" Having heard this, the enemy straightway fled, shuddering at the words and dreading any longer even to come near the man.

7. This was Anthony's first struggle against the devil, or rather this victory was the Savior's work in Anthony, "Who condemned sin in the flesh that the ordinance of the law might be fulfilled in us who walk not after the flesh but after the spirit." But neither did Anthony, although the evil one had fallen, henceforth relax his care and despise him; nor did the enemy as though conquered tease to lay snares for him. For again he went round as a lion seeking some occasion against him. But Anthony having learned from the Scriptures that the devices of the devil are many, zealously continued the discipline, reckoning that though the devil had not been able to deceive his heart by bodily pleasure, he would endeavor to ensnare him by other means. For the demon loves sin. Wherefore more and more he repressed the body and kept it in subjection, lest haply having conquered on one side, he should be dragged down on the other. He therefore planned to accustom himself to a severer mode of life. And many marveled, but he himself used to bear the labor easily; for the eagerness of soul, through the length of time it had abode in him, had wrought a good habit in him, so that taking but little initiation from others he showed great zeal in this matter. He kept vigil to such an extent that he often continued the whole night without sleep; and this not once but often, to the marvel of others. He ate once a day, after sunset, sometimes once in two days, and often even in four. His food was bread and salt, his drink, water only. Of flesh and wine it is superfluous even to speak, since no such thing was found with the other earnest men. A rush mat served him to sleep upon, but for the most part he lay upon the bare ground. He would not anoint himself with oil, saying it is necessary

for young men to be earnest in training and not to seek what would enervate the body; but they must accustom it to labor, mindful of the Apostle's words, "when I am weak, then am I strong." "For," said he, "the fiber of the soul is then sound when the pleasures of the body are diminished." And he had come to this truly wonderful conclusion, "that progress in virtue, and retirement from the world for the sake of it, ought not to be measured by time, but by desire and fixity of purpose." He at least gave no thought to the past, but day by day, as if he were at the beginning of his discipline, applied greater parts for advancement, often repeating to himself the saying of Paul, "Forgetting the things which are behind and stretching forward to the things which are before." He was also mindful of the words spoken by the prophet Elias, "the Lord lives before whose presence I stand today." For he observed that in saying "today" the prophet did not compute the time that had gone by: but daily as though ever commencing he eagerly endeavored to make himself fit to appear before God, being pure in heart and ever ready to submit to His counsel, and to Him alone. And he used to say to himself that from the life of the great Isaiah the hermit ought to see his own as in a mirror.

8. Thus tightening his hold upon himself, Anthony repaired to the tombs, which happened to be at a distance from the village; and having bid one of his acquaintances to bring him bread at intervals of many days, he entered one of the tombs, and the other having shut the door on him, he remained within alone. And when the enemy could not endure it, but was even fearful that in a short time Anthony would fill the desert with the discipline, coming one night with a multitude of demons, he so cut him with stripes that he lay on the ground speechless from the excessive pain. For he affirmed that the torture had been so excessive that no blows inflicted by man could ever have caused him such torment. But by the Providence of God—for the Lord never overlooks them that hope in Him—the next day his acquaintance came bringing him the loaves. And having opened the door and seeing him lying on the ground as though dead, he lifted him up and carried him to the church in the village, and laid him upon the ground. And many of his kinsfolk and the villagers sat around Anthony as round a corpse. But about midnight he came to himself and arose, and when be saw them all asleep and his comrade alone watching, he motioned with his head for him to approach, and asked him to carry him again to the tombs without waking anybody.

9. He was carried therefore by the man, and as he was wont, when the door was shut he was within alone. And he could not stand up on account of the blows, but he prayed as he lay. And after he had prayed, he said with a shout, "Here am I, Anthony; I flee not from your stripes, for even if you inflict more nothing shall separate rues from the love of Christ." And then he sang, "though a camp be set against me, my heart shall not be afraid." These were the thoughts and words of this ascetic. But the enemy, who hates good, marveling that after the blows he dared to return, called together his hounds and burst forth, "You see," said he, "that neither by the spirit of lust nor by blows did we stay the man, but that he braves us, let us attack him in another fashion." But changes of form for evil are easy for the devil, so in the night they made such a din that the whole of that place seemed to be shaken by an earthquake, and the demons as if breaking the four walls of the dwelling seemed to enter through them, coming in the likeness of beasts and creeping things. And the place was on a sudden filled with the forms of lions, bears, leopards, bulls, serpents, asps, scorpions, and wolves, and each of them was moving according to his nature. The lion was roaring, wishing to attack, the bull seeming to toss with its horns, the serpent writhing but unable to approach, and the wolf as it rushed on was restrained; altogether the noises of the apparitions, with their angry raging, were dreadful. But Anthony, stricken and goaded by them, felt bodily pains severer still. He lay watching, however, with unshaken soul, groaning from bodily anguish;

but his mind was clear, and as in mockery he said, "If there had been any power in you, it would have sufficed had one of you come, but since the Lord has made you weak you attempt to terrify me by numbers: and a proof of your weakness is that you take the shapes of brute beasts." And again with boldness he said, "If you are able, and have received power against me, delay not to attack; but if you are unable, why trouble me in vain? For faith in our Lord is a seal and a wall of safety to us." So after many attempts they gnashed their teeth upon him, because they were mocking themselves rather than him.

10. Nor was the Lord then forgetful of Anthony's wrestling, but was at hand to help him. So looking up he saw the roof as it were opened, and a ray of light descending to him. The demons suddenly vanished, the pain of his body straightway ceased, and the building was again whole. But Anthony feeling the help, and getting his breath again, and being freed from pain, besought the vision which had appeared to him, saying, "Where were you? Why did you not appear at the beginning to make my pains to cease?" And a voice came to him, "Anthony, I was here, but I waited to see your fight; wherefore since you have endured, and have not been worsted, I will ever be a succor to you, and will make your name known everywhere." Having heard this, Anthony arose and prayed, and received such strength that he perceived that he had more power in his body than formerly. And he was then about thirty-five years old.

JEROME: "ON RAISING A CHRISTIAN DAUGHTER" (LETTER TO LAETA)
Latin, Early Fifth Century

Among the most distinguished of the Latin Church Fathers was Jerome (c. 347–420), a leader in the (cenobite) monastic movement and translator of the *Vulgate*, the most widely received Latin translation of the Bible. This letter of Jerome is dated Anno Domini (in the year of the Lord)

403. It is addressed to Laeta, the mother of an infant girl, Paula, who has been named in honor of her grandmother, the founder of a convent of nuns at Bethlehem. Laeta had earlier written from Rome to ask for Jerome's advice on raising little Paula as "a virgin consecrated to Christ." In his response, Jerome instructs Laeta in great detail as to the child's training and education. Feeling some doubt, however, as to the possibility of raising a godly child in so worldly a city as Rome, Jerome recommends that Laeta send Paula to Bethlehem where she can be under the watchful eye of her grandmother and aunt, the elder Paula and Eustochium. Laeta later took Jerome's advice and sent the child to Bethlehem where little Paula eventually succeeded Eustochium as head of the nunnery founded by her grandmother.

> ### Questions for Guided Reading
> 1. What does Jerome conclude about growth in Christian maturity?
> 2. What military symbols depict the triumph of Christianity over Roman paganism?
> 3. How were monastic ideals and teaching techniques to assist in the education of a Christian child?
> 4. What role was Christian modeling to play in little Paula's education?

✦

The apostle Paul in his letter to the Corinthians—an immature church in Christ—has, in his teaching on holy discipline, commanded that "A woman who has an unbelieving husband, and who wishes to remain with her, should not leave him. For the unbelieving husband is sanctified by the believing wife, and the unbelieving wife is sanctified by the believing husband; otherwise, your children would be unclean but now are they holy" (1 Cor. 7:13–14). Now, whoever believes that up until now discipline has been slack, or that the Apostle's command permits too much freedom, then he or she ought to consider the household of your father—a man of the highest distinction and learning, but one still walking in darkness; then he or she will understand that Paul's advice is like good fruit growing out of a bitter root, or even precious spice sprung from weeds. You yourself,

Laeta, are the offspring of a mixed marriage; yet you and my friend Toxotius—Paula's faithful parents—are both Christian.

After all, who would ever have believed that to that corrupt bishop, Albinus, could be born (in answer to a mother's vows) a Christian granddaughter? And that her delighted grandfather might hear from the little one's faltering lips Christ's Alleluia? And that, after waiting for so many years, he would have the opportunity to see for himself one of God's own virgins? Our expectations have been fully gratified. The one unbeliever is sanctified by his holy and believing family. For, when a man is surrounded by a believing crowd of children and grandchildren, he is as good as a candidate for the faith. For myself, I believe that, if only Albinus had had as many Christian relatives when he was a younger man, then he himself might have been brought to faith in Christ. For though he may spit upon my letter and laugh at it, and though he may call me a fool or a madman, his son-in-law did the same before he came to believe! Christians are not born but made.

In spite of all its fine gold trimming, the Capitol is beginning to look dingy. Every temple in Rome is covered with soot and cobwebs. The city is stirred to its depths and the people rush past their half-ruined shrines to visit the tombs of the martyrs. Their "belief" has never yet matured into conviction, and it may yet disintegrate into mere shame.

I speak this way to you, Laeta my most devout daughter in Christ, to teach you first of all not to give up hope concerning your father's salvation. My hope is that the same faith which claims your daughter may have won your father as well, and I believe you may yet see blessings bestowed upon your entire family. You know the Lord's promise: "The things which are impossible with men are possible with God." It is never too late to change. The thief passed even from the cross to paradise. Nebuchadnezzar also, the king of Babylon, recovered his reason, even after he had been made like the beasts in body and in heart and had been compelled to live with the brutes in the wilderness. And didn't your own uncle Gracchus used to tell these old stories (which to unbelievers may well seem incredible)? As I recall, he himself was formerly a Prefect in Rome and the one who destroyed the Temple of Mithras and all the dreadful images in which so many worshipers were initiated into the cults of the Raven, the Bridegroom,

the Soldier, the Lion, the Perseus, the Sun, and Crab, and the Father? Didn't he destroy all these practices and claim for himself Christian baptism? Even in Rome itself paganism is being abandoned. Those who were once the exalted gods of the nations are now left to dwell under their lonely roofs with owls and pigeons. And the banners of the military are emblazoned with the sign of the Cross! The emperor's robes of purple and his crown sparkling with jewels are ornamented with representations of the shameful yet saving cross of Christ. Already the Serapis[1] has been removed and replace with the Christian insignia, and at Gaza, the pagan priest Marnas mourns in confinement and every moment expects to see his temple overturned. From India, from Persia, and from Ethiopia we daily welcome monks in crowds. The Armenian bowman has laid aside his quiver, the Huns learn the Psalter, the chilly Scythians are warmed with the glow of the faith. The Getae, ruddy and yellow-haired, carry tent-churches about with their armies: and perhaps their success in fighting against us may be due to the fact that they believe in the same religion.

Yes, I digress; and so while "spinning my pottery wheel," my hands have been molding a pitcher instead of making a flask as I intended. For, in answer to your prayers and those of the saintly Marcella, I wish to address you as a mother and to instruct you how to bring up our dear Paula, who has been consecrated to Christ before her birth and vowed to His service before her conception. Thus in our own day we have seen repeated the story told us in the Prophets, of Hannah, who though at first barren afterward became fruitful. You have exchanged a fertility bound up with sorrow for offspring which shall never die. For I am confident that having given to the Lord your first-born you will be the mother of sons. It is the first-born that is offered under the Law. Samuel and Samson are both instances of this, as is also John the Baptist who, when Mary came in, leaped for joy. For he heard the Lord speaking by the mouth of the Virgin and desired to break from his mother's womb to meet him. As then, too, since Paula has been born in answer to a promise, her parents should give her a training suitable to her birth. Samuel, as you know, was nurtured in the Temple, and John was trained in the wilderness. The first as a Nazarite wore his hair long,

---

1. Egyptian god of the underworld.

drank neither wine nor strong drink, and even in his childhood talked with God. The second shunned cities, wore a leather girdle, and had for his meat locusts and wild honey. Moreover, to signify that repentance which he was to preach, he was clothed in the spoils of the hump-backed camel. Thus must a soul be educated which is to be a temple of God. It must learn to hear nothing and to say nothing but what belongs to the fear of God. It must have no understanding of unclean words, and no knowledge of the world's songs. Its tongue must be steeped while still tender in the sweetness of the psalms. Boys with their lustful thoughts must be kept away from Paula: even her maids and female attendants must be separated from worldly associates. For if they have learned a little mischief, they may teach even more!

Buy for Paula a set of letters made of boxwood or of ivory and teach her the proper names of each one. Let her play with these, so that even her play may teach her something. And not only make her grasp the right order of the letters and see that she forms their names into a rhyme, but constantly test her by disarranging their order, placing the last letters in the middle and the middle ones at the beginning and so on, so that she can learn them all by sight as well as by sound. Moreover, so soon as she is able to work with the stylus and wax tablet, though her hands will be shaky for a while, guide her weak fingers by holding her hand in yours. You should also cut a few simple letters upon the tablet as a guide for her to trace—whatever keeps her from straying outside the lines. Offer prizes for good spelling and motivate her with little gifts such as children of her age delight in. And let her learn alongside another child—one who can serve as a suitable model and who will encourage a bit of competition whenever Paula sees the praise she receives. However, you must not scold Paula if she is slow to learn, rather, give her praise often and encourage any progress. In this way she may become self-motivated—being glad when she does better than others and inwardly regretting when they do better than she.

Above all, take care keep her lessons from becoming like drudgery, because a dislike for learning in childhood may continue into adulthood. Let her very first words, those which she tries bit by bit to put together and to pronounce—not be merely random. Rather, read often in her hearing the list of names found in the Gospels of the prophets and patriarchs, from Adam on-

ward. In this way while her tongue will be well-trained, her memory will be likewise developed.

Again, you must choose for her a master of approved years, life, and learning. A man of culture will not, I think, blush to do for a kinswoman or a highborn virgin what Aristotle did for King Philip's son when, descending to the level of an caretaker, he agreed to teach him his letters. Things must not be despised as of small account in the absence of which great results cannot be achieved. The very rudiments and first beginnings of knowledge sound differently in the mouth of an educated man and of an uneducated. Accordingly you must see that the child is not led away by the silly coaxing of women to form a habit of shortening long words or of decking herself with gold and purple. Of these habits one will spoil her conversation and the other her character. She must not therefore learn as a child what afterward she will have to unlearn. The eloquence of the Gracchi is said to have been largely due to the way in which from their earliest years their mother spoke to them. Hortensius became an orator while still on his father's lap. Early impressions are hard to erase from the mind, and once wool has been dyed purple who can restore it to its previous whiteness? Also, an unused jar keeps the taste and smell of that which fills it long after it has been emptied. The history of Greece teaches us that Alexander the Great, emperor of the entire world, was not able to outgrow the crude habits of speech and mannerisms which he picked up from his childhood tutor, Leonides. It seems that a child is always ready to imitate what is evil; and faults are quickly copied when there is no virtue to imitate.

Paula's nursemaid must be self-disciplined, neither wild nor given to gossip. Her tutor must be of excellent reputation, and her advisor of a serious manner. When she sees her grandfather she ought to embrace him and, whether he likes it or not, sing Alleluia in his ears. She ought also to show much affection to her grandmother and to smile sweetly to everyone, endearing herself to the family that they might rejoice in the possession of such a rosebud. Paula must come to realize what army she is enrolled in as a recruit, and what Captain it is under whose banner she is called to serve. Let her manner of dressing and behaving remind her to Whom she is pledged. Never pierce the ears or make up the face of a daughter consecrated to Christ! Do not hang gold or pearls about her neck or load her head with jewels, or by reddening her hair make it suggest the fires of hell! Let her pearls be of a spiritual sort, the kind she may sell in order to purchase the "pearl of great price."

Formerly, there was an aristocratic lady by the name of Praetextata who, against her mother's advice and at the request of her husband exchanged her proper dress and styled her neglected hair in a fashionable and worldly manner, hoping to rid herself of the appearance and reputation of a virgin of Christ. Soon a scowling angel appeared to her in a dream and, with threatening words, asked her: Have you willingly placed your husband's commands before those of Christ? Do you willingly placed sacrilegious hands upon the head of one who is God's virgin? Those very hands shall therefore wither, so that you may know by torment what you have done, and at the end of five months you shall be carried off to hell! Moreover, if you continue your wickedness, you shall lose both your husband your children." Now, all this came to pass as predicted, her premature death proving that she had delayed repentance for too long a time. So terribly does Christ punish those who violate His temple, and so jealously does he defend His precious jewels. I have related this story here not to gloat over tragic misfortunes, but to warn you that you must with much fear and carefulness keep the vow which you have made to God. We read of Eli the priest that he became displeasing to God on account of the sins of his children; and we are told that a man may not be made a bishop if his sons are loose and disorderly. On the other hand it is written of the woman that "she shall be saved in childbearing, if she continues in faith and charity and holiness with chastity" (1 Tim. 2:15). If then parents are responsible for their children even after they are grown and out of the home, how much more ought they to be responsible for them while still unweaned and weak, before they are able to discern between their right hand and their left: when, that is to say, they cannot yet distinguish good from evil? If you take precautions to save your daughter from the bite of a snake, why are you not equally careful to shield her from "the hammer of the whole earth" (Jer. 50:23)? to prevent her from drinking of the golden cup of Babylon? to keep her from going out with Dinah to see the daughters of a strange land? to save her from the tripping dance and from the trailing robe? No one administers drugs till be has rubbed the rim of the cup with honey! And, in order to deceive us, sin masquerades as virtue! Why, then, you may ask,

is it written that "the son shall not be punished for the sins of the father, neither shall the father be punished for the sins of the son," but "the soul that sins shall die" (Ezek. 18:4, 20)? My answer is that this passage refers to those who have reached the age of discretion, like the man described in the Gospel whose parents said, "He is of age . . . he shall speak for himself" (John 9:21). As long as the son is a child and thinks as a child and until he comes to years of discretion to choose between the two roads (to which the letter of Pythagoras points), his parents are responsible for his actions whether these be good or bad. But perhaps you think that, if they are not baptized, the children of Christians are responsible for their own sins; and that no guilt will be charged to parents who withhold baptism from their children— though these are too young even to request it. The truth is that, just as baptism ensures the salvation of the child, this in turn brings advantage to the parents. Whether one offers his firstborn on the "altar of sacrifice" or not is a matter of free choice. But now that you, Laeta, have offered up Paula, to neglect her would indeed prove disastrous for you. And, of course, you dedicated your little one even before she was conceived! Just remember, whoever offers a blemished sacrifice to God is guilty of sacrilege. How much more then shall she be punished who, though she offers a stainless soul on her own behalf, neglects her child?

When Paula comes to be a little older and begins to increase like her Spouse in wisdom and stature and in favor with God and man, let her go with her parents to the temple of her true Father but let her not come out of the temple with them. Let them seek her upon the world's highway amid the crowds and the throng of their kinsfolk, and let them find her nowhere but in the shrine of the scriptures, questioning the prophets and the apostles on the meaning of that spiritual marriage to which she is vowed. Let her imitate the retirement of Mary whom Gabriel found alone in her chamber and who was frightened, it would appear, by seeing a man there. Let the child emulate her of whom it is written that "the king's daughter is all glorious within" (Ps. 45:13). Wounded with love's arrow let her say to her beloved, "the king has brought me into his chambers" (Song 1:4). At no time let her wander off, lest the watchers of the city discover her, wound her, and remove the veil of her virginity. Rather, if anyone should knock at her door let her respond: "I have washed my feet, must I soil them again?" (Song 5:3). Let her not regularly dine with others, that is, at her parents' table, lest she see too many rich and savory dishes which may lead to gluttony. There are those, I realize, who think it wise to subject themselves to temptation in order to build up their resistance; but is it not better to avoid even the sight of a temptation? When I was a school boy I once heard it said that, "Whatever you allow to become a habit will soon tell on you." Let Paula learn even now not to care much for wine "wherein is excess." Even so, since ascetic practices are not healthy for young children, let her enjoy warm baths from time to time, and allow her to take a little wine for her stomach's sake. Allow her also to eat some meat, lest her feet grow weak even before they begin to run their course. But I emphasize these things by way of caution, and not as a command; we want neither to weaken Paula nor to teach her self-indulgence. After all, why shouldn't a Christian virgin do completely what others do half way?

The Jews, for example, refuse certain animals and products as articles of food, while among the Indians the Brahmans and among the Egyptians the Gymnosophists subsist altogether on porridge, rice, and apples. If mere glass repays so much labor, must not a pearl be worth more labor still? Paula has been born in response to a vow. Let her life be as the lives of those (Samuel, John the Baptist, etc.) who were born under the same conditions. If the grace given is the same in all their lives, the care taken ought to be so too. Let Paula be deaf to the sound of the organ, and not know even the uses of the pipe, the lyre, and the cithern. Let her daily work be to bring you blossoms which she has gathered from Scripture. Let her learn by heart many verses in the Greek, but let her be instructed also in Latin. For if tender lips are not trained in this early, the tongue is spoiled by foreign accents and its native speech debased by alien elements.

You must yourself be her mistress, a model on which she may form her childish conduct. Never in your own behavior nor her father's allow her to see something she cannot imitate without sinning. Remember both of you that you are the parents of a consecrated virgin, and that your example will teach her more than your commandments. Flowers are quick to fade and an ill wind soon withers the violet, the lily, and the crocus. Let her never appear in public unless accompanied by you. Let her never visit a church or a martyr's shrine unless with her mother. Let no young man greet her with smiles and no fancy boy with curled hair pay her compliments. If our little virgin goes to keep solemn eves and all-night vigils, fine, but she must never once stray from her mother's side. Neither should she favor one of her maids in order to become close friends or confidants with her. Let her rather choose for a friend not a lovely and well-dressed girl with a beautiful voice, but a serious one, pale and somber in her manner and dress. But let her take as her model some aged virgin of approved faith, character, and virginity, able to instruct her by word and by example.

Paula should rise at night to recite prayers and psalms; to sing hymns in the morning; at the third, sixth, and ninth hours to take her place in the line to do battle for Christ; and, lastly, in lighting her lamp to offer her evening sacrifice. In these occupations let her pass the day, and when night comes let it find her still engaged in them. With her, reading should follow prayer and then more prayer should follow reading. Time will seem to pass quickly when used in so many different ways.

Let her also learn how to spin wool, to hold the distaff, to put the basket in her lap, to turn the spinning wheel and to shape the yarn with her thumb. Teach her to shun silken fabrics, Chinese fleeces, and gold brocades; the clothing which she makes for herself should keep out the cold and not expose the body which it is supposed to cover. Let her food be herbs and wheaten bread with an occasional small fish or two. And, so that I may not spend more time on dietary regulations (a subject on which I have written more elsewhere), let her leave the table a little hungry—ready at a moment's notice to begin the reading or chanting. I strongly disapprove—especially for those of tender years—of long fasts in which week is added to week and during which even oil and apples are forbidden as food. I have learned by experience that "the hardest working mules head for the barn as soon as they grow tired." In the same way, our fasting may lead later on to stuffing ourselves—just like that of the worshippers of Isis and of Cybele who gobble up pheasants and turtle-doves piping hot in order to prepare themselves for the fast of Ceres. Those who fast regularly must pace themselves, lest after starting well they wear out half way through the journey.

However during the season of Lent, as I have written before now, those who practice self-denial should do their utmost, even as the charioteer tightens the reins and increases the speed of his horses. Still, there is one rule for those who live in the world and another for virgins and monks. The typical layman during Lent does injury to his stomach, and living like a snail on his own juices thinks only of the rich foods and feasting which follow lent. But with the virgin and the monk the case is different; after all, for them the journey continues even after the season of Lent has passed. A strict fast, if brief, is good, but longer fasts ought to be more moderate since after the former we may catch our breath but during the latter we have to continue on without a break.

Now, when you take short trips into the countryside, do not leave Paula behind. Leave her no power or capacity of living without you, and let her feel frightened when she is left to herself. Let her not converse with people of the world or associate with virgins indifferent to their vows. Let her not be present at the weddings of your slaves and let her take no part in the noisy games of the household. . . .

Let Paula's treasures be not silks or gems but manuscripts of the holy Scriptures; and in these let her think little of gold-edged pages, and Babylonian parchment, and arabesque patterns, and more of correctness and accurate punctuation. Let her begin by learning the psalms, and then let her gather rules of life out of the proverbs of Solomon. From Ecclesiastes let her gain the habit of despising the world and its vanities. Let her follow the example set in Job of virtue and of patience. Then let her pass on to the gospels and never entirely stop reading them once she has begun. Let her also drink in with a willing heart the Acts of the Apostles and the Epistles. As soon as she has enriched the storehouse of her mind with these treasures, let her commit to memory the prophets, the books of Moses, the Kings and of Chronicles, and also the rolls of Ezra and Esther. When she has done all these she may safely read the Song of Songs but not before: for, were she to read it at the beginning, she would fail to understand that, though it is written in fleshly words, it is a marriage song of a spiritual bride. And not understanding this she would suffer hurt from it. Let her generally avoid all apocryphal writings; yet, if she should begin to study these works, it ought to be on account of the wonderful miracles they describe and not the doctrines they teach. She must understand that those documents were not really written by the authors to whom they are attributed, that many errors have been introduced into them, and

that it requires great skill and patience to find the gold in the mud. She should always have Cyprian's writings in her hands. The letters of Athanasius and the treatises of Hilary she may go through without fear of stumbling. Let her take pleasure in the works and wits of any book which does not neglect the faith. But if she takes up any works other than those named here, she should read in order to judge them and not to live by them.

Now, Laeta, you may well ask, "How can I, a woman of the world, living at Rome, surrounded by a crowd, be able to keep all your suggestions?" If indeed you feel that way then by all means avoid a burden you think yourself unable to bear. What I mean is this: When you have weaned Paula as Isaac was weaned, and when you have clothed her as Samuel was clothed, then send her to Bethlehem to her grandmother and aunt; give up this most precious of gems, to be placed in Mary's chamber and to rest in the cradle where the infant Jesus cried. Let her be brought up in the monastery, let her be one among many virgins, let her learn to avoid swearing, let her regard lying as sacrilege, let her be ignorant of the world, let her live the angelic life, while in the flesh let her be without the flesh, and let her suppose that all human beings are like herself. To say nothing of the many other advantages, this choice will free you from the difficult task of minding her, and from the responsibility of guardianship. It is better to miss her once she is gone than to spend all your time fretting over her. After all, you cannot help but tremble as you watch what she says and to whom she says it, to whom she bows and whom she likes best to see. Hand her over to Eustochium while she is still but an infant and her every cry is a prayer for you. Paula will become Eustochium's companion in holiness now as well as her successor later. Let her gaze upon and love, let her "from her earliest years admire" one whose language and mannerisms and dress are an education in virtue. Let her also sit in the lap of her grandmother, and let this latter repeat to her granddaughter the lessons that she once bestowed upon her own child. Long experience has shown the elder Paula how to raise, preserve, and to instruct virgins; and daily woven into her crown is the mystic century which betokens the highest chastity. O happy virgin! happy Paula, daughter of Toxotius, who through the virtues of her grandmother and aunt is nobler in holiness than she is in lineage!

Yes, Laeta, were it possible for you with your own eyes

to see your mother-in-law and your sister, and to realize the mighty souls which enliven their small bodies, your own love of purity would lead you—even before your daughter—to free yourself from God's first decree of the law and to put yourself under His second dispensation of the Gospel. You would then lose your desire for other children and would offer up yourself to the service of God. But because "there is a time to embrace, and a time to refrain from embracing" (Eccl. 3:5), and because "the wife hath not power of her own body" (1 Cor. 7:4), and because the apostle says "Let every man abide in the same calling wherein he was called" in the Lord, and because he that is under the yoke ought so to run as not to leave his companion behind, I counsel you to pay back to the full in your offspring what meantime you defer paying in your own person. When Hannah had once offered in the tabernacle the son whom she had vowed to God she never took him back; for she thought it unbecoming that one who was to be a prophet should grow up in the same house with her who still desired to have other children. Accordingly after she had conceived him and given him birth, she did not venture to come to the temple alone or to appear before the Lord empty, but first paid to Him what she owed; and then, when she had offered up that great sacrifice, she returned home and because she had borne her firstborn for God, she was given five children for herself. Do you marvel at the happiness of that holy woman? Imitate her faith. Moreover, if you will only send Paula, I promise to be myself both a tutor and a foster father to her. Old as I am I will carry her on my shoulders and train her stammering lips; and my charge will be a far grander one than that of the worldly philosopher; for while he only taught a King of Macedon who was one day to die of Babylonian poison, I shall instruct the handmaid and bride of Christ who must one day be offered to her Lord in heaven.

AUGUSTINE: *RULE* (FOR MONASTIC LIFE)
Latin, A.D. 400

See page 71 for a biographical introduction of Augustine.
   Augustine's *Rule*, reprinted in its entirety here, is one of the earliest guides for monastic life.

Chapter I: Purpose and basis of common life

Before all else, dear brothers, love God and then your neighbor, because these are the chief commandments given to us.

1. The following are the precepts we order you living in the monastery to observe.
2. The main purpose for you having come together is to live harmoniously in your house, intent upon God in oneness of mind and heart.
3. Call nothing your own, but let everything be yours in common. Food and clothing shall be distributed to each of you by your superior, not equally to all, for all do not enjoy equal health, but rather according to each one's need. For so you read in the Acts of the Apostles that "they had all things in common and distribution was made to each one according to each one's need" (Acts 4:32–35).
4. Those who owned something in the world should be careful in wanting to share it in common once they have entered the monastery.
5. But they who owned nothing should not look for those things in the monastery that they were unable to have in the world. Nevertheless, they are to be given all that their health requires even if, during their time in the world, poverty made it impossible for them to find the very necessities of life. And those should not consider themselves fortunate because they have found the kind of food and clothing which they were unable to find in the world.
6. And let them not hold their heads high, because they associate with people whom they did not dare to approach in the world, but let them rather lift up their hearts and not seek after what is vain and earthly. Otherwise, monasteries will come to serve a useful purpose for the rich and not the poor, if the rich are made humble there and the poor are puffed up with pride.
7. The rich, for their part, who seemed important in the world, must not look down upon their brothers who have come into this holy brotherhood from a condition of poverty. They should seek to glory in the fellowship of poor

brothers rather than in the reputation of rich relatives. They should neither be elated if they have contributed a part of their wealth to the common life, nor take more pride in sharing their riches with the monastery than if they were to enjoy them in the world. Indeed, every other kind of sin has to do with the commission of evil deeds, whereas pride lurks even in good works in order to destroy them. And what good is it to scatter one's wealth abroad by giving to the poor, even to become poor oneself, when the unhappy soul is thereby more given to pride in despising riches than it had been in possessing them?

8. Let all of you then live together in oneness of mind and heart, mutually honoring God in yourselves, whose temples you have become.

Chapter II: Prayer

1. "Be diligent in prayer" (Col. 4:2) at the hours and times appointed.

2. In the Oratory no one should do anything other than that for which was intended and from which it also takes its name. Consequently, if there are some who might wish to pray there during their free time, even outside the hours appointed, they should not be hindered by those who think something else must be done there.

3. When you pray to God in Psalms and hymns, think over in your hearts the words that come from your lips.

4. Chant only what is prescribed for chant; moreover, let nothing be chanted unless it is so prescribed.

Chapter III: Moderation and self-denial

1. Subdue the flesh, so far as your health permits, by fasting and abstinence from food and drink. However, when someone is unable to fast, he should still take no food outside mealtimes unless he is ill.

2. When you come to table, listen until you leave to what is the custom to read, without disturbance or strife. Let not your mouths alone take nourishment but let your hearts too hunger for the words of God.

3. If those in more delicate health from their former way of life are treated differently in the matter of food, this should not be a source of annoyance to the others or appear unjust in the eyes of those who owe their stronger health to different habits of life. Nor should the healthier brothers deem them more fortunate for having food which they do not have, but rather consider themselves fortunate for having the good health which the others do not enjoy.

4. And if something in the way of food, clothing, and bedding is given to those coming to the monastery from a more genteel way of life, which is not given to those who are stronger, and therefore happier, then these latter ought to consider how far these others have come in passing from their life in the world down to this life of ours, though they have been unable to reach the level of frugality common to the stronger brothers. Nor should all want to receive what they see given in larger measure to the few, not as a token of honor, but as a help to support them in their weakness. This would give rise to a deplorable disorder—that in the monastery, where the rich are coming to bear as much hardship as they can, the poor are turning to a more genteel way of life.

5. And just as the sick must take less food to avoid discomfort, so too, after their illness, they are to receive the kind of treatment that will quickly restore their strength, even though they come from a life of extreme poverty. Their more recent illness has, as it were, afforded them what accrued to the rich as part of their former way of life. But when they have recovered their former strength, they should go back to their happier way of life which, because their needs are fewer, is all the more in keeping with God's servants. Once in good health, they must not become slaves to the enjoyment of food which was necessary to sustain them in their illness. For it is better to suffer a little want than to have too much.

Chapter IV: Safeguarding chastity, and fraternal correction

1. There should be nothing about your clothing to

attract attention. Besides, you should not seek to please by your apparel, but by a good life.

2. Whenever you go out, walk together, and when you reach your destination, stay together.

3. In your walk, deportment, and in all actions, let nothing occur to give offense to anyone who sees you, but only what becomes your holy state of life.

4. Although your eyes may chance to rest upon some woman or other, you must not fix your gaze upon any woman. Seeing women when you go out is not forbidden, but it is sinful to desire them or to wish them to desire you, for it is not by tough or passionate feeling alone but by one's gaze also that lustful desires mutually arise. And do not say that your hearts are pure if there is immodesty of the eye, because the unchaste eye carries the message of an impure heart. And when such hearts disclose their unchaste desires in a mutual gaze, even without saying a word, then it is that chastity suddenly goes out of their life, even though their bodies remain unsullied by unchaste acts.

5. And whoever fixes his gaze upon a woman and likes to have hers fixed upon him must not suppose that others do not see what he is doing. He is very much seen, even by those he thinks do not see him. But suppose all this escapes the notice of man; what will he do about God who sees from on high and from whom nothing is hidden? Or are we to imagine that he does not see because he sees with a patience as great as his wisdom? Let the religious man then have such fear of God that he will not want to be an occasion of sinful pleasure to a woman. Ever mindful that God sees all things, let him not desire to look at a woman lustfully. For it is on this point that fear of the Lord is recommended, where it is written: "An abomination to the Lord is he who fixes his gaze" (Prov. 27:20).

6. So when you are together in church and anywhere else where women are present, exercise a mutual care over purity of life. Thus, by mutual vigilance over one another will God, who dwells in you, grant you his protection.

7. If you notice in someone of your brothers this wantonness of the eye, of which I am speaking, admonish him at once so that the beginning of evil will not grow more serious but will be promptly corrected.

8. But if you see him doing the same thing again on some other day, even after your admonition, then whoever had occasion to discover this must report him as he would a wounded man in need of treatment. But let the offense first be pointed out to two or three so that he can be proven guilty on the testimony of these two or three and be punished with due severity. And do not charge yourselves with ill-will when you bring this offense to light. Indeed, yours in the greater blame if you allow your brothers to be lost through your silence when you are able to bring about their correction by your disclosure. If your brother, for example, were suffering a bodily wound that he wanted to hide for fear of undergoing treatment, would it not be cruel of you to remain silent and a mercy on your part to make this known? How much greater then is your obligation to make his condition known lest he continue to suffer a more deadly wound of the soul.

9. But if he fails to correct the fault despite this admonition, he should first be brought to the attention of the superior before the offense is made known to the others who will have to prove his guilt, in the event he denies the charge. Thus, corrected in private, his fault can perhaps be kept from the others. But should he feign ignorance, the others are to be summoned so that in the presence of all he can be proven guilty, rather than stand accused on the word of one alone. Once proven guilty, he must undergo salutary punishment according to the judgment of the superior or priest having the proper authority. If he refuses to submit to punishment, he shall be expelled from your brotherhood even if he does not withdraw of his own accord. For this too is not done out of cruelty, but from a sense of compassion so that many others may not be lost through his bad example.

10. And let everything I have said about not fixing one's gaze be also observed carefully and faithfully with regard to other offenses: to find

them out, to ward them off, to make them known, to prove and punish them: all out of love for man and a hatred of sin.

11. But if anyone should go so far in wrongdoing as to receive letters in secret from any woman, or small gifts of any kind, you ought to show mercy and pray for him if he confesses this of his own accord. But if the offense is detected and he is found guilty, he must be more severely chastised according to the judgment of the priest or superior.

Chapter V: The care of community goods and the treatment of the sick

1. Keep your clothing in one place in charge of one or two, or of as many as are needed to care for them and to prevent damage from moths. And just as you have your food from the one pantry, so, too, you are to receive your clothing from a single wardrobe. If possible, do not be concerned about what you are given to wear at the change of seasons, whether each of you gets back what he had put away or something different, providing no one is denied what he needs. If, however, disputes and murmuring arise on this account because someone complains that he received poorer clothing than he had before, and thinks it is beneath him to wear the kind of clothing worn by another, you may judge from this how lacking you are in that holy and inner garment of the heart when you quarrel over garments for the body. But if allowance is made for your weakness and you do receive the same clothing you had put away, you must still keep it in one place under the common charge.

2. In this way, no one shall perform any task for his own benefit but all your work shall be done for the common good, with greater zeal and more dispatch than if each one of you were to work for yourself alone. For charity, as it is written, "is not self-seeking" (1 Cor. 13:5) meaning that it places the common good before its own, not its own before the common good. So whenever you show greater concern for the common good than for your own, you may know that you are growing in charity. Thus,

let the abiding virtue of charity prevail in all things that minister to the fleeting necessities of life.

3. It follows, therefore, that if anyone brings something for their sons or other relatives living in the monastery, whether a garment or anything else they think is needed, this must not be accepted secretly as one's own but must be placed at the disposal of the superior so that, as common property, it can be given to whoever needs it. But if someone secretly keeps something given to him, he shall be judged guilty of theft.

4. Your clothing should be cleaned either by yourselves or by those who perform this service, as the superior shall determine, so that too great a desire for clean clothing may not be the source of interior stains on the soul.

5. As for bodily cleanliness too, a brother must never deny himself the use of the bath when his health requires it. But this should be done on medical advice, without complaining, so that even though unwilling, he shall do what has to be done for his health when the superior orders it. However, if the brother wishes it, when it might not be good for him, you must not comply with his desire, for sometimes we think something is beneficial for the pleasure it gives, even though it may prove harmful.

6. Finally, if the cause of a brother's bodily pain is not apparent, you make take the word of God's servant when he indicates what is giving him pain. But if it remains uncertain whether the remedy he likes is good for him, a doctor should be consulted.

7. When there is need to frequent the public baths or any other place, no fewer than two or three should go together, and whoever has to go somewhere must not go with those of his own choice but with those designated by the superior.

8. The care of the sick, whether those in convalescence or others suffering from some indisposition, even though free of fever, shall be assigned to a brother who can personally obtain from the pantry whatever he sees is necessary for each one.

9. Those in charge of the pantry, or of clothing and books, should render cheerful service to their brothers.

10. Books are to be requested at a fixed hour each day, and anyone coming outside that hour is not to receive them.

11. But as for clothing and shoes, those in charge shall not delay the giving of them whenever they are required by those in need of them.

Chapter VI: Asking pardon and forgiving offenses

1. You should either avoid quarrels altogether or else put an end to them as quickly as possible; otherwise, anger may grow into hatred, making a plank out of a splinter, and turn the soul into a murderer. For so you read: "Everyone who hates his brother is a murderer" (1 John 3:15).

2. Whoever has injured another by open insult, or by abusive or even incriminating language, must remember to repair the injury as quickly as possible by an apology, and he who suffered the injury must also forgive, without further wrangling. But if they have offended one another, they must forgive one another's trespasses for the sake of your prayers which should be recited with greater sincerity each time you repeat them. Although a brother is often tempted to anger, yet prompt to ask pardon from one he admits to having offended, such a one is better than another who, though less given to anger, finds it too hard to ask forgiveness. But a brother who is never willing to ask pardon, or does not do so from his heart, has no reason to be in the monastery, even if he is not expelled. You must then avoid being too harsh in your words, and should they escape your lips, let those same lips not be ashamed to heal the wounds they have caused.

3. But whenever the good of discipline requires you to speak harshly in correcting your subjects, then, even if you think you have been unduly harsh in your language, you are not required to ask forgiveness lest, by practicing too great humility toward those who should be your subjects, the authority to rule is undermined. But you should still ask forgiveness from the Lord of all who knows with what deep affection you love even those whom you might happen to correct with undue severity. Besides, you are to love another with a spiritual rather than an earthly love.

Chapter VII: Governance and obedience

1. The superior should be obeyed as a father with the respect due him so as not to offend God in his person, and, even more so, the priest who bears responsibility for you all.

2. But it shall pertain chiefly to the superior to see that these precepts are all observed and, if any point has been neglected, to take care that the transgression is not carelessly overlooked but is punished and corrected. In doing so, he must refer whatever exceeds the limit and power of his office, to the priest who enjoys greater authority among you.

3. The superior, for his part, must not think himself fortunate in his exercise of authority but in his role as one serving you in love. In your eyes he shall hold the first place among you by the dignity of his office, but in fear before God he shall be as the least among you. He must show himself as an example of good works toward all. "Let him admonish the unruly, cheer the fainthearted, support the weak, and be patient toward all" (1 Thess. 5:14). Let him uphold discipline while instilling fear. And though both are necessary, he should strive to be loved by you rather than feared, ever mindful that he must give an account of you to God.

4. It is by being more obedient, therefore, that you show mercy not only toward yourselves but also toward the superior whose higher rank among you exposes him all the more to greater peril.

Chapter VIII: Observance of the rule

1. The Lord grant that you may observe all these precepts in a spirit of charity as lovers of spiritual beauty, giving forth the good odor of Christ in the holiness of your lives: not as slaves living under the law but as men living in freedom under grace.

2. And that you may see yourselves in this little

book, as in a mirror, have it read to you once a week so as to neglect no point through forgetfulness. When you find that you are doing all that has been written, give thanks to the Lord, the Giver of every good. But when one of you finds that he has failed on any point, let him be sorry for the past, be on his guard for the future, praying that he will be forgiven his fault and not be led into temptation.

BENEDICT: *RULE* (FOR MONASTIC LIFE, ABRIDGED)
Latin, Early Sixth Century

Benedict was born about A.D. 480 to a wealthy and noble family from the small village of Nursia, near Spoleto, in Italy. Not long before Benedict's birth, the Roman Empire was conquered by the Germanic tribe, the Ostragoths. In addition to barbarian rule, the church of Benedict's day suffered the stress of an ongoing conflict between orthodox and Arian believers. At the age of twenty, Benedict left home to live the ascetic life of a hermit. For three years he lived alone in a cave. In time his disciplined commitment to the Christian life gained him a following of disciples. When his cave could no longer support what had become a growing community, Benedict and his followers moved to the remote village of Monte Cassino, where they banished local pagan worshipers and established a monastery. Soon, Benedict's sister, Scholastica, also settled in Monte Cassino and established a monastic community for women. Benedict is chiefly remembered for his *Rule*, a guide for every aspect of monastic life. Benedict's *Rule* served as a corrective to earlier, more severe approaches, while establishing two principles which in time became central to Benedictine monasticism: *permanence* (a monk must remain for life in the monastery in which he took his original vows) and *obedience* (to whatever may be commanded by the abbot). The monastic director, or abbot (the word means father), was also subject to the *Rule*, however, and was generally appointed to the oversight of a small community for life. During his lifetime Benedict established twelve monasteries of twelve monks each. For many centuries thereafter, his *Rule* was adopted and used by monasteries far beyond Monte Cassino. Most of what is known of the life of Benedict has come down to us from the *Dialogues* of Pope Gregory the Great.

Suggested Assignment: Compose a Community Rule

Reading a work like Benedict's *Rule* opens our eyes not merely to medieval monastic practices, but also to classical Christian concepts and disciplines: the elements of prayer, the role of discipline in spiritual formation, a daily schedule bounded by worship, and so on. As his prologue suggests, Benedict composed his *Rule* as a guide for "transforming our sinful ways and testing our love." As you read, consider where the elements of your own lifestyle and daily schedule empower or else defeat such objectives. Notice also the basic themes of the *Rule*: Membership in the community/joining (chap. 58); community decision making (chap. 3); Christian modeling and leadership (chap. 2); personal possessions, food, and clothing (chaps. 33, 39, 55); rules, regulations (chap. 5); living arrangements (chap. 22); and community worship (chaps. 8, 9, 16, etc.). Some or all of these elements provide a basis for a contemporary *Rule* for Christian community living. Compose your own *Rule* in the setting of your choice (i.e., Christians living together in a shared residence, whether in an urban, suburban, or rural setting).

✦

Prologue: A school for the Lord's service

Listen attentively my child and turn the ear of your heart toward your master's teachings. Gladly receive this advice, the counsel of a loving father, and consistently put it to use that you may turn back to the God from whom through complacency you have wandered. My rule is meant for you, whoever you may be, if you are prepared to surrender your will and take up the armor of obedience to do battle for Christ the king! Begin, then, by asking God to complete the good work he has begun in you so that he may never be grieved by our sinful ways; he who, through his great goodness counts us as one of his own. For at all times we ought to serve him with the good things he has given us so that he won't, as an angry Father, disinherit his children nor, as a dreaded Lord, angered by our sinful ways give us over to everlasting punishment like those wicked servants who fail to follow him to his glory. We are about to establish, therefore, a school for the Lord's service, the curriculum of which, we trust, will not prove too severe or burdensome. However, if justice should require that some of the practices outlined here greatly challenge you for the purpose of transforming your sinful ways and testing your love, you should not flee in fear from the way of salvation, which is found only through small gate and narrow way. After all, as one's way of life and one's faith progresses, so the Lord's path is followed and becomes the sweetest way of life. So then never forsaking His guidance and continuing in this Cenobitic way of life and teaching until death, through patience we participate in Christ's sufferings that we may be worthy companions in His kingdom.

Chapter I: Four kinds of monks

It is evident that there are four types of monks. The *Cenobites* are the first type; that is, those living in a monastery, serving under a rule or an abbot. The second type is that of the *Anchorites*; that is, the hermits, those who, not by the zeal of a recent conversion but by long endurance of life in a monastery, have learned to fight against the devil, having already been instructed by the encouragement of many. They, having been well-prepared in the army of brothers for the solitary fight of the hermit, being secure now without the consolation of another, are able, God helping them, to fight with their own hand or arm against the vices of the flesh or of their thoughts. Now a third and greatly inferior type of monks are the *Sarabaites* who, with no experience to guide them and no rule to try them "as gold is tried in a furnace" (Prov. 27:21) have a character as soft as lead. Their behavior reveals their continued loyalty to the world while their bald heads conceal their broken vows. *Sarabaites* congregate in private little flocks of two or three monks, occasionally alone and always without a shepherd. Their rule is to satisfy their own desires. For whatever they find pleasing they call holy, and whatever they dislike they consider sinful. Fourth and finally, there are those monks who are called *Gyravagues*. They live their lives as vagabonds, staying as guests for three to four days at a time in the cells of different monasteries and throughout the various provinces, ever wandering and never putting down roots, always seeking greater comfort and better food. These monks are even worse than the Sarabaites but it is better to keep silent than to say more about the wretched ways of living practiced by them. With God's help, then, let us proceed to describe the *Cenobitic* way of life.

Chapter II: The ideal abbott and prioress

An abbot or prioress who is worthy to govern a monastery should remember what his or her title signifies and live accordingly. For they are Christ's representative, called by His name, as the apostle says: "you received the Spirit of sonship, and by him we cry, Abba, Father" (Rom. 8:15). And so they should never teach, or decree, or order anything contrary to God's commands. Indeed, it should be evident to their disciples that their teaching is guided by divine justice. Let them be ever mindful of the fact that, at the awesome judgment of God, two matters will be weighed as in a balance: their teaching and the obedience of their disciples. The prioress and abbot must, therefore, be aware that the shepherd will bear the blame whenever the owner of the household finds that the sheep have yielded no profit. On the other hand, they shall be acquitted if they have diligently kept watch over an unruly and disobedient flock. Therefore, those who accept the name of abbot or prioress should guide the community with a twofold teaching, that is, to demonstrate in both words and actions all that is good and holy. For while those who are receptive to the commands of God may indeed be formally instructed, the rebellious and simple-minded need a living example. And again, whatever behavior these teachers forbid as contrary to God's law they must themselves avoid, so that after they have preached to others, they themselves will not be disqualified for the prize (1 Cor. 9:27), and so that God may never say to them, "What right have you to recite my laws or take my covenant on your lips? You hate my instruction and cast my words behind you" (Ps. 50:16–17). Remember also the words, "Why do you look at the speck of sawdust in your brother's eye and pay no attention to the plank in your own eye?" (Matt. 7:3).

Abbots and prioresses should take care to avoid showing favoritism to anyone in the monastery. No one should be more esteemed than anyone else, except those who excel in obedience and good works. And there is no reason why someone who is free-born should be esteemed more worthy than a former slave. Indeed, both abbot and prioress are free, as they see fit, to change anyone's rank as justice demands. Ordinarily, however, everyone should remain in their own social class since whether slave or free, we are all one in Christ (Gal. 3:28, Eph. 6:8), and since we are all called to serve God, who "does not show favoritism" (Rom. 2:11).

Abbots and prioresses must therefore show equal love for all and administer justice in accordance with each one's merit. In teaching, they must observe that method commanded by the apostle when he says: "correct, rebuke, and encourage" (2 Tim. 4:2). Which is to say, as the occasion may require, let them mingle encouragement with reproofs, and let them display both the sternness of master and the loving affection of a father. They must, of course, rebuke the undisciplined and restless more severely. But those who are obedient, gentle, and patient may be encouraged and persuaded to even greater obedience.

Chapter III: Community involvement in decision making

Whenever anything important must be transacted in the monastery, the abbot or prioress shall call the entire community together and explain the matter at hand. After carefully considering the advice of the brothers or sisters, the abbot or prioress shall ponder the matter on their own and do as they think best. Everyone should be called to the council because the Lord often reveals to a younger member what is best. But let each one offer advice with all humility, not presuming to defend an opinion arrogantly, and remembering that the final decision rests with the abbot or prioress. Just as it is proper for disciples to obey their teacher, so it is fitting for a teacher to make decisions with foresight and fairness.

Chapter IV: The instruments of good works

These are:

1. First of all, to love the Lord our God with all our heart, with all our soul, and with all our strength.
2. Then, to love our neighbor as ourselves.
3. Then, not to kill.
4. Not to commit adultery.
5. Not to steal.
6. Not to be covetous.
7. Not to bear false witness.
8. To respect everyone.
9. Not to do to another what one would not have done to oneself.
10. To deny oneself in order to follow Christ.
11. To discipline the body.
12. Not to be fond of pleasures.
13. To love fasting.
14. To give food to the poor.
15. To clothe the naked.
16. To visit the sick.
17. To bury the dead.
18. To come to the aid of those in trouble.
19. To comfort those in sadness.
20. To become a stranger to the ways of the world.
21. To like nothing better than the love of Christ.
22. Not to give in to anger.
23. Not to hold a grudge.
24. Not to make plans to deceive anyone.
25. Not to make a false peace.
26. Not to cease showing love.
27. Never to swear.
28. To speak truth with the heart and the lips.
29. Never to repay evil for evil.
30. Never to injure another, but to patiently suffer injuries.
31. To love one's enemies.
32. Not to speak ill of those who speak ill of you, but rather to speak well of them.
33. To do the right thing, even when it brings on persecution.
34. Not to be proud.
35. Not to drink much wine.
36. Not to be a glutton.
37. Not to oversleep.
38. Not to be lazy.
39. Not to be a complainer.
40. Not to criticize.
41. To put one's trust in God.
42. To attribute one's goodness to God alone.
43. To recognize one's evil nature.
44. To fear the day of judgment.
45. To be afraid of hell.
46. To desire life everlasting with a great, spiritual longing.
47. To be mindful of the nearness of one's death, daily.
48. To keep watch on one's actions every hour of the day.
49. To be aware that God sees everything.
50. To dash against Christ (as against a rock) evil thoughts which rise up in the mind.
51. To confess evil thoughts to one's spiritual father.

52. To guard one's lips from speaking evil and wicked words.
53. Not to be fond of talking too much.
54. Not to speak idle words, or those which cause laughter.
55. Not to love hilarity or loud laughter.
56. Willing to listen to sacred readings.
57. Often devoting oneself to prayer.
58. Daily with tears and sighs to confess to God in prayer one's past sins and to avoid repeating them.
59. Not to give in to the desires of the flesh, and to hate one's own inclinations.
60. In all things to obey the abbot's or prioress's commands.
61. Not to wish to be called holy before one is so, but to be holy first so as to be called such with truth.
62. To daily keep God's commandments in all one's behavior.
63. To love abstinence.
64. To hate no one.
65. Not to be jealous or envious.
66. Not to love quarreling.
67. To show no spirit of arrogance.
68. To respect the old.
69. To love the young.
70. To pray for one's enemies to experience the love of Christ.
71. To make peace with one's adversary before the sun sets.
72. And, never to despair of God's mercy.

Behold these are the tools of our spiritual craft. Once we have made use of them constantly day and night, and so have proved them at the day of judgment, then the Lord shall give to us that reward which he has promised, which "No eye has seen, no ear has heard, no mind has conceived what God has prepared for those who love him" (1 Cor. 2:9). Faithfully dwelling in the community, the workshop where all these instruments are employed is the cloister of the monastery.

Chapter V: Concerning obedience

The first step of humility is prompt obedience. This is expected of all who, by reason of the holy service they profess or out of the dread of hell and the anticipation of the glory of eternal life, hold nothing more dear than Christ. Such disciples obey the abbot's orders as if the command were from God Himself, and about such disciples the Lord has said: "As soon as they hear me, they obey me" (Ps. 18:44); Again, to his teachers he has said, "He who listens to you listens to me" (Luke 10:16). These people put aside their own concerns, abandon their own will, and leave their own business unfinished in order to follow His command. As soon as the teacher gives the instruction, then, the disciple quickly puts it into practice out of reverence for God, and both actions together are completed as swiftly as one.

Chapter VI: Concerning silence

Let us follow the counsel of the prophet who says, "I will watch my ways and keep my tongue from sin . . . I was silent and still, not even saying anything good" (Ps. 39:1–3). Here the prophet shows that there are times when even good words are better left unsaid, out of esteem for silence. And if this is so, how much more important is it to leave sinful things unsaid! Indeed, preserving silence is so vital that permission to speak should seldom be granted even to mature disciples, and no matter how edifying their words may be. As it is written, "When words are many, sin is not absent," (Prov. 10:19) and also, "The tongue has the power of life and death," (Prov. 18:21). The master should speak and teach; the disciple must be silent and listen. Whatever requests, therefore, are made of the abbot or prioress should be made with all humility and respectful submission. We absolutely condemn in all places any vulgarity and gossip and talk leading to laughter, and so we do not permit a disciple to speak that way.

Chapter VII: Concerning humility

The first step of humility is to "keep the reverence of God always before our eyes" (Ps. 36:2) and never forget it. The second step of humility is that we love not our own will nor take pleasure in the satisfaction of our desires; rather, we are to imitate Christ, as in his saying, "I have come not to do my own will but the will of Him who sent me" (John 6:38). The third step of humility is to submit ourselves to the abbot or prioress in obedience and for the sake of the love of God, again imitating Christ, of whom the apostle says, "He became obedient even unto death" (Phil. 2:8). The fourth step of humility is that, in obedience, our hearts quietly embrace suffering and endure it without weakening or seeking escape. As Scripture says, "He who stands firm to the end will be saved" (Matt. 10:22). The fifth step of humility is that we do not conceal from the abbot or prioress any sinful thoughts entering our hearts, or any wrongs committed in secret, but rather confess them humbly. For concerning this, the prophet exhorts us, "I acknowledged my sin to you and did not cover up my iniquity. I said, "I will confess my transgressions to the LORD," and "you forgave the guilt of my sin" (Ps. 32:5). The sixth step of humility is, that we are content with the lowest and most menial treatment, and regard ourselves as a poor and worthless worker in whatever task we are given, saying with the prophet, "I was senseless and ignorant; I was a brute beast before you. Yet I am always with you; you hold me by my right hand" (Ps. 73:22–23). The seventh step of humility is not only that we admit with our tongues but are also convinced in our hearts that we are inferior to all and of less value, humbling ourselves and saying with the prophet, "I am a worm and not a man, scorned by men and despised by the people" (Ps. 22:67), and again, "It was good for me to be afflicted so that I might learn your commandments" (Ps. 119:71). The eighth step of humility is that we do nothing except what the common rule of the monastery, or the example of his elders, urges us to do. The ninth step of humility is that we restrain our tongues from speaking and, keeping silent, we do not speak until spoken to. The tenth step of humility is that we be not ready, and easily inclined, to laugh. The eleventh step of humility is that, when we do speak, we do so slowly and without laughter, humbly and in all seriousness, using few and reasonable words, not speaking loudly. The twelfth step of humility is that we shall, not only in our hearts but also with our bodies, demonstrate humility toward all who see us, that is, as we work but also in the oratory, in the monastery, in the garden, on the road, and in the fields. Wherever we may be, whether sitting or walking or standing, let our heads be inclined and our gaze fixed upon the ground, remembering every hour that we are guilty of sinful ways. Let us imagine that we are already being presented before the tremendous judgment of God, saying to ourselves in our hearts the same as the publican described in the gospel who fixed his eyes on the earth, saying, "Lord I am unworthy even to lift mine eyes unto Heaven."

Chapter VIII: The divine offices at night

In the winter time, that is from the Calends of November until Easter, according to what is reasonable, they must rise at the eighth hour of the night, so that they rest a little more than half the night, and rise when they have already digested. But let the time that remains after vigils be kept for meditation by those brothers who are in any way behind with the Psalter or lessons. From Easter, moreover, until the aforesaid Calends of November, let the hour of keeping vigils be so arranged that, a short interval being observed in which the brethren may go out for the necessities of nature, the matins, which are always to take place with the dawning light, may straightway follow.

Chapter IX: How many psalms are said at night

In the winter first of all the verse shall be said: "Make haste oh God to deliver me; make haste to help me oh God." Then, secondly, there shall be said three times: "Oh Lord open Thou my lips and my mouth shall show forth Thy praise." To which is to be subjoined the third psalm and the Gloria. After this the ninety-fourth psalm is to be sung antiphonally or in unison. The Ambrosian chant shall then follow: then six psalms antiphonally. These having been said, the abbot shall, with the verse mentioned, give the blessing. And all being seated upon the benches, there shall be read in turn from the Scriptures—following out the analogy—three lessons; between which also three responses shall be sung. Two responses shall be said without the Gloria; but, after the third lesson, he who chants shall say the Gloria. And, when the cantor begins to say this, all shall straightway rise from their seats out of honor and reverence for the holy Trinity. Books, moreover, of the Old as well as the New Testament of Divine authority shall be read at the Vigils; but also expositions of them which have been made by the most celebrated orthodox teachers and catholic fathers. Moreover, after these three lessons with their responses, shall follow other six psalms to be sung with the Alleluia. After this a lesson of the Apostle shall follow, to be recited by heart; and verses and the supplication of the Litany, that is the Kyrie Eleison: and thus shall end the nocturnal vigils.

Chapter XVI: Divine service through the day

As the prophet says: "Seven times in the day so I praise Thee." Which sacred number of seven will thus be fulfilled by us if, at matins, at the first, third, sixth, ninth hours, at vesper time and at completorium we perform the duties of our service; for it is of these hours of the day that he said: "Seven times in the day do I praise Thee." For, concerning nocturnal vigils, the same prophet says: "At midnight I arose to confess unto thee." Therefore, at these times, let us give thanks to our Creator concerning the judgments of his righteousness; that is, at matins, at the first, third, sixth, ninth hours, at vesper time and at completorium we will rise and confess to him.

Chapter XXII: Sleeping quarters for the monks

They shall sleep separately in separate beds. They shall receive positions for their beds, after the manner of their characters, according to the dispensation of their abbot. If it can be done, they shall all sleep in one place. If, however, their number does not permit it, they shall rest, by tens or twenties, with elders who will concern themselves about them. A candle shall always be burning in that same cell until early in the morning. They shall sleep clothed, and girt with belts or with ropes; and they shall not have their knives at their sides while they sleep, lest perchance in a dream they should wound the sleepers. And let the monks be always on the alert; and, when the signal is given, rising without delay, let them hasten to mutually prepare themselves for the service of God with all gravity and modesty, however. The younger brothers shall not have beds by themselves, but interspersed among those of the elder ones. And when they rise for the service of God, they shall exhort each other mutually with moderation on account of the excuses that those who are sleepy are inclined to make.

Chapter XXXIII: Possessions of the monks

More than anything else is this special vice to be cut off root and branch from the monastery, that one should presume to give or receive anything without the order of the abbot, or should have anything of his own. He should have absolutely nothing: neither a book, nor tablets, nor a pen—nothing at all. For indeed it is not allowed to the monks to have their own bodies or wills in their own power. But all things necessary they must expect from the Father of the monastery; nor is it allowable to have anything which the abbot did not give or permit. All things shall be common to all, as it is written: "Let not any man presume or call anything his own." But if any one shall have been discovered delighting in this most evil vice: being warned once and again, if he do not amend, let him be subjected to punishment.

Chapter XXXIX: Daily meals

For the daily reflection of the sixth and of the ninth hours, two cooked dishes, on account of the infirmities of the different ones, are enough for all tables: so that whoever, perchance, cannot eat of one may partake of the other. Therefore let two cooked dishes suffice for all the brothers: and, if it is possible to obtain apples or growing vegetables, a third may be added. One full pound of bread shall suffice for a day, whether there be one refection, or a breakfast and a supper. But if they are going to have supper, the third part of that same pound shall be reserved by the cellarer, to be given back to those who are about to sup. But if, perchance, some greater labor shall have been performed, it shall be in the will and power of the abbot, if it is expedient, to increase anything; surfeiting above all things being guarded against, so that indigestion may never seize a monk: for nothing is so contrary to every Christian as surfeiting, as our Lord says: "Take heed to yourselves, lest your hearts be overcharged with surfeiting." But to the younger boys the same quantity shall not be served, but less than that to the older ones; moderation being observed in all things. But the eating of meat shall be abstained from altogether by every one, excepting for the weak and the sick.

Chapter XLV: Mistakes in the oratory

If any one, in saying a psalm, response, or antiphone or lesson, make a mistake; unless he humbles himself there before all, giving satisfaction, He shall be subjected to greater punishment, as one who was unwilling to correct by humility that in which he had erred by neglect. But children, for such a fault, shall not be whipped.

Chapter XLVIII: Daily manual labor

Idleness is the enemy of the soul. And therefore, at fixed times, the brothers ought to be occupied in manual labor; and again, at fixed times, in sacred reading. . . . There shall certainly be appointed one or two elders, who shall go round the monastery at the hours in which the brothers are engaged in reading, and see to it that no troublesome brother chance to be found who is open to idleness and trifling, and is not intent on his reading; being not only of no use to himself, but also stirring up others.

Chapter LV: Clothing and shoes

Vestments shall be given to the brothers according to the quality of the places where they dwell, or the temperature of the air. For in cold regions more is required; but in warm, less. This, therefore, is a matter for the abbot to decide. We nevertheless consider that for ordinary places there suffices for the monks a cowl and a gown apiece—the cowl, in winter hairy, in summer plain or old—and a working garment, on account of their labors, as clothing for the feet, shoes and boots.

Chapter LVIII: Receiving new brothers

When any new comer applies for conversion, an easy entrance shall not be granted him: but, as the apostle says, "Try the spirits if they be of God." Therefore, if he who comes perseveres in knocking, and is seen after four or five days to patiently endure the insults inflicted upon him, and the difficulty of gaining entrance, and to persist in his demand: entrance shall be allowed him, and he shall remain for a few days in the cell of the guests. After this, moreover, he shall be in the cell of the novices, where He shall meditate and eat and sleep. And an elder shall be appointed to him who is capable of saving souls, who shall altogether intently watch over him, and make it a care to see if he reverently seek God, if he be zealous in the service of God, in obedience, in suffering shame. And all the harshness and roughness of the means through which God is approached shall be told him in advance. If he promise perseverance in his steadfastness, after the lapse of two months this *Rule* shall be read to him in order, and it shall be said to him: Consider the law under which you wish to serve; if you are able to observe it, enter; but if you are not able, depart freely. If he remains firm in his desire to enter, then he shall return to the aforesaid cell of the novices; and again he shall be proven with all patience. And, after six months, the *Rule* shall be read to him again; that he may understand the nature of the life he is entering. And, if continues to stand firm, after another four months the same *Rule* shall once more be re-read to him. And if, having deliberated with himself, he shall promise to keep everything, and to obey all the commands that are laid upon him: then he shall be accepted into the congregation; knowing that it is decreed, by the law of the *Rule*, that from that day he shall not be allowed to depart from the monastery, nor to shake free his neck from the yoke of the *Rule*, which, after such lengthy deliberation, he was at liberty either to refuse or receive.

IGNATIUS OF LOYOLA: *SPIRITUAL EXCERCISES* (EXCERPT)
Latin, Sixteenth Century

The name of Ignatius of Loyola is synonymous with the Society of Jesus, or Jesuit Order, which he founded in 1534. After giving up a military career following injuries sustained in battle, Ignatius vowed to become a soldier of Christ, making confession and entering seclusion for a year during which he prayed fervently, fasted almost constantly, and received mystical visions which led him to compose the Spiritual Exercises. Ignatius later undertook pilgrimages to Rome and Jerusalem and studied theology at Paris. His career mission was to reform the church from within by way of education, greater appreciation for (and more frequent practice of) the sacraments, and preaching the Gospel to the pagan world. Ignatius was canonized—officially recognized by the Catholic Church as a "saint"—in 1622. The name, Spiritual Exercises, describes the examination of one's conscience and the processes of meditation, contemplation, and vocal and mental (silent) prayer.

Questions for Guided Reading
1. Why do you think these guidelines are called exercises? Are they well named?
2. How are these exercises organized or arranged?
3. Describe the role of the five senses and of the imagination in these meditation exercises.
4. Describe the role of Scripture in these exercises.
5. How might the regular practice of such exercises influence the practitioner?
6. What aspects of life besides meditation and devotion are addressed in this writing?

✦

Four Divisions: Four "Weeks" of Exercises

The division of these exercises is as follows: First, a consideration and contemplation on one's sins; Second, on the life of Christ our Lord up to the events of Palm Sunday; Third, the Passion of Christ our Lord; Fourth and finally, the Resurrection and Ascension, to be approached by means of the three Methods of Prayer (see below). Although one "week" is meant to correspond to each division, these weeks need not be precisely seven days. For, as it happens, some are slower, in the first week for example, to find what they seek—namely, contrition, sorrow and tears for their sins—and in the same way some are more diligent than others, and more acted on or tried by different spirits; it may, at times, be necessary to shorten the Week, and at other times to lengthen it. The same is true of all the other subsequent Weeks, seeking out the things according to the subject matter. However, the Exercises were designed to be experienced as a whole over the course of a month or so.

True Understanding

The Spiritual Exercises must be adapted to the dispositions of the persons who wish to receive them, that is, to their age, education, and ability, in order not to give to one who is uneducated or of little intelligence things he cannot easily bear and profit by. In all the following Spiritual Exercises, we use acts of the intellect in reasoning, and acts of the will in movements of the feelings: let us remark that, in the acts of the will, when we are speaking vocally or mentally with God our Lord, or with His Saints, greater reverence is required on our part than when we are using the intellect in understanding. It is not so much the knowing of the things found in these exercises as it is realizing and relishing them interiorly; this is what satisfies the soul.

Willingness Required

It is very helpful to him who is receiving the Exercises to enter into them with great courage and generosity toward his Creator and Lord, offering Him all his will and liberty, that His Divine Majesty may make use of his person and of all he has according to His most Holy Will.

Diligence Required

When he who is giving the Exercises sees that no spiritual movements, such as consolation or desolation, come to the soul of him who is exercising himself, and that he is not moved by different spirits, he ought to inquire carefully of him about the Exercises, whether he does them at their appointed times, and how. Let him ask in detail about each of these things.

It is easy to be in contemplation a full hour. For this reason, the person who is exercising himself, in order to act against the desolation and conquer the temptations, ought always to stay longer than the full hour; so as to accustom himself not only to resist the adversary, but even to overthrow him.

A person of education or ability who is taken up with public affairs or suitable business, ought to spend at least an hour and a half daily in these exercises.

Preparation

Immediately on recollecting that it is the time of the Exercise which I have to make, before I go, I remind myself where I am going and before Whom, and summarizing a little the Exercise which I have to make, I then enter into the Exercise.

Patience Required

If he who is giving the Exercises sees that he who is receiving them is in desolation and tempted, let him not be hard or dissatisfied with him, but gentle and indulgent, giving him courage and strength for the future, and laying bare to him the wiles of the enemy of human nature, and getting him to prepare and dispose himself for the consolation coming. If he who is giving the Exercises sees that he who is receiving them is in need of instruction about the desolation and wiles of the enemy—and the same of consolations—he may explain to him, as far as he needs them, the Rules of the First and Second Weeks for recognizing different spirits. The person who is making the Contemplation takes the true groundwork of the narrative, and, discussing and considering for himself, will find the events a little clearer—whether this comes through his own reasoning, or because his intellect is enlightened by the Divine power—he will get more spiritual relish and fruit, than if he who is giving the Exercises had much explained and amplified the meaning of the events.

Haste in Taking Vows

If he who is giving the Exercises sees that he who is receiving them is going on in consolation and with much fervor, he ought to warn him not to make any inconsiderate and hasty promise or vow. For, though one may justly influence another to embrace the religious life, in which he is understood to make vows of obedience, poverty and chastity,[2] and, although a good work done under vow is more meritorious than one done without it, one should carefully consider the circumstances and personal qualities of the individual and how much help or hindrance he is likely to find in fulfilling the thing he would want to promise.

Benefits of Spending Time Alone

Three chief benefits, among many others, follow from isolation. The first is that a man, by separating himself from many friends and acquaintances, and likewise from many not well-ordered affairs, to serve and praise God our Lord, merits no little in the sight of His Divine Majesty. The second is, that being thus isolated, and not having his understanding divided on many things, but concentrating his care on one only, namely, on serving his Creator and benefiting his own soul, he uses with greater freedom his natural powers, in seeking with diligence what he so much desires. The third: the more our soul finds itself alone and isolated, the more apt it makes itself to approach and to reach its Creator and Lord, and the more it so approaches Him, the more it disposes itself to receive graces and gifts from His Divine and Sovereign Goodness.

Specific Daily Examinations

Note that three times (and two examinations) are to be undertaken daily: The first time is in the morning, immediately on rising, when one ought to propose to guard himself with diligence against that particular sin or defect which he wants to correct and amend. The second time is after the midday meal, when one is to ask of God our Lord the grace to remember how many times he has fallen into that particular sin or defect, and to amend himself in the future. Here is the first Examination: asking account of his soul of that particular thing proposed, which he wants to correct and amend. Let him do this by reviewing his actions hour by hour, or period by period, commencing at the hour he rose, and continuing up to the hour and instant of the present examination. And let him note each time

he has fallen with a dot between the lines of the specific hour.

First Period   _____

                       _____

Second Period _____

Third Period _____

Then let him resolve anew to amend himself up to the second examination which he will make. During the third time, after the evening meal, a second examination will be made, in the same way, hour by hour, beginning from the time of the first examination and continuing up to the present.

First Week: Examination of Conscience and Confession

Principle and Foundation

Man is created to *praise*, reverence, and serve God our Lord, and by this means to save his soul. And the other things on the face of the earth are created for man and that they may help him in prosecuting the end for which he is created. From this it follows that man is to use them as much as they help him on to his end, and ought to rid himself of them so far as they hinder him as to it. For this it is necessary to make ourselves indifferent to all created things in all that is allowed to the choice of our free will and is not prohibited to it; so that, on our part, we want not health rather than sickness, riches rather than poverty, honor rather than dishonor, long rather than short life, and so in all the rest; desiring and choosing only what is most conducive for us to the end for which we are created.

Exercise: Meditation on Sin

Following a prayer of preparation, to *First* of all bring to memory all the sins of life, looking from year to year, or from period to period. To accomplish this, three things are helpful: first, to look at the place and the house where I have lived; second, the relations I have had with others; third, the occupation in which I have lived. *Second*, to weigh the sins, looking at the foulness and the malice which any mortal sin committed has in it, even

---

2. Note the three traditional vows of a monk.

supposing it were not forbidden. *Third*, to look at who I am, lessening myself by examples: Namely, how little I am in comparison to all men; next, how insignificant men are in comparison to all the Angels and Saints of Paradise; and finally, how little all of Creation is in comparison to God: (Then I alone, what can I be?). *Fourth*, to see all my bodily corruption and foulness, that is, to look on myself as a sore and ulcer, from which have sprung so many sins and so many iniquities and so very vile poison. *Fifth*, to consider what God is, against Whom I have sinned, according to His attributes; comparing them with their contraries in me—His Wisdom with my ignorance; His Omnipotence with my weakness; His Justice with my iniquity; His Goodness with my malice. *Sixth* and finally, an exclamation of wonder with deep feeling, going through all creatures, how they have left me in life and preserved me in it; the Angels, how, though they are the sword of the Divine Justice, they have endured me, and guarded me, and prayed for me; the Saints, how they have been engaged in interceding and praying for me; and the heavens, sun, moon, stars, and elements, fruits, birds, fishes and animals—and the earth, how it has not opened to swallow me up, creating new Hells for me to suffer in them forever!

Colloquy

Let me finish with a Colloquy of mercy, pondering and giving thanks to God our Lord that He has given me life up to now, proposing amendment, with His grace, for the future. "Our Father."

Types of Humility

It is very helpful to consider and mark the following three Manners of Humility, reflecting on them occasionally through all the day, and also making the Colloquies, as will be said later. *First Humility*. The first manner of Humility is necessary for eternal salvation; namely, that I so lower and so humble myself, as much as is possible to me, that in everything I obey the law of God, so that, even if they made me lord of all the created things in this world, nor for my own temporal life, I would not be in deliberation about breaking a Commandment, whether Divine or human, which binds me under mortal sin. *Second Humility*. The second is more perfect Humility than the first; namely, if I find myself at such a stage that I do not want, and feel no inclination to have, riches rather than poverty, to want

honor rather than dishonor, to desire a long rather than a short life—the service of God our Lord and the salvation of my soul being equal; and so not for all creation, nor because they would take away my life, would I be in deliberation about committing a venial sin. *Third Humility*. The third is most perfect Humility; namely, when—including the first and second, and the praise and glory of the Divine Majesty being equal—in order to imitate and be more actually like Christ our Lord, I want and choose poverty with Christ poor rather than riches, opprobrium with Christ replete with it rather than honors; and to desire to be rated as worthless and a fool for Christ, Who first was held as such, rather than wise or prudent in this world.

Second Week: Responding to the Temporal King by Meditating on the Eternal King

If we consider the call of the temporal King to his subjects to be important, how much more worthy of consideration is it to see Christ our Lord, King eternal, and before Him all the entire world, which and each one in particular He calls, and says: "It is My will to conquer all the world and all enemies and so to enter into the glory of My Father; therefore, whoever would like to come with Me is to labor with Me, that following Me in the pain, he may also follow Me in the glory."

The First Prelude: Using the sight of the imagination to see the Incarnation, Nativity, and Ministry of Christ our Lord. Second Prelude. The second, to ask for the grace which I want: it will be here to ask grace of our Lord that I may not be deaf to His call, but ready and diligent to fulfill His most Holy Will. First Point. The first Point is, to put before me a human king chosen by God our Lord, whom all Christian princes and men reverence and obey. Second Point. The second, to look how this king speaks to all his people, saying: It is my Will to conquer all the land of unbelievers. Therefore, whoever would like to come with me is to be content to eat as I, and also to drink and dress, etc., as I: likewise he is to labor like me in the day and watch in the night, etc., that so afterward he may have part with me in the victory, as he has had it in the labors." Third Point. The third, to consider what the good subjects ought to answer to a King so liberal and so kind, and hence, if any one did not accept the appeal of such a king, how deserving he would be of being censured by all the world, and held for a mean-spirited knight.

Use of the Five Senses in Meditation

To use the five senses of the imagination in the following way: First, to see the persons with the sight of the imagination, meditating and contemplating in particular the details about them and drawing some profit from the sight. Second, to hear with the hearing what they are, or might be, talking about and, reflecting on oneself, to draw some profit from it. Third, to smell and to taste with the smell and the taste the infinite fragrance and sweetness of the Divinity, of the soul, and of its virtues, and of all, according to the person who is being contemplated; reflecting on oneself and drawing profit from it. Fourth, to touch with the touch, as for instance, to embrace and kiss the places where such persons put their feet and sit, always seeing to my drawing profit from it. The first Exercise, on the Incarnation, will be made at midnight; the second at dawn; the third at the hour of Mass; the fourth at the hour of Vespers, and the fifth before the hour of supper, being for the space of one hour in each one of the five Exercises; and the same order will be taken in all the following.

Contemplating the Nativity

First Prelude: How Our Lady went forth from Nazareth, about nine months with child, as can be piously meditated, seated on an ass, and accompanied by Joseph and a maid, taking an ox, to go to Bethlehem to pay the tribute which Caesar imposed on all those lands. Second Prelude: See with the sight of the imagination the road from Nazareth to Bethlehem; considering the length and the breadth, and whether such road is level or through valleys or over hills; likewise looking at the place or cave of the Nativity, how large, how small, how low, how high, and how it was prepared. First Point: See the persons; that is, to see Our Lady and Joseph and the maid, and, after His Birth, the Child Jesus, I making myself a poor creature and a wretch of an unworthy slave, looking at them and serving them in their needs, with all possible respect and reverence, as if I found myself present; and then to reflect on myself in order to draw some profit. Second Point: Look, mark and contemplate what they are saying, and, reflecting on myself, to draw some profit. Third Point: Consider what they are doing, as going a journey and laboring, that the Lord may be born in the greatest poverty; and as a termination of so many labors—of hunger, of thirst, of heat and of cold, of injuries and affronts—that He may die on the Cross; and all this for me: then reflecting, to draw some spiritual profit. Finish with a Colloquy as in the preceding Contemplation, and with an "Our Father."

To Amend and Reform One's Life

It is to be noted that as to those who are settled in ecclesiastical office or in matrimony—whether they abound much or not in temporal goods—when they have no opportunity or have not a very prompt will to make election about the things which fall under an election that can be changed, it is very helpful, in place of making election, to give them a form and way to amend and reform each his own life and state. That is, putting his creation, life and state for the glory and praise of God our Lord and the salvation of his own soul, to come and arrive at this end, he ought to consider much and ponder through the Exercises and Ways of Election, as has been explained, how large a house and household he ought to keep, how he ought to rule and govern it, how he ought to teach and instruct it by word and by example; likewise of his means, how much he ought to take for his household and house; and how much to dispense to the poor and to other pious objects, not wanting nor seeking any other thing except in all and through all the greater praise and glory of God our Lord. For let each one think that he will benefit himself in all spiritual things in proportion as he goes out of his self-love, will and interest.

Prelude for Making Election (Decisions)

In every good election, as far as depends on us, the eye of our intention ought to be simple, only looking at what we are created for, namely, the praise of God our Lord and the salvation of our soul. And so I ought to choose whatever I do, that it may help me for the end for which I am created, not ordering or bringing the end to the means, but the means to the end: as it happens that many choose first to marry—which is a means—and secondarily to serve God our Lord in the married life—which service of God is the end. So, too, there are others who first want to have benefices, and then to serve God in them. They do not go straight to God but want God to come straight to their disordered tendencies, and consequently they make a means of the end, and an end of the means. What they had to take first, they take last; because first we have to set as our aim the wanting to serve God—which is the end—and secondarily, to take a benefice, or to marry, if it is more suitable to us—which is the means for the end. So, nothing ought to move me to take such means or to deprive myself of them, except only the service and praise of God our Lord and the eternal salvation of my soul.

Contemplation at Midnight: How Our Lord Went from Bethany to Jerusalem to the Last Supper

The first Prelude is to bring to memory the narrative which is how Christ our Lord sent two Disciples from Bethany to Jerusalem to prepare the Supper, and then He Himself went there with the other Disciples; and how, after having eaten the Paschal Lamb, and having supped, He washed their feet and gave His most Holy Body and Precious Blood to His Disciples, and made them a discourse, after Judas went to sell his Lord. The second, a composition, seeing the place. It will be here to consider the road from Bethany to Jerusalem, whether broad, whether narrow, whether level, etc.; likewise the place of the Supper, whether large, whether small, whether of one kind or whether of another. The third, to ask for what I want. It will be here grief, feeling and confusion because for my sins the Lord is going to the Passion. The first Point is to see the persons of the Supper, and, reflecting on myself, to see to drawing some profit from them. The second, to hear what they are talking about, and likewise to draw some profit from it. The third, to look at what they are doing, and draw some profit. The fourth, to consider that which Christ our Lord is suffering in His Humanity, or wants to suffer, according to the passage which is being contemplated, and here to commence with much vehemence and to force myself to grieve, be sad and weep, and so to labor through the other points which follow. The fifth, to consider how the Divinity hides Itself, that is, how It could destroy Its enemies and does not do it, and how It leaves the most sacred Humanity to suffer so very cruelly. The sixth, to consider how He suffers all this for my sins, etc.; and what I ought to do and suffer for Him. I will finish with a Colloquy to Christ our Lord, and, at the end, with an "Our Father."

Rules for Eating

The first rule is that it is well to abstain less from bread, because it is not a food as to which the appetite is used to act so inordinately, or to which temptation urges as in the case of the other foods. The second: Abstinence appears more convenient as to drinking, than as to eating bread. So, one ought to look much what is helpful to him, in order to admit it, and what does him harm, in order to discard it. The third: As to foods, one ought to have the greatest and most entire abstinence, because as the appetite is more ready to act inordinately, so temptation is more ready in making trial, on this head. And so abstinence in foods, to avoid disorder, can be kept in two ways, one by accustoming oneself to eat coarse foods; the other, if one takes delicate foods, by taking them in small quantity. The fourth: Guarding against falling into sickness, the more a man leaves off from what is suitable, the more quickly he will reach the mean which he ought to keep in his eating and drinking; for two reasons: the first, because by so helping and disposing himself, he will many times experience more the interior knowledge, consolations and Divine inspirations to show him the mean which is proper for him; the second, because if the person sees himself in such abstinence not with so great corporal strength or disposition for the Spiritual Exercises, he will easily come to judge what is more suitable to his bodily support. The fifth: While the person is eating, let him consider as if he saw Christ our Lord eating with His Apostles, and how He drinks and how He looks and how He speaks; and let him see to imitating Him. So that the principal part of the intellect shall occupy itself in the consideration of Christ our Lord, and the lesser part in the support of the body; because in this way he will get greater system and order as to how he ought to behave and manage himself. The sixth: Another time, while he is eating, he can take another consideration, either on the life of Saints, or on some pious Contemplation, or on some spiritual affair which he has to do, because, being intent on such thing, he will take less delight and feeling in the corporal food. The seventh: Above all, let him guard against all his soul being intent on what he is eating, and in eating let him not go hurriedly, through appetite, but be master of himself, as well in the manner of eating as in the quantity which he eats. The eighth: To avoid disorder, it is very helpful, after dinner or after supper, or at another hour when one feels no appetite for eating, to decide with oneself for the coming dinner or supper, and so on, each day, the quantity which it is suitable that he should eat. Beyond this let him not go because of any appetite or temptation, but rather, in order to conquer more all inordinate appetite and temptation of the enemy, if he is tempted to eat more, let him eat less.

CHAPTER 6

Reformation Theses, Catechisms, and Confessions

The seeds of the movement known as the Protestant Reformation were planted by Catholics reacting against abuses of authority within their own church. The anti-legalistic preaching of John Wycliffe in England (late 1300s) and of John Hus in Bohemia (early 1400s) signaled the beginnings of widespread unrest among Catholics with both the government and teachings of their church. This unrest was in turn fueled by corrupt practices such as simony (buying and selling church offices for profit), indulgences (the sale of official church documents granting forgiveness of sins), and the Inquisition (severe punishment of those who opposed the official teachings of the church). It was against the sale of indulgences that Martin Luther, a Catholic priest and professor of Scripture at Wittenburg University, posted his famous "Ninety-five Theses," condemning both its practice and the papal authority on which it rested; the date was October 31, 1517.

The distribution of Luther's theses by the recently invented printing press gave momentum to the reforming movement and this, together with a host of other social and economic factors, led to the establishment of the first evangelical (Protestant) Lutheran churches of Germany. Even at that early date there were a variety of Protestant sects and many opinions on how the Reformation should proceed. Radical Reformers who followed the teachings of the Swiss priest Ulrich Zwingli insisted on a complete break with the established Church and its practices, while Luther advocated a more moderate response. It would be difficult to exaggerate the impact on the Church of the revolutionary events of the fourteenth through the sixteenth centuries and the lives and writings of Reformers such as Bucer, Calvin, Erasmus, Hus, Luther, Melanchthon, Wycliffe, and Zwingli.

MARTIN LUTHER: "NINETY-FIVE THESES"
Latin, 1517

How could Christians of any era believe that sin could be forgiven through the purchase of a piece of paper—an indulgence? Few common people of the Medieval and Reformation eras could read; fewer still had copies of Scripture with which to refute false teaching. Most accepted whatever the priests taught. The early church belief in the merits of confessors and martyrs (that these could intercede on behalf of the sinful), coupled with fear of God's judgment and a growing belief in purgatory (a transition state where the dead were purged of sins committed while living), encouraged the belief that the outstanding faithfulness of some Christians—namely, the saints—could be converted to a type of currency acceptable before God and the Church to remit the debt of sin. The practice of granting indulgences was already common in the twelfth century A.D.[1] In Martin Luther's day a special plenary-edition indulgence (full forgiveness for all sins) was sold to raise funds for the re-construction of St. Peter's Basilica in Rome. In his "Ninety-five Theses" Martin Luther formally challenged the practice of buying and selling indulgences, but he did so in a manner appropriate to a university setting—by posting a series of scholastic theses for debate. While both Luther and his Catholic opponents believed that Christ had given the "keys" of forgiveness to the Church and its leaders (see Matt. 16:19), Luther condemned the church's practice of selling forgiveness.

---

1. E. A. Livingstone, ed., *The Oxford Dictionary of the Christian Church*, 3rd ed. (Oxford: Oxford University Press, 1997), 830.

Questions for Guided Reading

1. Compare Luther's understanding of repentance with the Catholic practice of penance.
2. What is the limit of the pope's power and authority in relation to forgiveness?
3. How has the doctrine of forgiveness of sins been corrupted through the promotion of indulgences?

Suggested Assignment: The "Ninety-five Theses" for Today

If Luther were alive today, which Church practices might he oppose? Choose one practice Luther might oppose and write a series of theses (statements) based on Scripture and reason in order to disqualify the practice. Test the clarity and persuasiveness of your theses by reading them to others. Were they convinced?

✦

1. When our Lord and Master Jesus Christ said, "Repent" (Matt. 4:17), he meant for a believer's entire life to be an act of repentance.
2. So then, "repentance" cannot be understood as referring to the sacrament of penance, that is, the act of confession and absolution administered by the priest.
3. Nor does it only refer to inward repentance; indeed, such inner repentance is worthless unless it produces an outward mortification of the flesh.
4. And so penance remains while self-hatred remains (that is, true inner repentance), namely until our entrance into the kingdom of heaven.
5. The Pope neither desires nor is able to remit (forgive) any penalties except those imposed by his own authority or that of the canons (church law).
6. The Pope has no power to remit guilt, except by declaring and confirming that it has been remitted by God; or, to be sure, by remitting guilt in cases reserved to his judgment. If he

neglected to observe these limitations the guilt would certainly remain unforgiven.

7. God remits guilt to no one unless at the same time he humbles him in all things and makes him submissive to the priest, God's vicar.
8. The canons of penance are imposed only on the living, and, according to the canons themselves, nothing should be imposed on the dying.
9. Therefore the Holy Spirit, acting through the Pope, is kind to us by granting exception to his decrees in the case of death or other necessity.
10. Those priests who, in the case of the dying, reserve canonical penalties for purgatory act ignorantly and wrongly.
11. Those tares (false teachings) which changed lawful penance into (a teaching about) purgatory must have been sown while the bishops slept (Matt. 13:25).
12. In former times canonical penalties were imposed, not after, but before absolution, as tests of true contrition.
13. The dying are freed by death from all penalties, are already dead as far as the canon laws are concerned, and have a right to be released from them.
14. Imperfect piety or love on the part of the dying person necessarily brings with it great fear; and the smaller the love, the greater the fear.
15. This fear or horror is sufficient in itself, to say nothing of other things, to constitute the penalty of purgatory, since it is very near to the horror of despair.
16. Hell, purgatory, and Heaven seem to differ, as do despair, near-despair, and assurance of safety.
17. It seems likely that for souls in purgatory love is increased in proportion as dread is diminished.
18. Furthermore, it does not seem proved, by reason or by Scripture, that souls in purgatory cannot earn merit or grow in love.
19. Nor does it seem proved that souls in purgatory, at least not all of them, may be sure of their eventual salvation, even if we ourselves have been inclined to believe this.
20. Therefore the Pope, when he uses the words "plenary remission of all penalties," does not

actually mean "all penalties," but only those he himself has imposed.

21. Thus those indulgence preachers err who say that a man is absolved from every penalty and saved by papal indulgences.

22. As a matter of fact, the Pope can forgive no penalty to souls in purgatory which, according to canon law, they should have paid in this life.

23. If remission of all penalties whatsoever could be granted to anyone at all, certainly it would be granted only to the most perfect, that is, to very few.

24. For this reason most people are necessarily deceived by that indiscriminate and high-sounding promise of release from penalty.

25. That power which the Pope has in general over purgatory corresponds to the power which any bishop or curate has in a particular way in his own diocese and parish.

26. The Pope does very well when he grants remission to souls in purgatory, not by the power of the keys, which he does not have, but through intercession.

27. Those who assert that a soul straightway flies out (of purgatory) as soon as the money clinks into the collection box, are preaching an invention of man.

28. Indeed, when money clinks in the collection box, greed and avarice are increased; but the intercession of the church is the will of God alone.

29. Who knows whether all souls in purgatory even desire to be redeemed? (Remember the story told about St. Severinus and St. Paschal.)

30. No one can be absolutely sure of the genuineness of his own repentance, and much less of having received plenary remission (full forgiveness of all sin).

31. The man who honestly purchases his indulgence is as rare as he who is truly repentant—and that is extremely rare!

32. Those who believe that they can be certain of their salvation because they have purchased an indulgence will be eternally damned, together with their teachers.

33. Men must especially be on guard against those who say that the Pope's pardons are that inestimable gift of God by which man is reconciled to him.

34. For the grace imparted by an indulgence relates only to penalties of sacramental satisfaction established by man.

35. They who teach that a repentant heart is not required of those who intend to buy souls out of purgatory or to buy confessional privileges preach unchristian doctrine.

36. Any truly repentant Christian has a right to full remission of penalty and guilt, even without indulgence letters.

37. Any true Christian, whether living or dead, participates in all the blessings of Christ and the church; and this is granted him by God, even without indulgence letters.

38. Nevertheless, papal remission and blessing are by no means to be disregarded, for they are, as I have said (Thesis 6), the proclamation of the divine remission.

39. How can the most skilled theologian teach both the importance of having a repentant heart and the effectiveness of indulgences?

40. A Christian who is truly contrite seeks and loves to pay penalties for his sins; the bounty of indulgences, however, relaxes penalties and causes men to hate them.

41. Papal indulgences must be preached with caution, lest people falsely believe they are better than good works motivated by love.

42. Christians should be taught that the Pope does not equate the buying of indulgences with works of mercy.

43. Christians should be taught that he who gives to the poor or lends to the needy does a better deed than he who buys indulgences.

44. Since love grows through works of love, this is how a man improves himself—not by indulgences.

45. Christians should be taught that he who sees a needy man and passes him by, yet gives his money for indulgences, does not buy papal indulgences but God's wrath.

46. Christians should be taught that, unless they have more money than they need, they must reserve enough for their family needs and by no means squander it on indulgences.

47. Christians should be taught that buying indulgences is a matter of free choice, and not commanded.

48. Christians should be taught that the Pope, by granting indulgences, needs their prayer more than money.

49. Christians should be taught that papal indulgences are useful only if they do not put their trust in them, but harmful if they lose their fear of God because of them.

50. Christians should be taught that if the Pope realized the percentage gleaned by indulgence peddlers, he would rather see St. Peter's Basilica burned to ashes than built up on the skin, flesh, and bones of his sheep.

51. Christians should be taught that the Pope would rather give his own money, even if he had to sell the St. Peter's Basilica, to those from whom the hawkers of indulgences take money.

52. It is vain to trust in salvation by indulgence letters, even though the indulgence commissary, or even the Pope, were to offer his soul as security.

53. They are the enemies of Christ and the Pope who forbid the preaching of the Word of God in those churches which do not permit the promotion of indulgences.

54. Injury is done to the Word of God when, in the same sermon, more time is devoted to preaching indulgences than to the Word.

55. If the Pope directs that indulgences (which are very insignificant) are to be celebrated with a single bell, a single procession, and a single ceremony, then the gospel (which is the very greatest thing), must be proclaimed with a hundred bells, a hundred processions, and a hundred ceremonies.

56. The true treasures of the church, out of which the Pope distributes indulgences, are not sufficiently discussed or known among the people of Christ.

57. It is at least clear that indulgences have no temporal value since they are not freely distributed but only collected by indulgence sellers.

58. Nor are they the merits of Christ and the saints, for, even without the Pope, the latter always work grace for the inner man, and the cross, death, and Hell for the outer man.

59. St. Lawrence said that the poor were the treasures of the church, but in speaking thus he was using the language of his own day.

60. Without rashness, we claim that the keys of the church, given by the merits of Christ, are that treasure.

61. For it is clear that the Pope's power is sufficient only for the remission of penalties imposed by himself.

62. The true treasure of the church is the most holy gospel of the glory and grace of God.

63. But this treasure is naturally most dreaded, for it makes the first to be last (Matt. 20:16).

64. On the other hand, the treasure of indulgences is naturally most acceptable, for it makes the last to be first.

65. Therefore the treasures of the gospel are nets with which one formerly fished for men of wealth.

66. The treasures of indulgences are nets with which one now fishes for the wealth of men.

67. Indulgences, according to the declarations of those who preach them, are the greatest graces; but "greatest" for them refers to the revenue they earn.

68. Indulgences are in fact the least significant graces when compared with the grace of God and the piety of the cross.

69. Bishops and curates are required to accept papal indulgences with all reverence.

70. Yet much more are they required to be certain they do not proclaim their own exaggerations than the Pope's commission.

71. Let him who speaks against the truth concerning papal indulgences be anathema and accursed.

72. But let him who guards against the lust and license of the indulgence preachers be blessed.

73. As the Pope rightly condemns those who oppose the sale of indulgences.

74. Much more shall he condemn those who use indulgences as a pretext to harm holy charity and truth.

75. To believe that papal indulgences are so great they could absolve any man is madness—as if

they could absolve a man who (to assume the impossible) had violated the mother of God.

76. We say on the contrary that papal indulgences cannot remove the very least of venial sins as far as guilt is concerned.

77. To say that even St. Peter, if he were now Pope, could not grant greater graces is blasphemy against St. Peter and the Pope.

78. We say on the contrary that even the present Pope, or any Pope whatsoever, has greater graces at his disposal, that is, the gospel, spiritual powers, gifts of healing, etc., as it is written in 1 Corinthians 12:28.

79. To say that the cross emblazoned with the papal coat of arms, and set up by the indulgence preachers is equal in worth to the cross of Christ is blasphemy.

80. The bishops, curates, and theologians who permit such talk to be spread among the people will have to answer for this.

81. The unrestricted preaching of indulgences makes it difficult even for learned men to rescue the reverence which is due the Pope from slander or from the shrewd questions of the laity.

82. For example: "Why doesn't the Pope simply forgive everyone in purgatory, for the sake of holy love and the dire need of the souls that are there, if he redeems an infinite number of souls for the sake of miserable money with which to build a church?" The former reason would be most just; the latter is most trivial.

83. And, "Why are funeral and anniversary masses for the dead continued and why does he not return or permit the withdrawal of money given for them, since it is wrong to pray for the redeemed?"

84. Again, "What sort of piety would allow a corrupt man and an enemy of God to purchase a redeemed soul and friendship with God, while failing to freely redeem a pious soul (who has no money to purchase an indulgence)?

86. Again, "Why doesn't the Pope—whose wealth exceeds the wealthiest—build St. Peter's Basilica with his own money than with the money of poor believers?"

87. Again, "What does the Pope offer those who, by

perfect repentance, already have a right to full remission and blessings?"

88. Again, "What greater blessing could come to the church than if the Pope were to bestow these remissions and blessings on every believer a hundred times a day, as he now does but once?"

89. Finally, "If the Pope uses indulgences only for the sake of the salvation of souls, and not for raising money, then why has he nullified the value of all indulgences and pardons previously granted?"

90. To suppress these considered objections from the laity and not to resolve them by giving reasons, is to expose the church and the Pope to the ridicule of their enemies and to make Christians unhappy.

91. If indulgences were preached as they ought to be, according to the spirit and intention of the Pope, then all these doubts would be resolved and, indeed, done away with.

92. Away, then, with all those prophets who say to the people of Christ, "Peace, peace," and there is no peace (Jer. 6:14)!

93. And farewell to all those prophets who say to the people of Christ, "Cross, cross," and there is no cross!

94. Christians should be exhorted to be diligent in following Christ, their Head, through pain, death, and Hell.

95. And so let them be confident of entering into heaven through many tribulations rather than through the false confidence of peace (Acts 14:22).

MARTIN LUTHER: *SHORTER CATECHISM*
German, 1529

Three central teachings of the Protestant Reformation—justification by faith, the supremacy of Scripture, and the priesthood of all believers—grew out of the experience of Martin Luther. Having lived as a Catholic monk, Luther had been taught that God awarded the grace necessary for salvation to those who earnestly strove for it. In contrast to this view of righteousness by works, Luther emphasized the scriptural teaching, found especially in the writings of the Apostle Paul, of the justification of believers by faith alone in Christ alone. Secondly, against the pope's claim to be final authority in matters of teaching and church government, Luther insisted that any claim that could not be proven by Scripture was to be abandoned. Finally, against the prevailing tendency to divide Christendom into spiritual (clergy) and temporal (laity) estates, Luther taught that all believers were responsible for their conduct before God, and that no one group enjoyed a special status before God; nor was anyone (i.e., the priest) able to mediate salvation for another. Luther believed strongly in the Christian education of all children. He wrote his *Shorter Catechism*, known as the "Jewel of the Reformation," to provide Christian parents with guidelines and a basic curriculum for teaching their children in the home. Luther encouraged reading instruction and the use of the catechism by pastors for the instruction of their flock and for all Christians as a daily devotional guide.

Questions for Guided Reading

1. Describe Luther's main complaints against and recommendation for gospel ministers.
2. What benefit is it to ministers that they are no longer under Catholicism, and in what ways should this help them in their devotion to God and study?
3. Now that the laity (non-priests, "common people") can read Scripture for themselves, are they benefiting?
4. According to Luther, how does his use of the catechism contrast with others?
5. What are the benefits of meditating on God's Word?
6. Identify the Old Testament passage, the Christian creed, and the New Testament prayer in this document.
7. Identify three articles of the creed and how they form a theological framework for it.
8. Identify the three sacraments described in this document.
9. What is the "sacrament of the altar"?
10. What is the expected context of this teaching (who teaches whom and where)?
11. Why do you suppose that Luther, who viewed

the rote prayers of monks as "burdensome babbling," taught people specific forms of prayer in this catechism?

Suggested Assignment: A Catechism for Today

After studying Luther's *Shorter Catechism* and answering the questions above, outline your own brief catechism for today's Christian. What would you name your catechism? What would it include and teach?

A faithful, earnest exhortation of Dr. Martin Luther to all Christians, but especially to all pastors and preachers, that they should daily exercise themselves in the catechism, which is a short summary and epitome of the entire holy Scripture, and that they may always teach the same.

We have many reasons for presenting the Catechism constantly in our lessons and sermons and for requiring others to teach it. However, many preachers and teachers are very negligent in this, disregarding both their call and this teaching; some for what are supposed to be important reasons and others from sheer laziness, as they have been accustomed to treat their duties under the Papacy. And although they now have everything that they are to preach and teach placed before them so abundantly, clearly, and easily, in so many excellent and helpful books, yet they are not so godly and honest as to buy these books, or even when they have them, to read them. Alas! They are altogether shameful gluttons and servants of their own bellies who ought to be swineherds and dog-tenders rather than caretakers of souls and pastors.[2] Indeed, no longer are they required to follow the unprofitable and burdensome babbling of the Seven Canonical Hours,[3] but is it too much to ask that they read a page or two, once in the morning, at noon, and in the evening from the Catechism, the Prayer-book, the New Testament, or elsewhere in the Bible, and pray the Lord's Prayer for themselves and their parishioners? Now, the common people regard the Gospel altogether

---

2. The harsh tone of this writing was typical of Luther's day.
3. A monk's daily life followed the schedule of the "divine office" of daily worship and recitations (see Benedict's *Rule*).

too lightly, and we accomplish nothing extraordinary even though we use all diligence. What, then, will be achieved if we shall be negligent and lazy as we were under the Papacy? To this there is added the shameful vice and secret infection of security and satiety, that is, that many regard the Catechism as a poor, mean teaching, which they can read through at one time, and then immediately know it, throw the book into a corner, and be ashamed, as it were, to read in it again. Yea, even among the nobility there may be found some louts and scrimps, who declare that there is no longer any need either of pastors or preachers; that we have everything in books, and every one can easily learn it by himself; and so they are content to let the parishes decay and become desolate, and pastors and preachers to suffer distress and hunger a plenty, just as it becomes crazy Germans to do. For we Germans have such disgraceful people, and must endure them.

I, too, am a doctor and preacher, as learned and experienced as all those may be who have such presumption and security; yet I do as a child who is being taught the Catechism, and every morning, and whenever I have time, I read and say, word for word, the Ten Commandments, the Creed, the Lord's Prayer, the Psalms, etc. And I must still read and study daily, and yet I cannot master it as I wish, but must remain a child and pupil of the Catechism, and am glad so to remain. And yet these delicate, fastidious fellows would with one reading promptly be doctors above all doctors, know everything and be in need of nothing. Well, this, too, is indeed a sure sign that they despise both their office and the souls of the people, yea, even God and His Word. They do not have to fall, they are already fallen all too horribly, they would need to become children, and begin to learn their alphabet, which they imagine that they have long since outgrown. Therefore I beg such lazy and presumptuous saints to be persuaded and believe for God's sake that they are not so learned or such great doctors as they imagine; and never to presume that they have finished learning this Catechism, or know it well enough in all points, even though they think that they know it ever so well. For though they should know and understand it perfectly (which, however, is impossible in this life), yet there are manifold benefits and fruits still to be obtained, if it be daily read and practiced in thought and speech; namely, that the Holy Ghost is present in such reading and repetition and meditation,

and bestows ever new and more light and devoutness, so that it is daily relished and appreciated better, as Christ promises [in Matt.18:20] "Where two or three are gathered together in My name, there am I in the midst of them." Besides, it is an exceedingly effective help against the devil, the world, and the flesh and all evil thoughts to be occupied with the Word of God, and to speak of it, and meditate upon it, so that the First Psalm declares those blessed who meditate upon the law of God day and night. Undoubtedly, you will not start a stronger incense or other fumigation against the devil than by being engaged upon God's commandments and words, and speaking, singing, or thinking of them. For this is indeed the true holy water and holy sign from which he flees, and by which he may be driven away. Now, for this reason alone you ought gladly to read, speak, think and treat of these things if you had no other profit and fruit from them than that by doing so you can drive away the devil and evil thoughts. For he cannot hear or endure God's Word; and God's Word is not some silly prattle but, as St. Paul says, "the power of God."

And if this were not sufficient to admonish us to read the Catechism daily, yet we should feel sufficiently constrained by the command of God alone, who solemnly enjoins in Deuteronomy 6:6ff. that we should always meditate upon His precepts, sitting, walking, standing, lying down, and rising, and have them before our eyes and in our hands as a constant mark and sign. Doubtless He did not so solemnly require and enjoin this without a purpose; but because He knows our danger and need, as well as the constant and furious assaults and temptations of devils, He wishes to warn, equip, and preserve us against them, as with a good armor against their fiery darts and with good medicine against their evil infection and suggestion. To this end may God grant His grace! Amen.

Part I: The Ten Commandments and the simple way a father should present them to his household

A.   The First Commandment: You must not have other gods.
Q.   What does this mean?
Ans.   We must fear, love, and trust God more than anything else.

B.   The Second Commandment: You must not misuse your God's name.

Q.   What does this mean?

Ans.   We must fear and love God, so that we will not use His name to curse, swear, cast a spell, lie or deceive, but will use it to call upon Him, pray to Him, praise Him and thank Him in all times of trouble.

C.   The Third Commandment: You must keep the Sabbath holy.

Q.   What does this mean?

Ans.   We must fear and love God, so that we will not look down on preaching or God's Word, but consider it holy, listen to it willingly, and learn it.

D.   The Fourth Commandment: You must honor your father and mother. [So that things will go well for you and you will live long on earth.][4]

Q.   What does this mean?

Ans.   We must fear and love God, so that we will neither look down on our parents or superiors nor irritate them, but will honor them, serve them, obey them, love them and value them.

E.   The Fifth Commandment: You must not kill.

Q.   What does this mean?

Ans.   We must fear and love God, so that we will neither harm nor hurt our neighbor's body, but help him and care for him when he is ill.

F.   The Sixth Commandment: You must not commit adultery.

Q.   What does this mean?

Ans.   We must fear and love God, so that our words and actions will be clean and decent and so that everyone will love and honor their spouses.

G.   The Seventh Commandment: You must not steal.

Q.   What does this mean?

Ans.   We must fear and love God, so that we will neither take our neighbor's money or property, nor acquire it by fraud or by selling him poorly made products, but will help him improve and protect his property and career.

H.   The Eighth Commandment: You must not tell lies about your neighbor.

Q.   What does this mean?

Ans.   We must fear and love God, so that we will not deceive by lying, betraying, slandering or ruining our neighbor's reputation, but will defend him, say good things about him, and see the best side of everything he does.

I.   The Ninth Commandment: You must not desire your neighbor's house.

Q.   What does this mean?

Ans.   We must fear and love God, so that we will not attempt to trick our neighbor out of his inheritance or house, take it by pretending to have a right to it, etc. but help him to keep and improve it.

J.   The Tenth Commandment: You must not desire your neighbor's wife, servant, maid, animals or anything that belongs to him.

Q.   What does this mean?

Ans.   We must fear and love God, so that we will not release his cattle, take his employees from him or seduce his wife, but urge them to stay and do what they ought to do.

K.   The Conclusion to the Commandments

Q.   What does God say to us about all these commandments?

Ans.   This is what He says: "I am the Lord Your God. I am a jealous God. I plague the grandchildren and great-grandchildren of those who hate me with their ancestor's sin. But I make

---

4.   Brackets in original.

whole those who love me for a thousand generations."

Q.   What does this mean?

Ans.   God threatens to punish everyone who breaks these commandments. We should be afraid of His anger because of this and not violate such commandments. But He promises grace and all good things to those who keep such commandments. Because of this, we too should love Him, trust Him, and willingly do what His commandments require.

Part II: The Apostles' Creed

I.   The First Article: On Creation
I believe in God the Almighty Father, Creator of Heaven and Earth.

Q.   What does this mean?

Ans.   I believe that God created me, along with all creatures. He gave to me: body and soul, eyes, ears and all the other parts of my body, my mind and all my senses and preserves them as well. He gives me clothing and shoes, food and drink, house and land, wife and children, fields, animals and all I own. Every day He abundantly provides everything I need to nourish this body and life. He protects me against all danger, shields and defends me from all evil. He does all this because of His pure, fatherly and divine goodness and His mercy, not because I've earned it or deserved it. For all of this, I must thank Him, praise Him, serve Him and obey Him. Yes, this is true!

II.   The Second Article: On Redemption
And in Jesus Christ, His only Son, our Lord, Who was conceived by the Holy Spirit, born of the Virgin Mary, suffered under Pontius Pilate, was crucified, died and was buried, descended to Hell, on the third day rose again from the dead, ascended to Heaven and sat down at the right hand of God the Almighty Father. From there He will come to judge the living and the dead.

Q.   What does this mean?

Ans.   I believe that Jesus Christ is truly God, born of the Father in eternity and also truly man, born of the Virgin Mary. He is my Lord! He redeemed me, a lost and condemned person, bought and won me from all sins, death and the authority of the Devil. It did not cost Him gold or silver, but His holy, precious blood, His innocent body—His death! Because of this, I am His very own, will live under Him in His kingdom and serve Him righteously, innocently and blessedly forever, just as He is risen from death, lives and reigns forever. Yes, this is true!

III.   The Third Article: On Becoming Holy
I believe in the Holy Spirit, the holy Christian Church, the community of the saints, the forgiveness of sins, the resurrection of the body, and an everlasting life. Amen.

Q.   What does this mean?

Ans.   I believe that I cannot come to my Lord Jesus Christ by my own intelligence or power. But the Holy Spirit called me by the Gospel, enlightened me with His gifts, made me holy and kept me in the true faith, just as He calls, gathers together, enlightens and makes holy the whole Church on earth and keeps it with Jesus in the one, true faith. In this Church, He generously forgives each day every sin committed by me and by every believer. On the last day, He will raise me and all the dead from the grave. He will give eternal life to me and to all who believe in Christ. Yes, this is true!

Part III: On the Lord's Prayer

I.   Introduction: Our Father, Who is in Heaven

Q.   What does this mean?

Ans.   In this introduction, God invites us to believe that He is our real Father and we are His real children, so that we will pray with trust and complete confidence, in the same way beloved children approach their beloved Father with their requests.

II. The First Request: May Your name be holy

Q. What does this mean?

Ans. Of course, God's name is holy in and of itself, but by this request, we pray that He will make it holy among us, too.

Q. How does this take place?

Ans. When God's Word is taught clearly and purely, and when we live holy lives as God's children based upon it. Help us, heavenly Father, to do this! But anyone who teaches and lives by something other than God's Word defiles God's name among us. Protect us from this, heavenly Father!

III. The Second Request: Your Kingdom come

Q. What does this mean?

Ans. Truly God's Kingdom comes by itself, without our prayer. But we pray in this request that it come to us as well.

Q. How does this happen?

Ans. When the heavenly Father gives us His Holy Spirit, so that we believe His holy Word by His grace and live godly lives here in this age and there in eternal life.

IV. The Third Request: May Your will be accomplished, as it is Heaven, so may it be on Earth

Q. What does this mean?

Ans. Truly, God's good and gracious will is accomplished without our prayer. But we pray in this request that it be accomplished among us as well.

Q. How does this happen?

Ans. When God destroys and interferes with every evil will and all evil advice, which will not allow God's Kingdom to come, such as the Devil's will, the world's will and will of our bodily desires. It also happens when God strengthens us by faith and by His Word and keeps living by them faithfully until the end of our

lives. This is His will, good and full of grace.

V. The Fourth Request: Give us our daily bread today

Q. What does this mean?

Ans. Truly, God gives daily bread to evil people, even without our prayer. But we pray in this request that He will help us realize this and receive our daily bread with thanksgiving.

Q. What does "daily bread" mean?

Ans. Everything that nourishes our body and meets its needs, such as: Food, drink, clothing, shoes, house, yard, fields, cattle, money, possessions, a devout spouse, devout children, devout employees, devout and faithful rulers, good government, good weather, peace, health, discipline, honor, good friends, faithful neighbors and other things like these.

VI. The Fifth Request: And forgive our guilt, as we forgive those guilty of sinning against us

Q. What does this mean?

Ans. We pray in this request that our heavenly Father will neither pay attention to our sins nor refuse requests such as these because of our sins and because we are neither worthy nor deserve the things for which we pray. Yet He wants to give them all to us by His grace, because many times each day we sin and truly deserve only punishment. Because God does this, we will, of course, want to forgive from our hearts and willingly do good to those who sin against us.

VII. The Sixth Request: And lead us not into temptation

Q. What does this mean?

Ans. God tempts no one, of course, but we pray in this request that God will protect us and save us, so that the Devil, the world and our bodily desires will neither deceive us nor seduce us into heresy, despair or other serious shame or vice, and so that we will win and be victorious in the end, even if they attack us.

VIII. The Seventh Request: But set us free from the Evil One

Q. What does this mean?

Ans. We pray in this request, as a summary, that our Father in Heaven will save us from every kind of evil that threatens body, soul, property and honor. We pray that when at last our final hour has come, He will grant us a blessed death, and, in His grace, bring us to Himself from this valley of tears.

IX. Amen.

Q. What does this mean?

Ans. That I should be certain that such prayers are acceptable to the Father in Heaven and will be granted, that He Himself has commanded us to pray in this way and that He promises to answer us. Amen. This means: Yes, yes it will happen this way.

Part IV: The Sacrament of Holy Baptism

I. Q. What is Baptism?

Ans. Baptism is not just plain water, but it is water contained within God's command and united with God's Word.

Q. Which Word of God is this?

Ans. The one which our Lord Christ spoke in the last chapter of Matthew: "Go into all the world, teaching all heathen nations, and baptizing them in the name of the Father, the Son and of the Holy Spirit."

II. Q. What does Baptism give? What good is it?

Ans. It gives the forgiveness of sins, redeems from death and the Devil, gives eternal salvation to all who believe this, just as God's words and promises declare.

Q. What are these words and promises of God?

Ans. Our Lord Christ spoke one of them in the last chapter of Mark: "Whoever believes and is baptized will be saved; but whoever does not believe will be damned."

III. Q. How can water do such great things?

Ans. Water doesn't make these things happen, of course. It is God's Word, which is with and in the water. Because, without God's Word, the water is plain water and not baptism. But with God's Word it is a Baptism, a grace-filled water of life, a bath of new birth in the Holy Spirit, as St. Paul said to Titus in the third chapter: "Through this bath of rebirth and renewal of the Holy Spirit, which He poured out on us abundantly through Jesus Christ, our Savior, that we, justified by the same grace are made heirs according to the hope of eternal life. This is a faithful saying."

IV. Q. What is the meaning of such a water Baptism?

Ans. It means that the old Adam in us should be drowned by daily sorrow and repentance, and die with all sins and evil lusts, and, in turn, a new person daily come forth and rise from death again. He will live forever before God in righteousness and purity.

Q. Where is this written?

Ans. St. Paul says to the Romans in chapter six: "We are buried with Christ through Baptism into death, so that, in the same way Christ is risen from the dead by the glory of the Father, thus also must we walk in a new life."

Part V: How one should teach the uneducated to confess

I. Q. What is confession?

Ans. Confession has two parts: First, a

person admits his sin; second, a person receives absolution or forgiveness from the confessor, as if from God Himself, without doubting it, but believing firmly that his sins are forgiven by God in Heaven through it.

II. Q. Which sins should people confess?
Ans. When speaking to God, we should plead guilty to all sins, even those we don't know about, just as we do in the "Our Father," but when speaking to the confessor, only the sins we know about, which we know about and feel in our hearts.

Q. Which are these?
Ans. Consider here your place in life according to the Ten Commandments. Are you a father? A mother? A son? A daughter? A husband? A wife? A servant? Are you disobedient, unfaithful or lazy? Have you hurt anyone with your words or actions? Have you stolen, neglected your duty, let things go or injured someone?

Part VI: The sacrament of the altar and the simple way a father should present it to his household

I. Q. What is the Sacrament of the Altar?
Ans. It is the true body and blood of our Lord Jesus Christ under bread and wine for us Christians to eat and to drink, established by Christ Himself.

II. Q. Where is that written?
Ans. The holy apostles Matthew, Mark and Luke and St. Paul write this: "Our Lord Jesus Christ, in the night on which He was betrayed, took bread, gave thanks, broke it, gave it to His disciples and said: 'Take! Eat! This is My body, which is given for you. Do this to remember Me.' In the same way He also took the cup after supper, gave thanks, gave it to them, and said: 'Take and drink from it, all of you. This cup is the New Covenant in my blood, which is shed for you to forgive sins. This do, as often as you drink it, to remember Me.'"

III. Q. What good does this eating and drinking do?
Ans. These words tell us: "Given for you" and "Shed for you to forgive your sins," namely, that the forgiveness of sins, life and salvation are given to us through these words in the sacrament. Because, where sins are forgiven, there is life and salvation as well.

IV. Q. How can physical eating and drinking do such great things?
Ans. Of course, eating and drinking do not do these things. These words, written here, do them: "given for you" and "shed for you to forgive sins." These words, along with physical eating and drinking are the important part of the sacrament. Anyone who believes these words has what they say and what they record, namely, the forgiveness of sins.

V. Q. Who, then, receives such a sacrament in a worthy way?
Ans. Of course, fasting and other physical preparations are excellent disciplines for the body. But anyone who believes these words, "Given for you," and "Shed for you to forgive sins," is really worthy and well prepared. But whoever doubts or does not believe these words is not worthy and is unprepared, because the words, "for you" demand a heart that fully believes.

Appendix: How a father should teach his household to conduct devotions

Morning Devotions

As soon as you get out of bed in the morning, you should bless yourself with the sign of the Holy Cross and say: "May the will of God, the Father, the Son and the Holy Spirit be done! Amen." Then, kneeling or standing, say the creed and pray the Lord's Prayer. If you wish, you may then pray this little prayer as well: "My heavenly Father, I thank You, through Jesus Christ, Your beloved Son, that You kept me safe from all evil and danger last night. Save me, I pray, today as well, from every evil and sin, so that all I do and the way that I live will please you. I put myself in your care, body and soul and all that I have. Let Your holy Angels be with me, so that the evil enemy will not gain power over me. Amen." After that, with joy go about your work and perhaps sing a song inspired by the Ten Commandments or your own thoughts.

Evening Devotions

When you go to bed in the evening, you should bless yourself with the sign of the Holy Cross and say: "May the will of God, the Father, the Son and the Holy Spirit be done! Amen." Then, kneeling or standing, say the creed and pray the Lord's Prayer. If you wish, then you may pray this little prayer as well: "My heavenly Father, I thank You, through Jesus Christ, Your beloved Son, that You have protected me, by Your grace. Forgive, I pray, all my sins and the evil I have done. Protect me, by Your grace, tonight. I put myself in your care, body and soul and all that I have. Let Your holy angels be with me, so that the evil enemy will not gain power over me. Amen." And after this, go to sleep immediately with joy!

How a Father Should Teach His Household to Return Thanks at Meals

The children and servants should come to the table modestly and with folded hands and say: "All eyes look to you, O Lord, and You give everyone food at the right time. You open Your generous hands and satisfy the hunger of all living things with what they desire."

After this, pray the Lord's Prayer and, finally, the following prayer: "Lord God, heavenly Father, bless us and these gifts, which we receive from Your generous hand, through Jesus Christ, our Lord. Amen."

PHILIP MELANCHTHON: *AUGSBURG CONFESSION*
German Text, 1530

The year after Luther posted his "Ninety-five Theses" (1517), Philip Melanchthon became professor of Greek at the same university (Wittenburg) and quickly embraced Reformation teachings. With Luther's permission, Melanchthon systematized these teachings in a "confession" presented to Emperor Charles V at Augsburg, Germany, in June of 1530. Readers will note the irenic tone of the confession (particularly in contrast to Luther's writing), intended to reduce Catholic offence. The *Confession* is reprinted here in its entirety.[5] Part 1 of the *Confession* is a summary in 21 articles of Lutheran doctrine, including the Reformers' response to elements of Catholic doctrine such as good works (XX) and the worship of saints (XXI). Part 2 clarifies and defends elements of Lutheran teaching that were especially subject to controversy.

The Confession of Faith which was submitted to His Imperial Majesty Charles V at the Diet of Augsburg in the Year 1530, by Philip Melanchthon, 1497–1560.

Preface to the Emperor Charles V

Most Invincible Emperor, Caesar Augustus, Most Clement Lord: Inasmuch as Your Imperial Majesty has summoned a Diet of the Empire here at Augsburg to deliberate concerning measures against the Turk, that most atrocious, hereditary, and ancient enemy of the Christian name and religion, in what way, namely, effectually to withstand his furor and assaults by strong and lasting military provision; and then also concerning dissensions in the matter of our holy religion and Christian Faith, that in this matter of religion the opinions and judgments of the parties might be heard in each other's presence; and considered and weighed among ourselves in mutual charity, leniency, and kindness, in order that, after the removal and correction of such things as have been treated and understood in a different manner in the writings on either side, these matters may be settled and brought back to one simple truth and

---

5. F. Bente and W. H. T. Dau, trans., *Triglot Concordia: The Symbolic Books of the Evangelical Lutheran Church* (St. Louis: Concordia, 1921), 37–95.

Christian concord, that for the future one pure and true religion may be embraced and maintained by us, that as we all are under one Christ and do battle under Him, so we may be able also to live in unity and concord in the one Christian Church. And inasmuch as we, the undersigned Elector and Princes, with others joined with us, have been called to the aforesaid Diet the same as the other Electors, Princes, and Estates, in obedient compliance with the Imperial mandate, we have promptly come to Augsburg, and (what we do not mean to say as boasting) we were among the first to be here.

Accordingly, since even here at Augsburg at the very beginning of the Diet, Your Imperial Majesty caused to be proposed to the Electors, Princes, and other Estates of the Empire, amongst other things, that the several Estates of the Empire, on the strength of the Imperial edict, should set forth and submit their opinions and judgments in the German and the Latin language, and since on the ensuing Wednesday, answer was given to Your Imperial Majesty, after due deliberation, that we would submit the Articles of our Confession for our side on next Wednesday, therefore, in obedience to Your Imperial Majesty's wishes, we offer, in this matter of religion, the Confession of our preachers and of ourselves, showing what manner of doctrine from the Holy Scriptures and the pure Word of God has been up to this time set forth in our lands, dukedoms, dominions, and cities, and taught in our churches.

And if the other Electors, Princes, and Estates of the Empire will, according to the said Imperial proposition, present similar writings, to wit, in Latin and German, giving their opinions in this matter of religion, we, with the Princes and friends aforesaid, here before Your Imperial Majesty, our most clement Lord are prepared to confer amicably concerning all possible ways and means, in order that we may come together, as far as this may be honorably done, and, the matter between us on both sides being peacefully discussed without offensive strife, the dissension, by God's help, may be done away and brought back to one true accordant religion; for as we all are under one Christ and do battle under Him, we ought to confess the one Christ, after the tenor of Your Imperial Majesty's edict, and everything ought to be conducted according to the truth of God; and this it is what, with most fervent prayers, we entreat of God. However, as regards the rest of the Electors, Princes, and Estates, who consti-

tute the other part, if no progress should be made, nor some result be attained by this treatment of the cause of religion after the manner in which Your Imperial Majesty has wisely held that it should be dealt with and treated namely, by such mutual presentation of writings and calm conferring together among ourselves, we at least leave with you a clear testimony, that we here in no wise are holding back from anything that could bring about Christian concord (such as could be effected with God and a good conscience), as also Your Imperial Majesty and, next, the other Electors and Estates of the Empire, and all who are moved by sincere love and zeal for religion, and who will give an impartial hearing to this matter, will graciously deign to take notice and to understand this from this Confession of ours and of our associates. Your Imperial Majesty also, not only once but often, graciously signified to the Electors, Princes, and Estates of the Empire, and at the Diet of Spires held A.D. 1526, according to the form of Your Imperial instruction and commission given and prescribed, caused it to be stated and publicly proclaimed that Your Majesty, in dealing with this matter of religion, for certain reasons which were alleged in Your Majesty's name, was not willing to decide and could not determine anything, but that Your Majesty would diligently use Your Majesty's office with the Roman Pontiff for the convening of a General Council. The same matter was thus publicly set forth at greater length a year ago at the last Diet which met at Spires. There Your Imperial Majesty, through His Highness Ferdinand, King of Bohemia and Hungary, our friend and clement Lord, as well as through the Orator and Imperial Commissioners caused this, among other things, to be submitted:

That Your Imperial Majesty had taken notice of; and pondered, the resolution of Your Majesty's Representative in the Empire, and of the President and Imperial Counselors, and the Legates from other Estates convened at Ratisbon, concerning the calling of a Council, and that your Imperial Majesty also judged it to be expedient to convene a Council; and that Your Imperial Majesty did not doubt the Roman Pontiff could be induced to hold a General Council, because the matters to be adjusted between Your Imperial Majesty and the Roman Pontiff were nearing agreement and Christian reconciliation; therefore Your Imperial Majesty himself signified that he would endeavor to secure the said

Chief Pontiff's consent for convening, together with your Imperial Majesty such General Council, to be published as soon as possible by letters that were to be sent out. If the outcome, therefore, should be such that the differences between us and the other parties in the matter of religion should not be amicably and in charity settled, then here, before Your Imperial Majesty we make the offer in all obedience, in addition to what we have already done, that we will all appear and defend our cause in such a general, free Christian Council, for the convening of which there has always been accordant action and agreement of votes in all the Imperial Diets held during Your Majesty's reign, on the part of the Electors, Princes, and other Estates of the Empire. To the assembly of this General Council, and at the same time to Your Imperial Majesty, we have, even before this, in due manner and form of law, addressed ourselves and made appeal in this matter, by far the greatest and gravest. To this appeal, both to Your Imperial Majesty and to a Council, we still adhere; neither do we intend nor would it be possible for us, to relinquish it by this or any other document, unless the matter between us and the other side, according to the tenor of the latest Imperial citation should be amicably and charitably settled, allayed, and brought to Christian concord; and regarding this we even here solemnly and publicly testify.

Article I: Of God

Our Churches, with common consent, do teach that the decree of the Council of Nicaea concerning the Unity of the Divine Essence and concerning the Three Persons, is true and to be believed without any doubting; that is to say, there is one Divine Essence which is called and which is God: eternal, without body, without parts, of infinite power, wisdom, and goodness, the Maker and Preserver of all things, visible and invisible; and yet there are three Persons, of the same essence and power, who also are coeternal, the Father, the Son, and the Holy Ghost. And the term "person" they use as the Fathers have used it, to signify, not a part or quality in another, but that which subsists of itself. They condemn all heresies which have sprung up against this article, as the Manichaeans, who assumed two principles, one Good and the other Evil—also the Valentinians, Arians, Eunomians, Mohammedans, and all such. They condemn also the Samosatenes, old and new, who, contending that there is but one Person, sophistically and impiously argue that the Word and the Holy Ghost are not distinct Persons, but that "Word" signifies a spoken word, and "Spirit" signifies motion created in things.

Article II: Of Original Sin

Also they teach that since the fall of Adam all men begotten in the natural way are born with sin, that is, without the fear of God, without trust in God, and with concupiscence; and that this disease, or vice of origin, is truly sin, even now condemning and bringing eternal death upon those not born again through Baptism and the Holy Ghost. They Condemn the Pelagians and others who deny that original depravity is sin, and who, to obscure the glory of Christ's merit and benefits, argue that man can be justified before God by his own strength and reason.

Article III: Of the Son of God

Also they teach that the Word, that is, the Son of God, did assume the human nature in the womb of the blessed Virgin Mary, so that there are two natures, the divine and the human, inseparably enjoined in one Person, one Christ, true God and true man, who was born of the Virgin Mary, truly suffered, was crucified, dead, and buried, that He might reconcile the Father unto us, and be a sacrifice, not only for original guilt, but also for all actual sins of men. He also descended into hell, and truly rose again the third day; afterward He ascended into heaven that He might sit on the right hand of the Father, and forever reign and have dominion over all creatures, and sanctify them that believe in Him, by sending the Holy Ghost into their hearts, to rule, comfort, and quicken them, and to defend them against the devil and the power of sin. The same Christ shall openly come again to judge the quick and the dead, etc., according to the Apostles' Creed.

Article IV: Of Justification

Also they teach that men cannot be justified before God by their own strength, merits, or works, but are freely justified for Christ's sake, through faith, when they believe that they are received into favor, and that their sins are forgiven for Christ's sake, who, by His death, has made satisfaction for our sins. This faith God imputes for righteousness in His sight (Rom. 3 and 4).

Article V: Of the Ministry

That we may obtain this faith, the Ministry of Teaching the Gospel and administering the Sacraments was instituted. For through the Word and Sacraments, as through instruments, the Holy Ghost is given, who works faith; where and when it pleases God, in them that hear the Gospel, to wit, that God, not for our own merits, but for Christ's sake, justifies those who believe that they are received into grace for Christ's sake. They condemn the Anabaptists and others who think that the Holy Ghost comes to men without the external Word, through their own preparations and works.

Article VI: Of New Obedience

Also they teach that this faith is bound to bring forth good fruits, and that it is necessary to do good works commanded by God, because of God's will, but that we should not rely on those works to merit justification before God. For remission of sins and justification is apprehended by faith, as also the voice of Christ attests: When ye shall have done all these things, say: We are unprofitable servants (Luke 17:10). The same is also taught by the Fathers. For Ambrose says: It is ordained of God that he who believes in Christ is saved, freely receiving remission of sins, without works, by faith alone.

Article VII: Of the Church

Also they teach that one holy Church is to continue forever. The Church is the congregation of saints, in which the Gospel is rightly taught and the Sacraments are rightly administered. And to the true unity of the Church it is enough to agree concerning the doctrine of the Gospel and the administration of the Sacraments. Nor is it necessary that human traditions, that is, rites or ceremonies, instituted by men, should be everywhere alike. As Paul says: One faith, one Baptism, one God and Father of all, etc. (Eph. 4:5–6).

Article VIII: What the Church Is

Although the Church properly is the congregation of saints and true believers, nevertheless, since in this life many hypocrites and evil persons are mingled therewith, it is lawful to use Sacraments administered by evil men, according to the saying of Christ: The Scribes and the Pharisees sit in Moses' seat, etc. (Matt. 23:2). Both the Sacraments and Word are effectual by reason of the institution and commandment of Christ, notwithstanding they be administered by evil men.

They condemn the Donatists, and such like, who denied it to be lawful to use the ministry of evil men in the Church, and who thought the ministry of evil men to be unprofitable and of none effect.

Article IX: Of Baptism

Of Baptism they teach that it is necessary to salvation, and that through Baptism is offered the grace of God, and that children are to be baptized who, being offered to God through Baptism are received into God's grace. They condemn the Anabaptists, who reject the baptism of children, and say that children are saved without Baptism.

Article X: Of the Lord's Supper

Of the Supper of the Lord they teach that the Body and Blood of Christ are truly present, and are distributed to those who eat the Supper of the Lord; and they reject those that teach otherwise.

Article XI: Of Confession

Of confession they teach that Private Absolution ought to be retained in the churches, although in confession an enumeration of all sins is not necessary. For it is impossible according to the Psalm: Who can understand his errors? (Ps. 19:12).

Article XII: Of Repentance

Of Repentance they teach that for those who have fallen after Baptism there is remission of sins whenever they are converted and that the Church ought to impart absolution to those thus returning to repentance. Now, repentance consists properly of these two parts: One is contrition, that is, terrors smiting the conscience through the knowledge of sin; the other is faith, which is born of the Gospel, or of absolution, and believes that for Christ's sake, sins are forgiven, comforts the conscience, and delivers it from terrors. Then good works are bound to follow, which are the fruits of repentance. They condemn the Anabaptists, who deny that those once justified can lose the Holy Ghost. Also those who contend that some may attain to such perfection in this life that they cannot sin. The Novatians also are condemned, who would not absolve such as had fallen after Baptism, though they returned to repentance. They also are rejected who do not teach that remission of sins comes through faith but command us to merit grace through satisfactions of our own.

Article XIII: Of the Use of the Sacraments

Of the Use of the Sacraments they teach that the Sacraments were ordained, not only to be marks of profession among men, but rather to be signs and testimonies of the will of God toward us, instituted to awaken and confirm faith in those who use them. Wherefore we must so use the Sacraments that faith be added to believe the promises which are offered and set forth through the Sacraments. They therefore condemn those who teach that the Sacraments justify by the outward act, and who do not teach that, in the use of the Sacraments, faith which believes that sins are forgiven, is required.

Article XIV: Of Ecclesiastical Order

Of Ecclesiastical Order they teach that no one should publicly teach in the Church or administer the Sacraments unless he be regularly called.

Article XV: Of Ecclesiastical Usages

Of Usages in the Church they teach that those ought to be observed which may be observed without sin, and which are profitable unto tranquility and good order in the Church, as particular holy-days, festivals, and the like. Nevertheless, concerning such things men are admonished that consciences are not to be burdened, as though such observance was necessary to salvation. They are admonished also that human traditions instituted to propitiate God, to merit grace, and to make satisfaction for sins, are opposed to the Gospel and the doctrine of faith. Wherefore vows and traditions concerning meats and days, etc., instituted to merit grace and to make satisfaction for sins, are useless and contrary to the Gospel.

Article XVI: Of Civil Affairs

Of Civil Affairs they teach that lawful civil ordinances are good works of God, and that it is right for Christians to bear civil office, to sit as judges, to judge matters by the Imperial and other existing laws, to award just punishments, to engage in just wars, to serve as soldiers, to make legal contracts, to hold property, to make oath when required by the magistrates, to marry a wife, to be given in marriage. They condemn the Anabaptists who forbid these civil offices to Christians. They condemn also those who do not place evangelical perfection in the fear of God and in faith, but in forsaking civil offices, for the Gospel teaches an eternal righteousness of the heart. Meanwhile, it does not destroy the State or the family, but very much requires that they be preserved as ordinances of God, and that charity be practiced in such ordinances. Therefore, Christians are necessarily bound to obey their own magistrates and laws save only when commanded to sin; for then they ought to obey God rather than men (Acts 5:29).

Article XVII: Of Christ's Return to Judgement

Also they teach that at the Consummation of the World Christ will appear for judgment and will raise up all the dead; He will give to the godly and elect eternal life and everlasting joys, but ungodly men and the devils He will condemn to be tormented without end. They condemn the Anabaptists, who think that there will be an end to the punishments of condemned men and devils. They condemn also others who are now spreading certain Jewish opinions, that before the resurrection of the dead the godly shall take possession of the kingdom of the world, the ungodly being everywhere suppressed.

Article XVIII: Of Free Will

Of Free Will they teach that man's will has some liberty to choose civil righteousness, and to work things subject to reason. But it has no power, without the Holy Ghost, to work the righteousness of God, that is, spiritual righteousness; since the natural man receiveth not the things of the Spirit of God (1 Cor. 2:14); but this righteousness is wrought in the heart when the Holy Ghost is received through the Word. These things are said in as many words by Augustine in his Hypognosticon, Book III: We grant that all men have a free will, free, inasmuch as it has the judgment of reason; not that it is thereby capable, without God, either to begin, or, at least, to complete aught in things pertaining to God, but only in works of this life, whether good or evil. "Good" I call those works which spring from the good in nature, such as, willing to labor in the field, to eat and drink, to have a friend, to clothe oneself, to build a house, to marry a wife, to raise cattle, to learn divers useful arts, or whatsoever good pertains to this life. For all of these things are not without dependence on the providence of God; yea, of Him and through Him they are and have their being. "Evil" I call such works as willing to worship an idol, to commit murder, etc. They condemn the Pelagians and others, who teach that without the Holy Ghost, by the power of nature alone, we are able to love God above all things; also to do the commandments of God as touching "the substance of the act." For, although nature is able in a manner to do the outward work (for it is able to keep the hands from theft and murder), yet it cannot produce the inward motions, such as the fear of God, trust in God, chastity, patience, etc.

Article XIX: Of the Cause of Sin

Of the Cause of Sin they teach that, although God does create and preserve nature, yet the cause of sin is the will of the wicked, that is, of the devil and ungodly men; which will, unaided of God, turns itself from God, as Christ says (John 8:44): When he speaketh a lie, he speaketh of his own.

Article XX: Of Good Works

Our teachers are falsely accused of forbidding good Works. For their published writings on the Ten Commandments, and others of like import, bear witness that they have taught to good purpose concerning all estates and duties of life, as to what estates of life and what works in every calling be pleasing to God. Concerning these things preachers heretofore taught but little, and urged only childish and needless works, as particular holy-days, particular fasts, brotherhoods, pilgrimages, services in honor of saints, the use of rosaries, monasticism, and such like. Since our adversaries have been admonished of these things, they are now unlearning them, and do not preach these unprofitable works as heretofore. Besides, they begin to mention faith, of which there was heretofore marvelous silence. They teach that we are justified not by works only, but they conjoin faith and works, and say that we are justified by faith and works. This doctrine is more tolerable than the former one, and can afford more consolation than their old doctrine. Forasmuch, therefore, as the doctrine concerning faith, which ought to be the chief one in the Church, has lain so long unknown, as all must needs grant that there was the deepest silence in their sermons concerning the righteousness of faith, while only the doctrine of works was treated in the churches, our teachers have instructed the churches concerning faith as follows: First, that our works cannot reconcile God or merit forgiveness of sins, grace, and justification, but that we obtain this only by faith when we believe that we are received into favor for Christ's sake, who alone has been set forth the Mediator and Propitiation (1 Tim. 2:6), in order that the Father may be reconciled through Him. Whoever, therefore, trusts that by works he merits grace, despises the merit and grace of Christ, and seeks a way to God without Christ, by human strength, although Christ has said of Himself: I am the Way, the Truth, and the Life (John 14:6). This doctrine concerning faith is everywhere treated by Paul (Eph. 2:8): By grace are ye saved through faith; and that not of yourselves; it is the gift of God, not of works, etc. And lest any one should craftily say that a new interpretation of Paul has been devised by us, this entire matter is supported by the testimonies of the Fathers. For Augustine, in many volumes, defends grace and the righteousness of faith, over against the merits of works. And Ambrose, in his *De Vocatione Gentium* (*On the Calling of the Nations*) says, "Redemption by the blood of Christ would become of little value, neither would the preeminence of man's works be superseded by the mercy of God, if justification, which is wrought through grace, were due to the merits going before, so as to be, not the free gift of a donor, but the reward due to the laborer." But, although this doctrine is despised by the inexperienced, nevertheless God-fearing and anxious consciences find by experience that it brings the greatest consolation, because consciences cannot be set at rest through any works, but only by faith, when they take the sure ground that for Christ's sake they have a reconciled God. As Paul teaches (Rom. 5:1), "Being justified by faith, we have peace with God." This whole doctrine is to be referred to that conflict of the terrified conscience; neither can it be understood apart from that conflict. Therefore inexperienced and profane men judge ill concerning this matter, who dream that Christian righteousness is nothing but civil and philosophical righteousness. Heretofore consciences were plagued with the doctrine of works; they did not hear the consolation from the Gospel. Some persons were driven by conscience into the desert, into monasteries hoping there to merit grace by a monastic life. Some also devised other works whereby to merit grace and make satisfaction for sins. Hence there was very great need to treat of, and renew, this doctrine of faith in Christ, to the end that anxious consciences should not be without consolation but that they might know that grace and forgiveness of sins and justification are apprehended by faith in Christ. Men are also admonished that here the term "faith" does not signify merely the knowledge of the history, such as is in the ungodly and in the devil, but signifies a faith which believes, not merely the history, but also the effect of the history—namely, this Article: the forgiveness of sins, to wit, that we have grace, righteousness, and forgiveness of sins through Christ. Now he that knows that he has a Father gracious to him through Christ, truly knows God; he knows also that God cares for him, and calls upon God; in a word, he is not without God, as the heathen. For devils and the ungodly are not able to believe this Article: the forgiveness of sins. Hence, they hate God as an enemy, call not upon Him, and expect no good from Him. Augustine also admonishes his readers concerning the word "faith," and teaches that the term "faith" is accepted in the Scriptures not for knowledge such as is in the ungodly but for confidence which consoles and encourages the terrified mind. Furthermore, it is taught on our part that it is necessary to do good works, not that we should trust to merit grace by them, but because it is the will of God. It is only by faith that forgiveness of sins is apprehended, and that, for nothing. And because through faith the Holy Ghost is received, hearts are renewed and endowed with new affections, so as to be able to bring forth good works. For Ambrose says: Faith is the mother of a good will and right doing. For man's powers without the Holy Ghost are full of ungodly affections, and are too weak to do works which are good in God's sight. Besides, they are in the power of the devil who impels men to diverse sins, to ungodly opinions, to open crimes. This we may see in the philosophers, who, although they endeavored to live an honest life could not succeed, but were defiled with many open crimes. Such is the feebleness of man when he is without faith and without the Holy Ghost, and governs himself only by human strength. Hence it may be readily seen that this doctrine is not to be charged with prohibiting good works, but rather the more to be commended, because it shows how we are enabled to do good works. For without faith human nature can in no wise do the works of the First or of the Second Commandment. Without faith it does not call upon God, nor expect anything from God, nor bear the cross, but seeks, and trusts in, man's help. And thus, when there is no faith and trust in God all manner of lusts and human devices rule in the heart. Wherefore Christ said, John 16:6: "Without Me ye can do nothing"; and the Church sings: "Lacking Thy divine favor, There is nothing found in man, Naught in him is harmless."

Article XXI: Of the Worship of the Saints

Of the Worship of Saints they teach that the memory of saints may be set before us, that we may follow their faith and good works, according to our calling, as the Emperor may follow the example of David in making war to drive away the Turk from his country; for both are kings. But the Scripture teaches not the invocation of saints or to ask help of saints, since it sets before us the one Christ as the Mediator, Propitiation, High Priest, and Intercessor. He is to be prayed to, and has promised that He will hear our prayer; and this worship He approves above all, to wit, that in all afflictions He be called upon (1 John 2:1): If any man sin, we have an Advocate with the Father, etc. This is about the Sum of our Doctrine, in which, as can be seen, there is nothing that varies from the Scriptures, or from the Church Catholic, or from the Church of Rome as known from its writers. This being the case, they judge harshly who insist that our teachers be regarded as heretics. There is, however, disagreement on certain Abuses, which have crept into the Church without rightful authority. And even in these, if there were some difference, there should be proper lenity on the part of bishops to bear with us by reason of the Confession which we have now reviewed; because even the Canons are not so severe as to demand the same rites everywhere, neither, at any time, have the rites of all churches been the same; although, among us, in large part, the ancient rites are diligently observed. For it is a false and malicious charge that all the ceremonies, all the things instituted of old, are abolished in our churches. But it has been a common complaint that some abuses were connected with the ordinary rites. These, inasmuch as they could not be approved with a good conscience, have been to some extent corrected.

Articles in Which Are Reviewed the Abuses Which Have Been Corrected

Inasmuch, then, as our churches dissent in no article of the faith from the Church Catholic, but only omit some abuses which are new, and which have been erroneously accepted by the corruption of the times, contrary to the intent of the Canons, we pray that Your Imperial Majesty would graciously hear both what has been changed, and what were the reasons why the people were not compelled to observe those abuses against their conscience. Nor should Your Imperial Majesty believe those who, in order to excite the hatred of men against our part, disseminate strange slanders among the people. Having thus excited the minds of good men, they have first given occasion to this controversy, and now endeavor, by the same arts, to increase the discord. For Your Imperial Majesty will undoubtedly find that the form of doctrine and of ceremonies with us is not so intolerable as these ungodly and malicious men represent. Besides, the truth cannot be gathered from common rumors or the revilings of enemies. But it can readily be judged that nothing would serve better to maintain the dignity of ceremonies, and to nourish reverence and pious devotion among the people than if the ceremonies were observed rightly in the churches.

Article XXII: Of Both Kinds in the Sacrament

To the laity are given both kinds in the Sacrament of the Lord's Supper, because this usage has the commandment of the Lord in Matthew 26:27: Drink ye all of it, where Christ has manifestly commanded concerning the cup that all should drink. And lest any man should craftily say that this refers only to priests, Paul in 1 Corinthians 11:27 recites an example from which it appears that the whole congregation did use both kinds. And this usage has long remained in the Church, nor is it known when, or by whose authority, it was changed; although Cardinal Cusanus mentions the time when it was approved. Cyprian in some places testifies that the blood was given to the people. The same is testified by Jerome, who says: The priests administer the Eucharist, and distribute the blood of Christ to the people. Indeed, Pope Gelasius commands that the Sacrament be not divided (dist. II., *De Consecratione*, cap. Comperimus). Only custom, not so ancient, has it otherwise. But it is evident that any custom introduced against the commandments of God is not to be allowed, as the Canons witness (dist. III., cap. Veritate, and the following chapters). But this custom has been received, not only against the Scripture, but also against the old Canons and the example of the Church. Therefore, if any preferred to use both kinds of the Sacrament, they ought not to have been compelled with offense to their consciences to do otherwise. And because the division of the Sacrament does not agree with the ordinance of Christ, we are accustomed to omit the procession, which hitherto has been in use.

Article XXIII: Of the Marriage of Priests

There has been common complaint concerning the examples of priests who were not chaste. For that reason also Pope Pius is reported to have said that there were certain causes why marriage was taken away from priests, but that there were far weightier ones why it ought to be given back; for so Platina writes. Since, therefore, our priests were desirous to avoid these open scandals, they married wives, and taught that it was lawful for them to contract matrimony. First, because Paul says (1 Cor. 7:2–9): To avoid fornication, let every man have his own wife. Also: It is better to marry than to burn. Secondly Christ says (Matt. 19:11): All men cannot receive this saying, where He teaches that not all men are fit to lead a single life; for God created man for procreation (Gen. 1:28). Nor is it in man's power, without a singular gift and work of God, to alter this creation. [For it is manifest, and many have confessed that no good, honest, chaste life, no Christian, sincere, upright conduct has resulted (from the attempt), but a horrible, fearful unrest and torment of conscience has been felt by many until the end.] Therefore, those who are not fit to lead a single life ought to contract matrimony. For no man's law, no vow, can annul the commandment and ordinance of God. For these reasons the priests teach that it is lawful for them to marry wives. It is also evident that in the ancient Church priests were married men. For Paul says (1 Tim. 3:2) that a bishop should be chosen who is the husband of one wife. And in Germany, four hundred years ago for the first time, the priests were violently compelled to lead a single life, who indeed offered such resistance that the Archbishop of Mayence, when about to publish the Pope's decree concerning this matter, was almost killed in the tumult raised by the enraged priests. And so harsh was the dealing in the matter that not only were marriages forbidden for the future, but also existing marriages were torn asunder, contrary to all laws, divine and human, contrary even to the Canons themselves, made not only by the Popes, but by most celebrated Synods. [Moreover, many God-fearing and intelligent people in high station are known frequently to have expressed misgivings that such enforced celibacy and depriving men of marriage (which God Himself has instituted and left free to men) has never produced any good results, but has brought on many great and evil vices and much iniquity.] Seeing also that, as the world is aging, man's nature is gradually growing weaker, it is well to guard that no more vices steal into Germany. Furthermore, God ordained marriage to be a help against human infirmity. The Canons themselves say that the old rigor ought now and then, in the latter times, to be relaxed because of the weakness of men; which it is to be wished were done also in this matter. And it is to be expected that the churches shall at some time lack pastors if marriage is any longer forbidden. But while the commandment of God is in force, while the custom of the Church is well known, while impure celibacy causes many scandals, adulteries, and other crimes deserving the punishments of just magistrates, yet it is a marvelous thing that in nothing is more cruelty exercised than against the marriage of priests. God has given commandment to honor marriage. By the laws of all well-ordered commonwealths, even among the heathen, marriage is most highly honored. But now men, and that, priests, are cruelly put to death, contrary to the intent of the Canons, for no other cause than marriage. Paul, in 1 Timothy 4:3, calls that a doctrine of devils which forbids marriage. This may now be readily understood when the law against marriage is maintained by such penalties. But as no law of man can annul the commandment of God, so neither can it be done by any vow. Accordingly, Cyprian also advises that women who do not keep the chastity they have promised should marry. His words are these (Book I, Epistle XI): But if they be unwilling or unable to persevere, it is better for them to marry than to fall into the fire by their lusts; they should certainly give no offense to their brethren and sisters. And even the Canons show some leniency toward those who have taken vows before the proper age, as heretofore has generally been the case.

Article XXIV: Of the Mass

Falsely are our churches accused of abolishing the Mass; for the Mass is retained among us, and celebrated with the highest reverence. Nearly all the usual ceremonies are also preserved, save that the parts sung in Latin are interspersed here and there with German hymns, which have been added to teach the people. For ceremonies are needed to this end alone that the unlearned be taught [what they need to know of Christ]. And not only has Paul commanded to use in the church a language understood by the people (1 Cor. 14:2), but it has also been so ordained by man's law. The people are accustomed to partake of the Sacrament together, if any be fit for it, and this also increases the reverence and devotion of public worship. For none are admitted except they be first examined. The people are also advised concerning the dignity and use of the Sacrament, how great consolation it brings anxious consciences, that they may learn to believe God, and to expect and ask of Him all that is good. [In this connection they are also instructed regarding other and false teachings on the Sacrament.] This worship pleases God; such use of the Sacrament nourishes true devotion toward God. It does not, therefore, appear that the Mass is more devoutly celebrated among our adversaries than among us. But it is evident that for a long time this also has been the public and most grievous complaint of all good men that Masses have been basely profaned and applied to purposes of lucre. For it is not unknown how far this abuse obtains in all the churches by what manner of men Masses are said only for fees or stipends, and how many celebrate them contrary to the Canons. But Paul severely threatens those who deal unworthily with the Eucharist when he says (1 Cor. 11:27): Whosoever shall eat this bread, and drink this cup of the Lord, unworthily, shall be guilty of the body and blood of the Lord. When, therefore our priests were admonished concerning this sin, Private Masses were discontinued among us, as scarcely any Private Masses were celebrated except for profit's sake.

Neither were the bishops ignorant of these abuses, and if they had corrected them in time, there would now be less dissension. Heretofore, by their own connivance, they suffered many corruptions to creep into the Church. Now, when it is too late, they begin to complain of the troubles of the Church, while this disturbance has been occasioned simply by those abuses which were so manifest that they could be borne no longer. There have been great dissensions concerning the Mass, concerning the Sacrament. Perhaps the world is being punished for such long-continued profanations of the Mass as have been tolerated in the churches for so many centuries by the very men who were both able and in duty bound to correct them. For in the Ten Commandments it is written (Exod. 20:7): The Lord will not hold him guiltless who takes His name in vain. But since the world began, nothing that God ever ordained seems to have been so abused for filthy lucre as the Mass. There was also added the opinion which infinitely increased Private Masses, namely that Christ, by His passion, had made satisfaction for original sin, and instituted the Mass wherein an offering should be made for daily sins, venial and mortal. From this has arisen the common opinion that the Mass takes away the sins of the living and the dead by the outward act. Then they began to dispute whether one Mass said for many were worth as much as special Masses for individuals, and this brought forth that infinite multitude of Masses. [With this work men wished to obtain from God all that they needed, and in the mean time faith in Christ and the true worship were forgotten.] Concerning these opinions our teachers have given warning that they depart from the Holy Scriptures and diminish the glory of the passion of Christ. For Christ's passion was an oblation and satisfaction, not for original guilt only, but also for all other sins, as it is written to the Hebrews (10:10): We are sanctified through the offering of Jesus Christ once for all. Also (10:14): By one offering He hath perfected forever them that are sanctified. [It is an unheard-of innovation in the Church to teach that Christ by His death made satisfaction only for original sin and not likewise for all other sin. Accordingly it is hoped that everybody will understand that this error has not been reproved without due reason.] Scripture also teaches that we are justified before God through faith in Christ, when we believe that our sins are forgiven for Christ's sake. Now if the Mass take away the sins of the living and the dead by the outward act justification comes of the work of Masses, and not of faith, which Scripture does not allow. But Christ commands us (Luke 22:19): "This do in remembrance of Me"; therefore the Mass was instituted that the faith of those who use the Sacrament should remember what benefits it receives through Christ, and cheer and comfort the anxious conscience. For to remember Christ is to remember His benefits, and to realize that they are truly offered unto us. Nor is it enough only to remember the history; for this also the Jews and the ungodly can remember. Wherefore the Mass is to be used to this end, that there the Sacrament [Communion] may be administered to them that have need of consola-

tion; as Ambrose says: Because I always sin, I am always bound to take the medicine. [Therefore this Sacrament requires faith, and is used in vain without faith.] Now, forasmuch as the Mass is such a giving of the Sacrament, we hold one communion every holy-day, and, if any desire the Sacrament, also on other days, when it is given to such as ask for it. And this custom is not new in the Church; for the Fathers before Gregory make no mention of any private Mass, but of the common Mass [the Communion] they speak very much. Chrysostom says that the priest stands daily at the altar, inviting some to the Communion and keeping back others. And it appears from the ancient Canons that some one celebrated the Mass from whom all the other presbyters and deacons received the body of the Lord; for thus the words of the Nicene Canon say: Let the deacons, according to their order, receive the Holy Communion after the presbyters, from the bishop or from a presbyter. And Paul (1 Cor. 11:33) commands concerning the Communion: "Tarry one for another, so that there may be a common participation." Forasmuch, therefore, as the Mass with us has the example of the Church, taken from the Scripture and the Fathers, we are confident that it cannot be disapproved, especially since public ceremonies, for the most part like those hitherto in use, are retained; only the number of Masses differs, which, because of very great and manifest abuses doubtless might be profitably reduced. For in olden times, even in churches most frequented, the Mass was not celebrated every day, as the Tripartite History (Book 9, chap. 33) testifies: Again in Alexandria, every Wednesday and Friday the Scriptures are read, and the doctors expound them, and all things are done, except the solemn rite of Communion.

Article XXV: Of Confession

Confession in the churches is not abolished among us; for it is not usual to give the body of the Lord, except to them that have been previously examined and absolved. And the people are most carefully taught concerning faith in the absolution, about which formerly there was profound silence. Our people are taught that they should highly prize the absolution, as being the voice of God, and pronounced by God's command. The power of the Keys is set forth in its beauty and they are reminded what great consolation it brings to anxious consciences, also, that God requires faith to believe such absolution as a voice sounding from heaven, and that such faith in Christ truly obtains and receives the forgiveness of sins. Aforetime satisfactions were immoderately extolled; of faith and the merit of Christ and the righteousness of faith no mention was made; wherefore, on this point, our churches are by no means to be blamed. For this even our adversaries must needs concede to us that the doctrine concerning repentance has been most diligently treated and laid open by our teachers. But of Confession they teach that an enumeration of sins is not necessary, and that consciences be not burdened with anxiety to enumerate all sins, for it is impossible to recount all sins, as the Psalm testifies, Psalm 19:13: Who can understand his errors? Also Jeremiah 17:9: The heart is deceitful; who can know it; but if no sins were forgiven, except those that are recounted, consciences could never find peace; for very many sins they neither see nor can remember. The ancient writers also testify that an enumeration is not necessary. For in the Decrees, Chrysostom is quoted, who says thus: I say not to you that you should disclose yourself in public, nor that you accuse yourself before others, but I would have you obey the prophet who says: "Disclose thy self before God." Therefore confess your sins before God, the true Judge, with prayer. Tell your errors, not with the tongue, but with the memory of your conscience, etc. And the Gloss (Of Repentance, Distinct. V, Cap. Consideret) admits that Confession is of human right only [not commanded by Scripture, but ordained by the Church]. Nevertheless, on account of the great benefit of absolution, and because it is otherwise useful to the conscience, Confession is retained among us.

Article XXVI: Of the Distinction of Meats

It has been the general persuasion, not of the people alone, but also of those teaching in the churches, that making Distinctions of Meats, and like traditions of men, are works profitable to merit grace, and able to make satisfactions for sins. And that the world so thought, appears from this, that new ceremonies, new orders, new holy-days, and new fastings were daily instituted, and the teachers in the churches did exact these works as a service necessary to merit grace, and did greatly terrify men's consciences, if they should omit any of these things. From this persuasion concerning traditions much detriment has resulted in the Church. First, the doctrine of grace and of the righteousness of

faith has been obscured by it, which is the chief part of the Gospel, and ought to stand out as the most prominent in the Church, in order that the merit of Christ may be well known, and faith, which believes that sins are forgiven for Christ's sake be exalted far above works. Wherefore Paul also lays the greatest stress on this article, putting aside the Law and human traditions, in order to show that Christian righteousness is something else than such works, to wit, the faith which believes that sins are freely forgiven for Christ's sake. But this doctrine of Paul has been almost wholly smothered by traditions, which have produced an opinion that, by making distinctions in meats and like services, we must merit grace and righteousness. In treating of repentance, there was no mention made of faith; only those works of satisfaction were set forth; in these the entire repentance seemed to consist. Secondly, these traditions have obscured the commandments of God, because traditions were placed far above the commandments of God. Christianity was thought to consist wholly in the observance of certain holy-days, rites, fasts, and vestures. These observances had won for themselves the exalted title of being the spiritual life and the perfect life. Meanwhile the commandments of God, according to each one's calling, were without honor namely, that the father brought up his offspring, that the mother bore children, that the prince governed the commonwealth—these were accounted works that were worldly and imperfect, and far below those glittering observances. And this error greatly tormented devout consciences, which grieved that they were held in an imperfect state of life, as in marriage, in the office of magistrate; or in other civil ministrations; on the other hand, they admired the monks and such like, and falsely imagined that the observances of such men were more acceptable to God. Thirdly, traditions brought great danger to consciences; for it was impossible to keep all traditions, and yet men judged these observances to be necessary acts of worship. Gerson writes that many fell into despair, and that some even took their own lives, because they felt that they were not able to satisfy the traditions, and they had all the while not heard any consolation of the righteousness of faith and grace. We see that the summists and theologians gather the traditions, and seek mitigations whereby to ease consciences, and yet they do not sufficiently unfetter, but sometimes entangle, consciences even more. And with the gathering of these traditions, the schools and sermons have been so much occupied that they have had no leisure to touch upon Scripture, and to seek the more profitable doctrine of faith, of the cross, of hope, of the dignity of civil affairs of consolation of sorely tried consciences. Hence Gerson and some other theologians have grievously complained that by these strivings concerning traditions they were prevented from giving attention to a better kind of doctrine. Augustine also forbids that men's consciences should be burdened with such observances, and prudently advises Januarius that he must know that they are to be observed as things indifferent; for such are his words. Wherefore our teachers must not be looked upon as having taken up this matter rashly or from hatred of the bishops, as some falsely suspect. There was great need to warn the churches of these errors, which had arisen from misunderstanding the traditions. For the Gospel compels us to insist in the churches upon the doctrine of grace, and of the righteousness of faith; which, however, cannot be understood, if men think that they merit grace by observances of their own choice. Thus, therefore, they have taught that by the observance of human traditions we cannot merit grace or be justified, and hence we must not think such observances necessary acts of worship. They add hereunto testimonies of Scripture. Christ, in Matthew 15:3, defends the Apostles who had not observed the usual tradition, which, however, evidently pertains to a matter not unlawful, but indifferent, and to have a certain affinity with the purifications of the Law, and says, "In vain do they worship Me with the commandments of men." He, therefore, does not exact an unprofitable service. Shortly after He adds: Not that which goes into the mouth defiles a man. So also Paul: The kingdom of God is not meat and drink. (Rom. 14:17) Let no man, therefore, judge you in meat, or in drink, or in respect of an holy-day (Col. 2:16), or of the Sabbath-day; also: If ye be dead with Christ from the rudiments of the world, why, as though living in the world, are ye subject to ordinances: Touch not, taste not, handle not! And Peter says (Acts 15:10): Why tempt ye God to put a yoke upon the neck of the disciples, which neither our fathers nor we were able to bear? But we believe that through the grace of the Lord Jesus Christ we shall be saved, even as they. Here Peter forbids to burden the consciences with many rites, either of Moses or of others. And in 1 Timothy 4:1–3 Paul calls the prohibition of meats a doctrine of devils; for it is against the Gospel to institute or to do such works that by them we may merit grace, or as though Christianity could not exist without such service of God. Here our adversaries object that our teachers are opposed to discipline and mortification of the flesh, as Jovinian. But the contrary may be learned from the writings of our teachers. For they have always taught concerning the cross that it behooves Christians to bear afflictions. This is the true, earnest, and unfeigned mortification, to wit, to be exercised with diverse afflictions, and to be crucified with Christ. Moreover, they teach that every Christian ought to train and subdue himself with bodily restraints, or bodily exercises and labors that neither satiety nor slothfulness tempt him to sin, but not that we may merit grace or make satisfaction for sins by such exercises. And such external discipline ought to be urged at all times, not only on a few and set days. So Christ commands (Luke 21:34): Take heed lest your hearts be overcharged with surfeiting; also Matthew 17:21: This kind goeth not out but by prayer and fasting. Paul also says (1 Cor. 9:27): I keep under my body and bring it into subjection. Here he clearly shows that he was keeping under his body, not to merit forgiveness of sins by that discipline, but to have his body in subjection and fitted for spiritual things, and for the discharge of duty according to his calling. Therefore, we do not condemn fasting in itself, but the traditions which prescribe certain days and certain meats, with peril of conscience, as though such works were a necessary service. Nevertheless, very many traditions are kept on our part, which conduce to good order in the Church, as the Order of Lessons in the Mass and the chief holy-days. But, at the same time, men are warned that such observances do not justify before God, and that in such things it should not be made sin if they be omitted without offense. Such liberty in human rites was not unknown to the Fathers. For in the East they kept Easter at another time than at Rome, and when, on account of this diversity, the Romans accused the Eastern Church of schism, they were admonished by others that such usages need not be alike everywhere. And Irenaeus says: Diversity concerning fasting does not destroy the harmony of faith; as also Pope Gregory intimates in Dist. XII, that such diversity does not violate the unity of the Church. And in the Tripartite History, Book 9, many examples of dissimilar rites are gathered, and the following statement is made: It was not the mind of the Apostles to enact rules concerning holy-days, but to preach godliness and a holy life [to teach faith and love].

Article XXVII: Of Monastic Vows

What is taught on our part concerning Monastic Vows, will be better understood if it be remembered what has been the state of the monasteries, and how many things were daily done in those very monasteries, contrary to the Canons. In Augustine's time they were free associations. Afterward, when discipline was corrupted, vows were everywhere added for the purpose of restoring discipline, as in a carefully planned prison. Gradually, many other observances were added besides vows. And these fetters were laid upon many before the lawful age, contrary to the Canons. Many also entered into this kind of life through ignorance, being unable to judge their own strength, though they were of sufficient age. Being thus ensnared, they were compelled to remain, even though some could have been freed by the kind provision of the Canons. And this was more the case in convents of women than of monks, although more consideration should have been shown the weaker sex. This rigor displeased many good men before this time, who saw that young men and maidens were thrown into convents for a living. They saw what unfortunate results came of this procedure, and what scandals were created, what snares were cast upon consciences! They were grieved that the authority of the Canons in so momentous a matter was utterly set aside and despised. To these evils was added such a persuasion concerning vows as, it is well known, in former times displeased even those monks who were more considerate. They taught that vows were equal to Baptism; they taught that by this kind of life they merited forgiveness of sins and justification before God. Yea, they added that the monastic life not only merited righteousness before God but even greater things, because it kept not only the precepts, but also the so-called "evangelical counsels." Thus they made men believe that the profession of monasticism was far better than Baptism, and that the monastic life was more meritorious than that of magistrates, than the life of pastors, and such like, who serve their calling in accordance with God's commands, without any man-made services. None of these things can be denied; for they appear in their own books. [Moreover, a person who has been thus ensnared and has entered a monastery learns little of Christ.] What, then, came to pass in the monasteries? Aforetime they were schools of theology and other branches, profitable to the Church; and thence pastors and bishops were obtained. Now it is another thing. It is needless to rehearse what is known to all. Aforetime they came together to learn; now they feign that it is a kind of life instituted to merit grace and righteousness; yea, they preach that it is a state of perfection, and they put it far above all other kinds of life ordained of God. These things we have rehearsed without odious exaggeration, to the end that the doctrine of our teachers on this point might be better understood. First, concerning such as contract matrimony, they teach on our part that it is lawful for all men who are not fitted for single life to contract matrimony, because vows cannot annul the ordinance and commandment of God. But the commandment of God is 1 Corinthians 7:2: To avoid fornication, let every man have his own wife. Nor is it the commandment only, but also the creation and ordinance of God, which forces those to marry who are not excepted by a singular work of God, according to the text Genesis 2:18: It is not good that the man should be alone. Therefore they do not sin who obey this commandment and ordinance of God. What objection can be raised to this? Let men extol the obligation of a vow as much as they list, yet shall they not bring to pass that the vow annuls the commandment of God. The Canons teach that the right of the superior is excepted in every vow; [that vows are not binding against the decision of the Pope;] much less, therefore, are these vows of force which are against the commandments of God. Now, if the obligation of vows could not be changed for any cause whatever, the Roman Pontiffs could never have given dispensation for it is not lawful for man to annul an obligation which is simply divine. But the Roman Pontiffs have prudently judged that leniency is to be observed in this obligation, and therefore we read that many times they have dispensed from vows. The case of the King of Aragon who was called back from the monastery is well known, and there are also examples in our own times. [Now, if dispensations have been granted for the sake of securing temporal interests, it is much more proper that they be granted on account of the distress of souls.] In the second place, why do our adversaries exaggerate the obligation or effect of a vow when, at the same time, they have not a word to say of the nature of the vow itself, that it ought to be in a thing possible, that it ought to be free, and chosen spontaneously and deliberately? But it is not unknown to what extent perpetual chastity is in the power of man. And how few are there who have taken the vow spontaneously and deliberately! Young maidens and men, before they are able to judge, are persuaded, and sometimes even compelled, to take the vow. Wherefore it is not fair to insist so rigorously on the obligation, since it is granted by all that it is against the nature of a vow to take it without spontaneous and deliberate action.

Most canonical laws rescind vows made before the age of fifteen; for before that age there does not seem sufficient judgment in a person to decide concerning a perpetual life. Another Canon, granting more to the weakness of man, adds a few years; for it forbids a vow to be made before the age of eighteen. But which of these two Canons shall we follow? The most part have an excuse for leaving the monasteries, because most of them have taken the vows before they reached these ages. Finally, even though the violation of a vow might be censured, yet it seems not forthwith to follow that the marriages of such persons must be dissolved. For Augustine denies that they ought to be dissolved (XXVII. Question 1, On Marriage), and his authority is not lightly to be esteemed, although other men afterward thought otherwise. But although it appears that God's command concerning marriage delivers very many from their vows, yet our teachers introduce also another argument concerning vows to show that they are void. For every service of God, ordained and chosen of men without the commandment of God to merit justification and grace, is wicked, as Christ says Matthew 16:9: In vain do they worship Me with the commandments of men. And Paul teaches everywhere that righteousness is not to be sought from our own observances and acts of worship, devised by men, but that it comes by faith to those who believe that they are received by God into grace for Christ's sake. But it is evident that monks have taught that services of man's making satisfy for sins and merit grace and justification. What else is this than to detract from the glory of Christ and to obscure and deny the righteousness of faith? It follows, therefore, that the vows thus commonly taken have been wicked services, and, consequently, are void. For a wicked vow, taken against the commandment of God, is not valid; for (as the Canon says) no vow ought to bind men to wickedness. Paul says, Galatians 5:4: Christ is become of no ef-fect unto you, whosoever of you are justified by the Law, ye are fallen from grace. To those, therefore, who want to be justified by their vows Christ is made of no effect, and they fall from grace. For also these who ascribe justification to vows ascribe to their own works that which properly belongs to the glory of Christ. Nor can it be denied, indeed, that the monks have taught that, by their vows and observances, they were justified, and merited forgiveness of sins, yea, they invented still greater absurdities, saying that they could give others a share in their works. If any one should be inclined to enlarge on these things with evil intent, how many things could he bring together whereof even the monks are now ashamed! Over and above this, they persuaded men that services of man's making were a state of Christian perfection. And is not this assigning justification to works? It is no light offense in the Church to set forth to the people a service devised by men, without the commandment of God, and to teach that such service justifies men. For the righteousness of faith, which chiefly ought to be taught in the Church, is obscured when these wonderful angelic forms of worship, with their show of poverty, humility, and celibacy, are east before the eyes of men. Furthermore, the precepts of God and the true service of God are obscured when men hear that only monks are in a state of perfection. For Christian perfection is to fear God from the heart, and yet to conceive great faith, and to trust that for Christ's sake we have a God who has been reconciled, to ask of God, and assuredly to expect His aid in all things that, according to our calling, are to be done; and meanwhile, to be diligent in outward good works, and to serve our calling. In these things consist the true perfection and the true service of God. It does not consist in celibacy, or in begging, or in vile apparel. But the people conceive many pernicious opinions from the false commendations of monastic life. They hear celibacy praised above measure; therefore they lead their married life with offense to their consciences. They hear that only beggars are perfect; therefore they keep their possessions and do business with offense to their consciences. They hear that it is an evangelical counsel not to seek revenge; therefore some in private life are not afraid to take revenge, for they hear that it is but a counsel, and not a commandment. Others judge that the Christian cannot properly hold a civil office or be a magistrate. There are on record examples of men who, forsaking marriage and the administration of the Commonwealth, have hid themselves in monasteries. This they called fleeing from the world, and seeking a kind of life which would be more pleasing to God. Neither did they see that God ought to be served in those commandments which He Himself has given and not in commandments devised by men. A good and perfect kind of life is that which has for it the commandment of God. It is necessary to admonish men of these things. And before these times, Gerson rebukes this error of the monks concerning perfection, and testifies that in his day it was a new saying that the monastic life is a state of perfection. So many wicked opinions are inherent in the vows, namely, that they justify, that they constitute Christian perfection, that they keep the counsels and commandments, that they have works of supererogation. All these things, since they are false and empty, make vows null and void.

Article XXVIII: Of Ecclesiastical Power

There has been great controversy concerning the Power of Bishops, in which some have awkwardly confounded the power of the Church and the power of the sword. And from this confusion very great wars and tumults have resulted, while the Pontiffs, emboldened by the power of the Keys, not only have instituted new services and burdened consciences with reservation of cases and ruthless excommunications, but have also undertaken to transfer the kingdoms of this world, and to take the Empire from the Emperor. These wrongs have long since been rebuked in the Church by learned and godly men. Therefore our teachers, for the comforting of men's consciences, were constrained to show the difference between the power of the Church and the power of the sword, and taught that both of them, because of God's commandment, are to be held in reverence and honor, as the chief blessings of God on earth. But this is their opinion, that the power of the Keys, or the power of the bishops, according to the Gospel, is a power or commandment of God, to preach the Gospel, to remit and retain sins, and to administer Sacraments. For with this commandment Christ sends forth His Apostles, John 20:21: As My Father hath sent Me, even so send I you. Receive ye the Holy Ghost. Whosoever sins ye remit, they are remitted unto them; and whosoever sins ye retain, they are retained. Mark 16:15: "Go preach the Gospel to every creature." This power is exercised only by teaching or preaching the Gospel and administering the Sacraments, according to their calling either to many or to individuals. For thereby are granted, not bodily, but eternal things, as eternal righteousness, the Holy Ghost, eternal life. These things cannot come but by the ministry of the Word and the Sacraments, as Paul says, Romans 1:16: The Gospel is the power of God unto salvation to every one that believeth. Therefore, since the power of the Church grants eternal things, and is exercised only by the ministry of the Word, it does not interfere with civil government; no more than the art of singing interferes with civil government. For civil government deals with other things than does the Gospel. The civil rulers defend not minds, but bodies and bodily things against manifest injuries, and restrain men with the sword and bodily punishments in order to preserve civil justice and peace. Therefore the power of the Church and the civil power must not be confounded. The power of the Church has its own commission to teach the Gospel and to administer the Sacraments. Let it not break into the office of another; Let it not transfer the kingdoms of this world; let it not abrogate the laws of civil rulers; let it not abolish lawful obedience; let it not interfere with judgments concerning civil ordinances or contracts; let it not prescribe laws to civil rulers concerning the form of the Commonwealth. As Christ says, John 18:33: My kingdom is not of this world; also Luke 12:14: Who made Me a judge or a divider over you? Paul also says, Philippians 3:20: Our citizenship is in heaven; 2 Corinthians 10:4: The weapons of our warfare are not carnal, but mighty through God to the casting down of imaginations. After this manner our teachers discriminate between the duties of both these powers, and command that both be honored and acknowledged as gifts and blessings of God. If bishops have any power of the sword, that power they have, not as bishops, by the commission of the Gospel, but by human law having received it of kings and emperors for the civil administration of what is theirs. This, however, is another office than the ministry of the Gospel. When, therefore, the question is concerning the jurisdiction of bishops, civil authority must be distinguished from ecclesiastical jurisdiction. Again, according to the Gospel or, as they say, by divine right, there belongs to the bishops as bishops, that is, to those to whom has been committed the ministry of the Word and the Sacraments, no jurisdiction except to forgive sins, to judge doctrine, to reject doctrines contrary to the Gospel, and to exclude from the communion of the Church wicked men, whose wickedness is known, and this without human force, simply by the Word. Herein the congregations of necessity and by divine right must obey them, according to Luke 10:16: He that heareth you heareth Me. But when they teach or ordain anything against the Gospel, then the congregations have a commandment of God prohibiting obedience, Matthew 7:15: Beware of false prophets; Galatians 1:8: Though an angel from heaven preach any other gospel, let him be accursed; 2 Corinthians 13:8: We can do nothing against the truth, but for the truth. Also: The power which the Lord hath given me to edification, and not to destruction. So, also, the Canonical Laws command (Part 2, Question 7 On Priests, and On Rejoicing). And Augustine (*Against the Letters of Petilian*): Neither must we submit to Catholic bishops if they chance to err, or hold anything contrary to the Canonical Scriptures of God. If they have any other power or jurisdiction, in hearing and judging certain cases, as of matrimony or of tithes, etc., they have it by human right, in which matters princes are bound, even against their will, when the ordinaries fail, to dispense justice to their subjects for the maintenance of peace. Moreover, it is disputed whether bishops or pastors have the right to introduce ceremonies in the Church, and to make laws concerning meats, holy-days and grades, that is, orders of ministers, etc. They that give this right to the bishops refer to this testimony John 16:12–13: I have yet many things to say unto you, but ye cannot bear them now. Howbeit when He, the Spirit of Truth, is come, He will guide you into all truth. They also refer to the example of the Apostles, who commanded to abstain from blood and from things strangled, Acts 15:29. They refer to the Sabbath-day as having been changed into the Lord's Day, contrary to the Decalog, as it seems. Neither is there any example whereof they make more than concerning the changing of the Sabbath-day. Great, say they, is the power of the Church, since it has dispensed with one of the Ten Commandments! But concerning this question it is taught on our part (as has been shown above) that bishops have no power to decree anything against the Gospel. The Canonical Laws teach the same thing (Part IX). Now, it is against Scripture to establish or require the observance of any traditions, to the end that by such observance we may make satisfaction for sins, or merit grace and righteousness. For the glory of Christ's merit suffers injury when, by such observances, we undertake to merit justification. But it is manifest that, by such belief, traditions have almost infinitely multiplied in the Church, the doctrine concerning faith and the righteousness of faith being meanwhile suppressed. For gradually more holy-days were made, fasts appointed, new ceremonies and services in honor of saints instituted, because the authors of such things thought that by these works they were meriting grace. Thus in times past the Penitential Canons increased, whereof we still see some traces in the satisfactions. Again, the authors of traditions do contrary to the command of God when they find matters of sin in foods, in days, and like things, and burden the Church with bondage of the law, as if there ought to be among Christians, in order to merit justification, a service like the Levitical, the arrangement of which God had committed to the Apostles and bishops. For thus some of them write; and the Pontiffs in some measure seem to be misled by the example of the law of Moses. Hence are such burdens, as that they make it mortal sin, even without offense to others, to do manual labor on holy-days, a mortal sin to omit the Canonical Hours, that certain foods defile the conscience, that fastings are works which appease God, that sin in a reserved case cannot be forgiven but by the authority of him who reserved it; whereas the Canons themselves speak only of the reserving of the ecclesiastical penalty, and not of the reserving of the guilt. Whence have the bishops the right to lay these traditions upon the Church for the ensnaring of consciences, when Peter (Acts 15:10), forbids to put a yoke upon the neck of the disciples, and Paul says (2 Cor. 13:10) that the power given him was to edification not to destruction? Why, therefore, do they increase sins by these traditions? But there are clear testimonies which prohibit the making of such traditions, as though they merited grace or were necessary to salvation. Paul says (Col. 2:16–23): Let no man judge you in meat, or in drink, or in respect of an holy-day, or of the new moon, or of the Sabbath-days. If ye be dead with Christ from the rudiments of the world, why, as though living in the world, are ye subject to ordinances (touch not; taste not; handle not, which all are to perish with the using) after the commandments and doctrines of men! Which things have indeed a show of wisdom. Also in Titus 1:14 he openly forbids traditions: Not giving heed to Jewish fables and commandments of men that turn from the truth. And Christ (Matt. 15:13–14) says of those who require traditions: Let them alone; they be blind leaders of the blind; and He rejects such services: Every plant which My Heavenly Father hath not planted shall be plucked up. If bishops have the right to burden churches with infinite traditions, and to ensnare consciences, why does Scripture so often prohibit to make, and to listen to, traditions? Why does it call them "doctrines of devils"? (1 Tim. 4:1). Did the Holy Ghost in vain forewarn of these things? Since, therefore, ordinances instituted as things necessary, or with an opinion of meriting grace, are contrary to the Gospel, it follows that it is not lawful for any bishop to institute or exact such services. For it is necessary that the doctrine of Christian liberty be preserved in the churches, namely, that the bondage of the Law is not necessary to justification, as it is written in Galatians 5:1: Be not entangled again with the yoke of bondage. It is necessary that the chief article of the Gospel be preserved, to wit, that we obtain grace freely by faith in Christ, and not for certain observances or acts of worship devised by men. What, then, are we to think of the Sunday and like rites in the house of God? To this we answer that it is lawful for bishops or pastors to make ordinances that things be done orderly in the Church, not that thereby we should merit grace or make satisfaction for sins, or that consciences be bound to judge them necessary services, and to think that it is a sin to break them without offense to others. So Paul ordains that women should cover their heads in the congregation(1 Cor. 11:5), that interpreters be heard in order in the church (1 Cor. 14:30), etc. It is proper that the churches should keep such ordinances for the sake of love and tranquility, so far that one do not offend another, that all things be done in the churches in order, and without confusion (1 Cor. 14:40; cf. Phil. 2:14); but so that consciences be not burdened to think that they are necessary to salvation, or to judge that they sin when they break them without offense to others; as no one will say that a woman sins who goes out in public with her head uncovered provided only that no offense be given. Of this kind is the observance of the Lord's Day, Easter, Pentecost, and like holy-days and rites. For those who judge that by the authority of the Church the observance of the Lord's Day instead of the Sabbath-day was ordained as a thing necessary, do greatly err. Scripture has abrogated the Sabbath-day; for it teaches that, since the Gospel has been revealed, all the ceremonies of Moses can be omitted. And yet, because it was necessary to appoint a certain day, that the people might know when they ought to come together, it appears that the Church designated the Lord's Day for this purpose; and this day seems to have been chosen all the more for this additional reason, that men might have an example of Christian liberty, and might know that the keeping neither of the Sabbath nor of any other day is necessary. There are monstrous disputations concerning the changing of the law, the ceremonies of the new law, the changing of the Sabbath-day, which all have sprung from the false belief that there must needs be in the Church a service like to the Levitical, and that Christ had given commission to the Apostles and bishops to devise new ceremonies as necessary to salvation. These errors crept into the Church when the righteousness of faith was not taught clearly enough. Some dispute that the keeping of the Lord's Day is not indeed of divine right, but in a manner so. They prescribe concerning holy-days, how far it is lawful to work. What else are such disputations than snares of consciences? For although they endeavor to modify the traditions, yet the mitigation can never be perceived as long as the opinion remains that they are necessary, which must needs remain where the righteousness of faith and Christian liberty are not known. The Apostles commanded (Acts 15:20) to abstain from blood. Who does now observe it? And yet they that do it not sin not; for not even the Apostles themselves wanted to burden consciences with such bondage; but they forbade it for a time, to avoid offense. For in this decree we must perpetually consider what the aim of the Gospel is. Scarcely any Canons are kept with exactness, and from day to day many go out of use even among those who are the most zealous advocates of traditions. Neither can due regard be paid to consciences unless this mitigation be observed, that we know that the Canons are kept without holding them to be necessary, and that no harm is done consciences, even though traditions go out of use. But the bishops might easily retain the lawful obedience of the people if they would not insist upon the observance of such traditions as cannot be kept with a good conscience. Now they command celibacy; they admit none unless they swear that they will not teach the pure doctrine of the Gospel. The churches do not ask that the bishops should restore concord at the expense of their honor; which, nevertheless, it would be proper for good pastors to do. They ask only that they would release unjust burdens which are new and have been received contrary to the custom of the Church Catholic. It may be that in the beginning there were plausible reasons for some of these ordinances; and yet they are not adapted to later times. It is also evident that some were adopted through erroneous conceptions. Therefore it would be befitting the clemency of the Pontiffs to mitigate them now, because such a modification does not shake the unity of the Church. For many human traditions have been changed in process of time, as the Canons themselves show. But if it be impossible to obtain a mitigation of such observances as cannot be kept without sin, we are bound to follow the apostolic rule (Acts 5:29), which commands us to obey God rather than men. Peter (1 Peter 5:3) forbids bishops to be lords, and to rule over the churches. It is not our design now to wrest the government from the bishops, but this one thing is asked, namely, that they allow the Gospel to be purely taught, and that they relax some few observances which cannot be kept without sin. But if they make no concession, it is for them to see how they shall give account to God for furnishing, by their obstinacy, a cause for schism.

Conclusion

These are the chief articles which seem to be in controversy. For although we might have spoken of more abuses, yet, to avoid undue length, we have set forth the chief points, from which the rest may be readily judged. There have been great complaints concerning indulgences, pilgrimages, and the abuse of excommunications. The parishes have been vexed in many ways by the dealers in indulgences. There were endless contentions between the pastors and the monks concerning the parochial right, confessions, burials, sermons on extraordinary occasions, and innumerable other things. Issues of this sort we have passed over so that the chief points in this matter, having been briefly set forth, might be the more readily understood. Nor has anything been here said or adduced to the reproach of any one. Only those things have been recounted whereof we thought that it was necessary to speak, in order that it might be understood that in doctrine and ceremonies nothing has been received on our part against Scripture or the Church Catholic. For it is manifest that we have taken most diligent care that no new and ungodly doctrine

should creep into our churches. The above articles we desire to present in accordance with the edict of Your Imperial Majesty, in order to exhibit our Confession and let men see a summary of the doctrine of our teachers. If there is anything that any one might desire in this Confession, we are ready, God willing, to present ampler information according to the Scriptures.

> Your Imperial Majesty's faithful subjects:
>   John, Duke of Saxony, Elector
>   George, Margrave of Brandenburg
>   Ernest, Duke of Lueneberg
>   Philip, Landgrave of Hesse
>   John Frederick, Duke of Saxony
>   Francis, Duke of Lueneburg
>   Wolfgang, Prince of Anhalt
>   Senate and Magistracy of Nuremburg
>   Senate of Reutlingen

THE WESTMINSTER SHORTER CATECHISM
English, 1647

Occupying a central place in the teaching ministry of the Presbyterian Church since its publication, this document is a restatement of the *Westminster Confession*—the profession of Presbyterian faith as declared by the historic Westminster Assembly in 1647. Note the Catechism's famous first question (on "man's chief end") and the effective form of all answers (which embody the question).

Q1. What is the chief end of man?
 A. Man's chief end is to glorify God, and to enjoy him forever.

Q2. What rule hath God given to direct us how we may glorify and enjoy him?
 A. The word of God, which is contained in the scriptures of the Old and New Testaments, is the only rule to direct us how we may glorify and enjoy him.

Q3. What do the scriptures principally teach?
 A. The scriptures principally teach what man is

to believe concerning God, and what duty God requires of man.

Q4. What is God?
A. God is a spirit, infinite, eternal, and unchangeable, in his being, wisdom, power, holiness, justice, goodness, and truth.

Q5. Are there more Gods than one?
A. There is but one only, the living and true God.

Q6. How many persons are there in the godhead?
A. There are three persons in the godhead; the Father, the Son, and the Holy Ghost; and these three are one God, the same in substance, equal in power and glory.

Q7. What are the decrees of God?
A. The decrees of God are his eternal purpose, according to the counsel of his will, whereby, for his own glory, he hath foreordained whatsoever comes to pass.

Q8. How doth God execute his decrees?
A. God executeth his decrees in the works of creation and providence.

Q9. What is the work of creation?
A. The work of creation is God's making all things of nothing, by the word of his power, in the space of six days, and all very good.

Q10. How did God create man?
A. God created man male and female, after his own image, in knowledge, righteousness, and holiness, with dominion over the creatures.

Q11. What are God's works of providence?
A. God's works of providence are his most holy, wise and powerful preserving and governing all his creatures, and all their actions.

Q12. What special act of providence did God exercise toward man in the estate wherein he was created?
A. When God had created man, he entered into a covenant of life with him, upon condition of perfect obedience; forbidding him to eat of the tree of the knowledge of good and evil, upon the pain of death.

Q13. Did our first parents continue in the estate wherein they were created?
A. Our first parents, being left to the freedom of their own will, fell from the estate wherein they were created, by sinning against God.

Q14. What is sin?
A. Sin is any want of conformity unto, or transgression of, the law of God.

Q15. What was the sin whereby our first parents fell from the estate wherein they were created?
A. The sin whereby our first parents fell from the estate wherein they were created was their eating the forbidden fruit.

Q16. Did all mankind fall in Adam's first transgression?
A. The covenant being made with Adam, not only for himself, but for his posterity; all mankind, descending from him by ordinary generation, sinned in him, and fell with him, in his first transgression.

Q17. Into what estate did the fall bring mankind?
A. The fall brought mankind into an estate of sin and misery.

Q18. Wherein consists the sinfulness of that estate whereinto man fell?
A. The sinfulness of that estate whereinto man fell consists in the guilt of Adam's first sin, the want of original righteousness, and the corruption of his whole nature, which is commonly called original sin; together with all actual transgressions which proceed from it.

Q19. What is the misery of that estate whereinto man fell?
A. All mankind by their fall lost communion with God, are under his wrath and curse, and so made liable to all miseries in this life, to death itself, and to the pains of hell forever.

Q20. Did God leave all mankind to perish in the estate of sin and misery?

A. God having, out of his mere good pleasure, from all eternity, elected some to everlasting life, did enter into a covenant of grace, to deliver them out of the estate of sin and misery, and to bring them into an estate of salvation by a redeemer.

Q21. Who is the redeemer of God's elect?

A. The only redeemer of God's elect is the Lord Jesus Christ, who, being the eternal Son of God, became man, and so was, and continueth to be, God and man in two distinct natures, and one person, forever.

Q22. How did Christ, being the Son of God, become man?

A. Christ, the Son of God, became man, by taking to himself a true body and a reasonable soul, being conceived by the power of the Holy Ghost in the womb of the virgin Mary, and born of her, yet without sin.

Q23. What offices doth Christ execute as our redeemer?

A. Christ, as our redeemer, executeth the offices of a prophet, of a priest, and of a king, both in his estate of humiliation and exaltation.

Q24. How doth Christ execute the office of a prophet?

A. Christ executeth the office of a prophet, in revealing to us, by his word and Spirit, the will of God for our salvation.

Q25. How doth Christ execute the office of a priest?

A. Christ executeth the office of a priest, in his once offering up of himself a sacrifice to satisfy divine justice, and reconcile us to God; and in making continual intercession for us.

Q26. How doth Christ execute the office of a king?

A. Christ executeth the office of a king, in subduing us to himself, in ruling and defending us, and in restraining and conquering all his and our enemies.

Q27. Wherein did Christ's humiliation consist?

A. Christ's humiliation consisted in his being born, and that in a low condition, made under the law, undergoing the miseries of this life, the wrath of God, and the cursed death of the cross; in being buried, and continuing under the power of death for a time.

Q28. Wherein consisteth Christ's exaltation?

A. Christ's exaltation consisteth in his rising again from the dead on the third day, in ascending up into heaven, in sitting at the right hand of God the Father, and in coming to judge the world at the last day.

Q29. How are we made partakers of the redemption purchased by Christ?

A. We are made partakers of the redemption purchased by Christ, by the effectual application of it to us by his Holy Spirit.

Q30. How doth the Spirit apply to us the redemption purchased by Christ?

A. The Spirit applieth to us the redemption purchased by Christ, by working faith in us, and thereby uniting us to Christ in our effectual calling.

Q31. What is effectual calling?

A. Effectual calling is the work of God's Spirit, whereby, convincing us of our sin and misery, enlightening our minds in the knowledge of Christ, and renewing our wills, he doth persuade and enable us to embrace Jesus Christ, freely offered to us in the gospel.

Q32. What benefits do they that are effectually called partake of in this life?

A. They that are effectually called do in this life partake of justification, adoption and sanctification, and the several benefits which in this life do either accompany or flow from them.

Q33. What is justification?

A. Justification is an act of God's free grace, wherein he pardoneth all our sins, and accepteth us as righteous in his sight, only for the righteousness of Christ imputed to us, and received by faith alone.

Q34. What is adoption?
A. Adoption is an act of God's free grace, whereby we are received into the number, and have a right to all the privileges of, the sons of God.

Q35. What is sanctification?
A. Sanctification is the work of God's free grace, whereby we are renewed in the whole man after the image of God, and are enabled more and more to die unto sin, and live unto righteousness.

Q36. What are the benefits which in this life do accompany or flow from justification, adoption and sanctification?
A. The benefits which in this life do accompany or flow from justification, adoption and sanctification, are, assurance of God's love, peace of conscience, joy in the Holy Ghost, increase of grace, and perseverance therein to the end.

Q37. What benefits do believers receive from Christ at death?
A. The souls of believers are at their death made perfect in holiness, and do immediately pass into glory; and their bodies, being still united to Christ, do rest in their graves till the resurrection.

Q38. What benefits do believers receive from Christ at the resurrection?
A. At the resurrection, believers being raised up in glory, shall be openly acknowledged and acquitted in the day of judgment, and made perfectly blessed in the full enjoying of God to all eternity.

Q39. What is the duty which God requireth of man?
A. The duty which God requireth of man is obedience to his revealed will.

Q40. What did God at first reveal to man for the rule of his obedience?

A. The rule which God at first revealed to man for his obedience was the moral law.

Q41. Where is the moral law summarily comprehended?
A. The moral law is summarily comprehended in the ten commandments.

Q42. What is the sum of the Ten Commandments?
A. The sum of the Ten Commandments is to love the Lord our God with all our heart, with all our soul, with all our strength, and with all our mind; and our neighbor as ourselves.

Q43. What is the preface to the Ten Commandments?
A. The preface to the Ten Commandments is in these words: "I am the Lord thy God, which have brought thee out of the land of Egypt, out of the house of bondage."

Q44. What doth the preface to the Ten Commandments teach us?
A. The preface to the Ten Commandments teacheth us that because God is the Lord, and our God, and redeemer, therefore we are bound to keep all his commandments.

Q45. Which is the first commandment?
A. The first commandment is "Thou shalt have no other gods before me."

Q46. What is required in the first commandment?
A. The first commandment requireth us to know and acknowledge God to be the only true God, and our God; and to worship and glorify him accordingly.

Q47. What is forbidden in the first commandment?
A. The first commandment forbiddeth the denying, or not worshiping and glorifying the true God as God, and our God; and the giving of that worship and glory to any other, which is due to him alone.

Q48. What are we specially taught by these words "before me" in the first commandment?
A. These words "before me" in the first

commandment teach us that God, who seeth all things, taketh notice of, and is much displeased with, the sin of having any other god.

Q49. Which is the second commandment?

A. The second commandment is "Thou shalt not make unto thee any graven image, or any likeness of anything that is in heaven above, or that is in the earth beneath, or that is in the water under the earth: thou shalt not bow down thyself to them, nor serve them: for I the Lord thy God am a jealous God, visiting the iniquity of the fathers upon the children unto the third and fourth generation of them that hate me; and showing mercy unto thousands of them that love me, and keep my commandments."

Q50. What is required in the second commandment?

A. The second commandment requireth the receiving, observing, and keeping pure and entire, all such religious worship and ordinances as God hath appointed in his word.

Q51. What is forbidden in the second commandment?

A. The second commandment forbiddeth the worshiping of God by images, or any other way not appointed in his word.

Q52. What are the reasons annexed to the second commandment?

A. The reasons annexed to the second commandment are, God's sovereignty over us, his propriety in us, and the zeal he hath to his own worship.

Q53. Which is the third commandment?

A. The third commandment is "Thou shalt not take the name of the Lord thy God in vain: for the Lord will not hold him guiltless that taketh his name in vain."

Q54. What is required in the third commandment?

A. The third commandment requireth the holy and reverent use of God's names, titles, attributes, ordinances, word and works.

Q55. What is forbidden in the third commandment?

A. The third commandment forbiddeth all profaning or abusing of anything whereby God maketh himself known.

Q56. What is the reason annexed to the third commandment?

A. The reason annexed to the third commandment is that however the breakers of this commandment may escape punishment from men, yet the Lord our God will not suffer them to escape his righteous judgment.

Q57. Which is the fourth commandment?

A. The fourth commandment is "Remember the Sabbath day, to keep it holy. Six days shalt thou labor, and do all thy work: but the seventh day is the Sabbath of the Lord thy God: in it thou shalt not do any work, thou, nor thy son, nor thy daughter, thy manservant, nor thy maidservant, nor thy cattle, nor thy stranger that is within thy gates: for in six days the Lord made heaven and earth, the sea, and all that in them is, and rested the seventh day: wherefore the Lord blessed the Sabbath day, and hallowed it."

Q58. What is required in the fourth commandment?

A. The fourth commandment requireth the keeping holy to God such set times as he hath appointed in his word; expressly one whole day in seven, to be a holy Sabbath to himself.

Q59. Which day of the seven hath God appointed to be the weekly Sabbath?

A. From the beginning of the world to the resurrection of Christ, God appointed the seventh day of the week to be the weekly Sabbath; and the first day of the week ever since, to continue to the end of the world, which is the Christian Sabbath.

Q60. How is the Sabbath to be sanctified?

A. The Sabbath is to be sanctified by a holy resting all that day, even from such worldly employments and recreations as are lawful on other days; and spending the whole time in the public and private exercises of God's worship, except so much as is to be taken up in the works of necessity and mercy.

Q61. What is forbidden in the fourth commandment?

A. The fourth commandment forbiddeth the omission or careless performance of the duties required, and the profaning the day by idleness, or doing that which is in itself sinful, or by unnecessary thoughts, words or works, about our worldly employments or recreations.

Q62. What are the reasons annexed to the fourth commandment?

A. The reasons annexed to the fourth commandment are, God's allowing us six days of the week for our own employments, his challenging a special propriety in the seventh, his own example, and his blessing the Sabbath day.

Q63. Which is the fifth commandment?

A. The fifth commandment is "Honor thy father and thy mother; that thy days may be long upon the land which the Lord thy God giveth thee."

Q64. What is required in the fifth commandment?

A. The fifth commandment requireth the preserving the honor, and performing the duties, belonging to every one in their several places and relations, as superiors, inferiors or equals.

Q65. What is forbidden in the fifth commandment?

A. The fifth commandment forbiddeth the neglecting of, or doing anything against, the honor and duty which belongeth to every one in their several places and relations.

Q66. What is the reason annexed to the fifth commandment?

A. The reason annexed to the fifth commandment is a promise of long life and prosperity (as far as it shall serve for God's glory and their own good) to all such as keep this commandment.

Q67. Which is the sixth commandment?

A. The sixth commandment is "Thou shalt not kill."

Q68. What is required in the sixth commandment?

A. The sixth commandment requireth all lawful endeavors to preserve our own life, and the life of others.

Q69. What is forbidden in the sixth commandment?

A. The sixth commandment forbiddeth the taking away of our own life, or the life of our neighbor unjustly, or whatsoever tendeth thereunto.

Q70. Which is the seventh commandment?

A. The seventh commandment is "Thou shalt not commit adultery."

Q71. What is required in the seventh commandment?

A. The seventh commandment requireth the preservation of our own and our neighbor's chastity, in heart, speech and behavior.

Q72. What is forbidden in the seventh commandment?

A. The seventh commandment forbiddeth all unchaste thoughts, words and actions.

Q73. Which is the eighth commandment?

A. The eighth commandment is "Thou shalt not steal."

Q74. What is required in the eighth commandment?

A. The eighth commandment requireth the lawful procuring and furthering the wealth and outward estate of ourselves and others.

Q75. What is forbidden in the eighth commandment?

A. The eighth commandment forbiddeth whatsoever doth or may unjustly hinder our own or our neighbor's wealth or outward estate.

Q76. Which is the ninth commandment?

A. The ninth commandment is "Thou shalt not bear false witness against thy neighbor."

Q77. What is required in the ninth commandment?
A. The ninth commandment requireth the maintaining and promoting of truth between man and man, and of our own and our neighbor's good name, especially in witness-bearing.

Q78. What is forbidden in the ninth commandment?
A. The ninth commandment forbiddeth whatsoever is prejudicial to truth, or injurious to our own or our neighbor's good name.

Q79. Which is the tenth commandment?
A. The tenth commandment is "Thou shalt not covet thy neighbor's house, thou shalt not covet thy neighbor's wife, nor his manservant, nor his maidservant, nor his ox, nor his ass, nor anything that is thy neighbor's."

Q80. What is required in the tenth commandment?
A. The tenth commandment requireth full contentment with our own condition, with a right and charitable frame of spirit toward our neighbor, and all that is his.

Q81. What is forbidden in the tenth commandment?
A. The tenth commandment forbiddeth all discontentment with our own estate, envying or grieving at the good of our neighbor, and all inordinate motions and affections to anything that is his.

Q82. Is any man able perfectly to keep the commandments of God?
A. No mere man since the fall is able in this life perfectly to keep the commandments of God, but doth daily break them in thought, word, and deed.

Q83. Are all transgressions of the law equally heinous?
A. Some sins in themselves, and by reason of several aggravations, are more heinous in the sight of God than others.

Q84. What doth every sin deserve?
A. Every sin deserveth God's wrath and curse, both in this life, and that which is to come.

Q85. What doth God require of us that we may escape his wrath and curse due to us for sin?
A. To escape the wrath and curse of God due to us for sin, God requireth of us faith in Jesus Christ, repentance unto life, with the diligent use of all the outward means whereby Christ communicateth to us the benefits of redemption.

Q86. What is faith in Jesus Christ?
A. Faith in Jesus Christ is a saving grace, whereby we receive and rest upon him alone for salvation, as he is offered to us in the gospel.

Q87. What is repentance unto life?
A. Repentance unto life is a saving grace, whereby a sinner, out of a true sense of his sin, and apprehension of the mercy of God in Christ, doth, with grief and hatred of his sin, turn from it unto God, with full purpose of, and endeavor after, new obedience.

Q88. What are the outward means whereby Christ communicateth to us the benefits of redemption?
A. The outward and ordinary means whereby Christ communicateth to us the benefits of redemption, are his ordinances, especially the word, sacraments, and prayer; all which are made effectual to the elect for salvation.

Q89. How is the word made effectual to salvation?
A. The Spirit of God maketh the reading, but especially the preaching, of the word, an effectual means of convincing and converting sinners, and of building them up in holiness and comfort, through faith, unto salvation.

Q90. How is the word to be read and heard, that it may become effectual to salvation?
A. That the word may become effectual to salvation, we must attend thereunto with diligence, preparation and prayer; receive it with faith and love, lay it up in our hearts, and practice it in our lives.

Q91. How do the sacraments become effectual means of salvation?

A. The sacraments become effectual means of salvation, not from any virtue in them, or in him that doth administer them; but only by the blessing of Christ, and the working of his Spirit in them that by faith receive them.

Q92. What is a sacrament?

A. A sacrament is a holy ordinance instituted by Christ; wherein, by sensible signs, Christ and the benefits of the new covenant are represented, sealed, and applied to believers.

Q93. Which are the sacraments of the New Testament?

A. The sacraments of the New Testament are baptism and the Lord's Supper.

Q94. What is baptism?

A. Baptism is a sacrament, wherein the washing with water in the name of the Father, and of the Son, and of the Holy Ghost, doth signify and seal our ingrafting into Christ, and partaking of the benefits of the covenant of grace, and our engagement to be the Lord's.

Q95. To whom is baptism to be administered?

A. Baptism is not to be administered to any that are out of the visible church, till they profess their faith in Christ, and obedience to him; but the infants of such as are members of the visible church are to be baptized.

Q96. What is the Lord's Supper?

A. The Lord's supper is a sacrament, wherein, by giving and receiving bread and wine according to Christ's appointment, his death is showed forth; and the worthy receivers are, not after a corporal and carnal manner, but by faith, made partakers of his body and blood, with all his benefits, to their spiritual nourishment and growth in grace.

Q97. What is required to the worthy receiving of the Lord's Supper?

A. It is required of them that would worthily partake of the Lord's Supper, that they examine themselves of their knowledge to discern the Lord's body, of their faith to feed upon him, of their repentance, love, and new obedience; lest, coming unworthily, they eat and drink judgment to themselves.

Q98. What is prayer?

A. Prayer is an offering up of our desires unto God, for things agreeable to his will, in the name of Christ, with confession of our sins, and thankful acknowledgment of his mercies.

Q99. What rule hath God given for our direction in prayer?

A. The whole word of God is of use to direct us in prayer; but the special rule of direction is that form of prayer which Christ taught his disciples, commonly called the Lord's Prayer.

Q100. What doth the preface of the Lord's Prayer teach us?

A. The preface of the Lord's prayer, which is "Our Father which art in heaven," teacheth us to draw near to God with all holy reverence and confidence, as children to a father able and ready to help us; and that we should pray with and for others.

Q101. What do we pray for in the first petition?

A. In the first petition, which is "Hallowed be thy name," we pray that God would enable us and others to glorify him in all that whereby he maketh himself known; and that he would dispose all things to his own glory.

Q102. What do we pray for in the second petition?

A. In the second petition, which is "Thy kingdom come," we pray that Satan's kingdom may be destroyed; and that the kingdom of grace may be advanced, ourselves and others brought into it, and kept in it; and that the kingdom of glory may be hastened.

Q103. What do we pray for in the third petition?

A. In the third petition, which is "Thy will be done in earth, as it is in heaven," we pray that God, by his grace, would make us able and willing to know, obey and submit to his will in all things, as the angels do in heaven.

Q104. What do we pray for in the fourth petition?

A. In the fourth petition, which is "Give us this day our daily bread," we pray that of God's free gift we may receive a competent portion of the good things of this life, and enjoy his blessing with them.

Q105. What do we pray for in the fifth petition?

A. In the fifth petition, which is "And forgive us our debts, as we forgive our debtors," we pray that God, for Christ's sake, would freely pardon all our sins; which we are the rather encouraged to ask, because by his grace we are enabled from the heart to forgive others.

Q106. What do we pray for in the sixth petition?

A. In the sixth petition, which is "And lead us not into temptation, but deliver us from evil," we pray that God would either keep us from being tempted to sin or support and deliver us when we are tempted.

Q107. What doth the conclusion of the Lord's Prayer teach us?

A. The conclusion of the Lord's prayer, which is "For thine is the kingdom, and the power, and the glory, forever, Amen," teacheth us to take our encouragement in prayer from God only, and in our prayers to praise him, ascribing kingdom, power and glory to him. And in testimony of our desire, and assurance to be heard, we say "Amen."

THIRTY-NINE ARTICLES OF RELIGION
English, 1563

In the first three decades of its existence—from the 1530s to the 1560s—the Church of England developed its doctrinal standards in contrast to the Catholic and Reformed Churches. Beginning with the *Ten Articles* published by Thomas Cranmer in 1536, various bishops, archdeacons,

and doctors of divinity (e.g., Hugh Latimer) offered revisions and additions to comprise the *Thirty-nine Articles* published in 1563. The version reprinted here is the revision of 1801 of the Episcopal Church in the United States. Like the version of 1563, these articles include creedal statements (articles 1–8), doctrinal statements (articles 9–18), institutional statements, including directions for corporate worship (articles 19–31), and miscellaneous articles relating to church traditions and discipline (articles 32–39).

◆

I. Of faith in the Holy Trinity

There is but one living and true God, everlasting, without body, parts, or passions; of infinite power, wisdom, and goodness; the Maker, and Preserver of all things both visible and invisible. And in unity of this Godhead there be three Persons, of one substance, power, and eternity; the Father, the Son, and the Holy Ghost.

II. Of the Word or Son of God, which was made very Man

The Son, which is the Word of the Father, begotten from everlasting of the Father, the very and eternal God, and of one substance with the Father, took Man's nature in the womb of the blessed Virgin, of her substance: so that two whole and perfect Natures, that is to say, the Godhead and Manhood, were joined together in one Person, never to be divided, whereof is one Christ, very God, and very Man; who truly suffered, was crucified, dead, and buried, to reconcile his Father to us, and to be a sacrifice, not only for original guilt, but also for actual sins of men

III. Of the going down of Christ into Hell

As Christ died for us, and was buried, so also is it to be believed, that he went down into Hell.

IV. Of the Resurrection of Christ

Christ did truly rise again from death, and took again his body, with flesh, bones, and all things appertaining to the perfection of Man's nature; wherewith he ascended into Heaven, and there sitteth, until he return to judge all Men at the last day.

V. Of the Holy Ghost

The Holy Ghost, proceeding from the Father and the Son, is of one substance, majesty, and glory, with the Father and the Son, very and eternal God.

VI. Of the Sufficiency of the Holy Scriptures for Salvation

Holy Scripture containeth all things necessary to salvation: so that whatsoever is not read therein, nor may be proved thereby, is not to be required of any man, that it should be believed as an article of the Faith, or be thought requisite or necessary to salvation. In the name of the Holy Scripture we do understand those canonical Books of the Old and New Testament, of whose authority was never any doubt in the Church.

Of the Names and Number of the Canonical Books.

Genesis	The First Book of Samuel	The Book of Esther
Exodus	The Second Book of Samuel	The Book of Job
Leviticus	The First Book of Kings	The Psalms
Numbers	The Second Book of Kings	The Proverbs
Deuteronomy	The First Book of Chronicles	Ecclesiastes or Preacher
Joshua	The Second Book of Chronicles	Cantica, or Songs of Solomon
Judges	The First Book of Esdras	Four Prophets the greater
Ruth	The Second Book of Esdras	Twelve Prophets the less

And the other Books (as Jerome says) the Church doth read for example of life and instruction of manners; but yet doth it not apply them to establish any doctrine; such are these following:

The Third Book of Esdras	The rest of the Book of Esther
The Fourth Book of Esdras	The Book of Wisdom
The Book of Tobias	Jesus the Son of Sirach
The Book of Judith	Baruch the Prophet

The Song of the Three Children	The Prayer of Manasses
The Story of Susanna	The First Book of Maccabees
Of Bel and the Dragon	The Second Book of Maccabees

All the Books of the New Testament, as they are commonly received, we do receive, and account them Canonical.

VII. Of the Old Testament

The Old Testament is not contrary to the New: for both in the Old and New Testament everlasting life is offered to Mankind by Christ, who is the only Mediator between God and Man, being both God and Man. Wherefore they are not to be heard, which feign that the old Fathers did look only for transitory promises. Although the Law given from God by Moses, as touching Ceremonies and Rites, do not bind Christian men, nor the Civil precepts thereof ought of necessity to be received in any commonwealth; yet notwithstanding, no Christian man whatsoever is free from the obedience of the Commandments which are called Moral.

VIII. Of the Creeds

The Nicene Creed, and that which is commonly called the Apostles' Creed, ought thoroughly to be received and believed: for they may be proved by most certain warrants of Holy Scripture.

The original Article given Royal assent in 1571 and reaffirmed in 1662, was titled "Of the Three Creeds; and began as follows, "The Three Creeds, Nicene Creed, Athanasius's Creed, and that which is commonly called the Apostles' Creed . . ."

IX. Of Original or Birth-Sin

Original sin standeth not in the following of Adam (as the Pelagians do vainly talk); but it is the fault and corruption of the Nature of every man, that naturally is engendered of the offspring of Adam; whereby man is very far gone from original righteousness, and is of his own nature inclined to evil, so that the flesh lusteth always contrary to the Spirit; and therefore in every person born into this world, it deserveth God's wrath and damnation. And this infection of nature doth remain, yea in them that are regenerated; whereby the lust of the flesh, called in Greek, *phronema sarkos* (which some do expound the wisdom, some sensuality, some the affection, some the desire, of the flesh), is not subject to the Law of God. And although there is no condemnation for them that believe and are baptized; yet the Apostle doth confess, that concupiscence and lust hath of itself the nature of sin.

X. Of Free-Will

The condition of Man after the fall of Adam is such, that he cannot turn and prepare himself, by his own natural strength and good works, to faith; and calling upon God. Wherefore we have no power to do good works pleasant and acceptable to God, without the grace of God by Christ preventing us, that we may have a good will, and working with us, when we have that good will.

XI. Of the Justification of Man

We are accounted righteous before God, only for the merit of our Lord and Saviour Jesus Christ by Faith, and not for our own works or deservings. Wherefore, that we are justified by Faith only, is a most wholesome Doctrine, and very full of comfort, as more largely is expressed in the Homily of Justification.

XII. Of Good Works

Albeit that Good Works, which are the fruits of Faith, and follow after Justification, cannot put away our sins, and endure the severity of God's judgment; yet are they pleasing and acceptable to God in Christ, and do spring out necessarily of a true and lively Faith insomuch that by them a lively Faith may be as evidently known as a tree discerned by the fruit.

XIII. Of Works before Justification

Works done before the grace of Christ, and the Inspiration of his Spirit, are not pleasant to God, forasmuch as they spring not of faith in Jesus Christ; neither do they make men meet to receive grace, or (as the School-authors say) deserve grace of congruity: yea rather, for that they are not done as God hath willed and commanded them to be done, we doubt not but they have the nature of sin.

XIV. Of Works of Supererogation

Voluntary Works besides, over and above, God's Commandments, which they call Works of Supereroga-tion, cannot be taught without arrogancy and impiety: for by them men do declare, that they do not only render unto God as much as they are bound to do, but that they do more for his sake, than of bounden duty is required: whereas Christ saith plainly (Luke 17:10) When ye have done all that are commanded to you, say, We are unprofitable servants.

XV. Of Christ alone without Sin

Christ in the truth of our nature was made like unto us in all things, sin only except, from which he was clearly void, both in his flesh, and in his spirit. He came to be the Lamb without spot, who, by sacrifice of himself once made, should take away the sins of the world; and sin (as Saint John saith) was not in him. But all we the rest, although baptized and born again in Christ, yet offend in many things; and if we say we have no sin, we deceive ourselves, and the truth is not in us.

XVI. Of Sin after Baptism

Not every deadly sin willingly committed after Baptism is sin against the Holy Ghost, and unpardonable. Wherefore the grant of repentance is not to be denied to such as fall into sin after Baptism. After we have received the Holy Ghost, we may depart from grace given, and fall into sin, and by the grace of God we may arise again, and amend our lives. And therefore they are to be condemned, which say, they can no more sin as long as they live here, or deny the place of forgiveness to such as truly repent.

XVII. Of Predestination and Election

Predestination to Life is the everlasting purpose of God, whereby (before the foundations of the world were laid) he hath constantly decreed by his counsel secret to us, to deliver from curse and damnation those whom he hath chosen in Christ out of mankind, and to bring them by Christ to everlasting salvation, as vessels made to honor. Wherefore, they which be endued with so excellent a benefit of God, be called according to God's purpose by his Spirit working in due season: they through Grace obey the calling: they be justified freely: they be made sons of God by adoption: they be made like the image of his only-begotten Son Jesus Christ: they walk religiously in good works, and at length, by God's mercy, they attain to everlasting felicity.

As the godly consideration of Predestination, and

our Election in Christ, is full of sweet, pleasant, and unspeakable comfort to godly persons, and such as feel in themselves the working of the Spirit of Christ, mortifying the works of the flesh, and their earthly members, and drawing up their mind to high and heavenly things, as well because it doth greatly establish and confirm their faith of eternal Salvation to be enjoyed through Christ as because it doth fervently kindle their love toward God: So, for curious and carnal persons, lacking the Spirit of Christ, to have continually before their eyes the sentence of God's Predestination, is a most dangerous downfall, whereby the Devil doth thrust them either into desperation, or into wretchlessness of most unclean living, no less perilous than desperation.

Furthermore, we must receive God's promises in such wise, as they be generally set forth to us in Holy Scripture: and, in our doings, that Will of God is to be followed, which we have expressly declared unto us in the Word of God.

XVIII. Of obtaining eternal Salvation only by the Name of Christ

They also are to be had accursed that presume to say, That every man shall be saved by the Law or Sect which he professeth, so that he be diligent to frame his life according to that Law, and the light of Nature. For Holy Scripture doth set out unto us only the Name of Jesus Christ, whereby men must be saved.

XIX. Of the Church

The visible Church of Christ is a congregation of faithful men, in which the pure Word of God is preached, and the Sacraments be duly ministered according to Christ's ordinance, in all those things that of necessity are requisite to the same.

As the Church of Jerusalem, Alexandria, and Antioch, have erred, so also the Church of Rome hath erred, not only in their living and manner of Ceremonies, but also in matters of Faith.

XX. Of the Authority of the Church

The Church hath power to decree Rites or Ceremonies, and authority in Controversies of Faith: and yet it is not lawful for the Church to ordain any thing that is contrary to God's Word written, neither may it so expound one place of Scripture, that it be repugnant to another. Wherefore, although the Church be a witness

and a keeper of Holy Writ, yet, as it ought not to decree any thing against the same, so besides the same ought it not to enforce any thing to be believed for necessity of Salvation.

XXI. Of the Authority of General Councils

General Councils may not be gathered together without the commandment and will of Princes. And when they be gathered together (forasmuch as they be an assembly of men, whereof all be not governed with the Spirit and Word of God), they may err, and sometimes have erred, even in things pertaining unto God. Wherefore things ordained by them as necessary to salvation have neither strength nor authority, unless it may be declared that they be taken out of holy Scripture.[6]

XXII. Of Purgatory

The Romish Doctrine concerning Purgatory, Pardons, Worshipping and Adoration, as well of Images as of Relics, and also Invocation of Saints, is a fond thing, vainly invented, and grounded upon no warranty of Scripture, but rather repugnant to the Word of God.

XXIII. Of Ministering in the Congregation

It is not lawful for any man to take upon him the office of public preaching, or ministering the Sacraments in the Congregation, before he be lawfully called, and sent to execute the same. And those we ought to judge lawfully called and sent, which be chosen and called to this work by men who have public authority given unto them in the Congregation, to call and send Ministers into the Lord's vineyard.

XXIV. Of Speaking in the Congregation in such a Tongue as the people understandeth

It is a thing plainly repugnant to the Word of God, and the custom of the Primitive Church to have public Prayer in the Church, or to minister the Sacraments, in a tongue not understood of the people.

XXV. Of the Sacraments

Sacraments ordained of Christ be not only badges or tokens of Christian men's profession, but rather they

---

6. The Twenty-first Article, included in the 1571 and 1622 texts, was omitted in the 1801 version, partly because of its local and civil nature, and also because the remaining parts of it were provided for in other articles.

be certain sure witnesses, and effectual signs of grace, and God's good will toward us, by the which he doth work invisibly in us, and doth not only quicken, but also strengthen and confirm our Faith in him.

There are two Sacraments ordained of Christ our Lord in the Gospel, that is to say, Baptism, and the Supper of the Lord.

Those five commonly called Sacraments, that is to say, Confirmation, Penance, Orders, Matrimony, and Extreme Unction, are not to be counted for Sacraments of the Gospel, being such as have grown partly of the corrupt following of the Apostles, partly are states of life allowed in the Scriptures, but yet have not like nature of Sacraments with Baptism, and the Lord's Supper, for that they have not any visible sign or ceremony ordained of God.

The Sacraments were not ordained of Christ to be gazed upon, or to be carried about, but that we should duly use them. And in such only as worthily receive the same, they have a wholesome effect or operation: but they that receive them unworthily, purchase to themselves damnation, as Saint Paul saith.

XXVI. Of the Unworthiness of the Ministers, which hinders not the effect of the Sacraments

Although in the visible Church the evil be ever mingled with the good, and sometimes the evil have chief authority in the Ministration of the Word and Sacraments, yet forasmuch as they do not the same in their own name, but in Christ's, and do minister by his commission and authority, we may use their Ministry, both in hearing the Word of God, and in receiving the Sacraments. Neither is the effect of Christ's ordinance taken away by their wickedness, nor the grace of God's gifts diminished from such as by faith, and rightly, do receive the Sacraments ministered unto them; which be effectual, because of Christ's institution and promise, although they be ministered by evil men.

Nevertheless, it appertaineth to the discipline of the Church, that inquiry be made of evil Ministers, and that they be accused by those that have knowledge of their offences; and finally, being found guilty, by just judgment be deposed.

XXVII. Of Baptism

Baptism is not only a sign of profession, and mark of difference, whereby Christian men are discerned from others that be not christened, but it is also a sign of Regeneration or New-Birth, whereby, as by an instrument, they that receive Baptism rightly are grafted into the Church; the promises of the forgiveness of sin, and of our adoption to be the sons of God by the Holy Ghost, are visibly signed and sealed, Faith is confirmed, and Grace increased by virtue of prayer unto God.

The Baptism of young Children is in any wise to be retained in the Church, as most agreeable with the institution of Christ.

XXVIII. Of the Lord's Supper

The Supper of the Lord is not only a sign of the love that Christians ought to have among themselves one to another, but rather it is a Sacrament of our Redemption by Christ's death: insomuch that to such as rightly, worthily, and with faith, receive the same, the Bread which we break is a partaking of the Body of Christ; and likewise the Cup of Blessing is a partaking of the Blood of Christ.

Transubstantiation (or the change of the substance of Bread and Wine) in the Supper of the Lord, cannot be proved by Holy Writ; but is repugnant to the plain words of Scripture, overthroweth the nature of a Sacrament, and hath given occasion to many superstitions.

The Body of Christ is given, taken, and eaten, in the Supper, only after an heavenly and spiritual manner. And the mean whereby the Body of Christ is received and eaten in the Supper, is Faith.

The Sacrament of the Lord's Supper was not by Christ's ordinance reserved, carried about, lifted up, or worshipped.

XXIX. Of the Wicked, which eat not the Body of Christ in the use of the Lord's Supper

The Wicked, and such as be void of a lively faith, although they do carnally and visibly press with their teeth (as Saint Augustine saith) the Sacrament of the Body and Blood of Christ; yet in no wise are they partakers of Christ: but rather, to their condemnation, do eat and drink the sign or Sacrament of so great a thing.

XXX. Of Both Kinds

The Cup of the Lord is not to be denied to the Lay-people: for both the parts of the Lord's Sacrament, by Christ's ordinance and commandment, ought to be ministered to all Christian men alike.

XXXI. Of the One Oblation of Christ Finished upon the Cross

The Offering of Christ once made is that perfect redemption, propitiation, and satisfaction, for all the sins of the whole world, both original and actual; and there is none other satisfaction for sin, but that alone. Wherefore the sacrifices of Masses, in the which it was commonly said, that the Priest did offer Christ for the quick and the dead, to have remission of pain or guilt, were blasphemous fables, and dangerous deceits.

XXXII. Of the Marriage of Priests

Bishops, Priests, and Deacons, are not commanded by God's Law, either to vow the estate of single life, or to abstain from marriage: therefore it is lawful for them, as for all other Christian men, to marry at their own discretion, as they shall judge the same to serve better to godliness.

XXXIII. Of Excommunicate Persons, How They Are to be Avoided

That person which by open denunciation of the Church is rightly cut off from the unity of the Church, and excommunicated, ought to be taken of the whole multitude of the faithful, as an Heathen and Publican, until he be openly reconciled by penance, and received into the Church by a Judge that hath authority thereunto.

XXXIV. Of the Traditions of the Church

It is not necessary that Traditions and Ceremonies be in all places one, or utterly like; for at all times they have been diverse, and may be changed according to the diversity of countries, times, and men's manners, so that nothing be ordained against God's Word. Whosoever, through his private judgment, willingly and purposely, doth openly break the Traditions and Ceremonies of the Church, which be not repugnant to the Word of God, and be ordained and approved by common authority, ought to be rebuked openly (that others may fear to do the like), as he that offendeth against the common order of the Church, and hurteth the authority of the Magistrate, and woundeth the consciences of the weak brethren.

Every particular or national Church hath authority to ordain, change, and abolish, Ceremonies or Rites of the Church ordained only by man's authority, so that all things be done to edifying.

XXXV. Of the Homilies

The Second Book of Homilies, the several titles whereof we have joined under this Article, doth contain a godly and wholesome Doctrine, and necessary for these times, as doth the former Book of Homilies, which were set forth in the time of Edward the Sixth; and therefore we judge them to be read in Churches by the Ministers, diligently and distinctly, that they may he understanded of the people.

Of the Names of the Homilies

1. Of the right Use of the Church.
2. Against Peril of Idolatry.
3. Of repairing and keeping clean of Churches.
4. Of good Works: first of Fasting.
5. Against Gluttony and Drunkenness.
6. Against Excess of Apparel.
7. Of Prayer.
8. Of the Place and Time of Prayer.
9. That Common Prayers and Sacraments ought to be ministered in a known tongue.
10. Of the reverend Estimation of God's Word.
11. Of Alms-doing.
12. Of the Nativity of Christ.
13. Of the Passion of Christ.
14. Of the Resurrection of Christ.
15. Of the worthy receiving of the Sacrament of the Body and Blood of Christ.
16. Of the Gifts of the Holy Ghost.
17. For the Rogation-days.
18. Of the State of Matrimony.
19. Of Repentance.
20. Against Idleness.
21. Against Rebellion.

XXXVI. Of Consecration of Bishops and Ministers

The Book of Consecration of Bishops, and Ordering of Priests and Deacons, as set forth by the General Convention of this Church in 1792, doth contain all things necessary to such Consecration and Ordering; neither hath it any thing that, of itself, is superstitious and ungodly. And, therefore, whosoever are consecrated or ordered according to said Form, we decree all such to be rightly, orderly, and lawfully consecrated and ordered.

XXXVII. Of the Power of the Civil Magistrates

The Power of the Civil Magistrate extendeth to all men, as well Clergy as Laity, in all things temporal; but hath no authority in things purely spiritual. And we hold it to be the duty of all men who are professors of the Gospel, to pay respectful obedience to the Civil Authority, regularly and legitimately constituted.[7]

XXXVIII. Of Christian Men's Goods, which are not common

The Riches and Goods of Christians are not common, as touching the right, title, and possession of the same; as certain Anabaptists do falsely boast. Notwithstanding, every man ought, of such things as he possesseth, liberally to give alms to the poor, according to his ability.

XXXIX. Of a Christian Man's Oath

As we confess that vain and rash Swearing is forbidden Christian men by our Lord Jesus Christ, and James his Apostle, so we judge, that Christian Religion doth not prohibit, but that a man may swear when the Magistrate requireth, in a cause of faith and charity, so it be done according to the Prophet's teaching in justice, judgment, and truth.

---

7. The original 1571, 1662 text of this Article reads as follows:

    "The King's Majesty hath the chief power in this Realm of England, and other his Dominions, unto whom the chief Government of all Estates of this Realm, whether they be Ecclesiastical or Civil, in all causes doth appertain, and is not, nor ought to be, subject to any foreign Jurisdiction. Where we attribute to the King's Majesty the chief government, by which Titles we understand the minds of some slanderous folks to be offended; we give not our Princes the ministering either of God's Word, or of the Sacraments, the which thing the Injunctions also lately set forth by Elizabeth our Queen do most plainly testify; but that only prerogative, which we see to have been given always to all godly Princes in holy Scriptures by God himself; that is, that they should rule all estates and degrees committed to their charge by God, whether they be Ecclesiastical or Temporal, and restrain with the civil sword the stubborn and evil-doers.

    "The Bishop of Rome hath no jurisdiction in this Realm of England.

    "The Laws of the Realm may punish Christian men with death, for heinous and grievous offences.

    "It is lawful for Christian men, at the commandment of the Magistrate, to wear weapons, and serve in the wars."

HEIDELBERG CATECHISM
German, 1563

This catechism presents a summary of the Reformed Christian faith in 129 questions and answers which are divided into three parts describing, respectively, the doctrines of Sin, "the misery of man" (questions 3–11); Salvation, "man's deliverance" (questions 12–85); and Service, "Of thankfulness" (questions 86–129). A "confession" of the Reformed faith, the Heidelberg Catechism was composed by request of Elector Frederick III, ruler of the Palatinate, Germany from 1559 to 1576, to settle the theological disputes of his province. Elector Frederick drew on the faculty of Sapienz College for this project, the primary responsibility (and credit) for publication falling to Zacharius Ursinius and Caspar Olevianus. This catechism was translated into many languages and its questions and answers have been memorized by countless children and adults since the sixteenth century.[8]

Questions for Guided Reading

1. What basic biblical creeds and confessions make up this catechism?

2. How does this catechism compare in content and organization with Luther's *Shorter Catechism*?

3. What sacraments are recognized by this catechism, and where does their description agree or disagree with your own understanding of these sacraments?

4. What are the "keys of the kingdom" according to this catechism, and how does their description compare with Luther's *Shorter Catechism*?

5. If you were to develop a catechism for children and youth, what would you include?

6. What are some benefits and drawbacks of having children memorize this catechism?

7. While many children memorize Scripture, few memorize the catechism these days; what's the difference, and what is lost or gained by this?

---

8. A contemporary children's version (at a fifth grade reading level) is published by the Christian Reformed Church and Reformed Church in America as *Q & A: A Summary of Biblical Teachings*, rev. ed, LiFE series [Living in Faith Everyday], 1998.

✦

Q1. What is thy only comfort in life and death?

A. That I with body and soul, both in life and death, am not my own, but belong unto my faithful Savior Jesus Christ; who, with his precious blood, has fully satisfied for all my sins, and delivered me from all the power of the devil; and so preserves me that without the will of my heavenly Father, not a hair can fall from my head; yea, that all things must be subservient to my salvation, and therefore, by his Holy Spirit, He also assures me of eternal life, and makes me sincerely willing and ready, henceforth, to live unto him.

Q2. How many things are necessary for thee to know, that thou, enjoying this comfort, mayest live and die happily?

A. Three; the first, how great my sins and miseries are; the second, how I may be delivered from all my sins and miseries; the third, how I shall express my gratitude to God for such deliverance.

The First Part: Of the Misery of Man

Q3. Whence knowest thou thy misery?

A. Out of the law of God.

Q4. What does the law of God require of us?

A. Christ teaches us that briefly, Matthew 22:37–40, "Thou shalt love the Lord thy God with all thy heart, with all thy soul, and with all thy mind, and with all thy strength. This is the first and the great commandment; and the second is like unto it, Thou shalt love thy neighbor as thyself. On these two commandments hang all the law and the prophets."

Q5. Canst thou keep all these things perfectly?

A. In no wise; for I am prone by nature to hate God and my neighbor.

Q6. Did God then create man so wicked and perverse?

A. By no means; but God created man good, and after his own image, in true righteousness and holiness, that he might rightly know God his Creator, heartily love him and live with him in eternal happiness to glorify and praise him.

Q7. Whence then proceeds this depravity of human nature?

A. From the fall and disobedience of our first parents, Adam and Eve, in Paradise; hence our nature is become so corrupt, that we are all conceived and born in sin.

Q8. Are we then so corrupt that we are wholly incapable of doing any good, and inclined to all wickedness?

A. Indeed we are; except we are regenerated by the Spirit of God.

Q9. Does not God then do injustice to man, by requiring from him in his law, that which he cannot perform?

A. Not at all; for God made man capable of performing it; but man, by the instigation of the devil, and his own willful disobedience, deprived himself and all his posterity of those divine gifts.

Q10. Will God suffer such disobedience and rebellion to go unpunished?

A. By no means; but is terribly displeased with our original as well as actual sins; and will punish them in his just judgment temporally and eternally, as he has declared, "Cursed is every one that continueth not in all things, which are written in the book of the law, to do them."

Q11. Is not God then also merciful?

A. God is indeed merciful, but also just; therefore his justice requires, that sin which is committed against the most high majesty of God, be also punished with extreme, that is, with everlasting punishment of body and soul.

The Second Part: Of Man's Deliverance

Q12. Since then, by the righteous judgment of God, we deserve temporal and eternal punishment, is there no way by which we may escape that punishment, and be again received into favor?

A. God will have his justice satisfied: and therefore we must make this full satisfaction, either by ourselves, or by another.

Q13. Can we ourselves then make this satisfaction?
A. By no means; but on the contrary we daily increase our debt.

Q14. Can there be found anywhere, one, who is a mere creature, able to satisfy for us?
A. None; for, first, God will not punish any other creature for the sin which man has committed; and further, no mere creature can sustain the burden of God's eternal wrath against sin, so as to deliver others from it.

Q15. What sort of a mediator and deliverer then must we seek for?
A. For one who is very man, and perfectly righteous; and yet more powerful than all creatures; that is, one who is also very God.

Q16. Why must he be very man, and also perfectly righteous?
A. Because the justice of God requires that the same human nature which has sinned, should likewise make satisfaction for sin; and one, who is himself a sinner, cannot satisfy for others.

Q17. Why must he in one person be also very God?
A. That he might, by the power of his Godhead sustain in his human nature, the burden of God's wrath; and might obtain for, and restore to us, righteousness and life.

Q18. Who then is that Mediator, who is in one person both very God, and a real righteous man?
A. Our Lord Jesus Christ: "who of God is made unto us wisdom, and righteousness, and sanctification, and redemption."

Q19. Whence knowest thou this?
A. From the holy gospel, which God himself first revealed in Paradise; and afterward published by the patriarchs and prophets, and represented by the sacrifices and other ceremonies of the law; and lastly, has fulfilled it by his only begotten Son.

Q20. Are all men then, as they perished in Adam, saved by Christ?
A. No; only those who are ingrafted into him, and, receive all his benefits, by a true faith.

Q21. What is true faith?
A. True faith is not only a certain knowledge, whereby I hold for truth all that God has revealed to us in his word, but also an assured confidence, which the Holy Ghost works by the gospel in my heart; that not only to others, but to me also, remission of sin, everlasting righteousness and salvation, are freely given by God, merely of grace, only for the sake of Christ's merits.

Q22. What is then necessary for a Christian to believe?
A. All things promised us in the gospel, which the articles of our catholic undoubted Christian faith briefly teach us.

Q23. What are these articles?
A. 1. I believe in God the Father, Almighty, Maker of heaven and earth: 2. And in Jesus Christ, his only begotten Son, our Lord: 3. Who was conceived by the Holy Ghost, born of the Virgin Mary: 4. Suffered under Pontius Pilate; was crucified, dead, and buried: He descended into hell: 5. The third day he rose again from the dead: 6. He ascended into heaven, and sitteth at the right hand of God the Father Almighty: 7. From thence he shall come to judge the quick and the dead: 8. I believe in the Holy Ghost: 9. I believe a holy catholic church: the communion of saints: 10. The forgiveness of sins: 11. The resurrection of the body: 12. And the life everlasting.

Q24. How are these articles divided?
A. Into three parts; the first is of God the Father, and our creation; the second of God the Son, and our redemption; the third of God the Holy Ghost, and our sanctification.

Q25. Since there is but one only divine essence, why speakest thou of Father, Son, and Holy Ghost?

A. Because God has so revealed himself in his word, that these three distinct persons are the one only true and eternal God.

Of God the Father

Q26. What believest thou when thou sayest, "I believe in God the Father, Almighty, Maker of heaven and earth"?

A. That the eternal Father of our Lord Jesus Christ (who of nothing made heaven and earth, with all that is in them; who likewise upholds and governs the same by his eternal counsel and providence) is for the sake of Christ his Son, my God and my Father; on whom I rely so entirely, that I have no doubt, but he will provide me with all things necessary for soul and body and further, that he will make whatever evils he sends upon me, in this valley of tears turn out to my advantage; for he is able to do it, being Almighty God, and willing, being a faithful Father.

Q27. What dost thou mean by the providence of God?

A. The almighty and everywhere present power of God; whereby, as it were by his hand, he upholds and governs heaven, earth, and all creatures; so that herbs and grass, rain and drought, fruitful and barren years, meat and drink, health and sickness, riches and poverty, yea, and all things come, not by chance, but by his fatherly hand.

Q28. What advantage is it to us to know that God has created, and by his providence does still uphold all things?

A. That we may be patient in adversity; thankful in prosperity; and that in all things, which may hereafter befall us, we place our firm trust in our faithful God and Father, that nothing shall separate us from his love; since all creatures are so in his hand, that without his will they cannot so much as move.

Of God the Son

Q29. Why is the Son of God called "Jesus," that is a Savior?

A. Because he saveth us, and delivereth us from our sins; and likewise, because we ought not to seek, neither can find salvation in any other.

Q30. Do such then believe in Jesus the only Savior, who seek their salvation and welfare of saints, of themselves, or anywhere else?

A. They do not; for though they boast of him in words, yet in deeds they deny Jesus the only deliverer and Savior; for one of these two things must be true, that either Jesus is not a complete Savior; or that they, who by a true faith receive this Savior, must find all things in him necessary to their salvation.

Q31. Why is he called "Christ," that is anointed?

A. Because he is ordained of God the Father, and anointed with the Holy Ghost, to be our chief Prophet and Teacher, who has fully revealed to us the secret counsel and will of God concerning our redemption; and to be our only High Priest, who by the one sacrifice of his body, has redeemed us, and makes continual intercession with the Father for us; and also to be our eternal King, who governs us by his word and Spirit, and who defends and preserves us in that salvation, he has purchased for us.

Q32. But why art thou called a Christian?

A. Because I am a member of Christ by faith, and thus am partaker of his anointing; that so I may confess his name, and present myself a living sacrifice of thankfulness to him: and also that with a free and good conscience I may fight against sin and Satan in this life and afterward I reign with him eternally, over all creatures.

Q33. Why is Christ called the "only begotten Son" of God, since we are also the children of God?

A. Because Christ alone is the eternal and natural Son of God; but we are children adopted of God, by grace, for his sake.

Q34. Wherefore callest thou him "our Lord"?

A. Because he hath redeemed us, both soul and body, from all our sins, not with silver or gold, but with his precious blood, and has delivered us from all the power of the devil; and thus has made us his own property.

Q35. What is the meaning of these words "He was conceived by the Holy Ghost, born of the Virgin Mary"?

A. That God's eternal Son, who is, and continues true and eternal God, took upon him the very nature of man, of the flesh and blood of the virgin Mary, by the operation of the Holy Ghost; that he might also be the true seed of David, like unto his brethren in all things, sin excepted.

Q36. What profit dost thou receive by Christ's holy conception and nativity?

A. That he is our Mediator; and with His innocence and perfect holiness, covers in the sight of God, my sins, wherein I was conceived and brought forth.

Q37. What dost thou understand by the words, "He suffered"?

A. That he, all the time that he lived on earth, but especially at the end of his life, sustained in body and soul, the wrath of God against the sins of all mankind: that so by his passion, as the only propitiatory sacrifice, he might redeem our body and soul from everlasting damnation, and obtain for us the favor of God, righteousness and eternal life.

Q38. Why did he suffer "under Pontius Pilate, as judge"?

A. That he, being innocent, and yet condemned by a temporal judge, might thereby free us from the severe judgment of God to which we were exposed.

Q39. Is there anything more in his being "crucified," than if he had died some other death?

A. Yes there is; for thereby I am assured, that he took on him the curse which lay upon me; for the death of the cross was accursed of God.

Q40. Why was it necessary for Christ to humble himself even "unto death"?

A. Because with respect to the justice and truth of God, satisfaction for our sins could be made no otherwise, than by the death of the Son of God.

Q41. Why was he also "buried"?

A. Thereby to prove that he was really dead.

Q42. Since then Christ died for us, why must we also die?

A. Our death is not a satisfaction for our sins, but only an abolishing of sin, and a passage into eternal life.

Q43. What further benefit do we receive from the sacrifice and death of Christ on the cross?

A. That by virtue thereof, our old man is crucified, dead and buried with him; that so the corrupt inclinations of the flesh may no more reign in us; but that we may offer ourselves unto him a sacrifice of thanksgiving.

Q44. Why is there added, "He descended into hell"?

A. That in my greatest temptations, I may be assured, and wholly comfort myself in this, that my Lord Jesus Christ, by his inexpressible anguish, pains, terrors, and hellish agonies, in which he was plunged during all his sufferings, but especially on the cross, has delivered me from the anguish and torments of hell.

Q45. What does the "resurrection" of Christ profit us?

A. First, by his resurrection he has overcome death, that he might make us partakers of that righteousness which he had purchased for us by his death; secondly, we are also by his power raised up to a new life; and lastly, the resurrection of Christ is a sure pledge of our blessed resurrection.

Q46. How dost thou understand these words, "He ascended into heaven"?

A. That Christ, in sight of his disciples, was taken up from earth into heaven; and that he continues there for our interest, until he comes again to judge the quick and the dead.

Q47. Is not Christ then with us even to the end of the world, as he has promised?

A. Christ is very man and very God; with respect to his human nature, he is no more on earth; but with respect to his Godhead, majesty, grace and spirit, he is at no time absent from us.

Q48. But if his human nature is not present, wherever his Godhead is, are not then these two natures in Christ separated from one another?

A. Not at all, for since the Godhead is illimitable and omnipresent, it must necessarily follow that the same is beyond the limits of the human nature he assumed, and yet is nevertheless in this human nature, and remains personally united to it.

Q49. Of what advantage to us is Christ's ascension into heaven?

A. First, that he is our advocate in the presence of his Father in heaven; secondly, that we have our flesh in heaven as a sure pledge that he, as the head, will also take up to himself, us, his members; thirdly, that he sends us his Spirit as an earnest, by whose power we "seek the things which are above, where Christ sitteth on the right hand of God, and not things on earth."

Q50. Why is it added, "and sitteth at the right hand of God"?

A. Because Christ is ascended into heaven for this end, that he might appear as head of his church, by whom the Father governs all things.

Q51. What profit is this glory of Christ, our head, unto us?

A. First, that by his Holy Spirit he pours out heavenly graces upon us his members; and then that by his power he defends and preserves us against all enemies.

Q52. What comfort is it to thee that "Christ shall come again to judge the quick and the dead"?

A. That in all my sorrows and persecutions, with uplifted head I look for the very same person, who before offered himself for my sake, to the tribunal of God, and has removed all curse from me, to come as judge from heaven: who shall cast all his and my enemies into everlasting condemnation, but shall translate me with all his chosen ones to himself, into heavenly joys and glory.

Of God the Holy Ghost

Q53. What dost thou believe concerning the Holy Ghost?

A. First, that he is true and coeternal God with the Father and the Son; secondly, that he is also given me, to make me by a true faith, partaker of Christ and all his benefits, that he may comfort me and abide with me for ever.

Q54. What believest thou concerning the "holy catholic church" of Christ?

A. That the Son of God from the beginning to the end of the world, gathers, defends, and preserves to himself by his Spirit and word, out of the whole human race, a church chosen to everlasting life, agreeing in true faith; and that I am and forever shall remain, a living member thereof.

Q55. What do you understand by "the communion of saints"?

A. First, that all and every one, who believes, being members of Christ, are in common, partakers of him, and of all his riches and gifts; secondly, that every one must know it to be his duty, readily and cheerfully to employ his gifts, for the advantage and salvation of other members.

Q56. What believest thou concerning "the forgiveness of sins"?

A. That God, for the sake of Christ's satisfaction, will no more remember my sins, neither my corrupt nature, against which I have to struggle all my life long; but will graciously impute to me the righteousness of Christ, that I may never be condemned before the tribunal of God.

Q57. What comfort does the "resurrection of the body" afford thee?

A. That not only my soul after this life shall be immediately taken up to Christ its head; but also, that this my body, being raised by the power of Christ, shall be reunited with my soul, and made like unto the glorious body of Christ.

Q58. What comfort takest thou from the article of "life everlasting"?

A. That since I now feel in my heart the beginning of eternal joy, after this life, I shall inherit perfect salvation, which "eye has not seen, nor ear heard, neither has it entered into the heart of man" to conceive, and that to praise God therein for ever.

Q59. But what does it profit thee now that thou believest all this?

A. That I am righteous in Christ, before God, and an heir of eternal life.

Q60. How are thou righteous before God?

A. Only by a true faith in Jesus Christ; so that, though my conscience accuse me, that I have grossly transgressed all the commandments of God, and kept none of them, and am still inclined to all evil; notwithstanding, God, without any merit of mine, but only of mere grace, grants and imputes to me, the perfect satisfaction, righteousness and holiness of Christ; even so, as if I never had had, nor committed any sin: yea, as if I had fully accomplished all that obedience which Christ has accomplished for me; inasmuch as I embrace such benefit with a believing heart.

Q61. Why sayest thou, that thou art righteous by faith only?

A. Not that I am acceptable to God, on account of the worthiness of my faith; but because only the satisfaction, righteousness, and holiness of Christ, is my righteousness before God; and that I cannot receive and apply the same to myself any other way than by faith only.

Q62. But why cannot our good works be the whole, or part of our righteousness before God?

A. Because, that the righteousness, which can be approved of before the tribunal of God, must be absolutely perfect, and in all respects conformable to the divine law; and also, that our best works in this life are all imperfect and defiled with sin.

Q63. What! do not our good works merit, which yet God will reward in this and in a future life?

A. This reward is not of merit, but of grace.

Q64. But does not this doctrine make men careless and profane?

A. By no means: for it is impossible that those, who are implanted into Christ by a true faith, should not bring forth fruits of thankfulness.

Of the Sacraments

Q65. Since then we are made partakers of Christ and all his benefits by faith only, whence does this faith proceed?

A. From the Holy Ghost, who works faith in our hearts by the preaching of the gospel, and confirms it by the use of the sacraments.

Q66. What are the sacraments?

A. The sacraments are holy visible signs and seals, appointed of God for this end, that by the use thereof, he may the more fully declare and seal to us the promise of the gospel, viz., that he grants us freely the remission of sin, and life eternal, for the sake of that one sacrifice of Christ, accomplished on the cross.

Q67. Are both word and sacraments, then, ordained and appointed for this end, that they may direct our faith to the sacrifice of Jesus Christ on the cross, as the only ground of our salvation?

A. Yes, indeed: for the Holy Ghost teaches us in the gospel, and assures us by the sacraments, that the whole of our salvation depends upon that one sacrifice of Christ which he offered for us on the cross.

Q68. How many sacraments has Christ instituted in the new covenant, or testament?

A. Two: namely, holy baptism, and the holy supper.

Of Holy Baptism

Q69. How art thou admonished and assured by holy baptism, that the one sacrifice of Christ upon the cross is of real advantage to thee?

A. Thus: That Christ appointed this external washing with water, adding thereto this promise, that I am as certainly washed by his blood and Spirit from all the pollution of my soul, that is, from all my sins, as I am washed externally with water, by which the filthiness of the body is commonly washed away.

Q70. What is it to be washed with the blood and Spirit of Christ?

A. It is to receive of God the remission of sins, freely, for the sake of Christ's blood, which he shed for us by his sacrifice upon the cross; and also to be renewed by the Holy Ghost, and sanctified to be members of Christ, that so we may more and more die unto sin, and lead holy and unblamable lives.

Q71. Where has Christ promised us, that he will as certainly wash us by his blood and Spirit, as we are washed with the water of baptism?

A. In the institution of baptism, which is thus expressed: "Go ye, therefore, and teach all nations, baptizing them in the name of the Father, and of the Son, and of the Holy Ghost," Matthew 28:19. And "he that believeth, and is baptized, shall be saved; but he that believeth not, shall be damned": Mark 16:16. This promise is also repeated, where the scripture calls baptism "the washing of regenerations" and the washing away of sins. Titus 3:5; Acts 22:16.

Q72. Is then the external baptism with water the washing away of sin itself?

A. Not at all: for the blood of Jesus Christ only, and the Holy Ghost cleanse us from all sin.

Q73. Why then does the Holy Ghost call baptism "the washing of regeneration," and "the washing away of sins"?

A. God speaks thus not without great cause, to-wit, not only thereby to teach us, that as the filth of the body is purged away by water, so our sins are removed by the blood and Spirit of Jesus Christ; but especially that by this divine pledge and sign he may assure us, that we are spiritually cleansed from our sins as really, as we are externally washed with water.

Q74. Are infants also to be baptized?

A. Yes: for since they, as well as the adult, are included in the covenant and church of God; and since redemption from sin by the blood of Christ, and the Holy Ghost, the author of faith, is promised to them no less than to the adult; they must therefore by baptism, as a sign of the covenant, be also admitted into the Christian church; and be distinguished from the children of unbelievers as was done in the old covenant or testament by circumcision, instead of which baptism is instituted in the new covenant.

Of the Holy Supper of Our Lord Jesus Christ

Q75. How art thou admonished and assured in the Lord's Supper, that thou art a partaker of that one sacrifice of Christ, accomplished on the cross, and of all his benefits?

A. Thus: That Christ has commanded me and all believers, to eat of this broken bread, and to drink of this cup, in remembrance of him, adding these promises: first, that his body was offered and broken on the cross for me, and his blood shed for me, as certainly as I see with my eyes, the bread of the Lord broken for me, and the cup communicated to me; and further, that he feeds and nourishes my soul to everlasting life, with his crucified body and shed blood, as assuredly as I receive from the hands of the minister, and taste with my mouth the bread and cup of the Lord, as certain signs of the body and blood of Christ.

Q76. What is it then to eat the crucified body, and drink the shed blood of Christ?

A. It is not only to embrace with believing heart all the sufferings and death of Christ and thereby to obtain the pardon of sin, and life eternal; but also, besides that, to become more and more united to his sacred body, by the Holy Ghost, who dwells both in Christ and in us; so that we, though Christ is in heaven and we on earth, are notwithstanding "flesh of his flesh and bone of his bone" and that we live, and are governed forever by one spirit, as members of the same body are by one soul.

Q77. Where has Christ promised that he will as certainly feed and nourish believers with his body and blood, as they eat of this broken bread, and drink of this cup?

A. In the institution of the supper, which is thus expressed: "The Lord Jesus, the same night in which he was betrayed, took bread, and when he had given thanks, he brake it, and said: eat, this is my body, which is broken for you; this do in remembrance of me. After the same manner also he took the cup, when he had supped, saying: this cup is the new testament in my blood; this do ye, as often as ye drink it, in remembrance of me. For, as often as ye eat this bread, and drink this cup, ye do show the Lord's death till he come" (1 Cor. 11:23–26). This promise is repeated by the holy apostle Paul, where he says "The cup of blessing which we bless, is it not the communion of the blood of Christ? The bread which we break, is it not the communion of the body of Christ? For we being many are one bread, and one body: for we are all partakers of that one bread" (1 Cor. 10:16–17).

Q78. Do then the bread and wine become the very body and blood of Christ?

A. Not at all: but as the water in baptism is not changed into the blood of Christ, neither is the washing away of sin itself, being only the sign and confirmation thereof appointed of God; so the bread in the Lord's supper is not changed into the very body of Christ; though agreeably to the nature and properties of sacraments, it is called the body of Christ Jesus.

Q79. Why then doth Christ call the bread "his body," and the cup "his blood," or "the new covenant in his blood"; and Paul the "communion of body and blood of Christ"?

A. Christ speaks thus, not without great reason, namely, not only thereby to teach us, that as bread and wine support this temporal life, so his crucified body and shed blood are the true meat and drink, whereby our souls are fed to eternal life; but more especially by these visible signs and pledges to assure us, that we are as really partakers of his true body and blood by the operation of the Holy Ghost as we receive by the mouths of our bodies these holy signs in remembrance of him; and that all his sufferings and obedience are as certainly ours, as if we had in our own persons suffered and made satisfaction for our sins to God.

Q80. What difference is there between the Lord's Supper and the popish mass?

A. The Lord's supper testifies to us, that we have a full pardon of all sin by the only sacrifice of Jesus Christ, which he himself has once accomplished on the cross; and, that we by the Holy Ghost are ingrafted into Christ, who, according to his human nature is now not on earth, but in heaven, at the right hand of God his Father, and will there be worshipped by us. But the mass teaches, that the living and dead have not the pardon of sins through the sufferings of Christ, unless Christ is also daily offered for them by the priests; and further, that Christ is bodily under the form of bread and wine, and therefore is to be worshipped in them; so that the mass, at bottom, is nothing else than a denial of the one sacrifice and sufferings of Jesus Christ, and an accursed idolatry.

Q81. For whom is the Lord's Supper instituted?

A. For those who are truly sorrowful for their sins, and yet trust that these are forgiven them for the sake of Christ; and that their remaining infirmities are covered by his passion and death; and who also earnestly desire to have their faith more and more strengthened, and their lives more holy; but hypocrites, and such as turn not to God with sincere hearts, eat and drink judgment to themselves.

Q82. Are they also to be admitted to this supper,

who, by confession and life, declare themselves unbelieving and ungodly?

A. No; for by this, the covenant of God would be profaned, and his wrath kindled against the whole congregation; therefore it is the duty of the Christian church, according to the appointment of Christ and his apostles, to exclude such persons, by the keys of the kingdom of heaven, till they show amendment of life.

Q83. What are the keys of the kingdom of heaven?

A. The preaching of the holy gospel, and Christian discipline, or excommunication out of the Christian church; by these two, the kingdom of heaven is opened to believers, and shut against unbelievers.

Q84. How is the kingdom of heaven opened and shut by the preaching of the holy gospel?

A. Thus: when according to the command of Christ, it is declared and publicly testified to all and every believer, that, whenever they receive the promise of the gospel by a true faith, all their sins are really forgiven them of God, for the sake of Christ's merits; and on the contrary, when it is declared and testified to all unbelievers, and such as do not sincerely repent, that they stand exposed to the wrath of God, and eternal condemnation, so long as they are unconverted: according to which testimony of the gospel, God will judge them, both in this, and in the life to come.

Q85. How is the kingdom of heaven shut and opened by Christian discipline?

A. Thus: when according to the command of Christ, those, who under the name of Christians, maintain doctrines, or practices inconsistent therewith, and will not, after having been often brotherly admonished, renounce their errors and wicked course of life, are complained of to the church, or to those, who are thereunto appointed by the church; and if they despise their admonition, are by them forbidden the use of the sacraments; whereby they are excluded from the Christian

church, and by God himself from the kingdom of Christ; and when they promise and show real amendment, are again received as members of Christ and his church.

The Third Part: Of Thankfulness

Q86. Since then we are delivered from our misery, merely of grace, through Christ, without any merit of ours, why must we still do good works?

A. Because Christ, having redeemed and delivered us by his blood, also renews us by his Holy Spirit, after his own image; that so we may testify, by the whole of our conduct, our gratitude to God for his blessings, and that he may be praised by us; also, that every one may be assured in himself of his faith, by the fruits thereof; and that, by our godly conversation others may be gained to Christ.

Q87. Cannot they then be saved, who, continuing in their wicked and ungrateful lives, are not converted to God?

A. By no means; for the holy scripture declares that no unchaste person, idolater, adulterer, thief, covetous man, drunkard, slanderer, robber, or any such like, shall inherit the kingdom of God.

Q88. Of how many parts does the true conversion of man consist?

A. Of two parts; of the mortification of the old, and the quickening of the new man.

Q89. What is the mortification of the old man?

A. It is a sincere sorrow of heart, that we have provoked God by our sins; and more and more to hate and flee from them.

Q90. What is the quickening of the new man?

A. It is a sincere joy of heart in God, through Christ, and with love and delight to live according to the will of God in all good works.

Q91. But what are good works?

A. Only those which proceed from a true faith, are performed according to the law of God, and to his glory; and not such as are founded on our imaginations, or the institutions of men.

Q92. What is the law of God?

A. God spake all these words, Exodus 20:1–17 and Deuteronomy 5:6–21, saying: "I am the LORD thy God, which have brought thee out of the land of Egypt, out of the house of bondage."

First commandment: Thou shalt have no other gods before me.

Second commandment: Thou shalt not make unto thee any graven image, or any likeness of any thing that is in heaven above, or that is in the earth beneath, or that is in the water under the earth. Thou shalt not bow down thyself to them, nor serve them; for I the LORD thy God am a jealous God, visiting the iniquity of the fathers upon the children unto the third and fourth generation of them that hate me, and shewing mercy unto thousands of them that love me, and keep my commandments.

Third commandment: Thou shalt not take the name of the LORD thy God in vain; for the LORD will not hold him guiltless that taketh his name in vain.

Fourth commandment: Remember the Sabbath day, to keep it holy. Six days shalt thou labour, and do all thy work; but the seventh day is the Sabbath of the LORD thy God: in it thou shalt not do any work, thou, nor thy son, nor thy daughter, thy manservant, nor thy maidservant, nor thy cattle, nor thy stranger that is within thy gates. For in six days the LORD made heaven and earth, the sea, and all that in them is, and rested the seventh day: wherefore the LORD blessed the Sabbath day, and hallowed it.

Fifth commandment: Honor thy father and thy mother: that thy days may be long upon the land which the LORD thy God giveth thee.

Sixth commandment: Thou shalt not kill.

Seventh commandment: Thou shalt not commit adultery.

Eighth commandment: Thou shalt not steal.

Ninth commandment: Thou shalt not bear false witness against thy neighbor.

Tenth commandment: Thou shalt not covet thy neighbor's house, thou shalt not covet thy neighbor's wife, nor his manservant, nor his maidservant, nor his ox, nor his ass, nor any thing that is thy neighbor's.

Q93. How are these commandments divided?

A. Into two tables; the first of which teaches us how we must behave toward God; the second, what duties we owe to our neighbor.

Q94. What does God enjoin in the first commandment?

A. That I, as sincerely as I desire the salvation of my own soul, avoid and flee from all idolatry, sorcery, soothsaying, superstition, invocation of saints, or any other creatures; and learn rightly to know the only true God; trust in him alone, with humility and patience submit to him; expect all good things from him only; love, fear, and glorify him with my whole heart; so that I renounce and forsake all creatures, rather than commit even the least thing contrary to his will.

Q95. What is idolatry?

A. Idolatry is, instead of, or besides that one true God, who has manifested himself in his word, to contrive, or have any other object, in which men place their trust.

Q96. What does God require in the second commandment?

A. That we in no wise represent God by images, nor worship him in any other way than he has commanded in his word.

Q97. Are images then not at all to be made?

A. God neither can, nor may be represented by any means: but as to creatures; though they may be represented, yet God forbids to make, or have any resemblance of them, either in order to worship them or to serve God by them.

Q98. But may not images be tolerated in the churches, as books to the laity?

A. No: for we must not pretend to be wiser than

God, who will have his people taught, not by dumb images, but by the lively preaching of his word.

Q99. What is required in the third commandment?

A. That we, not only by cursing or perjury, but also by rash swearing, must not profane or abuse the name of God; nor by silence or connivance be partakers of these horrible sins in others; and, briefly, that we use the holy name of God no otherwise than with fear and reverence; so that he may be rightly confessed and worshipped by us, and be glorified in all our words and works.

Q100. Is then the profaning of God's name, by swearing and cursing, so heinous a sin, that his wrath is kindled against those who do not endeavor, as much as in them lies, to prevent and forbid such cursing and swearing?

A. It undoubtedly is, for there is no sin greater or more provoking to God, than the profaning of his name; and therefore he has commanded this sin to be punished with death.

Q101. May we then swear religiously by the name of God?

A. Yes: either when the magistrates demand it of the subjects; or when necessity requires us thereby to confirm a fidelity and truth to the glory of God, and the safety of our neighbor: for such an oath is founded on God's word, and therefore was justly used by the saints, both in the Old and New Testament.

Q102. May we also swear by saints or any other creatures?

A. No; for a lawful oath is calling upon God, as the only one who knows the heart, that he will bear witness to the truth, and punish me if I swear falsely; which honor is due to no creature.

Q103. What does God require in the fourth commandment?

A. First, that the ministry of the gospel and the schools be maintained; and that I, especially on the Sabbath, that is, on the day of rest, diligently frequent the church of God, to hear his word, to use the sacraments, publicly to call upon the Lord, and contribute to the relief of the poor. Secondly, that all the days of my life I cease from my evil works, and yield myself to the Lord, to work by his Holy Spirit in me: and thus begin in this life the eternal Sabbath.

Q104. What does God require in the fifth commandment?

A. That I show all honor, love and fidelity, to my father and mother, and all in authority over me, and submit myself to their good instruction and correction, with due obedience; and also patiently bear with their weaknesses and infirmities, since it pleases God to govern us by their hand.

Q105. What does God require in the sixth commandment?

A. That neither in thoughts, nor words, nor gestures, much less in deeds, I dishonor, hate, wound, or kill my neighbor, by myself or by another: (a) but that I lay aside all desire of revenge: (b) also, that I hurt not myself, nor willfully expose myself to any danger. (c) Wherefore also the magistrate is armed with the sword, to prevent murder.

Q106. But this commandment seems only to speak of murder?

A. In forbidding murder, God teaches us, that he abhors the causes thereof, such as envy, hatred, anger, and desire of revenge; and that he accounts all these as murder.

Q107. But is it enough that we do not kill any man in the manner mentioned above?

A. No: for when God forbids envy, hatred, and anger, he commands us to love our neighbor as ourselves; to show patience, peace, meekness, mercy, and all kindness, toward him, and prevent his hurt as much as in us lies; and that we do good, even to our enemies.

Q108. What does the seventh commandment teach us?

A. That all uncleanness is accursed of God: and

that therefore we must with all our hearts detest the same, and live chastely and temperately, whether in holy wedlock, or in single life.

Q109. Does God forbid in this commandment only adultery and such like gross sins?

A. Since both our body and soul are temples of the holy Ghost, he commands us to preserve them pure and holy: therefore he forbids all unchaste actions, gestures, words, thoughts, desires, and whatever can entice men thereto.

Q110. What does God forbid in the eighth commandment?

A. God forbids not only those thefts, and robberies, which are punishable by the magistrate; but he comprehends under the name of theft all wicked tricks and devices, whereby we design to appropriate to ourselves the goods which belong to our neighbor: whether it be by force, or under the appearance of right, as by unjust weights, ells, measures, fraudulent merchandise, false coins, usury, or by any other way forbidden by God; as also all covetousness, all abuse and waste of his gifts.

Q111. But what does God require in this commandment?

A. That I promote the advantage of my neighbor in every instance I can or may; and deal with him as I desire to be dealt with by others: further also that I faithfully labor, so that I may be able to relieve the needy.

Q112. What is required in the ninth commandment?

A. That I bear false witness against no man, nor falsify any man's words; that I be no backbiter, nor slanderer; that I do not judge, nor join in condemning any man rashly, or unheard; but that I avoid all sorts of lies and deceit, as the proper works of the devil, unless I would bring down upon me the heavy wrath of God; likewise, that in judgment and all other dealings I love the truth, speak it uprightly and confess it; also that I defend and promote, as much as I am able, the honor and good character of my neighbor.

Q113. What does the tenth commandment require of us?

A. That even the smallest inclination or thought, contrary to any of God's commandments, never rise in our hearts; but that at all times we hate all sin with our whole heart, and delight in all righteousness.

Q114. But can those who are converted to God perfectly keep these commandments?

A. No: but even the holiest men, while in this life, have only a small beginning of this obedience; yet so, that with a sincere resolution they begin to live, not only according to some, but all the commandments of God.

Q115. Why will God then have the Ten Commandments so strictly preached, since no man in this life can keep them?

A. First, that all our lifetime we may learn more and more to know our sinful nature, and thus become the more earnest in seeking the remission of sin, and righteousness in Christ; likewise, that we constantly endeavor and pray to God for the grace of the Holy Spirit, that we may become more and more conformable to the image of God, till we arrive at the perfection proposed to us, in a life to come.

Q116. Why is prayer necessary for Christians?

A. Because it is the chief part of thankfulness which God requires of us: and also, because God will give his grace and Holy Spirit to those only, who with sincere desires continually ask them of him, and are thankful for them.

Q117. What are the requisites of that prayer, which is acceptable to God, and which he will hear?

A. First, that we from the heart pray to the one true God only, who has manifested himself in his word, for all things, he has commanded us to ask of him; secondly, that we rightly and thoroughly know our need and misery, that so we may deeply humble ourselves in the presence of his divine majesty; thirdly, that we be fully persuaded that he, notwithstanding that we are unworthy of it, will, for the sake of Christ our Lord, certainly hear our prayer, as he has promised us in his word.

Q118. What has God commanded us to ask of him?
A. All things necessary for soul and body; which Christ our Lord has comprised in that prayer he himself has taught us.

Q119. What are the words of that prayer?
A. Our Father which art in heaven, 1. Hallowed be thy name. 2. Thy kingdom come. 3. Thy will be done on earth, as it is in heaven. 4. Give us this day our daily bread. 5. And forgive us our debts, as we forgive our debtors. 6. And lead us not into temptation, but deliver us from evil. For thine is the kingdom, and the power, and the glory, for ever. Amen.

Q120. Why has Christ commanded us to address God thus: "Our Father"?
A. That immediately, in the very beginning of our prayer, he might excite in us a childlike reverence for, and confidence in God, which are the foundation of our prayer: namely, that God is become our Father in Christ, and will much less deny us what we ask of him in true faith, than our parents will refuse us earthly things.

Q121. Why is it here added, "Which art in heaven"?
A. Lest we should form any earthly conceptions of God's heavenly majesty, and that we may expect from his almighty power all things necessary for soul and body.

Q122. Which is the first petition?
A. "Hallowed be thy name"; that is, grant us, first, rightly to know thee, and to sanctify, glorify and praise thee, in all thy works, in which thy power, wisdom, goodness, justice, mercy and truth, are clearly displayed; and further also, that we may so order and direct our whole lives, our thoughts, words and actions, that thy name may never be blasphemed, but rather honored and praised on our account.

Q123. Which is the second petition?
A. "Thy kingdom come"; that is, rule us so by thy word and Spirit, that we may submit ourselves more and more to thee; preserve and increase thy church; destroy the works of the devil, and all violence which would exalt itself against thee; and also all wicked counsels devised against thy holy word; till the full perfection of thy kingdom take place, wherein thou shalt be all in all.

Q124. Which is the third petition?
A. "Thy will be done on earth as it is in heaven"; that is, grant that we and all men may renounce our own will, and without murmuring obey thy will, which is only good; that every one may attend to, and perform the duties of his station and calling, as willingly and faithfully as the angels do in heaven.

Q125. Which is the fourth petition?
A. "Give us this day our daily bread"; that is, be pleased to provide us with all things necessary for the body, that we may thereby acknowledge thee to be the only fountain of all good, and that neither our care nor industry, nor even thy gifts, can profit us without thy blessing; and therefore that we may withdraw our trust from all creatures, and place it alone in thee.

Q126. Which is the fifth petition?
A. "And forgive us our debts as we forgive our debtors"; that is, be pleased for the sake of Christ's blood, not to impute to us poor sinners, our transgressions, nor that depravity, which always cleaves to us; even as we feel this evidence of thy grace in us, that it is our firm resolution from the heart to forgive our neighbor.

Q127. Which is the sixth petition?
A. "And lead us not into temptation, but deliver us from evil"; that is, since we are so weak in ourselves, that we cannot stand a moment; and besides this, since our mortal enemies, the devil, the world, and our own flesh, cease not to assault us, do thou therefore preserve and strengthen us by the power of thy Holy Spirit, that we may not be overcome in this spiritual

warfare, but constantly and strenuously may resist our foes, till at last we obtain a complete victory.

Q128. How dost thou conclude thy prayer?
A. "For thine is the kingdom, and the power, and the glory, forever"; that is, all these we ask of thee, because thou, being our King and almighty, art willing and able to give us all good; and all this we pray for, that thereby not we, but thy holy name, may be glorified for ever.

Q129. What does the word "Amen" signify?
A. "Amen" signifies, it shall truly and certainly be: for my prayer is more assuredly heard of God, than I feel in my heart that I desire these things of him.

CHAPTER 7

Writings of the Protestant Reformers

This chapter, while continuing the theme of Reformation, adds essays to the catechisms of chapter 6. Writings included here are the heritage of Lutheran, Reformed, and Arminian perspectives.

MARTIN LUTHER: "THREE WALLS OF THE ROMANISTS" (FROM *ADDRESS TO THE CHRISTIAN NOBILITY OF THE GERMAN NATION*)
German, 1520

See page 183 for an introduction to Martin Luther.

Questions for Guided Reading
1. What three walls, according to Luther, has the church hierarchy erected?
2. How do these walls prevent helpful reform within the church?
3. On what basis does Luther oppose each of the three walls (with what arguments)?
4. What view of the "keys of the church" does Luther express here?
5. Identify two of the three central principles of the Protestant Reformation found in this address (see *Introduction to Shorter Catechism*).

✦

The Romanists, with great skill, have built three walls around themselves behind which they have so far avoided any sort of reform; and this has been the cause of terrible corruption throughout all Christendom. First, when pressed by the temporal (governmental) authority, they have made decrees and said that the temporal power has no jurisdiction over them since spiritual authority is above the temporal authority. Second, when the attempt is made to correct them from Scriptures; they raise the objection that the interpretation of the Scriptures is the right of the Pope alone. Third, if anyone threatens to convene a church council to look into the matter, they answer with the fable that no one can call a church council except the Pope. In this way they have slyly stolen from us our three rods that they may go unpunished, and have hidden themselves within the safe stronghold of these three walls, that they may practice all the mischievousness and wickedness which we now see. Even when they have been compelled to hold a church council they have weakened its power in advance by requiring the princes, on oath, to allow things to remain the same. Moreover, they have given the Pope full authority over all the decisions of the council so that the out-come is always the same whether one council or many councils meet the will of the Pope is enforced and the council becomes little more than a sham! Not only this, they have also intimidated both kings and princes making them believe it would be an offense against God not to obey them in all these crafty deceptions. Now God help us, and give us one of the trumpets with which the walls of Jericho were over-thrown, that we may blow down these walls of straw and paper, and may set free the Christian rods for the punishment of sin, bringing to light the craft and deceit of the devil, to the end that through punishment we may reform ourselves, and once more attain God's favor.

The First Wall

Against the first wall, then, we will direct our first attack. It is a ridiculous lie that the Pope, bishops, priests, and monks are referred to as the spiritual estate, while princes, lords, craftsmen, and farmers are called the temporal estate. That is indeed a fine bit of lying and hypocrisy that no one should be convinced by since all Christians are truly of the spiritual estate, and there is no difference among them at all but that of office. As Paul says (1 Cor. 12:12), We are all one body, yet every member has its own work, where by it serves every other, all because we have one baptism, one Gospel, one faith, and are all alike Christians. Baptism, Gospel, and faith alone make us spiritual and a Christian people. The fact that the Pope or a bishop anoints, ordains, consecrates, confers tonsures, or prescribes dress unlike that of the laity makes no one spiritual—though it may make him a hypocrite or an idol worshiper! Rather, through baptism all of us are consecrated to priesthood, as St. Peter says in 1 Peter 2:9, You are a royal priesthood, a priestly kingdom, and the book of Revelation (Rev. 5:10) says, You have made us by your blood to be priests and kings. For the consecration of the Pope or the bishop alone makes no one a priest, nor gives anyone the right to say mass or preach a sermon or offer absolution. Therefore when the bishop consecrates the mass, it is as if those gathered for worship—all of whom are equal before God—have chosen him to represent them before God, and they could just as easily choose anyone in the congregation to do the same. It would also be like a king with ten sons who, though they are all equal heirs to the throne, chose one among them to rule the rest on their behalf. To offer a more clear example, if a small group of faithful Christian laymen were taken captive and left in the wilderness, and none of them was a priest or had been consecrated by bishop, they would be free to choose one of their number—whether married or unmarried—and charge him with the office of baptizing, of saying mass, of absolving and of preaching. Such a man would be as much priest as if all the bishops together with the Pope had consecrated him! That is why in cases of necessity anyone can baptize and give absolution, which would be impossible unless we were all priests. This great grace and power of baptism and of the Christian Estate they have nearly destroyed and caused us to forget through Canon law. In ancient times Christians elected bishops and priests from among themselves.

This is how Saints Augustine, Ambrose, and Cyprian became bishops. Only later did ordination come to be confirmed through the administration of other bishops with all the pomp which now attends. So then, since temporal authorities are baptized with the same baptism and have the same faith and Gospel as we, we must grant that they too are priests and bishops, and count their office one which has a proper and a useful place in the Christian community. For whoever comes out the water of baptism can boast that he is already consecrated priest, bishop, and pope, though it is not proper that every one should exercise the office. Indeed, just because we are all in like manner priests, no one must put himself forward and undertake, without our consent and election, to do what is in the power of all of us. For what is common to all, no one dare take upon himself without the will and the command of the community; and should it happen that one chosen for such an office were deposed for misconduct, he would then be just what he was before he held office. Therefore a priest in Christendom is simply an office holder. While he is in office, he has authority; when deposed, he is a peasant or a townsman like the rest. Beyond all doubt, then, a priest is no longer a priest when he is deposed. But now the bishops have regulated even this, so that a deposed priest is considered higher that a mere layman. They even state that a priest can never become a layman, or be anything other than a priest. All this is mere talk and man-made law! From all this it follows that there is really no difference between laymen and priests, princes and bishops, between spirituals and temporals, as they call them, except that of office and work, but not of estate. For they are all of the same estate—true priests, bishops and popes—though they are not all engaged in the same work, just as all priests and monks do not do the same work. This is also the teaching of St. Paul in Romans 12:4 and 1 Corinthians 12:12, and of St. Peter in 1 Peter 2:9, as I have said above, viz., that we are all one body of Christ, the Head, all members one of another. Christ does not have two different bodies, one temporal and the other spiritual. He is one Head and has One body. Therefore, just as those who are now called priests, bishops or popes are neither different from other Christians nor superior to them, except that they are charged with the administration of the Word of God and the sacraments, which is their work and office, so it is with the temporal authorities, they bear sword and rod with which to punish the evil and to protect the good. A cobbler, a smith, a fanner, each has the work and office of his trade, and yet they are all alike consecrated priests and bishops, and everyone by means of his own work or office must benefit and serve every other, that in this way many kinds of work may be done for the bodily and spiritual welfare of the community, even as all the members of the body serve one another. Consider: how Christian is the decree that says that the temporal power is not above the spiritual estate and may not punish it? That is like saying that the hand shall lend no aid when the eye is suffering. Isn't it unnatural, not to say unchristian, that one member should not help another and prevent its destruction? Indeed, the more honorable the member, the more others should help. I say then, since the temporal power is ordained of God to punish evil-doers and to protect them that do well, it should therefore be left free to do its duty without interference through the entire body of Christ without respect of persons, whether it affect pope, bishops, priests, monks, nuns or anybody else. For the mere fact that the temporal power is less regarded than has the office of preachers or confessors should not keep them from their duties. Again, the Christian temporal power should exercise its office without interference, regardless even if against a pope, a bishop or a priest; whoever is guilty, let him suffer. All that the canon law has said to the contrary is sheer invention of Roman presumption. For St. Paul has said to all Christians, "Let every soul (which I take to mean the Pope's soul also) be subject unto the higher powers; for they bear not the sword in vain, but are the ministers of God for the punishment of evildoers, and for the praise of them that do well" (Rom. 13:1–4). St. Peter also says, "Submit yourselves unto every ordinance of man for the Lord s sake, for so is the will of God" (1 Peter 2:13–15). The Apostles also prophesied that some men shall come to despise the temporal authorities—and this is what has happened through the Canon law. So then, I think this first paper-wall is overthrown, since the temporal power has become a member of the body of Christendom, and is also of the spiritual estate even though its work is of a temporal nature. Therefore its work should extend freely and without hindrance to all the members of the whole body; it should punish and use force whenever guilt deserves or necessity demands, without regard to Pope, bishops and priests, let them hail threats and bans as much as they will. Again, it is intolerable that in the canon law so much importance is attached to the freedom, life and property of the clergy, as though the laity were not also as spiritual and as good Christians as they, or as if they did not belong to the Church. Why are your life and limb, your property and honor so free, and not mine? We are all Christians, and have baptism, faith, Spirit and all things alike. If a priest is killed, the land is laid under interdict—why not when a peasant is killed? From where does this great distinction between those who are equally Christians come? Only from human laws and inventions!

The Second Wall

Now the second wall is more flimsy and worthless. The Romanists consider themselves the only masters of Holy Scripture, even though they learn nothing from it all their lives. They assume for themselves sole authority, and by deceptive words they want to persuade us that the Pope, whether he be a bad man or a good man, is inerrant in matters of faith, yet they cannot prove a single letter of this. And this is why so many heretical and unchristian ordinances have found their way into canon law. For since they believe that the Holy Spirit never leaves them, in spite of their wickedness and ignorance, they are bold enough to decree whatever they desire. And if it they did indeed rule by the Holy Spirit and without erring, what need would there be for the Holy Scriptures? Why not just burn them and be satisfied with the unlearned lords at Rome, who are possessed of the Holy Spirit (although the Holy Spirit fills only faithful hearts)! Unless I had read it myself, I would not have believed that the devil would make such outrageous claims at Rome, and find a following. But not to fight them with mere words, we will quote the Scriptures. St. Paul says in 1 Corinthians 14:30: If to anyone something better is revealed, though he be sitting and listening to another in God's Word, then the first, who is speaking, shall hold his peace and give place. What would be the use of this commandment if we were only to believe him who does the talking or who has the highest seat? Christ also says in John 6:45 regarding Christians that they shall all be taught of God. Thus it may well happen that the Pope and his followers are wicked men, and no true Christians, not taught of God, not having true understanding. On the other hand, an ordinary man may have true understanding; why then should we not follow him? Has not the Pope made many mistakes? Who can help Christendom when the Pope errs if we are not able to trust one who has the Scriptures on his side, more than the Pope? Therefore it is a wickedly invented fable and they cannot produce a letter in defense of it, that the interpretation of Scripture or the confirmation of its interpretation belongs to the Pope alone. They have themselves usurped this power; and although they allege that this power was given to Peter when the keys were given to him, it is plain enough that the keys were not given to Peter alone, but to the whole Church. Moreover, the keys were not ordained for doctrine or government, but only for the binding and loosing of sin. The usurping of any further authority on the basis of the keys is mere invention. And Christ's word to Peter (Luke 22:32) I have prayed for you that your faith shall not fail, cannot be applied to the Pope since the majority of the popes have been without faith, as they must themselves confess. Besides, it is not only for Peter that Christ prayed, but also for all Apostles and Christians, as he says in John 17:9, 20: Father, I pray for those whom you have given me, and not for these only, but for all who believe on me through their word. Is this not clear enough? Just think of it! The Romanists must admit that there are faithful Christians among us who have the true faith, Spirit, understanding, word and mind of Christ. Why, then, should we follow the Pope, who has neither faith nor Spirit? That would be to deny the whole faith and the Christian Church as well. After all, if The Creed is correct when it says, I believe one holy Christian Church, then the Pope cannot be the only one who is right. Otherwise the prayer would have to say: I believe in the Pope at Rome, and so reduce the Christian Church to one man, which would be nothing more than a devilish and hellish error. Besides, if we are all priests, as was said above, and all have one faith, one Gospel, one sacrament, why should we not also have the power to test and judge what is correct or incorrect in matters of faith? What becomes of the words of Paul in 1 Corinthians 2:15: He that is spiritual judges all things, yet he himself is judged by no one, and in 2 Corinthians 4:13: We have all the same Spirit of faith? Why, then,

should not each of us Christians be able to perceive what is of faith and what is not, at least as well as does an unbelieving pope? All these and many other passages should make us bold and free, and we should not allow the Spirit of liberty, as Paul calls Him, to be frightened off by the fabrications of the popes, but we ought rather to go boldly forward to test all that they do, according to our interpretation of the Scriptures, which rests on faith, and compel them to follow not their own interpretation, but the one that is better. In ancient times Abraham had to listen to Sarah, although she was in more complete subjection to him than we are to anyone on earth. Balaam's donkey also was wiser than the prophet himself. If God then spoke through a donkey against a prophet, why should He not be able even now to speak by a righteous man against the Pope? In like manner St. Paul rebukes St. Peter as a man in error. Therefore it is necessary for every Christian to espouse the cause of the faith, to understand and defend it, and to rebuke errors.

The Third Wall

The third wall falls of itself when the first two are down. For when the Pope acts contrary to the Scriptures, it is our duty to stand by the Scriptures, to reprove him, and to constrain him, according to the word of Christ in Matthew 18:15, If your brother sins against you, go and tell him alone; if he does not listen to you, then take someone with you; if he still will not listen, then tell it to the Church; if he still will not listen, then consider him a heathen. Here every member is commanded to care for every other. How much rather should we do this when the member that does evil is a ruling member, and by his evil-doing is the cause of much harm and offense to the rest! But if I am to accuse him before the Church, I must bring the Church together. And on this point they have no basis in Scripture for their argument that the Pope alone may convene a church council or confirm its actions; for this is based merely upon their own laws, which are valid only in so far as they are not injurious to Christendom or contrary to the laws of God. When the Pope deserves punishment, church law goes out of force, since it is injurious to Christendom not to punish him by means of a council. Thus we read in Acts 15:6 that it was not St. Peter who called the Apostolic Council, but the Apostles and elders. If, then, that right had belonged to St. Peter alone, the council would not have been a Christian council, but a heretical council. Even the Council of Nicaea, the most famous of all, was neither called nor confirmed by the Bishop of Rome, but by the Emperor Constantine, and many other emperors after him did likewise, yet these councils were the most Christian of all. But if the Pope alone had the right to call councils, then all those councils must have been heretical.

Moreover, if I consider the recent councils that the Pope has created, I find that they have done nothing of special importance. Therefore, when necessity demands, and the Pope is an offense to Christendom, the first man who is able should, being a faithful member of the whole body, do what he can to bring about a truly free council. No one can do this so well as the temporal authorities, especially since now they also are fellow-Christians, fellow-priests, fellow-spirituals, and fellow-lords over all things. So, whenever it is necessary or profitable, they should freely exercise the authority that God has given them above every man. Would not it be an unnatural thing if a fire broke out in a city and everybody were to stand by and allow it to burn because nobody had the authority of the mayor? In such case, is it not the duty of every citizen to arouse and call the rest? How much more then should this be done in the spiritual city of Christ, if a fire of offense breaks out, whether in the papal government, or anywhere else? In the same way, if the enemy attacks a city, he who first rouses the others deserves honor and thanks; why then should he not deserve honor who makes known the presence of the enemy from hell, awakens the Christians, and calls them together? But all their boasts of an authority whom no one ought to opposed amounts to nothing. No Christian has been granted the authority to hurt other Christians, or to prevent the resistance of such injury. There is no rightful authority in the Church except that which edifies. Therefore, if the Pope were to use his authority to prevent the calling of a free council, and in this manner became a hindrance to the edification of the Church, we should disregard him and his authority; and if he were to hurl his bans and thunderbolts, we should despise his conduct as that of a madman, and relying on God, hurl back the ban on him, and coerce him as best we could. For this presumptuous authority of his is nothing; he has no such authority, and he is quickly overthrown by a text of Scripture; for Paul says to the Corinthians (2 Cor. 10:8) that God has given authority for building up, not destroying, the church. Who can disregard this passage? It is only the power of the devil and of the Antichrist which resist the things that serve for the edification of Christendom; and this we must opposed with all our life and possessions and strength. Even though a miracle were to be done in the Popes behalf against the temporal powers, or though someone were to be stricken with a plague—which they claim sometimes happened—it should be considered only the work of the devil, because of the weakness of our faith in God. Christ Himself prophesied in Matthew 24:23–24 that There shall come in my name false Christs and false prophets to do signs and wonders, and to deceive even the elect, and Paul says in 2 Thessalonians 2:9, that the Antichrist shall, through the power of Satan, be mighty in lying wonders. Let us, therefore, hold on to this: No Christian authority can do anything against Christ; as St. Paul says, 2 Corinthians 13:8: We can do nothing authoritatively against Christ, but only for Christ. Whoever works against Christ is none other than the power of the Antichrist and of the devil, even though it were to rain and hail wonders and plagues. Wonders and plagues prove nothing, especially in these last evil times, for which all the Scriptures prophesy false wonders. Therefore we must cling with firm faith to the words of God, and then the devil will cease from wonders. So I hope that the false, lying terror with which the Romans have this long time made our conscience timid and stupid, has been allayed. They, like all of us, are subject to the temporal sword; they have no power to interpret the Scriptures by mere authority, without learning; they have no authority to prevent a councilor, in sheer wantonness, to pledge it, bind it, or take away its liberty; but if they do this, they are in truth the communion of Antichrist and of the devil, and have nothing at all of Christ except the name.

PHILIP MELANCHTHON: *LOCI COMMUNES*
German, 1521

The first work of Protestant systematic theology, Melanchthon's *Loci Communes* was written as a summary of key Christian doctrines and was intended to supersede theological works such as Lombard's *Sentences*. For a biographical introduction to Melanchthon, see page 195.

✦

Let us bring this whole discussion of law, gospel, and faith together under several theses:

1. The law is the doctrine that commands what is and what is not to be done.
2. The gospel is the promise of the grace of God.
3. The law demands impossible things such as the love of God and our neighbor.
4. Those who try to keep the law by their natural powers or free will simulate only the external works; they do not give expression to those attitudes which the law demands.
5. Therefore, they do not satisfy the law, but they are hypocrites, whitewashed tombs, as Christ calls them in Matthew 23:27. Galatians 3:10 says: For all who rely on the works of the law are under a curse.
6. Therefore, it is not the function of the law to justify.
7. But the proper function of the law is to reveal sin and especially to confound the conscience. Romans 3:20: Through the law comes knowledge of sin.
8. To a conscience acknowledging sin and confounded by the law, the gospel reveals Christ.
9. Thus John reveals Christ at the very time he preaches repentance: Behold the Lamb of God, who takes away the sin of the world (John 1:29).
10. The faith by which we believe the gospel showing us Christ and by which Christ is received as the one who has placated the Father and through whom grace is given, this faith is our righteousness. John 1:12: But to all who received him, who believed in his name, he gave power to become Children of God.
11. If it is actually faith alone that justifies, there is clearly no regard for our merits or our works, bought only for the merits of Christ.
12. This faith calms and gladdens the heart. Romans 5:1: Therefore, since we are justified by faith, we have peace.
13. The result of faith is that for such a great blessing, the forgiveness of sins because of Christ, we love God in return. Therefore, love for God is a fruit of faith.
14. This same faith causes us to be ashamed of having offended such a kind and generous father.
15. Therefore, it causes us to abhor our flesh with its evil desires.
16. Human reason neither fears God nor believes him, but is utterly ignorant of him and despises him. We know this from Psalm 14:1: The fool says in his heart, "There is no God." Luke 16:31: "If they do not hear Moses and the prophets, neither will they be convinced if someone should rise from the dead." Here Christ points out that the human heart does not believe the word of God. This madness of the human heart is what Solomon railed at in the whole book of Ecclesiastes as can be seen from Ecclesiastes 8:11: Because sentence against an evil deed is not executed speedily, the heart of the sons of men is fully set to do evil.
17. Because the human heart is utterly ignorant of God, it turns aside to its own counsels and desires, and sets itself up in the place of God.
18. When God confounds the human heart through the law with a sense of sin, it does not yet know God, that is, it does not know his goodness and therefore hates him as if he were a tormentor.
19. When God comforts and consoles the human heart through the gospel by showing it Christ, then finally it knows God, for it recognizes both his power and his goodness. This is what Jeremiah 9:24 means: But let him who glories glory in this, that . . . he knows me.
20. The heart of him who has believed the gospel and come to know the goodness of God is now fortified so that it trusts in God and fears him and consequently abhors the thoughts of the human heart.
21. Peter said very fittingly in Acts 15:9 that hearts are cleansed by faith.
22. Mercy is revealed through the promises.
23. Sometimes material things are promised, and at other times spiritual.

24. In the law, material things such as the Land of Canaan, the Kingdom, etc. are promised.

25. The gospel is the promise of grace or the forgiveness of sins through Christ.

26. All material promises are dependent on the promise of Christ.

27. For the first promise was a promise of grace or Christ. It is found in Genesis 3:15: He shall bruise your head. This means that the seed of Eve will crush the kingdom of the serpent plotting against our heel; that is, Christ will crush sin and death.

28. This was renewed in the promise made to Abraham: By your descendants shall all the nations of the earth be blessed (Gen. 22:18).

29. Therefore, since Christ was to be born of the descendants of Abraham, the promises added to the law about the possession of the earth, etc. were obscure promises of the Christ who was to come. For those material things were promised to the people until the promised seed should be born, lest they perish and in order that in the meantime God might indicate his mercy by material things and might thereby exercise the faith of his people.

30. By Christ's birth the promises to mankind were consummated, and the forgiveness of sins, for which Christ had to be born, was openly made known.

31. The promises of the Old Testament are signs of the Christ to come and also of the promise of grace to be broadcast at some future time. The gospel, the very promise of grace, has already been made known.

32. Just as that man does not know God who knows only that he exists but does not know either his power or his mercy, so also that man does not believe who believes only that God exists but does not believe both in his power and his mercy.

33. He really believes, therefore, who, looking beyond the threats, believes the gospel also, who fixes his face on the mercy of God or on Christ, the pledge of divine mercy.

So much on faith; we shall add certain things on love a little later after we have dealt with the difference between the law and gospel.

MARTIN LUTHER: "OF JUSTIFICATION" (FROM *TABLE TALK*)
German, 1529–1546

Table Talk brings together Luther's occasional talks and observations as recorded by friends and colleagues through the years. See page 183 for an introduction to Martin Luther.

◆

Part CCXCII

It is impossible for a papist to understand this article: I believe the forgiveness of sins. For the papists are drowned in their opinions, as I also was when among them, of the cleaving to or inherent righteousness. The Scripture names the faithful, saints and people of God. It is a sin and shame that we should forget this glorious and comfortable name and title. But the papists are such direct sinners, that they will not be reckoned sinners; and again, they will neither be holy nor held so to be. And in this sort it goes on with them untoward and crosswise, so that they neither believe the Gospel which comforts, nor the law which punishes.

But here one may say: the sins which we daily commit offend and anger God; how then can we be holy? Answer: A mother's love to her child is much stronger than the distaste of the scurf upon the child's head. Even so, God's love toward us is far stronger than our uncleanness. Therefore, though we be sinners, yet we lose not thereby our childhood, neither do we fall from grace by reason of our sins.

Another may say; we sin without ceasing, and where sin is, there the Holy Spirit is not; therefore we are not holy, because the Holy Spirit is not in us, which makes holy. Answer: The text says plainly; The Holy Ghost shall glorify me. Now where Christ is, there is the Holy Spirit. Now Christ is in the faithful, although they have and feel, and confess sins, and with sorrow of heart complain thereof, therefore sins do not separate Christ from those that believe.

The God of the Turks helps no longer or further, as they think, than as they are godly people; in like manner also the God of the papists. So when Turk and papist begin to feel their sins and unworthiness, as in time of trial and temptation, or in death, then they tremble and despair.

But a true Christian says: I believe in Jesus Christ my Lord and Savior, who gave himself for my sins, and is at God's right hand, and intercedes for me; fall I into sin, as, alas! oftentimes I do, I am sorry for it; I rise again, and am an enemy unto sin. So that we plainly see, the true Christian faith is far different from the faith and religion of the Pope and Turk. But human strength and nature are not able to accomplish this true Christian faith without the Holy Spirit. It can do no more than take refuge in its own deserts.

But he that can say: I am a child of God through Christ, who is my righteousness, and despairs not, though he be deficient in good works, which always fail us, he believes rightly. But grace is so great that it amazes a human creature, and is very difficult to be believed. Insomuch that faith gives the honor to God, that he can and will perform what he promised, namely, to make sinners righteous, Rom. 4, though 'tis an exceeding hard matter to believe that God is merciful unto us for the sake of Christ. O! Man's heart is too strait and narrow to entertain or take hold of this.

Part CCXCIII

All men, indeed, are not alike strong, so that in some many faults, weaknesses, and offences, are found; but these do not hinder them of sanctification, if they sin not of evil purposes and premeditation, but only out of weakness. For a Christian, indeed, feels the lusts of the flesh, but he resists them, and they have not dominion over him; and although, now and then, he stumbles and falls into sin, yet it is forgiven him, whom he raises again, and holds on to Christ, who will not That the lost sheep be hunted away, but he sought after.

Part CCXCIV

Why do Christians make use of their natural wisdom and understanding, seeing it must be set aside in matters of faith, as not only not understanding them, but also as striving against them?

Answer: The natural wisdom of a human creature in matters of faith, until he be regenerate and born anew, is altogether darkness, knowing nothing in divine cases. But in a faithful person, regenerate and enlightened by the Holy Spirit, through the Word, it is a fair and glorious instrument, and work of God: for even as all God's gifts, natural instruments, and expert faculties,

are hurtful to the ungodly, even so are they wholesome and saving to the good and godly.

The understanding, through faith, receives life from faith; that which was dead, is made alive again; like as our bodies, in light day, when it is clear and bright, and better disposed, rise, move, walk, etc., more readily and safely than they do in the dark night, so it is with human reason, which strives not against faith, when enlightened, but rather furthers and advances it.

So the tongue, which before blasphemed God, now lauds, extols, and praises God and his grace, as my tongue, now it is enlightened, is now another manner of tongue than it was in popedom; a regeneration done by the Holy Ghost through the Word.

A sanctified and upright Christian says: My wife, my children, my art, my wisdom, my money and wealth, help and avail me nothing in heaven; yet I cast them not away nor reject them when God bestows such benefits upon me, but part and separate the substance from the vanity and foolery which cleave thereunto. Gold is and remains gold as well when a strumpet carries it about her, as when 'tis with an honest, good, and godly woman. The body of a strumpet is even as well God's creature, as the body of an honest matron. In this manner ought we to part and separate vanity and folly from the thing and substance, or from the creature given and God who created it.

Part CCXCV

Upright and faithful Christians ever think they are not faithful, nor believe as they ought; and therefore they constantly strive, wrestle, and are diligent to keep and to increase faith, as good workmen always see that something is wanting in their workmanship. But the botchers think that nothing is wanting in what they do, but that everything is well and complete. Like as the Jews conceive they have the Ten Commandments at their fingers end, whereas, in truth, they neither learn nor regard them.

Part CCXCVI

Truly it is held for presumption in a human creature that he dare boast of his own proper righteousness of faith; 'tis a hard matter for a man to say: I am the child of God, and am comforted and solaced through the immeasurable grace and mercy of my heavenly Father. To do this from the heart, is not in every man's power.

Therefore no man is able to teach pure and aright touching faith, nor to reject the righteousness of works, without sound practice and experience. St Paul was well exercised in this art; he speaks more vilely of the law than any arch heretic can speak of the sacrament of the altar, of baptism, or than the Jews have spoken thereof; for he names the law, the ministration of death, the ministration of sin, and the ministration of condemnation; yea, he holds all the works of the law, and what the law requires, without Christ, dangerous and hurtful, which Moses, if he had then lived, would doubtless have taken very ill at Paul's hands. It was, according to human reason, spoken too scornfully.

Part CCXCVII

Faith and hope are variously distinguishable. And, first, in regard of the subject, wherein everything subsists: faith consists in a person's understanding, hope in the will; these two cannot be separated; they are like the two cherubim over the mercy seat. Secondly, in regard of the office; faith indicates, distinguishes, and teaches, and is the knowledge and acknowledgment; hope admonishes, awakens, hears, expects, and suffers. Thirdly, in regard to the object: faith looks to the word or promise, which is truth; but hope to that which the Word promises, which is the good or benefit. Fourthly, in regard of order in degree: faith is first, and before all adversities and troubles, and is the beginning of life. Heb. 11. But hope follows after, and springs up in trouble. Rom. 5. Fifthly, by reason of the contrariety: faith fights against errors and heresies; it proves and judges spirits and doctrines. But hope strives against troubles and vexations, and among the evil it expects good.

Faith in divinity, is the wisdom and providence, and belongs to the doctrine. But hope is the courage and joyfulness in divinity, and pertains to admonition. Faith is the dialectica, for it is altogether prudence and wisdom; hope is the rhetorica, an elevation of the heart and mind. As wisdom without courage is futile, even so faith without hope is nothing worth; for hope endures and overcomes misfortune and evil. And as a joyous valor without understanding is but rashness, so hope without faith is spiritual presumption. Faith is the key to the sacred Scriptures, the right Cabata or exposition, which one receives of tradition, as the prophets left this doctrine to their disciples. 'Tis said St Peter wept whenever he thought of the gentleness with which Jesus taught. Faith is given from one to another, and remains continually in one school. Faith is not a quality, as the schoolmen say, but a gift of God.

Part CCXVIII

Everything that is done in the world is done by hope. No husbandman would sow one grain of corn, if he hoped not it would grow up and become seed; no bachelor would marry a wife, if he hopes not to have children; no merchant or tradesman would set himself to work, if he did not hope to reap benefit thereby, etc. How much more, then, does hope urge us on to everlasting life and salvation?

Part CCXCIX

Faith's substance is our will; its manner is that we take hold on Christ by divine instinct; its final cause and fruit, that it purifies the heart, makes us children of God, and brings with it the remission of sins.

Part CCC

Adam received the promise of the woman's seed ere he had done any work or sacrifice, to the end God's truth might stand fast—namely, that we are justified before God altogether without works, and obtain forgiveness of sins merely by grace. Whoso is able to believe this well and steadfastly, is a doctor above all the doctors in the world.

Part CCCI

Faith is not only necessary, that thereby the ungodly may become justified and saved before God, and their hearts be settled in peace, but it is necessary in every other respect. St Paul says: Now that we are justified by faith, we have peace with God through our Lord Jesus Christ.

Part CCCII

Joseph of Arimathea had a faith in Christ, like as the apostles had; he thought Christ would have been a worldly and temporal potentate; therefore he took care of him as a good friend, and buried him honorably. He believed not that Christ should raise again from death, and become a spiritual and everlasting king.

Part CCCIII

When Abraham shall rise again at the last day, then he will chide us for our unbelief, and will say: I had not the hundredth part of the promises which ye have, and yet I believed. That example of Abraham exceeds all human natural reason, who, overcoming the paternal love he bore toward his only son, Isaac, was all obedient to God, and against the law of nature, would have sacrificed that son. What, for the space of three days, he felt in his breast, how his heart yearned and panted, what hesitations and trials he had, cannot be expressed.

Part CCCIV

All heretics have continually failed in this one point, that they do not rightly understand or know the article of justification. If we had not this article certain and clear, it were impossible we could criticize the Pope's false doctrine of indulgences and other abominable errors, much less be able to overcome greater spiritual errors and vexations. If we only permit Christ to be our Savior, then we have won, for he is the only girdle which clasps the whole body together, as St Paul excellently teaches. If we look to the spiritual birth and substance of a true Christian, we shall soon extinguish all deserts of good works; for they serve us to no use, neither to purchase sanctification, nor to deliver us from sin, death, devil, or hell.

Little children are saved only by faith, without any good works; therefore faith alone justifies. If God's power be able to effect that in one, then he is also able to accomplish it in all; for the power of the child effects it not, but the power of faith; neither is it done through the child's weakness or disability; for then that weakness would be merit of itself, or equivalent to merit. It is a mischievous thing that we miserable, sinful wretches will upbraid God, and hit him in the teeth with our works, and think thereby to be justified before him; but God will not allow it.

Part CCCV

This article, how we are saved, is the chief of the whole Christian doctrine, to which all divine disputations must be directed. All the prophets were chiefly engaged upon it, and sometimes much perplexed about it. For when this article is kept fast and sure by a constant faith, then all other articles draw on softly after, as that of the Holy Trinity, etc. God has declared no article so plainly and openly as this, that we are saved only by Christ; though he speaks much of the Holy Trinity, yet he dwells continually upon this article of the salvation of our souls; other articles are of great weight, but this surpasses all.

Part CCCVI

A Capuchin says: wear a grey coat and a hood, a rope round thy body, and sandals on thy feet.[1] A Cordelier says: put on a black hood; an ordinary papist says: do this or that work, hear mass, pray, fast, give alms, etc. But a true Christian says: I am justified and saved only by faith in Christ, without any works or merits of my own; compare these together, and judge which is the true righteousness.

Part CCCVII

Christ says: The spirit is willing, but the flesh is weak; St Paul also says: the spirit willingly would give itself wholly unto God, would trust in him, and be obedient; but natural reason and understanding, flesh and blood, resist and will not go forward. Therefore our Lord God must needs have patience and bear with us. God will not put out the glimmering flax; the faithful have as yet but only the first fruits of the spirit; they have not the fulfilling, but the tenth.

Part CCCVIII

I well understand that St Paul was also weak in faith, whence he boasted and said, I am a servant of God, and an apostle of Jesus Christ. An angel stood by him at sea, and comforted him, and when he came to Rome, he was comforted as he saw the brethren come out to meet him. Hereby we see what the communion and company does of such as fear God. The Lord commanded the disciples to remain together in one place, before they received the Holy Ghost, and to comfort one another; for Christ well knew that adversaries would assault them.

Part CCCIX

A Christian must be well armed, grounded, and furnished with sentences out of God's Word, that so he may stand and defend religion and himself against the devil, in case he should be asked to embrace another doctrine.

---

1. Capuchin and Cordelier are monastic orders.

Part CCCX

When at the last day we shall live again, we shall blush for shame, and say to ourselves: fie on thee, in that thou hast not been more courageous, bold, and strong to believe in Christ, and to endure all manner of adversities, crosses, and persecutions, seeing his glory is so great. If I were now in the world, I would not stick to suffer ten thousand times more.

Part CCCXI

Although a man knew, and could do as much as the angels in heaven, yet all this would not make him a Christian, unless he knew Christ and believed in him. God says: Let not the wise man glory in his wisdom, neither let the mighty man glory in his might; let not the rich man glory in his riches; but let him that glories, glory in this, that he understands and knows me, that I am the Lord, which doth exercise lovingkindness, judgment, and righteousness, etc.

Part CCCXII

The article of our justification before God is as with a son who is born heir to all his father's goods, and comes not thereunto by deserts, but naturally, or ordinary course. But yet, meantime, his father admonishes him to do such and such things, and promises him gifts to make him the more willing. As when he says to him: if thou wilt be good, be obedient, study diligently, then I will buy thee a fine coat; or, come hither to me, and I will give thee an apple. In such sort does he teach his son industry; though the whole inheritance belongs unto him of course, yet will he make him, by promises, pliable and willing to do what he would have done.

Even so God deals with us; he is loving unto us with friendly and sweet words, promises us spiritual and temporal blessings, though everlasting life is presented unto thee who believe in Christ, by mere grace and mercy, gratis, without any merits, works, or worthinesses.

And this ought we to teach in the church and in the assembly of God, that God will have upright and good works, which he has commanded, not such as we ourselves take in hand, of our own choice and devotion, or well meaning, as the friars and priests teach in popedom, for such works are not pleasing to God, as Christ says: In vain do they worship me, teaching for doctrines the commandments of men, etc. We must teach of good works, yet always so that the article of justification remain pure and unfalseified. For Christ neither can nor will endure any beside himself; he will have the bride alone; he is full of jealousy.

Should we teach: if thou believes, thou shalt be saved, whatsoever thou doest; that were stark naught; for faith is either false or feigned, or, though it be upright, yet is eclipsed, when people wittingly and willfully sin against God's command. And the Holy Spirit, which is given to the faithful, departs by reason of evil works done against the conscience, as the example of David sufficiently testifies.

Part CCCXIII

As to ceremonies and ordinances, the kingdom of love must have precedence and government, and not tyranny. It must be a willing, not a halter love; it must altogether be directed and construed for the good and profit of the neighbor; and the greater he that governs, the more he ought to serve according to love.

Part CCCXIV

The love toward our neighbor must be like the pure and chaste love between bride and bridegroom, where all faults are connived at and borne with, and only the virtues regarded.

Part CCCXV

Do you believe? Then you will speak boldly. Do you speak boldly? Then you will suffer. Do you suffer? Then you will be comforted. For faith, the confession thereof, and the cross, follow one upon another.

Give and it shall be given unto you: this is a fine maxim, and makes people poor and rich; it is that which maintains my house. I would not boast, but I well know what I give away in the year. If my gracious lord and master, the prince elector, should give a gentleman two thousand florins, this should hardly answer to the cost of my housekeeping for one year; and yet I have but three hundred florins a year, but God blesses these and makes them suffice.

There is in Austria a monastery, which, in former times, was very rich, and remained rich so long as it was charitable to the poor; but when it ceased to give, then it became indigent, and is so to this day. Not long since, a poor man went there and solicited alms, which was denied him; he demanded the cause why they refused to give for God's sake? The porter of the monastery answered:

We are become poor; whereupon the mendicant said: The cause of your poverty is this: you had formerly in this monastery two brethren, the one named Date (give), and the other Dabitur (it shall be given you). The former you threw out; the other went away of himself.

We are bound to help one's neighbor in three ways: with giving, lending, and selling. But no man gives; every one scrapes and claws all to himself; each would willingly steal, but give nothing, and lend but upon usury. No man sells unless he can outsell his neighbor; so, Dabitur is gone, and our Lord God will bless us no more so richly. Beloved, he that desires to have anything, must also give: a liberal hand was never in want, or empty.

Part CCCXVII

Desert is a work nowhere to be found, for Christ gives a reward by reason of the promise. If the prince elector should say to me: Come to the court, and I will give thee one hundred florins, I perform a work in going to the court, yet I receive not the gift by reason of my work in going thither, but by reason of the promise the prince made me.

Part CCCXVIII

I marvel at the madness and bitterness of Wetzell, in undertaking to write so much against the Protestants, assailing us without rhyme or reason, and, as we say, getting a case out of hedge; as where he rages against this principle of ours, that the works and acts of a farmer, husbandman, or any other good and godly Christian, if done in faith, are far more precious in the sight of God, than all the works of monks, friars, nuns, etc. This poor, ignorant fellow gets very angry against us, regarding not the works which God has commanded and imposed upon each man in his vocation, state and calling. He heeds only superstitious practices, devised for show and effect, which God neither commands nor approves of.

St Paul, in his epistles, wrote of good works and virtues more energetically and truthfully than all the philosophers; for he extols highly the works of godly Christians, in their respective vocations and callings. Let Wetzell know that David's wars and battles were more pleasing to God than the fastings and prayings even of the holiest of the old monks, setting aside altogether the works of the monks of our time, which are simply ridiculous.

Part CCCXIX

I never work better than when I am inspired by anger; when I am angry, I can write, pray, and preach well, for then my whole temperament is quickened, my understanding sharpened, and all mundane vexations and temptations depart.

Part CCCXX

Dr. Justus Jonas asked me if the thoughts and words of the prophet Jeremiah were Christianlike, when he cursed the day of his birth. I said: We must now and then wake up our Lord God with such words. Jeremiah had cause to murmur in this way. Did not our Savior Christ say: O faithless and perverse generation! How long shall I be with you, and suffer you? Moses also took God in hand, where he said: Wherefore hast thou afflicted thy servant? Have I conceived all this people? Have I begotten them?

Part CCCXXI

A man must needs be plunged in bitter affliction when in his heart he means good, and yet is not regarded. I can never get rid of these cogitations, wishing I had never begun this business with the Pope. So, too, I desire myself rather dead than to hear or see God's Word and his servants condemned; but 'tis the frailty of our nature to be thus discouraged.

They who condemn the movement of anger against antagonists, are theologians who deal in mere speculations; they play with words, and occupy themselves with subtleties, but when they are aroused, and take a real interest in the matter, they are touched sensibly.

Part CCCXXII

In quietness and in confidence shall be your strength. This sentence I expounded thus: If thou intendest to vanquish the greatest, the most abominable and wickedest enemy, who is able to do thee mischief both in body and soul, and against whom you prepare all sorts of weapons, but canst not overcome; then know that there is a sweet and loving physical herb to serve thee, named Patienta.

Thou wilt say: how may I attain this physic? Take unto thee faith, which says: no creature can do me mischief without the will of God. In case thou receives hurt and mischief by thine enemy, this is done by the sweet and gracious will of God, in such sort that the enemy hurts himself a thousand times more than he does thee. Hence flows unto us, a Christian, the love which says: I will, instead of the evil which mine enemy does unto me, do him all the good I can; I will heap coals of fire upon his head. This is the Christian armor and weapon, wherewith to beat and overcome those enemies that seem to be like huge mountains. In a word, love teaches to suffer and endure all things.

Part CCCXXIII

A certain honest and God-fearing man at Wittenberg, told me, that though he lived peaceably with every one, hurt no man, was ever quiet, yet many people were enemies unto him. I comforted him in this manner: Arm thyself with patience, and be not angry though they hate thee; what offence, I pray, do we give the devil? What ails him to be so great an enemy unto us? Only because he has not that which God has; I know no other cause of his vehement hatred toward us. If God give thee to eat, eat; if he causes thee to fast, be resigned thereto; gives he the honors? Take them; hurt or shame? Endure it; casts he thee into prison? Murmur not; will he make thee a king? Obey him; casts he thee down again? Heed it not.

Part CCCXXIV

Patience is the most excellent of the virtues, and, in Sacred Writ, highly praised and recommended by the Holy Ghost. The learned heathen philosophers applaud it, but they do not know its genuine basis, being without the assistance of God. Epictetus, the wise and judicious Greek, said very well: Suffer and abstain.

Part CCCXXV

It was the custom of old, in burying the dead, to lay their heads toward the sun-rising, by reason of a spiritual mystery and signification therein manifested; but this was not an enforced law. So all laws and ceremonies should be free in the church, and not be done on compulsion, being things which neither justify nor condemn in the sight of God, but are observed merely for the sake of orderly discipline.

Part CCCXXVI

The righteousness of works and hypocrisy are the most mischievous diseases born in us, and not easily expelled, especially when they are confirmed and settled upon us by use and practice; for all mankind will have dealings with Almighty God, and dispute with him, according to their human natural understanding, and will make satisfaction to God for their sins, with their own strength and self-chosen works. For my part, I have so often deceived our Lord God by promising to be upright and good, that I will promise no more, but will only pray for a happy hour, when it shall please God to make me good.

Part CCCXXVII

A popish priest once argued with me in this manner: Evil works are damned, therefore good works justify. I answered: Your argument is worthless since it concludes, ratione contrariorum (contrary to reason), things that are not in connection; evil works are evil in complete measure, because they proceed from a heart that is altogether spoiled and evil; but good works, yea, even in an upright Christian, are incompletely good; for they proceed out of a weak obedience but little recovered and restored. Whoso can say from his heart, I am a sinner, but God is righteous; and who, at the point of death, from his heart can say; Lord Jesus Christ, I commit my spirit into thy hands, may assure himself of true righteousness, and that he is not of the number of those that blaspheme God, in relying upon their own works and righteousness.

JOHN CALVIN: "ON JUSTIFICATION BY FAITH" (FROM *INSTITUTES OF THE CHRISTIAN RELIGION*)
Latin, 1530s

For a biographical introduction to John Calvin, see page 151. Book 3, chapter 2 of the *Institutes* follows.

1. I trust I have now sufficiently shown how man's only resource for escaping from the curse of the law, and recovering salvation, lies in faith; and also what the nature of faith is, what the benefits which it confers, and the fruits which it produces. The whole may be thus summed up: Christ given to us by the kindness of God is apprehended and possessed by faith,

by means of which we obtain in particular a twofold benefit; first, being reconciled by the righteousness of Christ, God becomes, instead of a judge, an indulgent Father; and, secondly, being sanctified by his Spirit, we aspire to integrity and purity of life. This second benefit—viz. regeneration—appears to have been already sufficiently discussed. On the other hand, the subject of justification was discussed more cursorily, because it seemed of more consequence first to explain that the faith by which alone, through the mercy of God, we obtain free justification, is not destitute of good works; and also to show the true nature of these good works on which this question partly turns. The doctrine of Justification is now to be fully discussed, and discussed under the conviction, that as it is the principal ground on which religion must be supported, so it requires greater care and attention. For unless you understand first of all what your position is before God, and what is the judgment which he passes upon you, you have no foundation on which your salvation can be laid, or on which piety toward God can be reared. The necessity of thoroughly understanding this subject will become more apparent as we proceed with it.

2. Lest we should stumble at the very threshold (this we should do were we to begin the discussion without knowing what the subject is), let us first explain the meaning of the expressions, *To be justified in the sight of God; to be Justified by faith or by works.* A man is said to be justified in the sight of God when in the judgment of God he is deemed righteous, and is accepted on account of his righteousness; for as iniquity is abominable to God, so neither can the sinner find grace in his sight, so far as he is and so long as he is regarded as a sinner. Hence, wherever sin is, there also are the wrath and vengeance of God. He, on the other hand, is justified who is regarded not as a sinner, but as righteous, and as such stands acquitted at the judgment seat of God, where all sinners are condemned. As an innocent man when charged before an impartial judge who decides according to his innocence is said to be justified

by the judge, so a man is said to be justified by God when, removed from the catalogue of sinners, he has God as the witness and assertor of his righteousness. In the same manner, a man will be said to be justified by works, if in his life there can be found a purity and holiness which merits an attestation of righteousness at the throne of God, or if by the perfection of his works he can answer and satisfy the divine justice. On the contrary, a man will be justified by faith when, excluded from the righteousness of works, he by faith lays hold of the righteousness of Christ, and clothed in it appears in the sight of God not as a sinner, but as righteous. Thus we simply interpret justification, as the acceptance with which God receives us into his favor as if we were righteous; and we say that this justification consists in the forgiveness of sins and the imputation of the righteousness of Christ (see sec. 21 and 23).

3. In confirmation of this there are many clear passages of Scripture. First, it cannot be denied that this is the proper and most usual signification of the term. But as it were too tedious to collect all the passages, and compare them with each other, let it suffice to have called the reader's attention to the fact: he will easily convince himself of its truth. I will only mention a few passages in which the justification of which we speak is expressly handled. First, when Luke relates that all the people that heard Christ "acknowledged God's justice" (Luke 7:29), and when Christ declares, that "Wisdom is justified of all her children" (Luke 7:35), Luke means not that they conferred righteousness which always dwells in perfection with God, although the whole world should attempt to wrest it from him, nor does Christ mean that the doctrine of salvation is made just: this it is in its own nature; but both modes of expression are equivalent to attributing due praise to God and his doctrine. On the other hand, when Christ upbraids the Pharisees for justifying themselves (Luke 16:15), he means not that they acquired righteousness by acting properly, but that they ambitiously courted a reputation for righteousness of which they

were destitute. Those acquainted with Hebrew understand the meaning better: for in that language the name of wicked is given not only to those who are conscious of wickedness, but to those who receive sentence of condemnation. Thus, when Bathsheba says, "I and my son Solomon shall be counted offenders," she does not acknowledge a crime, but complains that she and her son will be exposed to the disgrace of being numbered among reprobates and criminals (1 Kings 1:21). It is, indeed, plain from the context, that the term even in Latin must be thus understood—viz. *relatively*—and does not denote any quality. In regard to the use of the term with reference to the present subject, when Paul speaks of the Scripture, "foreseeing that God would justify the heathen through faith" (Gal. 3:8), what other meaning can you give it than that God imputes righteousness by faith? Again, when he says "that he (God) might be just, and the justifier of him who believeth in Jesus" (Rom. 3:26), what can the meaning be, if not that God, in consideration of their faith, frees them from the condemnation which their wickedness deserves? This appears still more plainly at the conclusion, when he exclaims, "Who shall lay anything to the charge of God's elect? It is God that justifieth. Who is he that condemneth? It is Christ that died, yea rather, that is risen again, who is even at the right hand of God, who also maketh intercession for us" (Rom. 8:33–34). For it is just as if he had said, Who shall accuse those whom God has acquitted? Who shall condemn those for whom Christ pleads? To *justify*, therefore, is nothing else than to acquit from the charge of guilt, as if innocence were proved. Hence, when God justifies us through the intercession of Christ, he does not acquit us on a proof of our own innocence, but by an imputation of righteousness, so that though not righteous in ourselves, we are deemed righteous in Christ. Thus it is said, in Paul's discourse in the Acts, "Through this man is preached unto you the forgiveness of sins; and by him all that believe are justified from all things from which ye could not be justified by the law of Moses"

(Acts 13:38–39). You see that after remission of sins justification is set down by way of explanation; you see plainly that it is used for acquittal; you see how it cannot be obtained by the works of the law; you see that it is entirely through the interposition of Christ; you see that it is obtained by faith; you see, in fine, that satisfaction intervenes, since it is said that we are justified from our sins by Christ. Thus when the publican is said to have gone down to his house "justified" (Luke 18:14), it cannot be held that he obtained this justification by any merit of works. All that is said is, that after obtaining the pardon of sins he was regarded in the sight of God as righteous. He was justified, therefore, not by any approval of works, but by gratuitous acquittal on the part of God. Hence Ambrose elegantly terms confession of sins "legal justification" (Ambrose on Ps. 118, sermon 10).

4. Without saying more about the term, we shall have no doubt as to the thing meant if we attend to the description which is given of it. For Paul certainly designates justification by the term *acceptance*, when he says to the Ephesians, "Having predestinated us unto the adoption of children by Jesus Christ to himself, according to the good pleasure of his will, to the praise of the glory of his grace, wherein he has made us accepted in the Beloved" (Eph. 1:5–6). His meaning is the very same as where he elsewhere says, "being justified freely by his grace" (Rom. 3:24). In the fourth chapter of the Epistle to the Romans, he first terms it the *imputation of* righteousness, and hesitates not to place it in forgiveness of sins: "Even as David also describeth the blessedness of the man unto whom God imputeth righteousness without works, saying, Blessed are they whose iniquities are forgiven," etc. (Rom. 4:6–8). There, indeed, he is not speaking of a part of justification, but of the whole. He declares, moreover, that a definition of it was given by David, when he pronounced him *blessed* who has obtained the *free* pardon of his sins. Whence it appears that this righteousness of which he speaks is simply opposed to judicial guilt. But the most satisfactory passage on this

subject is that in which he declares the sum of the Gospel message to be reconciliation to God, who is pleased, through Christ, to receive us into favor by not imputing our sins (2 Cor. 5:18–21). Let my readers carefully weigh the whole context. For Paul shortly after adding, by way of explanation, in order to designate the mode of reconciliation, that Christ who knew no sin was made sin for us, undoubtedly understands by reconciliation nothing else than justification. Nor, indeed, could it be said, as he elsewhere does, that we are made righteous "by the obedience of Christ" (Rom. 5:19), were it not that we are deemed righteous in the sight of God in him and not in ourselves.

JOHN CALVIN: "ON THE LORD'S SUPPER" (FROM *INSTITUTES OF THE CHRISTIAN RELIGION*)
Latin, 1530s

For a biographical introduction to John Calvin, see page 151. Book 4, chapter 17 of the *Institutes* follows.

✦

1. After God has once received us into his family, it is not that he may regard us in the light of servants, but of sons, performing the part of a kind and anxious parent, and providing for our maintenance during the whole course of our lives. And, not contented with this, he has been pleased by a pledge to assure us of his continued liberality. To this end, he has given another sacrament to his Church by the hand of his only begotten Son—viz., a spiritual feast, at which Christ testifies that he himself is living bread (John 6:51), on which our souls feed, for a true and blessed immortality.

Now, as the knowledge of this great mystery is most necessary, and, in proportion to its importance, demands an accurate exposition, and Satan, in order to deprive the Church of this inestimable treasure, long ago introduced, first

mists, and then darkness to obscure its light, and stirred up strife and contention to alienate the minds of the simple from a relish for this sacred food, and in our age, also, has tried the same artifice, I will proceed, after giving a simple summary adapted to the capacity of the ignorant, to explain those difficulties by which Satan has tried to ensnare the world.

First, then, the signs are bread and wine, which represent the invisible food which we receive from the body and blood of Christ. For as God, regenerating us in baptism, ingrafts us into the fellowship of his Church, and makes us his by adoption, so we have said that he performs the office of a provident parent, in continually supplying the food by which he may sustain and preserve us in the life to which he has begotten us by his word.

Moreover, Christ is the only food of our soul, and, therefore, our heavenly Father invites us to him, that, refreshed by communion with him, we may ever and anon gather new vigour until we reach the heavenly immortality.

But as this mystery of the secret union of Christ with believers is incomprehensible by nature, he exhibits its figure and image in visible signs adapted to our capacity, nay, by giving, as it were, earnests and badges, he makes it as certain to us as if it were seen by the eye; the familiarity of the similitude giving it access to minds however dull, and showing that souls are fed by Christ just as the corporeal life is sustained by bread and wine. We now therefore, understand the end which this mystical benediction has in view—viz., to assure us that the body of Christ was once sacrificed for us, so that we may now eat it, and, eating, feel within ourselves the efficacy of that one sacrifice—that his blood was once shed for us so as to be our perpetual drink. This is the force of the promise which is added, "Take, eat; this is my body, which is broken for you" (Matt. 26:26, etc.). The body which was once offered for our salvation we are enjoined to take and eat, that, while we see ourselves made partakers of it, we may safely conclude that the virtue of that death will be efficacious in us. Hence he terms the cup the covenant in his blood. For the covenant which he once sanctioned by his blood he in a manner renews, or rather continues, in so far as regards the confirmation of our faith, as often as he stretches forth his sacred blood as drink to us.

2. Pious souls can derive great confidence and delight from this sacrament, as being a testimony that they form one body with Christ, so that everything which is his they may call their own. Hence it follows, that we can confidently assure ourselves, that eternal life, of which he himself is the heir, is ours, and that the kingdom of heaven, into which he has entered, can no more be taken from us than from him; on the other hand, that we cannot be condemned for our sins, from the guilt of which he absolves us, seeing he has been pleased that these should be imputed to himself as if they were his own. This is the wondrous exchange made by his boundless goodness. Having become with us the Son of Man, he has made us with himself sons of God. By his own descent to the earth he has prepared our ascent to heaven. Having received our mortality, he has bestowed on us his immortality. Having undertaken our weakness, he has made us strong in his strength. Having submitted to our poverty, he has transferred to us his riches. Having taken upon himself the burden of unrighteousness with which we were oppressed, he has clothed us with his righteousness.

3. To all these things we have a complete attestation in this sacrament, enabling us certainly to conclude that they are as truly exhibited to us as if Christ were placed in bodily presence before our view, or handled by our hands. For these are words which can never lie nor deceive—Take, eat, drink. This is my body, which is broken for you: this is my blood, which is shed for the remission of sins. In bidding us take, he intimates that it is ours: in bidding us eat, he intimates that it becomes one substance with us: in affirming of his body that it was broken, and of his blood that it was shed for us, he shows that both were not so much his own as ours, because he took and laid down both, not for his own advantage, but for our salvation.

And we ought carefully to observe, that the chief, and almost the whole energy at the sacrament consists in these words, It is broken for you; it is shed for you. It would not be of much importance to us that the body and blood of the Lord are now distributed, had they not once been set forth for our redemption and salvation. Wherefore they are represented under bread and wine, that we may learn that they are not only ours but intended to nourish our spiritual life; that is, as we formerly observed, by the corporeal things which are produced in the sacrament, we are by a kind of analogy conducted to spiritual things.

Thus when bread is given as a symbol of the body of Christ, we must immediately think of this similitude. As bread nourishes, sustains, and protects our bodily life, so the body of Christ is the only food to invigorate and keep alive the soul. When we behold wine set forth as a symbol of blood, we must think that such use as wine serves to the body, the same is spiritually bestowed by the blood of Christ; and the use is to foster, refresh, strengthen, and exhilarate. For if we duly consider what profit we have gained by the breaking of his sacred body, and the shedding of his blood, we shall clearly perceive that these properties of bread and wine, agreeably to this analogy, most appropriately represent it when they are communicated to us.

4. Therefore, it is not the principal part of a sacrament simply to hold forth the body of Christ to us without any higher consideration, but rather to seal and confirm that promise by which he testifies that his flesh is meat indeed, and his blood drink indeed, nourishing us unto life eternal, and by which he affirms that he is the bread of life, of which, whosoever shall eat, shall live for ever—I say, to seal and confirm that promise, and in order to do so, it sends us to the cross of Christ, where that promise was performed and fulfilled in all its parts. For we do not eat Christ duly and savingly unless as crucified, while with lively apprehension we perceive the efficacy of his death. When he called himself the bread of life, he did not

take that appellation from the sacrament, as some perversely interpret; but such as he was given to us by the Father, such he exhibited himself when becoming partaker of our human mortality he made us partakers of his divine immortality; when offering himself in sacrifice, he took our curse upon himself, that he might cover us with his blessing, when by his death he devoured and swallowed up death, when in his resurrection he raised our corruptible flesh, which he had put on, to glory and incorruption.

5. It only remains that the whole become ours by application. This is done by means of the gospel, and more clearly by the sacred Supper, where Christ offers himself to us with all his blessings, and we receive him in faith. The sacrament, therefore, does not make Christ become for the first time the bread of life; but, while it calls to remembrance that Christ was made the bread of life that we may constantly eat him, it gives us a taste and relish for that bread, and makes us feel its efficacy. For it assures us, first, that whatever Christ did or suffered was done to give us life; and, secondly, that this quickening is eternal; by it we are ceaselessly nourished, sustained, and preserved in life. For as Christ could not have been the bread of life to us if he had not been born, if he had not died and risen again; so he could not now be the bread of life, were not the efficacy and fruit of his nativity, death, and resurrection, eternal. All this Christ has elegantly expressed in these words, "The bread that I will give is my flesh, which I will give for the life of the world" (John 6:51; cf. 6:52); doubtless intimating, that his body will be as bread in regard to the spiritual life of the soul, because it was to be delivered to death for our salvation, and that he extends it to us for food when he makes us partakers of it by faith. Wherefore he once gave himself that he might become bread, when he gave himself to be crucified for the redemption of the world; and he gives himself daily, when in the word of the gospel he offers himself to be partaken by us, inasmuch as he was crucified, when he seals that offer by the sacred mystery of the Supper, and when he accomplishes inwardly what he externally designates.

Moreover, two faults are here to be avoided. We must neither, by setting too little value on the signs, dissever them from their meanings to which they are in some degree annexed, nor by immoderately extolling them, seem somewhat to obscure the mysteries themselves.

That Christ is the bread of life by which believers are nourished unto eternal life, no man is so utterly devoid of religion as not to acknowledge. But all are not agreed as to the mode of partaking of him. For there are some who define the eating of the flesh of Christ, and the drinking of his blood, to be, in one word, nothing more than believing in Christ himself. But Christ seems to me to have intended to teach something more express and more sublime in that noble discourse, in which he recommends the eating of his flesh—viz. that we are quickened by the true partaking of him, which he designated by the terms eating and drinking, lest any one should suppose that the life which we obtain from him is obtained by simple knowledge. For as it is not the sight but the eating of bread that gives nourishment to the body, so the soul must partake of Christ truly and thoroughly, that by his energy it may grow up into spiritual life.

Meanwhile, we admit that this is nothing else than the eating of faith, and that no other eating can be imagined. But there is this difference between their mode of speaking and mine.

According to them, to eat is merely to believe; while I maintain that the flesh of Christ is eaten by believing, because it is made ours by faith, and that that eating is the effect and fruit of faith; or, if you will have it more clearly, according to them, eating is faith, whereas it rather seems to me to be a consequence of faith. The difference is little in words, but not little in reality. For, although the apostle teaches that Christ dwells in our hearts by faith (Eph. 3:17), no one will interpret that dwelling to be faith. All see that it explains the admirable effect of faith, because to it, it is owing that believers have Christ dwelling in them. In this way, the Lord was pleased, by calling himself the bread of life, not only to teach that our salvation is treasured up in the faith of his death and resurrection, but also, by virtue of true communication with him, his life passes into us and becomes ours, just as bread when taken for food gives vigor to the body.

6. When Augustine, whom they claim as their patron, wrote, that we eat by believing, all he meant was to indicate that that eating is of faith, and not of the mouth. This I deny not; but I at the same time add, that by faith we embrace Christ, not as appearing at a distance, but as uniting himself to us, he being our head, and we his members. I do not absolutely disapprove of that mode of speaking; I only deny that it is a full interpretation, if they mean to define what it is to eat the flesh of Christ. I see that Augustine repeatedly used this form of expression, as when he said (De Doct. Christ. Lib. 3), "Unless ye eat the flesh of the Son of Man" is a figurative expression enjoining us to have communion with our Lord's passion, and sweetly and usefully to treasure in our memory that his flesh was crucified and wounded for us. Also when he says, "These three thousand men who were converted at the preaching of Peter (Acts 2:41), by believing, drank the blood which they had cruelly shed." But in very many other passages he admirably commends faith for this, that by means of it our souls are not less refreshed by the communion of the blood of Christ, than our bodies with the bread which they eat. The very same thing is said by Chrysostom, "Christ makes us his body, not by faith only, but in reality." He does not mean that we obtain this blessing from any other quarter than from faith: he only intends to prevent any one from thinking of mere imagination when he hears the name of faith.

I say nothing of those who hold that the Supper is merely a mark of external professions because I think I sufficiently refuted their error when I treated of the sacraments in general

(chap. 14, sec. 13). Only let my readers observe, that when the cup is called the covenant in blood (Luke 22:20), the promise which tends to confirm faith is expressed. Hence it follows, that unless we have respect to God, and embrace what he offers, we do not make a right use of the sacred Supper.

7. I am not satisfied with the view of those who, while acknowledging that we have some kind of communion with Christ, only make us partakers of the Spirit, omitting all mention of flesh and blood. As if it were said to no purpose at all, that his flesh is meat indeed, and his blood is drink indeed; that we have no life unless we eat that flesh and drink that blood; and so forth. Therefore, if it is evident that full communion with Christ goes beyond their description, which is too confined, I will attempt briefly to show how far it extends, before proceeding to speak of the contrary vice of excess. For I shall have a longer discussion with these hyperbolical doctors, who, according to their gross ideas, fabricate an absurd mode of eating and drinking, and transfigure Christ, after divesting him of his flesh, into a phantom: if, indeed, it be lawful to put this great mystery into words, a mystery which I feel, and therefore freely confess that I am unable to comprehend with my mind, so far am I from wishing any one to measure its sublimity by my feeble capacity. Nay, I rather exhort my readers not to confine their apprehension within those too narrow limits, but to attempt to rise much higher than I can guide them. For whenever this subject is considered, after I have done my utmost, I feel that I have spoken far beneath its dignity. And though the mind is more powerful in thought than the tongue in expression, it too is overcome and overwhelmed by the magnitude of the subject. All then that remains is to break forth in admiration of the mystery, which it is plain that the mind is inadequate to comprehends or the tongue to express. I will, however, give a summary of my view as I best can, not doubting its truth, and therefore trusting that it will not be disapproved by pious breasts.

8. First of all, we are taught by the Scriptures that

Christ was from the beginning the living Word of the Father, the fountain and origin of life, from which all things should always receive life. Hence John at one time calls him the Word of life, and at another says, that in him was life; intimating, that he, even then pervading all creatures, instilled into them the power of breathing and living.

He afterward adds, that the life was at length manifested, when the Son of God, assuming our nature, exhibited himself in bodily form to be seen and handled. For although he previously diffused his virtue into the creatures, yet as man, because alienated from God by sin, had lost the communication of life, and saw death on every side impending over him, he behaved, in order to regain the hope of immortality, to be restored to the communion of that Word. How little confidence can it give you, to know that the Word of God, from which you are at the greatest distance, contains within himself the fullness of life, whereas in yourself, in whatever direction you turn, you see nothing but death? But ever since that fountain of life began to dwell in our nature, he no longer lies hid at a distance from us, but exhibits himself openly for our participation. Nay, the very flesh in which he resides he makes vivifying to us, that by partaking of it we may feed for immortality. "I," says he, "am that bread of life"; "I am the living bread which came down from heaven"; "And the bread that I will give is my flesh, which I will give for the life of the world" (John 6:48, 51). By these words he declares, not only that he is life, inasmuch as he is the eternal Word of God who came down to us from heaven, but, by coming down, gave vigor to the flesh which he assumed, that a communication of life to us might thence emanate.

Hence, too, he adds, that his flesh is meat indeed, and that his blood is drink indeed: by this food believers are reared to eternal life. The pious, therefore, have admirable comfort in this, that they now find life in their own flesh. For they not only reach it by easy access, but have it spontaneously set forth before them. Let

them only throw open the door of their hearts that they may take it into their embrace, and they will obtain it.

9. The flesh of Christ, however, has not such power in itself as to make us live, seeing that by its own first condition it was subject to mortality, and even now, when endued with immortality, lives not by itself. Still it is properly said to be life-giving, as it is pervaded with the fullness of life for the purpose of transmitting it to us. In this sense I understand our Savior's words as Cyril interprets them, "As the Father has life in himself, so has he given to the Son to have life in himself" (John 5:26). For there properly he is speaking not of the properties which he possessed with the Father from the beginning, but of those with which he was invested in the flesh in which he appeared. Accordingly, he shows that in his humanity also fullness of life resides, so that every one who communicates in his flesh and blood, at the same time enjoys the participation of life.

The nature of this may be explained by a familiar example. As water is at one time drunk out of the fountain, at another drawn, at another led away by conduits to irrigate the fields, and yet does not flow forth of itself for all these uses, but is taken from its source, which, with perennial flow, ever and anon sends forth a new and sufficient supply; so the flesh of Christ is like a rich and inexhaustible fountain, which transfuses into us the life flowing forth from the Godhead into itself. Now, who sees not that the communion of the flesh and blood of Christ is necessary to all who aspire to the heavenly life?

Hence those passages of the apostle: The Church is the "body" of Christ; his "fullness." He is "the head," "from whence the whole body fitly joined together, and compacted by that which every joint supplieth," "maketh increase of the body" (Eph. 1:23 and 4:15–16). Our bodies are the "members of Christ" (1 Cor. 6:15). We perceive that all these things cannot possibly take place unless he adheres to us wholly in body and spirit. But the very close connection which unites us to his flesh, he illustrated with still more splendid epithets, when he said that we "are members of his body, of his flesh, and of his bones" (Eph. 5:30). At length, to testify that the matter is too high for utterance, he concludes with exclaiming, "This is a great mystery" (Eph. 5:32). It were, therefore, extreme infatuation not to acknowledge the communion of believers with the body and blood of the Lord, a communion which the apostle declares to be so great, that he chooses rather to marvel at it than to explain it.

10. The sum is that the flesh and blood of Christ feed our souls just as bread and wine maintain and support our corporeal life. For there would be no aptitude in the sign, did not our souls find their nourishment in Christ. This could not be, did not Christ truly form one with us, and refresh us by the eating of his flesh, and the drinking of his blood.

But though it seems an incredible thing that the flesh of Christ, while at such a distance from us in respect of place, should be food to us, let us remember how far the secret virtue of the Holy Spirit surpasses all our conceptions, and how foolish it is to wish to measure its immensity by our feeble capacity. Therefore, what our mind does not comprehend let faith conceive—viz. that the Spirit truly unites things separated by space.

That sacred communion of flesh and blood by which Christ transfuses his life into us, just as if it penetrated our bones and marrow, he testifies and seals in the Supper, and that not by presenting a vain or empty sign, but by there exerting an efficacy of the Spirit by which he fulfils what he promises. And truly the thing there signified he exhibits and offers to all who sit down at that spiritual feast, although it is beneficially received by believers only who receive this great benefit with true faith and heartfelt gratitude.

For this reason the apostle said, "The cup of blessing which we bless, is it not the communion of the blood of Christ? The bread which we break, is it not the communion of the body of Christ?" (1 Cor. 10:16). There is no ground to object that the expression is figurative, and gives the sign the name of the thing signified. I admit, indeed, that the breaking of bread is a symbol, not the reality. But this being admitted, we duly infer from the exhibition of the symbol that the thing itself is exhibited. For unless we would charge God with deceit, we will never presume to say that he holds forth an empty symbol. Therefore, if by the breaking of bread the Lord truly represents the partaking of his body, there ought to be no doubt whatever that he truly exhibits and performs it. The rule which the pious ought always to observe is, whenever they see the symbols instituted by the Lord, to think and feel surely persuaded that the truth of the thing signified is also present. For why does the Lord put the symbol of his body into your hands, but just to assure you that you truly partake of him? If this is true, let us feel as much assured that the visible sign is given us in seal of an invisible gift as that his body itself is given to us.

11. I hold then (as has always been received in the Church, and is still taught by those who feel aright), that the sacred mystery of the Supper consists of two things—the corporeal signs, which, presented to the eye, represent invisible things in a manner adapted to our weak capacity, and the spiritual truth, which is at once figured and exhibited by the signs.

When attempting familiarly to explain its nature, I am accustomed to set down three things—the thing meant, the matter which depends on it, and the virtue or efficacy consequent upon both. The thing meant consists in the promises which are in a manner included in the sign. By the matter, or substance, I mean Christ, with his death and resurrection. By the effect, I understand redemption, justification, sanctification, eternal life, and all the other benefits which Christ bestows upon us.

Moreover, though all these things have respect to faith, I leave no room for the cavil, that when I say Christ is conceived by faith, I mean that he is only conceived by the intellect and imagination. He is offered by the promises not that we may stop short at the sight, or mere knowledge of him, but that we may enjoy true communion with him. And, indeed, I see not how any one can expect to have redemption and righteousness in the cross of Christ, and life in his death, without trusting first of all to true communion with Christ himself. Those blessings could not reach us, did not Christ previously make himself ours.

I say then, that in the mystery of the Supper, by the symbols of bread and wine, Christ, his body and his blood, are truly exhibited to us, that in them he fulfilled all obedience, in order to procure righteousness for us, first, that we might become one body with him; and, secondly, that being made partakers of his substance, we might feel the result of this fact in the participation of all his blessings.

JACOBUS ARMINIUS: "ON PREDESTINATION," "ON THE PROVIDENCE OF GOD," AND "ON THE FREE WILL OF MEN"
Latin, Late Sixteenth Century

The Dutch Reformed theologian known as "Arminius" was Jacob Harmenszoon (1559–1609) who studied under Theodore Beza and was professor of theology at Leiden University.

✦

ON PREDESTINATION
(SECTIONS 1–10)

[I. On Predestination]The first and most important article in religion on which I have to offer my views, and which for many years past has engaged my attention, is the Predestination of God, that is, the Election of men to salvation, and the Reprobation of them to destruction. Commencing with this article, I will first explain what is taught concerning it, both in discourses and writings, by certain persons in our Churches, and in the University of Leyden. I will afterward declare my own views and thoughts on the same subject, while I show my opinion on what they advance.

1. What Is Taught Concerning Predestination

On this article there is no uniform and simple opinion among the teachers of our Churches; but there is some variation in certain parts of it in which they differ from each other.

1. The first opinion, which I reject, but which is espoused by those [Supralapsarians] who assume the very highest ground of this. The opinion of those who take the highest ground on this point, as it is generally contained in their writings, is to this effect:

"(1)   God by an eternal and immutable decree has predestinated, from among men (whom he did not consider as being then created, much less as being fallen), certain individuals to everlasting life, and others to eternal destruction, without any regard whatever to righteousness or sin, to obedience or disobedience, but purely of his own good pleasure, to demonstrate the glory of his justice and mercy; or (as others assert), to demonstrate his saving grace, wisdom and free uncontrollable power.

"(2)   In addition to this decree, God has pre-ordained certain determinate means which pertain to its execution, and this by an eternal and immutable decree. These means necessarily follow by virtue of the preceding decree, and necessarily bring him who has been predestinated, to the end which has been fore-ordained for him. Some of these means belong in common both to the decree of election and that of rejection, and others of them are specially restricted to the one decree or to the other.

"(3)   The means common to both the decrees, are three: the first is, the creation of man in the upright [or erect] state of original righteousness, or after the image and likeness of God in righteousness and true holiness. The second is, the permission of the fall of Adam, or the ordination of God that man should sin, and become corrupt or vitiated. The third is, the loss or the removal of original righteousness and of the image of God, and a being concluded under sin and condemnation.

"(4)   For unless God had created some men, he would not have had any upon whom he might either bestow eternal life, or superinduce everlasting death. Unless he had created them in righteousness and true holiness, he would himself have been the author of sin, and would by this means have possessed no right either to punish them to the praise of his justice, or to save them to the praise of his mercy. Unless they had themselves sinned, and by the demerit of sin had rendered themselves guilty of death, there would have been no room for the demonstration either of justice or of mercy.

"(5)   The means pre-ordained for the execution of the decree of election, are also these three. The first is, the pre-ordination, or the giving of Jesus Christ as a Mediator and a Savior, who might by his meet deserve, [or purchase,] for all the elect and for them only, the lost righteousness and life, and might communicate them by his own power [or virtue]. The second is, the call [or vocation] to faith outwardly by the word, but inwardly by his Spirit, in the mind, affections and will; by an operation of such efficacy that the elect person of necessity yields assent and obedience to the vocation, in so much that it is not possible for him to do otherwise than believe and be obedient to this vocation. From hence arise justification and sanctification through the blood of Christ and his Spirit, and from them the existence of all good works, and all that manifestly by means of the same force and necessity. The third is, that which keeps and preserves the elect in faith, holiness, and a zeal for good works; or, it is the gift of perseverance; the virtue of which is such, that believing and elect

persons not only do not sin with a full and entire will, or do not fall away totally from faith and grace, but it likewise is neither possible for them to sin with a full and perfect will, nor to fall away totally or finally from faith and grace.

"(6)   The two last of these means [vocation and perseverance,] belong only to the elect who are of adult age. But God employs a shorter way to salvation, by which he conducts those children of believers and saints who depart out of this life before they arrive at years of maturity; that is, provided they belong to the number of the elect (who are known to God alone), for God bestows on them Christ as their Savior, and gives them to Christ, to save them by his blood and Holy Spirit, without actual faith and perseverance in it [faith]; and this he does according to the promise of the covenant of grace, I will be a God unto you, and unto your seed after you.

"(7)   The means pertaining to the execution of the decree of reprobation to eternal death, are partly such as peculiarly belong to all those who are rejected and reprobate, whether they ever arrive at years of maturity or die before that period; and they are partly such as are proper only to some of them. The mean that is common to all the reprobate, is desertion in sin, by denying to them that saving grace which is sufficient and necessary to the salvation of any one. This negation [or denial,] consists of two parts. For, in the first place, God did not will that Christ should die for them [the reprobate,] or become their Savior, and this neither in reference to the antecedent will of God (as some persons call it), nor in reference to his sufficient will, or the value of the price of reconciliation; because this price was not offered for reprobates, either with respect to the decree of God, or its virtue and efficacy.

(1) But the other part of this negation [or denial] is, that God is unwilling to communicate the Spirit of Christ to reprobates, yet without communication they can neither be made partakers of Christ nor of his benefits.

"(8)   The mean which belongs properly only to some of the reprobates, is obduration, [or the act of hardening,] which befalls those of them who have attained to years of maturity, either because they have very frequently and enormously sinned against the law of God, or because they have rejected the grace of the gospel.

(1)   To the execution of the first species of induration, or hardening, belong the illumination of their conscience by means of knowledge, and its conviction of the righteousness of the law. For it is impossible that this law should not necessarily detain them in unrighteousness, to render them inexcusable.

(2)   For the execution of the second species of induration, God employs a call by the preaching of his gospel, which call is inefficacious and insufficient both in respect to the decree of God, and to its issue or event. This calling is either only an external one, which it is neither in their desire nor in their power to obey. Or it is likewise an internal one, by which some of them may be excited in their understandings to accept and believe the things which they hear; but yet it is only with such a faith as that with which the devils are endowed when they believe and tremble. Others of them are excited and conducted still further, so as to desire in a certain measure to taste the heavenly gift. But the latter are, of all others, the most unhappy, because they are raised up on high, that they may be brought down with a heavier fall. And this fate it is impossible for them to escape, for they must of necessity return to their vomit, and depart or fall away from the faith.

"(9)   From this decree of Divine election and reprobation, and from this administration of the means which pertain to the execution of both of them, it follows, that the elect are necessarily saved, it being impossible for them to perish—and that the reprobate are necessarily damned, it being impossible for them to be saved; and all this from the absolute purpose [or determination] of God, which is altogether antecedent to all things, and to all those causes which are either in things themselves or can possibly result from them."

These opinions concerning predestination are considered, by some of those who advocate them, to be the foundation of Christianity, salvation and of its certainty. On these sentiments they suppose, "is founded the sure and undoubted consolation of all believers, which is capable of rendering their consciences tranquil; and on them also depends the praise of the grace of God, so that if any contradiction be offered to this doctrine, God is necessarily deprived of the glory of his grace, and then the merit of salvation is attributed to the free will of man and to his own powers and strength, which ascription savors of Pelagianism."

These then are the causes which are offered why the advocates of these sentiments labor with a common anxiety to retain the purity of such a doctrine in their churches and why they oppose themselves to all those innovations which are at variance with them.

2. My Sentiments on the Preceding Scheme of Predestination

But, for my own part, to speak my sentiments with freedom, and yet with a salvo in favor of a better judgment, I am of opinion, that this doctrine of theirs contains many things that are both false and impertinent, and at an utter disagreement with each other; all the instances of which, the present time will not permit me to recount, but I will subject it to an examination only in those parts which are most prominent and extensive. I shall, therefore, propose to myself four principal heads, which are of the greatest importance in this doctrine; and when I have in the first place explained of what kind they are, I will afterward declare more fully the judgment and sentiments which I have formed concerning them. They are the following:

"(1) That God has absolutely and precisely decreed to save certain particular men by his mercy or grace, but to condemn others by his justice: and to do all this without having any regard in such decree to righteousness or sin, obedience or disobedience, which could possibly exist on the part of one class of men or of the other.

"(2) That, for the execution of the preceding decree, God determined to create Adam, and all men in him, in an upright state of original righteousness; besides which he also ordained them to commit sin that they might thus become guilty of eternal condemnation and be deprived of original righteousness.

"(3) That those persons whom God has thus positively willed to save, he has decreed not only to salvation but also to the means which pertain to it; (that is, to conduct and bring them to faith in Christ Jesus, and to perseverance in that faith ;) and that He also in reality leads them to these results by a grace and power that are irresistible, so that it is not possible for them to do otherwise than believe, persevere in faith, and be saved.

"(4) That to those whom, by his absolute will, God has fore-ordained to perdition, he has also decreed to deny that grace which is necessary and sufficient for salvation, and does not in reality confer it upon them; so that they are neither placed in a possible condition nor in any capacity of believing or of being saved."

After a diligent contemplation and examination of these four heads, in the fear of the Lord, I make the following declaration respecting this doctrine of predestination.

3. I Reject This Predestination for the Following Reasons:

Section I

Because it is not the foundation of Christianity, of Salvation, or of its certainty.

1. It is not the foundation of Christianity:
    (1) For this Predestination is not that decree of God by which Christ is appointed by God to be the Savior, the Head, and the Foundation of those who will be made heirs of salvation. Yet that decree is the only foundation of Christianity.
    (2) For the doctrine of this Predestination is not that doctrine by which, through faith, we as lively stones are built up into Christ, the only corner stone, and are inserted into him as the members of the body are joined to their head.
2. It is not the foundation of Salvation:
    (1) For this Predestination is not that decree of the good pleasure of God in Christ Jesus on which alone our salvation rests and depends.
    (2) The doctrine of this Predestination is not the foundation of Salvation: for it is not "the power of God to salvation to every one that believeth": because through it "the righteousness of God" is not "revealed from faith to faith."
3. Nor is it the foundation of the certainty of salvation: For that is dependent upon this decree, "they who believe, shall be saved": I believe, therefore, I shall be saved. But the doctrine of this Predestination embraces within itself neither the first nor the second member of the syllogism.

This is likewise confessed by some persons in these words: "we do not wish to state that the knowledge of this [Predestination] is the foundation of Christianity or of salvation, or that it is necessary to salvation in the same manner as the doctrine of the Gospel," etc.

Section II

This doctrine of Predestination comprises within it neither the whole nor any part of the Gospel. For, according to the tenor of the discourses delivered by John and Christ, as they are described to us by the Evangelist, and according to the doctrine of the Apostles and Christ after his ascension, the Gospel consists partly of an injunction to repent and believe, and partly of a promise to bestow forgiveness of sins, the grace of the Spirit, and life eternal. But this Predestination belongs neither to the injunction to repent and believe, nor to the annexed promise. Nay, this doctrine does not even teach what kind of men in general God has predestinated, which is properly the doctrine of the Gospel; but it embraces within itself a certain mystery, which is known only to God, who is the Predestinater, and in which mystery are comprehended what particular persons and how many he has decreed to save and to condemn. From these premises I draw a further conclusion, that this doctrine of Predestination is not necessary to salvation, either as an object of knowledge, belief, hope, or performance. A Confession to this effect has been made by a certain learned man, in the theses which he has proposed for discussion on this subject, in the following words: "Wherefore the gospel cannot be simply termed the book or the revelation of Predestination, but only in a relative sense. Because it does not absolutely denote either the matter of the number or the form; that is, it neither declares how many persons in particular, nor (with a few exceptions) who they are, but only the description of them in general, whom God has predestinated."

Section III

This doctrine was never admitted, decreed, or approved in any Council, either general or particular, for the first six hundred years after Christ.

1. Not in the General Council of Nice, in which sentence was given against Arius and in favor of the Deity and Consubstantiality of the Son of God. Not in the first Council of Constantinople, in which a decree was passed against Macedonius, respecting the Deity of the Holy Spirit. Not in the Council of Ephesus, which determined against Nestorius and in favor of the Unity of the Person of the Son of God. Not in that of Chalcedon, which condemned Eutyches and determined "that in one and the same person of our Lord Jesus Christ, there were two distinct natures, which differ from each other in their essence." Not in the second Council of Constantinople, in which Peter, Bishop of Antioch, and Anthymus, Bishop of Constantinople, with certain other persons, were condemned for having asserted "that the Father had likewise suffered," as well as the Son. Nor in the third Council of Constantinople, in which the Monothelites were condemned for having asserted "that there was only one will and operation in Jesus Christ."

2. But this doctrine was not discussed or confirmed in particular Councils, such as that of Jerusalem, Orange, or even that of Mela in Africa, which was held against Pelagius and his errors, as is apparent from the articles of doctrine which were then decreed both against his person and his false opinions.

But so far was Augustine's doctrine of Predestination from being received in those councils, that when Celestinus, the Bishop of Rome, who was his contemporary, wrote to the Bishops of France, and condemned the doctrines of the Pelagians, he concluded his epistle in these words: "but as we dare not despise, so neither do we deem it necessary to defend the more profound and difficult parts of the questions which occur in this controversy, and which have been treated to a very great extent by those who opposed the heretics. Because we believe, that whatever the writings according to the forementioned rules of the Apostolic See have taught us, is amply sufficient for confessing the grace of God, from whose work, credit and authority not a little must be subtracted or withdrawn," etc. In reference to the rules which were laid down by Celestinus in that epistle, and which had been decreed in the three preceding particular Councils, we shall experience no difficulty in agreeing together about them, especially in regard to those matters which are necessary to the establishment of grace in opposition to Pelagius and his errors.

Section IV

None of those Doctors or Divines of the Church, who held correct and orthodox sentiments for the first six hundred years after the birth of Christ, ever brought this doctrine forward or gave it their approval. Neither was it professed and approved by a single individual of those who showed themselves the principal and keenest defenders of grace against Pelagius. Of this description, it is evident, were St. Jerome, Augustine, the author of the treatise titled, *De Vocatione Gentium*, ["The calling of the Gentiles,"] Prosper of Aquitaine, Hilary, Fulgentius, and Orosius. This is very apparent from their writings.

Section V

It neither agrees nor corresponds with the Harmony of those confessions which were printed and published together in one volume at Geneva, in the name of the Reformed and Protestant Churches. If that harmony of Confessions be faithfully consulted, it will appear that many of them do not speak in the same manner concerning Predestination; that some of them only incidentally mention it; and that they evidently never once touch upon those heads of the doctrine, which are now in great repute and particularly urged in the preceding scheme of Predestination, and which I have already adduced. Nor does any single Confession deliver this doctrine in the same manner as it has just now been propounded by me. The Confessions of Bohemia, England and Wirtemburgh, and the first Helvetian [Swiss] Confession, and that of the four cities of Strasburgh, Constance, Memmingen, and Lindau, make no mention of this Predestination. Those of Basle and Saxony, only take a very cursory notice of it in three words. The Augustan Confession speaks of it in such a manner as to induce the Genevan editors to think, that some annotation was necessary on their part, to give us a previous warning. The last of the Helvetian [Swiss] Confessions, to which a great portion of the Reformed Churches have expressed their assent and which they have subscribed, likewise speaks of it in such a strain as makes me very desirous to see what method can possibly be adopted to give it any accordance with that doctrine of Predestination which I have just now advanced. Yet this [Swiss] Confession is that which has obtained the approbation of the Churches of Geneva and Savoy.

Section VI

Without the least contention or caviling, it may very properly be made a question of doubt, whether this doctrine agrees with the Belgic Confession and the Heidelberg Catechism; as I shall briefly demonstrate.

1. In the Fourteenth Article of the Dutch Confession, these expressions occur: "Man knowingly and willingly subjected himself to sin, and, consequently, to death and cursing, while he lent an ear to the deceiving words and impostures of the devil," etc. From this sentence I conclude, that man did not sin on account of any necessity through a preceding decree of Predestination: which inference is diametrically opposed to that doctrine of Predestination against which I now contend. Then, in the Sixteenth Article, which treats of the eternal election of God, these words are contained: "God showed himself Merciful, by delivering from damnation, and by saving, those persons whom, in his eternal and immutable counsel and cording to his gratuitous goodness, he chose in Christ Jesus our Lord, without any regard to their works. And he showed himself just, in leaving others in that their fall and perdition into which they had precipitated themselves." It is not obvious to me, how these words are consistent with this doctrine of Predestination.

2. In the twentieth question of the Heidelberg Catechism, we read: "salvation through Christ is not given [restored] to all them who had perished in Adam, but to those only who are engrafted into Christ by the faith, and who embrace his benefits." From this sentence I infer, that God has not absolutely Predestinated any men to salvation; but that he has in his decree considered [or looked upon] them as believers. This deduction is at open conflict with the first and third points of this Predestination. In the fifty-fourth question of the same Catechism, it is said: "I believe that, from the beginning to the end of the world, the Son of God out of the entire race of mankind doth by his word and Spirit gather or collect unto himself a company chosen unto eternal life and agreeing together in the true faith."

In this sentence "election to eternal life," and "agreement in the faith," stand in mutual juxtaposition; and in such a manner, that the latter is not rendered subordinate to the former, which, according to these sentiments on Predestination ought to have been done. In that case the words should have been placed in the following order: "the son of God calls and gathers to himself, by his word and Spirit, a company chosen to eternal life that they may believe and agree together in the true faith."

Since such are the statements of our Confession and Catechism, no reason whatever exists, why those who embrace and defend these sentiments on Predestination, should either violently endeavor to obtrude them on their colleagues and on the Church of Christ; or why they should take it amiss, and put the worst construction upon it, when any thing is taught in the Church or University that is not exactly accordant with their doctrine, or that is opposed to it.

Section VII

I affirm that this doctrine is repugnant to the Nature of God, but particularly to those Attributes of his nature by which he performs and manages all things, his wisdom, justice, and goodness.

1. It is repugnant to his wisdom in three ways.
    (1) Because it represents God as decreeing something for a particular end [or purpose] which neither is nor can be good: which is, that God created something for eternal perdition to the praise of his justice.
    (2) Because it states, that the object which God proposed to himself by this Predestination, was, to demonstrate the glory of his mercy and justice: But this glory he cannot demonstrate, except by an act that is contrary at once to his mercy and his justice, of which description is that decree of God in which he determined that man should sin and be rendered miserable.
    (3) Because it changes and inverts the order of the two-fold wisdom of God,

as it is displayed to us in the Scriptures. For it asserts, that God has absolutely predetermined to save men by the mercy and wisdom that are comprehended in the doctrine of the cross of Christ, without having foreseen this circumstance, that it was impossible for man (and that, truly, through his own fault) to be saved by the wisdom which was revealed in the law and which was infused into him at the period of his creation: When the scripture asserts, on the contrary, "that it pleased God by the foolishness of preaching to save them that believe"; that is, "by the doctrine of the cross, after that in the wisdom of God the world by wisdom knew not God" (1 Cor. 1:21).

2. It is repugnant to the justice of God, not only in reference to that attribute denoting in God a love of righteousness and a hatred of iniquity, but also in reference to its being a perpetual and constant desire in him to render to every one that which is his due.
    (1) It is at variance with the first of these ideas of justice in the following manner: Because it affirms, that God has absolutely willed to save certain individual men, and has decreed their salvation without having the least regard to righteousness or obedience: The proper inference from which, is, that God loves such men far more than his own justice [or righteousness.]
    (2) It is opposed to the second idea of his justice: Because it affirms, that God wishes to subject his creature to misery (which cannot possibly have any existence except as the punishment of sin), although, at the same time, he does not look upon [or consider] the creature as a sinner, and therefore as not obnoxious either to wrath or to punishment. This is the manner in which it lays down the position, that God has willed to give to the creature not only something which does not

belong to it, but which is connected with its greatest injury. Which is another act directly opposed to his justice. In accordance, therefore, with this doctrine, God, in the first place, detracts from himself that which is his own, [or his right,] and then imparts to the creature what does not belong to it, to its great misery and unhappiness.

3. It is also repugnant to the Goodness of God. Goodness is an affection [or disposition] in God to communicate his own good so far as his justice considers and admits to be fitting and proper. But in this doctrine the following act is attributed to God, that, of himself, and induced to it by nothing external, he wills the greatest evil to his creatures; and that from all eternity he has pre-ordained that evil for them, or pre-determined to impart it to them, even before he resolved to bestow upon them any portion of good. For this doctrine states, that God willed to damn; and, that he might be able to do this, he willed to create; although creation is the first egress [or going forth] of God's goodness toward his creatures. How vastly different are such statements as these from that expansive goodness of God by which he confers benefits not only on the unworthy, but also on the evil, the unjust and on those who are deserving of punishment, which trait of Divine beneficence in our Father who is in heaven, we are commanded to imitate (Matt. 5:45).

Section VIII

Such a doctrine of Predestination is contrary to the nature of man, in regard to his having been created after the Divine image in the knowledge of God and in righteousness, in regard to his having been created with freedom of will, and in regard to his having been created with a disposition and aptitude for the enjoyment of life eternal. These three circumstance, respecting him, may be deduced from the following brief expressions: "Do this, and live" (Rom. 10:5); "In the day that thou eatest thereof, thou shalt surely die" (Gen. 2:17). If man be deprived of any of these qualifications, such admonitions as these cannot possibly be effective in exciting him to obedience.

1. This doctrine is inconsistent with the Divine image, which consists of the knowledge of God and holiness. For according to this knowledge and righteousness man was qualified and empowered, he was also laid under an obligation to know God, to love, worship, and serve him. But by the intervention, or rather by the prevention, of this Predestination, it was pre-ordained that man should be formed vicious and should commit sin, that is, that he should neither know God, love, worship, nor serve him; and that he should not perform that which by the image of God, he was well qualified and empowered to do, and which he was bound to perform. This is tantamount to such a declaration as the following, which any one might make: "God did undoubtedly create man after his own image, in righteousness and true holiness; but, notwithstanding this, he fore-ordained and decreed, that man should become impure and unrighteous, that is, should be made conformable to the image of Satan."

2. This doctrine is inconsistent with the freedom of the will, in which and with which man was created by God. For it prevents the exercise of this liberty, by binding or determining the will absolutely to one object, that is, to do this thing precisely, or to do that. God, therefore, according to this statement, may be blamed for the one or the other of these two things (with which let no man charge his Maker!), either for creating man with freedom of will, or for hindering him in the use of his own liberty after he had formed him a free agent. In the former of these two cases, God is chargeable with a want of consideration, in the latter with mutability. And in both, with being injurious to man as well as to himself.

3. This Predestination is prejudicial to man in regard to the inclination and capacity for the eternal fruition of salvation, with which he was endowed at the period of his creation. For, since by this Predestination it has been pre-determined, that the greater part of mankind shall not be made partakers of salvation, but shall fall into everlasting condemnation, and

since this predetermination took place even before the decree had passed for creating man, such persons are deprived of something, for the desire of which they have been endowed by God with a natural inclination. This great privation they suffer, not in consequence of any preceding sin or demerit of their own, but simply and solely through this sort of Predestination.

Section IX

This Predestination is diametrically opposed to the Act of Creation.

1. For creation is a communication of good according to the intrinsic property of its nature. But, creation of this description, whose intent or design is, to make a way through itself by which the reprobation that had been previously determined may obtain its object, is not a communication of good. For we ought to form our estimate and judgment of every good from the mind and intention of Him who is the Donor and from the end to which or on account of which it is bestowed. In the present instance, the intention of the Donor would have been, to condemn, which is an act that could not possibly affect any one except a creature; and the end or event of creation would have been the eternal perdition of the creature. In that case creation would not have been a communication of any good, but a preparation for the greatest evil both according to the very intention of the Creator and the actual issue of the matter; and according to the words of Christ, "it had been good for that man, if he had never been born!" (Matt. 26:24).

2. Reprobation is an act of hatred, and from hatred derives its origin. But creation does not proceed from hatred; it is not therefore a way or means, which belongs to the execution of the decree of reprobation.

3. Creation is a perfect act of God, by which he has manifested his wisdom, goodness and omnipotence: It is not therefore subordinate to the end of any other preceding work or action of God. But it is rather to be viewed as that act of God, which necessarily precedes and is antecedent to all other acts that he can possibly either decree or undertake. Unless God had formed a previous conception of the work of creation, he could not have decreed actually to undertake any other act; and until he had executed the work of creation, he could by no means have completed any other operation.

4. All the actions of God which tend to the condemnation of his creatures, are strange work or foreign to him; because God consents to them, for some other cause that is quite extraneous. But creation is not an action that is foreign to God, but it is proper to him. It is eminently an action most appropriate to Him, and to which he could be moved by no other external cause, because it is the very first of the Divine acts, and, till it was done, nothing could have any actual existence, except God himself; for every thing else that has a being, came into existence through this action.

5. If creation be the way and means through which God willed the execution of the decree of his reprobation, he was more inclined to will the act of reprobation than that of creation; and he consequently derived greater satisfaction from the act of condemning certain of his innocent creatures, than in the act of their creation.

6. Lastly. Creation cannot be a way or means of reprobation according to the absolute purpose of God: because, after the creation was completed, it was in the power of man still to have remained obedient to the divine commands, and not to commit sin; to render this possible, while God had on one part bestowed on him sufficient strength and power, he had also on the other placed sufficient impediments; a circumstance most diametrically opposed to a Predestination of this description.

Section X

This doctrine is at open hostility with the Nature of Eternal Life, and the titles by which it is signally distinguished in the Scriptures. For it is called "the inheritance of the sons of God" (Titus 3:7); but those alone are the sons of God, according to the doctrine of the Gospel, "who believe in the name of Jesus Christ" (John 1:12). It is also called, "the reward of obedience" (Matt. 5:12), and of "the labor of love" (Heb. 6:10); "the recompense of those who fight the good fight and who run well, a crown of righteousness," etc. (Rev. 2:10; 2 Tim. 4:7–8). God therefore has not, from his own absolute decree, without any consideration or regard whatever to faith and obedience, appointed to any man, or determined to appoint to him, life eternal.

ON THE PROVIDENCE OF GOD

I consider Divine Providence to be that solicitous, continued, and universally present inspection and oversight of God, according to which he exercises a general care over the whole world, but evinces a particular concern for all his [intelligent] creatures without any exception, with the design of preserving and governing them in their own essence, qualities, actions, and passions, in a manner that is at once worthy of himself and suitable to them, to the praise of his name and the salvation of believers. In this definition of Divine Providence, I by no means deprive it of any particle of those properties which agree with it or belong to it; but I declare that it preserves, regulates, governs and directs all things and that nothing in the world happens fortuitously or by chance. Beside this, I place in subjection to Divine Providence both the free-will and even the actions of a rational creature, so that nothing can be done without the will of God, not even any of those things which are done in opposition to it; only we must observe a distinction between good actions and evil ones, by saying, that God both wills and performs good acts, but that He only freely permits those which are evil. Still farther than this, I very readily grant, that even all actions whatever, concerning evil, that can possibly be devised or invented, may be attributed to Divine Providence Employing solely one caution, not to conclude from this concession that God is the cause of sin. This I have testified with sufficient clearness, in a certain disputation concerning the Righteousness and Efficacy of Divine Providence concerning things that are evil, which was discussed at Leyden on two different occasions, as a divinity-act, at which I presided. In that disputation, I endeavored to ascribe to God whatever actions concerning sin I could possibly conclude from the scriptures to belong to him; and I proceeded to such a length in my attempt, that some persons thought proper on that account to charge me with having made God the author of sin. The same serious allegation has likewise been often produced against me, from the pulpit, in the city of Amsterdam, on account of those very theses; but with what show of justice such a charge was made, may be evident to any one, from the contents of my written answer to those Thirty-one Articles formerly mentioned, which have been falsely imputed to me, and of which this was one.

ON THE FREE WILL OF MAN

This is my opinion concerning the free-will of man: In his primitive condition as he came out of the hands of his creator, man was endowed with such a portion of knowledge, holiness and power, as enabled him to understand, esteem, consider, will, and to perform the true good, according to the commandment delivered to him. Yet none of these acts could he do, except through the assistance of Divine Grace. But in his lapsed and sinful state, man is not capable, of and by himself, either to think, to will, or to do that which is really good; but it is necessary for him to be regenerated and renewed in his intellect, affections or will, and in all his powers, by God in Christ through the Holy Spirit, that he may be qualified rightly to understand, esteem, consider, will, and perform whatever is truly good. When he is made a partaker of this regeneration or renovation, I consider that, since he is delivered from sin, he is capable of thinking, willing and doing that which is good, but yet not without the continued aids of Divine Grace.

FIVE ARTICLES OF REMONSTRANCE
Dutch, 1610

This summary of Arminian teaching was signed and circulated by followers of Jacob Arminius after his death in 1610. Arminius and his followers opposed strict Calvinist teachings, especially the doctrines that Christ died only for the elect, and that for these elect God's grace was irresistible (i.e., they had no choice in the matter, neither could they lose their salvation). The Articles were distributed along with pleas for tolerance toward Arminians, but both were condemned by Calvinists at the Synod of Dort in 1618.[2]

Questions for Guided Reading

1. What is prevenient grace, and what is its role in salvation according to these articles?
2. Calvinists taught that Christ died only for the elect—those whom God elected (chose for salvation) before the fall of Adam and Eve; what do these articles teach by contrast?
3. Calvinists also taught that it was impossible for the elect to resist God's grace (i.e., to say no to salvation); how do these articles contrast with that teaching?
4. What do these articles teach about the possibility of losing one's standing with God (backsliding)?

◆

These Articles thus set out and delivered the Remonstrants deem agreeable to the word of God, suitable for edification and, on this subject, sufficient for salvation. So that it is not needful, and tends not to edification, to rise higher or to descend lower.

1. That God, by an eternal and unchangeable purpose in Jesus Christ his Son, before the foundations of the world were laid, determined to save, out of the human race which had fallen into sin, in Christ, for Christ's sake and through Christ, those who through the grace of the Holy Spirit shall believe on the same his Son and shall through the same grace persevere in this same faith and obedience of faith even to the end; and on the other hand to leave under sin and wrath the contumacious and unbelieving and to condemn them as aliens from Christ, according to the word of the Gospel in John 3:36 and other passages of Scripture.

2. That, accordingly, Jesus Christ, the Savior of the world, died for all men and for every man, so that he has obtained for all, by his death on the cross, reconciliation and remission of sins; yet so that no one is partaker of this remission except the believers (John 3:16 and 1 John 2:2).

3. That man has not saving grace of himself, nor of the working of his own free-will, inasmuch as in his state of apostasy and sin he can for himself and by himself think nothing that is good—nothing, that is, truly good, such as saving faith is, above all else. But that it is necessary that by God, in Christ and through his Holy Spirit he be born again and renewed in understanding, affections and will and in all his faculties, that he may be able to understand, think, will, and perform what is truly good, according to the Word of God (John 15:5).

4. That this grace of God is the beginning, the progress and the end of all good; so that even the regenerate man can neither think, will nor effect any good, nor withstand any temptation to evil, without grace precedent (or prevenient), awakening, following and cooperating. So that all good deeds and all movements toward good that can be conceived must be ascribed to the grace of God in Christ. But with respect to the mode of operation, grace is not irresistible; for it is written of many that they resisted the Holy Spirit (Acts 7, etc.).

5. That those who are grafted into Christ by a true faith, and have thereby been made partakers of his life-giving Spirit, are abundantly endowed with power to strive against Satan, sin, the world and their own flesh, and to win the victory; always, be it understood, with the help of the grace of the Holy Spirit, with Jesus Christ assisting them in all temptations, through his Spirit; stretching out his hand to them and (providing only that they are themselves prepared for the fight, that they entreat his aid and do not fail to help themselves) propping and upbuilding them so that by no guile or violence of Satan can they be led astray or plucked from Christ's hands (John 10:28). But for the question whether they are not able through sloth or negligence to forsake the

---

2. A critical edition of these articles is in part 4 of Jaroslav Pelikan and Valerie Hotchkiss, eds., *Creeds and Confessions of the Reformation Era*, vol. 2 of *Creeds and Confessions of Faith in the Christian Tradition* (New Haven: Yale University Press, 2003).

beginning of their life in Christ, to embrace again this present world, to depart from the holy doctrine once delivered to them, to lose their good conscience and to neglect grace—this must be the subject of more exact inquiry in the Holy Scriptures, before we can teach it with full confidence of our mind.

FRANCIS TURRETIN: "THE NECESSITY OF THE ATONEMENT" (FROM *INSTITUTES OF ELENCTIC THEOLOGY*)
Latin, 1679–1685

Francis Turretin (1623–1687) was a Protestant scholastic theologian who followed and developed the teachings of John Calvin. Originally "A Historical Sketch of Opinions on the Atonement . . .", this translation of Turretin's writings on the atonement was first published by James R. Wilson in Philadelphia in 1817. The best available text of Turretin's *Institutes* is that of James T. Dennison Jr. (Phillipsburg, NJ: P & R Publishing, 1997).

The Priesthood of Christ, according to the Apostle Paul and the types of the Jewish ritual, is divided into two parts: the atonement which he made to divine justice, and his intercession in heaven (1 John 2:2; Heb. 9:12). The necessity of such an atonement, which is the foundation of all practical piety and all Christian hopes, must therefore be firmly established, and defended against the fiery darts of Satan, with which it is attacked by innumerable adversaries.

Upon this subject, the opinions of divines may be classed under three heads:

1. That of the Socinians, who not only deny that an atonement was made, but affirm that it was not at all necessary, since God both could and would pardon sin, without any satisfaction made to his justice.

2. That of those who distinguish between an absolute and a hypothetical necessity; and in opposition to the Socinians maintain the latter, while they deny the former. By a hypothetical necessity they mean that which flows from the divine decree, God has decreed that an atonement is to be made, therefore it is necessary. To this they also add a necessity of fitness; as the commands of God have been transgressed, it is fit that satisfaction should be made, that the transgressor may not pass with impunity. Yet they deny that it was absolutely necessary, as God, they say, might have devised some other way of pardon than through the medium of an atonement. This is the ground taken by Augustine in his book on the Trinity. Some of the reformers who wrote before the time of Socinus adopt the opinions of that father.

3. That of those who maintain its absolute necessity; affirming that God neither has willed, nor could have willed to forgive sins, without a satisfaction made to his justice. This, the common opinion of the orthodox, is our opinion.

Various errors are maintained on this point by our opponents. The removal of the grounds upon which they rest will throw light upon the whole subject. They err in their views of the nature of sin, for which a satisfaction is required; of the satisfaction itself; of the character of God to whom it is to be rendered; and of Christ by whom it is rendered.

1. Of sin, which renders us guilty, and binds us over to punishment as hated of God. It may be viewed as a debt which we are bound to pay to divine justice, in which sense the law is called a hand-writing (Col. 2:14), as a principle of enmity, whereby we hate God and he becomes our enemy: as a crime against the government of the universe by which, before God, the supreme governor and judge, we become deserving of everlasting death and malediction. Whence, sinners are expressly called debtors (Matt. 6:12); enemies to God, both actively and passively (Col. 1:21); and guilty before God (Rom. 3:19). We, therefore, infer that three things were necessary in order to our redemption; the payment of the debt contracted by sin, the appeasing of the divine wrath, and the expiation of guilt.

2. From the preceding remarks, the nature of the satisfaction which sin requires may be easily perceived. That which we are chiefly to attend to in sin being its criminality, satisfaction has relation to the penalty enacted against it by the Supreme Judge.

But here we must attend to a twofold payment, which is noticed by jurists. One which, by the very deed of payment, sets at liberty the debtor, and annuls the obligation, whether the payment is made by the debtor in his own person, or by a surety in his name; another in which the fact of payment is not sufficient to liberate the debtor because the payment is not precisely that which is demanded in the obligation, but all equivalent. In this case, though the creditor of such payment has a right to refuse the acceptance of it, yet if he admits it and esteems it a payment, it is a satisfaction. The former of these takes place in a pecuniary, the latter in a penal debt. In a pecuniary transaction, the fact of the payment of the sum due frees the debtor, by whomsoever the payment is made. Respect here is had, not to the person paying but to the payment only. Whence, the creditor, having been paid the full amount due, is not said to have treated with indulgence the debtor, or to have forgiven the debt. But in penal matters the case is different. The debt rewards not things, but persons; not what is paid, so much as him who pays; i.e., that the transgressor may be punished. For as the law demands individual personal obedience, so it demands individual personal suffering. In order that the guilty person may be released through an atonement made by another in his stead, the governor or judge must pass a decree to that effect. That decree or act of the judge is, in relation to the law, called relaxation, and in relation to the debtor or guilty person, pardon; for his personal suffering is dispensed with, and in its place a vicarious suffering accepted. But because, in the subject under discussion, sin has not a relation to debt only, but also to punishment, satisfaction is not of that kind, which by the act itself frees the debtor. To effect this there must be an act of pardon passed by the Supreme Judge, because that is not precisely paid, i.e., a personal enduring of the penalty, which the law demands, but a vicarious suffering only. Hence we discover how perfectly accordant remission and satisfaction are with each other, notwithstanding the outcry made by the enemy respecting their supposed discrepancy. Christ made the *satisfaction* in his life and at his death, and God, by accepting this satisfaction, provides for *remission*. The satisfaction respects Christ, from whom God demands a punishment, not numerically, but in kind, the same with that which we owed. Pardon respects believers, who are freed from punishment in their own persons, while a vicarious suffering is accepted. Hence we see how admirably mercy is tempered with justice. Justice is exercised against sin, and mercy toward the sinner; an atonement is made to the divine justice by a surety, and God mercifully pardons us.

3. This reasoning is greatly fortified from a consideration of *the relations in which God stands to the sinner.* He may be viewed in a threefold relation: as the creditor; as the Lord and party offended; and as the judge and ruler. But though both the former relations must be attended to in this matter, yet the third is to be chiefly considered. God here is not merely a creditor, who may at pleasure remit what is his due, nor merely the party offended who may do as he will with his own claims without injury to any one; but he is also a judge and rectoral governor, to whom alone pertains the infliction of punishment upon offenders, and the power of remitting the penal sanction of the law. This all jurists know belongs to the chief magistrate alone. The creditor may demand his debt, and the party offended reparation for the offence or indemnity for his loss; but the judge alone has the power to compel payment, or exact punishment. Here lies the capital error of our adversaries, who maintain that God is to be considered merely in the light of a creditor, who is at liberty to exact or remit the punishment at pleasure. It is however certain, that God sustains the character of judge and ruler of

the world, who has the rights of sovereignty to maintain, and professes himself to be the guardian and avenger of his laws; and hence he possesses not only the claims of a creditor, which he might assert or remit at pleasure, but also the right of government and of punishment, which is naturally indispensable. We must, however, in the punishment itself, distinguish accurately between the enforcing of the penalty, and the manner and circumstances under which it is enforced, as they are things widely different. Punishment may be viewed generally; and in this respect the right of Heaven to inflict it is indispensable, being founded in the divine justice. If there be such an attribute as justice belonging to God, then sin must have its due, which is punishment. But as to the manner and circumstances of the punishment, the case is altogether different. They are not essential to that attribute. They are to be arranged according to his will and pleasure. It may seem fit to the goodness of God that there should be, in relation to time, a delay of punishment; in relation to degree, a mitigation of it; and in relation to persons, a substitution. For although the person sinning deserves punishment and might suffer it with the strictest justice, yet such punishment is not necessarily indispensable. For reasons of great importance, it may be transferred to a surety. In this sense, it is said by divines that sin is of necessity punished impersonally, but every sinner is not therefore of necessity to be punished personally. Through the singular mercy of God some may be exempted from punishment, by the substitution of a surety in their stead.

But that we may conceive it possible for God to do this, he must not be considered as an inferior judge appointed by law. An officer of that character cannot remit anything of the rigor of the law by transferring the punishment from the actual offender to another person. God must be viewed in his true character, as a supreme judge who giveth account of none of his matters, who will satisfy his justice by the punishment of sin, and who, through his infinite wisdom and unspeakable mercy, determines to do this in such a way as shall relax somewhat of the extreme rigor of punishment, by admitting a substitute and letting the sinner go free. Hence we discover to whom the atonement is to be made; whether to the devil (as Socinus, with a sneer, asks), or to God, as sovereign judge. For as the devil is no more than the servant of God, the keeper of the prison, who has no power over sinners, unless by the just judgment of God, the atonement is not to be made to this executor of the divine vengeance, but to the Supreme Ruler, who primarily and principally holds them in durance. We may add that it is a gratuitous and false supposition, that in the suffering of punishment, there must be some person to whom the punishment shall be rendered, as in a pecuniary debt. It is sufficient that there is a judge, who may exact it in order to support the majesty of the State, and maintain the order of the empire.

4. The *person who makes the atonement* is here to be considered. As sin is to be viewed in the threefold light of debt, enmity, and crime; and God in the threefold light of creditor, party offended, and judge; so Christ must put on a threefold relation corresponding to all these. He must sustain the character of a Surety, for the payment of the debt. He must be a Mediator, a peace-maker, to take away the enmity of the parties and reconcile us to God. He must be a Priest and victim, to substitute himself in our room, and make atonement, by enduring the penal sanction of the law. Again: that such an atonement may be made, two things are requisite: 1. That the same *nature* which sins shall make restitution. 2. That the consideration given must possess infinite value, in order to the removal of the infinite demerit of sin.

In Christ, two natures were necessary for the making of an atonement: a human nature, to suffer, and a divine nature, to give the requisite value to his sufferings. Moreover, we must demonstrate how it is possible, in consistency with justice, to substitute an innocent person, as Christ was. In our room;

because such a substitution, at first view, appears to be not only unusual, but also unjust. Though a substitution, which is common in a pecuniary debt, rarely occurs in penal transactions; nay, is sometimes prohibited, as was the case among the Romans, because no one is master of his own life, and because the commonwealth would suffer loss in such cases—yet it was not unknown among the heathen. We have an example of it in Damon and Pythias; two intimate friends, one of whom voluntarily entered himself bail for the other to Dionysius in a capital cause. Curtius, Codrus, and Brutus devoted themselves for their country. The right of punishing hostages, when princes fail in their promises, has been recognized by all nations. Hence hostages are called *anti-psukoi* substitutes. To this Paul alludes, when he says, "For a good man some would even dare to die" (Rom. 5:7). The Holy Scriptures often give it support, not only from the imputation of sin, by which one bears the punishment due to another, but from the public use of sacrifices, in which the victim was substituted in the place of the sinner and suffered death in his stead. Hence the imposition of hands, and the confession of sins over the head of the victims.

But, that such a substitution may be made without the slightest appearance of injustice, various conditions are requisite in the substitute or surety, all which are found in Christ. 1. A common nature, that sin may be punished in the same nature which is guilty (Heb. 2:14). 2. The consent of the will, that he should voluntarily take the burden upon himself: "Lo, I come to do thy will" (Heb. 10:9). 3. Power over his own life, so that he may rightfully determine respecting it, "No one taketh away my life, but I lay it down of myself, for I have power to lay it down, and take it up again" (John 10:18). 4. The power of bearing the punishment due to us, and of freeing both himself and us from the power of death; because, if he himself could be holden of death, he could free no one from its dominion. That Christ possesses this power, no one doubts. 5. Holiness and immaculate purity, that, being polluted by no sin, he might not have to offer sacrifice for himself, but for us only (Heb. 7:26–27).

Under these conditions, it was not unjust for Christ to substitute himself in our room, while he is righteous and we unrighteous. By this act no injury is done to any one. Not to Christ, for he voluntarily took the punishment upon himself, and had the right to decide concerning his own life and death, and also power to raise himself from the dead. Not to God the judge, for he willed and commanded it; nor to his natural justice, for the Surety satisfied this by suffering the punishment which demanded it. Not to the empire of the universe, by depriving an innocent person of life, for Christ, freed from death, lives for evermore; or by the life of the surviving sinner injuring the kingdom of God, for he is converted and made holy by Christ. Not to the divine law, for its honor has been maintained by the perfect fulfillment of all its demands, through the righteousness of the Mediator; and, by our legal and mystical union, he becomes one with us, and we one with him. Hence he may justly take upon him our sin and sorrows, and impart to us his righteousness and blessings. So there is no abrogation of the law, no derogation from its claims; as what we owed is transferred to the account of Christ, to be paid by him.

These preliminary remarks we have thought necessary, in order to the lucid discussion of the question concerning the necessity of the atonement. We now proceed to inquire whether it was necessary that Christ should satisfy for us, as well absolutely, in relation to the divine justice, as hypothetically, on the ground of a divine decree: whether it was absolutely necessary, in order to our salvation, that an atonement should be made, God not having the power to pardon our sins without a satisfaction, or whether it was rendered necessary only by the divine decree? The Socinians, indeed, admit no kind of necessity. Some of the old divines, and some members of the Reformed Church, contend for a hypothetical necessity only. They think it sufficient for the refutation of the heretic. But we, with the great body of the orthodox, contend for both. We do not urge a necessity simply natural, such as that of fire to burn, which is involuntary, and admits of no modification in its exercise. It is a moral and rational necessity for which we plead; one which, as it flows from the holiness and justice of God, and cannot be exercised any other way than freely and voluntarily, admits of various modifications, provided there is no infringement of the natural rights of Deity. That there is such a necessity is evinced by many arguments.

1. The vindicatory justice of God. That such an attribute is natural and essential to God, has been proved at large elsewhere. This avenging justice belongs to God as a judge, and he can no more dispense with it than he can cease to be a judge or deny himself; though, at the same time, he exercises it freely. It does not consist in the exercise of a gratuitous power, like mercy, by which, whether it be exercised or not, injustice is done to no one. It is that attribute by which God gives to every one his due, and from the exercise of which, when proper objects are presented, he can no more abstain, than he can do what is unjust. This justice is the constant will of punishing sinners, which in God cannot be inefficient, as his majesty is supreme and his power infinite. And hence the infliction of punishment upon the transgressor or his surety is inevitable. No objection to this can be drawn from the liberty of God, for that is exercised only in matters of positive enactment, not in such as are of natural right: nor from his mercy, because that, while it may free the sinner from punishment, does not demand that sin shall not be punished.

2. The nature of sin, which is a moral evil and essentially opposed to holiness, forms another argument. The connection between it and physical evil is natural and necessary. As physical or penal evil cannot exist without moral evil, either personal or imputed, so there cannot be moral evil without producing natural evil. Moral and physical good, or holiness and happiness, are united together by the wisdom, as well as by the goodness and justice of God; so that a good man must be happy, for goodness is a part of the divine image. The wicked must be miserable, because God is just; and this the rather, because when God gives blessings to the righteous, he does it of his own bounty, without any merit on their part; but when he punishes the sinner, he renders to him precisely what he has merited by his sins.

3. The sanction of the Law, which threatens death to the sinner (Deut. 27:29; Gen. 2:17; Exod. 18:20; Rom. 1:18–32; 6:23). Since God is true and cannot lie, these threatenings must necessarily be executed either upon the sinner, or upon some one in his stead. In vain do our opponents reply that the threatening is hypothetical, not absolute, and may be relaxed by repentance. This is a gratuitous supposition. That such a condition is either expressed or understood, neither has been nor can be proved. Nay, as the penal sanction of the law is a part of the law itself, which is natural and indispensable, this sanction must also be immutable. With the judicial threatenings of the law, we must not confound particular and economical comminations, or such as are paternal and evangelical, which are denounced against men to recall them to repentance. Such threatenings may be recalled in case of penitence. Of this kind were those denounced against Hezekiah (Isa. 38) and against Nineveh (Jonah 3).

4. The Preaching of the Gospel, which announces the violent and painful death of the Mediator and Surety on the cross, is another argument which power fully confirms the necessity of that event. For we cannot believe that God would multiply sufferings unnecessarily. His goodness and wisdom do not permit us to harbor an idea that the Father could expose his most innocent and beloved Son to an excruciating and ignominious death, without a necessity which admits of no relaxation. The only necessity which can be possibly imagined here is that of making an atonement to the divine justice for our sins. Everyone must perceive that it was absolutely necessary. I know that our opponents affect to produce various other reasons for the accursed death of the cross, such as to confirm Christ's doctrine, and to set an example of all kinds of virtue, especially of charity and constancy! But since Christ had confirmed his doctrines by numerous stupendous miracles and through his life had given the most illustrious examples of every human virtue, who could believe that God, for that one cause alone, would expose his only begotten Son to such dire torments? Therefore, without all doubt, there was another cause for that dispensation, to wit: a regard for the honor of

his justice. To this the Holy Spirit bears witness by the Apostle Paul (Rom. 3:5) who affirms that God hath set forth Christ to be a propitiation for our sins to declare his righteousness, which was inexorable, and did not suffer our sins to be pardoned on any other terms, than by the intervention of the death of Christ. Again: if God was able and willing by his word alone without any atonement to pardon our sins, why does the Apostle Paul so often and emphatically refer our justification and salvation to the blood of Christ? "We are justified—by the redemption which is in his blood" (Rom. 3:24). We have redemption through his blood; the remission of sins (Eph. 1:7). He hath reconciled all things to himself by the blood of Christ (Col. 1:20). Now there was no need that his blood should be shed if remission depended solely upon the divine will. On this supposition, the apostle would rashly and falsely affirm, what he often affirms, that the blood of bulls and of goats, that is, the sacrifices under the law, could not take away sins; and that the oblation of Christ alone could if there was no need of any purgation, but penitence alone was sufficient to *take away sin*, that is, the guilt of sin, without any sacrifice, the apostle's assertion is groundless. What could be taken away without any sacrifice at all could surely be removed by legal sacrifices. If the divine will alone is necessary, why is it that Paul never refers to it, but always ascends to the nature of things, as when he asserts that it was impossible for the blood of bulls to take away sins? Surely it must be because sin is so hateful to God, that its stain can be washed away by nothing less than the blood of the Son of God.

5.   If there was no necessity that Christ should die, the greatness of God's love in not sparing his own Son, but delivering him up for us all, which the apostle commends, will be not a little diminished. If there was no obstacle on the part of justice, in the way of our salvation, it would indeed have been great grace in God to have forgiven our sins. But it would have fallen far short of that stupendous love which, though justice inexorable stood in the way, removed, by means found in the treasures of infinite wisdom, all impediments to our redemption, displaying a most amiable harmony between justice and mercy. Nor can Christ be said to have appeased the wrath of God, if he, without demanding any satisfaction, could by a mere volition have laid aside his own wrath.

6.   Finally, our opinion relative to the necessity of an atonement does not, in the least, derogate from any of the Divine Perfections. Not from God's absolute Power, because he can neither deny himself nor any of his attributes, nor can he act in such a way as to give the appearance of delighting in sin, by holding communion with the sinner. Not from the Freedom of his Will, because he can will nothing contrary to his justice and holiness, which would be injured should sin go unpunished. Not from his boundless Mercy, for this is exercised toward the sinner, though punishment is inflicted on the Surety. On the contrary, it makes a glorious display of the most illustrious of the divine perfections: of his Holiness, on account of which he can have no communion with the sinner, until, by an atonement, his guilt is removed and his pollution purged; of his Justice, which inexorably demands punishment of sin; of his Wisdom, in reconciling the respective claims of justice and mercy; and of his Love, in not sparing his own Son in order that he might spare us.

CHAPTER 8

Hermeneutics

The term hermeneutics comes from the Greek *hermeneuein* which means to interpret, translate, or explain. Hermeneutical principles or frameworks are used to guide the understanding of Scripture. In fact, such principles and frameworks are found in Scripture itself wherever an Old Testament passage is drawn on to explain something in the New Testament. In Romans 5:14, for example, we read that Adam "is a type of Him who was to come" (i.e., Christ). Here Paul describes the first Adam as foreshadowing the future Adam (Christ), an approach known as typology, where Adam is the type (Greek *typos*) and Christ is the antitype (*antitypos*) corresponding (in this case antithetically) to the type. While most documents found in this chapter explicitly describe hermeneutical principles, the first document—the Rule of Faith—merely implies such a principle by supplying the theological standard by which all Scripture was to be interpreted. Origen's "Threefold Interpretation of Scripture" soon followed, distinguishing literal from spiritual or mystical interpretations, and Augustine's *On Christian Teaching* opened the floodgate for the discussion of many hermeneutical issues. On the basis of these and other church Fathers, Medieval expositors employed a fourfold approach to interpretation, emphasizing, in turn, historical (literal), allegorical, tropological (moral), and anagogical (future-oriented) understandings. Aquinas, in the excerpt from his *Summa Theologica* included here, affirms that a single word in Scripture can have several senses, and clarifies their use. Finally, Martin Luther's exegesis of Scripture demonstrates his familiarity with and adaptation of the fourfold approach.

THE RULE OF FAITH (*REGULA FIDEI*)
Greek, Second Century A.D.

The rise of theological heresies in the second century made necessary an authoritative guideline for the right interpretation of Scripture. An essential summary of Christian doctrine, the *Rule of Faith* provided a standard—though not static—guideline, which appears in various forms in the church fathers. Compare the two examples of the *Rule of Faith* below, noting (1) the role of the Trinity, (2) the specific ministry and roles of Jesus, (3) the means of salvation, and (4) the life and proper response of faith.

THE RULE OF FAITH CITED BY JUSTIN MARTYR (*FIRST APOLOGY*, CHAPTER 13)

. . . We worship the Maker of this universe, and affirm, as we have been taught, that He needs no blood sacrifice, no libations, and no incense. Yet we praise to the utmost of our power through prayer and thanksgiving for all He supplies. We have been instructed that the only honor worthy of Him is not to consume by fire what He has created for our nurture, but to use it for the good of ourselves and the needy, and, with thankful voices, to offer Him thanks through prayers and hymns for our creation, for preserving our health, for the changes of the seasons, and petition Him for eternal life through faith in Him. Our teacher in these things is Jesus Christ, who was born for this purpose, who was crucified under Pontius Pilate, procurator of Judea during the reign of Tiberius Caesar. And we will demonstrate that our worship of Him is reasonable, since we have learned that He is the Son of the living God Himself, second only to the Father, and after whom the prophetic Spirit in the third. On account of this they say we are deranged: that we hold a crucified man up next to the unchangeable and eternal God, Creator of everything, yet this because they cannot discern the mystery that lies herein. To this mystery, then, we now ask you to turn your attention as we endeavor to clarify it for you.

THE RULE OF FAITH CITED BY IRENAEUS (*AGAINST HERESIES*, 1.10.1)

The Church, though dispersed through the whole world, even to the ends of the earth, has received from the Apostles and their disciples this faith: [She believes] in one God, the Father Almighty, Maker of heaven, and earth, and the sea, and all things that are in them; and in one Christ Jesus, the Son of God, who became incarnate for our salvation; and in the Holy Spirit, who proclaimed through the prophets the dispensations of God, and the advents, and the birth from a virgin, and the passion, and the resurrection from the dead, and the ascension into heaven in the flesh of the beloved Christ Jesus, our Lord, and His [future] manifestation from heaven in the glory of the Father to gather all things in one, and to raise up anew all flesh of the whole human race, in order that to Christ Jesus, our Lord, and God, and Savior, and King, according to the will of the invisible Father, every knee should bow, of things in heaven, and things in earth, and things under the earth, and that every tongue should confess to Him, and that He should execute just judgment toward all; Yet, that He may send into everlasting fire the spiritual forces of wickedness, together with the angels who transgressed and became apostates, the ungodly, the unrighteous, and the wicked and profane among men; but that He may bestow life on the righteous and holy, those who have kept His commandments and have persevered in His love—both those who did so from the beginning and those who did so after their repentance—as an act of grace, clothing them with everlasting glory.

ORIGEN: "THREEFOLD INTERPRETATION OF SCRIPTURE" (FROM *ON FIRST PRINCIPLES*)
Greek, Late Second Century A.D.

For a biographical introduction to Origen, see page 93.

Questions for Guided Reading
1. What are the three "senses" or aspects of Scripture, and what does each represent?
2. How does a study of numbers, and particularly the number 6, enlighten Scriptural study?
3. What if a passage has neither a literal nor a logical interpretation, what then?
4. What role do apparent contradictions and historical problems in Scripture serve in our understanding?

◆

It appears to us that the right way of approaching the Scriptures and gathering their meaning is found in the writings themselves. As Solomon in the Proverbs says, "Behold, you are to portray these things to yourself threefold in counsel and knowledge, so that you can answer in truth those who question you." Now the simple person is, first of all, edified by what we may call the flesh of the Scripture—the name being given to the obvious (literal) interpretation. Those who begin to make further progress in understanding and are able to perceive something more are edified by the soul of Scripture. Finally, those who are perfect, of whom the apostle says: "We speak wisdom among the perfect; yet a wisdom not of this world, nor of the rulers of this world, which are coming to nothing; but we speak God's wisdom hidden in a mystery, the wisdom which God foreordained before the worlds unto our glory," these are edified by that spiritual law, which has "a shadow of the things to come," as if by the Spirit. Just as man, therefore, is said to consist of body, soul, and spirit, so also does Holy Scripture, which has been bestowed by the divine bounty for man's salvation. We must certainly not forget, however, that there are some passages of Scripture in which this that we call the body (or flesh), that is, the logical and literal meaning, is not found; and there are also passages where those meanings which we have called the soul and the spirit are alone to be looked for. I believe this is taught in the gospels, when six waterpots are said to be set there for the purifying of the Jews, containing two or three measures each (John 2:6). For those who are said by the apostle Paul to be Jews inwardly (Rom. 2:29) are purified through the word of Scripture by receiving in some cases two measures, that is, by accepting the soul meaning and the spiritual meaning in accordance with what we have said above, and in other cases three measures, when the reading also retains for the edification of the hearers a bodily meaning, namely the literal one. And the six waterpots are mentioned in allusion to those who are being purified while living in the world. For we read that this world and all that is in it were completed in six days, which is a perfect number.[1] The value which there is in the first or literal meaning is evident from the multitude of Christians who accept the faith simply and without doubt. This requires no long argument because it is obvious to all. But of the kind of explanation which we have spoken of above as the soul of Scripture, many illustrations are given us by the apostle Paul. For example, in his epistle to the Corinthians he says, "As it is written, do not muzzle the ox that treads out the grain." Then in explaining how this precept ought to be understood, he adds: "Is for oxen that God is concerned? Or does he not speak entirely for our sake? It was indeed written for our sakes, for whoever plows should plow in hope and whoever threshes should thresh in hope of a share in the crop" (1 Cor. 9:9–10). But a spiritual explanation is one that is able to show of what heavenly things those who are Jews according to the flesh serve as an image, or of what good things to come the law serves as a shadow, or whenever we ask what is that wisdom hidden in a mystery, which God foreordained before the world for our glory, which none of the rulers of this world understood (1 Cor 2:7–8) . . . studies of this kind succeed only with the utmost purity and sobriety and through nights of watching, by which means one may be able to trace out the deeply hidden meaning of the Spirit of God, concealed in the language of an ordinary narrative which points in a different direction, and that so one might become a sharer of the Spirit's knowledge and a partaker of His

divine counsel. For in no other way can the soul reach perfection of knowledge except by being inspired with the truth of divine wisdom. Now, divine wisdom has arranged for certain stumbling-blocks and interruptions of the historical sense to be found in Scripture, by inserting in their midst a number of impossibilities and incongruities, that the very interruption of the narrative might present a barrier to the reader and lead him to refuse to proceed along the pathway of the ordinary meaning. We know this because the aim of the Holy Spirit was mainly to preserve the spiritual meaning. Then too, whenever he found that things which had been done in history could be harmonized with the spiritual meaning, he composed in a single narrative a texture comprising both kinds of meaning, always, however, concealing the secret sense more deeply. And it even happens that the Spirit has mingled a few things by which the historical order of the narrative is interrupted and broken, with the object of turning and calling the attention of the reader, by the impossibility of the literal sense, to an examination of the inner meaning.

AUGUSTINE: *ON CHRISTIAN DOCTRINE* (EXCERPTS)
Latin, Late Fourth Century A.D.

See page 71 for a biographical introduction to Augustine. He began this work soon after his appointment as Bishop in A.D. 396, out of his evident concern to identify principles of Scripture interpretation. From the title, doctrina "sums up the entire field of Christian knowledge . . . gathered from its three sources: Scripture, tradition, and the living authority of the church" and is therefore the very first advanced work of Christian education produced by the church.[2] Patterning his work after the grammatical manuals of classical antiquity, Augustine here describes a cautious appropriation of hermeneutical concepts and skills in the understanding and teaching of Scripture. As in his other writings, some of the more interesting and enlightening points are found in asides and many sections hold more for the careful reader than

---

1. A "perfect number" is equal to the sum of its factors (e.g., 6 = 1 x 2 x 3) and carried allegorical significance for the Greeks.

2. John Rotell, ed. *Teaching Christianity.* In *The Works of Saint Augustine: A Translation for the 21st Century* (Hyde Park, NY: New City Press, 1996), 11. The best contemporary translation and notes for *De Doctrina Christiana* are found in this work, translated by Edmond Hill.

the chapter titles may at first suggest. J. F. Shaw's translation On Christian Doctrine (Edinburgh: T & T Clark, 1873) is the basis of the following paraphrase. Included here are Book 1 in its entirety and two key chapters from Book 2. This work is numbered by chapters and sections, following standard editions of Augustine, but that numbering does not always coincide.

Augustine divides his work into two parts: one relating to the discovery, the other to the expression, of the true sense of Scripture. He shows that to discover the meaning we must attend both to "things" (i.e., content) and to their "signs" (by which he refers to letters, spoken and written words, pictures, gestures, etc.). It is necessary, he points out, to know what should be taught to Christians and exactly how it is best taught. In this first book he addresses content ("things"), which he divides into three classes—things to be enjoyed, things to be used, and things which we use and enjoy. The only object which ought to be enjoyed is the triune God, who is our highest good and true happiness. Although our sinful nature would keep us from enjoying God, "the word was made flesh, so that our sins might be taken away. And if our sins are remitted and our souls renewed by grace, we may await with hope the resurrection of the body to eternal glory; if not, we shall be raised to everlasting punishment." Having expounded the content of faith, Augustine goes on to show that all objects, except God, are for our "use." For, though some of these things may be "loved," yet our love is not to rest in them, but must point ultimately to God. And we ourselves are not objects of enjoyment to God. Even though he "uses" us, he does so for our own advantage. He then goes on to show that love—the love of God for his own sake and the love of our neighbor for God's sake—is the fulfillment and the end of all Scripture. Faith, hope, and love are, finally, essential graces for whoever would rightly understand and explain the Holy Scriptures.

✦

BOOK I

Chapter I: Understanding Scripture and communicating its meaning to others

There are two things upon which all interpretation of Scripture depends: discovering the proper meaning, and then communicating the meaning that has been discovered. First we will consider the discovery process, then the communication of the meaning—a great challenge to carry out, indeed even to attempt. And such an attempt would be presumptuous if I were counting on my own strength; but since my hope of accomplishing the work rests on Him who has already supplied me with many thoughts on this subject, I do not fear but that He will go on to supply what is yet wanting when once I have begun to use what He has already given. For a possession which is not diminished by being shared with others, if it is possessed and not shared, is not yet possessed as it ought to be possessed. The Lord says "Whoever has shall be given more" (Mark 4:25). He will give, then, to those who have; that is to say, if they use freely and cheerfully what they have received, He will add to and perfect His gifts. The loaves in the miracle were only five and seven in number before the disciples began to divide them among the hungry people. But when once they began to distribute them, though the wants of so many thousands were satisfied, they filled baskets with the fragments that were left. Now, just as that bread increased in the very act of breaking it, so those thoughts which the Lord has already given to me with a view to undertaking this work will, as soon as I begin to impart them to others, be multiplied by His grace, so that, in this very work of distribution in which I have engaged, so far from incurring loss and poverty, I shall be made to rejoice in a marvelous increase of wealth.

Chapter II: Things and their signs

All instruction is either about things or their signs; but notice that things are learned by means of their signs. I am using the word "thing" in a strict sense, to signify that which is never employed as a sign of anything else: for example, wood, stone, cattle, and other things of that kind. Not, however, the wood which we read Moses cast into the bitter waters to make them sweet, nor the stone which Jacob used as a pillow, nor the ram which Abraham offered up instead of his son; for these, though they are things, are also signs of other things. There are signs of another kind, those which are never employed except as signs: for example, words. No one uses words except as signs of something else; and this is what I mean by signs: those things which are used to indicate something else. Accordingly, every sign is also a thing; for what is not a thing is nothing at all. Every thing, however, is not also a sign. And so, in regard to this distinction between things and signs, I shall, when I speak of things, speak in such a way that even if some of them may be used as signs also, that will not interfere with the division of the subject according to which I am to discuss things first and signs afterward. We must know things in themselves, not what other things they are signs of.

Chapter III: Some things are for use, others for enjoyment

There are some things which are to be enjoyed while others which are to be used, and vice versa. Those things which are objects of enjoyment make us happy. Those things which are objects of use assist, and support us in our efforts to pursue happiness. Having access to both enjoyable and useful things, if we attempt to enjoy things we ought to use, we may become ensnared in a love of lesser things, lagging behind or else turning aside from the pursuit of the real and proper objects of enjoyment.

Chapter IV: The difference between use and enjoyment

To enjoy a thing is to rest with satisfaction in it for its own sake. To use, on the other hand, is to employ whatever means are at one's disposal to obtain what one desires, if it is a proper object of desire; for an unlawful use ought rather to be called an abuse. Suppose, then, we were wanderers in a strange country , and could not live happily away from our fatherland, and that we felt wretched in our wandering, and wishing to put an end to our misery, determined to return home. We find, however, that we must make use of some means of transportation, either by land or water, to reach home where our enjoyment begins. Now, the beauty of the country through which we pass and the very pleasure of the trip charm our hearts. And the things we ought to use become objects of enjoyment. So we become unwilling to hurry the end of our journey and are diverted from the home whose delights would truly make us happy. And this is a parable of our mortal lives. We have wandered far from God and if we wish to return to our Father's home, this world must be used, not enjoyed, so that the invisible things of God may be clearly seen, being understood by the things that are made (Rom. 1:20).

Therefore, by means of what is material and temporary we may grasp the spiritual and eternal.

Chapter V: The Trinity is the true object of enjoyment

The true objects of enjoyment, then, are the Father and the Son and the Holy Spirit, who are at the same time the Trinity, one Being, supreme above all, and common to all who enjoy Him (that is, if He is an object, and not rather the cause of all objects, or indeed even if He is the cause of all). For it is not easy to find a name that will suitably express so great an excellence, unless it is better to speak in this way: The Trinity, one God, from whom are all things, through whom are all things, in whom are all things (Rom. 11:36). Thus the Father and the Son and the Holy Spirit, and each of these by Himself, is God, and at the same time they are all one God; and each of them by Himself is a complete substance, and yet they are all one substance. The Father is not the Son nor the Holy Spirit; the Son is not the Father nor the Holy Spirit; the Holy Spirit is not the Father nor the Son: but the Father is only Father, the Son is only Son, and the Holy Spirit is only Holy Spirit. To all three belong the same eternity, the same unchangeableness, the same majesty, the same power. In the Father is unity, in the Son equality, in the Holy Spirit the harmony of unity and equality; and these three attributes are all one because of the Father, all equal because of the Son, and all harmonious because of the Holy Spirit.

Chapter VI: God is ineffable

Have I fully expressed God's nature or praise? No, not in the least. I want to speak about God but God is inexpressible. Nor is it correct to call God "inexpressible," since to call Him "inexpressible" is to speak of Him. So the contradiction arises: if the inexpressible cannot be expressed, it is not inexpressible if it can be called inexpressible. Now this contradiction should simply be avoided by silence rather than explained away by speech. And yet God, although nothing worthy of His greatness can be said of Him, has condescended to accept the worship of human mouths. Indeed, He desires us by means of our own words to rejoice in His praise. This is why He is called *Deus* (God). For the sound of those two syllables in itself conveys no true knowledge of His nature; yet all who know the Latin tongue are led, when that sound reaches their ears, to think of a nature supreme in excellence and eternal in existence.

Chapter VII: What everyone should understand by the term "God"

Whoever ponders the one supreme God of gods, even if he believes in the existence of other gods, calls them by that name and worships them as gods, in pondering he is attempting to grasp the very nature of that than which nothing more excellent or exalted exists. And since humans are moved by various kinds of good-some of which are sense-related while others are essentially rational, those (people) who are inclined to trust their eyes, ears and other senses, imagine that either the heavens or the brightest object in the heavens is the God of gods. When such thinking attempts to press beyond the visible cosmos, it pictures a dazzling brightness, or else conceives vaguely of infinity or of the most beautiful form imaginable—which is represented in the form of the human body. Even if he imagines there is no one supreme God but many gods of equal rank, these too are conceived as possessing shape and form according to his view of excellence. Those, however, who by intelligence reach a conception of God (as supreme), place Him above all visible and bodily natures, and even above all intelligent and spiritual natures that are subject to change. All, however, strive to exalt the excellence of God. Nor can one be found who believes that any being to whom there exists a superior is God. And so all believe that God is that which excels in dignity all other objects.

Chapter VIII: God is esteemed above all because He is unchangeable wisdom

All who think about God must think of Him as something living—indeed, as life itself. For whatever bodily form one considers, it is life that animates and gives the body value, and it is life, regardless of the body's splendor, that is valued above the bodily form. So then, when one considers the nature of the life itself, if it be mere nutritive life without sensibility such as that of plants, then it is considered inferior to sentient life such as that of cattle, and intelligent life such as that of humankind is, of course, placed higher still. But even intelligent life is subject to change such that some sort of unchangeable life must rank higher. Those who have become wise, for example, were unwise prior to becoming wise. Yet wisdom itself was never unwise and can never be so. Those who have never glimpsed unchangeable wisdom could never with entire confidence prefer a life which is unchangeably wise to one that is subject to change. This will be evident, if we consider that the very rule of truth by which they affirm the unchangeable life to be the more excellent, is itself unchangeable: and they cannot find such a rule, except by going beyond their own nature; for they find nothing in themselves that is not subject to change.

Chapter IX: Everyone recognizes the superiority of unchangeable to variable wisdom

Now then, no one asks, "How do you know that a life of unchangeable wisdom is preferable to one of change?" because that very truth is unchangeably fixed in the minds of all, and presented to our common contemplation. And the one who does not see it is like a blind man in the sun, for whom the splendor of light profits nothing. The one, on the other hand, who sees but shrinks back from this truth is weak in his mental vision from dwelling too long among the shadows of the flesh. And so humans are driven back from their native land by contrary blasts of evil habits, and they pursue lower and less valuable objects in preference to that which they own to be more excellent and more worthy.

Chapter X: To see God the soul must be purified

Since it is our duty fully to enjoy the truth which lives unchangeably, and since the triune God takes counsel in this truth for the things which He has made, the soul must be purified so that it may have power to perceive that light, and to rest in it when it is perceived. And let us look upon this purification as a kind of journey or voyage to our native land. For it is not by change of place that we can come nearer to Him who is in every place, but by the cultivation of pure desires and virtuous habits.

Chapter XI: Wisdom becoming incarnate is, for us, a pattern of purification

Now we would be completely incapable of such cultivation (see above) had not Wisdom condescended to adapt Himself to our weakness, and to show us a pattern of holy life in the form of our own humanity. Yet, since we when we come to Him do wisely, He when He came to us was considered by proud men to have done very foolishly. And since we when we come to Him become strong, He when He came to us was looked upon as weak. But "the foolishness of God is wiser than men; and the weakness of God is stronger than men" (1 Cor. 1:25). And thus, though Wisdom was Himself our home, He made Himself also the way by which we should reach our home.

Chapter XII: How the wisdom of God came to us

And though He is everywhere present to the inner eye when it is sound and clear, He condescended to make Himself manifest to the outward eye of those whose inward sight is weak and dim. "For after that, in the wisdom of God, the world by wisdom knew not God, it pleased God by the foolishness of preaching to save them that believe" (1 Cor. 1:21).

12. Not then in the sense of traversing space, but because He appeared to mortal men in the form of mortal flesh, He is said to have come to us. For He came to a place where He had always been, seeing that "He was in the world, and the world was made by Him." But, because men, who in their eagerness to enjoy the creature instead of the Creator had grown into the likeness of this world, and are therefore most appropriately named "the world," did not recognize Him, therefore the evangelist says, "and the world knew Him not." Thus, in the wisdom of God, the world by wisdom knew not God. Why then did He come, seeing that He was already here, except that it pleased God through the foolishness of preaching to save them that believe?

Chapter XIII: The Word was made flesh

In what way did He come but this, "The Word was made flesh, and dwelt among us"? Just as when we speak, in order that what we have in our minds may enter through the ear into the mind of the heart, the word which we have in our hearts becomes an outward sound and is called speech; and yet our thought does not lose itself in the sound, but remains complete in itself, and takes the form of speech without being modified in its own nature by the change: so the Divine Word, though suffering no change of nature, yet became flesh that He might dwell among us.

Chapter XIV: How the wisdom of God healed man: Likes and opposites

13. Moreover as the use of remedies is the way to health, so this remedy took up sinners to heal and restore them. And just as surgeons, when they bind up wounds, do not do so in a careless manner but carefully and with neatness in the binding, so Wisdom, our medicine, by His assumption of humanity adapted to our wounds, cures some of them by their opposites, some of them by their likes. And just as he who ministers to an injury in some cases applies contraries, as cold to hot, moist to dry, etc., and in other cases applies likes, as a round cloth to a round wound, or an oblong cloth to an oblong wound, and does not fit the same bandage to all limbs, but puts like to like; in the same way the Wisdom of God in healing man has applied Himself to his cure, being Himself healer and medicine both in one. Seeing, then, that humanity fell through pride, He restored him through humility. We were ensnared by the wisdom of the serpent: we are set free by the foolishness of God. Moreover, just as the former was called wisdom, but was in reality the folly of those who despised God, so the latter is called foolishness, but is true wisdom in those who overcome the devil. We used our immortality so badly as to incur the penalty of death: Christ used His mortality so well as to restore us to life. The disease was brought in through a woman's corrupted soul: the remedy came through a woman's virgin body. To the same class of opposite remedies it belongs, that our vices are cured by the example of His virtues. On the other hand, the following are, as it were, bandages made in the same shape as the limbs and wounds to which they are applied: He was born of a woman to deliver us who fell through a woman: He came as a man to save us who are men, as a mortal to save us who are mortals, by death to save us who were dead. And those who can follow out the matter more fully, who are not hurried on by the necessity of carrying out a set undertaking, will find many other points of instruction in considering the remedies, whether opposites or likes, employed in the medicine of Christianity.

Chapter XV: Faith is supported by the resurrection and ascension of Christ, and is stimulated by His coming to judge

14. The belief of the resurrection of our Lord from the dead, and of His ascension into heaven, has strengthened our faith by adding a great buttress of hope. For it clearly "shows how freely He laid down His life for us when He had it in His power thus to take it up again.

With what assurance, then, is the hope of believers animated, when they reflect how great He was who suffered so great things for them while they were still in unbelief. And when anyone looks for Him to come from heaven as the judge of the living and dead, it strikes great terror into the careless, so that they betake themselves to diligent preparation, and learn by holy living to desire His approach, instead of quaking at it on account of their evil deeds. And what tongue can tell, or what imagination can conceive, the reward He will bestow at the last, when we consider that for our comfort in this earthly journey He has given us so freely of His Spirit, that in the adversities of this life we may retain our confidence in, and love for, Him whom as yet we do not see; and that He has also given to each gifts suitable for the building up of His Church, that we may do what He points out as right to be done, not only without a murmur, but even with delight?

Chapter XVI: Christ purifies His church

15. For the Church is His body, as the apostle's teaching shows us; and it is even called His spouse. His body, then, which has many members, and all performing different functions, He holds together in the bond of unity and love, which is its true health. Moreover He exercises it in the present time, and purges it with many wholesome afflictions, so that when He has transplanted it from this world to the eternal world, He may take it to Himself as His bride, without spot or wrinkle, or any such thing.

Chapter XVII: Christ, by forgiving our sins, opened our way home

16. Further, when we are on the way, and that not a way that lies through space, but through a change of affections, and one which the guilt of our past sins like a hedge of thorns barred against us, what could He, who was willing to lay Himself down as the way by which we should return, do that would be still gracious and more merciful, except to forgive us all our sins, and by being crucified for us to remove the stern decrees that barred the door against our return?

Chapter XVIII: The keys are given to the Church

17. He has given, therefore, the keys to His Church, that whatsoever it should bind on earth might be bound in heaven, and whatsoever it should loose on earth might be loosed in heaven; that is to say, that whosoever in the Church should not believe that his sins are remitted, they should not be remitted to him; but that whosoever should believe and should repent, and turn from his sins, should be saved by the same faith and repentance on the ground of which he is received into the bosom of the Church. For he who does not believe that his sins can be pardoned, falls into despair, and becomes worse as if no greater good remained for him than to be evil, when he has ceased to have faith in the results of his own repentance.

Chapter XIX: Bodily and spiritual death and resurrection

18. Furthermore, as there is a kind of death of the soul, which consists in the putting away of former habits and former ways of life, and which comes through repentance, so also the death of the body consists in the dissolution of the former principle of life. And just as the soul, after it has put away and destroyed by repentance its former habits, is created anew after a better pattern, so we must hope and believe that the body, after that death which we all owe as a debt contracted through sin, shall at the resurrection be changed into a better form; not that flesh and blood shall inherit the kingdom of God (for that is impossible), but that this corruptible shall put on incorruption, and this mortal shall put on immortality. And thus the body, being the source of no uneasiness because it can feel no want, shall be animated by a spirit perfectly pure and happy, and shall enjoy unbroken peace.

Chapter XX: The resurrection to eternal judgment

19. Now he whose soul does not die to this world and begin here to be conformed to the truth, falls when the body dies into a more terrible death, and shall revive, not to change his earthly for a heavenly habitation, but to endure the penalty of his sin.

Chapter XXI: Neither body nor soul are extinguished at death

And so faith clings to the assurance, and we must believe that it is so in fact, that neither the human soul nor the human body suffers complete extinction, but that the wicked rise again to endure inconceivable punishment, and the good to receive eternal life.

Chapter XXII: God alone is to be enjoyed

20. Among all these things, then, those only are the true objects of enjoyment which we have spoken of as eternal and unchangeable. The rest are for use, that we may be able to arrive at the full enjoyment of the former. We, however, who enjoy and use other things are things ourselves. For a great thing truly is man, made after the image and similitude of God, not as respects the mortal body in which he is clothed, but as respects the rational soul by which he is exalted in honor above the beasts. And so it becomes an important question, whether humans ought to enjoy, or to use, themselves, or to do both. For we are commanded to love one another: but it is a question whether human is to be loved by human for his own sake, or for the sake of something else. If it is for his own sake, we enjoy him; if it is for the sake of something else, we use him. It seems to me, then, that he is to be loved for the sake of something else. For if a thing is to be loved for its own sake, then in the enjoyment of it consists a happy life, the hope of which at least, if not yet the reality, is our comfort in the present time. But a curse is pronounced on him who places his hope in humanity.

21. Neither ought anyone to have joy in himself, if you look at the matter clearly, because no one ought to love even himself for his own sake, but for the sake of Him who is the true object of enjoyment. For no human is in so good a state as when his whole life is a journey toward the unchangeable life, and his affections are entirely fixed upon that. If, however, he loves himself for his own sake, he does not look at himself in relation to God, but turns his mind in upon himself, and so is not occupied with anything that is unchangeable. And thus he does not enjoy himself at his best, because he is better when his mind is fully fixed upon, and his affections wrapped up in, the unchangeable good, than when he turns from that to enjoy even himself. Therefore if you ought not to love even yourself for your own sake, but for His in whom your love finds its most worthy object, no other man has a right to be angry if you love him too for God's sake. For this is the law of love that has been laid down by Divine authority: "Thou shalt love thy neighbor as thyself"; but, "Thou shalt love God with all thy heart, and with all thy soul, and with all thy mind": so that you are to concentrate all your thoughts, your whole life and your whole intelligence upon Him from whom you derive all that you bring. For when He says, "With all thy heart, and with all thy soul, and with all thy mind," He means that no part of our life is to be unoccupied, and to afford room, as it were, for the wish to enjoy some other object, but that whatever else may suggest itself to us as an object worthy of love is to be borne into the same channel in which the whole current of our affections flows. Whoever, then, loves his neighbor rightly, should urge him to love God with his whole heart, and soul, and mind. For in this way, loving his neighbor as himself, a man turns the whole current of his love both for himself and his neighbor into the channel of the love of God, which suffers no stream to be drawn off from itself by whose diversion its own volume would be diminished.

Chapter XXIII: Man needs no command to love himself and his own body

22. Those things which are objects of use are not all, however, to be loved, but only those that are either united with us in a common relation to God, such as a man or an angel, or are so related to us as to need the goodness of God through our instrumentality, such as the body. For assuredly the martyrs did not love the wickedness of their persecutors, although they used it to attain the favor of God. As, then, there are four kinds of things that are to be loved—first, that which is above us; second, ourselves; third, that which is on a level with us; fourth, that which is beneath us—no precepts need be given about the second and fourth of these. For, however far a man may fall away from the truth, he still continues to love himself, and to love his own body. The soul which flies away from the unchangeable Light, the Ruler of all things, does so that it may rule over itself and over its own body; and so it cannot but love both itself and its own body.

23. Moreover, it thinks it has attained something very great if it is able to lord it over its companions, that is, other humans. For it is inherent in the sinful soul to desire above all things, and to claim as due to itself, that which is properly due to God only. Now such love of itself is more correctly called hate. For it is not just that it should desire what is beneath it to be obedient to it while itself will not obey its own superior; and most justly has it been said, "He who loves iniquity hates his own soul." And accordingly the soul becomes weak, and endures much suffering about the mortal body. For, of course, it must love the body, and be grieved at its corruption;

and the immortality and incorruptibility of the body spring out of the health of the soul. Now the health of the soul is to cling steadfastly to the better part, that is, to the unchangeable God. But when it aspires to lord it even over those who are by nature its equals—that is, its fellow-men—this is a reach of arrogance utterly intolerable.

Chapter XXIV: No one hates his own flesh

24. No man, then, hates himself. On this point, indeed, no question was ever raised by any sect. But neither does any man hate his own body. For the apostle says truly, "No man ever yet hated his own flesh." And when some people say that they would rather be without a body altogether, they entirely deceive themselves. For it is not their body, but its corruptions and its heaviness, that they hate. And so it is not no body, but an uncorrupted and very light body, that they want. But they think a body of that kind would be no body at all, because they think such a thing as that must be a spirit. And as to the fact that they seem to scourge their bodies by abstinence and toil, those who do this in the right spirit do not do so to get rid of their body, but that they may have it in subjection and ready for every needful work. For they strive by a kind of toilsome exercise of the body itself to root out those lusts that are hurtful to the body, that is, those habits and affections of the soul that lead to the enjoyment of unworthy objects. They are not destroying themselves; they are taking care of their health.

25. Those, on the other hand, who do this in a perverse spirit, make war upon their own body as if it were a natural enemy. And in this matter they are led astray by a mistaken interpretation of what they read: "The flesh lusts against the spirit, and the spirit against the flesh, and these are contrary the one to the other." For this is said of the carnal habit not yet mastered, against which the spirit lusts, not to destroy the body, but to eradicate the lust of the body, i.e., its evil habit, and thus to make it subject to the spirit, which is what the order of nature demands. For as, after the resurrection, the body, having become wholly subject to the spirit, will live in perfect peace to all eternity; even in this life we must make it an object to have the carnal habit changed for the better, so that its inordinate affections may not war against the soul. And until this shall take place, "the flesh lusts against the spirit, and the spirit against

the flesh"; the spirit struggling, not in hatred, but for the mastery, because it desires that what it loves should be subject to the higher principle; and the flesh struggling, not in hatred, but because of the bondage of habit which it has derived from its parent stock, and which has grown in upon it by a law of nature till it has become inveterate. The spirit, then, in subduing the flesh, is working as it were to destroy the ill-founded peace of an evil habit, and to bring about the real peace which springs out of a good habit. Nevertheless, not even those who, led astray by false notions, hate their bodies would be prepared to sacrifice one eye, even supposing they could do so without suffering any pain, and that they had as much sight left in one as they formerly had in two, unless some object was to be attained which would overbalance the loss. This and other indications of the same kind are sufficient to show those who candidly seek the truth how well-founded is the statement of the apostle when he says, "No man ever yet hated his own flesh." He adds too, "but nourishes and cherishes it, even as the Lord the Church."

Chapter XXV: That he loves something more does not mean a man hates his body

26. Man, therefore, ought to be taught the due measure of loving, that is, in what measure he may love himself so as to be of service to himself. For that he does love himself, and does desire to do good to himself, nobody but a fool would doubt. He is to be taught, too, in what measure to love his body, so as to care for it wisely and within due limits. For it is equally manifest that he loves his body also, and desires to keep it safe and sound. And yet a man may have something that he loves better than the safety and soundness of his body. For many have been found voluntarily to suffer both pains and amputations of some of their limbs that they might obtain other objects which they valued more highly. But no one is to be told not to desire the safety and health of his body because there is something he desires more. For the miser, though he loves money, buys bread for himself—that is, he gives away money that he is very fond of and desires to heap up—but it is because he values more highly the bodily health which the bread sustains. It is superfluous to argue longer on a point so very plain, but this is just what the error of wicked men often compels us to do.

Chapter XXVI: The command to love God and our neighbors includes a command to love ourselves

27. Seeing, then, that there is no need of a command that every man should love himself and his own body, seeing, that is, that we love ourselves, and what is beneath us but connected with us, through a law of nature which has never been violated, and which is common to us with the beasts (for even the beasts love themselves and their own bodies), it only remained necessary to lay injunctions upon us in regard to God above us, and our neighbor beside us. "You shall love," He says, "the Lord your God with all your heart, and with all your soul, and with all your mind; and you shall love your neighbor as yourself. On these two commandments hang all the law and the prophets." Thus the end of the commandment is love, and that twofold, the love of God and the love of our neighbor. Now, if you take yourself in your entirety, that is, soul and body together, and your neighbor in his entirety, soul and body together (for a human is comprised of soul and body), you will find that none of the classes of things that are to be loved is overlooked in these two commandments. For though, when the love of God comes first, and the measure of our love for Him is prescribed in such terms that it is evident all other things are to find their center in Him, nothing seems to be said about our love for ourselves; yet when it is said, "You shall love your neighbor as yourself," it at once becomes evident that our love for ourselves has not been overlooked.

Chapter XXVII: The order of love

28. Now he is a man of just and holy life who forms an unprejudiced estimate of things, and keeps his affections also under strict control, so that he neither loves what he ought not to love, nor fails to love what he ought to love, nor loves that more which ought to be loved less, nor loves that equally which ought to be loved either less or more, nor loves that less or more which ought to be loved equally. No sinner is to be loved as a sinner; and every human is to be loved as a human for God's sake; but God is to be loved for His own sake. And if God is to be loved more than any human, each man ought to love God more than himself. Likewise we ought to love another person better than our own body, because all things are to be loved in reference to God, and another person can have fellowship with us in the enjoyment of

God, whereas our body cannot; for the body only lives through the soul, and it is by the soul that we enjoy God.

Chapter XXVIII: How to decide whom to help

29. Furthermore, men are to be loved equally. But since you cannot do good to all, you are to pay special regard to those who, by the accidents of time, or place, or circumstance, are brought into closer connection with you. Or, suppose that you had a great deal of some commodity, and felt bound to give it away to somebody who had none, and that it could not be given to more than one person; if two persons presented themselves, neither of whom had either from need or relationship a greater claim upon you than the other, you could do nothing fairer than choose by lot to which you would give what could not be given to both. Just so among men: since you cannot consult for the good of them all, you must take the matter as decided for you by a sort of lot, according as each man happens for the time being to be more closely connected with you.

Chapter XXIX: Desire and work for the conversion of all

30. Now of all who can with us enjoy God, we love partly those to whom we render services, partly those who render services to us, partly those who both help us in our need and in turn are helped by us, partly those upon whom we confer no advantage and from whom we look for none. We ought to desire, however, that they should all join with us in loving God, and all the assistance that we either give them or accept from them should tend to that one end. For in the theaters, dens of iniquity though they be, if someone is fond of a particular actor, and enjoys him as a great or even as the very greatest good, he is fond of all who join with him in admiration of his favorite, not for their own sakes, but for the sake of him whom they admire in common; and the more fervent he is in his admiration, the more he works in every way he can to secure new admirers for him, and the more anxious he becomes to show him to others; and if he find anyone comparatively indifferent, he does all he can to excite his interest by urging his favorite's merits: if, however, he meet with anyone who opposes him, he is exceedingly displeased by such a man's contempt of his favorite, and strives in every way he can to remove it. Now, if this be so, what does it become us to do who live in the fellowship of

the love of God, the enjoyment of whom is true happiness of life, to whom all who love Him owe both their own existence and the love they bear Him, concerning whom we have no fear that anyone who comes to know Him will be disappointed in Him, and who desires our love, not for any gain to Himself, but that those who love Him may obtain an eternal reward, even Himself whom they love? And hence it is that we love even our enemies. For we do not fear them, seeing they cannot take away from us what we love; but we pity them rather, because the more they hate us the more are they separated from Him whom we love. For if they would turn to Him, they must of necessity love Him as the supreme good, and love us too as partakers with them in so great a blessing.

Chapter XXX: Are angels our neighbors, too?

31. There arises further in this connection a question about angels. For they are happy in the enjoyment of Him whom we long to enjoy; and the more we enjoy Him in this life as through a glass darkly, the more easy do we find it to bear our pilgrimage, and the more eagerly do we long for its termination. But it is not irrational to ask whether in those two commandments is included the love of angels also. For that He who commanded us to love our neighbor made no exception, as far as men are concerned, is shown both by our Lord Himself in the Gospel, and by the Apostle Paul. For when the man to whom our Lord delivered those two commandments, and to whom He said that on these hang all the law and the prophets, asked Him, "And who is my neighbor?" He told him of a certain man who, going down from Jerusalem to Jericho, fell among thieves, and was severely wounded by them, and left naked and half dead. And He showed him that nobody was neighbor to this man except him who took pity upon him and came forward to relieve and care for him. And the man who had asked the question admitted the truth of this when he was himself interrogated in turn. To whom our Lord says, "Go and do likewise"; teaching us that he is our neighbor whom it is our duty to help in his need, or whom it would be our duty to help if he were in need. Whence it follows, that he whose duty it would be in turn to help us is our neighbor. For the name "neighbor" is a relative one, and no one can be neighbor except to a neighbor. And, again, who does not see that no exception is made of anyone as a person

to whom the offices of mercy may be denied when our Lord extends the rule even to our enemies? "Love your enemies, do good to them that hate you."

32. And so also the Apostle Paul teaches when he says: "For this, 'You shall not commit adultery, You shall not kill, You shall not steal, You shall not bear false witness, You shall not covet'; and if there be any other commandment, it is briefly comprehended in this saying, namely, You shall love thy neighbor as thyself. Love works no ill to his neighbor." Whoever then supposes that the apostle did not embrace every man in this precept, is compelled to admit, what is at once most absurd and most pernicious, that the apostle thought it no sin, if a person were not a Christian or were an enemy, to commit adultery with his wife, or to kill him, or to covet his goods. And as nobody but a fool would say this, it is clear that every man is to be considered our neighbor, because we are to work no ill to any man.

33. But now, if every one to whom we ought to show, or who ought to show to us, the offices of mercy is by right called a neighbor, it is manifest that the command to love our neighbor embraces the holy angels also, seeing that so great offices of mercy have been performed by them on our behalf, as may easily be shown by turning the attention to many passages of Holy Scripture. And on this ground even God Himself, our Lord, desired to be called our neighbor. For our Lord Jesus Christ points to Himself under the figure of the man who brought aid to him who was lying half dead on the road, wounded and abandoned by the robbers. And the Psalmist says in his prayer, "I behaved myself as though he had been my friend or brother." But as the Divine nature is of higher excellence than, and far removed above, our nature, the command to love God is distinct from that to love our neighbor. For He shows us pity on account of His own goodness, but we show pity to one another on account of His; that is, He pities us that we may fully enjoy Himself; we pity one another that we may fully enjoy Him.

Chapter XXXI: God uses rather than enjoys us

34. And on this ground, when we say that we enjoy only that which we love for its own sake, and that nothing is a true object of enjoyment except that which makes us happy, and that all other things are for use, there seems still to be something that requires explanation. For God loves us, and Holy Scripture frequently

sets before us the love He has toward us. In what way then does He love us? As objects of use or as objects of enjoyment? If He enjoys us, He must be in need of good from us, and no sane person will say that; for all the good we enjoy is either Himself, or what comes from Himself. And no one can be ignorant or in doubt as to the fact that the light stands in no need of the glitter of the things it has itself lit up. The Psalmist says most plainly, "I said to the Lord, You are my God, for You need not my goodness." He does not enjoy us then, but makes use of us. For if He neither enjoys nor uses us, I am at a loss to discover in what way He can love us.

Chapter XXXII: In what ways God uses humans

35. But neither does He use after our fashion of using. For when we use objects, we do so with a view to the full enjoyment of the goodness of God. God, however, in His use of us, has reference to His own goodness. For it is because He is good we exist; and so far as we truly exist we are good. And, further, because He is also just, we cannot with impunity be evil; and so far as we are evil, so far is our existence less complete. Now He is the first and supreme existence, who is altogether unchangeable, and who could say in the fullest sense of the words, "I AM that I AM," and "You shall say to them, I AM has sent me to you"; so that all other things that exist, both owe their existence entirely to Him, and are good only so far as He has given it to them to be so. That use, then, which God is said to make of us has no reference to His own advantage, but to ours only; and, so far as He is concerned, has reference only to His goodness. When we take pity upon a man and care for him, it is for his advantage we do so; but somehow or other our own advantage follows by a sort of natural consequence, for God does not leave the mercy we show to him who needs it to go without reward. Now this is our highest reward, that we should fully enjoy Him, and that all who enjoy Him should enjoy one another in Him.

Chapter XXXIII: In what way humans are enjoyed

36. For if we find our happiness complete in one another, we stop short upon the road, and place our hope of happiness in human or angel. Now the proud person and the proud angel presume this for themselves, and are glad to have the hope of others fixed upon them. But, on the contrary, the holy person and the holy angel, even when we are weary and anxious to stay with them and rest in them, set themselves to recruit our energies with the provision which they have received of God for us or for themselves; and then urge us thus refreshed to go on our way toward Him, in the enjoyment of whom we find our common happiness. For even the apostle exclaims, "Was Paul crucified for you? or were you baptized in the name of Paul?" and again: "Neither is he that plants anything, neither he that waters; but God that gives the increase." And the angel admonishes the man who is about to worship him, that he should rather worship Him who is his Master, and under whom he himself is a fellow-servant.

37. But when you have joy of a human in God, it is God rather than the human that you enjoy. For you enjoy Him by whom you are made happy, and you rejoice to have come to Him in whose presence you place your hope of joy. And accordingly, Paul says to Philemon, "Yes brother, let me have joy of you in the Lord." For if he had not added "in the Lord," but had only said, "Let me have joy of you," he would have implied that he fixed his hope of happiness upon him, although even in the immediate context to "enjoy" is used in the sense of to "use with delight." For when the thing that we love is near us, it is a matter of course that it should bring delight with it. And if you pass beyond this delight, and make it a means to that which you are permanently to rest in, you are using it, and it is an abuse of language to say that you enjoy it. But if you cling to it, and rest in it, finding your happiness complete in it, then you may be truly and properly said to enjoy it. And this we must never do except in the case of the Blessed Trinity, who is the Supreme and Unchangeable Good.

Chapter XXXIV: Christ is the way to God

38. And mark that even when He who is Himself the Truth and the Word, by whom all things were made, had been made flesh that He might dwell among us, the apostle yet says: "Although we have known Christ according to the flesh, from now on we no longer know in this way." For Christ, desiring not only to give the possession to those who had completed the journey, but also to be Himself the way to those who were just setting out, determined to take a fleshly body. So the expression, "The Lord created me in the beginning of His way," that is, that those who wished to come might begin their journey in Him. The apostle, therefore,

although still on the way, and following after God who called him to the reward of His heavenly calling, yet forgetting those things which were behind, and pressing on toward those things which were before, had already passed over the beginning of the way, and had now no further need of it; yet by this way all must commence their journey who desire to attain to the truth, and to rest in eternal life. For He says: "I am the way, and the truth, and the life," that is, by me men come, to me they come, in me they rest. For when we come to Him, we come to the Father also, because through an equal an equal is known; and the Holy Spirit binds, and as it were seals us, so that we are able to rest permanently in the supreme and unchangeable Good. And thus we may learn how essential it is that nothing should detain us on the way, when not even our Lord Himself, so far as He has condescended to be our way, is willing to detain us, but wishes us rather to press on; and, instead of weakly clinging to temporal things, even though these have been put on and worn by Him for our salvation, to pass over them quickly, and to struggle to attain unto Himself, who has freed our nature from the bondage of temporal things, and has set it down at the right hand of His Father.

Chapter XXXV: The aim and fulfillment of Scripture is love of God and our neighbor

39. Of all, then, that has been said since we entered upon the discussion about things, this is the sum: that we should clearly understand that the fulfillment and the end of the Law, and of all Holy Scripture, is the love of an object which is to be enjoyed, and the love of an object which can enjoy that other in fellowship with ourselves. For there is no need of a command that each. man should love himself. The whole temporal dispensation for our salvation, therefore, was framed by the providence of God that we might know this truth and be able to act upon it; and we ought to use that dispensation, not with such love and delight as if it were a good to rest in, but with a transient feeling rather, such as we have toward the road, or carriages, or other things that are merely means. Perhaps some other comparison can be found that will more suitably express the idea that we are to love the things by which we are borne only for the sake of that toward which we are borne.

Chapter XXXVI: No scriptural interpretation that builds us up in love is entirely deceptive or harmful even if inaccurate; but it should be corrected

40. Whoever, then, thinks that he understands the Holy Scriptures, or any part of them, but puts such an interpretation upon them as does not tend to build up this twofold love of God and our neighbor, does not yet understand them as he ought. If, on the other hand, one draws a meaning from them that may be used for building up in love, even though he does not happen upon the precise meaning which the (scriptural) author intended, his error is not harmful, and he is not guilty of deception. For there is involved in deception the intention to say what is false; and we find plenty of people who intend to deceive, but nobody who wishes to be deceived. Since, then, the one who knows practices deceit, and the ignorant man is practiced upon, it is quite clear that in any particular case the one who is deceived is better than he who deceives, seeing that it is better to suffer than to commit injustice. Now everyone who lies commits an injustice; and if anyone thinks that a lie is ever useful, he must think that injustice is sometimes useful. For no liar keeps faith in the matter about which he lies. He wishes, of course, that the one to whom he lies should place confidence in him; and yet he betrays his confidence by lying to him. Now everyone who breaks faith is unjust. Either, then, injustice is sometimes useful (which is impossible), or a lie is never useful.

41. Whoever takes another meaning out of Scripture than the writer intended, goes astray, but not through any falsehood in Scripture. Nevertheless, as I was going to say, if his mistaken interpretation tends to build up love, which is the end of the commandment, he goes astray in much the same way as one who by mistake leaves the high road, but still reaches through the fields the same place to which the road leads. He is to be corrected, however, and to be shown how much better it is not to leave the straight road, lest, if he get into a habit of going astray, he may sometimes take cross roads, or even go in the wrong direction altogether.

Chapter XXXVII: Dangers of mistaken interpretation

For if he takes up rashly a meaning which the author whom he is reading did not intend, he often falls in with other statements which he cannot harmonize with this meaning. And if he admits that these statements are true and certain, then it follows that the meaning he had put upon the former passage cannot be the true one: and so it comes to pass, one can hardly tell how, that, out of love for his own opinion, he begins to feel more angry with Scripture than he is with himself. And if he should once permit that evil to creep in, it will utterly destroy him. "For we walk by faith, not by sight." Now faith will totter if the authority of Scripture begin to shake. And then, if faith totter, love itself will grow cold. For if a man has fallen from faith, he must necessarily also fall from love; for he cannot love what he does not believe to exist. But if he both believes and loves, then through good works, and through diligent attention to the precepts of morality , he comes to hope also that he shall attain the object of his love. And so these are the three things to which all knowledge and all prophecy are subservient: faith, hope, love.

Chapter XXXVIII: Love never fails

42. But sight shall displace faith; and hope shall be swallowed up in that perfect bliss to which we shall come: love, on the other hand, shall wax greater when these others fail. For if we love by faith that which as yet we see not, how much more shall we love it when we begin to see! And if we love by hope that which as yet we have not reached, how much more shall we love it when we reach it! For there is this great difference between things temporal and things eternal, that a temporal object is valued more before we possess it, and begins to prove worthless the moment we attain it, because it does not satisfy the soul, which has its only true and sure resting-place in eternity: an eternal object, on the other hand, is loved with greater ardor when it is in possession than while it is still an object of desire, for no one in his longing for it can set a higher value on it than really belongs to it, so as to think it comparatively worthless when he finds it of less value than he thought; on the contrary, however high the value any man may set upon it when he is on his way to possess it, he will find it, when it comes into his possession, of higher value still.

Chapter XXXIX: Three sufficient graces: faith, hope, and love

43. And thus one who is resting on faith, hope and love, and who keeps a firm hold upon these, needs only to teach Scripture. So, many live without copies of the Scriptures, even in solitude, on the strength of these three graces. So that in their case, I think, the saying is already fulfilled: "Whether there be prophecies, they shall fail; whether there be tongues, they shall cease; whether there be knowledge, it shall vanish away." Yet by means of these instruments (as they may be called), so great an edifice of faith and love has been built up in them, that, holding to what is perfect, they do not seek for what is only in part perfect of course, I mean, so far as is possible in this life; for, in comparison with the future life, the life of no just and holy person is perfect here. Therefore the apostle says: "Now abides faith, hope, love, these three; but the greatest of these is love"; because, when one reaches the eternal world, while the other two graces will fail, love will remain greater and more assured.

Chapter XL: What type of reader Scripture demands

44. And, therefore, if one fully understands that "the end of the commandment is charity, out of a pure heart, and of a good conscience, and of faith unfeigned," and is bent upon making all his understanding of Scripture to bear upon these three graces, one may come to the interpretation of these books with an easy mind. For while the apostle says "love," he adds "out of a pure heart," to provide against anything being loved but that which is worthy of love. And he joins with this "a good conscience," in reference to hope; for, if one has the burden of a bad conscience, he despairs of ever reaching that which he believes in and loves. And in the third place he says: "and of genuine faith." For if our faith is free from all hypocrisy, then we both abstain from loving what is unworthy of our love, and by living uprightly we are able to indulge the hope that our hope shall not be in vain. For these reasons I have been anxious to speak about the objects of faith, as far as I thought it necessary for my present purpose; for much has already been said on this subject in other volumes, either by others or by myself. And so let this be the end of the present book. In the next I shall discuss, as far as God shall give me light, the subject of signs.

BOOK II

Chapter XLI: What kind of spirit is necessary for studying holy Scripture?

62. When a student of Holy Scriptures is prepared as I have suggested and begins his study, let him constantly meditate on the Apostle's statement, "Knowledge puffs up, but love edifies" (1 Cor. 8:1). Whatever riches he may bring with him out of Egypt, unless he has kept the Passover he will not be safe. Now then, Christ is our Passover sacrificed for us (1 Cor. 5:7), and there is nothing this sacrifice teaches more clearly than the call He himself offers to those toiling in Egypt under Pharaoh: "Come to me all you who labor and are heavy laden and I will give you rest. Take my yoke upon you and learn of me; for I am meek and lowly in heart, and you will find rest for your souls. For my yoke is easy and my burden is light" (Matt. 11:28–30). To whom else would this yoke seem light-weight but the meek and lowly in heart, whom knowledge does not puff up but love edifies? Recall that those who first celebrated the Passover (in type and shadow), as they marked their door-posts with the blood of the lamb, did so with hyssop. Although this is a meek and lowly herb, nothing is stronger and more penetrating than its roots. In this way we too are "rooted and grounded in love, and able to comprehend with all saints what is the breadth and length and depth and height," that is, to comprehend the cross of our Lord—the breadth of which is indicated by the cross-bar constricting the hands, and its length from the ground up to the cross-bar on which the torso from the head downward is fixed, its height from the crossbar to the top on which the head rests, and its depth by that which lies hidden, buried in the earth. By the sign of the cross all Christian action is symbolized—to do good works in Christ, to remain steadfast in Him, to hope for heaven, and not to desecrate the sacraments. Purified by all this we shall be able to know "the love of Christ which surpasses knowledge," in which He through whom all things were made is equal to the Father, "so that we may be filled with all the fullness of God" (Eph. 3:17–19). Hyssop also possesses a purifying property, to keep the lungs from swelling with pride, that is, from becoming puffed up with knowledge about those riches brought out from Egypt. "Purge me with hyssop," the Psalmist says, "and I shall be clean; wash me, and I shall be whiter than snow. Let me hear joy and gladness." Then in order to show that hyssop points to purification from pride, he adds, "that the bones You have broken may rejoice" (Ps. 51:7–8).

Chapter XLII: Scripture compared with pagan works

63. Poor as the gold, silver, and garments from Egypt were in comparison with the riches attained at Jerusalem and which reached their summit during Solomon's kingdom, meager also is the knowledge gathered from pagan books when compared with Holy Scripture. Whatever found outside of them is to be condemned if hurtful, but if useful it will also be found in them. After you have found everything of use that is also found in others' books, you will discover much more that can be learned nowhere else but in the wonderful sublimity and simplicity of the Scriptures. When, therefore, the reader has grasped the instruction of book 2 such that unknown signs are no longer a hindrance; when he becomes meek and lowly of heart, subject to the easy yoke of Christ, fitted with His light burden, rooted and grounded and built up in faith, so that knowledge cannot puff him up, let him then consider the ambiguous signs in Scripture, about which I shall now, in a third book, endeavor to say what the Lord has been pleased to grant me.

THOMAS AQUINAS: "TREATISE ON SACRED DOCTRINE" (FROM *SUMMA THEOLOGICA*)
Latin, Late Thirteenth Century

For a biographical introduction to Thomas Aquinas, see page 107.

Question I: The Nature and Extent of Sacred Doctrine
Article X: Whether in Holy Scripture a word may have several senses

Objection I

It seems that in Holy Writ a word cannot have several senses, historical or literal, allegorical, tropological or moral, and anagogical. For many different senses in one text produce confusion and deception and destroy all force of argument. Hence no argument, but only fallacies, can be deduced from a multiplicity of propositions. But Holy Writ ought to be able to state the truth without any fallacy. Therefore in it there cannot be several senses to a word.

Objection II

Further, Augustine says (in *On the Usefulness of Believing*, 3) that "the Old Testament has a fourfold division as to history, etiology, analogy and allegory." Now these four seem altogether different from the four divisions mentioned in the first objection. Therefore it does not seem fitting to explain the same word of Holy Writ according to the four different senses mentioned above.

Objection III

Further, besides these senses, there is the parabolical, which is not one of these four.

On the contrary, Gregory says (*Magna Moralia* 20, 1): "Holy Writ by the manner of its speech transcends every science, because in one and the same sentence, while it describes a fact, it reveals a mystery."

I answer that, The author of Holy Writ is God, in whose power it is to signify His meaning, not by words only (as man also can do), but also by things themselves. So, whereas in every other science things are signified by words, this science has the property, that the things signified by the words have themselves also a signification. Therefore that first signification whereby words signify things belongs to the first sense, the historical or literal. That signification whereby things signified by words have themselves also a signification is called the spiritual sense, which is based on the literal, and presupposes it. Now this spiritual sense has a threefold division. For as the Apostle says (Heb. 10:1) the Old Law is a figure of the New Law, and Dionysius says (*Celestial Hierarchy*, 1) "the New Law itself is a figure of future glory." Again, in the New Law, whatever our Head has done is a type of what we ought to do. Therefore, so far as the things of the Old Law signify the things of the New Law, there is the allegorical sense; so far as the things done in Christ, or so far as the things which signify Christ, are types of what we ought to do, there is the moral sense. But so far as they signify what relates to eternal glory, there is the anagogical sense. Since the literal sense is that which the author intends, and since

the author of Holy Writ is God, Who by one act comprehends all things by His intellect, it is not unfitting, as Augustine says (*Confessions*, 12), if, even according to the literal sense, one word in Holy Writ should have several senses.

Reply to Objection I

The multiplicity of these senses does not produce equivocation or any other kind of multiplicity, seeing that these senses are not multiplied because one word signifies several things, but because the things signified by the words can be themselves types of other things. Thus in Holy Writ no confusion results, for all the senses are founded on one—the literal—from which alone can any argument be drawn, and not from those intended in allegory, as Augustine says (Epistle 48). Nevertheless, nothing of Holy Scripture perishes on account of this, since nothing necessary to faith is contained under the spiritual sense which is not elsewhere put forward by the Scripture in its literal sense.

Reply to Objection II

These three—history, etiology, analogy—are grouped under the literal sense. For it is called history, as Augustine expounds (Epistle 48), whenever anything is simply related; it is called etiology when its cause is assigned, as when Our Lord gave the reason why Moses allowed the putting away of wives—namely, on account of the hardness of men's hearts; it is called analogy whenever the truth of one text of Scripture is shown not to contradict the truth of another. Of these four, allegory alone stands for the three spiritual senses. Thus Hugh of St. Victor (*On the Sacraments of the Christian Faith*, 4, 4) includes the anagogical under the allegorical sense, laying down three senses only—the historical, the allegorical, and the tropological.

Reply to Objection III

The parabolical sense is contained in the literal, for by words things are signified properly and figuratively. Nor is the figure itself, but that which is figured, the literal sense. When Scripture speaks of God's arm, the literal sense is not that God has such a member, but only what is signified by this member, namely operative power. Hence it is plain that nothing false can ever underlie the literal sense of Holy Writ.

MARTIN LUTHER: LECTURES ON SCRIPTURE
German, 1515–1544

Martin Luther's commentaries on Scripture offer readers clear examples of the Medieval, fourfold approach to interpreting Scripture—the historical (literal), allegorical, tropological (moral), and anagogical (future-oriented) understandings—but also of his own special adaptation of these methods, together with his rationale for employing them. Commentaries on several passages, composed at various times in the Reformer's career, are reprinted here by permission of Concordia Publishing House. All rights reserved.[3]

FROM FIRST LECTURES ON THE PSALMS, PSALMS 1–75

Preface to the Glosses

I will sing with the spirit and I will sing with mind also (1 Cor. 14:15). To sing with the spirit is to sing with spiritual devotion and emotion. This is said in opposition to those who sing only with the flesh. And these appear in a twofold sense: the first are those who with an unsettled and weary heart sing only with the tongue and the mouth. The second are those who indeed sing with a cheerful and devout heart but are still enjoying it more in a carnal way, as, for example, taking pleasure in the voice, the sound, the staging, and the harmony. They act as boys usually do, not concerned about the meaning or the fruit of the spirit that is to be raised up to God. In the same way, to sing with the mind is to sing

with the spiritual understanding. And there are likewise two opposites of these: the first are those who understand nothing of what they sing, as nuns are said to read the Psalter. The others are those who have a carnal understanding of the Psalms, like the Jews, who always apply the Psalms to ancient history apart from Christ. But Christ has opened the mind of those who are His so that they might understand the Scriptures. More often however the spirit enlightens the mind, the emotions, the intellect, yes, also vice versa, because the spirit lifts up to the place where the illuminating light is, whereas the mind assigns a place to the emotions. Therefore both are required, but the elevated spirit it better, etc.

Jerusalem:	allegorically: the good people
	tropologically: virtues
	anagogically: rewards
Babylon:	allegorically: the bad people
	tropologically: vices
	anagogically: punishments

Mount Zion		The killing letter	The life-giving spirit concerning the Babylonian ecclesiastical body
	historically:	the land of Canaan	The people living in Zion
	allegorically:	the synagogue or a prominent person in it	the church or any teacher, bishop, or prominent man in it
	tropologically:	the righteousness of the Pharisees and of the Law	the righteousness of faith or of some other prominent matter
	anagogically:	the future glory after the flesh	the eternal glory in the heavens

In the Scriptures, therefore, no allegory, tropology, anagogy is valid, unless the same truth is expressly stated historically elsewhere. Otherwise Scripture would become a mockery. But one must indeed take in an allegorical sense only what is elsewhere stated historically, as mountain in the sense of righteousness in the

3. Oswald, Hilton C. (ed), *First Lectures on the Psalms, I, Psalms 1–75*, Luther's Works, vol. 10 (St. Louis: Concordia Publishing House, 1974). Used with Permission of Concordia Publishing House. All rights reserved.

Pelikan, Jaroslav (ed), *Selected Psalms, III*, Luther's Works, vol. 14 (St. Louis: Concordia Publishing House, 1958). Used with Permission of Concordia Publishing House. All rights reserved.

Pelikan, Jaroslav (ed), *Lectures on Genesis, Chapters 6–14*. Luther's Works, vol. 2 (St. Louis: Concordia Publishing House, 1960). Used with Permission of Concordia Publishing House. All rights reserved.

Pelikan, Jaroslav (ed), *Lectures on Isaiah, Chapters 1–39*, Luther's Works, vol. 16 (St. Louis: Concordia Publishing House, 1969). Used with Permission of Concordia Publishing House. All rights reserved.

Pelikan, Jaroslav (ed), *Lectures on Galatians 1535, Chapters 1–4*, Luther's Works, vol. 26 (St. Louis: Concordia Publishing House, 1963). Used with Permission of Concordia Publishing House. All rights reserved.

Psalms 36:6: "Thy righteousness is like the mountains of God." For that reason it is best to distinguish the spirit from the letter in the Sacred Scriptures, for this is what makes one a theologian indeed and the church has this only from the Holy Spirit, not from human understanding. Thus Psalm 72 says: "May He have dominion from sea to sea." Before the Spirit's revelation no one could know this dominion means a spiritual dominion, especially because he adds "from sea to sea" according to the historical sense. Therefore those who interpret this dominion as referring to the flesh and to earthly majesty have the killing letter, but others have the life giving spirit.

For that reason I often understand the Psalms as referring to the Jews, because we know that what the Law says it speaks to those who are under the Law (Rom. 3:19).

PREFACE OF JESUS CHRIST, SON OF GOD AND OUR LORD, TO THE PSALTER OF DAVID

"I am the door if anyone enters by Me he will be saved, and will go in and out and find pasture" (John 10:9).

"The words of the Holy One, the True One, who has the key of David, who opens and no one shall shut, who shuts and no one opens" (Rev. 3:7).

"In the roll of the book it is written of Me" (Ps. 40:7).

"Even what I have told you from the beginning" (John 8:25).

"Therefore My people shall know My name; therefore in that day they shall know that it is I who speak; here am I" (Isa. 52:6).

The First Witness: Moses

"If Thy presence will not go with me, do not carry us up from here" (Exod. 33:15).

"And the Lord said, 'My presence will go with you, and I will give you rest'" (Exod. 33:14).

The Second Witness: Zechariah the Prophet

"The Lord [Jesus Christ] is the eye, [the light and the vision] of man and all the tribes of Israel" (cf. Zech. 9:1).

The Third Witness: Peter the Apostle

"In all the prophets who have spoken, from Samuel and those who came afterwards, also proclaimed these days" (Acts 3:24).

The Fourth Witness: Paul the Apostle

"For I decided to know nothing among you except Jesus Christ and Him crucified" (1 Cor. 2:2).

From these we draw the following guidelines for this dark, yet holy labyrinth:

Every prophecy and every prophet must be understood as referring to Christ the Lord, except where it is clear from plain words where someone else is spoken of. For thus He Himself says: "Search the Scriptures, . . . and it is they that bear witness to Me" (John 5:39). Otherwise it is most certain that the searchers will not find what they are searching for. For that reason some explain very many psalms not prophetically but historically, following certain Hebrew rabbis who are falsifiers and inventors of Jewish vanities. No wonder, because they are far away from Christ (that is, from the truth). "But we have the mind of Christ," says the apostle (1 Cor. 2:16).

Whatever is said literally concerning the Lord Jesus Christ as to His person must be understood allegorically of a help that is like Him and of the church conformed to Him in all things. And at the same time this must be understood tropologically of any spiritual and inner man against his flesh and the outer man. Let this be made plain by means of examples. "Blessed is the man who walks not, etc." (Ps. 1:1). Literally this means that the Lord Jesus made no concessions to the designs of the Jews and of the evil and adulterous age that existed in His time. Allegorically it means that the holy church did not agree to the evil designs of persecutors, heretics, and ungodly Christians. Tropologically this means that the spirit of man did not accede to the persuasions and suggestions of the inimical flesh and of the ungodly stirrings of the body of sin. Thus also Psalm 2:1 says: "Why do the nations conspire, etc." Literally this refers to the raging of the Jews and Gentiles against Christ during His suffering. Allegorically it is directed against tyrants, heretics, and ungodly leaders of the church. Tropologically it has to do with tyranny, temptation, and tempest of the carnal and outer man who provokes and torments the spirit as the dwelling place of Christ. Thus, Psalm 3:1 reads: "O Lord, how many are my foes." This is literally Christ's complaint concerning the Jews, His enemies. Allegorically it is a complaint and accusation of the church regarding tyrants, heretics, etc. But tropologically it is a complaint, or prayer, of the devout and afflicted spirit placed into trials. In their own way we must also judge in other places, lest we become burdened with a closed book and receive no food.

FROM WORKS ON THE FIRST TWENTY-TWO PSALMS, PSALMS 1 AND 2
1519–1521

Psalm 1

1. Blessed is the man who walks not in the counsel of the ungodly.

The search for personal blessedness is common to all men. There is no one who does not desire to fare well or hate to fare badly. And yet all men, whoever they are, have strayed from the knowledge of true blessedness, most of all those who have made a special search for it, such as the philosophers, the best of whom have identified it with virtue or virtuous works. Thus they have made themselves more miserable than others and have robbed themselves equally of the blessings of this life and the next; for although the common people are grossly out of their mind to strive for blessedness in the pleasures of the flesh, they at least have partaken of the good things of this life. However, the psalmist, speaking from heaven, rejects the efforts of all men and gives a unique definition of blessedness which is unknown to everyone: Blessed is he who loves the Law of God. This is a short definition; but it is one which contradicts all human reason, particularly that of the wise. But first let us consider matters that are grammatical and yet theological.

The Hebrew speaks in the plural, 'ašrē, "blessed people" or "blessed things." Thus: Blessed are the affairs of man who does not stray; as if he wanted to say: All things go well with that man who, etc. Why do you argue? Why do you draw empty conclusions? This is that unique pearl; and if a man can find it by loving the Law of God and being separate from the ungodly, all his affairs are in excellent shape. But if he does not make this discovery, he will search in vain for all good things. For just as to the pure all things are pure (Titus 1:5), so to those who love all things are lovely, and to the good all things are good. In general: As you are, so God is to you, to say nothing of creatures. Since God is pure to the pure, perverse to the perverse, and holy to the holy,

there is nothing good to him who is evil and nothing pleasant to him to whom the Law of God is unpleasant. "Man" is used in the Scriptures in a threefold way. It signifies age, sex, or humanity. It is used for age in 1 Corinthians 13:11: 'When I became a man, I gave up childish ways"; for sex in Matthew 1:16: "Jacob was the father of Joseph, the husband of Mary," and in John 4:16: "Go, call your husband"; and for humanity in 1 Samuel 26:15: "And David said to Abner, 'Are you not a man?'" And in this third sense man is called blessed here, so that the female sex is not excluded from the blessing.

"He has departed" or better, the Hebrew *Lo hālăk* "he has not walked, not entered, not approached," which the Greek renders as *ouk eporeuthei*. It is well known that in the manner of the Scriptures "to walk" and "to approach" are figures of speech, meaning "to live" or "to associate," as in Psalm 15:2: "He who walks blamelessly," and in Psalm 101:6: "He who walks in the way that is blameless shall minister unto me." Similarly in Romans 8: 1, 4: "There is no condemnation for those who walk not according to the flesh."

Here "counsel" is undoubtedly used in place of "principles," or "doctrines," since no human association exists unless it is constructed and maintained according to certain principles and laws. With this word the psalmist rebukes the pride and the corrupt arrogance of the ungodly. For first of all they disdain to walk in the Law of the Lord but follow their own counsel. And then he calls it a counsel, which sounds like wisdom and the right way and thus would be free from error. For this is the corruption of the ungodly, that in their own eyes they are wise, and that among themselves they disguise their errors with the appearance of wisdom and the right way. For if they attacked men with manifest error, it would not be a great praise of blessedness not to walk with them. For he does not say: "in the foolishness of the wicked" or "in the error of sinners." Therefore he warns us most earnestly to beware of the appearance of goodness, so that the satanic angel, disguised as an angel of light (2 Cor. 11:14), does not seduce us by his cunning. But the counsel of the wicked is placed in contrast to the Law of the Lord, so that we learn to beware of the wolves in sheep's clothing. They are quick to counsel everyone, to teach everyone, to help everyone, whereas there is nothing of which they are less capable.

The "ungodly," which the Hebrew terms *rāšā'*, was rightly interpreted by St. Hilary as one having evil feelings about God. For ungodliness is, strictly speaking, the crime of unbelief and is committed in the heart. But it is expressed capriciously and in various ways. Thus you must always have these two opposites in mind: faith in God and godlessness, just as the Law of God and the counsel of man. For when we deal with piety and impiety, we are dealing, not with behavior but with attitudes, that is, with the source of the behavior. Thus whoever rightly believes in God can do nothing but good and lead a good life. And even though the righteous falls seven times a day, he will rise again just as often (Prov. 24:16). But the wicked fall into evil and do not rise again. Because they are unbelievers, they do no good works at all. Everything they do has a beautiful cast, but it is the shadow of Behemoth (Job 40:15), with which they deceive themselves and attract the simple. Therefore he is godly who lives by faith, and he is ungodly who lives in unbelief.

Now we are able to see the sinner. This is the outward way of the wicked, for you cannot see counsel or the wicked man concealed in the heart. Therefore he speaks of the works, the conduct, and the endeavors in which they are outwardly active, and he calls this their way, so that counsel appears in application and, as the saying goes, in practice; and the evil which they think inwardly they do outwardly. Truly this way, as I have said, is always much more pleasing in appearance than the way of the godly. For anyone can easily avoid crude sinners without this guide, or at least recognize them.

"Has stood" means stubbornness, a stiff neck, in which the proud excuse themselves with words of malice; for they have become incorrigible in their godlessness, since they consider it piety. For "to stand" means, in Scriptural metaphor, "to be steadfast," as in Romans 14:4: "It is before his own master that he stands or falls. And he will be upheld, for the Master is able to make him stand," Therefore the Hebrew word for column, like the Latin word for statue, comes from the concept of standing. For this is the fixation of the ungodly, that to themselves they seem to live a righteous life and shine before others with their beautiful works. "Seat," "to sit in the seat," is to instruct, to be a master or teacher. For example, in Matthew 23:2: "The scribes sit on Moses' seat," etc. Thus to sit on a throne is to reign or be a king, just as it frequently appears in the Books of Kings; "to sit on a seat of state" is to be a ruler, and "to sit on a bench" is to be a judge.

Although "pestilence" is not a literal translation, it is a very adequate expression; for the Hebrew refers to mockers or to the scornful. Now they are the scornful whom he accuses throughout the Psalter as the deceitful and the deceitful tongue, as those who, under the appearance of sound doctrine, administer the poison of their false teaching. And no bodily pestilence is as contagious for the body as the teaching of godlessness is for the soul. In the words of the apostle (2 Tim. 2:17): "And their talk will eat its way like gangrene." But just as the wise are called the soundness of the world (Wisd. of Sol. 6:26), so the ungodly are justly called the pestilence of the world. Indeed, what more pernicious deceit is there than to give a deadly poison to souls hungry for pure truth?

In accordance with universal use in the church, therefore—which distinguishes the good life as to faith and morals, the former determining godly and ungodly, and the latter sinners and saints—the psalmist here describes two states. And to them he adds a third. For since ungodliness had no other goal after it had infected man inwardly in his attitude and outwardly in his behavior, it burst forth to drag others along into the same perdition. It was not content with its own ungodly attitude and wicked conduct unless it taught ungodliness also to others. So much for the grammar.

This is to be especially noted about Scripture, how prudently it refrains from mentioning sects and persons. For without a doubt this psalm deals primarily with the Jewish people, as the apostle says, "to the Jew first, and also to the Greek" (Rom. 1:16), and Romans 3:19: "Now we know that whatever the Law says, it speaks to those who are under the Law." Yet it does not say: "Blessed are the Jews, or blessed is this one or that one." Neither does it say "in the counsel of this or that people," but absolutely: "Blessed is the man . . . the counsel of the ungodly . . . the way of the sinners . . . the seat of the scornful," etc., whoever these may be; for there is no respect of persons with God (Gal. 2:6).

And this was most necessary so that the Word of God, because it is eternal, should apply to all men of all times. For although in the course of time customs, people, places, and usages may vary, godliness and ungodliness remain the same through all the ages. Thus we see the prophets opposed to the false prophets, apostles against the pseudoapostles, church fathers against the heretics, all using the same Scriptures; yet neither the prophets nor the apostles nor the doctors nor their adversaries are named, but only the terms "godly" and "ungodly" appear.

Furthermore, this is done so that, if the name of a person were added, others should not imagine that what is called evil does not apply to them, or that what is called good applies to them alone. Thus the Jews referred to themselves whatever blessing was promised to the seed of Abraham and Israel, while, as I have said, this psalm was certainly directed first against them. Therefore we, too, like the holy fathers, apply the psalm to that generation which is contemporaneous with us. In fact, we should rather follow as the psalmist leads; for he reproves all the wicked. Not that he is forced into that pattern, but we find him doing this.

Therefore the psalmist says: "Blessed is the man who does not go astray," that is, when so many thousands of the ungodly are about us that it is possible to say (Ps. 12: 1): "Help, Lord, for there is no longer any that is godly; for the faithful have vanished from among the sons of men." And also with Micah 7:2: "The godly man has perished from the earth, and there is none upright among men." Is not he blessed and truly a man strong in faith who does not walk with the great throng on the broad way, who suffers much abuse and evil and still does not consent to walk with them, and who is not deceived by the attractive counsel of the ungodly which would lead even the elect astray (Matt. 24:24)? It is a great thing when a man is not overcome by riches, pleasures, and honors; but it is an even greater victory when a man overcomes the reasoning and the glittering righteousness of the ungodly, by which pure faith is attacked most of all.

However, it should be noted that the words of the psalm are words of faith, that they do not speak of men according to what one sees on the outside. For then (as I have said) no one would consider them ungodly. The prophet speaks in the spirit, where also that is godless (because it is empty of faith) which among men is the holiest of all. Thus Ecclesiastes 8:10: "Then I saw the wicked buried; they used to go in and out of the holy place and were praised in the city where they had done such things." And Psalm 37:35: "I have seen a wicked man overbearing, and towering like a cedar of Lebanon." These are terrible things, for who would look for ungodliness there, and so deeply?

But listen! This psalm does not reproach merely the ungodly and the sinners, for every man apart from Christ is ungodly and a sinner, but mainly those who are double sinners. They not only fail to recognize themselves as ungodly but, besides this, devise a counsel in which they might move and give their wickedness a bright coloring. Therefore he does not say: Blessed is he who does not walk as an ungodly man or stand as a sinner, but: Who does not walk in the counsel of the ungodly and in the way of the sinners. For they are not satisfied with being ungodly, but they also want to be righteous and holy by giving their ungodliness the appearance of godliness.

Now whom do you think this means in our time? I would not dare name such persons, lest I draw upon myself the implacable enmity of certain priests, monks, and bishops. For the generations of the ungodly have always been most intolerant of the Word of God and have filled heaven with martyrs for no other reason than that they maintained that by it they were doing God a service (John 16:2). They looked on themselves as fighting for the godly when they stubbornly accused the truly pious of ungodliness.

LECTURES ON ISAIAH, CHAPTERS 1–39
1534

Preface to the Prophet Isaiah

Two things are necessary to explain the prophet. The first is a knowledge of grammar, and this may be regarded as having the greatest weight. The second is more necessary, namely, a knowledge of the historical background, not only as an understanding of the events themselves as expressed in letters and syllables but as at the same time embracing rhetoric and dialectic, so that the figures of speech and the circumstances may be carefully heeded. Therefore, having command of the grammar in the first place, you must quickly move on to the histories, namely, what those kings under whom Isaiah prophesied did; and these matters must be carefully examined and thoroughly studied.

The chief and leading theme of all the prophets is their aim to keep the people in eager anticipation of the coming Christ. Thus Moses, too, although he teaches many things that should be done, nevertheless always points to the well-known words in Deuteronomy 18:15, where he also keeps the people in eager anticipation of Christ the Teacher, who will come with that authority with which He is endowed in His own right, yes, who will come as the chief Teacher and Disposer. Likewise in our time, too, whatever we teach and establish in the church, we do with a view to getting the people to await the coming of the Savior. Here we must not act in an ungodly manner, but we must live sober, upright, and godly lives (Titus 1:8; 2:12), not, however, as if we always had to stay here ("for here we have no lasting city" [Heb. 13:14] but through Christ we should await another life to come after this life). Whoever knows this will not feel ashamed of the reading and preaching in the course of which the histories must constantly be observed and treated. The prophets must be read in such a way that we prepare ourselves for the coming of Christ. But although the majority of the prophets do speak about a physical kingdom, yet they do (however tersely) lead to Christ. For this reason we must pay more attention to the designs and intentions of the prophets than to their words. Thus, therefore, Isaiah has much to say about his people and the physical kingdom; he condemns sins in one place and praises righteousness in another, and it seems that almost the entire prophecy is directed toward the people. Meanwhile, however, he also prepares the hearts of the people and causes them to look forward to the coming reign of Christ. Thus Peter says (1 Peter 1: 10): "The prophets . . . searched and inquired about this salvation." The rule and government of that particular people teaches how they were helped and protected by God at one time and forsaken and punished at another, and the prophet intersperses these accounts with references to Christ and to us. We read these things as an example for us who must expect the same treatment if we live in the same way. Hence we are taught here to lead a good life in faith and love, and our faith rests on clear prophecies when we see those things that were foretold by God so many centuries ago.

LECTURES ON GALATIANS, CHAPTERS 1–4
1535

22. *For it is written that Abraham had two sons, one by a slave and one by a free woman.*

23. *But the son of the slave was born according to the flesh, the son of the free woman through promise.*

It is as though Paul were saying: "You have forsaken grace, faith, and Christ; and you have defected to the Law, wanting to be under it and to gain wisdom from it. Therefore I shall discuss the Law with you. I ask you to look at it carefully. You will find that Abraham had two sons, Ishmael by Hagar and Isaac by Sarah.

Both were true sons of Abraham. Ishmael was the true son of Abraham no less than Isaac was; for both were born of the same father, the same flesh, the same seed. Then what was the difference between them?" The difference, Paul says, is not that one mother was a free woman and the other a slave—although this does contribute to the allegory—but that Ishmael, who was born of the slave, was born according to the flesh, that is, apart from the promise and the Word of God, while Isaac was not only born of the free woman but also in accordance with a promise. "So what? Still Isaac was born of the seed of Abraham, just as Ishmael was." "I grant this. Both were sons of the same father. And yet there is a difference. Even though Isaac was born of the flesh, this was preceded by God's promising and naming him." No one but Paul has ever observed this difference, which he gathered this way on the basis of the text of Genesis.

When Hagar conceived and gave birth to Ishmael, there was no voice or Word of God that predicted this; but with Sarah's permission Abraham went in to Hagar the slave, whom Sarah, because she was barren, gave him as his wife, as Genesis testifies. For Sarah had heard that by the promise of God Abraham was to have an offspring of his own body, and she hoped to become the mother of this offspring. But when she had been waiting anxiously for many years after the promise and saw that the realization of the promise was being postponed, she thought that she had been disappointed of her hope. Therefore the saintly woman gave in to the honor of her husband and resigned her right to another, that is, to the slave. Yet she did not permit her husband to marry another wife outside their home; but she gave him her slave in marriage, so that she might obtain children by the slave. For this is what the narrative in Genesis 16:1–2 says: "Sarai, Abram's wife, bore him no children. She had an Egyptian maid whose name was Hagar; and Sarai said to Abram: 'Behold now, the Lord has prevented me from bearing children; go in to my maid; it may be that I shall obtain children by her.'"

It was an act of great humility for Sarai to demean herself this way and to bear this trial of faith with such equanimity. She thought to herself: "God is not a liar. What He has promised to my husband He will certainly perform. But perhaps God does not want me to be the mother of this offspring. I shall not envy Hagar this honor. Let my lord go in to her; perhaps I can obtain children by her." Therefore Ishmael was born without the Word, solely at the request of Sarah herself. Here there was no Word of God that commanded or promised Abraham a son; but everything happened by chance, as Sarah's words indicate: "It may be," she says, "that I shall obtain children by her." Since there was no statement from God that preceded, as there was when Sarah gave birth to Isaac, but only the statement of Sarah, it is abundantly clear that Ishmael was Abraham's son only according to the flesh and without the Word; therefore he was expected and born by chance, like any other child.

Paul noticed this. And in Romans 9:7 he carefully sets forth this argument, which he repeats here as part of the allegory; and he comes to the powerful conclusion that not all the sons of Abraham are sons of God. For Abraham has sons of two kinds: those who are born jointly of him and of the Word or promise of God, as Isaac was; and those who are born of him without the Word of God, as Ishmael was. With this argument, which is like Christ's argument in Matthew 3:9 and John 8:37, Paul stops the mouths of the proud Jews, who boast that they are the offspring and children of Abraham. It is as though he were to say: "It does not follow: 'I am the genuine offspring of Abraham; therefore I am a child of God. Esau was a genuine child; therefore he was an heir.' No, those who want to be sons of Abraham must be children of promise over and above their physical birth, and they must believe. In the last analysis, those who have the promise and believe are the true sons of Abraham and, consequently, of God."

But because Ishmael was not promised to Abraham by God, he was a son only according to the flesh, not according to the promise. Therefore he was expected and born by chance, like other children.

For no mother knows whether she is going to have a child; or if she senses that she is pregnant, she still does not know whether it will be a boy or a girl. But Isaac was named definitely in Genesis 17:19. "Sarah your wife," the angel said to Abraham, "shall bear you a son, and you shall call his name Isaac." Here both the son and the mother are explicitly named. Thus for the humility with which Sarah yielded her right and suffered the contempt of Hagar (Gen. 16:4) God granted her the honor of being the mother of the promised son.

24. Now this is an allegory.

Allegories do not provide solid proofs in theology; but, like pictures, they adorn and illustrate a subject. For if Paul had not proved the righteousness of faith against the righteousness of works by more substantial arguments, he would not have accomplished anything with this allegory. But because he has already fortified his case with more solid arguments—based on experience, on the case of Abraham, on the evidence of Scripture, and on analogy—now, at the end of the argument, he adds an allegory as a kind of ornament. For it is very fine, once the foundation has been properly laid and the case has been firmly established, to add some kind of allegory. Just as a picture is an ornament for a house that has already been constructed, so an allegory is a kind of illumination of an oration or of a case that has already been established on other grounds.

LECTURES ON GENESIS, CHAPTERS 6–14
1544

11. Now the earth was corrupt in God's sight, and the earth was filled with violence.

Lyra comments on this passage—perhaps because of the opinion of the rabbis—that the birds and the rest of the animals had also departed from their nature and crossbred with various kinds. But I do not believe this. Among the beasts the creation or nature stayed the way it was created. They did not fall by sinning, as man did. No, they were created merely for this physical life. Therefore they do not hear the Word, and the Word does not concern itself with them; they are altogether without the Law of the First and the Second Table. Hence these words must be applied only to man.

That even the animals bore the punishment of sin and perished by the Flood, together with mankind, happened because God wanted to destroy man completely, not only in body and soul but also with his possessions and the dominion with which he had been created. Examples of similar punishments occur in the Old Testament. In the sixth chapter of Daniel the enemies of Daniel are thrown into the lions' pit, together with their wives, children, and their entire household (6:24). The same thing happened in Numbers 16, when Korah, Dathan, and Abiram perished (16:32). Something similar is also what Christ states in the Gospel (Matt. 18:25) of the king who commands his servant to be sold, together with his wife, his children, and all his possessions.

In this very same manner not only the human beings but also all their possessions were destroyed by the Flood, that there might be full and complete punishment for sin. The beasts of the field and the birds of the heaven were created for mankind; these are the wealth and the possessions of men. Accordingly, the animals perished, not because they sinned but because God wanted man to perish among and together with all those things that he had on the earth.

Here Moses expressly adds the clause, "The earth was corrupt in God's sight," in order to indicate that in the sight of his age Noah was treated and regarded as a stupid and worthless person. In contrast, the world appeared to itself most holy and most righteous; it assumed that it had adequate reasons for persecuting Noah, especially so far as the First Table and the worship of God were concerned. To be sure, the Second Table likewise gives rise to pretense and hypocrisy; but there is no comparison with the First. An adulterer, a thief, and a murderer can remain hidden for a time, but not forever. But the sins against the First Table usually remain hidden under the guise of saintliness until God reveals them. Ungodliness never wants to be considered and actually to be ungodliness; it strives to be praised for piety and godliness. It embellishes its forms of worship to such a degree that in comparison with them the true forms of worship and true godliness are filthy.

The verb šāḥă (corrupt) is very common in Holy Scripture, and it is striking.

Moses also employs it in Deuteronomy 31:29: "I know that after my death you will surely act corruptly; and turn aside from the way"; and David, in Psalm 14:3: "All are corrupt and have become detestable." Furthermore, both passages are really speaking of sins against the First Table; that is, they charge those who are saintliest in appearance with false worship of God and with false doctrine. It is impossible for an ungodly life not to follow in the wake of false doctrine.

When Moses states that the earth was corrupt in the sight of God, he clearly points out the contrast, namely, that the hypocrites and tyrants were of the opinion that what Noah taught and did was wrong, but that they taught and did everything in the saintliest manner. But, says Moses, the opposite was true. The earth, that is, the entire world, or all human beings, was corrupt, namely, so far as the First Table is concerned, they did not have the true Word or the true worship. This distinction in regard to the First and Second Table is very much to my liking and has undoubtedly been pointed out by the Holy Spirit.

Moreover, by his addition—"And the earth was filled with violence"—he indicates that this is the unvarying sequence of events: after the Word has been lost, and faith has ceased to exist, and tradition and *ethelothreskeia* (voluntary worship) as Paul calls them (Col. 2:23), flourish in place of the true forms of worship, acts of violence and a shameful life follow.

The word ḥāmās properly denotes violence, force, and harm, with disregard of all law and equity, when anyone may do what he pleases, and whatever things are done are done not by law but by force. If this was their kind of life, someone may say, how could they maintain an outward reputation for saintliness and righteousness? As though indeed one did not have similar examples before one's eyes today! What has the world ever seen that is crueler than the Turks? Nevertheless, they adorn all their brutality with the name of God and godliness.

Thus the popes have not only seized for themselves the wealth of the world, but they have filled the church itself with endless errors and blasphemous doctrines. They live in unspeakable voluptuousness; and when they wish, they sow dissension in the hearts of kings and give ample occasion for war and bloodshed. Nevertheless, in the midst of these very blasphemies and infamous deeds they claim the right to the name and designation "the saintliest"; they boast that they are the vicars of Christ, the successors of Peter, etc.

Accordingly, the greatest wrongs are associated with the designation of holiness, church, true religions, etc. If anyone should express disapproval, he is immediately clubbed with the curse of excommunication and is condemned as a heretic and an enemy of God and the church. Next to the Roman popes and their confederates there is no people that prides itself more on its godliness and righteousness than the Turks, who despise Christians as idolaters but regard themselves as the saintliest and wisest of men. And yet what else is their life and godliness than endless murder, robbery, depredation, and other awful crimes?

The examples of the present time, therefore, show how those two incompatibles can exist side by side: the utmost godliness is paired with the greatest abominations, the utmost violence with the appearance of righteousness. This is also the reason why men become so hardened and smug, and do not look for the punishment they have deserved because of their sins.

12. And God saw the earth, and behold, it was corrupt; for all flesh had corrupted their way upon the earth.

Because God's wrath is so dreadful and because the destruction of all flesh, with the exception of eight souls, is already imminent, the language of Moses is somewhat richer in this passage and makes use of repetitions, which, nevertheless, are not purposeless but have their special emphasis. He stated previously that the earth was corrupt; now, as in the orderly progress of a trial, he states that God saw this and gave thought to the punishment. In this manner he depicts the order, as it were, according to which God customarily proceeds.

Today spiritual-minded people are right in their conviction that the pope is the Antichrist and rages madly against the Word and the kingdom of Christ. But the very people who have this conviction are unable to bring about an improvement in this ungodliness. Ungodliness grows daily, and the contempt of godliness becomes greater from day to day. It is then that they reflect: "What is God doing? Why does He not punish His enemies? Is He asleep and not interested at all in human affairs?" The delay of the judgment is torture for the godly. They themselves are unable to bring aid to religion in its distress; and they see that God, who is able to do so, connives at the raging of the popes, who are smugly sinning against both the First and the Second Table.

CHAPTER 9

The Great Awakening

In New England in the 1730s and 1740s among Congregational and Reformed churches, a series of remarkable gatherings took place, revivals marked by preaching that emphasized God's righteous wrath directed at sinners, and accompanied by an urgent call for hearers to repent and to seek God's mercy through Christ's atoning sacrifice. The spiritual awakening in America paralleled an evangelical revival in Great Britain under the preaching of Anglican Church ministers George Whitefield (1714–1770) and John Wesley (1703–1791); both movements were preceded by the advent of pietism—a renewal of fervent, heart-felt worship and Christian living—in Germany and elsewhere in Europe. The mutually reinforcing nature of these movements is apparent: John Wesley's exposure to Moravian pietism prompted his quest for a transforming spiritual experience, and this in turn launched his remarkable preaching career. Likewise, George Whitefield traveled to America where his preaching is believed to have sparked the awakening there. While in America, Whitefield preached to large crowds in the cities of Philadelphia, New York, Boston, and elsewhere. During his tours, Whitefield met with a young minister, Gilbert Tennent, and stayed in the home of Jonathan Edwards. These and many other Christian leaders of their day witnessed the hand of God in bringing about an extended period of dramatic spiritual renewal amidst conditions of moral degradation, cold formality in the churches, and widespread spiritual apathy. This chapter contains some of the key documents of the period, including leading Pietist Philip Jacob Spener's critique of the church of his day; Jonathan Edwards's report on the progress of the revival ("A Faithful Narrative") and his best known sermon, "Sinners in the Hands of an Angry God"; Gilbert Tennent's "The Dangers of an Unconverted Ministry"; a sermon on "Free Grace" by John Wesley; two letters that passed between Wesley and Whitefield concerning their theological differences; and Wesley's "Plain Account of Christian Perfection."

PHILIP JACOB SPENER: *PIOUS LONGINGS* (EXCERPT)
Latin, 1675

We preachers in our estate need reformation as much as any estate can ever need it.

As chief pastor of the Lutheran Church at Frankfort, Germany (1666–1686), Spener's deep concern for the rekindling of the spiritual life of the Church, among both the ordained and the laity, accompanied the movement known as Pietism. According to Theodore Tappert, Spener's *Pious Longings* (*Pia Desideria*), "falls naturally into three parts," including (1) a critique of the problems of the Church of Spener's day, (2) scriptural encouragement for the Church's reform, and (3) Spener's specific proposals for such a reform. A portion of the first proposal in part 3 is reprinted here from the first English translation.[1]

---

1. From pages 87–89 of *Pia Desideria* by Philip Spener, translated by Theodore Tappert, copyright © 1964 Fortress Press. Used by permission of Augsburg Fortress Publishers.

Thought should be given to the more extensive use of the Word of God among us. We know that by nature we have no good in us. If there is to be any good in us, it must be brought about by God. To this end the Word of God is the powerful means, since faith must be rekindled through the gospel, and the law provides the rules for good works and many wonderful impulses to attain them. The more at home the Word of God is among us, the more we shall bring about faith and its fruits.

It may appear that the Word of God has sufficiently free course among us inasmuch as at various places (as in this city [Frankfurt am Main]) there is daily or frequent preaching from the pulpit. When we reflect further on the matter, however, we shall find that with respect to this first proposal, more is needed. I do not at all disapprove of the preaching of sermons in which a Christian congregation is instructed by the reading and exposition of a certain text, for I myself do this. But I find that this is not enough. In the first place, we know that "all Scripture is inspired by God and profitable for teaching, for reproof, for correction, and for training in righteousness" (2 Tim. 3:16). Accordingly all Scripture, without exception, should be known by the congregation if we are all to receive the necessary benefit. If we put together all the passages of the Bible which in the course of many years are read to a congregation in one place, they will comprise only a very small part of the Scriptures which have been given to us. The remainder is not heard by the congregation at all, or is heard only insofar as one or another verse is quoted or alluded to in sermons, without, however, offering any understanding of the entire context, which is nevertheless of the greatest importance. In the second place, the people have little opportunity to grasp the meaning of the Scripture except on the basis of those passages which may have been expounded to them, and even less do they have opportunity to become as practiced in them as edification requires. Meanwhile, although solitary reading of the Bible at home is in itself a splendid and praiseworthy thing, it does not accomplish enough for most people.

It should therefore be considered whether the church would not be well advised to introduce the people to Scripture in still other ways than through the customary sermons on the appointed lessons. This might be done, first of all, by diligent reading of the Holy Scriptures, especially of the New Testament. It would not be difficult for every housefather to keep a Bible or at least a New Testament handy and read from it every day or, if they cannot read to have somebody else read.

Then a second thing would be desirable in order to encourage people to read privately, namely, that where the practice can be introduced the books of the Bible be read one after another, at specified times in the public service, without further comment (unless one wished to add brief summaries). This would be intended for the edification of all, but especially of those that cannot read at all, or cannot read easily or well or of those who do not own a copy of the Bible.

For a third thing it would perhaps not be inexpedient (and I set this down for further and more mature reflection) to reintroduce the ancient and apostolic kind of church meetings. In addition our customary services with preaching, other assemblies would also be held in the manner in which Paul describes them in 1 Corinthians 14:26–40. One person would not rise to preach (although this practice would be continued at other times), but others who have been blessed with gifts and knowledge would also speak and present their pious opinions on the proposed subject to the judgement of the rest, doing all this in such a way as to avoid disorder and strife. This might conveniently be done by having several ministers (in places where a number of them live in a town) meet together by having several members of a congregation who have a fair knowledge of God or desire to increase their knowledge meet under the leadership of a minister, take up the Holy Scriptures, read aloud from them, and fraternally discuss each verse in order to discover its simple meaning and whatever may be useful for the edification of all. Anybody who is not satisfied with his understanding of a matter should be permitted to express his doubts and seek further explanation. On the other hand, those (including the ministers) who have made more progress should be allowed the freedom to state how they understand each passage. Then all that has been contributed, insofar as it accords with the sense of the Holy Spirit in the Scriptures, should be carefully considered by the rest, especially by the ordained ministers, and applied to the edification of the whole meeting. Everything should be arranged with an eye to the glory of God, to the spiritual growth of the participants, and therefore also to their limitations. Any threat of meddlesomeness, quarrelsomeness, self-seeking, or something else of this sort should be guarded against and tactfully cut off especially by the preachers who retain leadership in these meetings.

JONATHAN EDWARDS: "A FAITHFUL NARRATIVE OF THE SURPRISING WORK OF GOD" (EXCERPTS)
English, 1737

Jonathan Edwards (1703–1758) was an American Congregational minister and missionary whose preaching and writing helped to start and guide the First Great Awakening. Edwards also served briefly as the president of the College of New Jersey (later Princeton University), and is considered to have been one of America's foremost philosophical thinkers.

Edwards's "Faithful Narrative" was written to report on the progress of the revival and to demonstrate objectively its genuineness as true work of God in the hearts of the people. Following an introduction (part 1), Edwards describes in minute detail the spiritual and psychological effects that the revival had on various participants, together with his general conclusions about its impact (part 2); he then concludes with detailed spiritual vignettes of two participants, an adult woman and a child (part 3). Excerpts from the introduction and part 2 are reprinted here, along with part 3 in its entirety. The text printed here is based on *The Works of President Edwards in Four Volumes* (New York: Robert Carter and Brothers, 1879). For the best available text see The Works of Jonathan Edwards series, vol. 4, ed. C. C. Goen (Yale University Press, 1972).

◆

From the Introduction

The people of the country, in general, I suppose, are as sober, orderly, and good sort of people, as in any part of New England; and I believe they have been preserved the freest by far of any part of the country, from error, and variety of sects and opinions. Our being so far within the land, at a distance from sea-ports, and in a corner of the country, has doubtless been one reason why we have not been so much corrupted with vice, as most other parts. But without question, the religion and good order of the county, and purity in doctrine, has, under God, been very much owing to the great abilities, and eminent piety of my venerable and honored grandfather Stoddard. . . .

At the latter end of the year 1733, there appeared a very unusual flexibleness, and yielding to advice, in our young people. It had been too long their manner to make the evening after the sabbath, [It must be noted, that it has never been our manner, to observe the evening that follows the sabbath, but that which precedes it, as part of the holy time], and after our public lecture, to be especially the times of their mirth, and company-keeping. But a sermon was now preached on the sabbath before the lecture, to show the evil tendency of the practice, and to persuade them to reform it; and it was urged on heads of families that it should be a thing agreed upon among them, to govern their families, and keep their children at home, at these times. It was also more privately moved, that they should meet together the next day, in their several neighborhoods, to know each other's minds; which was accordingly done, and the notion complied with throughout the town. But parents found little or no occasion for the exercise of government in the case. The young people declared themselves convinced by what they had heard from the pulpit, and were willing of themselves to comply with the counsel that had been given: and it was immediately, and, I suppose, almost universally, complied with; and there was a thorough reformation of these disorders thenceforward, which has continued ever since.

Presently after this, there began to appear a remarkable religious concern at a little village belonging to the congregation called Pascommuck, where a few families were settled, at about three miles distance from the main body of the town. At this place, a number of persons seemed to be savingly wrought upon. In the April following, anno 1734, there happened a very sudden and awful death of a young man in the bloom of his youth; who being violently seized with a pleurisy, and taken immediately very delirious, died in about two days; which (together with what was preached publicly on that occasion) much affected many young people. This was followed with another death of a young married woman, who had been considerably exercised in mind, about the salvation of her soul, before she was ill, and was in great distress in the beginning of her illness; but seemed to have satisfying evidences of God's mercy to her, before her death; so that she died very full of comfort, in a most earnest and moving manner warning and counselling others. This seemed to contribute to render solemn the spirits of many young persons; and there began evidently to appear more of a religious concern on people's minds.

In the fall of the year I proposed it to the young people, that they should agree among themselves to spend the evenings after lectures in social religion, and to that end divide themselves into several companies to meet in various parts of the town; which was accordingly done, and those meetings have been since continued, and the example imitated by elder people. This was followed with the death of an elderly person, which was attended with many unusual circumstances, by which many were much moved and affected. . . .

From Section II: The manner of conversion various, yet bearing a great analogy

I therefore proceed to give an account of the manner of persons being wrought upon; and here there is a vast variety, perhaps as manifold as the subjects of the operation; but yet in many things there is a great analogy in all. Persons are first awakened with a sense of their miserable condition by nature, the danger they are in of perishing eternally, and that it is of great importance to them that they speedily escape and get into a better state. Those who before were secure and senseless, are made sensible how much they were in the way to ruin, in their former courses. Some are more suddenly seized with convictions—it may be, by the news of others' conversion, or some thing they hear in public, or in private conference—their consciences are smitten, as if their hearts were pierced through with a dart. Others are awakened more gradually, they begin at first to be something more thoughtful and considerate, so as to come to a conclusion in their minds, that it is their best and wisest way to delay no longer, but to improve the present opportunity. They have accordingly set themselves seriously to meditate on those things that have the most awakening tendency, on purpose to obtain convictions; and so their awakenings have increased, till a sense of their misery, by God's Holy Spirit setting in therewith, has had fast hold of them. Others who before had been somewhat religious, and concerned for their salvation, have been awakened in a new manner; and made sensible that their slack and dull way of seeking, was never like to attain that purpose.

These awakenings when they have first seized on

persons, have had two effects; one was, that they have brought them immediately to quit their sinful practices; and the looser sort have been brought to forsake and dread their former vices and extravagances. When once the Spirit of God began to be so wonderfully poured out in a general way through the town, people had soon done with their old quarrels, backbitings, and intermeddling with other men's matters. The tavern was soon left empty, and persons kept very much at home; none went abroad unless on necessary business, or on some religious account, and every day seemed in many respects like a Sabbath-day. The other effect was, that it put them on earnest application to the means of salvation, reading, prayer, meditation, the ordinances of God's house, and private conference; their cry was, What shall we do to be saved? The place of resort was now altered, it was no longer the tavern, but the minister's house that was thronged far more than ever the tavern had been wont to be.

There is a very great variety, as to the degree of fear and trouble that persons are exercised with, before they attain any comfortable evidences of pardon and acceptance with God. Some are from the beginning carried on with abundantly more encouragement and hope than others. Some have had ten times less trouble of mind than others, in whom yet the issue seems to be the same. Some have had such a sense of the displeasure of God, and the great danger they were in of damnation, that they could not sleep at nights; and many have said that when they have laid down, the thoughts of sleeping in such a condition have been frightful to them; they have scarcely been free from terror while asleep, and they have awakened with fear, heaviness, and distress still abiding on their spirits. It has been very common, that the deep and fixed concern on persons' minds, has had a painful influence on their bodies, and given disturbance to animal nature. The awful apprehensions persons have had of their misery, have for the most part been increasing, the nearer they have approached to deliverance; though they often pass through many changes and alterations in the frame and circumstances of their minds. Sometimes they think themselves wholly senseless, and fear that the Spirit of God has left them, and that they are given up to judicial hardness; yet they appear very deeply exercised about that fear, and are in great earnest to obtain convictions again.

Together with those fears, and that exercise of mind

which is rational, and which they have just ground for, they have often suffered many needless distresses of thought, in which Satan probably has a great hand, to entangle them, and block up their way. Sometimes the distemper of melancholy has been evidently mixed; of which, when it happens, the tempter seems to take great advantage, and puts an unhappy bar in the way of any good effect. One knows not how to deal with such persons; they turn every thing that is said to them the wrong way, and most to their own disadvantage. There is nothing that the devil seems to make so great a handle of, as a melancholy humor; unless it be the real corruption of the heart.

But it is very remarkable, that there has been far less of this mixture at this time of extraordinary blessing, than there was wont to be in persons under awakenings at other times; for it is evident that many who before had been exceedingly involved is such difficulties, seemed now strangely to be set at liberty. Some persons who had before, for a long time, been exceedingly entangled with peculiar temptations of one sort or other, unprofitable and hurtful distresses, were soon helped over former stumbling-blocks, that hindered their progress towards saving good; convictions have wrought more kindly, and they have been successfully carried on in the way to life. And thus Satan seemed to be restrained, till towards the latter end of this wonderful time, when God's Holy Spirit was about to withdraw.

Many times persons under great awakenings were concerned, because they thought they were not awakened, but miserable, hard-hearted, senseless, sottish creatures still, and sleeping upon the brink of hell. The sense of the need they have to be awakened, and of their comparative hardness, grows upon them with their awakenings; so that they seem to themselves to be very senseless, when indeed most sensible. There have been some instances of persons who have had as great a sense of their danger and misery as their natures could well subsist under, so that a little more would probably have destroyed them; and yet they have expressed themselves much amazed at their own insensibility and sottishness at such an extraordinary time.

Persons are sometimes brought to the borders of despair, and it looks as black as midnight to them a little before the day dawns in their souls. Some few instances there have been, of persons who have had such a sense of God's wrath for sin, that they have been overborne;

and made to cry out under an astonishing sense of their guilt, wondering that God suffers such guilty wretches to live upon earth, and that he doth not immediately send them to hell. Sometimes their guilt doth so stare them in the face, that they are in exceeding terror for fear that God will instantly do it; but more commonly their distresses under legal awakenings have not been to such a degree. In some, these terrors do not seem to be so sharp, when near comfort, as before; their convictions have not seemed to work so much that way, but to be led further down into their own hearts, to a further sense of their own universal depravity and deadness in sin.

The corruption of the heart has discovered itself in various exercises, in the time of legal convictions; sometimes it appears in a great struggle, like something roused by an enemy, and Satan, the old inhabitant, seems to exert himself, like a serpent disturbed and enraged. Many in such circumstances, have felt a great spirit of envy towards the godly, especially towards those who are thought to have been lately converted, and most of all towards acquaintances and companions, when they are thought to be converted. Indeed, some have felt many heart-risings against God, and murmurings at His way of dealing with mankind, and His dealings with themselves in particular. It has been much insisted on, both in public and private, that persons should have the utmost dread of such envious thoughts; which if allowed tend exceedingly to quench the Spirit of God, if not to provoke Him finally to forsake them. And when such a spirit has much prevailed, and persons have not so earnestly strove against it as they ought to have done, it has seemed to be exceedingly to the hindrance of the good of their souls. But in some other instances, where persons have been much terrified at the sight of such wickedness in their hearts, God has brought good to them out of evil; and made it a means of convincing them of their own desperate sinfulness, and bringing them off from all self-confidence.

The drift of the Spirit of God in His legal strivings with persons, has seemed most evidently to be, to bring to a conviction of their absolute dependence on His sovereign power and grace, and an universal necessity of a mediator. This has been effected by leading them more and more to a sense of their exceeding wickedness and guiltiness in His sight; their pollution, and the insufficiency of their own righteousness; that they can in no wise help themselves, and that God would be wholly just and righteous in rejecting them and all that they do, and in casting them off for ever. There is however a vast variety as to the manner and distinctness of such convictions.

As they are gradually more and more convinced of the corruption and wickedness of their hearts, they seem to themselves to grow worse and worse, harder and blinder, and more desperately wicked, instead of growing better. They are ready to be discouraged by it, and oftentimes never think themselves so far off from good as when they are nearest. Under the sense which the Spirit of God gives them of their sinfulness, they often think that they differ from all others; their hearts are ready to sink with the thought that they are the worst of all, and that none ever obtained mercy who were so wicked as they.

When awakenings first begin, their consciences are commonly most exercised about their outward vicious course, or other acts of sin; but afterwards are much more burdened with a sense of heart-sins, the dreadful corruption of their nature, their enmity against God, the pride of their hearts, their unbelief, their rejection of Christ, the stubbornness and obstinacy of their wills; and the like. In many, God makes much use of their own experience, in the course of their awakenings and endeavors after saving good, to convince them of their own vile emptiness and universal depravity.

Very often, under first awakenings, when they are brought to reflect on the sin of their past lives, and have something of a terrifying sense of God's anger, they set themselves to walk more strictly, and confess their sins, and perform many religious duties, with a secret hope of appeasing God's anger, and making up for the sins they have committed. And oftentimes, at first setting out, their affections are so moved, that they are full of tears, in their confessions and prayers; which they are ready to make very much of, as though they were some atonement, and had power to move correspondent affections in God too. Hence they are for a while big with expectation of what God will do for them; and conceive they grow better apace, and shall soon be thoroughly converted. But these affections are but short-lived; they quickly find that they fail, and then they think themselves to be grown worse again. They do not find such a prospect of being soon converted, as they thought: instead of being nearer, they seem to be further off; their

hearts they think are grown harder, and by this means their fears of perishing greatly increase. But though they are disappointed, they renew their attempts again and again; and still as their attempts are multiplied, so are their disappointments. All fails, they see no token of having inclined God's heart to them, they do not see that He hears their prayers at all, as they expected He would; and sometimes there have been great temptations arising hence to leave off seeking, and to yield up the case. But as they are still more terrified with fears of perishing, and their former hopes of prevailing on God to be merciful to them in a great measure fail, sometimes their religious affections have turned into heart risings against God, because He will not pity them, and seems to have little regard to their distress, and piteous cries, and to all the pains they take. They think of the mercy God has shown to others; how soon and how easily others have obtained comfort, and those too who were worse than they, and have not labored so much as they have done; and sometimes they have had even dreadful blasphemous thoughts, in these circumstances.

But when they reflect on these wicked workings of heart against God—if their convictions are continued, and the Spirit of God is not provoked utterly to forsake them—they have more distressing apprehensions of the anger of God towards those whose hearts work after such a sinful manner about Him; and it may be, have great fears that they have committed the unpardonable sin, or that God will surely never show mercy to them who are such vipers; and are often tempted to leave off in despair. But then perhaps by something they read or hear of the infinite mercy of God, and all-sufficiency of Christ for the chief of sinners, they have some encouragement and hope renewed; but think that as yet they are not fit to come to Christ; they are so wicked that Christ will never accept them. And then it may be they set themselves upon a new course of fruitless endeavors, in their own strength, to make themselves better, and still meet with new disappointments. They are earnest to inquire what they shall do. They do not know but there is something else to be done, in order to their obtaining converting grace, that they have never done yet. It may be they hope that they are something better than they were; but then the pleasing dream all vanishes again. If they are told that they trust too much to their own strength and righteousness, they cannot unlearn this practice all at once, and find not yet the appearance of any good, but all looks as dark as midnight to them. Thus they wander about from mountain to hill, seeking rest, and finding none. When they are beat out of one refuge, they fly to another; till they are as it were debilitated, broken, and subdued with legal humblings; in which God gives them a conviction of their own utter helplessness and insufficiency, and discovers the true remedy in a clearer knowledge of Christ and His gospel.

When they begin to seek salvation, they are commonly profoundly ignorant of themselves; they are not sensible how blind they are; and how little they can do towards bringing themselves to see spiritual things aright, and towards putting forth gracious exercises in their own souls. They are not sensible how remote they are from love to God, and other holy dispositions, and how dead they are in sin. When they see unexpected pollution in their own hearts, they go about to wash away their own defilements, and make themselves clean; and they weary themselves in vain, till God shows them that it is in vain, and that their help is not where they have sought it. But some persons continue wandering in such a kind of labyrinth, ten times as long as others, before their own experience will convince them of their insufficiency; and so it appears not to be their own experience only, but the convincing influence of God's Holy Spirit with their experience, that attains the effect. God has of late abundantly shown that He does not need to wait to have men convinced by long and often repeated fruitless trials; for in multitudes of instances He has made a shorter work of it. He has so awakened and convinced persons' consciences, and made them so sensible of their exceeding great vileness, and given them such a sense of His wrath against sin, as has quickly overcome all their vain self-confidence, and borne them down into the dust before a holy and righteous God. . . .

Section III: This work further illustrated in particular instances

But to give a clear idea of the nature and manner of the operation of God's Spirit, in this wonderful effusion of it, I would give an account of two particular instances. The first is an adult person, a young woman whose name was Abigail Hutchinson. I fix upon her especially, because she is now dead, and so it may be more fit to speak freely of her than of living instances: though I am under far greater disadvantages, on other accounts, to give a full and clear narrative of her experiences, than I might of some others; nor can any account be given but what has been retained in the memories of her friends, of what they have heard her express in her lifetime. She was of an intelligent family: there could be nothing in her education that tended to enthusiasm, but rather to the contrary extreme. It is in no-wise the temper of the family to be ostentatious of experiences, and it was far from being her temper. She was, before her conversion, to the observation of her neighbors, of a sober and inoffensive conversation; and was a still, quiet, reserved person. She had long been infirm of body, but her infirmity had never been observed at all to incline her to be notional or fanciful, or to occasion any thing of religious melancholy.

She was under awakenings scarcely a week, before there seemed to be plain evidence of her being savingly converted. She was first awakened in the winter season, on Monday, by something she heard her brother say of the necessity of being in good earnest in seeking regenerating grace, together with the news of the conversion of the young woman before mentioned, whose conversion so generally affected most of the young people here. This news wrought much upon her, and stirred up a spirit of envy in her towards this young woman, whom she thought very unworthy of being distinguished from others by such a mercy; but withal it engaged her in a firm resolution to do her utmost to obtain the same blessing.

Considering with herself what course she should take, she thought that she had not a sufficient knowledge of the principles of religion to render her capable of conversion; whereupon she resolved thoroughly to search the Scriptures; and accordingly immediately began at the beginning of the Bible, intending to read it through. She continued thus till Thursday: and then there was a sudden alteration, by a great increase of her concern in an extraordinary sense of her own sinfulness, particularly the sinfulness of her nature, and wickedness of her heart. This came upon her, as she expressed it, as a flash of lightning, and struck her into an exceeding terror. Upon which she left off reading the Bible, in course, as she had begun; and turned to the New Testament, to see if she could not find some relief there for her distressed soul. Her great terror, she said, was, that she had sinned against God: her distress grew more and more for three days; until she saw nothing but blackness of darkness before her, and her very flesh trembled for fear of God's wrath: she wondered and was astonished at herself, that she had been so concerned for her body, and had applied so often to physicians to heal that, and had neglected her soul. Her sinfulness appeared with a very awful aspect to her, especially in three things; viz. her original sin, and her sin in murmuring at God's providence—in the weakness and afflictions she had been under—and in want of duty to parents, though others had looked upon her to excel in dutifulness.

On Saturday, she was so earnestly engaged in reading the Bible and other books, that she continued in it, searching for something to relieve her, till her eyes were so dim that she could not know the letters. While she was thus engaged in reading, prayer, and other religious exercises, she thought of those words of Christ, wherein He warns us not to be as the heathen, that think they shall be heard for their much speaking; which, she said, led her to see that she had trusted to her own prayers and religious performances, and now she was put to a nonplus, and knew not which way to turn herself, or where to seek relief. While her mind was in this posture, her heart, she said, seemed to fly, to the minister for refuge, hoping that he could give her some relief.

She came the same day to her brother, with the countenance of a person in distress, expostulating with him, why he had not told her more of her sinfulness, and earnestly inquiring of him what she should do. She seemed that day to feel in herself an enmity against the Bible, which greatly affrighted her. Her sense of her own exceeding sinfulness continued increasing from Thursday till Monday and she gave this account of it: That it had been her opinion, till now, she was not guilty of Adam's sin, nor any way concerned in it, because she was not active in it; but that now she saw she was guilty of that sin, and all over defiled by it; and the sin which she brought into the world with her, was alone sufficient to condemn her. On the Sabbath-day she was so ill, that her friends thought it best that she should not go to public worship, of which she seemed very desirous: but when she went to bed on the Sabbath night, she took up a resolution, that she would the next morning go to the minister, hoping to find some relief there.

As she awakened on Monday morning, a little before day, she wondered within herself at the easiness and calmness she felt in her mind, which was of that kind she never felt before. As she thought of this, such words as these were in her mind: "The words of the Lord are pure words, health to the soul, and marrow to the bones," and then these words, "The blood of Christ cleanses from all sin," which were accompanied with a lively sense of the excellency of Christ, and His sufficiency to satisfy for the sins of the whole world. She then thought of that expression, "It is a pleasant thing for the eyes to behold the sun," which words then seemed to her to be very applicable to Jesus Christ. By these things her mind was led into such contemplations and views of Christ, as filled her exceeding full of joy. She told her brother, in the morning, that she had seen (i.e., in realizing views by faith) "Christ the last night," and that she had "really thought that she had not knowledge enough to be converted"; but, says she, "God can make it quite easy!" On Monday she felt all day a constant sweetness in her soul. She had a repetition of the same discoveries of Christ three mornings together, and much in the same manner, at each time, waking a little before day; but brighter and brighter every day. At the last time, on Wednesday morning, while in the enjoyment of a spiritual view of Christ's glory and fullness, her soul was filled with distress for Christless persons, to consider what a miserable condition they were in.

She felt a strong inclination immediately to go forth to warn sinners; and proposed it the next day to her brother to assist her in going from house to house; but her brother restrained her, by telling her of the unsuitableness of such a method. She told one of her sisters that day, that she loved "all mankind, but especially the people of God." Her sister asked her why she loved all mankind. She replied, "Because God has made them." After this, there happened to come into the shop where she was at work, three persons who were thought to have been lately converted: her seeing of them, as they stepped in one after another, so affected her, and so drew forth her love to them, that it overcame her, and she almost fainted. When they began to talk of the things of religion, it was more than she could bear; they were obliged to cease on that account. It was a very frequent thing with her to be overcome with the flow of affection to them whom she thought godly, in conversation with them, and sometimes only at the sight of them. She had many extraordinary discoveries of the glory of God and Christ; sometimes, in some particular attributes, and sometimes in many. She gave an account, that once, as those four words passed through her mind, wisdom, justice, goodness, and truth, her soul was filled with a sense of the glory of each of these divine attributes, but especially the last. "Truth," said she, "sunk the deepest!" And, therefore, as these words passed, this was repeated, "truth, truth!" Her mind was so swallowed up with a sense of the glory of God's truth and other perfections, that she said, "it seemed as though her life was going," and that she saw "it was easy with God to take away her life by discoveries of Himself."

Soon after this she went to a private religious meeting, and her mind was full of a sense and view of the glory of God all the time. When the exercise was ended, some asked her concerning what she had experienced, and she began to give an account, but as she was relating it, it revived such a sense of the same things, that her strength failed, and they were obliged to take her and lay her upon the bed.

Afterwards she was greatly affected, and rejoiced with these words, "Worthy is the Lamb that was slain!" She had several days together a sweet sense of the excellency and loveliness of Christ in His meekness, which disposed her continually to be repeating over these words, which were sweet to her, meek and lowly in heart, meek and lowly in heart. She once expressed herself to one of her sisters to this purpose, that she had continued whole days and whole nights, in a constant ravishing view of the glory of God and Christ, having enjoyed as much as her life could bear. Once, as her brother was speaking of the dying love of Christ, she told him, she had such a sense of it, that the mere mentioning of it was ready to overcome her. . . .

But I now proceed to the other instance, that of the little child before mentioned. Her name is Phebe Bartlet, daughter of William Bartlet. I shall give the account as I took it from the mouth of her parents, whose veracity none who know them doubt of. She was born in March, 1731. About the latter end of April, or beginning of May, 1735, she was greatly affected by the talk of her brother, who had been hopefully converted a little before, at about eleven years of age, and then seriously talked to her about the great things of religion.

Her parents did not know of it at that time, and were not wont, in the counsels they gave to their children, particularly to direct themselves to her, being so young, and, as they supposed, not capable of understanding. But after her brother had talked to her, they observed her very earnestly listen to the advice they gave to the other children; and she was observed very constantly to retire, several times in a day, as was concluded, for secret prayer. She grew more and more engaged in religion, and was more frequent in her closet; till at last she was wont to visit it five or six times a day: and was so engaged in it, that nothing would at any time divert her from her stated closet exercises. Her mother often observed and watched her, when such things occurred as she thought most likely to divert her, either by putting it out of her thoughts, or otherwise engaging her inclinations; but never could observe her to fail. She mentioned some very remarkable instances.

She once of her own accord spake of her unsuccessfulness, in that she could not find God, or to that purpose. But on Thursday, the last day of July, about the middle of the day, the child being in the closet, where it used to retire, its mother heard it speaking aloud; which was unusual, and never had been observed before. And her voice seemed to be as of one exceedingly importunate and engaged; but her mother could distinctly hear only these words, spoken in a childish manner, but with extraordinary earnestness, and out of distress of soul, "pray, blessed Lord, give me salvation! I pray, beg, pardon all my sins!"

When the child had done prayer, she came out of the closet, sat down by her mother, and cried out aloud. Her mother very earnestly asked her several times what the matter was, before she would make any answer; but she continued crying, and writhing her body to and fro, like one in anguish of spirit. Her mother then asked her, whether she was afraid that God would not give her salvation. She then answered, "Yes, I am afraid I shall go to hell!" Her mother then endeavored to quiet her, and told her she would not have her cry, she must be a good girl, and pray every day, and she hoped God would give her salvation. But this did not quiet her at all; she continued thus earnestly crying, and taking on for some time, till at length she suddenly ceased crying, and began to smile, and presently said with a smiling countenance, "Mother, the kingdom of heaven is come to me!"

Her mother was surprised at the sudden alteration, and at the speech; and knew not what to make of it; but at first said nothing to her. The child presently spake again, and said, "There is another come to me, and there is another, there is three"; and being asked what she meant, she answered, "One is, Thy will be done, and there is another, Enjoy Him for ever"; by which it seems, that when the child said, "There is three come to me";

she meant three passages of her catechism that came to her mind. After the child had said this, she retired again into her closet, and her mother went over to her brother's, who was next neighbor; and when she came back, the child, being come out of the closet, meets her mother with this cheerful speech: "I can find God now!" referring to what she had before complained of, that she could not find God.

Then the child spoke again and said, "I love God!" Her mother asked her how well she loved God, whether she loved God better than her father and mother. She said yes. Then she asked her, whether she loved God better than her little sister Rachel. She answered, "Yes, better than any thing!" Then her elder sister, referring to her saying she could find God now, asked her where she could find God. She answered "In heaven." "Why," said she, "have you been in heaven?" "No," said the child. By this it seems not to have been any imagination of any thing seen with bodily eyes, that she called God, when she said, "I can find God now."

Her mother asked her whether she was afraid of going to hell, and if that had made her cry. She answered, "Yes, I was; but now I shan't." Her mother asked her, whether she thought that God had given her salvation: she answered, "Yes." Her mother asked her. When? She answered, "Today." She appeared all that afternoon exceeding cheerful and joyful. One of the neighbors asked her, how she felt herself. She answered, "I feel better than I did." The neighbor asked her, what made her feel better. She answered, "God makes me."

That evening, as she lay a-bed, she called one of her little cousins to her, who was present in the room, as having something to say to him; and when he came, she told him, that heaven was better than earth. The next day, her mother asked her what God made her for? She answered, "To serve him"; and added, "Every body should serve God, and get an interest in Christ." The same day the elder children, when they came home from school, seemed much affected with the extraordinary change that seemed to be made in Phebe. And her sister Abigail standing by, her mother took occasion to counsel her, now to improve her time, to prepare for another world. On which Phebe burst out in tears, and cried out, "Poor Nabby!" Her mother told her, she would not have to cry; she hoped that God would give Nabby salvation; but that did not quiet her, she continued earnestly crying for some time. When she had in a measure ceased, her sister Eunice being by her, she burst out again, and cried, "Poor Eunice!" and cried exceedingly; and when she had almost done, she went into another room, and there looked upon her sister Naomi: and burst out again, crying, "Poor Amy!" Her mother was greatly affected at such a behavior in a child, and knew not what to say to her.

One of the neighbors coming in a little after, asked her what she had cried for. She seemed at first backward to tell the reason: her mother told her she might tell that person, for he had given her an apple: upon which she said, she cried because she was afraid they would go to hell. At night, a certain minister, who was occasionally in the town, was at the house, and talked with her of religious things. After he was gone, she sat leaning on the table, with tears running from her eyes; and being asked what made her cry, she said, "I was thinking about God."

The next day, being Saturday, she seemed a great part of the day to be in a very affectionate frame, had four turns of crying and seemed to endeavor to curb herself, and hide her tears, and was very backward to talk of the occasion. On the Sabbath-day she was asked, whether she believed in God; she answered, *Yes*. And being told that Christ was the Son of God, she made ready answer, and said, *I know it*. From this time there appeared a very remarkable abiding change in the child. She has been very strict upon the Sabbath; and seems to long for the Sabbath-day before it comes, and will often in the week time be inquiring how long it is to the Sabbath-day, and must have the days between particularly counted over, before she will be contented. She seems to love God's house, and is very eager to go thither. . . .

Honored Sir, With humble respect,
Your obedient Son and Servant,
Jonathan Edwards.
Northampton,
November 6, 1736.

GILBERT TENNENT: "THE DANGERS OF AN UNCOVERTED MINISTRY" (ABRIDGED)
English, 1740

Gilbert Tennent (1703–1764), a contemporary of Jonathan Edwards, was educated by his father and prepared for ministry in the "Log College" (later Princeton University), which he, William, established for the preparation of Presbyterian clergy. The younger Tennent supported British evangelist George Whitefield's 1740 preaching tour of New England (which sparked the Great Awakening) and came to Boston to follow up Whitefield's work. Some Boston clergymen were highly critical of the growing revival, and Gilbert Tennent's most highly publicized sermon was apparently aimed at these critics. Parts 1 and 2 and the opening portion of part 3 are reprinted here.

And Jesus, when He came out, saw much people
and was moved with compassion towards them,
because they were as sheep not having a shepherd.
(Mark 6:34)

✦

As a faithful ministry is a great ornament, blessing, and comfort, to the church of God (even the feet of such messengers are beautiful), so, on the contrary, an ungodly ministry is a great curse and judgment. These caterpillars labor to devour every green thing.

There is nothing that may more justly call forth our saddest sorrows, and make all our powers and passions mourn in the most doleful accents, the most incessant, insatiable, and deploring agonies, than the melancholy case of such who have no faithful ministry! This truth is set before our minds in a strong light in the words that I have chosen now to insist upon, in which we have an account of our Lord's grief with the causes of it.

We are informed that our dear Redeemer was moved with compassion towards them. The original word signifies the strongest and most vehement pity, issuing from the innermost bowels. But what was the cause of this great and compassionate commotion in the heart of Christ? It was because He saw much people as sheep having no shepherd. Why, had the people then no teachers? O yes! They had heaps of Pharisee-teachers that came out, no doubt, after they had been at the feet of Gamaliel the usual time, and according to the acts,

cannons, and traditions of the Jewish church. But, notwithstanding the great crowds of these orthodox, letter-learned, and regular Pharisees, our Lord laments the unhappy case of that great number of people who, in the days of His flesh, had no letter guides, because those were as good as none (in many respects), in our Savior's judgment. For all them, the people were as sheep without a Shepherd.

From the words of our text, the following proposition offers itself to our consideration: that the case of such is much to be pitied who have no other but Pharisee-shepherds, or unconverted teachers.

In discoursing upon this subject, I would:

I. Inquire into the characters of the old Pharisee-teachers.
II. Show why the case of such people who have no better should be pitied. And,
III. Show how pity should be expressed upon this mournful occasion!

First, I am to inquire into the characters of the old Pharisee-teachers. No, I think the most notorious branches of their character were these: pride, policy, malice, ignorance, covetousness, and bigotry to human inventions in religious matters.

The old Pharisees were very proud and conceited. They loved the uppermost seats in the synagogues and to be called "Rabbi." They were masterly and positive in their assertions, as if knowledge must die with them. They looked upon others who differed from them, and the common people, with an air of disdain and, especially any who had a respect for Jesus and His doctrine. They disliked them and judged them accursed.

The old Pharisee-shepherds were as crafty as foxes. They tried by all means to ensnare our Lord by their captious questions, and to expose Him to the displeasure of the state while, in the meantime, by sly and sneaking methods, they tried to secure for themselves the favor of the Grandees and the people's displeasure, and this they obtained to their satisfaction (John 7:48).

But while they exerted the craft of foxes, they did not forget to breathe forth the cruelty of wolves in a malicious aspersing of the person of Christ, and in a violent opposing of the truths, people, and power of His religion. Yes, the most stern and strict of them were the ringleaders of the party. Witness Saul's journey to

Damascus, with letters from the chief priest to bring bound to Jerusalem all that he could find of The Way. It's true that the Pharisees did not proceed to violent measures with our Savior and His disciples just at first; but that was not owing to their good nature, but their policy, for they feared the people. They must keep the people in their interests. Aye, that was the main chance, the compass that directed all their proceedings and, therefore, such sly cautious methods must be pursued as might consist herewith. They wanted to root vital religion out of the world, but they found it beyond their thumb.

Although some of the old Pharisee-shepherds had a very fair and strict outside, yet they were ignorant of the New Birth. Witness Rabbi Nicodemus, who talked like a fool about it. Hear how our Lord cursed those plastered hypocrites in Matthew 23:27–28: "Woe unto you, Scribes and Pharisees, hypocrites; for ye are like whited sepulchres, which indeed appear beautiful outward, but are within full of dead bones and of all uncleanness. Even so ye also appear righteous unto men, but within ye are full of hypocrisy and iniquity." Aye, if they had but a little of the learning then in fashion, and a fair outside, they were presently put into the priest's office, though they had no experience of the New Birth. O sad!

The old Pharisees, for all their long prayers and other pious pretenses, had their eyes, with Judas, fixed upon the bag. Why, they came into the priest's office for a piece of bread. They took it up as a trade and, therefore, endeavored to make the best market of it they could. O shame!

It may be further observed that the Pharisee-teachers in Christ's time were great bigots to small matters in religion. Matthew 23:23: "Woe unto you, Scribes and Pharisees, hypocrites; for ye pay tithe of mind, and anise, and cummin, and have omitted the weightier matters of the Law, judgment, mercy, and faith." The Pharisees were fired with a party-zeal. They compassed sea and land to make a proselyte; and yet, when he was made, they made him twofold more the child of hell than themselves. They were also bigoted to human inventions in religious matters. Paul himself, while he was a natural man, was wonderfully zealous for the traditions of the Fathers. Aye, those poor, blind guides, as our Lord testifies, strained at a gnat and swallowed a camel.

And what a mighty respect they had for the Sabbath Day, insomuch that Christ and His disciples must be charged with the breach thereof for doing works of mercy and necessity! Ah, the rottenness of these hypocrites! It was not so much respect to the Sabbath as malice against Christ; that was the occasion of the charge. They wanted some plausible pretense to offer against Him in order to blacken His character.

And what a great love had they in pretense to those pious prophets who were dead before they were born while, in the meantime, they were persecuting the Prince of Prophets! Hear how the King of the Church speaks to them upon this head, Matthew 23:29–33: "Woe unto you Scribes and Pharisees, hypocrites; because ye build the tombs of the prophets, and garnish the sepulchres of the righteous; and say, If we had been in the days of our fathers, we would not have been partakers with them in the blood of the prophets. Ye serpents, ye generation of vipers, how can ye escape the damnation of hell?"

The second general head of discourse is to show why much people, who have no better than the old Pharisee-teachers, are to be pitied:

1. Natural men have no call of God to the ministerial work under the gospel dispensation. Isn't it a principal part of the ordinary call of God to the ministerial work to aim at the glory of God and, in subordination thereunto, the good of souls as their chief marks in their undertaking that work? And can any natural man on earth do this? No! No! Every skin of them has an evil eye, for no cause can produce effects above its own power. Are not wicked men forbidden to meddle in things sacred? Psalm 50:16: "But unto the wicked, God says, 'What hast thou to do to declare My statutes, or that thou should take My covenant in thy mouth?'" Now, are not all unconverted men wicked men? Does not the Lord Jesus inform us in John 10:1 that "he who enters not by the door into the sheepfold, but climbs up some other way, the same is a thief and a robber?" In the ninth verse, Christ tells us that He is the Door, and that if any man enters in by Him, he shall be saved by Him, i.e., by faith in Him, says (Matthew) Henry. Hence we read of a "door of faith" being opened to the Gentiles (Acts 14:22).

   It confirms that salvation is annexed to the

entrance before mentioned. Remarkable is that saying of our Savior in Matthew 4:9: "Follow Me, and I will make you fishers of men." See, our Lord will not make men ministers till they follow Him. Men who do not follow Christ may fish faithfully for a good name, and for worldly self, but not for the conversion of sinners to God. Is it reasonable to suppose that they will be earnestly concerned for others' salvation when they slight their own? Our Lord reproved Nicodemus for taking upon himself the office of instructing others while he himself was a stranger to the New Birth. John 3:10: "Art thou a master of Israel, and knows not these things?" The Apostle Paul (1 Tim. 1:12) thanks God for counting him faithful, and putting him into the ministry, which plainly supposes that God Almighty does not send Pharisees and natural men into ministry; for how can those men be faithful who have no faith? It's true, men may put themselves into the ministry through unfaithfulness or mistake. Credit and money may draw them, and the devil may drive them into it, knowing by long experience of what special service they may be to his kingdom in that office; but God does not send such hypocritical varlets.

Hence Timothy was directed by the Apostle Paul to commit the ministerial work to faithful men (2 Tim. 2:2), and do not those qualifications necessary for church-officers, specified in 1 Timothy 3:2–3, 9–11 and Titus 1:7–8 plainly suppose converting grace? How else can they avoid being greedy of filthy lucre? How else can they hold the mystery of faith in a pure conscience and be faithful in all things? How else can they be lovers of good, sober, just, holy, temperate?

2. The ministry of natural men is uncomfortable to gracious souls. The enmity that is put between the seed of the woman and the seed of the serpent will, now and then, be creating jars. And no wonder; for as it was of old, so it is now: "He that was born after the flesh, persecuteth him that was born after the Spirit." This enmity is not one grain less in unconverted ministers than in others; though it is possible it may

be better polished with wit and rhetoric, and gilded with the specious names of zeal, fidelity, peace, good order, and unity.

Natural men, not having true love to Christ or the souls of their fellow-creatures, find their discourses are cold and sapless, and, as it were, freeze between their lips. And not being sent of God, they lack the divine authority with which the faithful ambassadors of Christ are clothed, who herein resemble their blessed Master of whom it is said, "He taught as one having authority, and not as the scribes" (Matt. 7:29).

And Pharisee-teachers, having no experience of a special work of the Holy Ghost upon their own souls, are therefore neither inclined to nor fitted for discoursing frequently, clearly, and pathetically upon such important subjects. The application of their discourses is either short or indistinct and general. They do not distinguish the precious from the vile, and divide not to every man his portion, according to the apostolic direction to Timothy. No! They carelessly offer a common mess to their people, and leave it to them to divide it among themselves as they see fit. This is, indeed, their general practice, which is bad enough; but sometimes they do worse by misapplying the Word through ignorance or anger. They often strengthen the hands of the wicked by promising him life. They comfort people before they convince them, sow before they plow, and are busy in raising a fabric before they lay a foundation. These foolish builders do but strengthen men's carnal security by their soft, selfish, cowardly discourses. They do not have the courage or honesty to thrust the nail of terror into sleeping souls.

Nay, sometimes they strive with all their might to fasten terror into the hearts of the righteous, and so to make those sad whom God would not have made sad! And this happens when pious people begin to suspect their hypocrisy, for which they have good reason, I may add that, inasmuch as Pharisee-teachers seek after righteousness, as it were, by the works of the law themselves, they therefore do not distinguish as they ought between Law and Gospel in their discourses to others. They keep driving, driving, to duty, duty, under this notion that it will recommend natural men to the favor of God, or entitle them to the promises of grace and salvation. And thus those blind guides fix a deluded world upon the false foundation of their own righteousness, and so exclude them from the dear Redeemer.

All the doings of unconverted men not proceeding from the principles of faith, love, and a new nature, nor being directed to the divine glory as their highest end, but flowing from, and tending to, self as their principle and end, are, doubtless, damnably wicked in their manner of performance, and deserve the wrath and curse of a sin-avenging God. Neither can any other encouragement be justly given them but that, in the way of duty, there is a peradventure of probability or obtaining mercy.

And natural men, lacking the experience of those spiritual difficulties which pious souls are exposed to in this vale of tears, do not know how to speak a word to the weary in season. Their prayers are also cold; little child-like love to God or pity to poor perishing souls runs through their veins. Their conversation has nothing of the savor of Christ, neither is it perfumed with the spices of heaven. They seem to make as little distinction in their practice as preaching. They love those unbelievers that are kind to them better than many Christians, and choose them for companions, contrary to Psalms 15:4; 119:115 and Galatians 6:10. Poor Christians are stunted and starved who are put to feed on such bare pastures, on such "dry nurses," as Rev. Mr. (Arthur) Hildersham justly calls them. It's only when the wise virgins sleep that they can bear with those dead dogs who can't bark; but when the Lord revives His people, they can't but abhor them. O! It is ready to break their very hearts with grief, to see how lukewarm those Pharisee-teachers are in their public discourses, while sinners are sinking into damnation in multitudes! But:

3. The ministry of natural men is, for the most part, unprofitable, which is confirmed by a three-fold evidence of Scripture, reason, and experience. Such as the Lord sends not, He Himself assures us, shall not profit the people at all (Jer. 23:32). Matthew Poole justly glosses upon this passage of sacred Scripture thus, "None can expect God's blessing upon their ministry that are not called and sent of God into the ministry." And right reason will inform us how unfit instruments they are to negotiate that work they pretend to. Is a blind man fit to be a guide in a very dangerous way? Is a dead man fit to bring others to life? A mad man fit to cast out devils? A rebel, an enemy to God, fit to be sent on an embassy of peace to bring rebels into a state of friendship with God? A captive bound in the massy chains of darkness and guilt, a proper person to set others at liberty? A leper, or one that has plague-sores upon him, fit to be a good physician? Is an ignorant rustic that has never been at sea in his life fit to be a pilot, to keep vessels from being dashed to pieces upon rocks and sand-banks? Isn't an unconverted minister like a man who would teach others to swim before he has learned it himself, and so is drowned in the act and dies like a fool?

I may add that sad experience verifies what has been now observed concerning the unprofitableness of the ministry of unconverted men. Look into the congregations of unconverted ministers, and see what a sad security reigns there; not a soul convinced that can be heard of for many years together, and yet the ministers are easy, for they say they do their duty! Aye, a small matter will satisfy us in the lack of that which we have no great desire after, but when persons have their eyes opened and their hearts set upon the work of God, they are not so soon satisfied with their doings, and with lack of success for a time. O! They mourn with Micah that they are as those that gather the summer-fruits, as the grape-gleaning of the vintage. Mr. (Richard) Baxter justly observes that those who speak about their doings in the aforesaid manner are likely to do little good to the Church of God. But many Ministers (as Mr. Bracel observes) think the gospel flourishes among them when the people are in peace, and many come to hear the Word and to the Sacrament. If, with the other, they get the salaries well-paid, then it is fine times indeed in their opinion! O sad! And they are full of hopes that they do good, though they know nothing about it. But what comfort can a conscientious man, who travails in birth that Christ may be formed in His hearer's hearts, take from what he knows not? Will a hungry stomach be satisfied with dreams about meat? I believe not, though, I confess, a full one may.

What if some instances could be shown of unconverted ministers being instrumental in convincing persons of their lost state? The thing is very rare and extraordinary. And, for what I know, as many instances may be given of Satan's convincing persons by his temptations. Indeed, it's a kind of chance-medley, both in respect of the father and his children, when any such event happens. And isn't this the reason why a work of conviction and conversion has been so rarely heard of for a long time in the churches till of late, that the bulk of her spiritual guides were stone-blind and stone-dead?

4. The ministry of natural men is dangerous, both in respect of the doctrines and practice of piety. The doctrines of original sin, justification by faith alone, and the other points of Calvinism, are very cross to the grain of unrenewed nature. And though men, by the influence of a good education and hopes of preferment, may have the edge of their natural enmity against them blunted, yet it's far from being broken or removed. It's only the saving grace of God that can give us a true relish for those nature-humbling doctrines; and so effectually secure us from being infected by the contrary. Is not the carnality of the ministry one great cause of the general spread of Arminianism, Socinianism, Arianism, and Deism, at this day through the world?

And alas! What poor guides are natural ministers to those who are under spiritual trouble? They either slight such distress altogether and call it "melancholy," or "madness," or daub those that are under it with untempered mortar. Our Lord assures us that the salt which has lost its savor is good for nothing. Some say, "It genders worms and vermin." Now, what savor have Pharisee-ministers? In truth, a very stinking one, both in the nostrils of God and good men. "Be these moral Negroes never so white in the mouth (as one expresses it), yet will they hinder instead of helping others in at the strait gate." Hence is that threatening of our Lord against them in Matthew 23:13: "Woe unto you, Scribes and Pharisees, hypocrites; for ye shut up the Kingdom of Heaven against men; for ye neither go in yourselves, nor suffer those that are entering to go in."

Pharisee-teachers will, with the utmost hate, oppose the very work of God's Spirit upon the souls of men, and labor by all means to blacken it, as well as the Instruments, which the Almighty improves to promote the same if it comes near their borders, and interferes with their credit or interest. Thus did the Pharisees deal with our Savior.

If it is objected against what has been offered under this general head of discourse, that Judas was sent by Christ, I answer:

(1) That Judas's ministry was partly legal, inasmuch as, during that period, the disciples were subject to Jewish observances and sent only to the house of Israel (Matt. 10:5–6). And in that they waited after Christ's resurrection for another mission (Acts 1:4), which we find they obtained, and that was different from the former (Matt. 28:19).

(2) Judas's ministry was extraordinarily necessary in order to fulfil some ancient prophesies concerning him (Acts 1:16–18, 20; John 13:18). I fear that the abuse of this instance has brought many Judases into the ministry whose chief desire, like their great grandfather, is to finger the pence and carry the bag. But let such hireling, murderous hypocrites take care that they don't feel the force of a halter in this world, and an aggravated damnation in the next.

Again, if it is objected that Paul rejoiced that the gospel was preached, though of contention and not sincerely, I answer this: the expression signifies the apostle's great self-denial! Some labored to eclipse his fame and character by contentious preaching, thinking thereby to afflict him; but they were mistaken. As to that, he was easy; for he had long before learned to die to his own reputation. The apostle's rejoicing was comparative only. He would rather that Christ should be preached out of envy than not at all, especially considering the gross ignorance of the doctrinal knowledge of the gospel which prevailed almost universally in that age of the world. Besides, the apostle knew that that trial should be sanctified to him to promote his spiritual progress in goodness and, perhaps, prove a means of procuring his temporal freedom; and, therefore, he would rejoice. It is certain, we may both rejoice and mourn in relation to the same thing upon different accounts without any contradiction.

But the third general head was to show how pity should be expressed upon this mournful occasion. My brethren, we should mourn over those who are destitute of faithful ministers and sympathize with them. Our bowels should be moved with the most compassionate tenderness over those dear fainting souls that are as "sheep having no Shepherd," and that after the example of our blessed Lord.

Dear sirs! We should also most earnestly pray for them that the compassionate Savior may preserve them by His mighty power, through faith, unto salvation; support their sinking spirits under the melancholy uneasiness of a dead ministry; sanctify and sweeten to them the dry morsels they get under such blind men, when they have none better to repair to.

And more especially, my brethren, we should pray to the Lord of the harvest to send forth faithful laborers into His harvest, seeing that the harvest truly is plenteous, but the laborers are few. And, O sirs, how humble, believing, and importunate should we be in this petition! O! Let us follow the Lord day and night with cries, tears, pleadings, and groanings upon this account! For God knows there is great necessity of it. O! Thou Fountain of mercy and Father of pity, pour forth upon Thy poor children a Spirit of prayer for the obtaining of this important mercy! Help, help, O Eternal God and Father, for Christ's sake!

And indeed, my brethren, we should join our endeavors to our prayers. The most likely method to stock the church with a faithful ministry, in the present situation of things, the public academies being so much corrupted and abused generally, is to encourage private schools, or seminaries of learning, which are under the care of skilful and experienced Christians; in which those only should be admitted who, upon strict examination have, in the judgment of a reasonable charity, the plain evidences of experimental religion. Pious and experienced youths, who have a good natural capacity, and great desires after the ministerial work, from good motives, might be sought for, and found up and down in the country, and put to private schools of the Prophets, especially in such places where the public ones are not.

This method, in my opinion, has a noble tendency. It builds up the church for the coming of His Kingdom. The church should be ready, according to their ability, to give something, from time to time, for the support of such poor youths who have nothing of their own. And truly, brethren, this charity to the souls of men is the most noble kind of charity. O! If the love of God is in you, it will constrain you to do something to promote so noble and necessary a work. It looks hypocritical to go no further, when other things are required, than cheap prayer. Don't think it much if the Pharisees should be offended at such a proposal; these subtle, selfish hypocrites are wont to be scared about their credit and their kingdom. And truly they are both little worth, for all the bustle they make about them. If they could help it, they wouldn't let one faithful man come into the ministry; and, therefore, their opposition is an encouraging sign. Let all the followers of the Lamb stand up and act for God against all opposers. Who is upon God's side? Who?

JOHN WESLEY: "FREE GRACE"
English, 1740

Concurrent with the Great Awakening in America was the Methodist revival of Great Britain, the two greatest exponents of which were John Wesley and George Whitefield. Not long into the revivals that sprang up under the outdoor preaching of both evangelists, theological differences between the two became apparent. While Whitefield held a Reformed theological perspective, emphasizing the doctrine of predestination as a "doctrine of grace," Wesley, with his High Anglican background, allowed much more latitude for the working of human free will in salvation. It appeared for a time that both would downplay their theological differences in the interest of Christian unity and the advancement of the revival. At a certain point, however, Wesley began to oppose the doctrine of predestination in his preaching—in particular through his sermon "Free Grace," preached at Bristol. To this Whitefield felt obliged to respond, and so letters between the two revivalists were exchanged. Wesley's sermon #128, from the edition of 1872, is reprinted here, along with two letters later published by Whitefield himself (in the interest of transparency) with an introduction (see pages 328–40).

He that spared not his own Son, but delivered him up for us all, how shall he not with him also freely give us all things? (Rom. 8:32)

✦

How freely does God love the world! While we were yet sinners, "Christ died for the ungodly." While we were "dead in our sin," God "spared not his own Son, but delivered him up for us all." And how freely with him does he "give us all things!" Verily, FREE GRACE is all in all!

The grace or love of God, whence cometh our salvation, is FREE IN ALL, and FREE FOR ALL.

I. It is free in all to whom it is given.
II. The doctrine of predestination is not a doctrine of God.
III. Predestination destroys the comfort of religion, the happiness of Christianity.
IV. This uncomfortable doctrine also destroys our zeal for good works.
V. Furthermore, the doctrine of predestination has a direct and manifest tendency to overthrow the whole Christian Revelation.
VI. And at the same time, makes that Revelation contradict itself.
VII. Predestination is a doctrine full of blasphemy.

I.

First. It is free in all to whom it is given. It does not depend on any power or merit in man; no, not in any degree, neither in whole, nor in part. It does not in anywise depend either on the good works or righteousness of the receiver; not on anything he has done, or anything he is. It does not depend on his endeavors. It does not depend on his good tempers, or good desires, or good purposes and intentions; for all these flow from the free grace of God; they are the streams only, not the fountain. They are the fruits of free grace, and not the root. They are not the cause, but the effects of it. Whatsoever good is in man, or is done by man, God is the author and doer of it. Thus is his grace free in all; that is, no way depending on any power or merit in man, but on God alone, who freely gave us his own Son, and "with him freely giveth us all things."

But it is free for ALL, as well as IN ALL. To this some have answered, "No: It is free only for those whom God hath ordained to life; and they are but a little flock. The greater part of God hath ordained to death; and it is not free for them. Them God hateth; and, therefore, before they were born, decreed they should die eternally. And this he absolutely decreed; because so was his good pleasure; because it was his sovereign will. Accordingly, they are born for this—to be destroyed body and soul in hell. And they grow up under the irrevocable curse of God, without any possibility of redemption; for what grace God gives, he gives only for this, to increase, not prevent, their damnation."

1. This is that decree of predestination. But methinks I hear one say, "This is not the predestination which I hold: I hold only the election of grace. What I believe is not more than this—that God, before the foundation of the world, did elect a certain number of men to be justified, sanctified, and glorified. Now, all these will be saved, and none else; for the rest of mankind God leaves to themselves: So they follow the imaginations of their own hearts, which are only evil continually, and, waxing worse and worse, are at length justly punished with everlasting destruction."

2. Is this all the predestination which you hold? Consider; perhaps this is not all. Do not you believe God ordained them to this very thing? If so, you believe the whole degree; you hold predestination in the full sense which has been above described. But it may be you think

you do not. Do not you then believe, God hardens the hearts of them that perish: Do not you believe, he (literally) hardened Pharaoh's heart; and that for this end he raised him up, or created him? Why, this amounts to just the same thing. If you believe Pharaoh, or any one man upon earth, was created for this end, to be damned, you hold all that has been said of predestination. And there is no need you should add, that God seconds his decree, which is supposed unchangeable and irresistible, by hardening the hearts of those vessels of wrath whom that decree had before fitted for destruction.

3. Well, but it may be you do not believe even this; you do not hold any decree of reprobation; you do not think God decrees any man to be damned, nor hardens, irresistibly fits him, for damnation; you only say, "God eternally decreed, that all being dead in sin, he would say to some of the dry bones, Live, and to others he would not; that, consequently, these should be made alive, and those abide in death; these should glorify God by their salvation, and those by their destruction."

4. Is not this what you mean by the election of grace? If it be, I would ask one or two questions: Are any who are not thus elected saved? Or were any, from the foundation of the world? Is it possible any man should be saved unless he be thus elected? If you say, "No," you are but where you were; you are not got one hair's breadth farther; you still believe, that, in consequence of an unchangeable, irresistible decree of God, the greater part of mankind abide in death, without any possibility of redemption; inasmuch as none can save them but God, and he will not save them. You believe he hath absolutely decreed not to save them; and what is this but decreeing to damn them? It is, in effect, neither more nor less; it comes to the same thing; for if you are dead, and altogether unable to make yourself alive, then, if God has absolutely decreed he will make only others alive, and not you, he hath absolutely decreed your everlasting death; you are absolutely consigned to damnation. So then, though you use softer words than some, you mean the self-same thing; and God's decree concerning the election of grace, according to your account of it, amounts to neither more nor less than what others call God's decree of reprobation.

5. Call it therefore by whatever name you please, election, preterition, predestination, or reprobation, it comes in the end to the same thing. The sense of all is plainly this—by virtue of an eternal, unchangeable, irresistible decree of God, one part of mankind are infallibly saved, and the rest infallibly damned; it being impossible that any of the former should be damned, or that any of the latter should be saved.

6. But if this be so, then is all preaching vain? It is needless to them that are elected; for they, whether with preaching or without, will infallibly be saved. Therefore, the end of preaching—to save souls—is void with regard to them; and it is useless to them that are not elected, for they cannot possibly be saved: They, whether with preaching or without, will infallibly be damned. The end of preaching is therefore void with regard to them likewise; so that in either case our preaching is vain, as your hearing is also vain.

II.

This then, is a plain proof that the doctrine of predestination is not a doctrine of God, because it makes void the ordinance of God; and God is not divided against himself.

A second is, that it directly tends to destroy that holiness which is the end of all the ordinances of God. I do not say, none who hold it are holy; (for God is of tender mercy to those who are unavoidably entangled in errors of any kind;) but that the doctrine itself, that every man is either elected or not elected from eternity, and that the one must inevitably be saved, and the other inevitably damned, has a manifest tendency to destroy holiness in general; for it wholly takes away those first motives to follow after it, so frequently proposed in Scripture, the hope of future reward and fear of punishment, the hope of heaven and fear of hell. That these shall go away into everlasting punishment, and those into life eternal, is not motive to him to struggle for life who believes his lot is cast already; it is not reasonable for him so to do, if he thinks he is unalterably adjudged either to life or death. You will say, "But he knows not whether it is life or death." What then?—this helps not the matter; for if a sick man knows that he must unavoidably die, or unavoidably recover, though he knows not which, it is unreasonable for him to take any physic at all. He might justly say (and so I have heard some speak, both in bodily sickness and in spiritual), "If I am ordained to life, I shall live; if to death, I shall die; so I need not trouble myself about it." So directly does this doctrine tend to shut the very gate of holiness in general—to hinder unholy men from ever approaching thereto, or striving to enter in thereat.

1. As directly does this doctrine tend to destroy several particular branches of holiness. Such are meekness and love,—love, I mean, of our enemies,—of the evil and unthankful. I say not, that none who hold it have meekness and love (for as is the power of God, so is his mercy;) but that it naturally tends to inspire, or increase, a sharpness or eagerness of temper, which is quite contrary to the meekness of Christ; as then especially appears, when they are opposed on this head. And it as naturally inspires contempt or coldness towards those whom we suppose outcast from God. "O but," you say, "I suppose no particular man a reprobate." You mean you would not if you could help it: But you cannot help sometimes applying your general doctrine to particular persons: The enemy of souls will apply it for you. You know how often he has done so. But you rejected the thought with abhorrence. True; as soon as you could; but how did it sour and sharpen your spirit in the mean time! You well know it was not the spirit of love which you then felt towards that poor sinner, whom you supposed or suspected, whether you would or no, to have been hated of God from eternity.

III.

Thirdly. This doctrine tends to destroy the comfort of religion, the happiness of Christianity. This is evident as to all those who believe themselves to be reprobated, or who only suspect or fear it. All the great and precious promises are lost to them; they afford them no ray of comfort: For they are not the elect of God; therefore they have neither lot nor portion in them. This is an effectual bar to their finding any comfort or happiness, even in that religion whose ways are designed to be "ways of pleasantness, and all her paths peace."

1. And as to you who believe yourselves the elect of God, what is your happiness? I hope, not a notion, a speculative belief, a bare opinion of any kind; but a feeling possession of God in your heart, wrought in you by the Holy Ghost, or, the witness of God's Spirit with your spirit that you are a child of God. This, otherwise termed "the full assurance of faith," is the true ground of a Christian's happiness. And it does indeed imply a full assurance that all your past sins are forgiven, and that you are now a child of God. But it does not necessarily imply a full assurance of our future perseverance. I do not say this is never joined to it, but that it is not necessarily implied therein; for many have the one who have not the other.

2. Now, this witness of the Spirit experience shows to be much obstructed by this doctrine; and not only in those who, believing themselves reprobated, by this belief thrust it far from them, but even in them that have tasted of that good gift, who yet have soon lost it again, and fallen back into doubts, and fears, and darkness, horrible darkness, that might be felt! And I appeal to any of you who hold this doctrine, to say, between God and your own hearts, whether you have not often a return of doubts and fears concerning your election or perseverance! If you ask, "Who has not?" I answer, Very few of those that hold this doctrine; but many, very many, of those that hold it not, in all parts of the earth; many of these have enjoyed the uninterrupted witness of his Spirit, the continual light of his countenance, from the moment wherein they first believed, for many months or years, to this day.

3. That assurance of faith which these enjoy excludes all doubt and fear, it excludes all kinds of doubt and fear concerning their future perseverance; though it is not properly, as was said before, an assurance of what is future, but

only of what now is. And this needs not for its support a speculative belief, that whoever is once ordained to life must live; for it is wrought from hour to hour, by the mighty power of God, "by the Holy Ghost which is given unto them." And therefore that doctrine is not of God, because it tends to obstruct, if not destroy, this great work of the Holy Ghost, whence flows the chief comfort of religion, the happiness of Christianity.

4. Again: How uncomfortable a thought is this, that thousands and millions of men, without any preceding offense or fault of theirs, were unchangeably doomed to everlasting burnings! How peculiarly uncomfortable must it be to those who have put on Christ! To those who, being filled with bowels of mercy, tenderness, and compassion, could even "wish themselves accursed for their brethren's sake!"

IV.

Fourthly. This uncomfortable doctrine directly tends to destroy our zeal for good works. And this it does, First, as it naturally tends (according to what was observed before) to destroy our love to the greater part of mankind, namely, the evil and unthankful. For whatever lessens our love, must go far to lessen our desire to do them good. This it does, Secondly, as it cuts off one of the strongest motives to all acts of bodily mercy, such as feeding the hungry, clothing the naked, and the like,—viz., the hope of saving their souls from death. For what avails it to relieve their temporal wants, who are just dropping into eternal fire? "Well; but run and snatch them as brands out of the fire." Nay, this you suppose impossible. They were appointed thereunto, you say, from eternity, before they had done either good or evil. You believe it is the will of God they should die. And "who hath resisted his will?" But you say you do not know whether these are elected or not. What then? If you know they are the one or the other,—that they are either elected or not elected, all your labour is void and vain. In either case, your advice, reproof, or exhortation is as needless and useless as our preaching. It is needless to them that are elected; for they will infallibly be saved without it. It is useless to them that are not elected; for with or without it they will infallibly be damned; therefore you cannot consistently with your principles take

any pains about their salvation. Consequently, those principles directly tend to destroy your zeal for good works; for all good works; but particularly for the greatest of all, the saving of souls from death.

V.

But, fifthly, this doctrine not only tends to destroy Christian holiness, happiness, and good works, but hath also a direct and manifest tendency to overthrow the whole Christian Revelation. The point which the wisest of the modern unbelievers most industriously labour to prove, is, that the Christian Revelation is not necessary. They well know, could they once show this, the conclusion would be too plain to be denied, "If it be not necessary, it is not true." Now, this fundamental point you give up. For supposing that eternal, unchangeable decree, one part of mankind must be saved, though the Christian Revelation were not in being, and the other part of mankind must be damned, notwithstanding that Revelation. And what would an infidel desire more? You allow him all he asks. In making the gospel thus unnecessary to all sorts of men, you give up the whole Christian cause. "O tell it not in Gath! Lest the daughters of the uncircumcised rejoice; lest the sons of unbelief triumph!"

VI.

And as this doctrine manifestly and directly tends to overthrow the whole Christian Revelation, so it does the same thing, by plain consequence, in making that Revelation contradict itself. For it is grounded on such an interpretation of some texts (more or fewer it matters not) as flatly contradicts all the other texts, and indeed the whole scope and tenor of Scripture. For instance: The assertors of this doctrine interpret that text of Scripture, "Jacob have I loved, but Esau have I hated," as implying that God in a literal sense hated Esau, and all the reprobated, from eternity. Now, what can possibly be a more flat contradiction than this, not only to the whole scope and tenor of Scripture, but also to all those particular texts which expressly declare, "God is love?" Again: They infer from that text, "I will have mercy on whom I will have mercy" (Rom. 4:15), that God is love only to some men, viz., the elect, and that he hath mercy for those only; flatly contrary to which is the whole tenor of Scripture, as is that express declaration in particular, "The Lord is loving unto every man; and his mercy is over all his works" (Ps. 114:9). Again: They infer from that and the like texts, "It is not of him that willeth, nor of him that runneth, but of God that showeth mercy" that he showeth mercy only to those to whom he had respect from all eternity. Nay, but who replieth against God now? You now contradict the whole oracles of God, which declare throughout, "God is no respecter of persons" (Acts 10:34): "There is no respect of persons with him" (Rom. 2:11). Again: from that text, "The children being not yet born, neither having done any good or evil, that the purpose of God according to election might stand, not of works, but of him that calleth; it was said unto her," unto Rebecca, "The elder shall serve the younger"; you infer, that our being predestinated, or elect, no way depends on the foreknowledge of God. Flatly contrary to this are all the scriptures; and those in particular, "Elect according to the foreknowledge of God" (1 Peter 1:2); "Whom he did foreknow, he also did predestinate" (Rom. 8:29).

1. And "the same Lord over all is rich" in mercy "to all that call upon him" (Rom. 10:12). But you say, "No; he is such only to those for whom Christ died. And those are not all, but only a few, whom God hath chosen out of the world; for he died not for all, but only for those who were 'chosen in him before the foundation of the world'" (Eph. 1:4). Flatly contrary to your interpretation of these scriptures, also, is the whole tenor of the New Testament; as are in particular those texts:—"Destroy not him with thy meat, for whom Christ died" (Rom. 14:15)—a clear proof that Christ died, not only for those that are saved, but also for them that perish: He is "the Saviour of the world" (John 4:42); He is "the Lamb of God that taketh away the sins of the world" (John 1:29); "He is the propitiation, not for our sins only, but also for the sins of the whole world" (1 John 2:2); "He," the living God, "is the Savior of all men" (1 Tim. 4:10); "He gave himself a ransom for all" (1 Tim. 2:6); "He tasted death for every man" (Heb. 2:9).

2. If you ask, "Why then are not all men saved?" the whole law and the testimony answer, First, Not because of any decree of God; not because it is his pleasure they should die; for, "As I live," saith the Lord God, "I have no pleasure in the death of him that dieth" (Ezek. 18:3, 32). Whatever be the cause of their perishing, it cannot be his will, if the oracles of God are true; for they declare, "He is not willing that any should perish, but that all should come to repentance" (2 Peter 3:9); "He willeth that all men should be saved." And they, Secondly, declare what is the cause why all men are not saved, namely, that they will not be saved: So our Lord expressly, "Ye will not come unto me that ye may have life" (John 5:40). "The power of the Lord is present to heal" them, but they will not be healed. "They reject the counsel," the merciful counsel, "of God against themselves," as did their stiff-necked forefathers. And therefore are they without excuse; because God would save them, but they will not be saved: This is the condemnation, "How often would I have gathered you together, and ye would not!" (Matt. 23:37).

VII.

Thus manifestly does this doctrine tend to overthrow the whole Christian Revelation, by making it contradict itself; by giving such an interpretation of some texts, as flatly contradicts all the other texts, and indeed the whole scope and tenor of Scripture;—an abundant proof that it is not of God. But neither is this all: For, Seventhly, it is a doctrine full of blasphemy; of such blasphemy as I should dread to mention, but that the honour of our gracious God, and the cause of his truth, will not suffer me to be silent. In the cause of God, then, and from a sincere concern for the glory of his great name, I will mention a few of the horrible blasphemies contained in this horrible doctrine. But first, I must warn every one of you that hears, as ye will answer it at the great day, not to charge me (as some have done) with blaspheming, because I mention the blasphemy of others. And the more you are grieved with them that do thus blaspheme, see that ye "confirm your love towards them: the more, and that your heart's desire, and continual prayer to God, be, "Father, forgive them; for they know not what they do!"

1. This premised, let it be observed, that this doctrine represents our blessed Lord, "Jesus

Christ the righteous," "the only begotten Son of the Father, full of grace and truth," as an hypocrite, a deceiver of the people, a man void of common sincerity. For it cannot be denied, that he everywhere speaks as if he was willing that all men should be saved. Therefore, to say he was not willing that all men should be saved, is to represent him as a mere hypocrite and dissembler. It cannot be denied that the gracious words which came out of his mouth are full of invitations to all sinners. To say, then, he did not intend to save all sinners, is to represent him as a gross deceiver of the people. You cannot deny that he says, "Come unto me, all ye that are weary and heavy laden." If, then, you say he calls those that cannot come; those whom he knows to be unable to come; those whom he can make able to come, but will not; how is it possible to describe greater insincerity? You represent him as mocking his helpless creatures, by offering what he never intends to give. You describe him as saying one thing, and meaning another; as pretending the love which his had not. Him, in "whose mouth was no guile," you make full of deceit, void of common sincerity;—then especially, when, drawing nigh the city, He wept over it, and said, "O Jerusalem, Jerusalem, thou killest the prophets, and stonest them that are sent unto thee; how often would I have gathered thy children together,—and ye would not" (Greek: *kai ouk eitheleisatei*). Now, if you say, they would, but he would not, you represent him (which who could hear?) as weeping crocodiles' tears; weeping over the prey which himself had doomed to destruction!

2. Such blasphemy this, as one would think might make the ears of a Christian to tingle! But there is yet more behind; for just as it honours the Son, so doth this doctrine honour the Father. It destroys all his attributes at once: It overturns both his justice, mercy, and truth; yea, it represents the most holy God as worse than the devil, as both more false, more cruel, and more unjust. More false; because the devil, liar as he is, hath never said, "He willeth all men to be saved": More unjust; because the devil

cannot, if he would, be guilty of such injustice as you ascribe to God, when you say that God condemned millions of souls to everlasting fire, prepared for the devil and his angels, for continuing in sin, which, for want of that grace he will not give them, they cannot avoid: And more cruel; because that unhappy spirit "seeketh rest and findeth none"; so that his own restless misery is a kind of temptation to him to tempt others. But God resteth in his high and holy place; so that to suppose him, of his own mere motion, of his pure will and pleasure, happy as he is, to doom his creatures, whether they will or no, to endless misery, is to impute such cruelty to him as we cannot impute even to the great enemy of God and man. It is to represent the high God (he that hath ears to hear let him hear!) as more cruel, false, and unjust than the devil!

3. This is the blasphemy clearly contained in the horrible decree of predestination! And here I fix my foot. On this I join issue with every assertor of it. You represent God as worse than the devil; more false, more cruel, more unjust. But you say you will prove it by Scripture. Hold! What will you prove by Scripture? That God is worse than the devil? It cannot be. Whatever that Scripture proves, it never proved this; whatever its true meaning be. This cannot be its true meaning. Do you ask, "What is its true meaning then?" If I say, "I know not," you have gained nothing; for there are many scriptures the true sense whereof neither you nor I shall know till death is swallowed up in victory. But this I know, better it were to say it had no sense, than to say it had such a sense as this. It cannot mean, whatever it mean besides, that the God of truth is a liar. Let it mean what it will, it cannot mean that the Judge of all the world is unjust. No scripture can mean that God is not love, or that his mercy is not over all his works; that is, whatever it prove beside, no scripture can prove predestination.

4. This is the blasphemy for which (however I love the persons who assert it) I abhor the doctrine of predestination, a doctrine, upon the supposition of which, if one could possibly

suppose it for a moment (call it election, reprobation, or what you please, for all comes to the same thing), one might say to our adversary, the devil, "Thou fool, why dost thou roar about any longer? Thy lying in wait for souls is as needless and useless as our preaching. Hearest thou not, that God hath taken thy work out of thy hands; and that he doeth it much more effectually? Thou, with all thy principalities and powers, canst only so assault that we may resist thee; but He can irresistibly destroy both body and soul in hell! Thou canst only entice; but his unchangeable decrees, to leave thousands of souls in death, compels them to continue in sin, till they drop into everlasting burnings. Thou temptest; He forceth us to be damned; for we cannot resist his will. Thou fool, why goest thou about any longer, seeking whom thou mayest devour? Hearest thou not that God is the devouring lion, the destroyer of souls, the murderer of men? Moloch caused only children to pass though the fire: and that fire was soon quenched; or, the corruptible body being consumed, its torment was at an end; but God, thou are told, by his eternal decree, fixed before they had done good or evil, causes, not only children of a span long, but the parents also, to pass through the fire of hell, the 'fire which never shall be quenched; and the body which is cast thereinto, being now incorruptible and immortal, will be ever consuming and never consumed, but 'the smoke of their torment,' because it is God's good pleasure, 'ascendeth up for ever and ever.'"

5. O how would the enemy of God and man rejoice to hear these things were so! How would he cry aloud and spare not! How would he lift up his voice and say, "To your tents, O Israel! Flee from the face of this God, or ye shall utterly perish! But whither will ye flee? Into heaven? He is there, Down to hell? He is there also. Ye cannot flee from an omnipresent, almighty tyrant. And whether ye flee or stay, I call heaven, his throne, and earth, his footstool, to witness against you, ye shall perish, ye shall die eternally. Sing, O hell, and rejoice, ye that are under the earth! For God, even the mighty God, hath spoken, and devoted to death thousands of souls, from the rising of the sun unto the going down thereof! Here, O death, is they sting! They shall not, cannot escape; for the mouth of the Lord hath spoken it. Here, O grave is thy victory. Nations yet unborn, or ever they have done good or evil are doomed never to see the light of life, but thou shalt gnaw upon them for ever and ever! Let all those morning stars sing together, who fell with Lucifer, son of the morning! Let all the sons of hell shout for joy! For the decree is past, and who shall disannul it?"

6. Yea, the decree is past; and so it was before the foundation of the world. But what decree? Even this: "I will set before the sons of men 'life and death, blessing, cursing.' And the soul that chooseth life shall live, as the soul that chooseth death shall die." This decree whereby "whom God did foreknow, he did predestinate," was indeed from everlasting; this, whereby all who suffer Christ to make them alive are "elect according to the foreknowledge of God," now standeth fast, even as the moon, and as the faithful witnesses in heaven; and when heaven and earth shall pass away, yet this shall not pass away; for it is as unchangeable and eternal as is the being of God that gave it. This decree yields the strongest encouragement to abound in all good works and in all holiness; and it is a well-spring of joy, of happiness also, to our great and endless comfort. This is worthy of God; it is every way consistent with all the perfections of his nature. It gives us the noblest view both of his justice, mercy, and truth. To this agrees the whole scope of the Christian Revelation, as well as all the parts thereof. To this Moses and all the Prophets bear witness, and our blessed Lord and all his Apostles. Thus Moses, in the name of his Lord: "I call heaven and earth to record against you this day, that I have set before you life and death, blessing and cursing; therefore choose life, that thou and thy seed may live." Thus Ezekiel: "choose life, that thou and thy seed may live"; Thus Ezekiel: (To cite one Prophet for all) "The soul that sinneth,

it shall die: The son shall not bear" eternally, "the iniquity of the father. The righteousness of the righteous shall be upon him, and the wickedness of the wicked shall be upon him" (18:20). Thus our blessed Lord: "If any man thirst, let him come unto me and drink" (John 7:37). Thus his great Apostle, St. Paul: "God commandeth all men everywhere to repent"— "all men everywhere" (Acts 17:30); every man in every place, without any exception either of place or person. Thus St. James: "If any of you lack wisdom, let him ask of God, who giveth to all men liberally, and upbraideth not, and it shall be given him" (James 1:5). Thus St. Peter: "The Lord is not willing that any should perish, but that all should come to repentance" (2 Peter 3:9). And thus St. John: "If any man sin, we have an Advocate with the Father; and he is the propitiation for our sins; and not for ours only, but for the sins of the whole world" (1 John 2:1–2).

7. O hear ye this, ye that forget God! Ye cannot charge your death upon him! "'Have I any pleasure at all that the wicked should die?' saith the Lord God" (Ezek. 18:23ff.). "Repent, and turn from all your transgressions; so iniquity shall not be your ruin. Cast away from you all your transgressions where by ye have transgressed,—for why will ye die, O house of Israel? For I have no pleasure in the death of him that dieth, saith the Lord God. Wherefore turn yourselves, and live ye." "As I live, saith the Lord God, I have no pleasure in the death of the wicked.—Turn ye, turn ye from your evil ways; for why will ye die, O house of Israel?" (Ezek. 33:11).

GEORGE WHITEFIELD AND JOHN WESLEY: LETTERS
English, 1740

See pages 320–21 for background information on the letters between George Whitefield and John Wesley regarding Wesley's sermon titled "Free Grace."

But when Peter was come to Antioch, I withstood him to the face, because he was to be blamed. (Gal. 2:11)

Whitefield's Preface to the Letters

I am very well aware what different effects publishing this letter against the dear Mr. Wesley's sermon will produce. Many of my friends who are strenuous advocates for universal redemption will immediately be offended. Many who are zealous on the other side will be much rejoiced. They who are lukewarm on both sides and are carried away with carnal reasoning will wish this matter had never been brought under debate.

The reasons I have given at the beginning of the letter, I think are sufficient to satisfy all of my conduct herein. I desire therefore that they who hold election would not triumph, or make a party on one hand (for I detest any such thing)—and that they who are prejudiced against that doctrine be not too much concerned or offended on the other.

Known unto God are all his ways from the beginning of the world. The great day will discover why the Lord permits dear Mr. Wesley and me to be of a different way of thinking. At present, I shall make no enquiry into that matter, beyond the account which he has given of it himself in the following letter, which I lately received from his own dear hands.

Wesley's Letter to Whitefield, from London, August 9, 1740

My dear Brother,

I thank you for yours, May the 24th. The case is quite plain. There are bigots both for predestination and against it. God is sending a message to those on either side. But neither will receive it, unless from one who is of their own opinion. Therefore, for a time you are suffered to be of one opinion, and I of another. But when his time is come, God will do what man cannot, namely, make us both of one mind. Then persecution will flame out, and it will be seen whether we count our lives dear unto ourselves, so that we may finish our course with joy.

I am, my dearest brother,
Ever yours,
J. Wesley

Thus, my honored friend, I heartily pray God to hasten the time, for his being clearly enlightened into all the doctrines of divine revelation, that we may thus be closely united in principle and judgment as well as heart and affection. And then if the Lord should call us to it, I care not if I go with him to prison, or to death. For like Paul and Silas, I hope we shall sing praises to God, and count it our highest honor to suffer for Christ's sake, and to lay down our lives for the brethren.

Whitefield's Letter to Wesley, from Bethesda in Georgia, December 24, 1740

Reverend and very dear Brother,

God only knows what unspeakable sorrow of heart I have felt on your account since I left England last. Whether it be my infirmity or not, I frankly confess, that Jonah could not go with more reluctance against Nineveh, than I now take pen in hand to write against you. Was nature to speak, I had rather die than do it; and yet if I am faithful to God, and to my own and others' souls, I must not stand neutral any longer. I am very apprehensive that our common adversaries will rejoice to see us differing among ourselves. But what can I say? The children of God are in danger of falling into error. Nay, numbers have been misled, whom God has been pleased to work upon by my ministry, and a greater number are still calling aloud upon me to show also my opinion. I must then show that I know no man after the flesh, and that I have no respect to persons, any further than is consistent with my duty to my Lord and Master, Jesus Christ.

This letter, no doubt, will lose me many friends: and for this cause perhaps God has laid this difficult task upon me, even to see whether I am willing to forsake all for him,

or not. From such considerations as these, I think it my duty to bear a humble testimony, and earnestly to plead for the truths which, I am convinced, are clearly revealed in the Word of God. In the defense whereof I must use great plainness of speech, and treat my dearest friends upon earth with the greatest simplicity, faithfulness, and freedom, leaving the consequences of all to God.

For some time before, and especially since my last departure from England, both in public and private, by preaching and printing, you have been propagating the doctrine of universal redemption. And when I remember how Paul reproved Peter for his dissimulation, I fear I have been sinfully silent too long. O then be not angry with me, dear and honored Sir, if now I deliver my soul, by telling you that I think in this you greatly err.

'Tis not my design to enter into a long debate on God's decrees. I refer you to Dr. Edwards his *Veritas Redux*,[2] which, I think is unanswerable—except in a certain point, concerning a middle sort between elect and reprobate, which he himself in effect afterwards condemns.

I shall only make a few remarks upon your sermon, titled "Free Grace." And before I enter upon the discourse itself, give me leave to take a little notice of what in your Preface you term an indispensable obligation to make it public to all the world. I must own, that I always thought you were quite mistaken upon that head.

The case (you know) stands thus: When you were at Bristol, I think you received a letter from a private hand, charging you with not preaching the gospel, because you did not preach up election. Upon this you drew a lot: the answer was "preach and print." I have often questioned, as I do now, whether in so doing, you did not tempt the Lord. A due exercise of religious prudence, without [the drawing of] a lot, would have directed you in that matter. Besides, I never heard that you

---

2. *Veritas Redux*, or "Truth Restored" by John Edwards of Cambridge.

enquired of God, whether or not election was a gospel doctrine.

But, I fear, taking it for granted [that election was not a biblical truth], you only enquired whether you should be silent or preach and print against it.

However this be, the lot came out "preach and print"; accordingly you preached and printed against election. At my desire, you suppressed the publishing of the sermon whilst I was in England; but you soon sent it into the world after my departure. O that you had kept it in! However, if that sermon was printed in answer to a lot, I am apt to think, one reason why God should so suffer you to be deceived, was, that hereby a special obligation might be laid upon me, faithfully to declare the Scripture doctrine of election, that thus the Lord might give me a fresh opportunity of seeing what was in my heart, and whether I would be true to his cause or not; as you could not but grant, he did once before, by giving you such another lot at Deal.

The morning I sailed from Deal for Gibraltar [February 2, 1738], you arrived from Georgia. Instead of giving me an opportunity to converse with you, though the ship was not far off the shore, you drew a lot, and immediately set forward to London. You left a letter behind you, in which were words to this effect: "When I saw [that] God, by the wind which was carrying you out, brought me in, I asked counsel of God. His answer you have enclosed." This was a piece of paper, in which were written these words, "Let him return to London."

When I received this, I was somewhat surprised. Here was a good man telling me he had cast a lot, and that God would have me return to London. On the other hand, I knew my call was to Georgia, and that I had taken leave of London, and could not justly go from the soldiers, who were committed to my charge. I betook myself with a friend to prayer. That passage in 1 Kings 13 was powerfully impressed upon my soul, where we are told that the Prophet was slain by a lion when he

was tempted to go back (contrary to God's express order) upon another Prophet's telling him God would have him do so. I wrote you word that I could not return to London. We sailed immediately.

Some months after, I received a letter from you at Georgia, wherein you wrote words to this effect: "Though God never before gave me a wrong lot, yet, perhaps, he suffered me to have such a lot at that time, to try what was in your heart." I should never have published this private transaction to the world, did not the glory of God call me to it. It is plain you had a wrong lot given you here, and justly, because you tempted God in drawing one. And thus I believe it is in the present case. And if so, let not the children of God who are mine and your intimate friends, and also advocates for universal redemption, think that doctrine true—because you preached it up in compliance with a lot given out from God.

This, I think, may serve as an answer to that part of the Preface to your printed sermon, wherein you say, "Nothing but the strongest conviction, not only that what is here advanced is the truth as it is in Jesus, but also that I am indispensably obliged to declare this truth to all the world." That you believe what you have written to be truth, and that you honestly aim at God's glory in writing, I do not in the least doubt. But then, honored Sir, I cannot but think you have been much mistaken in imagining that your tempting God, by casting a lot in the manner you did could lay you under an indispensable obligation to any action, much less to publish your sermon against the doctrine of predestination to life.

I must next observe, that as you have been unhappy in printing at all upon such an imaginary warrant, so you have been as unhappy in the choice of your text. Honored Sir, how could it enter into your heart to choose a text to disprove the doctrine of election out of Romans 8, where this doctrine is so plainly asserted? Once I spoke with a Quaker upon this subject, and he had no other way of evading the force of the Apostle's assertion than by saying, "I believe Paul was in the wrong." And another friend lately, who was once highly prejudiced against election, ingenuously confessed that he used to think St. Paul himself was mistaken, or that he was not truly translated.

Indeed, honored Sir, it is plain beyond all contradiction that St. Paul, through the whole of Romans 8, is speaking of the privileges of those only who are really in Christ. And let any unprejudiced person read what goes before and what follows your text, and he must confess the word "all" only signifies those that are in Christ. And the latter part of the text plainly proves, what, I find, dear Mr. Wesley will, by no means, grant. I mean the final perseverance of the children of God: "He that spared not his own Son, but delivered him up for us all, [i.e., all Saints] how shall he not with him also freely give us all things?" (Rom. 8:32). [He shall give us] grace, in particular, to enable us to persevere, and every thing else necessary to carry us home to our Father's heavenly kingdom.

Had any one a mind to prove the doctrine of election, as well as of final perseverance, he could hardly wish for a text more fit for his purpose than that which you have chosen to disprove it! One who did not know you would suspect that you were aware of this, for after the first paragraph, I scarce know whether you have mentioned [the text] so much as once through your whole sermon.

But your discourse, in my opinion, is as little to the purpose as your text, and instead of warping, does but more and more confirm me in the belief of the doctrine of God's eternal election.

I shall not mention how illogically you have proceeded. Had you written clearly, you should first, honoured Sir, have proved your proposition: "God's grace is free to all." And then by way of inference [you might have] exclaimed against what you call the horrible decree. But you knew that people (because Arminianism, of late, has so much abounded among us) were generally prejudiced against

the doctrine of reprobation, and therefore thought if you kept up their dislike of that, you could overthrow the doctrine of election entirely. For, without doubt, the doctrine of election and reprobation must stand or fall together.

But passing by this, as also your equivocal definition of the word grace, and your false definition of the word free, and that I may be as short as possible, I frankly acknowledge: I believe the doctrine of reprobation, in this view, that God intends to give saving grace, through Jesus Christ, only to a certain number, and that the rest of mankind, after the fall of Adam, being justly left of God to continue in sin, will at last suffer that eternal death which is its proper wages.

This is the established doctrine of Scripture, and acknowledged as such in the seventeenth article of the Church of England, as Bishop Burnet himself confesses. Yet dear Mr. Wesley absolutely denies it.

But the most important objections you have urged against this doctrine as reasons why you reject it, being seriously considered, and faithfully tried by the Word of God, will appear to be of no force at all. Let the matter be humbly and calmly reviewed, as to the following heads:

First, you say that if this be so (i.e., if there be an election) then is all preaching vain: it is needless to them that are elected; for they, whether with preaching or without, will infallibly be saved. Therefore, the end of preaching to save souls is void with regard to them. And it is useless to them that are not elected, for they cannot possibly be saved. They, whether with preaching or without, will infallibly be damned. The end of preaching is therefore void with regard to them likewise. So that in either case our preaching is vain, and your hearing also vain. Page 10, paragraph 9.

O dear Sir, what kind of reasoning—or rather sophistry—is this! Hath not God, who hath appointed salvation for a certain number, appointed also the preaching of the Word as a means to bring them to it? Does anyone hold election in any other sense? And if so, how is preaching needless to them that are elected, when the gospel is designated by God himself to be the power of God unto their eternal salvation? And since we know not who are elect and who reprobate, we are to preach promiscuously to all. For the Word may be useful, even to the non-elect, in restraining them from much wickedness and sin. However, it is enough to excite to the utmost diligence in preaching and hearing, when we consider that by these means, some, even as many as the Lord hath ordained to eternal life, shall certainly be quickened and enabled to believe. And who that attends, especially with reverence and care, can tell but he may be found of that happy number?

Second, you say that the doctrine of election and reprobation directly tends to destroy holiness, which is the end of all the ordinances of God. For (says the dear mistaken Mr. Wesley) "it wholly takes away those first motives to follow after it, so frequently proposed in Scripture. The hope of future reward, and fear of punishment, the hope of heaven, and the fear of hell, et cetera."

I thought that one who carries perfection to such an exalted pitch as dear Mr. Wesley does, would know that a true lover of the Lord Jesus Christ would strive to be holy for the sake of being holy, and work for Christ out of love and gratitude, without any regard to the rewards of heaven, or fear of hell. You remember, dear Sir, what Scougal says, "Love's a more powerful motive that does them move." But passing by this, and granting that rewards and punishments (as they certainly are) may be motives from which a Christian may be honestly stirred up to act for God, how does the doctrine of election destroy these motives? Do not the elect know that the more good works they do, the greater will be their reward? And is not that encouragement enough to set them upon, and cause them to persevere in working for Jesus Christ? And how does the doctrine of election destroy holiness? Who ever preached any other election than what the

Apostle preached, when he said, "Chosen . . . through sanctification of the Spirit?" (2 Thess. 2:13). Nay, is not holiness made a mark of our election by all that preach it? And how then can the doctrine of election destroy holiness?

The instance which you bring to illustrate your assertion, indeed, dear Sir, is quite impertinent. For you say, "If a sick man knows that he must unavoidably die or unavoidably recover, though he knows not which, it is not reasonable to take any physic at all." Dear Sir, what absurd reasoning is here? Were you ever sick in your life? If so, did not the bare probability or possibility of your recovering, though you knew it was unalterably fixed that you must live or die, encourage you to take physic? For how did you know but that very physic might be the means God intended to recover you by?

Just thus it is as to the doctrine of election. I know that it is unalterably fixed (one may say) that I must be damned or saved; but since I know not which for a certainty, why should I not strive, though at present in a state of nature, since I know not but this striving may be the means God has intended to bless, in order to bring me into a state of grace?

Dear Sir, consider these things. Make an impartial application, and then judge what little reason you had to conclude the tenth paragraph, page 12, with these words: "So directly does this doctrine tend to shut the very gate of holiness in general, to hinder unholy men from ever approaching thereto, or striving to enter in thereat."

"As directly," you say, "does the doctrine tend to destroy several particular branches of holiness, such as meekness, love, etc." I shall say little, dear Sir, in answer to this paragraph. Dear Mr. Wesley perhaps has been disputing with some warm narrow-spirited men that held election, and then he infers that their warmth and narrowness of spirit was owing to their principles? But does not dear Mr. Wesley know many dear children of God, who are predestinarians, and yet are meek, lowly, pitiful, courteous, tender-hearted, kind, of a catholic spirit, and hope to see the most vile and profligate of men converted? And why? Because they know God saved themselves by an act of his electing love, and they know not but he may have elected those who now seem to be the most abandoned.

But, dear Sir, we must not judge of the truth of principles in general, nor of this of election in particular, entirely from the practice of some that profess to hold them. If so, I am sure much might be said against your own. For I appeal to your own heart, whether or not you have not felt in yourself, or observed in others, a narrow-spiritedness, and some disunion of soul respecting those that hold universal redemption. If so, then according to your own rule, universal redemption is wrong, because it destroys several branches of holiness, such as meekness, love, et cetera. But not to insist upon this, I beg you would observe that your inference is entirely set aside by the force of the Apostle's argument, and the language which he expressly uses in Colossians 3:12–13: "Put on therefore, as the elect of God, holy and beloved, bowels of mercies, kindness, humbleness of mind, meekness, longsuffering; forbearing one another, and forgiving one another, if any man have a quarrel against any: even as Christ forgave you, so also do ye."

Here we see that the Apostle exhorts them to put on bowels of mercy, kindness, humbleness of mind, meekness, long-suffering, et cetera, upon this consideration: namely, because they were elect of God. And all who have experientially felt this doctrine in their hearts feel that these graces are the genuine effects of their being elected of God.

But perhaps dear Mr. Wesley may be mistaken in this point, and call that passion which is only zeal for God's truths. You know, dear Sir, the Apostle exhorts us to "contend earnestly for the faith once delivered to the saints" (Jude 3). Therefore you must not condemn all that appear zealous for the doctrine of election as narrow-spirited, or persecutors, just because they think it their duty to oppose you. I am sure, I love you in the bowels of Jesus Christ, and think I could lay down my life for your sake; but yet, dear Sir, I cannot help strenuously opposing your errors upon this important subject, because I think you warmly, though not designedly, oppose the truth, as it is in Jesus. May the Lord remove the scales of prejudice from off the eyes of your mind and give you a zeal according to true Christian knowledge!

Third, says your sermon, "This doctrine tends to destroy the comforts of religion, the happiness of Christianity, et cetera."

But how does Mr. Wesley know this, who never believed election? I believe they who have experienced it will agree with our seventeenth article, that "the godly consideration of predestination, and election in Christ, is full of sweet, pleasant, unspeakable comfort to godly persons, and such as feel in themselves the working of the Spirit of Christ, mortifying the works of the flesh, and their earthly members, and drawing their minds to high and heavenly things, as well because it does greatly establish and confirm their faith of eternal salvation, to be enjoyed through Christ, as because it doth fervently kindle their love towards God," et cetera.

This plainly shows that our godly reformers did not think election destroyed holiness or the comforts of religion. As for my own part, this doctrine is my daily support. I should utterly sink under a dread of my impending trials, were I not firmly persuaded that God has chosen me in Christ from before the foundation of the world, and that now being effectually called, he will allow no one to pluck me out of his almighty hand.

You proceed thus: "This is evident as to all those who believe themselves to be reprobate, or only suspect or fear it; all the great and precious promises are lost to them; they afford them no ray of comfort."

In answer to this, let me observe that none living, especially none who are desirous of salvation, can know that they are not of the number of God's elect. None but the unconverted, can have any just reason so much as to fear it. And would dear Mr. Wesley give comfort, or dare you apply the precious promises of the gospel, being children's bread, to men in a natural state, while they continue so? God forbid! What if the doctrine of election and reprobation does put some upon doubting? So does that of regeneration. But, is not this doubting a good means to put them upon searching and striving; and that striving, a good means to make their calling and their election sure?

This is one reason among many others why I admire the doctrine of election and am convinced that it should have a place in gospel ministrations and should be insisted on with faithfulness and care. It has a natural tendency to rouse the soul out of its carnal security. And therefore many carnal men cry out against it. Whereas universal redemption is a notion sadly adapted to keep the soul in its lethargic sleepy condition, and therefore so many natural men admire and applaud it.

Your thirteenth, fourteenth and fifteenth paragraphs come next to be considered. "The witness of the Spirit," you say, "experience shows to be much obstructed by this doctrine."

But, dear Sir, whose experience? Not your own; for in your journal, from your embarking for Georgia, to your return to London, you seem to acknowledge that you have it not, and therefore you are no competent judge in this matter. You must mean then the experience of others. For you say in the same paragraph, "Even in those who have tasted of that good gift, who yet have soon lost it again," (I suppose you mean lost the sense of it again) "and fallen back into doubts and fears and darkness, even horrible darkness that might be felt, et cetera." Now, as to the darkness of desertion, was not this the case of Jesus Christ himself, after he had received an unmeasurable unction of the Holy Ghost? Was not his soul exceeding sorrowful, even unto death, in the garden? And was he not surrounded with a horrible darkness, even a darkness that might be felt, when on the cross he cried out, "My God! My God! Why hast thou forsaken me?"

And that all his followers are liable to the same, is it not evident from Scripture? For, says the Apostle, "He was tempted in all things like as we are" (Heb. 4:15) so that he himself might be able to succor those that are tempted (Heb. 2:18). And is not their liableness thereunto consistent with that conformity to him in suffering, which his members are to bear (Phil. 3:10)? Why then should persons falling into darkness, after they have received the witness of the Spirit, be any argument against the doctrine of election?

"Yet," you say, "many, very many of those that hold it not, in all parts of the earth, have enjoyed the uninterrupted witness of the Spirit, the continual light of God's countenance, from the moment wherein they first believed, for many months or years, to this very day." But how does dear Mr. Wesley know this? Has he consulted the experience of many, very many in all parts of the earth? Or could he be sure of what he hath advanced without sufficient grounds, would it follow that their being kept in this light is owing to their not believing the doctrine of election? No, this [doctrine], according to the sentiments of our church, "greatly confirms and establishes a true Christian's faith of eternal salvation through Christ," and is an anchor of hope, both sure and steadfast, when he walks in darkness and sees no light; as certainly he may, even after he hath received the witness of the Spirit, whatever you or others may unadvisedly assert to the contrary.

Then, to have respect to God's everlasting covenant, and to throw himself upon the free distinguishing love of that God who changeth not, will make him lift up the hands that hang down, and strengthen the feeble knees.

But without the belief of the doctrine of election, and the immutability of the free love of God, I cannot see how it is possible that any should have a comfortable assurance of eternal salvation. What could it signify to a man whose conscience is thoroughly awakened, and who is warned in good earnest to seek deliverance from the wrath to come, though he should be assured that all his past sins be forgiven, and that he is now a child of God; if notwithstanding this, he may hereafter become a child of the devil, and be cast into hell at last? Could such an assurance yield any solid, lasting comfort to a person convinced of the corruption and treachery of his own heart, and of the malice, subtlety, and power of Satan? No! That which alone deserves the name of a full assurance of faith is such an assurance as emboldens the believer, under the sense of his interest in distinguishing love, to give the challenge to all his adversaries, whether men or devils, and that with regard to all their future, as well as present, attempts to destroy—saying with the Apostle,

"Who shall lay any thing to the charge of God's elect? It is God that justifieth. Who is he that condemneth? It is Christ that died, yea rather, that is risen again, who is even at the right hand of God, who also maketh intercession for us. Who shall separate us from the love of Christ? Shall tribulation, or distress, or persecution, or famine, or nakedness, or peril, or sword? As it is written, For thy sake we are killed all the day long; we are accounted as sheep for the slaughter. Nay, in all these things we are more than conquerors through him that loved us. For I am persuaded, that neither death, nor life, nor angels, nor principalities, nor powers, nor things present, nor things to come, nor height, nor depth, nor any other creature, shall be able to separate us from the love of God, which is in Christ Jesus our Lord" (Rom. 8:33–39).

This, dear Sir, is the triumphant language of every soul that has attained a full assurance of faith. And this assurance can only arise from a belief of God's electing everlasting love. That many have an assurance they are in Christ today, but take no thought for, or are not assured they shall be in him tomorrow—nay to all eternity—is rather their imperfection and unhappiness than their privilege. I pray God to bring all such to a sense of his eternal love, that they may no longer build upon their own faithfulness, but on the unchangeableness of that God whose gifts and callings are without repentance. For those whom God has once justified, he also will glorify.

I observed before, dear Sir, it is not always a safe rule to judge of the truth of principles from people's practice. And therefore, supposing that all who hold universal redemption in your way of explaining it, after they received faith, enjoyed the continual uninterrupted sight of God's countenance, it does not follow that this is a fruit of their principle. For that I am sure has a natural tendency to keep the soul in darkness for ever, because the creature thereby is taught that his being kept in a state of salvation is owing to his own free will. And what a sandy foundation is that for a poor creature to build his hopes of perseverance upon? Every relapse into sin, every surprise by temptation, must throw him "into doubts and fears, into horrible darkness, even darkness that may be felt."

Hence it is that the letters which have been lately sent me by those who hold universal redemption are dead and lifeless, dry and inconsistent, in comparison of those I receive from persons on the contrary side. Those who settle in the universal scheme, though they might begin in the Spirit (whatever they may say to the contrary), are ending in the flesh, and building up a righteousness founded on their own free will: whilst the others triumph in hope of the glory of God, and build upon God's never-failing promise and unchangeable love, even when his sensible presence is withdrawn from them.

But I would not judge of the truth of election by the experience of any particular persons: if I did (O bear with me in this foolishness of boasting) I think I myself might glory in election. For these five or six years I have received the witness of God's Spirit; since that, blessed be God, I have not doubted a quarter of an hour of a saving interest in Jesus Christ: but with grief and humble shame I do acknowledge, I have fallen into sin often since that. Though I do not—dare not—allow of any one transgression, yet hitherto I have not been (nor do I expect that while I am in this present world I ever shall be) able to live one day perfectly free from all defects and sin. And since the Scriptures declare that there is not a just man upon earth (no, not among those of the highest attainments in grace) that doeth good and sinneth not (Eccl. 7:20), we are sure that this will be the case of all the children of God.

The universal experience and acknowledgement of this among the godly in every age is abundantly sufficient to confute the error of those who hold in an absolute sense that after a man is born again he cannot commit sin. Especially since the Holy Spirit condemns the persons who say they have no sin as deceiving themselves, as being destitute of the truth, and as making God a liar (1 John 1:8, 10). I have been also in heaviness through manifold temptations, and expect to be often so before I die. Thus were the Apostles and primitive Christians themselves. Thus was Luther, that man of God, who, as far as I can find, did not peremptorily, at least, hold election; and the great John Arndt was in the utmost perplexity, but a quarter of an hour before he died, and yet he was no predestinarian.

And if I must speak freely, I believe your fighting so strenuously against the doctrine of election and pleading so vehemently for a sinless perfection are among the reasons or culpable causes, why you are kept out of the liberties of the gospel, and from that full assurance of faith which they enjoy, who have experimentally tasted, and daily feed upon God's electing, everlasting love.

But perhaps you may say, that Luther and Arndt were no Christians, at least very weak ones. I know you think meanly of Abraham, though he was eminently called the friend of God: and, I believe, also of David, the man after God's own heart. No wonder, therefore, that in a letter you sent me not long since, you should tell me that no Baptist or Presbyterian writer whom you have read knew anything of the liberties of Christ. What? Neither Bunyan,

Henry, Flavel, Halyburton, nor any of the New England and Scots divines? See, dear Sir, what narrow-spiritedness and want of charity arise from your principles, and then do not cry out against election any more on account of its being "destructive of meekness and love."

Fourth, I shall now proceed to another head. Says the dear Mr. Wesley, "How uncomfortable a thought is this, that thousands and millions of men, without any preceding offence or fault of theirs, were unchangeably doomed to everlasting burnings?"

But who ever asserted, that thousands and millions of men, without any preceding offence or fault of theirs, were unchangeably doomed to everlasting burnings? Do not they who believe God's dooming men to everlasting burnings, also believe, that God looked upon them as men fallen in Adam? And that the decree which ordained the punishment first regarded the crime by which it was deserved? How then are they doomed without any preceding fault? Surely Mr. Wesley will own God's justice in imputing Adam's sin to his posterity. And also, after Adam fell, and his posterity in him, God might justly have passed them all by, without sending his own Son to be a savior for any one. Unless you heartily agree to both these points, you do not believe original sin aright. If you do own them, then you must acknowledge the doctrine of election and reprobation to be highly just and reasonable. For if God might justly impute Adam's sin to all, and afterwards have passed by all, then he might justly pass by some. Turn on the right hand, or on the left; you are reduced to an inextricable dilemma. And, if you would be consistent, you must either give up the doctrine of the imputation of Adam's sin, or receive the amiable doctrine of election, with a holy and righteous reprobation as its consequent. For whether you can believe it or not, the Word of God abides faithful: "The election hath obtained it, and the rest were blinded" (Rom. 11:7).

Your seventeenth paragraph, page 16, I pass

over. What has been said on the ninth and tenth paragraphs, with a little alteration, will answer it. I shall only say, it is the doctrine of election that most presses me to abound in good works. I am willing to suffer all things for the elect's sake. This makes me to preach with comfort, because I know salvation does not depend on man's free will, but the Lord makes willing in the day of his power, and can make use of me to bring some of his elect home, when and where he pleases.

But, Fifth, you say, "This doctrine has a direct manifest tendency to overthrow the whole Christian religion. " For," say you, "supposing that eternal, unchangeable decree, one part of mankind must be saved, though the Christian revelation were not in being."

But, dear Sir, how does that follow? Since it is only by the Christian revelation that we are acquainted with God's design of saving his church by the death of his Son. Yea, it is settled in the everlasting covenant that this salvation shall be applied to the elect through the knowledge and faith of him. As the prophet says in Isaiah 53:11, "By his knowledge shall my righteous servant justify many." How then has the doctrine of election a direct tendency to overthrow the whole Christian revelation? Who ever thought that God's declaration to Noah, that seed-time and harvest should never cease, could afford an argument for the neglect of plowing or sowing? Or that the unchangeable purpose of God, that harvest should not fail, rendered the heat of the sun, or the influence of the heavenly bodies unnecessary to produce it? No more does God's absolute purpose of saving his chosen preclude the necessity of the gospel revelation, or the use of any of the means through which he has determined the decree shall take effect. Nor will the right understanding, or the reverent belief of God's decree, ever allow or suffer a Christian in any case to separate the means from the end, or the end from the means.

And since we are taught by the revelation itself that this was intended and given by God as a means of bringing home his elect, we therefore receive it with joy, prize it highly, use it in faith, and endeavor to spread it through all the world, in the full assurance, that wherever God sends it, sooner or later, it shall be savingly useful to all the elect within its call.

How then, in holding this doctrine, do we join with modern unbelievers in making the Christian revelation unnecessary? No, dear Sir, you mistake. Infidels of all kinds are on your side of the question. Deists, Arians, and Socinians arraign God's sovereignty and stand up for universal redemption. I pray God that dear Mr. Wesley's sermon, as it has grieved the hearts of many of God's children, may not also strengthen the hands of many of his most avowed enemies!

Here I could almost lie down and weep. "Tell it not in Gath, publish it not in the streets of Askelon; lest the daughters of the Philistines rejoice, lest the daughters of the uncircumcised triumph" (2 Sam. 1:20).

Further, you say, "This doctrine makes revelation contradict itself." For instance, say you, "The assertors of this doctrine interpret that text of Scripture, 'Jacob have I loved, but Esau have I hated,' as implying that God, in a literal sense, hated Esau and all the reprobates from eternity!" And, when considered as fallen in Adam, were they not objects of his hatred? And might not God, of his own good pleasure, love or show mercy to Jacob and the elect— and yet at the same time do the reprobate no wrong? But you say, "God is love." And cannot God be love, unless he shows the same mercy to all?

Again, says dear Mr. Wesley, "They infer from that text, 'I will have mercy on whom I will have mercy,' that God is merciful only to some men, viz the elect; and that he has mercy for those only, flatly contrary to which is the whole tenor of the Scripture, as is that express declaration in particular, 'The Lord is loving to every man, and his mercy is over all his works.'"

And so it is, but not his saving mercy. God

is loving to every man: he sends his rain upon the evil and upon the good. But you say, "God is no respecter of persons" (Acts 10:34). No! For every one, whether Jew or Gentile, that believeth on Jesus, and worketh righteousness, is accepted of him. "But he that believeth not shall be damned" (Mark 16:16). For God is no respecter of persons, upon the account of any outward condition or circumstance in life whatever; nor does the doctrine of election in the least suppose him to be so. But as the sovereign Lord of all, who is debtor to none, he has a right to do what he will with his own, and to dispense his favours to what objects he sees fit, merely at his pleasure. And his supreme right herein is clearly and strongly asserted in those passages of Scripture, where he says, "Moses, I will have mercy on whom I will have mercy, and I will have compassion on whom I will have compassion" (Rom. 9:15: Exod. 33:19).

Further, from the text, "the children being not yet born, neither having done any good or evil, that the purpose of God according to election might stand, not of works, but of him that calleth; it was said unto her [Rebekah], "The elder shall serve the younger" (Rom. 9:11–12)—you represent us as inferring that our predestination to life in no way depends on the foreknowledge of God.

But who infers this, dear Sir? For if foreknowledge signifies approbation, as it does in several parts of Scripture, then we confess that predestination and election do depend on God's foreknowledge. But if by God's foreknowledge you understand God's foreseeing some good works done by his creatures as the foundation or reason of choosing them and therefore electing them, then we say that in this sense predestination does not any way depend on God's foreknowledge.

But I referred you, at the beginning of this letter, to Dr. Edwards's *Veritas Redux* [*Truth Restored*], which I recommended to you also in a late letter, with Elisha Coles on God's Sovereignty. Be pleased to read these, and also the excellent sermons of Mr. Cooper of

Boston in New England (which I also sent you) and I doubt not but you will see all your objections answered. Though I would observe, that after all our reading on both sides the question, we shall never in this life be able to search out God's decrees to perfection. No, we must humbly adore what we cannot comprehend, and with the great Apostle at the end of our enquiries cry out, "O the depth of the riches both of the wisdom and knowledge of God! how unsearchable are his judgments, and his ways past finding out! For who hath known the mind of the Lord? or who hath been his counsellor?" (Rom. 11:33–34)—or with our Lord, when he was admiring God's sovereignty, "Even so, Father: for so it seemed good in thy sight" (Matt. 11:26).

However, it may not be amiss to take notice, that if those texts, "The Lord is . . . not willing that any should perish, but that all should come to repentance" (2 Peter 3:9) and "I have no pleasure in the death of the wicked; but that the wicked turn from his way and live" (Ezek. 33:11)—and such like—be taken in their strictest sense, then no one will be damned.

But here's the distinction. God taketh no pleasure in the death of sinners, so as to delight simply in their death; but he delights to magnify his justice, by inflicting the punishment which their iniquities have deserved. As a righteous judge who takes no pleasure in condemning a criminal, may yet justly command him to be executed, that law and justice may be satisfied, even though it be in his power to procure him a reprieve.

I would hint further, that you unjustly charge the doctrine of reprobation with blasphemy, whereas the doctrine of universal redemption, as you set it forth, is really the highest reproach upon the dignity of the Son of God, and the merit of his blood. Consider whether it be not rather blasphemy to say as you do, "Christ not only died for those that are saved, but also for those that perish."

The text you have misapplied to gloss over this, see explained by Ridgely, Edwards, Henry; and I purposely omit answering your texts myself so that you may be brought to read such treatises, which, under God, would show you your error. You cannot make good the assertion that Christ died for them that perish without holding (as Peter Bohler, one of the Moravian brethren, in order to make out universal redemption, lately frankly confessed in a letter) that all the damned souls would hereafter be brought out of hell. I cannot think Mr. Wesley is thus minded. And yet unless this can be proved, universal redemption, taken in a literal sense, falls entirely to the ground. For how can all be universally redeemed, if all are not finally saved?

Dear Sir, for Jesus Christ's sake, consider how you dishonor God by denying election. You plainly make salvation depend not on God's free grace, but on man's free-will. And if thus, it is more than probable, Jesus Christ would not have had the satisfaction of seeing the fruit of his death in the eternal salvation of one soul. Our preaching would then be vain, and all invitations for people to believe in him would also be in vain.

But, blessed be God, our Lord knew for whom he died. There was an eternal compact between the Father and the Son. A certain number was then given him as the purchase and reward of his obedience and death. For these he prayed (John 17:9), and not for the world. For these elect ones, and these only, he is now interceding, and with their salvation he will be fully satisfied.

I purposely omit making any further particular remarks on the several last pages of your sermon. Indeed had not your name, dear Sir, been prefixed to the sermon, I could not have been so uncharitable as to think you were the author of such sophistry. You beg the question, in saying that God has declared (notwithstanding you own, I suppose, some will be damned) that he will save all—i.e., every individual person. You take it for granted (for solid proof you have none) that God is unjust, if he passes by any, and then you exclaim against the "horrible decree": and yet, as I before hinted, in holding the doctrine

of original sin, you profess to believe that he might justly have passed by all.

Dear, dear Sir, O be not offended! For Christ's sake be not rash! Give yourself to reading. Study the covenant of grace. Down with your carnal reasoning. Be a little child; and then, instead of pawning your salvation, as you have done in a late hymn book, if the doctrine of universal redemption be not true; instead of talking of sinless perfection, as you have done in the preface to that hymn book, and making man's salvation to depend on his own free will, as you have in this sermon; you will compose a hymn in praise of sovereign distinguishing love. You will caution believers against striving to work a perfection out of their own hearts, and print another sermon the reverse of this, and title it "Free Grace Indeed." Free, not because free to all; but free, because God may withhold or give it to whom and when he pleases.

Till you do this, I must doubt whether or not you know yourself. In the meanwhile, I cannot but blame you for censuring the clergy of our church for not keeping to their articles, when you yourself by your principles, positively deny the ninth, tenth and seventeenth.

Dear Sir, these things ought not so to be. God knows my heart, as I told you before, so I declare again, nothing but a single regard to the honor of Christ has forced this letter from me. I love and honor you for his sake; and when I come to judgment, will thank you before men and angels, for what you have, under God, done for my soul.

There, I am persuaded, I shall see dear Mr. Wesley convinced of election and everlasting love. And it often fills me with pleasure to think how I shall behold you casting your crown down at the feet of the Lamb, and as it were filled with a holy blushing for opposing the divine sovereignty in the manner you have done.

But I hope the Lord will show you this before you go hence. O how do I long for that day! If the Lord should be pleased to make use of this letter for that purpose, it would abundantly rejoice the heart of, dear and honored Sir,

Your affectionate, though unworthy brother and servant in Christ,
George Whitefield

JONATHAN EDWARDS: "SINNERS IN THE HANDS OF AN ANGRY GOD"
English, 1741

For an introduction to Jonathan Edwards, see "A Faithful Narrative" on page 307. Jonathan Edwards preached of "Sinners in the Hands of an Angry God" to his home congregation in Northampton, Massachusetts. This best known of Edward's sermons includes the infamous passage,

The God that holds you over the pit of hell, much as one holds a spider, or some loathsome insect, over the fire, abhors you, and is dreadfully provoked; his wrath towards you burns like a fire; he looks upon you as worthy of nothing else, but to be cast into the fire; he is of purer eyes than to bear to have you in his sight; you are ten thousand times so abominable in his eyes as the most hateful venomous serpent is in ours. You have offended him infinitely more than ever a stubborn rebel did his prince: and yet tis nothing but his hand that holds you from falling into the fire every moment: 'tis to be ascribed to nothing else, that you did not go to hell last night . . . but that God's hand has held you up: there is no other reason to be given why you hadn't gone to hell since you have sat here in the house of God, provoking his pure eyes by your sinful wicked manner of attending his solemn worship: yea, there is nothing else that is to be given as a reason why you don't this very moment drop down into hell. Oh sinner! Consider the fearful danger you are in.

For the setting and impact of this sermon, the reader is referred to the biography of Edwards by George Marsden

([Yale University Press, 2003], 214–26). The complete sermon is reprinted here. Note that Edwards quotes from the King James Bible.

Their foot shall slide in due time. (Deut. 32:35)

◆

In this verse is threatened the vengeance of God on the wicked unbelieving Israelites, who were God's visible people, and who lived under the means of grace; but who, notwithstanding all God's wonderful works towards them, remained (as v. 28) void of counsel, having no understanding in them. Under all the cultivations of heaven, they brought forth bitter and poisonous fruit; as in the two verses next preceding the text. The expression I have chosen for my text, Their foot shall slide in due time, seems to imply the following doings, relating to the punishment and destruction to which these wicked Israelites were exposed.

1. That they were always exposed to destruction; as one that stands or walks in slippery places is always exposed to fall. This is implied in the manner of their destruction coming upon them, being represented by their foot sliding. The same is expressed, Psalm 73:18: "Surely thou didst set them in slippery places; thou castedst them down into destruction."

2. It implies, that they were always exposed to sudden unexpected destruction. As he that walks in slippery places is every moment liable to fall, he cannot foresee one moment whether he shall stand or fall the next; and when he does fall, he falls at once without warning: Which is also expressed in Psalm 73:18, 19. "Surely thou didst set them in slippery places; thou castedst them down into destruction: How are they brought into desolation as in a moment!"

3. Another thing implied is, that they are liable to fall of themselves, without being thrown down by the hand of another; as he that stands or walks on slippery ground needs nothing but his own weight to throw him down.

4. That the reason why they are not fallen already, and do not fall now, is only that God's appointed time is not come. For it is said,

that when that due time, or appointed time comes, their foot shall slide. Then they shall be left to fall, as they are inclined by their own weight. God will not hold them up in these slippery places any longer, but will let them go; and then at that very instant, they shall fall into destruction; as he that stands on such slippery declining ground, on the edge of a pit, he cannot stand alone, when he is let go he immediately falls and is lost.

The observation from the words that I would now insist upon is this. "There is nothing that keeps wicked men at any one moment out of hell, but the mere pleasure of God." By the mere pleasure of God, I mean his sovereign pleasure, his arbitrary will, restrained by no obligation, hindered by no manner of difficulty, any more than if nothing else but God's mere will had in the least degree, or in any respect whatsoever, any hand in the preservation of wicked men one moment.

The truth of this observation may appear by the following considerations.

1. There is no want of power in God to cast wicked men into hell at any moment. Men's hands cannot be strong when God rises up. The strongest have no power to resist him, nor can any deliver out of his hands.—He is not only able to cast wicked men into hell, but he can most easily do it. Sometimes an earthly prince meets with a great deal of difficulty to subdue a rebel, who has found means to fortify himself, and has made himself strong by the numbers of his followers. But it is not so with God. There is no fortress that is any defense from the power of God. Though hand join in hand, and vast multitudes of God's enemies combine and associate themselves, they are easily broken in pieces. They are as great heaps of light chaff before the whirlwind; or large quantities of dry stubble before devouring flames. We find it easy to tread on and crush a worm that we see crawling on the earth; so it is easy for us to cut or singe a slender thread that any thing hangs by: thus easy is it for God, when he pleases, to cast his enemies down to hell. What are we, that we should think to stand before him, at whose

rebuke the earth trembles, and before whom the rocks are thrown down?

2. They deserve to be cast into hell; so that divine justice never stands in the way, it makes no objection against God's using his power at any moment to destroy them. Yea, on the contrary, justice calls aloud for an infinite punishment of their sins. Divine justice says of the tree that brings forth such grapes of Sodom, "Cut it down, why cumbereth it the ground?" Luke 13:7. The sword of divine justice is every moment brandished over their heads, and it is nothing but the hand of arbitrary mercy, and God's mere will, that holds it back.

3. They are already under a sentence of condemnation to hell. They do not only justly deserve to be cast down thither, but the sentence of the law of God, that eternal and immutable rule of righteousness that God has fixed between him and mankind, is gone out against them, and stands against them; so that they are bound over already to hell. John 3:18. "He that believeth not is condemned already." So that every unconverted man properly belongs to hell; that is his place; from thence he is, John 8:23: "Ye are from beneath." And thither he is bound; it is the place that justice, and God's word, and the sentence of his unchangeable law assign to him.

4. They are now the objects of that very same anger and wrath of God, that is expressed in the torments of hell. And the reason why they do not go down to hell at each moment, is not because God, in whose power they are, is not then very angry with them; as he is with many miserable creatures now tormented in hell, who there feel and bear the fierceness of his wrath. Yea, God is a great deal more angry with great numbers that are now on earth: yea, doubtless, with many that are now in this congregation, who it may be are at ease, than he is with many of those who are now in the flames of hell.

So that it is not because God is unmindful of their wickedness, and does not resent it, that he does not let loose his hand and cut them off. God is not altogether such an one as themselves, though they may imagine him to be so. The wrath of God burns against them, their damnation does not slumber; the pit is prepared, the fire is made ready, the furnace is now hot, ready to receive them; the flames do now rage and glow. The glittering sword is whet, and held over them, and the pit hath opened its mouth under them.

5. The devil stands ready to fall upon them, and seize them as his own, at what moment God shall permit him. They belong to him; he has their souls in his possession, and under his dominion. The scripture represents them as his goods, Luke 11:12. The devils watch them; they are ever by them at their right hand; they stand waiting for them, like greedy hungry lions that see their prey, and expect to have it, but are for the present kept back. If God should withdraw his hand, by which they are restrained, they would in one moment fly upon their poor souls. The old serpent is gaping for them; hell opens its mouth wide to receive them; and if God should permit it, they would be hastily swallowed up and lost.

6. There are in the souls of wicked men those hellish principles reigning, that would presently kindle and flame out into hell fire, if it were not for God's restraints. There is laid in the very nature of carnal men, a foundation for the torments of hell. There are those corrupt principles, in reigning power in them, and in full possession of them, that are seeds of hell fire. These principles are active and powerful, exceeding violent in their nature, and if it were not for the restraining hand of God upon them, they would soon break out, they would flame out after the same manner as the same corruptions, the same enmity does in the hearts of damned souls, and would beget the same torments as they do in them. The souls of the wicked are in scripture compared to the troubled sea, Isaiah 57:20. For the present, God restrains their wickedness by his mighty power, as he does the raging waves of the troubled sea, saying, "Hitherto shalt thou come, but no further"; but if God should withdraw that restraining power, it would soon carry all before it. Sin is the ruin and misery of the soul; it is destructive in its nature; and if God should leave it without restraint, there would need nothing else to make the soul perfectly miserable. The corruption of the heart of man is immoderate and boundless in its fury; and while wicked men live here, it is like fire pent up by God's restraints, whereas if it were let loose, it would set on fire the course of nature; and as the heart is now a sink of sin, so if sin was not restrained, it would immediately turn the soul into a fiery oven, or a furnace of fire and brimstone.

7. It is no security to wicked men for one moment, that there are no visible means of death at hand. It is no security to a natural man, that he is now in health, and that he does not see which way he should now immediately go out of the world by any accident, and that there is no visible danger in any respect in his circumstances. The manifold and continual experience of the world in all ages, shows this is no evidence, that a man is not on the very brink of eternity, and that the next step will not be into another world. The unseen, unthought-of ways and means of persons going suddenly out of the world are innumerable and inconceivable. Unconverted men walk over the pit of hell on a rotten covering, and there are innumerable places in this covering so weak that they will not bear their weight, and these places are not seen. The arrows of death fly unseen at noon-day; the sharpest sight cannot discern them. God has so many different unsearchable ways of taking wicked men out of the world and sending them to hell, that there is nothing to make it appear, that God had need to be at the expense of a miracle, or go out of the ordinary course of his providence, to destroy any wicked man, at any moment. All the means that there are of sinners going out of the world, are so in God's hands, and so universally and absolutely subject to his power and determination, that it does not depend at all the less on the mere will of God, whether sinners shall at any moment go to hell, than if means were never made use of, or at all concerned in the case.

8. Natural men's prudence and care to preserve

their own lives, or the care of others to preserve them, do not secure them a moment. To this, divine providence and universal experience do also bear testimony. There is this clear evidence that men's own wisdom is no security to them from death; that if it were otherwise we should see some difference between the wise and politic men of the world, and others, with regard to their liableness to early and unexpected death: but how is it in fact? Ecclesiastes 2:16. "How dieth the wise man? Even as the fool."

9. All wicked men's pains and contrivance which they use to escape hell, while they continue to reject Christ, and so remain wicked men, do not secure them from hell one moment. Almost every natural man that hears of hell, flatters himself that he shall escape it; he depends upon himself for his own security; he flatters himself in what he has done, in what he is now doing, or what he intends to do. Every one lays out matters in his own mind how he shall avoid damnation, and flatters himself that he contrives well for himself, and that his schemes will not fail. They hear indeed that there are but few saved, and that the greater part of men that have died heretofore are gone to hell; but each one imagines that he lays out matters better for his own escape than others have done. He does not intend to come to that place of torment; he says within himself, that he intends to take effectual care, and to order matters so for himself as not to fail.

But the foolish children of men miserably delude themselves in their own schemes, and in confidence in their own strength and wisdom; they trust to nothing but a shadow. The greater part of those who heretofore have lived under the same means of grace, and are now dead, are undoubtedly gone to hell; and it was not because they were not as wise as those who are now alive: it was not because they did not lay out matters as well for themselves to secure their own escape. If we could speak with them, and inquire of them, one by one, whether they expected, when alive, and when they used to hear about hell ever to be the subjects of that

misery: we doubtless, should hear one and another reply, "No, I never intended to come here: I had laid out matters otherwise in my mind; I thought I should contrive well for myself: I thought my scheme good. I intended to take effectual care; but it came upon me unexpected; I did not look for it at that time, and in that manner; it came as a thief: Death outwitted me: God's wrath was too quick for me. Oh, my cursed foolishness! I was flattering myself, and pleasing myself with vain dreams of what I would do hereafter; and when I was saying, Peace and safety, then suddenly destruction came upon me."

10. God has laid himself under no obligation, by any promise to keep any natural man out of hell one moment. God certainly has made no promises either of eternal life, or of any deliverance or preservation from eternal death, but what are contained in the covenant of grace, the promises that are given in Christ, in whom all the promises are yea and amen. But surely they have no interest in the promises of the covenant of grace who are not the children of the covenant, who do not believe in any of the promises, and have no interest in the Mediator of the covenant.

So that, whatever some have imagined and pretended about promises made to natural men's earnest seeking and knocking, it is plain and manifest, that whatever pains a natural man takes in religion, whatever prayers he makes, till he believes in Christ, God is under no manner of obligation to keep him a moment from eternal destruction.

So that, thus it is that natural men are held in the hand of God, over the pit of hell; they have deserved the fiery pit, and are already sentenced to it; and God is dreadfully provoked, his anger is as great towards them as to those that are actually suffering the executions of the fierceness of his wrath in hell, and they have done nothing in the least to appease or abate that anger, neither is God in the least bound by any promise to hold them up one moment; the devil is waiting for them, hell is gaping for them, the flames gather and flash about them, and would fain lay hold on them, and swallow them up; the fire pent up in their own hearts is struggling to break out: and they have no interest in any Mediator, there are no means within reach that can be any security to them. In short, they have no refuge, nothing to take hold of, all that preserves them every moment is the mere arbitrary will, and uncovenanted, unobliged forbearance of an incensed God.

Application

The use of this awful subject may be for awakening unconverted persons in this congregation. This that you have heard is the case of every one of you that are out of Christ. That world of misery, that lake of burning brimstone, is extended abroad under you. There is the dreadful pit of the glowing flames of the wrath of God; there is hell's wide gaping mouth open; and you have nothing to stand upon, nor any thing to take hold of, there is nothing between you and hell but the air; it is only the power and mere pleasure of God that holds you up.

You probably are not sensible of this; you find you are kept out of hell, but do not see the hand of God in it; but look at other things, as the good state of your bodily constitution, your care of your own life, and the means you use for your own preservation. But indeed these things are nothing; if God should withdraw his band, they would avail no more to keep you from falling, than the thin air to hold up a person that is suspended in it.

Your wickedness makes you as it were heavy as lead, and to tend downwards with great weight and pressure towards hell; and if God should let you go, you would immediately sink and swiftly descend and plunge into the bottomless gulf, and your healthy constitution, and your own care and prudence, and best contrivance, and all your righteousness, would have no more influence to uphold you and keep you out of hell, than a spider's web would have to stop a falling rock. Were it not for the sovereign pleasure of God, the earth would not bear you one moment; for you are a burden to it; the creation groans with you; the creature is made subject to the bondage of your corruption, not willingly; the sun does not willingly shine upon you to give you light to serve sin and Satan; the earth does not willingly yield her increase to satisfy your lusts; nor is it willingly a stage for your wickedness to be acted upon; the air does not willingly serve you for breath to maintain the flame of life in your vitals, while you spend your life in the service of God's enemies. God's creatures are good, and were made for men to serve God with, and do not willingly subserve to any other purpose, and groan when they are abused to purposes so directly contrary to their nature and end. And the world would spew you out, were it not for the sovereign hand of him who hath subjected it in hope. There are black clouds of God's wrath now hanging directly over your heads, full of the dreadful storm, and big with thunder; and were it not for the restraining hand of God, it would immediately burst forth upon you. The sovereign pleasure of God, for the present, stays his rough wind; otherwise it would come with fury, and your destruction would come like a whirlwind, and you would be like the chaff of the summer threshing floor.

The wrath of God is like great waters that are dammed for the present; they increase more and more, and rise higher and higher, till an outlet is given; and the longer the stream is stopped, the more rapid and mighty is its course, when once it is let loose. It is true, that judgment against your evil works has not been executed hitherto; the floods of God's vengeance have been withheld; but your guilt in the mean time is constantly increasing, and you are every day treasuring up more wrath; the waters are constantly rising, and waxing more and more mighty; and there is nothing but the mere pleasure of God, that holds the waters back, that are unwilling to be stopped, and press hard to go forward. If God should only withdraw his hand from the flood-gate, it would immediately fly open, and the fiery floods of the fierceness and wrath of God, would rush forth with inconceivable fury, and would come upon you with omnipotent power; and if your strength were ten thousand times greater than it is, yea, ten thousand times greater than the strength of the stoutest, sturdiest devil in hell, it would be nothing to withstand or endure it.

The bow of God's wrath is bent, and the arrow made ready on the string, and justice bends the arrow at your heart, and strains the bow, and it is nothing but the mere pleasure of God, and that of an angry God, without any promise or obligation at all, that keeps the arrow one moment from being made drunk with your blood. Thus all you that never passed under a great change of heart, by the mighty power of the Spirit of God upon your souls; all you that were never born again, and made new creatures, and raised from being dead in sin, to a state of new, and before altogether unexperienced light and life, are in the hands of an angry God. However you may have reformed your life in many things, and may have had religious affections, and may keep up a form of religion in your families and closets, and in the house of God, it is nothing but his mere pleasure that keeps you from being this moment swallowed up in everlasting destruction. However unconvinced you may now be of the truth of what you hear, by and by you will be fully convinced of it. Those that are gone from being in the like circumstances with you, see that it was so with them; for destruction came suddenly upon most of them; when they expected nothing of it, and while they were saying, Peace and safety: now they see, that those things on which they depended for peace and safety, were nothing but thin air and empty shadows.

The God that holds you over the pit of hell, much as one holds a spider, or some loathsome insect over the fire, abhors you, and is dreadfully provoked: his wrath towards you burns like fire; he looks upon you as worthy of nothing else, but to be cast into the fire; he is of purer eyes than to bear to have you in his sight; you are ten thousand times more abominable in his eyes, than the most hateful venomous serpent is in ours. You have offended him infinitely more than ever a stubborn rebel did his prince; and yet it is nothing but his hand that holds you from falling into the fire every moment. It is to be ascribed to nothing else that you did not go to hell the last night; that you were suffered to awake again in this world, after you closed your eyes to sleep. And there is no other reason to be given, why you have not dropped into hell since you arose in the morning, but that God's hand has held you up. There is no other reason to be given why you have not gone to hell, since you have sat here in the house of God, provoking his pure eyes by your sinful wicked manner of attending his solemn worship. Yea, there is nothing else that is to be given as a reason why you do not this very moment drop down into hell.

O sinner! Consider the fearful danger you are in: it is a great furnace of wrath, a wide and bottomless pit, full of the fire of wrath, that you are held over in the hand of that God, whose wrath is provoked and incensed as much against you, as against many of the damned in hell. You hang by a slender thread, with the flames of divine wrath flashing about it, and ready every moment to singe it, and burn it asunder; and you have no interest in any Mediator, and nothing to lay hold of to save yourself, nothing to keep off the flames of wrath, nothing of your own, nothing that you ever have done, nothing that you can do, to induce God to spare you one moment. And consider here more particularly:

1. Whose wrath it is: it is the wrath of the infinite God. If it were only the wrath of man, though it were of the most potent prince, it would be comparatively little to be regarded. The wrath of kings is very much dreaded, especially of absolute monarchs, who have the possessions and lives of their subjects wholly in their power, to be disposed of at their mere will. Proverbs 20:2. "The fear of a king is as the roaring of a lion: Whoso provoketh him to anger, sinneth against his own soul." The subject that very much enrages an arbitrary prince, is liable to suffer the most extreme torments that human art can invent, or human power can inflict. But the greatest earthly potentates in their greatest majesty and strength, and when clothed in their greatest terrors, are but feeble, despicable worms of the dust, in comparison of the great and almighty Creator and King of heaven and earth. It is but little that they can do, when most enraged, and when they have exerted the utmost of their fury. All the kings of the earth, before God, are as grasshoppers; they are nothing, and less than nothing: both their love and their hatred is to be despised. The wrath of the great King of kings, is as much more terrible than theirs, as his majesty is greater. Luke 12:4–5. "And I say unto you, my friends, Be not afraid of them that kill the body, and after that, have no more that they can do. But I will forewarn you whom you shall fear: fear him, which after he hath killed, hath power to cast into hell: yea, I say unto you, Fear him."

2. It is the fierceness of his wrath that you are exposed to. We often read of the fury of God; as in Isaiah 59:18, "According to their deeds, accordingly he will repay fury to his adversaries." So Isaiah 66:15. "For behold, the Lord will come with fire, and with his chariots

like a whirlwind, to render his anger with fury, and his rebuke with flames of fire." And in many other places. So, Revelation 19:15, we read of "the wine press of the fierceness and wrath of Almighty God." The words are exceeding terrible. If it had only been said, "the wrath of God," the words would have implied that which is infinitely dreadful: but it is "the fierceness and wrath of God." The fury of God! The fierceness of Jehovah! Oh, how dreadful must that be! Who can utter or conceive what such expressions carry in them! But it is also "the fierceness and wrath of Almighty God." As though there would be a very great manifestation of his almighty power in what the fierceness of his wrath should inflict, as though omnipotence should be as it were enraged, and exerted, as men are wont to exert their strength in the fierceness of their wrath. Oh! Then, what will be the consequence! What will become of the poor worms that shall suffer it! Whose hands can be strong? And whose heart can endure? To what a dreadful, inexpressible, inconceivable depth of misery must the poor creature be sunk who shall be the subject of this!

Consider this, you that are here present, that yet remain in an unregenerate state. That God will execute the fierceness of his anger, implies, that he will inflict wrath without any pity. When God beholds the ineffable extremity of your case, and sees your torment to be so vastly disproportioned to your strength, and sees how your poor soul is crushed, and sinks down, as it were, into an infinite gloom; he will have no compassion upon you, he will not forbear the executions of his wrath, or in the least lighten his hand; there shall be no moderation or mercy, nor will God then at all stay his rough wind; he will have no regard to your welfare, nor be at all careful lest you should suffer too much in any other sense, than only that you shall not suffer beyond what strict justice requires. Nothing shall be withheld, because it is so hard for you to bear. Ezekiel 8:18, "Therefore will I also deal in fury: mine eye shall not spare, neither will I have pity; and though they cry in mine ears with a loud voice, yet I will not hear them." Now God stands ready to pity you; this is a day of mercy; you may cry now with some encouragement of obtaining mercy. But when once the day of mercy is past, your most lamentable and dolorous cries and shrieks will be in vain; you will be wholly lost and thrown away of God, as to any regard to your welfare. God will have no other use to put you to, but to suffer misery; you shall be continued in being to no other end; for you will be a vessel of wrath fitted to destruction; and there will be no other use of this vessel, but to be filled full of wrath. God will be so far from pitying you when you cry to him, that it is said he will only "laugh and mock," Proverbs 1:25–26, etc.

How awful are those words, Isaiah 63:3, which are the words of the great God, "I will tread them in mine anger, and will trample them in my fury, and their blood shall be sprinkled upon my garments, and I will stain all my raiment." It is perhaps impossible to conceive of words that carry in them greater manifestations of these three things, namely, contempt and hatred, and fierceness of indignation. If you cry to God to pity you, he will be so far from pitying you in your doleful case, or showing you the least regard or favor, that instead of that, he will only tread you under foot. And though he will know that you cannot bear the weight of omnipotence treading upon you, yet he will not regard that, but he will crush you under his feet without mercy; he will crush out your blood, and make it fly, and it shall be sprinkled on his garments, so as to stain all his raiment. He will not only hate you, but he will have you, in the utmost contempt: no place shall be thought fit for you, but under his feet to be trodden down as the mire of the streets.

The misery you are exposed to is that which God will inflict to that end, that he might show what that wrath of Jehovah is. God hath had it on his heart to show to angels and men, both how excellent his love is, and also how terrible his wrath is. Sometimes earthly kings have a mind to show how terrible their wrath is, by the extreme punishments they would execute on those that would provoke them. Nebuchadnezzar, that mighty and haughty monarch of the Chaldean empire, was willing to show his wrath when enraged with Shadrach, Meshech, and Abednego; and accordingly gave orders that the burning fiery furnace should be heated seven times hotter than it was before; doubtless, it was raised to the utmost degree of fierceness that human art could raise it. But the great God is also willing to show his wrath, and magnify his awful majesty and mighty power in the extreme sufferings of his enemies. Romans 9:22, "What if God, willing to show his wrath, and to make his power known, endure with much long-suffering the vessels of wrath fitted to destruction?" And seeing this is his design, and what he has determined, even to show how terrible the unrestrained wrath, the fury and fierceness of Jehovah is, he will do it to effect. There will be something accomplished and brought to pass that will be dreadful with a witness. When the great and angry God hath risen up and executed his awful vengeance on the poor sinner, and the wretch is actually suffering the infinite weight and power of his indignation, then will God call upon the whole universe to behold that awful majesty and mighty power that is to be seen in it. Isaiah 33:12–14, "And the people shall be as the burnings of lime, as thorns cut up shall they be burnt in the fire. Hear ye that are far off, what I have done; and ye that are near, acknowledge my might. The sinners in Zion are afraid; fearfulness hath surprised the hypocrites," etc.

Thus it will be with you that are in an unconverted state, if you continue in it; the infinite might, and majesty, and terribleness of the omnipotent God shall be magnified upon you, in the ineffable strength of your torments. You shall be tormented in the presence of the holy angels, and in the presence of the Lamb; and when you shall be in this state of suffering, the glorious inhabitants of heaven shall go forth and look on the awful spectacle, that they may see what the wrath and fierceness of the Almighty is; and when they have seen it, they will fall down and adore that great power and majesty. Isaiah 66:23–24, "And it shall come to pass, that from one new moon to another, and from one Sabbath to another, shall all flesh come to worship before me, saith the Lord. And they shall go forth and look upon the carcasses of the men that have transgressed against me; for their worm shall not die, neither shall their fire be quenched, and they shall be an abhorring unto all flesh."

4. It is everlasting wrath. It would be dreadful to suffer this fierceness and wrath of Almighty God one moment; but you must suffer it to all eternity. There will be no end to this exquisite horrible misery. When you look forward, you shall see a long for ever, a boundless duration before you, which will swallow up your thoughts, and amaze your soul; and you will absolutely despair of ever having any deliverance, any end, any mitigation, any rest at all. You will know certainly that you must wear out long ages, millions of millions of ages, in wrestling and conflicting with this almighty merciless vengeance; and then when you have so done, when so many ages have actually been spent by you in this manner, you will know that all is but a point to what remains. So that your punishment will indeed be infinite. Oh, who can express what the state of a soul in such circumstances is! All that we can possibly say about it, gives but a very feeble, faint representation of it; it is inexpressible and inconceivable: For "who knows the power of God's anger?"

How dreadful is the state of those that are daily and hourly in the danger of this great wrath and infinite misery! But this is the dismal case of every soul in this congregation that has not been born again, however moral and strict, sober and religious, they may otherwise be. Oh that you would consider it, whether you be young or old! There is reason to think, that there are many in this congregation now hearing this discourse that will actually be the subjects of this very misery to all eternity. We know not who they are, or in what seats they sit, or what thoughts they now have. It may be they are now at ease, and hear all these things without much disturbance, and are now flattering themselves that they are not the persons, promising themselves that they shall escape. If we knew that there was one person, and but one, in the whole congregation, that was to be the subject of this misery, what an awful thing would it be to think of! If we knew who it was, what an awful sight would it be to see such a person! How might all the rest of the congregation lift up a lamentable and bitter cry over him! But, alas! Instead of one, how many is it likely will remember this discourse in hell? And it would be a wonder, if some that are now present should not be in hell in a very short time, even before this year is out. And it would be no wonder if some persons, that now sit here, in some seats of this meeting-house, in health, quiet and secure, should be there before to-morrow morning. Those of you that finally continue in a natural condition that shall keep out of hell longest will be there in a little time! Your damnation does not slumber; it will come swiftly, and, in all probability, very suddenly upon many of you. You have reason to wonder that you are not already in hell. It is doubtless the case of some whom you have seen and known, that never deserved hell more than you, and that heretofore appeared as likely to have been now alive as you. Their case is past all hope; they are crying in extreme misery and perfect despair; but here you are in the land of the living and in the house of God, and have an opportunity to obtain salvation. What would not those poor damned hopeless souls give for one day's opportunity such as you now enjoy!

And now you have an extraordinary opportunity, a day wherein Christ has thrown the door of mercy wide open, and stands in calling and crying with a loud voice to poor sinners; a day wherein many are flocking to him, and pressing into the kingdom of God. Many are daily coming from the east, west, north and south; many that were very lately in the same miserable condition that you are in, are now in a happy state, with their hearts filled with love to him who has loved them, and washed them from their sins in his own blood, and rejoicing in hope of the glory of God. How awful is it to be left behind at such a day! To see so many others feasting, while you are pining and perishing! To see so many rejoicing and singing for joy of heart, while you have cause to mourn for sorrow of heart, and howl for vexation of spirit! How can you rest one moment in such a condition? Are not your souls as precious as the souls of the people at Suffield,[3] where they are flocking from day to day to Christ?

Are there not many here who have lived long in the world, and are not to this day born again? and so are aliens from the commonwealth of Israel, and have done nothing ever since they have lived, but treasure up wrath against the day of wrath? Oh, sirs, your case, in an especial manner, is extremely dangerous. Your guilt and hardness of heart is extremely great. Do you not see how generally persons of your years are passed over and left, in the present remarkable and wonderful dispensation of God's mercy? You had need to consider yourselves, and awake thoroughly out of sleep. You cannot bear the fierceness and wrath of the infinite God. And you, young men, and young women, will you neglect this precious season which you now enjoy, when so many others of your age are renouncing all youthful vanities, and flocking to Christ? You especially have now an extraordinary opportunity; but if you neglect it, it will soon be with you as with those persons who spent all the precious days of youth in sin, and are now come to such a dreadful pass in blindness and hardness. And you, children, who are unconverted, do not you know that you are going down to hell, to bear the dreadful wrath of that God, who is now angry with you every day and every night? Will you be content to be the children of the devil, when so many other children in the land are converted, and

---

3. A nearby town experiencing revival.

are become the holy and happy children of the King of kings?

And let every one that is yet out of Christ, and hanging over the pit of hell, whether they be old men and women, or middle aged, or young people, or little children, now harken to the loud calls of God's word and providence. This acceptable year of the Lord, a day of such great favors to some, will doubtless be a day of as remarkable vengeance to others. Men's hearts harden, and their guilt increases apace at such a day as this, if they neglect their souls; and never was there so great danger of such persons being given up to hardness of heart and blindness of mind. God seems now to be hastily gathering in his elect in all parts of the land; and probably the greater part of adult persons that ever shall be saved, will be brought in now in a little time, and that it will be as it was on the great out-pouring of the Spirit upon the Jews in the apostles' days; the election will obtain, and the rest will be blinded. If this should be the case with you, you will eternally curse this day, and will curse the day that ever you was born, to see such a season of the pouring out of God's Spirit, and will wish that you had died and gone to hell before you had seen it.

Now undoubtedly it is, as it was in the days of John the Baptist, the axe is in an extraordinary manner laid at the root of the trees, that every tree which brings not forth good fruit, may be hewn down and cast into the fire.

Therefore, let every one that is out of Christ, now awake and fly from the wrath to come. The wrath of Almighty God is now undoubtedly hanging over a great part of this congregation: Let every one fly out of Sodom: "Haste and escape for your lives, look not behind you, escape to the mountain, lest you be consumed."

JOHN WESLEY: *A PLAIN ACCOUNT OF CHRISTIAN PERFECTION* (ABRIDGED)
English, 1777

". . . to be inwardly and outwardly devoted to God; all devoted in heart and life."
—John Wesley

This is a defense of the doctrine of "entire sanctification," describing the experiential and biblical basis for the doctrine, and offering Wesley's best advice for growth in the Christian life—in faith, purity, integrity, and also in outward testimony. The work is laid out as a development both of Wesley's own thinking and of the Methodist movement. It is, therefore, something of an itinerary of Wesley's spiritual journey and provides some details of the early history of the movement. The writing is not only rich in scriptural citations but also includes letters of testimony, advice on the role and value of class meetings, and a number of both John Wesley's and Charles Wesley's poems and hymn lyrics. For a brief summary of the main propositions of *A Plain Account*, see section 26, below. *A Plain Account* was first edited and published by Thomas Jackson in 1872 in The Works of John Wesley (vol. 11, pp. 366–446).

◆

1. What I purpose in the following papers is, to give a plain and distinct account of the steps by which I was led, during a course of many years, to embrace the doctrine of Christian perfection. This I owe to the serious part of mankind, those who desire to know all "the truth as it is in Jesus." And these only are concerned in questions of this kind. To these I would nakedly declare the thing as it is, endeavouring all along to show, from one period to another, both what I thought, and why I thought so.

2. In the year 1725, being in the twenty-third year of my age, I met with Bishop Taylor's *Rule and Exercises of Holy Living and Dying*. In reading several parts of this book, I was exceedingly affected; that part in particular which relates to purity of intention. Instantly I resolved to dedicate all my life to God, all my thoughts, and words, and actions; being thoroughly convinced, there was no medium; but that every part of my life (not some only) must either be a sacrifice to God, or myself, that is, in effect, to the devil. Can any serious person doubt of this, or find a medium between serving God and serving the devil?

3. In the year 1726, I met with Kempis's *Christian's Pattern*. The nature and extent of inward religion, the religion of the heart, now appeared to me in a stronger light than ever it had done before. I saw, that giving even

all my life to God (supposing it possible to do this) and go no farther would profit me nothing, unless I gave my heart, yea, all my heart, to him. I saw, that "simplicity of intention, and purity of affection," one design in all we speak or do, and one desire ruling all our tempers, are indeed "the wings of the soul," without which she can never ascend to the mount of God.

4. A year or two after, Mr. Law's *Christian Perfection* and *Serious Call* were put into my hands. These convinced me, more than ever, of the absolute impossibility of being half a Christian; and I determined, through his grace (the absolute necessity of which I was deeply sensible of) to be all-devoted to God, to give him all my soul, my body, and my substance. Will any considerate man say, that this is carrying matters too far? or that anything less is due to Him who has given Himself for us, than to give Him ourselves, all we have, and all we are?

5. In the year 1729, I began not only to read, but to study, the Bible, as the one, the only standard of truth, and the only model of pure religion. Hence I saw, in a clearer and clearer light, the indispensable necessity of having "the mind which was in Christ," and of "walking as Christ also walked"; even of having, not some part only, but all the mind which was in him; and of walking as he walked, not only in many or in most respects, but in all things. And this was the light, wherein at this time I generally considered religion, as an uniform following of Christ, an entire inward and outward conformity to our Master. Nor was I afraid of anything more, than of bending this rule to the experience of myself; or of other men; of allowing myself in any the least disconformity to our grand Exemplar.

6. On January 1, 1733, I preached before the University in St. Mary's church, on "the Circumcision of the Heart"; an account of which I gave in these words: "It is that habitual disposition of soul which, in the sacred writings, is termed holiness; and which directly implies, the being cleansed from sin 'from all filthiness both of flesh and spirit'; and, by consequence the being endued with those virtues which were in Christ Jesus the being so 'renewed in the image of our mind,' as to be 'perfect as our Father in heaven is perfect.'"

In the same sermon I observed, "'Love is the fulfill-

ing of the law, the end of the commandment.' It is not only 'the first and great' command, but all the commandments in one. 'Whatsoever things are just, whatsoever things are pure, if there be any virtue, if there be any praise,' they are all comprised in this one word, love. In this is perfection, and glory, and happiness: The royal law of heaven and earth is this, 'Thou shall love the Lord thy God with all thy heart, and with all thy soul, and with all thy mind, and with all thy strength.' The one perfect good shall be your one ultimate end. One thing shall ye desire for its own sake,—the fruition of Him who is all in all. One happiness shall ye propose to your souls, even an union with Him that made them, the having 'fellowship with the Father and the Son,' the being 'joined to the Lord in one spirit.' One design ye are to pursue to the end of time,—the enjoyment of God in time and in eternity. Desire other things so far as they tend to this; love the creature, as it leads to the Creator. But in every step you take, be this the glorious point that terminates your view. Let every affection, and thought and word, and action, be subordinate to this. Whatever ye desire or fear, whatever ye seek or shun, whatever ye think, speak, or do, be it in order to your happiness in God, the sole end, as well as source, of your being." I concluded in these words: "Here is the sum of the perfect law, the circumcision of the heart. Let the spirit return to God that gave it, with the whole train of its affections.—Other sacrifices from us he would not, but the living sacrifice of the heart hath he chosen. Let it be continually offered up to God through Christ, in flames of holy love. And let no creature be suffered to share with him; for he is a jealous God. His throne will he not divide with another; he will reign without a rival. Be no design, no desire admitted there, but what has Him for its ultimate object. This is the way wherein those children of God once walked, who being dead still speak to us: 'Desire not to live but to praise his name; let all your thoughts, words, and works tend to his glory.' 'Let your soul be filled with so entire a love to Him that you may love nothing but for his sake.' 'Have a pure intention of heart, a steadfast regard to his glory in all you actions.' For then, and not till then, is that 'mind in us, which was also in Christ Jesus,' when in every motion of our heart, in every word of our tongue, in every work of our hands, we 'pursue nothing but in relation to him, and in subordination to his pleasure'; when we too neither think, nor speak, nor act, to fulfil 'our own will, but the will of Him that sent us'; when, 'whether we eat or drink, or whatever we do,' we do it all 'to the glory of God.'"

It may be observed, this sermon was composed the first of all my writings which have been published. This was the view of religion I then had, which even then I scrupled not to term perfection. This is the view I have of it now, without any material addition or diminution. And what is there in it, which any man of understanding, who believes the Bible, can object to? What can he deny, without flatly contradicting the Scripture? What retrench, without taking from the word of God?

7. In the same sentiment did my brother and I remain (with all those young gentlemen in derision termed Methodists) till we embarked for America, in the latter end of 1735. It was the next year, while I was at Savannah, that I wrote the following lines:—Is there a thing beneath the sun, that strives with thee my heart to share? Ah! tear it thence, and reign alone, The Lord of every motion there! In the beginning of the year 1738, as I was returning from thence, the cry of my heart was, O grant that nothing in my soul May dwell, but thy pure love alone! O may thy love possess me whole, My joy, my treasure, and my crown! Strange fires far from my heart remove; My every act, word, thought, be love! I never heard that any one objected to this. And indeed who can object? Is not this the language, not only of every believer, but of every one that is truly awakened? But what have I wrote, to this day, which is either stronger or plainer?

8. In August following, I had a long conversation with Arvid Gradin, in Germany. After he had given me an account of his experience, I desired him to give me, in writing, a definition of "the full assurance of faith," which he did in the following words:—*Requies in sanguine Christi; firma fiducia in Deum, et persuasio de gratia divina; tranquillitas mentis summa, atque serenitas et pax; cum absentia omnis desiderii carnalis, et cessatione peccatorum etiam internorum* ("Repose in the blood of Christ; a firm confidence in God, and persuasion of his favour; the highest tranquillity, serenity, and peace of mind, with a deliverance from every fleshly desire, and a cessation of all, even inward sins"). This was the first account I ever heard from any living man, of what I had before learned myself from the oracles of God, and had

been praying for (with the little company of my friends), and expecting, for several years.

9. In 1739, my brother and I published a volume of *Hymns and Sacred Poems*. In many of these we declared our sentiments strongly and explicitly. So, for example, "Turn the full stream of nature's tide; Let all our actions tend To thee, their source; thy love the guide, Thy glory be the end. Earth then a scale to heaven shall be; Sense shall point out the road; The creatures all shall lead to thee, And all we taste be God." Again, "Lord, arm me with thy Spirit's might, Since I am call'd by thy great name: In thee my wand'ring thoughts unite, Of all my works be thou the aim: Thy love attend me all my days, And my sole business be thy praise." Again, "Eager for thee I ask and pant, So strong the principle divine, Carries me out with sweet constraint, Till all my hallow'd soul be thine; Plunged in the Godhead's deepest sea, And lost in thine immensity!" Once more, "Heavenly Adam, life divine, Change my nature into thine; Move and spread throughout my soul, Actuate and fill the whole." It would be easy to cite many more passages to the same effect. But these are sufficient to show, beyond contradiction, what our sentiments then were.

10. The first tract I ever wrote expressly on this subject was published in the latter end of this year. That none might be prejudiced before they read it, I gave it the indifferent title of "The Character of a Methodist." In this I described a perfect Christian, placing in the front, "Not as though I had already attained." Part of it I subjoin without any alteration:

"A Methodist is one who loves the Lord his God with all his heart, with all his soul, with all his mind, and with all his strength. God is the joy of his heart, and the desire of his soul, which is continually crying, 'Whom have I in heaven but thee? and there is none upon earth whom I desire besides thee.' My God and my all! 'Thou art the strength of my heart, and my portion for ever.' He is therefore happy in God; yea, always happy, as having in him a well of water springing up unto everlasting life, and over-flowing his soul with peace and joy. Perfect love living now cast out fear, he rejoices evermore. Yea, his joy is full, and all his bones cry out, 'Blessed be the God and Father of our Lord Jesus Christ, who, according to his abundant mercy, hath begotten me again unto a living hope of an inheritance incorruptible and undefiled, reserved in heaven for me.'

"And he, who hath this hope, thus full of immortality, in everything giveth thanks, as knowing this (whatsoever it is) is the will of God in Christ Jesus concerning him. From him therefore he cheerfully receives all, saying, 'Good is the will of the Lord'; and whether he giveth or taketh away, equally blessing the name of the Lord. Whether in ease or pain, whether in sickness or health, whether in life or death, he giveth thanks from the ground of the heart to Him who orders it for good; into whose hands he hath wholly committed his body and soul, 'as into the hands of a faithful Creator.' He is therefore anxiously 'careful for nothing,' as having 'cast all his care on Him that careth for him'; and 'in all things' resting on him, after 'making his request known to him with thanksgiving.'

"For indeed he 'prays without ceasing'; at all times the language of his heart is this, 'Unto thee is my mouth, though without a voice; and my silence speaketh unto thee.' His heart is lifted up to God at all times, and in all places. In this he is never hindered, much less interrupted, by any person or thing. In retirement or company, in leisure, business, or conversation, his heart is ever with the Lord. Whether he lie down, or rise up, 'God is in all his thoughts': He walks with God continually; having the loving eye of his soul fixed on him, and everywhere 'seeing Him that is invisible.'

"And loving God, he 'loves his neighbour as himself'; he loves every man as his own soul. He loves his enemies, yea, and the enemies of God. And if it be not in his power to 'do good to them that hate' him, yet he ceases not to 'pray for them,' though they spurn his love, and still 'despitefully use him, and persecute him.'

"For he is 'pure in heart'. Love has purified his heart from envy, malice, wrath, and every unkind temper. It has cleansed him from pride, whereof 'only cometh contention'; and he hath now 'put on bowels of mercies, kindness, humbleness of mind, meekness, long-suffering.' And indeed all possible ground for contention, on his part, is cut off. For none can take from him what he desires, seeing he 'loves not the world, nor any of the things of the world'; but 'all his desire is unto God, and to the remembrance of his name.'

"Agreeable to this his one desire, is this one design of his life; namely, 'to do, not his own will, but the will of Him that sent him.' His one intention at all times and in all places is, not to please himself, but Him whom his soul loveth. He hath a single eye; and because his 'eye is single, his whole body is full of light. The whole is light, as when the bright shining of a candle doth enlighten the house.' God reigns alone; all that is in the soul is 'holiness to the Lord.' There is not a motion in his heart but is according to his will. Every thought that arises points to him, and is in 'obedience to the law of Christ.'

"And the tree is known by its fruits. For, as he loves God, so he 'keeps his commandments'; not only some, or most of them, but all, from the least to the greatest. He is not content to 'keep the whole law and offend in one point,' but has in all points 'a conscience void of offence towards God, and towards man.' Whatever God has forbidden, he avoids; whatever God has enjoined, he does. 'He runs the way of God's commandments,' now He bath set his heart at liberty. It is his glory and joy so to do; it is his daily crown of rejoicing, to 'do the will of God on earth, as it is done in heaven.'

"All the commandments of God he accordingly keeps, and that with all his might; for his obedience is in proportion to his love, the source from whence it flows. And therefore, loving God with all his heart, he serves him with all his strength; he continually presents his soul and 'body a living sacrifice, holy, acceptable to God'; entirely and without reserve devoting himself, all he has, all he is, to his glory. All the talents he has, he constantly employs according to his Master's will; every power and faculty of his soul, every member of his body."

"By consequence, 'whatsoever he doeth, it is all to the glory of God.' In all his employments of every kind, he not only aims at this, which is implied in having a single eye, but actually attains it; his business and his refreshments, as well as his prayers, all serve to this great end. Whether he 'sit in the house, or walk by the way,' whether he lie down, or rise up, he is promoting, in all he speaks or does, the one business of his life. Whether he put on his apparel, or labour, or eat and drink, or divert himself from too wasting labour, it all tends to advance the glory of God, by peace and good-will among men. His one invariable rule is this: 'Whatsoever ye do, in word or deed, do it all in the name of the Lord Jesus, giving thanks to God, even the Father, through him.'

"Nor do the customs of the world at all hinder his 'running the race which is set before him.' He cannot therefore 'lay up treasures upon earth,' no more than he can take fire into his bosom. He cannot speak evil of his neighbour, any more than he can lie either for God or man. He cannot utter an unkind word of any one; for love keeps the door of his lips. He cannot 'speak idle words; no corrupt conversation' ever 'comes out of his mouth'; as is all that is not 'good to the use of edifying,' not fit to 'minister grace to the hearers.' But 'whatsoever things are pure, whatsoever things are lovely, whatsoever things are justly of good report,' he thinks, speaks, and acts, 'adorning the doctrine of God our Saviour in all things.'"

These are the very words wherein I largely declared, for the first time, my sentiments of Christian perfection. And is it not easy to see, (1) That this is the very point at which I aimed all along from the year 1725; and more determinately from the year 1730, when I began to be *homo unius libri*, "a man of one book," regarding none, comparatively, but the Bible? Is it not easy to see, (2) That this is the very same doctrine which I believe and teach at this day; not adding one point, either to that inward or outward holiness which I maintained eight-and-thirty years ago? And it is the same which, by the grace of God, I have continued to teach from that time till now; as will appear to every impartial person from the extracts subjoined below.

11. I do not know that any writer has made any objection against that tract to this day; and for some time, I did not find much opposition upon the head, at least, not from serious persons. But after a time, a cry arose, and, what a little surprised me, among religions men, who affirmed, not that I stated perfection wrong, but that "there is no perfection on earth"; nay, and fell vehemently on my brother and me for affirming the contrary. We scarce expected so rough an attack from these; especially as we were clear on justification by faith, and careful to ascribe the whole of salvation to the mere grace of God. But what most surprised us, was, that we were said to "dishonour Christ" by asserting that he "saveth to the uttermost," by maintaining he will reign in our hearts alone, and subdue all things to himself.

12. I think it was in the latter end of the year 1740, that I had a conversation with Dr. Gibson, then Bishop of London, at Whitehall. He asked me what I meant by perfection. I told him without any disguise or reserve. When I ceased speaking, he said, "Mr. Wesley, if this be all you mean, publish it to all the world. If any one then can confute what you say, he may have free leave." I answered, "My Lord, I will"; and accordingly wrote and published the sermon on Christian perfection.

In this I endeavoured to show, (1) In what sense Christians are not, (2) In what sense they are, perfect.

"(1)   In what sense they are not. They are not perfect in knowledge. They are not free from ignorance, no, nor from mistake. We are no more to expect any living man to be infallible, than to be omniscient. They are not free from infirmities, such as weakness or slowness of understanding, irregular quickness or heaviness of imagination. Such in another kind are impropriety of language, ungracefulness of pronunciation; to which one might add a thousand nameless defects, either in conversation or behaviour. From such infirmities as these none are perfectly freed till their spirits return to God; neither can we expect till then to be wholly freed from temptation; for 'the servant is not above his master.' But neither in this sense is there any absolute perfection on earth. There is no perfection of degrees, none which does not admit of a continual increase.

"(2) In what sense then are they perfect? Observe, we are not now speaking of babes in Christ, but adult Christians (though) even babes in Christ are so far perfect as not to commit sin. This St. John affirms expressly; and it cannot be disproved by the examples of the Old Testament. For what, if the holiest of the ancient Jews did sometimes commit sin? We cannot infer from hence, that 'all Christians do and must commit sin as long as they live.' But does not the Scripture say, 'A just man sinneth seven times a day?' It does not. Indeed it says, 'A just man falleth seven times.' But this is quite another thing; for, First, the words, a day, are not in the text. Secondly, here is no mention of falling into sin at all. What is here mentioned, is, falling into temporal affliction. But elsewhere Solomon says, 'There is no man that sinneth not.' Doubtless thus it was in the days of Solomon; yea, and from Solomon to Christ there was then no man that sinned not. But whatever was the case of those under the law, we may safely affirm, with St. John, that, since the gospel was given, 'he that is born of God sinneth not.'

"The privileges of Christians are in nowise to be measured by what the Old Testament records concerning those who were under the Jewish dispensation; seeing the fulness of time is now come, the Holy Ghost is now given, the great salvation of God is now brought to men by the revelation of Jesus Christ. The kingdom of heaven is now set up on earth, concerning which the Spirit of God declared of old time (so far is David from being the pattern or standard of Christian perfection), 'He that is feeble among them, at that day, shall be as David, and the house of David shall be as the angel of the Lord before them' (Zech. 12:8).

"But the Apostles themselves committed sin; Peter by dissembling, Paul by his sharp contention with Barnabas. Suppose they did, will you argue thus: 'If two of the Apostles once committed sin, then all other Christians, in all ages, do and must commit sin as long as they live?' Nay, God forbid we should thus speak. No necessity of sin was laid upon them; the grace of God was surely sufficient for them. And it is sufficient for us at this day.

"But St. James says, 'In many things we offend all.' True, but who are the persons here spoken of? Why, those 'many masters' or teachers whom God had not sent; not the Apostle himself, nor any real Christian. That in the word we, used by a figure of speech, common in all other as well as the inspired writings, the Apostle could not possibly include himself, or any other true believer, appears, First, from the ninth verse, 'Therewith bless we God, and therewith curse we men.' Surely not we Apostles! Not we believers! Secondly, from the words preceding the text: 'My brethren, be not many masters,' or teachers, 'knowing that we shall receive the greater condemnation. For in many things we offend all.' We! Who? Not the Apostles nor true believers, but they who were to 'receive the greater condemnation,' because of those many offences. Nay, Thirdly, the verse itself proves, that 'we offend all,' cannot be spoken either of all men or all Christians. For in it immediately follows the mention of a man who 'offends not,' as the we first mentioned did; from whom therefore he is professedly contradistinguished, and pronounced a 'perfect man.'

"But St. John himself says, 'If we say that we have no sin, we deceive ourselves'; and, 'If we say we have not sinned, we make him a liar, and his word is not in us.' I answer, (1) The tenth verse fixes the sense of the eighth: 'If we say we have no sin,' in the former, being explained by, 'If we say we have not sinned,' in the latter, verse. (2) The point under consideration is not, whether we have or have not sinned heretofore; and neither of these verses asserts that we do sin, or commit sin now. (3) The ninth verse explains both the eighth and tenth: 'If we confess our sins, he is faithful and just to forgive us our sins, and to cleanse us from all unrighteousness.' As if he had said, 'I have before affirmed, the blood of Christ cleanseth from all sin.' And no man can say, 'I need it not; I have no sin to be cleansed, from.' If we say, we have no sin, that we have not sinned, 'we deceive ourselves, and make God a liar.' But if we confess our sins, he is faithful and just, not only 'to forgive us our sins,' but also 'to cleanse us from all unrighteousness,' that we may 'go and sin no more.' In conformity, therefore, both to the doctrine of St. John, and the whole tenor of the New Testament, we fix this conclusion: A Christian is so far perfect, as not to commit sin.

"This is the glorious privilege of every Christian, yea, though he be but a babe in Christ. But it is only of grown Christians it can be affirmed, they are in such a sense perfect, as, Secondly, to be freed from evil thoughts and evil tempers. First, from evil or sinful thoughts. Indeed, whence should they spring? 'Out of the heart of man,' if at all, 'proceed evil thoughts.' If, therefore, the heart be no longer evil, then evil thoughts no longer proceed out of it: For 'a good tree cannot bring forth evil fruit.' And as they are freed from evil thoughts, so likewise from evil tempers. Every one of these can say, with St. Paul, 'I am crucified with Christ; nevertheless I live; yet not I, but Christ liveth in me'—words that manifestly describe a deliverance from inward as well as from outward sin. This is expressed both negatively, 'I live not,' my evil nature, the body of sin, is destroyed; and positively, 'Christ liveth in me,' and therefore all that is holy, and just, and good. Indeed, both these, 'Christ liveth in me,' and, 'I live not,' are inseparably connected. For what communion hath light with darkness, or Christ with Belial? He, therefore, who liveth in these Christians hath 'purified their hearts by faith'; insomuch that every one that has Christ in him, 'the hope of glory, purifieth himself even as he is pure.' He is purified from pride; for Christ was lowly in heart: He is pure from desire and self-will; for Christ desired only to do the will of his Father: And he is pure from anger, in the common sense of the word; for Christ was meek and gentle. I say, in the common sense of the word; for he is angry at sin, while he is grieved for the sinner. He feels a displacency at every offence against God, but only tender compassion to the offender. Thus doth Jesus save his people from their sins, not only from outward sins, but from the sins of their hearts. 'True,' say some, 'but not till death, not in this world.' Nay, St. John says, 'Herein is our love made perfect, that we may have boldness in the day of judgment; because, as he is, so are we in this world.' The Apostle here, beyond all contradiction, speaks of himself and other living Christians, of whom he flatly affirms, that, not only at or after death, but 'in this world,' they are 'as their Master.'

"Exactly agreeable to this are his words in the first chapter: 'God is light, and in him is no darkness at all. If we walk in the light, as he is in the light, we have fellowship one with another, and the blood of Jesus Christ his Son cleanseth us from all sin.' And again: 'If we confess our sins, he is faithful and just to forgive us our sins, and to cleanse us from all unrighteousness.' Now, it is evident, the Apostle here speaks of a deliverance wrought in this world: For he saith not, The blood of Christ *will* cleanse (at the hour of death, or in the day of judgment), but it 'cleanseth,' at the time present, us living Christians from all sin. And it is equally evident, that if any sin remain, we are not cleansed from all sin. If any unrighteousness remain in the soul, it is not cleansed from all, unrighteousness. Neither let any say that this relates to justification only, or the cleansing us from the guilt of sin: First, because this is confounding together what the Apostle clearly distinguishes, who mentions, first, to forgive us our sins, and then to cleanse us from all unrighteousness. Secondly, because this is asserting justification by works, in the strongest sense possible; it is making all inward, as well as all outward, holiness, necessarily previous to justification. For if the cleansing here spoken of is no other than the cleansing us from the guilt of sin, then we are not cleansed from guilt, that is, not justified, unless on condition of walking 'in the light, as he is in the light.' It remains, then, that Christians are saved in this world from all sin, from all unrighteousness; that they are now in such a sense perfect, as not to commit sin, and to be freed from evil thoughts and evil tempers. It could not be, but that a discourse of this kind, which directly contradicted the favourite opinion of many, who were esteemed by others, and possibly esteemed themselves, some of the best of Christians (whereas, if these things were so, they were not Christians at all), should give no small offence. Many answers or animadversions (criticisms), therefore, were expected; but I was agreeably disappointed. I do not know that any appeared; so I went quietly on my way. . . ."

17. On Monday, June 25, 1744, our First Conference began; six Clergymen and all our Preachers being present. The next morning we seriously considered the doctrine of sanctification, or perfection. The questions asked concerning it, and the substance of the answers given, were as follows:

"Q.	What is it to be sanctified?

Ans.	To be renewed in the image of God, 'in righteousness and true holiness.

Q.	What is implied in being a perfect Christian?

Ans.	The loving God with all our heart, and mind, and soul. (Deut. 6:5)

Q.	Does this imply, that all inward sin is taken away?

Ans.	Undoubtedly; or how can we be Said to be 'saved from all our uncleannesses?' (Ezek. 36:29)"

Our Second Conference began August 1,1745. The next morning we spoke of sanctification as follows:

"Q.	When does inward sanctification begin?

Ans.	In the moment a man is justified. (Yet sin remains in him, yea, the seed of all sin, till he is sanctified throughout.) From that time a believer gradually dies to sin, and grows in grace.

Q.	Is this ordinarily given till a little before death?

Ans.	It is not, to those who expect it no sooner.

Q.	But may we expect it sooner?

Ans.	Why not? For, although we grant, (1) That the generality of believers, whom we have hitherto known, were not so sanctified till near death; (2) That few of those to whom St. Paul wrote his Epistles were so at that time; nor, (3) He himself at the time of writing his former Epistles; yet all this does not prove, that we may not be so today.

Q.	In what manner should we preach sanctification?

Ans.	Scarce at all to those who are not pressing forward: To those who are, always by way of promise; always drawing, rather than driving."

Our Third Conference began Tuesday, May 13, 1746. In this we carefully read over the Minutes of the two preceding Conferences, to observe whether anything contained therein might be retrenched or altered on more mature consideration. But we did not see cause to alter in any respect what we had agreed upon before.

Our Fourth Conference began on Tuesday, June the 16th, 1747. As several persons were present, who did not believe the doctrine of perfection, we agreed to examine it from the foundation. In order to this, it was asked,

"Q.	How much is allowed by our brethren who differ from us with regard to entire sanctification?

Ans.	They grant, (1) That every one must be entirely sanctified in the article of death. (2) That till then a believer daily grows in grace, comes nearer and nearer to perfection. (3) That we ought to be continually pressing after it, and to exhort all others so to do.

Q.	What do we allow them?

Ans.	We grant, (1) That many of those who have died in the faith, yea, the greater part of those we have known, were not perfected in love till a little before their death. (2) That the term sanctified is continually applied by St. Paul to all that were justified. (3) That by this term alone, he rarely, if ever, means saved from all sin. (4) That, consequently, it is not proper to use it in that sense, without adding the word wholly, entirely, or the like. (5) That the inspired writers almost continually speak of or to those who were justified, but very rarely of or to those who were wholly sanctified. [That is, unto those alone, exclusive of others; but they speak to them, jointly with others, almost continually.] (6) That, consequently, it behooves us to speak almost continually of the state of justification; but more rarely, [More rarely, I allow; but yet in some places very frequently, strongly, and explicitly.] at least in full and explicit terms, concerning entire sanctification.

Q.	What then is the point where we divide?

Ans.	It is this: Should we expect to be saved from all sin before the article of death?

Q.	Is there any clear Scripture promise of this, that God will save us from all sin?

Ans. There is: He shall redeem Israel from all his sins. (Psalm 130:8)

This is more largely expressed in the prophecy of Ezekiel: 'Then will I sprinkle clean water upon you, and ye shall be clean; from all your filthiness and from all your idols will I cleanse you: I will also save you from all your uncleannesses' (Ezek. 36:25, 29). No promise can be more clear. And to this the Apostle plainly refers in that exhortation: 'Having these promises, let us cleanse ourselves from all filthiness of flesh and spirit, perfecting holiness in the fear of God' (2 Cor. 7:1). Equally clear and express is that ancient promise: 'The Lord thy God will circumcise thy heart, and the heart of thy seed, to love the Lord thy God with all thy heart and with all thy soul' (Deut. 30:6).

Q. But does any assertion answerable to this occur in the New Testament?

Ans. There does, and that laid down in the plainest terms. So 1 John 3:8: 'For this purpose the Son of God was manifested, that he might destroy the works of the devil'; the works of the devil, without any limitation or restriction; but all sin is the work of the devil. Parallel to which is the assertion of St. Paul: 'Christ loved the Church, and gave himself for it, that he might present it to himself a glorious Church, not having spot or wrinkle, or any such thing, but that it might be holy and without blemish' (Eph. 5:25–27). And to the same effect is his assertion in the eighth of the Romans, verses 3, 4: 'God sent his Son, that the righteousness of the law might be fulfilled in us, who walk not after the flesh, but after the spirit.'

Q. Does the New Testament afford any farther ground for expecting to be saved from all sin?

Ans. Undoubtedly it does; both in those prayers and commands, which are equivalent to the strongest assertions.

Q. What prayers do you mean?

Ans. Prayers for entire sanctification; which, were there no such thing, would be mere mockery of God. Such in particular are, (1) 'Deliver us from evil.' Now, when this is done, when we are delivered from all evil, there can be no sin remaining. (2) 'Neither pray I for these alone, but for them also who shall believe on me through their word; that they all may be one; as thou, Father, art in me and I in thee, that they also may be one in us; I in them, and thou in me, that they may be made perfect in one' (John 17:20–23). (3) 'I bow my knees unto the God and Father of our Lord Jesus Christ, that he would grant you, that ye,' 'being rooted and grounded in love, may be able to comprehend, with all saints, what is the breadth, and length, and depth, and height, and to know the love of Christ, which passeth knowledge; that ye may be filled with all the fulness of God' (Eph. 3:14ff). (4) 'The very God of peace sanctify you wholly. And I pray God, your whole spirit, soul, and body, may be preserved blameless unto the coming of our Lord Jesus Christ' (1 Thess. 5:23).

Q. What command is there to the same effect?

Ans. (1) 'Be ye perfect, as your Father who is in heaven is perfect' (Matt. 5:48). (2) 'Thou shalt love the Lord thy God with all thy heart, and with all thy soul, and with all thy mind' (Matt. 12:37). But if the love of God fill all the heart, there can be no sin therein.

Q. But how does it appear that this is to be done before the article of death?

Ans. (1) From the very nature of a command, which is not given to the dead, but to the living. Therefore, 'Thou shalt love God with all thy heart,' cannot mean, Thou shalt do this when thou diest; but, while thou livest. (2) From express texts of Scripture: (i) 'The grace of God, that bringeth salvation, hath appeared to all men; teaching us that, having renounced ungodliness and worldly lusts, we should live soberly, righteously, and godly in this present world; looking for the glorious appearing of our Lord Jesus Christ, who gave himself for us, that he might redeem us from all iniquity, and purify unto himself a peculiar people, zealous of good works' (Titus 2:11–14). (ii) 'He hath raised up an horn of salvation for us, to perform the mercy promised to our fathers; the oath which he sware to our father Abraham, that he would grant unto us, that we, being delivered out of the hands of our enemies, should serve him without fear, in holiness and righteousness before him, all the days of our life' (Luke 1:69ff).

Q. Is there any example in Scripture of persons who had attained to this?

Ans. Yes; St. John, and all those of whom he says, 'Herein is our love made perfect, that we may have boldness in the day of judgment; because, as he is, so are we in this world' (1 John 4:17).

Q. Can you show one such example now? Where is he that is thus perfect?

Ans. To some that make this inquiry one might answer, If I knew one here, I would not tell you; for you do not inquire out of love. You are like Herod; you only seek the young child to slay it. But more directly we answer: There are many reasons why there should be few, if any, indisputable examples. What inconveniences would this bring on the person himself, set as a mark for all to shoot at! And how unprofitable would it be to gainsayers! 'For if they hear not Moses and the Prophets,' Christ and his Apostles, 'neither would they be persuaded though one rose from the dead.'

Q. Are we not apt to have a secret distaste to any who say they are saved from all sin?

Ans. It is very possible we may, and that upon several grounds; partly from a concern for the good of souls, who may be hurt if these are not what they profess; partly from a kind of implicit envy at those who speak of higher attainments than our own; and partly from our natural slowness and unreadiness of heart to believe the works of God.

Q. Why may we not continue in the joy of faith till we are perfected in love?

Ans. Why indeed? since holy grief does not quench this joy; since even while we are under the cross, while we deeply partake of the sufferings of Christ, we may 'rejoice with joy unspeakable.'"

From these extracts it undeniably appears, not only what was mine and my brother's judgment, but what was the judgment of all the Preachers in connexion with us, in the years 1744, 45, 46 and 47. Nor do I remember that, in any one of these Conferences, we had one dissenting voice; but whatever doubts any one had when we met, they were all removed before we parted. . . .

26. In the year 1764, upon a review of the whole subject, I wrote down the sum of what I had observed in the following short propositions:

"(1) There is such a thing as perfection; for it is again and again mentioned in Scripture.

(2) It is not so early as justification; for justified persons are to 'go on unto perfection' (Heb. 6:1).

(3) It is not so late as death; for St. Paul speaks of living men that were perfect (Phil. 3:15).

(4) It is not absolute. Absolute perfection belongs not to man, nor to angels, but to God alone.

(5) It does not make a man infallible: None is infallible, while he remains in the body.

(6) Is it sinless? It is not worth while to contend for a term. It is 'salvation from sin.'

(7) It is perfect love (1 John 4:18). This is the essence of it; its properties, or inseparable fruits, are, rejoicing evermore, praying without ceasing, and in everything giving thanks (1 Thess. 5:16ff).

(8) It is improvable. It is so far from lying in an indivisible point, from being incapable of increase, that one perfected in love may grow in grace far swifter than he did before.

(9) It is amissible, capable of being lost; of which we have numerous instances. But we were not thoroughly convinced of this, till five or six years ago.

(10) It is constantly both preceded and followed by a gradual work.

(11) But is it in itself instantaneous or not? In examining this, let us go on step by step. An instantaneous change has been wrought in some believers: None can deny this. Since that

change, they enjoy perfect love; they feel this, and this alone; they rejoice evermore, pray without ceasing, and in everything give thanks. Now, this is all that I mean by perfection; therefore, these are witnesses of the perfection which I preach. But in some this change was not instantaneous. They did not perceive the instant when it was wrought. It is often difficult to perceive the instant when a man dies; yet there is an instant in which life ceases. And if ever sin ceases, there must be a last moment of its existence, and a first moment of our deliverance from it. But if they have this love now, they will lose it. They may; but they need not. And whether they do or no, they have it now; they now experience what we teach. They now are all love; they now rejoice, pray, and praise without ceasing. However, sin is only suspended in them; it is not destroyed. Call it which you please. They are all love today; and they take no thought for the morrow. But this doctrine has been much abused. So has that of justification by faith. But that is no reason for giving up either this or any other scriptural doctrine. When you wash your child, as one speaks, throw away the water; but do not throw away the child. But those who think they are saved from sin say they have no need of the merits of Christ. They say just the contrary. Their language is, 'Every moment, Lord, I want The merit of thy death!' They never before had so deep, so unspeakable, a conviction of the need of Christ in all his offices as they have now. Therefore, all our Preachers should make a point of preaching perfection to believers constantly, strongly, and explicitly; and all believers should mind this one thing, and continually agonize for it."

26. I have now done what I proposed. I have given a plain and simple account of the manner wherein I first received the doctrine of perfection, and the sense wherein I received, and wherein I do receive, and teach it to this day. I have declared the whole and every part of what I mean by that scriptural expression. I have drawn the picture of it at full length, without either disguise or covering. And I would now ask any impartial person, What is there so frightful herein? Whence is all this outcry, which, for these twenty years and upwards, has been made throughout the kingdom; as if all Christianity were destroyed, and all religion torn up by the roots? Why is it, that the very name of perfection has been cast out of the mouths of Christians; yea, exploded and abhorred, as if it contained the most pernicious heresy? Why have the Preachers of it been hooted at, like mad dogs, even by men that fear God; nay, and by some of their own children, some whom they, under God, had begotten through the gospel? What reason is there for this, or what pretence? Reason; sound reason, there is none. It is impossible there should. But pretences there are, and those in great abundance. Indeed, there is ground to fear that, with some who treat us thus, it is mere pretence; that it is no more than a copy of their countenance, from the beginning to the end. They wanted, they sought, occasion against me; and here they found what they sought. "This is Mr. Wesley's doctrine! He preaches perfection!" He does; yet this is not his doctrine any more than it is yours, or any one's else, that is a Minister of Christ. For it is His doctrine, peculiarly, emphatically His; it is the doctrine of Jesus Christ. Those are his words, not mine: "Ye shall therefore be perfect, as your Father who is in heaven is perfect." And who says, ye shall not; or, at least, not till your soul is separated from the body? It is the doctrine of St. Paul, the doctrine of St. James, of St. Peter, and St. John; and no otherwise Mr. Wesley's, than as it is the doctrine of every one who preaches the pure and the whole gospel. I tell you, as plain as I can speak, where and when I found this. I found it in the oracles of God, in the Old and Now Testament; when I read them with no other view or desire but to save my own soul. But whosoever this doctrine is, I pray you, what harm is there in it? Look at it again; survey it on every side, and that with the closest attention. In one view, it is purity of intention, dedicating all the life to God. It is the giving God all our heart; it is one desire and design ruling all our tempers. It is the devoting, not a part, but all our soul, body, and substance to God. In another view, it is all the mind which was in Christ, enabling us to walk as Christ walked. It is the circumcision of the heart from all filthiness, all inward as well as outward pollution. It is a renewal of the heart in the whole image of God, the full likeness of Him that created it. In yet another, it is the loving God with all our heart, and our neighbour

as ourselves. Now, take it in which of these views you please (for there is no material difference), and this is the whole and sole perfection, as a train of writings prove to a demonstration, which I have believed and taught for these forty years, from the year 1725 to the year 1765.

28. Now let this perfection appear in its native form, and who can speak one word against it? Will any dare to speak against loving the Lord our God with all our heart, and our neighbour as ourselves? against a renewal of heart, not only in part, but in the whole image of God? Who is he that will open his mouth against being cleansed from all pollution both of flesh and spirit; or against having all the mind that was in Christ, and walking in all things as Christ walked? What man, who calls himself a Christian, has the hardiness to object to the devoting, not a part, but all our soul, body, and substance to God? What serious man would oppose the giving God all our heart, and the having one design ruling all our tempers? I say, again, let this perfection appear in its own shape, and who will fight against it? It must be disguised before it can be opposed. It must be covered with a bear-skin first, or even the wild beasts of the people will scarce be induced to worry it. But whatever these do, let not the children of God any longer fight against the image of God. Let not the members of Christ say anything against having the whole mind that was in Christ. Let not those who are alive to God oppose the dedicating all our life to Him. Why should you who have his love shed abroad in your heart withstand the giving him all your heart? Does not all that is within you cry out, "O who that loves can love enough?" What pity that those who desire and design to please him should have any other design or desire! much more, that they should dread, as a fatal delusion, yea, abhor as an abomination to God, the having this one desire and design ruling every temper! Why should devout men be afraid of devoting all their soul, body, and substance to God? Why should those who love Christ count it a damnable error, to think we may have all the mind that was in him? We allow, we contend, that we are justified freely through the righteousness and the blood of Christ. And why are you so hot against us, because we expect likewise to be sanctified wholly through his Spirit? We look for no favour either from the open servants of sin, or from those who have only the form of religion. But how long will you who worship God in spirit, who are "circumcised with the circumcision not made with hands," set our battle in array against those who seek a entire circumcision of heart, who thirst to be cleansed "from all filthiness of flesh and spirit," and to "perfect holiness in the fear of God?" Are we your enemies, because we look for a full deliverance from that "carnal mind which is enmity against God?" Nay, we are your brethren, your fellow-labourers in the vineyard of our Lord, your companions in the kingdom and patience of Jesus. Although this we confess (if we are fools therein, yet as fools bear with us), we do expect to love God with all our heart, and our neighbour as ourselves. Yea, we do believe, that he will in this world so cleanse the thoughts of our hearts, by the inspiration of his Holy Spirit, that we shall perfectly love him, and worthily magnify his holy name.

Select Bibliography

PRIMARY SOURCES, ONLINE

Christian Classics Ethereal Library, http://www.ccel.org.

Edwards, Jonathan, works, http://www.edwards.yale.edu/.

Heidelberg Catechism, http://www.reformed.org/documents/heidelberg.html.

Medieval Sourcebook, The, http://www.fordham.edu/halsall/sbook.html#12.

Wesley, John, works, http://gbgm-umc.org/umhistory/wesley/.

PRIMARY SOURCES, PRINTED

Aquinas, St. Thomas. *Summa Theologica*. London: Blackfriars, 1964.

Ehrman, Bart, and A. Jacobs. *Christianity in Late Antiquity: A Reader*, New York: Oxford, 2004.

Elder, E. R., ed. The Cistercian Fathers Series. Kalamazoo, MI: Cistercian, 1970–.

Halton, T. P., ed. *The Fathers of the Church*. Washington, D.C.: Catholic University of America, 1953–.

Lake, K., trans. *Apostolic Fathers*. Cambridge, MA: Harvard University Press, 1977.

McGinn, Bernard, ed. *Luther's Works*. St. Louis: Concordia Publishing House, 1955–1976.

Payne, Richard. *Classics of Western Spirituality*. New York: Paulist Press, 1978.

Pelikan, J., and V. Hotchkiss, eds. *Creeds and Confessions of Faith in the Christian Tradition*. New Haven: Yale, 2003.

Rotelle, John E. *The Works of Saint Augustine: A Translation for the 21st Century*. Multiple vols. Hyde Park: New City, 1997.

SECONDARY SOURCES

Ahlstrom, Sydney. *A Religious History of the American People*. New Haven: Yale, 1972.

Chadwick, Henry. *The Church in Ancient Society*. New York: Oxford University Press, 2003.

Christian History and Biography. Journal published by *Christianity Today*.

Church History. Journal published by the American Society of Church History.

Davies, J. G. *New Westminster Dictionary of Liturgy and Worship*. Philadelphia: Westminster, 1986.

Di Berardino, A., ed. *Encyclopedia of the Early Church*. 2 vols. New York: Oxford Press, 1992.

Esler, Philip. *The Early Christian World*. 2 vols. New York: Routledge, 2000.

Ferguson, E., ed. *Encyclopedia of Early Christianity*. New York: Garland Publishers, 1990.

Frend, W. H. C. *The Early Church*. Minneapolis: Fortress, 1982.

Gaustad, E., and Leigh Schmidt. *The Religious History of America*. San Francisco: Harper, 2002.

Gilson, Etienne. *The Christian Philosophy of Saint Augustine*. New York: Random House, 1960.

Hillerbrand, Hans., ed. *The Encyclopedia of Protestantism*. 4 vols. New York: Routledge, 2004.

———. *The Oxford Encyclopedia of the Reformation*. 4 vols. New York: Oxford Press, 1996.

Kelly, J. F. *The World of the Early Christians*. Collegeville, MN: Liturgical Press, 1997.

Kelly, J. N. D. *Golden Mouth: The Story of John Chrysostom*. Grand Rapids: Baker, 1995.

Leclercq, Jean. *The Love of Learning and the Desire for God: A Study of Monastic Culture*. New York: Fordham, 1961.

Livingstone, E. A., ed. *The Oxford Dictionary of the Christian Church*. 3rd ed. New York: Oxford, 1997.

Marsden, George. *Jonathan Edwards: A Life*. New Haven: Yale, 2003.

Maus, C. P. *The Church and the Fine Arts*. New York: Harper & Brothers, 1960.

McKechnie, Paul. *The First Christian Centuries*. Downers Grove: InterVarsity Press, 2001.

Meade, Frank, and S. Hill. *Handbook of Denominations in the United States*. 10th ed. Nashville: Abingdon, 1995.

Oberman, H. A. *Luther: Man Between God and the Devil*. New York: Doubleday, 1990.

O'Meara, Dominic, ed. *Neoplatonism and Christian Thought*. Albany: SUNY Press, 1982.

Pelikan, Jaroslav. *The Christian Tradition: A History of the Development of Doctrine*. 5 vols. Chicago: University of Chicago, 1978.

Peterson, S. L. *Timeline Charts of the Western Church*. Grand Rapids: Zondervan, 1999.

Piltz, Anders. *The World of Medieval Learning*. Oxford: Blackwell, 1981.

Quasten, Johannes. *Patrology*. 4 vols. 1963–1995.

Rudolph, L. C. *Hoosier Faiths: A History of Indiana Churches and Religious Groups*. Bloomington: Indiana University Press, 1995.

Strayer, J. R., ed. *Dictionary of the Middle Ages*. 13 vols. New York: Charles Scribner's Sons, 1989.

Tomlin, G. *Luther and His World*. Downers Grove, IL: InterVarsity Press, 2002.

Vallee, G. *The Shaping of Christianity*. New York: Paulist, 1999.

TAKE A LOOK AT CHRISTIAN HISTORY
FROM OTHER PERSPECTIVES

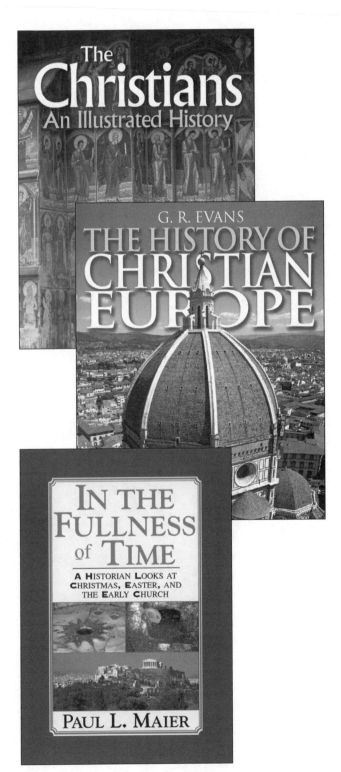

The Christians
An Illustrated History
Tim Dowley

The Christians: An Illustrated History is an extravagantly illustrated survey of the development of Christianity from the time of Jesus to the present day. Writing in an accessible, topical style, Tim Dowley covers subjects that continue to influence the church and society today. Dowley also surveys key figures such as Paul, Justin Martyr, Augustine, Innocent III, Peter Abelard, Francis of Assisi, Martin Luther, D. L. Moody, Karl Barth, C. S. Lewis, and others. The book is international in scope and is illustrated throughout with four-color art, photographs, maps, charts, and sidebar material.

978-0-8254-6256-6 | 176 pages | $24.99 | Hardcover

The History of Christian Europe
G. R. Evans

Beginning with the spread of Jesus' teachings and the apostles' ministry throughout the Roman world, G. R. Evans shows how Christianity transformed not only the thinking but also the social structures of Europe. In *The History of Christian Europe*, Evans traces Christianity's influence across the centuries, from its earliest days, through the East/West schism, Reformation, and Counter-Reformation, to its development in the scientific age of the seventeenth and eighteenth centuries and its place in the modern world. The narrative is complemented by sidebars highlighting key events and concepts, such as monastic life, icons, Darwin's *The Origin of Species*, prophecy, the slave trade, and the influence of psychology.

978-0-8254-7827-7 | 224 pages | $34.95 | Hardcover

In the Fullness of Time
A Historian Looks at Christmas, Easter, and the Early Church
Paul L. Maier

Maier's impressive research and brilliant insights correlate history, archaeology, and the New Testament text in this classic trilogy on early Christianity. Full-color photographs and illustrations help recreate the world, the mood, the people, and the events of the early years of faith.

978-0-8254-3329-0 | 384 pages | $24.99 | Hardcover

MORE SOURCES THAT TELL THE STORY OF THE CHURCH'S HISTORY

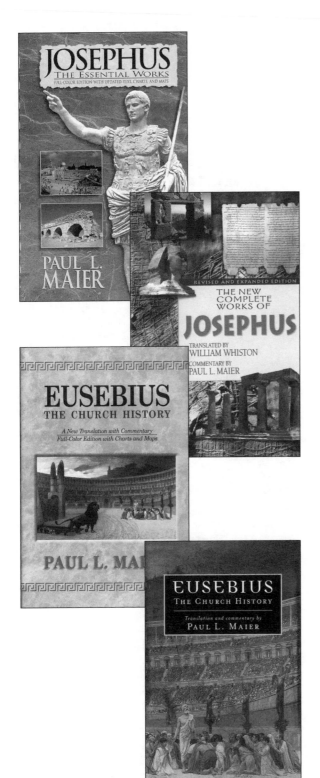

Josephus: The Essential Works
Flavius Josephus; Paul L. Maier, editor and translator

Josephus's *The Jewish Antiquities* and *The Jewish War* take on a brilliant new dimension in this revised edition of the award-winning translation and condensation, now with full-color photographs, charts, and maps.

978-0-8254-3260-6 | 416 pages | $25.99 | Hardcover

The New Complete Works of Josephus
Flavius Josephus; William Whiston, translator; Paul L. Maier, commentator

No source, other than the Bible itself, provides more relevant information on the first century than the work of Flavius Josephus. This edited version updates the original eighteenth-century language; includes commentary by the award-winning author and historian, Dr. Paul L. Maier; features more than forty photographs of ancient sites and artifacts mentioned by Josephus; cross-references numbers throughout to the Greek text of Josephus in the Loeb Classical Library; and offers revised indexes of subjects and Old Testament texts.

978-0-8254-2948-4 | 1152 pages | $19.99 | Paperback
978-0-8254-2924-8 | 1152 pages | $24.99 | Hardcover

Eusebius: The Church History
Eusebius; Paul L. Maier, editor and translator

Next to *Josephus*, *Eusebius* is the most widely consulted reference work on the early church. Much of our knowledge of the first three centuries of Christianity—the terrible persecutions, the courageous martyrs, and the theological controversies—come from the writings of this first-century historian. This translation includes more than 150 color photographs, maps, and charts.

978-0-8254-3328-3 | 416 pages | $26.99 | Hardcover

Eusebius: The Church History
Eusebius; Paul L. Maier, editor and translator

This highly affordable paperback edition includes Maier's best-selling translation, historical commentary on each book of *The Church History*, and ten maps and illustrations. Often called the "Father of Church History," Eusebius recorded crucial information about the lives of Jesus' disciples, the development of the New Testament, Roman politics, and the persecution of early Christians.

978-0-8254-3307-8 | 368 pages | $15.99 | Paperback